Mahalia Jackson and the Black Gospel Field

Mahalia Jackson and the Black Gospel Field

MARK BURFORD

OXFORD
UNIVERSITY PRESS

OXFORD

UNIVERSITY PRESS

Oxford University Press is a department of the University of Oxford. It furthers
the University's objective of excellence in research, scholarship, and education
by publishing worldwide. Oxford is a registered trade mark of Oxford University
Press in the UK and certain other countries.

Published in the United States of America by Oxford University Press
198 Madison Avenue, New York, NY 10016, United States of America.

© Oxford University Press 2019

This volume is published with the generous support of the AMS 75 PAYS Endowment of
the American Musicological Society, funded in part by the National Endowment for the
Humanities and the Andrew W. Mellon Foundation.

Library of Congress Cataloging-in-Publication Data
Names: Burford, Mark, 1967- author.
Title: Mahalia Jackson and the black gospel field / Mark Burford.
Description: New York, NY: Oxford University Press, [2018] | Includes
bibliographical references and index.
Identifiers: LCCN 2018005596 | ISBN 9780190634902 (hardcover: alk. paper) |
ISBN 9780190634926 (epub)
Subjects: LCSH: Jackson, Mahalia, 1911-1972. | African American gospel
singers—United States—Biography. | Gospel singers—United
States—Biography. | African Americans—Music—History and criticism. |
Gospel music—History and criticism.
Classification: LCC ML420.J17 B87 2018 | DDC 782.25/4092 [B] —dc23
LC record available at https://lccn.loc.gov/2018005596

1 3 5 7 9 8 6 4 2

Printed by Sheridan Books, Inc., United States of America

To Michael, Marcia, Melinda,
and above all Mom

In memory of Corliss Askew Watkins
(1955–2018)

Contents

Preface

TWO DAYS AFTER Christmas 2015, I attended a wedding reception in Oakland, California, for the daughter of long-time family friends. While I was exchanging pleasantries with the father of the bride, he became visibly excited upon finding out that I was writing a book on gospel singer Mahalia Jackson. A musician, an English professor, and a Christian, he asked what my angle was. I told him that I was studying Jackson's career in the decade after World War II, considering how during this period Jackson became an international, multi-mediated celebrity through her increasingly high profile concerts, radio and television appearances, and commercial recordings, all the while maintaining her street cred as an active "church singer," as she liked to describe herself. Having encountered many people who had never heard of Mahalia Jackson—invariably my students, though also, more often than I expected, friends and acquaintances intrigued that I was writing a book on black gospel music but whose faces went blank when I mentioned Jackson's name—I couldn't help but find his fascination gratifying. "It is remarkable, when you think about it," he said, scanning Jackson's luminous career in his mind. "Why her?"

As scholars across the disciplines know all too well, the most fundamental questions, even rhetorical ones, can often be the most fruitful. As I continued to weave together a sprawling body of research material on Jackson and her singular positioning within the history of black gospel music, the question "Why her?" continuously generated complex answers. Taken at face value, "Why her?" seemed to ask how Jackson, among the multitude of extraordinary vocalists who sang gospel music and other religious songs in African American churches across the country, was able to attain such visibility and global resonance as an artist and as a cultural symbol. The capacity for Jackson's voice and prowess as a performer to stir listeners, devout and nonbeliever alike, is an inescapable threshold, but it quickly became clear that this was just a starting point. Jackson's rise to national prominence in the 1940s and 1950s was inextricably and reciprocally bound up with post-war shifts in mass mediation, civil rights aspirations, and early Cold War ideology that gave new cultural-political salience to black vernacular and religious expression. Preparing the way for Jackson's reception and prestige as a gospel singer even more directly were a personal biographical narrative charting her journey from New Orleans to Chicago in the midst of the Great Depression, her entrepreneurial panache, an interconnected network of influential white, media-connected advocates, and the myriad overlapping organizational structures affiliated with the black Baptist church.

I might have also, however, heard the question "Why her?" another way: How did I find my way to a study of Mahalia Jackson and her transformative place within the black gospel field? These days I am admittedly a backslider, but I was born and raised in the bosom of a close-knit congregation at Philadelphian Seventh-Day Adventist Church in San Francisco. A fundamentalist Protestant denomination popularly known for strict sundown-to-sundown observance of the Sabbath on Saturday and for a "health message" involving a dietary regimen that forbids eating pork and shellfish, Seventh-Day Adventists experienced a recent fifteen minutes of fame when black Adventist neurosurgeon Ben Carson ran as a Republican candidate in the 2016 U.S. presidential election and was eventually appointed secretary of Housing and Urban Development in the Trump administration. Philadelphian was especially welcoming to immigrants from circum-Caribbean countries like Jamaica, the Bahamas, Guyana, and especially Panama, my mother's birthplace before she came, on her own, to San Francisco as a seventeen-year-old "looking for a better life." The rest of the church membership was made up primarily of transplants from the South. My father, for instance, raised Baptist in Columbus, Texas, moved to San Francisco as a young adult and became a member of Philadelphian when he married my mother. I'm not sure how much dad's heart was ever into churchgoing; he stuck it out at Philadelphian for several years and even became a deacon, but he was no longer attending by the time I was born, so my childhood Saturdays unfailing meant church with mom.

My experience at Philadelphian always made me wonder whenever I encountered conventional wisdom and popular stereotypes about the "black church." There was never any question in my mind that I attended a black church, if a West Indian–accented one. At any given time, you could count the white congregants in the sanctuary on one hand, when there were any at all. Still, I was aware that other black churches worshipped on different days and in different ways. Black Adventists are typically buttoned-down church folk. Our pastors delivered the sermon with bookish decorum, for the most part withholding fire and brimstone. Our choir rendered anthems and spirituals accompanied by the piano and Philadelphian's majestic organ and the congregation sang straight out of the hymnal. The occasional visitor from one of those Sunday black churches, hand-waving during the preaching and clapping at the end of musical selections instead of offering the customary hearty "Amen," was usually easy to spot—and if you missed a clue, conspicuous sideways glances from Philadelphian's matrons would let you know. Except for a brief moment in the late 1970s when a new member tried to organize a youth choir—James Cleveland's "God Is" and Walter Hawkins's "Jesus Christ is the Way" may have been our one and only performance—I have no recollection of hearing anything resembling what I understood then and recognize now to be gospel singing in church, and certainly not at home. When, somewhat as a provocation, I asked my mother if she knew who Mahalia Jackson was, she furrowed her brow and shot me a wry look—"Who doesn't know Mahalia Jackson?"—then went on to describe her as that Baptist woman who "got all whipped up and excited and did all that carrying on" when she sang. For all intents and purposes, black gospel music, in style or in substance, was outside of my experience, a keystone of musical worship for other black denominations perhaps, but not ours.

Or so I thought. As I got to know gospel in later years, first as a fan and subsequently as a music historian, I came to realize that if gospel was not explicitly a part of my musical landscape as a black churchgoer, it was not wholly unfamiliar. As a listener, I came to gospel by following black singing voices backward in time, reversing my way through influences on the music I loved. In high school and college, my friends and I were avid devotees of roots reggae. Drawn especially to the singing and wondering where it came from, I discovered sublime rocksteady crooners like Alton Ellis, Pat Kelly, Phyllis Dillon, and Ken Booth and, in turn, their indebtedness to 1960s soul. From there, it was an inevitable next step to gospel, whereupon I realized that I had found what was, for me, the mother lode in terms of the vocality that resonated with me most. I began to devour the music, reveling obsessively in a stockpile of compilations of music by male quartets, women's and mixed groups, choirs, and soloists spanning the 1920s through the 1970s, and as I listened I found myself repeatedly saying to myself: "Wait, I know that song. . . . We used to sing that song." My perception of the remoteness of gospel music from *my* black church experience, based on styles of worship, was confounded by a growing awareness of shared histories, evidenced by the circulation of repertory and the familiarity of recognizably African American vocal strategies.

This is not to say that Philadelphian was a gospel church after all. But my recognition of the connectedness of the presumably discrete captures the spirit of this book, which considers black gospel as a field of broad possibilities linking a diverse range of church denominations, personal beliefs, musical styles, individual desires, strategic goals, performance contexts, cultural producers, and economic stakes. I hope to make black gospel more legible in these terms. Jackson, whom her friend Harry Belafonte once called "the single most powerful black woman in the United States," represented one of these possibilities, though one uniquely complicated by a sense of her being at once exemplary of and an exceptional case within the black gospel field.[1] Following Jackson's early career, through scrutiny of the available literature, combing mainstream and black-targeted press, digging through archival collections, and, most enjoyably, close listening, led me to an even greater appreciation of her extraordinary personal resources and resourcefulness as a vocal artist and as an African American woman in post-war U.S. society, while also revealing the all-too-human qualities often veiled by routine assertions of her iconic status. At the same time, following Jackson, whose star shone so brightly, helps to illuminate intimate spaces of a black gospel field with which her every activity was so densely interwoven, a field that came to make a permanent, metamorphic impact on American music and culture. Why her? The chapters that follow seek to answer that question.

Acknowledgments

WRITING THIS BOOK would not have been possible without the contributions of many people in numerous ways, both large and small.

I first owe thanks to my home institution, Reed College, which has been consistently supportive of my research. I don't think I ever heard a "No" from the Dean of Faculty's office when I asked for funding for trips to New Orleans and other archives around the country. I am also deeply appreciative of the Reed College Library, directed by Dena Hutto and her predecessor Vickie Hanawalt, which has been exceedingly generous in acquiring any resources I asked for, especially the complete (and not inexpensive) Proquest Historical Black Newspaper Database that has been essential to my research. A special thanks goes to librarians Jim Holmes, Erin Connor, and Bruce Van Buskirk, who have unfailingly granted my incessant requests for recordings and other media. Lastly, I am grateful to my valued colleagues in Reed's Music Department, Virginia Hancock, David Schiff, Morgan Luker, John Cox, and Denise VanLeuven, from whom I learn something new on a regular basis.

In working on this book, I received integral support from outside funding and research assistants. I benefited greatly from a Dena Epstein Award from the Music Library Association and a Diane Woest Fellowship in the Arts and Humanities from the Historic New Orleans Collection. I was honored by the opportunity to conduct interviews with Carl Bean, Otis Clay, Alice McClarity, Lewis Merenstein, Ronald Merenstein, Garnett Mimms, Therman Ruth Jr., Howard Tate, and the recently deceased George Avakian, who plays a significant role in the latter stages of the book's story. My students at Reed had a significant impact on this project through their assistance with transcription of these interviews and additional research: a big thank you to Wolfgang Black, Nora Jones, and Katharina Schwaiger, and especially to Reuben de la Huerga for the major task of transcribing Bill Russell's journal.

More informal contacts have been indispensible to my thinking about this project and have shepherded me through the process of research and writing. The opportunity to have gotten to know, consult, and converse with Tony Heilbut and Bob Marovich, both whom have forgotten more about gospel than I will ever know, has been a privilege, not to mention a rod and a staff. I know of few people more passionate about black gospel music than Glen Smith, who talked shop with me, shared rare recordings, and opened my eyes to the Historic New Orleans Collection. A byproduct of this project is what has became a love affair with Mahalia Jackson's hometown of New Orleans, where I spent extended periods of time learning as much walking the streets as I did sitting in archives. I am indebted to New Orleans geographer Richard Campanella and Pointe Coupée historian Brian Costello, who took the time to meet with me and share their singular expertise and who gave me insights and leads that greatly furthered my understanding of the region. The hospitality, insider knowledge, and friendship of Jennifer Growden, Stephen Haedicke, Annie Whitson, Tom Worrell, and Sue Mobley made New Orleans feel like home in ways for which I will always be grateful. A very special acknowledgment goes to Professors Randy Sanders of Southeastern Louisiana University and Matt Sakakeeny of Tulane University, who have become cherished friends and interlocutors and who will always be at the forefront of my mind when I think of what it means to miss New Orleans.

Seemingly small favors often paid big dividends. My thanks to the late, great photographer Don Hunstein for introducing me to the Sony Archives; to David Hinckley for making the connection to the family of Thermon Ruth Sr.; to Reverend Christopher Jackson for making available J. Robert Bradley materials; to Dino Gankendorff, who facilitated contact with the Mahalia Jackson Family Estate; to Gerry Zahavi for pointing me toward helpful Jackson interviews; to Gema Interiano of SOFA Entertainment for granting me access to rare archival video; to Renette Hall of the *Louisiana Weekly*; to James Abbington for allowing me to tap his inexhaustible knowledge of black religious music; and to Loreta Garrett, historian of National Convention of Gospel Choirs and Choruses for sharing her intimate knowledge of that extraordinary and still thriving institution.

Oxford University Press has been a supportive partner throughout the process of bringing this book into existence. I am indebted to Editor-in-Chief of Humanities and Executive Editor of Music Suzanne Ryan for her work on this project and for her consistent encouragement and faith since I was a graduate student; editorial assistants Victoria Kouznetsov and Eden Piacitelli for keeping the train moving; and the anonymous reviewers and Thomas Brothers, who provided valuable feedback at the early and final draft stages, respectively. The book benefited from me being able to give test runs of some of the material. For these opportunities, I would like to express my gratitude to David Metzer and Hedy Law at the University of British Columbia, David Dominique at the College of William and Mary, and the American Musicological Society. Suggestions and clarifying explanations from Glenda Goodman, Marc Schneiberg, Albin Zak, and my partner in many a music-historical kitchen table conversation Andy Flory are reflected in the pages that follow. I would also like to thank four senior scholars in the field of musicology whose support and encouragement over the years has been particularly meaningful: Walter Frisch, Tammy Kernodle, Jeffrey Magee, and Guthrie Ramsey.

What would archival researchers do without librarians and the collections they oversee with such exquisite care and illuminating insight? This would have been a very different and greatly diminished book without the cumulative help I received from the staff of numerous archives, including Che Williams at the Sony Entertainment Photograph Archive; Brenda Nelson-Strauss at the Archives of African American Music and Culture at Indiana University; Gino Francesconi at the Carnegie Hall Archives; Chantel Clark in Special Collections at the Fisk University Library; Christina Bryant and the staff at the Louisiana Division/City Archives at the New Orleans Public Library; Roger Williams at the Chicago Public Library; Ezra Wheeler at the Memphis Music Hall of Fame; Brigitte Billeaudeaux in Special Collections at the University of Memphis Libraries; and Richard Boursey at Yale University's Gilmore Music Library. Two archives in particular deserve special mention for their singular roles in shaping the chapters that follow. I owe a huge debt to Lynn Abbott at the Hogan Jazz Archive at Tulane University not only for the opportunity to pick his brain about gospel but for going out of his way to provide me with access to deep vault materials in their collections. I will be eternally grateful for Lynn's indefatigable legwork tracking down the research materials of Mahalia Jackson biographer Laurraine Goreau, which became an indispensible primary source. I am also appreciative of the assistance of the rest of the Hogan staff, Director Bruce Boyd Raeburn, Alaina Hébert, and Nicole Shibata. Finally, I would like to express my deepest appreciation for the Historic New Orleans Collection. This began as a very different project and my discovery of the Mahalia Jackson Papers in the William Russell Collection fundamentally changed what the book was about and forced me to reimagine what it could be. The competence, professionalism, patience, and accommodation of the staff at the HNOC's Williams Research Center, directed by Alfred Lemmon, was unparalleled. I would like to thank especially Daniel Hammer, Rebecca Smith, Jennifer Navarre, Matt Farah, Robert Ticknor, Mary Lou Eichorn, and Eric Seiferth for their invaluable help over a period of five years combing through the Russell collection.

Mahalia Jackson and the Black Gospel Field

I
_____

Introduction

"MISS JACKSON AND HER ART (GOSPEL SINGING)"

HOSTED BY ED Sullivan, CBS's *Toast of the Town* offered viewers the motley assortment of acts expected of a something-for-everybody 1950s television variety show. In 1948, the network tapped the telegenically awkward Irish American gossip columnist to become the producer and face of what was soon to be renamed the *Ed Sullivan Show*. After tentative beginnings and against stiff competition from NBC's *Colgate Comedy Hour*, the program, the first of its kind on CBS, rode Sullivan's ambition and extensive entertainment industry connections on the way to becoming a "nationwide Sunday night addiction." The January 20, 1952, episode of *Toast of the Town* featured a presentation of the 1951 New York Film Critics Circle awards (*A Streetcar Named Desire* was the year's big winner) and a short set by the Phil Spitalny Hour of Charm All-Girl Orchestra, fronted by Spitalny's "fiddling Frau" Evelyn playing her "magic violin." Filling out the vaudeville-style lineup were an opening number starring Hal LeRoy with a company of dancers hoofing to a medley of George Gershwin tunes and, the entertainment trade magazine *Variety* mentioned in passing, "two quick pace-changers in John Tio's talking parrot and gospel singer Mahalia Jackson."[1]

For the forty-year-old Jackson (1911–1972), a Baptist-born-and-bred but Pentecostal-friendly Chicago resident originally from New Orleans, this was a symbolically important milestone in a career that had already advanced beyond any reasonable expectations. The twelve months leading up to her national television debut on *Toast of the Town* unfolded with an unheard-of string of achievements for a black gospel artist. Jackson managed her regular appearances at myriad stops along the black gospel highway in 1951—the CIO Union Hall in Muskegon, Michigan, Booker T. Washington High School in Norfolk, Virginia, the Atlanta City Auditorium, the seventy-fourth National Baptist Convention in Oklahoma City, and her own twenty-fifth anniversary gala concert at the Chicago Coliseum in October, among a slew of other programs. But her name and voice had also begun to circulate in ways that indicated something new afoot for Jackson and for post-war black gospel music, a story that this book seeks to tell. Jazz writers on both sides of the Atlantic who were fans of her recordings for Apollo Records developed an enthusiasm for Jackson described by gospel historian Anthony Heilbut as a "cultist following." In March 1951, Jackson received a Grand Prix du Disque, awarded by a committee of influential French music critics, for her Apollo single "I Can Put My Trust in Jesus." In the fall, Jackson was invited to appear at the "Definitions in Jazz" roundtable at the Music Inn in Lenox, Massachusetts, to demonstrate for an eminent gathering of scholars and aficionados the roots of jazz in black religious song. And there were yet other less-than-expected points of contact in 1951: a Chicago concert featuring Jackson and members of the leftist folk song organization People's Artists in April, her second appearance at a sold-out Carnegie Hall in October, and a ranking of sixth on *Jet* magazine's year-end list of the country's "best girl singers," behind only Sarah Vaughan, Ella Fitzgerald, Dinah Washington, Billie Holiday, and Ruth Brown. Just a month after Jackson's *Toast of the Town* appearance, the Gospel Train, an ambitious package headlined by Jackson and the Ward Singers, kicked off a planned thirty-concert coast-to-coast tour, "the highest priced religious concert unit ever assembled," black newspapers marveled.[2]

But an appearance on the Sullivan show in the still early years of television was another thing entirely. "Everybody in show business had heard about this tremendous Negro singer," Sullivan remembered two decades afterward, perhaps generously, and he "gave her a date immediately." Presenting Jackson also reflected Sullivan's sensitivity to the racial politics of early television.

> There had been a lot of comment about her and we always tried to make sure that we'd have Negro representation on the show. At that time the Negroes were in an uproar. They said the whites were monopolizing TV, that producers of TV shows were apparently scared to put a Negro on because of the Southern reaction. Well, the Southern reaction was as great as the Northern reaction toward her and the other ones.[3]

Sullivan had a solid track record of booking black acts. One press report called his show the "biggest single vehicle" for promoting African American talent on television. The Ink Spots, the popular vocal harmony group who were the first black performers on *Toast of the Town*, appeared as early as the second episode and others followed in uncommonly regular succession. Sullivan went so far as to insist that the intimacy of televisual mediation had the potential to become a uniquely powerful mechanism for social justice: "Television subtly has supplied ten-league boots to the Negro in his fight to win what the Constitution of this country guarantees as his birthright. It has taken his long fight to the living rooms of Americans' homes where public opinion is formed." TV was especially important as a socializing force for "the white children, who finally will lay Jim Crow to rest."[4]

Jackson's performance had further significance for being the first appearance by a black gospel singer on national television. As was so often the case throughout her early career when she was invited to appear in pop-cultural settings, Jackson was presented as both an outstanding individual artist and as a stand-in for the entire black gospel field. Accordingly, her performances bridged members of black church communities for whom gospel singing was a virtual daily presence, those in the broader public who experienced gospel as a piquant musical and cultural curiosity, and all positions in between. With a responsibility to represent, and not simply to provide Sullivan show producers with a diverting change of pace, Jackson was determined to do it right. She was irate when she arrived for the Sunday morning rehearsal to the news that a smoothly flowing production required that she would be backed by music director Ray Block's studio orchestra and not her usual piano and organ. "She was mad as hell" when "I didn't want to give her my only organ," Sullivan recalled, and Jackson stormed past CBS crew members to knock on Sullivan's dressing room door, finding him "in his BVDs" but getting her organ.[5] In light of these contexts, and as a means of introduction, we might not only think about Jackson's performance as part of the slate of acts that Sunday evening, but also imagine how it may have been understood as part of the black gospel field. What would it look like to fully account for and position Jackson's *Toast of the Town* appearance as a gospel performance, and what might it tell us about black gospel music at mid-century?

"These Are They"

Coming abruptly out of his plug for show sponsor Lincoln-Mercury, Sullivan's introduction of Jackson was complimentary, but characteristically clunky:

> There's a young singer—not a young singer, it's a middle-aged Negro star. She's acclaimed as the greatest gospel singer in the country. On three occasions she's come into New York's Carnegie Hall by herself. Packs the place. So tonight, we're going to present this New Orleans singer. Her name is Mahalia Jackson. She's going to sing for you a gospel song, "These Are They." Here is Mahalia Jackson. So let's have a nice welcome for her though, would you?[6]

Jackson stood spotlighted in front of the stage curtain, hands clasped, her dark robe streaked with a light-colored sash bound at her left shoulder. Her selection for gospel's big moment in the national spotlight, "These Are They," was written by William Herbert Brewster (1897–1987), the African American pastor of East Trigg Baptist Church in Memphis for nearly six decades and a prolific sacred song composer.[7] Brewster's learned, Bible-based lyric narrates an episode from the story of the exiled John of Patmos, to whom the voice of God dictated the eschato-logical vision in the Book of Revelation. This included a promise of being "sealed," a guarantee of grace at the final judgment for those of steadfast faith amid oppressive persecution.

Verse
    It was on a Lord's day morning
    Out on a lonely isle
    In the beauty of the dawning
    As John was in exile
    He heard a voice resounding
    Across the rolling sea
    Like mighty billows bounding
    John fell down on his knee
Chorus
    These are they from every nation
    Who have washed their garments white
    Coming up through great tribulation
    To a land of pure delight.[8]

"These Are They" was a relatively new gospel composition, published only in 1949, though it was surely introduced in performance earlier. Performed with a change in both tempo and meter—its slow triple-meter verse setting up a faster chorus in four—the song was apparently a centerpiece of Jackson's repertory at the time: along with "Move On Up a Little Higher" and "Just Over the Hill," "These Are They" was one of the three songs that she programmed for her gala twenty-fifth anniversary concert at the Chicago Coliseum three months earlier.[9] Soon after it appeared as sheet music, the song was documented on record by a cluster of performances featuring four respected female gospel leads: Frances Steadman, Queen C. Anderson, Dorothy Love Coates, and Jackson, who recorded the song for Apollo sixteen months before she sang it live for Sullivan's audience. The newness of the song that Jackson chose to showcase on the national stage is significant because it marks a seam linking the familiar and the remote in post-war black gospel reception. "These Are They" undoubtedly would have been un-known to the overwhelming majority of Sullivan's viewers, some of whom may have heard it as a venerable "Negro spiritual," while also giving members of black Baptist circles the satisfaction of recognizing a recent hit that was a roof-raising vehicle for some of gospel's elite divas.

At the same time, Jackson's television rendition of "These Are They" departed from these other recorded performances of the song in subtle but salient ways that focus our ears on various strategies for delivering a gospel song and offer a sense of the field and its performance practices. All four recordings take distinguishable liberties with the melody, structure, and especially the words. The 1949 recording by Steadman with the Mary Johnson Davis Gospel Singers bypassed the verse entirely and launched directly into the chorus. By contrast, the performances by Anderson with the Brewster Singers in 1950 and by Coates in 1951 with her own group, the Original Gospel Harmonettes, included at least part of Brewster's verse (Coates only sings the second half), making the mid-song shift in character an essential feature of both records. The Anderson-Brewster performance, accompanied by piano, organ, and drums, dramatically exaggerates the song's tempo change, exploding out of the gate at the arrival of the chorus and nearly tripling the tempo from 58 beats per minute (bpm) to 172, abruptly transforming a stately gospel ballad into a driving "shout" number. Coates and the Harmonettes also emphasize a pronounced contrast while lending the song a distinctly different flavor: powerful supporting choral harmonies and an even slower opening tempo (36 bpm) give the shortened verse an epic grandeur that yields to the irresistible and more modern sounding swing of the chorus.[10]

The Steadman, Anderson, and Coates recordings feature a lead singer supported by backing vocalists, presenting distinct arrangement possibilities. In the chorus, Anderson and Coates both employ the bread-and-butter gospel device of an interpolated vamp or "drive" section, an extended looping passage of call-and-response between the lead and backing singers over restricted harmonic movement that interrupts the continuation of the song's melody and chord progression with a "record-skipping," groove-building stasis. The vamps on these two records include a roll call of "nations," the naming of the twelve 12,000-member tribes of Israel, that Brewster lifted directly from the seventh chapter of Revelation. The singers then drop back into the chorus.

Tribe of Judah . . .

Twelve thousand

Tribe of Reuben . . .

Twelve thousand

Tribe of Gad . . .

Twelve thousand

Tribe of Aser . . .

Twelve thousand

Tribe of Nephtalim . . .

Twelve thousand

Tribe of Manasses . . .

	Twelve thousand
Tribe of Simeon . . .	
	Twelve thousand
Tribe of Levi . . .	
	Twelve thousand
Tribe of Issachar . . .	
	Twelve thousand
Tribe of Zabulon . . .	
	Twelve thousand
Tribe of Joseph . . .	
	Twelve thousand
Tribe of Benjamin . . .	
	Twelve thousand
These are they . . .	

It is difficult not to fold a black nation into those "coming up through great tribulation" to be sealed, bringing stories of the "burdens they had borne" to God's throne, as Brewster describes in the second verse. Such a connection points toward an interpretation of the song's message as a sermonic, scripture-based call for civil rights.[11]

Jackson's performances of "These Are They" for Apollo and on the Sullivan show stand apart from the contemporaneous Steadman, Anderson, and Coates recordings most conspicuously because she performs as a soloist, but also because of her crafty handling of both the verse's scene-setting narrative and the chorus's exhilarating release and promise of salvation. The absence of backing singers and the slow tempo of the verse leave ample space that Jackson, in understated dialogue with pianist Mildred Falls and the anonymous organist, exploits to phrase the lyric and repeat words as she desires. Jackson's composure on *Toast of the Town* is notable and impressive, as she worked the darkened audience like a confident pro, glancing from side to side with no sign of nervousness. On the Sullivan show, she was the consummate storyteller, subtly gesturing with her hands almost in the manner of a musical theater performer to highlight the isolation of the deserted island, the rolling sea, awestruck John falling to his knees, and most conspicuously the cleansing of the garments, which Jackson depicted with a pantomime of scrubbing clothes on a washboard, an activity she knew all too well. This physical movement seemed to goose Jackson's energy, conviction, and comfort, as she indulged herself the vernacular pronunciation "washin' dey garments." The interpolated hand claps, touch of growl, and brief moment of dancing with herself accentuated the emotional payoff of a line that she clearly relished swinging as forcefully as she could:

Oh, they're comin' on up, comin' on up
Through great tribulay-ayyy-shun-nuh . . . !

After taking her time in the verse, Jackson, exhibiting her characteristically idiosyncratic handling of the words, cut to the chase in the chorus, abandoning
the final line and thus the end rhyme of Brewster's poem to instead sing "Well,
we're gonna march all around my God's throne," a lyric borrowed from a very
similar gospel song, Charles Bridges's "I Am Bound for Canaan Land."[12] Her delivery of the chorus most closely matched the ministerial authority of Coates's
performance in its propulsive swing, which Jackson liked to call "bounce." In this
sense, the rhythmic commitment of Jackson's darting attacks and cutoffs and her
strong, sustained notes in the television performance more than compensated
for the dynamic solo-group interaction on the Steadman, Anderson, and Coates
recordings and surpassed even the more regular phrasing on Jackson's Apollo
side. On record, Jackson simply repeated the chorus, but on the Sullivan show she
drifted slightly toward the audience, as if tempted to "walk the floor" like she
might at a church program, and sang a new verse drawn from Isaiah 63. Jackson
used word repetition to further ratchet up the rhythmic energy before bringing the
song to a close with a dramatic slowing down in the final line:

Well, well, you know Isaiah said he saw
Saw the Lamb of God, Mary's holy baby
He had his dyed, his dyed, dyed garments on, dyed garments on
He was comin' on up, comin' on up through great tribulation
Well, we've got to march all around my God's throne, yeah

Jackson was in extraordinary voice that Sunday night. "She gave a tremendous
performance," Sullivan remembered. "My personal reaction was that she should
be in opera." The sheer muscularity of her singing and her total command of the
performance space—cameras caught the almost flirty glance shot heavenward at
the line "He was comin' on up"—produced a document of Jackson's artistry at the
height of her power and of a national coming out of sorts for black gospel singing.

Exceptionalism

Like all nationally mediated black performances in the early television era,
Jackson's appearance on *Toast of the Town* mattered significantly to African
Americans. One of Jackson's closest associates, singer Brother John Sellers, who
was mentored by Jackson, characterized her performance on the show as a dividing line in her career. By 1950, "a lot of people would see Mahalia, but they,"

Sellers remembered, referring to the broader entertainment industry, "didn't pay attention to her. . . .She was really big among the church people—but she hadn't did the *Ed Sullivan Show* then." In an interview three years later, another Jackson friend and gospel-singing protégé, Princess Stewart, told a newspaper reporter that her ambition was "to reach the heights of Mahalia Jackson and to sing on Ed Sullivan's *Toast of the Town*." In September 1952, popular Dayton, Ohio, disc jockey Harold "Brother James" Wright was praised for his "expert promotion" of a Jackson concert when he billed the gospel singer as a *Toast of the Town* artist, "reminding the public of her successful appearance early this year on the nation-spanning Ed Sullivan telecast." An emotionally overwhelmed Jackson was greeted in Dayton with a parade that reportedly drew 50,000—dwarfing the recent reception for President Truman, locals said—and a sold-out concert at the city's largest venue, 5,000-seat Memorial Hall.[13]

The black press also recognized the moment as newsworthy. A captioned photo in the *New York Amsterdam News* showed Jackson shaking hands with Brooklyn Dodgers infielder Jackie Robinson, who broke the color line in Major League Baseball in 1947: "Real point of the get-together here is because Jackie Robinson wanted to congratulate Miss Jackson on her recent debut on television via the Ed Sullivan Show. Her appearance was the first time a gospel singer has appeared on a nationally televised video show." Commentators on Jackson's television engagement ranged from *Baltimore Afro-American* columnist E. B. Rea, who simply noted "Mahalia Jackson, gospel singer, made her coast-to-coast debut on Ed Sullivan's *Toast of the Town*," to S. W. Garlington, managing editor and entertainment writer for the *Amsterdam News*, who offered a more extensive postmortem. Perhaps recognizing that opportunities to showcase black talent via a powerful new medium were precious, Garlington, though willing to cut Sullivan some slack, expressed disappointment that the host failed to grasp the significance of being the first to introduce not just a "tremendous Negro singer" but an entire stylistic category, black gospel singing, to a national television audience.

> Mahalia Jackson, the Queen of Gospel Singers, was seen on the Ed Sullivan "Toast of the Town" variety presentation Sunday: but Ed, who is usually very nice to his guests, didn't treat her right. His introduction of Miss Jackson and her art (Gospel singing), and the way the cameras worked on her, and the general lack of build-up certainly did her no good. Since Sullivan has heretofore been an O.K. guy, here's hoping he will have her back and give her a proper build-up, so that the general public (those who do not understand Gospel music) can have a fair chance to judge what makes Mahalia truly great in her respective field.[14]

Sullivan's description of the forty-year-old singer as "a middle-aged Negro" and his hurried transition to Spitalny over the sustained applause for Jackson's performance without acknowledging her in any way must have struck some as a bit gauche. But Garlington's dissatisfaction with Sullivan's prepping of the audience for what they were going to see and hear betrayed his recognition that *Toast of the Town* was presenting both an individual and a heavily racialized musical practice. Curiously, Garlington makes no mention whatsoever of Jackson's cracking performance, leaving one to wonder if flattering production and Sullivan's imprimatur were a prerequisite for white Americans being able to "understand" the music. We can almost discern his lack of confidence that the art of gospel singing and Jackson's "truly great" ability as a practitioner of the art had a "fair chance" of standing on their own feet in the shadow of stereotypical notions about black musical performance, or perhaps his anxiety that the performance *would* speak for itself, but with a less than comely dialect. Nonetheless, Garlington's sense that a "proper build-up" of Jackson and the reception of black gospel singing by the "general public" were joined at the hip is a provocative lead worth following.

The Sullivan show might seem like a counterintuitive place to begin a book on Mahalia Jackson and black gospel music, but as my unpacking of her appearance on *Toast of the Town* hopefully shows, this moment, approached with a commitment to accounting for as much as we possibly can, introduces a bounty of issues that help illuminate post-war gospel: the production and circulation of gospel repertory; the documentation of gospel music on record; gospel's various ensembles and performance approaches; how biblical scripture becomes gospel song and how, through performance, this shared repertory becomes personal testimony; the professional aspirations of gospel singers; the reception of gospel singing by African Americans beyond the context of the black church; questions of race, representation, and mediation; the salience of both collective protest and individual prestige in the black freedom struggle; and, not least, the place of U.S. popular culture *within*, not in opposition to, the black gospel music field. Jackson's nationally televised performance also suggests two avenues for thinking about her career and the field of black gospel music in the decade following World War II. Both of these trajectories are linked to perennial claims of exceptionalism about black gospel music and about Jackson.

By "black gospel music" I refer specifically to a repertory of songs, distinct from traditional "Negro spirituals," that began to be consciously promoted in novel ways by African American musicians and entrepreneurs around 1930 and proliferated more extensively after World War II; to the improvisatory, Pentecostal-influenced singing style that became popularized by singers of both these songs and earlier repertory; to the institutions and agents, both church-affiliated and independent, that supported their production and circulation; and to the black religious subjects and fan base that shaped the aesthetic, evangelical, cultural, and entertainment ideals that gave the music its value. I intentionally tend toward a definition that emphasizes production, dissemination, and reception. A host of other writers have productively detailed musical components commonly associated with African American–identified singing styles that Pearl Williams-Jones has called "in large measure the essence of gospel." Williams-Jones and Horace Clarence Boyer, both of whom were gospel singers, have highlighted such elements as expressive use of vocal timbre, melodic ornamentation, pitch fluidity, a flux between a sharply chiseled pulse and elastically rendered rhythm, quasi-sermonic phrasing, and textual interpolation.[15] The cataloguing of these features has served an important function, often forming the basis of a reading of black gospel as a register of West African cultural retentions that result in an African American vernacular distinctiveness, as a "crystallization of a black aesthetic" and a "symbol of ethnicity," in the words of Williams-Jones and Mellonee Burnim, respectively. Historian Penny Von Eschen communicates this commonly held view when she describes gospel musicians as "artists whose performance style is emblematic of black particularity."[16] The reviewer for *Variety* represented gospel singing—along with Tio's talking parrot—as a "pace-changer," which in vaudeville terms suggests a performance that breaks the established routine, adds variety, represents a discernible shift from what came before, and serves as preparation for something to come. But black gospel singing as a "change of pace" also suggests a performance perceived as separable from its broader context, as something to be enjoyed almost like the earmarked pleasure of an *amuse-bouche* set off from the meat-and-potatoes familiarity of what are often perceived to be conventional cultural forms. Sonically and experientially, black religious performativity is something else.

Because of this exceptionalism, Garlington urged, it took dedicated work to equip "those who do not understand Gospel music" with a frame of reference that would give them a sufficiently "fair chance to judge" the music. This fascination with the exceptionalism of black religious musical performativity extends as far back as the arrival of black Africans in the Americas and in many ways has never left us.[17] For many listeners, part of the work of "black gospel music" has been to conjure difference, whether for the purpose of legitimizing oppressive, racialized hierarchies of power and subordination or to marshal politically progressive cultural nationalist energies. The question of why practices of African American church music have been continuously present and audible throughout U.S. history yet often remain knowable to many observers only through the *frisson* of cultural distinctiveness is one of the curiosities that intrigues me about black gospel singing, which began to circulate within U.S. popular culture in new and transformative ways after World War II.

Some readers will undoubtedly and perhaps justifiably question my choice to address black gospel apart from white traditions of gospel music, in particular

those styles identified since the 1970s as "Southern gospel."[18] Among those calling
for a less segregated history of gospel music is musicologist Stephen Shearon, a
historian of Christian sacred music who was a major contributor to the recently
revised entry on gospel music in the *Grove Dictionary of Music and Musicians*, a
cornerstone reference source in the field. In light of the "confusion" caused by
the fact that "gospel music" was already in circulation in the United States as early
as the second half of the nineteenth century and the perception that "many fans
of African American gospel are convinced absolutely that Thomas A. Dorsey is
'The Father of Gospel Music,'" Shearon argues, "it becomes clear that we have
a problem." It is essentially a problem of nomenclature that "reflects the contemporaneous understandings of persons in the Christian music industry, *not
that of historians*" (emphasis in the original). As a remedy, Shearon seeks a more
"coherent narrative of gospel music history in America," one that acknowledges
gospel's "various cultural and stylistic manifestations and the relationships between them." Making the claim—an extraordinary and debatable one, I think—
that "prior to the mid-1970s few, if any, distinctions appear to have been made
between the music of the various gospel music cultures," Shearon calls upon
music historians to solve "the obvious problems inherent in the present historiography" by adopting the umbrella term "Gospel music phenomenon." Such a cor-
rective "likely would mean that the term 'gospel music' would be reserved for the
phenomenon as a whole, and additional qualifiers or more-specific terminology
would be developed to refer to specific traditions and styles in a way that explains,
too, the relationships between them."[19] Black gospel matters, some say? *All* gospel
matters, Shearon seems to counter.

Shearon's plea is legitimate and well meaning, though its hoped-for intervention strikes my ears and sensibilities as curiously muddying both the spirit
and letter of gospel music historiography. First, the "problem" of Dorsey's identification as the "Father of Gospel Music" is an unnecessary straw man. Surely
this honorific is intended not to credit him with inventing "gospel music" from
scratch but rather to convey Dorsey's central role in catalyzing the modern black
gospel song movement, above all for his leadership in establishing gospel choirs
in Chicago's Baptist churches and cofounding the National Convention of Gospel
Choirs and Choruses in 1932. As late as mid-century, many African Americans
still considered "black gospel" a new and modern music phenomenon, and not
because they didn't know their history. Kenneth Morris, a respected Chicago-
based composer, arranger, and publisher who was influential among black church
musicians, undoubtedly had Dorsey in mind when in 1949 he noted "the enormous popularity and public reception" of modern gospel music, "due in a great
part to the exemplary efforts of the pioneers in this field, who have sacrificed their
time and efforts to make this new type of music popular." Black newspapers also
lauded Dorsey, who "blazed the trail, pioneered the field, made a new market,

and brought to the churches throughout America new life and spirit through his gospel songs."[20] It is indeed true, as Shearon reminds us, that the eclectic Connecticut-born composer Charles Ives incorporated "gospel songs" into some of his modernist compositions, most of which were written before 1918. But in a field of musicology already overwhelmingly white in constituency and Eurocentric in orientation, the far greater benefit for fellow scholars and our students would be to shed *more* clarifying light on Dorsey's distinctive achievements and influence—No, he was not a Swing Era trombonist—instead of casting his reception as a conundrum in need of being solved by a heroic cavalry of music historians.

Shearon's call also strikes me as rooted in a problematic distinction between what he calls the "fundamentals of gospel music history" and historiographical concoctions. It is a distinction that privileges the intellectual abstraction of style history over the messiness of cultural politics and that too conveniently shunts the vagaries of racial separation, partially reflected in the "various cultural and stylistic manifestations" of gospel music, onto the music industry. To be sure, stylistic categories are more often than not the product of market-driven fiction—if a fiction that musicians have had to apprehend to make their livelihood—but no more or less so than the belief that shared musical features and repertory trump lived social realities. Because of *de jure* and *de facto* segregation, African Americans and whites across the nation did, and still do—despite concerted efforts toward "racial reconciliation" within Christian ministries in recent decades—by and large, worship separately.[21] Yet African Americans resourcefully developed publishing and performance networks so that gospel songs penned by black composers could see the light of day. Singers cultivated styles of performance that spoke both to the evangelical aims of this repertory and to the expectations of audiences who often made sense of the cultural specificity of these activities by understanding them as somehow articulate of the experiences of black people living in the United States. Thinking laterally among traditions of American gospel music and bringing to light heretofore obscured stories about race, region, and religion, as Shearon hopes to do, is a notably valuable, even valiant, endeavor. But doing so need not efface the still much needed work of critically assessing how African Americans negotiated their identities as Christian subjects and as raced U.S. citizens in the process of developing a recognizably distinct style and practice—black gospel music—that has had enormous global impact. Whatever the interrelationships that constitute the broader "Gospel music phenomenon" and notwithstanding the discursive complexity and potentially new questions we might bring to interrogating "black gospel music," the latter, precisely because of its dogged exceptionalism, both real and imagined, presents itself to me as a viable and essential object of independent study. What the hurts of history have put asunder cannot so unproblematically be joined together.

Jackson's live performance of "These Are They" on *Toast of the Town* invites us to consider a second exceptionalism: Jackson's own situatedness with respect to the black gospel field more broadly. "When Mahalia appeared on national shows, she would sing songs that everyone knew. Spirituals or inspirational songs like 'I Believe,'" said Heilbut, an influential gospel historian, critic, and producer. "But in one of her earliest appearances on national television—on, of all places, the *Ed Sullivan Show*—she sings with the power that had wrecked churches in Chicago."[22] Holding up Jackson's *Toast of the Town* performance as a rare instance of the real Jackson singing real gospel where you would least expect to find either—thus distinguishing the black-cultural Jackson known among Chicago church folk from the pop-cultural Jackson "everyone knew"—Heilbut calls attention to the persistent question of how to assess Jackson's performances over the course of a near half-century-long career within the broader field of gospel.

What did people mean when they called Jackson the "Queen of the Gospel Singers"? What exactly was she the "Queen" of? After migrating from New Orleans to Chicago in late 1931 at the age of twenty, Jackson sang in the choir at Greater Salem Baptist Church and in a pioneering gospel group, the Johnson Singers, before going on to perform almost exclusively as a soloist. Jackson built her reputation gradually on the Chicago church circuit and as a traveling song-plugger for Dorsey. She made her first commercial recordings for Decca in 1937 but her true breakthrough came in early 1948 with the unprecedented response to her double-sided single for independent label Apollo Records, "Move On Up a Little Higher," which outsold Apollo's better promoted jazz, rhythm and blues, and pop releases on the way, reportedly, to becoming black gospel's first million-seller. Between 1946 and 1950, Jackson was presented by New York gospel promoter Johnny Myers in a series of concerts at Harlem's Golden Gate Auditorium and at several additional local concerts scheduled to meet the overwhelming demand. Jackson's name was still largely unknown among white audiences, other than discophile connoisseurs, but the enthusiasm generated by her Apollo recordings and her New York triumphs brought her extraordinary acclaim as a soloist among black gospel fans nationwide (Figures 1.1 and 1.2).

In the fall of 1954, Jackson left Apollo to become a radio, television, and recording artist for the CBS network and its subsidiary Columbia Records. Major label production and coast-to-coast distribution dramatically heightened Jackson's visibility among audiences beyond her black church base. Yet over time, the rub of Jackson's church roots and pop-cultural celebrity made her a field-straddling anomaly: a singer who was recognized as an extraordinary artist and marketed as the premier exemplar of black gospel music yet whose commercially successful religious albums for Columbia often featured a production style and a repertory of middle-of-the-road religious pop that made some dyed-in-the-wool gospel lovers, and at times even Jackson herself, long for the good old days. Thus in some accounts, we find Jackson cast as both representing and misrepresenting the black gospel field, selling gospel to the world while selling out herself. The

FIG. 1.1 Mahalia Jackson singing at Gillis Memorial Church in Baltimore, February 1949. Gillis pastor Rev. Theodore C. Jackson listens in the far left background. Photograph by Paul Henderson. Maryland Historical Society, HEN.00.A2-254.

Queen's "regal status had obviously isolated her," Heilbut argues.[23] The long arc of Jackson's career, and in particular its exceptional dimensions, has, in short, both affirmed and been complicated by what is indicated by the signifier "black gospel music."

Black Gospel Scholarship in Word and in Sound

For many of her admirers, Jackson's eminence as a gospel singer is taken for granted. Publicity materials for a 2015 symposium in her hometown of New Orleans proclaimed: "Mahalia Jackson defined gospel music in the 1940s and she went on to become the most powerful voice in the history of sacred music in America."[24] But the meanings of Jackson's qualitatively distinct fame as a gospel singer—success that places her, it would seem, in an exceptional position within the black gospel field—remains an unsettled and looming question in gospel literature, a body of work that presents a wealth of opportunities for future scholars. With its still thriving practice and its transformative impact on popular music since the 1950s, black gospel singing has generated an ample bibliography. The

FIG. I.2 Mahalia Jackson in performance at Gillis Memorial Church in Baltimore, February 1949. The predominance of women in the pews is striking. Photograph by Paul Henderson. Maryland Historical Society, HEN.01.11-053.

past forty years have seen a number of historical studies[25] as well as monographs and edited collections on individual singers, groups, and composers,[26] and on individual styles of gospel music, especially male quartet singing.[27] There have also been a healthy number of studies focusing on local gospel traditions[28] and on the cultural-historical interpretation of black gospel.[29] Ethnomusicologist Mellonee Burnim deserves special mention for her prolific research and publications on various aspects of black gospel music history and practice.[30]

Somewhat paradoxically, because of the sheer number of groups that were recorded by independent labels and the relative inaccessibility of these limited-release records in the present day, recordings—and their fastidious collection—have been the lifeblood of documenting pre-1980 gospel and they too belong to this body of scholarship. Devoted gospel discophiles in the United States and in Europe continue to play an indispensible role in knowledge production about black gospel music. Fans and scholars have been heavily reliant upon those record collectors who have spearheaded a steady stream of compilation releases organized by artist, region, record label, or personal taste. Most influential have been those focusing on gospel music recorded in the two decades following World War

II, a period commonly celebrated in literature and in commercial marketing as the "Golden Age of Gospel," during which black gospel attained unprecedented productivity, visibility, popularity, and, some gospel aficionados insist, artistic heights. Opal Louis Nation's Pewburner Records has offered the broadest and most systematically organized catalogue of reissued material, but it is only one of many introductions to recordings from black gospel's "Golden Age."[31]

Radio shows with hosts spinning "vintage" or "classic" black gospel records have also provided important opportunities for exposure to historical recordings and connoisseurial expertise. Foremost among these are Linwood Heath's *Precious Memories* on WNAP in Philadelphia, Robert Marovich's *Gospel Memories* on WLUW in Chicago, Kevin Nutt's *Sinner's Crossroads* out of WFMU in Jersey City, New Jersey, and Mike McGonigal's *'Buked and Scorned* on KXRY in Portland, Oregon. Launched for the purpose of "reinstituting gospel's central place within the history of American popular music," Gospel Roots of Rock and Soul, an ambitious project funded by the Pew Center for Arts and Heritage and involving Heath, Marovich, and other prominent advocates of the music, will culminate in a national radio documentary, scheduled for 2019.[32] A significant recent development in recording-based "Golden Age" gospel scholarship is the Black Gospel Restoration Project at Baylor University, directed by Professor of Journalism, Public Relations, and New Media Robert Darden. Darden established the archive in 2005 "to identify, acquire, preserve, record and catalogue the most at-risk music from the black gospel music tradition" with an ultimate goal of housing "a copy of every song released by every black gospel artist or group" from 1940 to 1980.[33] Cedric Hayes and Robert Laughton's massive discography of black gospel recorded since World War II, now in its third edition, has become an indispensible tool for gospel researchers faced with the onerous task of establishing the dating of and personnel on often obscure releases.[34]

By a considerable margin, writers have devoted more attention to Mahalia Jackson than any other single black gospel figure, though even in her case the pickings are slim and increasingly dated. Jackson has been the subject of three book-length studies: *Movin' On Up* (1966), an autobiography written with journalist Evan McLeod Wylie; *Just Mahalia, Baby: The Mahalia Jackson Story* (1975), published shortly after Jackson's death by journalist and personal assistant Laurraine Goreau; and filmmaker Jules Schwerin's *Got to Tell It: Mahalia Jackson, Queen of Gospel* (1992).[35] The as-told-to autobiography would seem to offer the unique value of the singer's perspective on the contours of her own career, though the reader must proceed with caution in light of Jackson's reported frustration with Wylie's misinterpretation of her oral history and introduction of misinformation. Despite the scant scholarly literature, Jackson has been a strikingly popular subject for biographies targeting younger readers.[36] She has also been the focus of at least seven staged musicals.[37] Jewish African American singer Joshua

Nelson has marketed himself as the "prince of kosher gospel" on the strength of his performances as a Mahalia Jackson vocal impersonator.

Goreau's 600-page book is by far the most comprehensive account since the author, who identifies herself as "Jackson's personally chosen biographer," interviewed over a hundred family members, friends, and associates whose memories were fresh, even raw, because of Jackson's recent death. Indeed, Goreau (1918–1985) reproduced the signatures of eight of Jackson's kin on the back cover as confirmation that the book was "stamped with approval by her closest blood relatives." Judging from the transcripts of her interviews, Goreau was not knowledgeable about gospel music beyond what her informants told her, and the lack of either citations or an index makes the volume a tricky one to navigate. Reading *Just Mahalia, Baby* can also chafe because of Goreau's writing style. An aspiring dramatist, Goreau, who was white, used self-consciously colloquial language, fragmentary phrasing, ungrammatical syntax, and deliberate misspellings to mimic the manner and spontaneity of Jackson's speaking voice—a rare instance of vernacular *non*fiction—resulting in a narrative voice that confronts the reader with the nagging distraction of authorial performance. A passage from the book describing Jackson's early years in Chicago is representative.

> Weekends, catch the train with Dorsey, sing, meet the people, make it back in time for school. No homework. Thank You Jesus! And Ike a peaceable man. Bad enough with the snow and now Big Alice to be seen to, feel so bad. Watch her medicine, the doctor said. They did, Halie and John between them. Big Alice grew worse. Pneumonia, the doctor said. Stay with her then—school have to wait. Halie's anyway; she made John keep on.[38]

A reader might also be troubled by strong hints of Goreau's racial fascination, suggested, to give just one example, by an observation about how "a grin lit her smooth brown skin" as Jackson shared anecdotes.[39] Nonetheless, gospel scholars are deeply indebted to Goreau for a book full of extraordinary detail, insider information, and vital leads salvaged from likely oblivion. *Just Mahalia, Baby* has been the single most valuable source on Jackson's life and career to date and it is indispensable reading for any serious researcher working on Jackson. The recent recovery of Goreau's papers by the Hogan Jazz Archive, including most of her recorded interviews and transcripts, presents fresh opportunities for direct study of her sources in a form closer to their own words.

Schwerin's book on Jackson represents the author's "personal impressions and reactions to the curve and events of her life," inspired by his "lifelong obsession" with her voice. The book is not without merit, drawing on interviews that Schwerin conducted with Jackson for the purpose of making a documentary film. Beyond Jackson, Schwerin's principal sources are two figures that were particularly close to the singer early in her career, Brother John Sellers and Studs Terkel. Commendably, the author devotes considerable attention to Jackson's long-time accompanist Mildred Falls. Over the course of the book, however, Schwerin's credibility crumbles in the face of an often misguided, shoot-from-the-hip representation of Jackson and her character. This is most alarming when Schwerin discusses Jackson's appearance in Douglas Sirk's 1958 remake of the 1934 movie *Imitation of Life*.

The plots of both films focus on the relationship between two single mothers—one white, the other black—and the fate of the "tragic mulatto" daughter of the latter. In the earlier version, black actress Louise Beavers plays Delilah Johnson, who works as a maid for Bea Pullman, the white protagonist played by Claudette Colbert. Not surprisingly for its time, Beavers is asked to deliver a performance trafficking heavily in mammy and Aunt Jemima stereotypes. Delilah's character, renamed Annie Johnson and played by Juanita Moore, is revised significantly in the later film, which is built around a more socially level relationship with her employer Lora Meredith, played by Lana Turner. According to Moore, producer Ross Hunter pitched the role of Annie to Jackson and persuaded her to audition, but Jackson rejected the part. Jackson did make a cameo appearance in the final climactic scene, singing the traditional spiritual "Soon I Will Be Done with the Trouble of This World" at Annie's funeral. Schwerin's bizarre analysis lays bare the inescapable conclusion that he did not bother to watch the film. He is unaware of Sirk's makeover of Delilah and incorrectly reports Jackson's role and the song that she sang—apparently at her own funeral—yet moralizes self-righteously about Jackson's "decision" to play a demeaning character.

> Mahalia's role was that of the Louise Beaver update, a segregation-era caricature of the happy "colored" servant. For the big, pivotal scene, the studio hired a Hollywood church and added a mob of screaming extras. Mahalia was persuasive when she sang, delivering a robust rendition of the 23rd Psalm from the pulpit. In the funeral scene she cried, magnificent and voluptuous, on cue.
>
> I never did get the chance to ask her whether she thought that the Hollywood money justified her ill-advised performance in the movie.[40]

It is difficult to decide which is more infuriating: that Schwerin, in a book on a major figure of twentieth-century American music, would approach the delicate question of racial representation with such cavalier negligence, or the fact that, having not seen the film, he simply *presumed* that Jackson would play the "voluptuous" mammy-fied maid—perhaps revealing Schwerin's "impressions" of Jackson—and then cast aspersions on Jackson's personal ethics for doing so. This is particularly troubling because, as I discuss in Chapter 9, the real-life Jackson had to carefully negotiate historically situated anxieties of some African Americans that she might be perceived by white observers as fulfilling this very stereotype. To corroborate his reading of the film, Schwerin goes on to claim, again incorrectly, that in 1957 Jackson was "costumed as a rocking-chair, bandana-head Mammy" in a television appearance with Bing Crosby and Dean Martin. In fact, on the show, Jackson, who sang her often-performed medley of Gershwin's "Summertime" and the spiritual "Sometimes I Feel Like a Motherless Child," is not wearing a headscarf, her only "costume" is a dark-colored dress, and Crosby and Martin are also seated in rocking chairs. Elsewhere, Schwerin writes: "Mahalia was no reader so she *could not* have read the seminal novel of Ralph Ellison, *Invisible Man*"— meaning, presumably, that she "could not have read" the Bible either. In another example of Schwerin's underestimation of his subjects, he recycles the stubbornly resilient canard about the dedicated and formally trained civil rights activist Rosa Parks: "Until the evening of December 1, she was a non-political woman. But this evening she was especially tired."[41]

I delineate this remiss—Schwerin's paternalistic tone and blithe comfort with making things up as he goes along—because his book, now a quarter of a century old, is the most recent monograph on Jackson, pointing to the urgent necessity for more critical, more original, and less impressionistic scholarship on Jackson and on black gospel music, driven by more intellectually ambitious questions. Gerald Early concluded his review of *Got to Tell It* for the *Washington Post* with a caustic but on-the-mark rejoinder on the behalf of subjects who deserve better: "It is, frankly, time to end such nonsense and get down to the business of the serious study of important black artists."[42] Undermining this serious business has been the issue of verifiable sourcing that continues to bedevil gospel scholarship. Despite their respective strengths and contributions, without which the present book would not have been possible, none of the five cornerstone sources on Jackson that present-day researchers have come to rely upon—Goreau, Jackson and Wylie, Heilbut, Schwerin, and Boyer's *The Golden Age of Gospel*—have any citations whatsoever, forcing researchers to take the author at his or her word on often crucial issues. It is encouraging to see the recent appearance of new interpretive and historical work on Jackson, but more is needed.[43] This book endeavors to continue closing that gap.

The Legacy of The Gospel Sound

Occupying a center of gravity within black gospel scholarship is what undoubtedly remains the most influential book on gospel music. Reckoning with its enduring legacy helps to clarify the present book's project. First published in 1971, updated over the course of four editions, and still in print, Anthony Heilbut's *The Gospel Sound: Good News and Bad Times* can be counted among a cluster of foundational books published during a conspicuously fecund period in the 1960s and 1970s that fundamentally shaped existing narratives about American popular music.[44] Born in 1940 in New York to a family of German-Jewish émigrés from Berlin, Heilbut received his PhD in English literature from Harvard in 1966, writing his dissertation on the prose works of D. H. Lawrence. It was during an appointment as assistant professor at Hunter College and New York University that the precocious thirty-year-old wrote *The Gospel Sound*. He has since published books on the cultural impact of German refugee artists and intellectuals in the United States and on writer Thomas Mann, as well as a recent collection of essays on U.S. popular culture with penetrating studies on Aretha Franklin and on the gay and lesbian closet, hardly a closed one, within the black gospel world.[45] As a resource on the history of black gospel music, *The Gospel Sound* is rivaled only by Boyer's *The Golden Age of Gospel*. The latter book, by virtue of Boyer having been both an accomplished gospel performer in the 1950s and 1960s and a productive scholar during his long tenure as a music professor at the University of Massachusetts–Amherst, has also been distinctly influential, particularly among academy-based music scholars.[46]

Along with his deep familiarity with the music, Heilbut's close and sustained personal and professional relationships with the artists themselves—relationships that make the gospel figures he discusses feel more like fully formed, three-dimensional people—are the most valuable currency and source of authority in his writing. In his view, this position made him a singular and singularly valuable commentator on the music. "When my gospel book appeared," Heilbut has written, "I received hostile glances from black cultural nationalists, who viewed me as an interloper, and white intellectuals, who thought I was slumming. The singers themselves were more welcoming."[47] As a teenager, Heilbut "graduated from R&B to gospel," making himself a regular at gospel programs in Harlem. He later launched a still active career as a gospel record producer responsible for albums by several of the heroes in his book as well as compilations of historic recordings that are important contributions to black gospel discography. His most recent is an important collection of rare live recordings by Jackson. The nexus of writing and record production was central to Heilbut's work from his initial foray as a gospel scholar. Publication of *The Gospel Sound* was accompanied by the release of two companion double-LPs for Columbia Records, the first co-produced with John Hammond.[48]

The Gospel Sound is built from individual chapters on influential "Golden Age" gospel singers—almost all of whom, with the possible exception of Mahalia Jackson, undoubtedly remain unfamiliar to most Americans today—and contextualizing excursions on the Holiness church, life on the road, and the gospel radio and recording industries. As reviewers noted upon its publication, *The Gospel Sound* was the first full-length study of black gospel music. In some ways, this was not surprising: in sharp contrast with jazz, blues, and country, the modern black gospel movement was among the least reliably documented and journalistically covered vernacular musics in the United States. But one of Heilbut's core arguments was that the neglect of gospel music communities was far from coincidental. A host of factors conspired to prevent gospel's master practitioners from receiving the attention they deserved: the fundamental insularity of the black church, principled rejection of modern trends by the truly faithful, the "impenetrable mystique" of Pentecostal styles of worship, intellectual disdain for traditional gospel on the part of African American youth, the failure of gospel fans to support their own, exploitation by music industry profiteers and derivative crossover singers, and, underlying it all, the general disregard for and social invisibility of poor, urban black people.

Unfamiliarity with black gospel beyond African American communities and white insiders like Heilbut made the music "the best-kept secret of ghetto culture," but it also revealed a tragic side of the story. *The Gospel Sound* is both an unapologetic expression of fandom—Heilbut describes himself as a "gospel monomaniac"—and an unflinching manifesto. Black gospel music is "the most important black musical form since jazz" (xxix) and "gospel voices are easily the most phenomenal outside of opera" (xiii). The two dominant forms of popular music when the book was written, soul and rock, were inconceivable without gospel, Heilbut insists. And yet its artists, especially the music's pioneers, soldiered on, unacknowledged and unremunerated: "A few gospel publishers and promoters have made fortunes, but for most of the singers, gospel pays like unskilled labor" (257). Emphasis on the poverty of black gospel singers, "the most underpaid" artists in America (xi), and the rugged hardship of gospel singing as a means of subsistence is in many ways a lynchpin of the book's rhetorical strategy, enabling Heilbut to pursue several narrative threads. Bessie Griffin and Dorothy Love Coates are identified, respectively, as "the barefoot girl" who "was one of the best black singers in America" (137) and as "a poor black asserting herself against all odds" (169). Running in parallel with Heilbut's praise of the singers he most admires is commentary on the injustice of true artistic talent unrewarded, the aesthetic bankruptcy of popular music's lucrative paydays, the paradox of gospel's obscurity despite its omnipresence, and black gospel as a vital "hidden transcript" of ghetto life and politics.[49]

Heilbut's view of black gospel as a critique of modern bourgeois society is detectable in his open admiration for the noble asceticism of gospel's most devout singers, who, though deserving economic prosperity, in the end inspire others to distrust worldliness and contemporary trends. Sallie Martin, one of the earliest organizers of the gospel singing movement in Chicago in the 1930s and later in Los Angeles, "apparently has little faith in modern ways, politics or gospel," Heilbut concludes in his opening chapter. "Sallie will keep being herself, singing the old songs, criticizing the new ways, pushing people to live right" (17). In this

regard, Heilbut also betrays his impatience with late-1960s iterations of black nationalist politics. Soul? "We invented it," an unidentified witness sniffed. "All this
mess you hear calling itself soul ain't nothing but warmed-over gospel" (xi). At its
best, gospel is organic, not processed, "a world complete unto itself" with "a distinctive language, special rhythms, [and] a complex sense of ritual and decorum"
that are emblematic of "its own very superior aesthetic standards."

For Heilbut, there are clear boundaries that call for censure, or at least elu-
cidation, when they are crossed. When Alex Bradford, leader of one of the most
popular gospel groups in the 1950s, refers to his "magnanimous Savior," Heilbut
explains how Bradford occasionally "gets worldly on you, throwing around a large
vocabulary" (145). Sallie Martin and fellow gospel pioneer Willie Mae Ford Smith
insisted that studying church-produced literature is central to their spiritual practice: "Reading? That's all I do," said Martin, with Smith adding: "Holiness is like
going to college." Heilbut was dubious. "One suspects the publications are a bourgeois trapping, curiously contrary to the anti-intellectual bias of the earlier saints,"
he determines, projecting a different sense of virtue. "The very considerable wisdom
of the saints clearly doesn't come from books" (180–81). Arguing passionately and
persuasively for the sublime artistry and far-reaching influence of gospel singing,
and for Heilbut's own social outlook, *The Gospel Sound* seeks to educate readers
about a sequestered music's innovators and cultural settings while also, confronted
with the contagion of flawed American taste, urging sharp discrimination between
originals and pale imitations, transcendent folk artists and pop-cultural decadents,
the steadfast and the sell-outs, the gospel church and "the world."

The Gospel Sound merits special attention because it is difficult to exaggerate
how central the book and its author have been in the production of knowledge
about black gospel music for nearly a half-century. For readers and listeners new
to the music, and even some already familiar with it, Heilbut was perhaps the first
commentator to delineate the meaningful distinction between quartet and gospel
singing in print. *The Gospel Sound* highlights star quartet lead singers, including
Ira Tucker of the Dixie Hummingbirds, R. H. Harris and Sam Cooke of the Soul
Stirrers, Julius Cheeks of the Sensational Nightingales, and Claude Jeter of the
Swan Silvertones; the gospel groups of Clara Ward, Alex Bradford, Dorothy Love
Coates, and DeLois Barrett Campbell; as well as such respected soloists as Willie
Mae Ford Smith, Mahalia Jackson, Marion Williams, and Bessie Griffin, among
other prominent artists and songwriters. Heilbut's projects as a gospel music pro-
ducer have paid homage to, and in some cases revived, the careers of several of
these singers. His astute, if sharply opinionated, critical commentary continues to
be cited by writers verbatim and obituaries for major gospel artists still often quote
Heilbut clarifying their significance.

Heilbut's ability to stimulate and sustain conversation about black gospel has
been particularly impressive. When *The Gospel Sound* first appeared, he claims,

"the assertion that gospel singing supplied the roots for much of contemporary music was not widely accepted; today it seems a received truth" (vii). His most recent book earned extensive national attention for its bold rebuke of what he perceives to be the hypocrisy of black churches that vigorously denounce homosexuality from the pulpit while building its institutions on the financial success of the music of queer men and women who have been the backbone of gospel music.[50] Heilbut's body of work as a writer, producer, and public intellectual has been a powerful, taste-shaping epistemological touchstone, offering listeners valuable guidance toward what they need to know about gospel. My own discovery of the Heilbut quartet compilation *Kings of the Gospel Highway* still stands as a personally impactful encounter with the music. Heilbut is fully aware of his improbable stature as a power broker of gospel knowledge and seems to relish the role. "People are amazed that a German Jewish atheist would be supposedly the world's expert on gospel music," he reflected in a 1996 interview. "And because nothing had ever been written on the subject, I had the pleasure of being able to define things."[51]

Indeed, *The Gospel Sound*'s most inescapable accolade, and a basis for its ongoing authority, is that it is "definitive." The book is rarely referenced without being identified in these terms. In 1991, music critic Robert Christgau wrote that *The Gospel Sound* was "still the definitive—and damn near only—study of the subject twenty years after it first came out." In a 2012 National Public Radio interview, R. J. Smith made the case better than Heilbut himself ever could: "You wrote the definitive overview of gospel music, *The Gospel Sound*, in 1971. You shaped the official story, and the book is still considered something of a standard text." This consensus on the legacy of *The Gospel Sound* can, however, mask certain respects in which its influence and reputation are as complicated as they are extensive and well deserved. Most obvious is a question pertaining less specifically to Heilbut than to the problematics of "master-narratives" identified by Jean-François Lyotard and other postmodernist critics who questioned the tidy power of sweeping definitive accounts, particularly the heterogeneity of human activity that is often sacrificed to the "official story" of metanarratives, a point to which I will return shortly.[52]

The more relevant implications of Heilbut's densely knotted personal musical tastes, commercial activity, and public identity as "the world's expert on gospel music" extend beyond the question of constructing a canon. Heilbut's gospel writing reverberates with a skepticism toward most popular music, particularly in light of his insistence that the very best features of post-war popular music are directly indebted to black gospel. "Singers today still live off the mannerisms developed by the gospel pioneers," Heilbut writes. "Meanwhile, soul radio is booming with decadent versions of the joyful noises gospel invented" (xxx, 275). *The Gospel Sound*'s most scathing vitriol is reserved for the popular music industry itself, the "petty capitalists," "bloodsuckers," and "rock hustlers" who make up "the show-business juggernaut" that engineered the "commercial take-over of gospel."

Heilbut would likely argue, perhaps justifiably and certainly admirably, that his commitment both to producing knowledge about gospel and to maintaining his position of authority has been an important counterweight to the appropriations and distortions of a music business that exploits the work of musicians, especially the black and the poor, by profiting from a derivative, commodified form of their art that erases the identity of the true innovators. Keeping the reception of black gospel on a short leash also communicates Heilbut's concerns over the question of aesthetic judgment. A real challenge to many casual listeners approaching the music is that the sound of many gospel recordings from the 1940s and 1950s, especially quartet performances, remain within a relatively narrow stylistic band-width and can therefore, despite delicious nuances, at a surface level exhibit a basic sonic sameness. Frustration over the tendency of some to enthuse over what he considers an average or even mediocre performance simply because it showcases expected "mannerisms" and fills the right phenomenological prescription—hand clappin', hallelujah shoutin' excitement by singing black bodies—seems to drive Heilbut's determination to steer listeners toward performers and performances that he believes are genuinely worthy of praise.

More suggestive, however, is Heilbut's palpable disappointment when discussing gospel singers who have, in his view, sold their birthright and cashed in on sleeping with the enemy. *The Gospel Sound* grapples continually, though most often only implicitly, with the tension between an appreciation for the her-metic purity of "real" gospel, untainted by "the world," and a desire to see its just compensation and fame in the public sphere as great art. It is highly suggestive that in writing *The Gospel Sound* Heilbut was almost grudgingly forced to recon-cile the myriad ways gospel singers themselves perceived and navigated the re-lationship between their religious convictions and their socioeconomic desires, between their identification with gospel singing and their catholic musical tastes, between the functions of black religion and the form, fashion, and finan-cial realities of commercialized popular music. Ultimately, even acknowledging *The Gospel Sound*'s indisputable importance, I find that in telling the story that the Heilbut of 1971 found most important—one emphasizing cultural insularity and an idealist conception of transcendent art—many concerns and dynamics that I believe are central to a fuller understanding of the post-war black gospel field fall by the wayside. This suggests to me that what twenty-first-century black gospel scholarship needs most is not a newly burnished definitive account but, rather, more stories. Questions regarding boundaries, values, prestige, and the complexity of subject positions that insistently percolate to the surface in *The Gospel Sound* help to pinpoint the fundamental issues that animate the present book.

The Black Gospel Field

This book addresses two interconnected subjects. It is a study focusing primarily on Mahalia Jackson's life and career as a gospel singer up through her first year as a CBS and Columbia Records artist in 1954–1955. The story ends here because, as I show in my final chapters, it represents a seam in Jackson's career, marked by the end of her radio and television shows, her work with her first producers at Columbia, Mitch Miller and George Avakian, a conspicuous broadening of her audience that made her a public figure in a qualitatively different way, and a bout of life-threatening illness that forced a reset of her professional activity. But I also hope to stimulate thinking about black gospel music as a field of cultural production. A core principle of field analysis—a premise that I believe yields a less predetermined picture of post-war gospel—is the necessity of assessing the agents, institutions, practices, points of contestation, and forms of capital within an area of cultural production in relational terms. Considering gospel as a "field" accounts for a fuller scope of Jackson's work as a gospel singer while at the same time assesses her position, however singular, within a realm encompassing the activities of countless others. Thinking of Jackson and the gospel field reciprocally also helps to tackle a frustrating methodological problem. Documentation of black gospel, even on recordings, is spotty—Darden estimates that 75 percent of gospel records made from the 1940s to the 1970s have been lost—and with precious few sources to work with, writing on the music has, by necessity, been heavily anecdotal. Fortunately, the rapid ascent of Jackson's career from 1946 through 1955 generated considerable coverage in print and other public media, enabling us to recover some of the texture of black gospel during a period when her professional career and her successes were deeply interwoven with local and national gospel communities.

Within the post-war music industry, references to a "spiritual field" or "gospel field" were common, simply indicating the market for commercially recorded and concert-produced black religious music. Jackson identified herself as among the pioneers who steered a transition from "these gospel singers who didn't do nothing but sing in the church" to "this field that we have created." But here I consider gospel as a "field" in a second sense. Some readers will recognize the field analysis that I am describing as drawing on the ideas of French sociologist Pierre Bourdieu. As anthropologists Paul Silverstein and Jane Goodman have suggested, scholars since the 1970s have found Bourdieu's theories of practice to be "good to think with," and though I am guided more by the methodological spirit than the theoretical letter of Bourdieu's work, several of his foundational ideas have stimulated questions and lines of inquiry that I pursue in the chapters that follow.[53]

A basic principle of Bourdieu's theories of practice and cultural production, one that has hovered spectrally in the background of most gospel literature to date, is the importance of the relations among a diversity of individuated agents, particular works, specific performance practices, values, sources of prestige, and political and economic dynamics within a field. When these issues have been addressed, the tendency has been to use them to define people, performances, and attitudes in or out of the category "real gospel," to separate the wheat from the tares, as Jackson sang on her first record. Bourdieu's dictum "To think in terms of a field is to think relationally" invites more agents and activities into the picture while also pushing us to consider how the picture changes once a field's boundaries are determined relationally instead of prescriptively. What, for instance, would it mean for our understanding of gospel to think of Jackson's performance in New York on a nationally televised Sunday night variety show as part of the same field of cultural production as a Sunday morning performance by Chicago's Pilgrim Baptist Church choir led by Dorsey? How might each performance matter differently to gospel singers, gospel fans, and black church congregations, and with respect to each other? Employing a field analysis approach oriented toward thinking relationally will, I believe, encourage gospel scholars, as David Schwartz has suggested, "to define the broadest possible range of factors that shape behavior rather than delimit a precise area of activity" or "narrow prematurely the range of their investigation." This openness is something I consciously strive to maintain throughout this book. If at times this inclusivity results in what might be for some a disconcerting decentering of the black church, hopefully it has the benefit of foregrounding a richer spectrum of desires on the part of black gospel's performers, producers, and consumers.[54]

Two features of field analysis will anchor my discussion of Jackson and postwar black gospel: a cultural field as a space of possible positions, and the work of species of capital within the field, particularly field-specific forms of prestige. Field analysis of black gospel music highlights internal differences among constituents who orient themselves by means of what Bourdieu refers to as "position-takings." The possibilities are open-ended and vast—too open-ended, some critics of field analysis argue. Within gospel, positions in the field—singer, accompanist, director, evangelist, popular entertainer, recording artist, competitor, curator, business entrepreneur, impresario, fan, "Queen"—can be static or change over time, be driven by spiritual beliefs or material ambition, and/or facilitate business or pleasure. But accounting for the diversity of positions allows us to consider how the field of black gospel presented itself to each agent less as a cultural template than as an unstable "space of possibilities" shaped by multiple factors. As the four recordings of "These Are They" discussed above suggest, we can include specific performances as representing discrete positions as well. Cooperation and contestation among agents occupying different positions in the field produce the distinctive dynamics that define a particular field while also potentially reshaping it. Indeed, changes over time—in this case, the nature, cause, and effect of transformations in the gospel field in the decade following World War II—is one of the developments that I seek to highlight.

Perhaps the most widely influential concept in Bourdieu's theory of cultural production is capital, which in its most basic sense he defines as "species of power . . . whose possession commands access to the specific profits that are at stake in the field." As a form of power, capital, whether economic, cultural, or symbolic, is diversely differentiated. Bourdieu explains the working of capital in a field through the elaborate but elucidating analogy of a parlor game that employs chips, "a pile of tokens of different colors, each color corresponding to a given species of capital." Unlike poker chips, however, capital is qualitative as well as quantitative. Qualitatively different possessions of capital, even when they might be quantitatively equivalent, determine how one plays the game.

> [P]layers can play to increase or conserve their capital . . . but they can also get in it to transform, partially or completely, the immanent rules of the game. They can, for instance, work to change the relative value of tokens of different colors, the exchange rate between various species of capital, through strategies aimed at discrediting the form of capital upon which the force of their opponents rests . . . and to valorize the species of capital they preferentially possess.[55]

The concept of prestige and its diverse forms is a productive way of assessing how species of capital operate in the black gospel field. I would identify four principal forms of prestige that I believe agents in the gospel field recognize and attribute to singers: devout integrity, charismatic artistry, recognition, and pop-cultural cachet. These function as a means through which gospel singers can accrue respect, admiration, esteem, and other specific profits, including, though not limited to, financial reward.

Devout Integrity

It is hard to imagine a gospel singer who would not claim that they sing first and foremost to the glory of the God he or she serves, whether through testifying about a personal relationship with the divine, seeking to inspire this personal connection in others, or communicating a song's religious message. When singers publicly attest from the floor during a program "I don't sing for form or fashion or for outside show," we see how this ethos functions almost as an ante to enter the game. A form of prestige that I will call "devout integrity" is thus conferred upon a singer who persuasively demonstrates his or her religious conviction and sincerity of purpose when singing gospel and, whether they are singing or not, consistently presents theirself in a manner others recognize as a "good Christian" in their day-to-day life. When Heilbut speaks of R. H. Harris as "the most spiritual man on the road," or identifies the woefully under-recorded Willie Mae Ford Smith as "the greatest of the 'anointed singers,' the ones who live by the spirit and sing to save souls," it is the prestige of devout integrity that he is ascribing to these individuals. The rejection of monetary reward often undergirds the economy of this form of prestige. Noting "the acclaim that soul singers get while gospel singers starve," Heilbut gives Dorothy Love Coates the final word: "Sure those singers get more money, but there's some money so dirty you hate to touch it." Indeed, by coincidence or by mistake, Heilbut attributes almost the exact same quote to Willie Mae Ford Smith ("I need money, I need money *bad*, but there's some money so dirty that you hate to touch it").[56] Jackson herself built a reputation of devout integrity through repeated public rejections of offers to sing secular music or perform in nightclubs, accruing prestige through a self-narrative that, paradoxically, she was able to parlay into considerable wealth as a professional gospel singer, exemplifying what Bourdieu called the "double reality" of symbolic capital.

Charismatic Artistry

Even when it is most fundamentally a form of testimony or evangelism, gospel singing is musical performance, and singers accrue the most conspicuously available prestige through dynamic performances on programs and on record. Gospel audiences are inseparably bound up with this second form of capital, which I call "charismatic artistry," since it is the reception of a performance or an artist who can "flat out sing" that confers this prestige. For most, the impact of the singing matters most, and gospel literature revels in stories and legends about the effect of great performances on an audience, from barely perceptible but hair-raising vocal inflections to such theatrical gestures as blind singers leaping from church balconies, all in an effort to "take the house." Part of the seductive pleasure of Heilbut's gospel writing comes from the shared intimacy and immediacy of accounts of charismatic artistry, allowing us, for instance, to savor anecdotes about how the power of Bessie Griffin's singing "literally killed people," as enraptured listeners at programs were, we are told, mortally stricken by the sound of her voice.[57] In practice, charismatic artistry bleeds into devout integrity, or vice versa, as gospel singers speak of "making the spirit come," or singing to audiences amid white-uniformed deaconesses standing by to assist members of the congregation who "get happy" when the spiritual presence of a performance fills them to overflowing.

For many post-war gospel singers, charismatic artistry was often more technical than spectacle. An innovative style, or simply stylishness, could be acquired through close study. Robert Marovich has characterized gospel programs as "lecture halls" that "served as classrooms for emerging singers and musicians," particularly in cases—Church of God in Christ (COGIC) churches, for instance, where hymnbooks were less often used during worship—in which music literacy was not a requisite skill.[58] Meticulous observation of respected artists was the core curriculum of a gospel classroom. Several outstanding quartet singers I have interviewed, including Otis Clay, Garnett Mimms, and Howard Tate, all of whom enjoyed successful crossover to popular music, expressed their deep admiration for Ira Tucker, lead singer of the Dixie Hummingbirds. Clay earned the nickname "Little Tucker" for modeling his vocal and visual style so closely on the singer. According to Therman Ruth Jr., Tucker drove crowds wild during shows at Harlem's Apollo Theater with his signature move of shedding his suit jacket at climactic moments of his performance. Mimms remembered marveling at how Tucker, "a real master in changing up and making himself sound different," would showcase his vocal dexterity. Tate received his gospel education listening to elite quartet leads at the Metropolitan Opera House in Philadelphia, known locally as the Met: "I would go down there every time they came to town to listen at them, very close, so that I could pick up on their music and what they were doing and how they executed their voice into the style they were singing. . . .I didn't go to music school, but they were my teachers."[59]

In an art form in which affecting the audience was a goal of performance technique, stagecraft was an inescapable component of gospel practice. Reverend Doctor Isaac Whittmon remembered that in "us[ing] programs for schooling" he "watched everything," including "how they would move from one song to the other song." Pastor Stephen Hawkins, who recorded as child gospel star "Little Stevie" Hawkins in the 1960s, remembered Jackson's televisual presence as an inspiring object of fascination.

> Mahalia Jackson when she would be on television every year, we would stay up late to see her sing. She would be singing on TV and you could see the seriousness of it and how she would handle it and the way she would move. . . .So, you know, when you're looking and you're studying different people, you not only study *what* they do but you study what *causes* them to do it.[60]

As Bourdieu's poker game analogy suggests, there are exchange rates between forms of prestige. A singer—Sallie Martin comes most immediately to mind—who is legitimated as possessing unassailable devout integrity can garner a reputation for charismatic artistry because of the persuasiveness of their performance, even if, at face value, their vocal talent, technical skill, or sheer virtuosity falls recognizably short of singers like Tucker or Jackson. "Martin's voice was not the most beautiful pipe in the organ," Marovich writes, but "watching Sallie Martin sing was like watching the stern church mother get happy."[61]

Recognition

Devout integrity and charismatic artistry are the available forms of prestige most often focused upon by writers on black gospel music. Other types of prestige further open up our thinking about gospel as a field of cultural production. A third species of gospel prestige is "recognition," the strong form of which is fame, the weaker form being differing types of acknowledgment. In the case of black gospel, recognition first emerged through a local, in-group dynamic well before the music went national. For gospel historians, the narrative of how the movement led by Dorsey, Theodore Frye, Magnolia Lewis Butts, and other members of the "gospel nexus" in Chicago achieved its decisive breakthrough in the 1930s is a story of how the musical worship valued by Southern migrants, by virtue of the stunning breadth of its appeal across congregations, was recognized as legitimate—or at least indispensible for building church membership—among Chicago's established old-line "landmark" churches.[62] Broader recognition subsequently came in many varieties: press coverage; the aura of mediated performances on recordings, on radio, and on television; the quantity and quality of performance opportunities; high-profile tours; billing on gospel programs (as in vaudeville, where one appeared on a program lineup communicated status); or symbolic "victory" in a gospel song battle.

Newspaper reports constantly referenced the prestige of recognition not only in the escalating coverage of Jackson—the "nationally known gospel singer" who is "without a doubt, the most outstanding spiritual singer of the present era" and "is being groomed for a network radio show"—but of other gospel singers as well. If in certain contexts singing to the glory of God was the most salient positioning, in others, celebrity, fame, and reputation, whether local or national, could represent the most immediate attraction for some singers, fans, and commentators, even if admitting as much was impolitic. In fact, from a certain perspective, particularly that of the black press, recognition beyond black communities, among "those who do not understand gospel music," was one of the most important implications of the growing popularity of black gospel singing. Recognition could also help garner a related and more collectively felt form of prestige: racial honor, or a sense of pride at a high level of attainment by black artists. It is clear that to many African Americans, Jackson's appearance on *Toast of the Town* indicated a level of individual recognition that was a powerful source of collective prestige in the form of racial honor.

Pop-Cultural Cachet

As Heilbut discusses, for the overwhelming majority, gospel singing was not a highly remunerative vocation. But when attained, success in material and economic terms was most often linked to the interface of gospel with popular culture.

What I call "pop-cultural cachet," a fourth type of prestige, is less strictly a matter of achieving financial reward than it is a highly specific sense of value suggested by such factors as record and sheet music sales, audience draw, or earnings. These apply to individual singers and groups but also to the gospel field itself. Singers were often identified by the fact that they had a hit record (by gospel standards). The astonishing success of "Move On Up a Little Higher," which sold in great volumes, catapulted Jackson to international recognition, but it also transformed the field by coaxing many more gospel singers to relax their ambivalence toward recording. As Jackson said, "Move On Up" taught gospel singers and the music industry that "you could take religious songs and sing them just like you sing in the church, put them on records, and people would buy 'em."[63]

Attendance and box office figures for gospel extravaganzas—more concretely comprehensible evidence of pop-cultural cachet than a "hit" record—were documented in music trade publications and re-reported enthusiastically in black newspapers. Earnings and attendance numbers were noteworthy to a black press than ran numerous articles trumpeting with considerable relish: "Yessir . . . GOSPEL SINGING is BIG business." African American newspapers enthusiastically promoted the 1952 Gospel Train and reported production costs in the neighborhood of $100,000, with Jackson alone said to have been paid "a juicy $3,000 weekly guarantee" as star of the show.[64] The reality of financial reward, or lack thereof, for the singers themselves is less my concern than the fact that the citing of packed stadiums and auditoriums and eye-popping box office receipts indicates that the prestige of pop-cultural cachet mattered in field-specific ways to gospel singers and their fans.

JACKSON'S SIGNIFICANCE AS an artist and as a public figure merits a study with her as its focus. As she came to prominence in the 1940s and 1950s, her voice was repeatedly compared to the late vaudeville blues singer Bessie Smith by commentators who seized upon her recollection that she closely studied Smith's records when she was growing up in New Orleans. These were most often jazz critics, for whom the representation of Jackson as a latter-day Bessie Smith made the gospel singer legible as a living embodiment of origin myths identifying the blues and black church music as an aesthetic dyad that was the heart, soul, and fountainhead of genuine jazz. But she was also embraced by the entertainment industries as a symbol of religious sincerity and racial rapprochement in the midst of a Cold War in which "godless communism" was the adversary and Jim Crow was an "Achilles heel."[65] Most often, Jackson was expected to represent black gospel music at its best and most genuine, though there was an implicit expectation that she would in fact represent on many levels: African American cultural history, the United States' Judeo-Christian heritage, black respectability politics, the American Dream. Jackson's negotiation of these multiple axes of representation is one of this book's major narrative threads. The period considered here also marked several broader transitions that intersect with Jackson's work as a professional singer within a changing black gospel field: from the ancestral hermeneutics of the Negro spiritual to the modern identity of black gospel; from the dominance of sheet music to the popularization of mobile performances on recordings; from radio to early television; from the last heyday of the American Left to a Cold War that fostered a revival of national religious identity. These years also saw shifting strategies in the black freedom struggle that gave new and perpetually contested salience to African American culture. The fault lines of difference and sameness, of social embeddedness and aesthetic transcendence, of materiality and spirit, are the crux of some of the larger questions probed in what follows, including perhaps the most fundamental one: Under what conditions can black culture and black bodies be recognized?

The unfolding of Jackson's early life and career—her family history in the Reconstruction Era South, her upbringing in New Orleans, her migration to Chicago, and her coming to unparalleled fame as a gospel singer in the 1940s and 1950s—placed her in an exceptional yet integral position within the black gospel field, though it remains a story half told.

2

Family Affairs, Part I

THE CLARKS OF LOUISIANA

THE RECENTLY RECOVERED trove of research material compiled in the early 1970s by Laurraine Goreau, Mahalia Jackson's indefatigable biographer, is housed at the Hogan Jazz Archive on the campus of Tulane University in Uptown New Orleans. Created in 1958 as the Archive of New Orleans Jazz and later renamed in honor of its founding director, Tulane history professor William Ransom Hogan, the archive has since 1998 resided on the third floor of Joseph Merrick Jones Hall. The building's namesake was among New Orleans's most respected citizens. Jones was a prominent attorney who went on to become a political speechwriter for the U.S. State Department, an editor of *Fortune* magazine, and the longtime president of the board for his alma mater Tulane.[1] It was Jones who announced the controversial 1963 desegregation of the university, only to be killed months later under mysterious circumstances in a house fire some suspected to be arson.

After spending the day combing the Hogan's impressive holdings in Jones Hall, a researcher can freshen up and head downtown to catch a show at the Mahalia Jackson Theater in the heart of Louis Armstrong Park. Opened in 1973 as the New Orleans Theater for the Performing Arts, the 2,100-seat venue was renamed in Jackson's honor in 1993 by unanimous vote of the New Orleans City Council. But there is a deeper history linking these two New Orleans landmarks. Joseph Merrick Jones was the great-grandson of Edwin T. Merrick, a chief justice of the Louisiana Supreme court, and the grandson of Civil War officer David T. Merrick. The two elder Merricks were owners of adjacent plantations in the Central Louisiana parish of Pointe Coupée (pronounced poynt koo-PEE) and it was on this land that Paul and Celia Clark, Jackson's maternal grandparents, were born into slavery and raised their family for decades after emancipation before migrating to New Orleans shortly after the turn of the century. Thus it is one of the characteristically provocative twists of U.S. racial history that an esteemed

Louisiana clan became slaveholding overseers of the family of a woman who became an even more glamorously celebrated daughter of New Orleans.

This chapter offers a narrative of the Clark family history from the their residence on the Merricks' Pointe Coupée plantation to Jackson's move from New Orleans to Chicago. But this and the following chapter also raise methodological questions regarding black gospel scholarship and writing on Jackson in particular. The principal source of information on the Clarks and Jackson's childhood in New Orleans is Goreau's 1975 biography *Just Mahalia, Baby*, based on a flurry of interviews that the author conducted mostly within two years of Jackson's death. As indispensible as Goreau's work has been for all subsequent writing on Jackson, gospel scholars have, I believe, engaged her book too uncritically, largely taking its claims and conclusions at face value. The surviving transcripts and recordings of Goreau's interviews at the Hogan Jazz Archive, from which I quote liberally, extend an opportunity to study Goreau's research materials and read them against the eventual rendering of this research as a biographical narrative. Doing so reveals clear and influential choices Goreau made in telling her story, choices that often pertain to facts as fundamental as the year of Jackson's birth. Though I do hope to offer as informed a reading of the evidence as possible and refine our understanding of certain details, I am also interested in suggesting why these seemingly pedantic quibbles matter and in highlighting what they might reveal about Jackson and our habits when we "do" black gospel scholarship.

Merricks and Clarks in Pointe Coupée

David Thomas Merrick was a junior at Centenary College in Jackson, Louisiana, when he left school to enlist in the Confederate army, attaining the rank of captain.[2] The war left him disabled when during combat a Minié ball passed completely through his head; his life was spared only by a miraculous surgery. After the South's surrender, Merrick began life as a cotton farmer, purchasing the Belair plantation at the extreme northwestern edge of Pointe Coupée Parish. Named by the French before Louisiana came under the control of Spain with the signing of the Treaty of Paris in 1763, Pointe Coupée (literally "cut point") had been occupied by Houma and Tunica Native American tribes for millennia. The Atchafalaya, Choctaw for "long river," registered the area's long indigenous presence that was abruptly ended by European colonization. Bordered to the east by the Mississippi River and to the west by the Atchafalaya, Pointe Coupée has been defined geographically and impacted historically by a complex handoff of river flows that brings three powerful waterways into confluence. The Red River completes its 1,300-mile journey by emptying into the Atchafalaya, the fifth largest river in North America by discharge and a major distributary of the Mississippi River. The Atchafalaya then flows onward 140 miles south to the Gulf of Mexico. For

Pointe Coupéeans like David Merrick, whose family plantation still sits today on the banks of the Atchafalaya, adjacency to these mighty rivers meant easy transport of harvested crops to market but also the seasonal threat of devastating flood, both of which figured into Jackson's family history.

Merrick was preceded as a plantation owner in Upper Pointe Coupée by his father, Edwin Thomas Merrick, who as a thirty-year-old Yankee lawyer from Massachusetts married fifteen-year-old Louisianan Caroline Thomas and adopted the South as his home. Edwin and Caroline made their residence in her native East Feliciana, two parishes to the west of Pointe Coupée, then purchased the Myrtle Grove plantation on the Atchafalaya as a second home for them, their four children, and, according to the 1860 slave schedule, the sixty-one African Americans who were their legal property.[3] When Edwin Merrick was elected the third chief justice of the Louisiana Supreme Court in 1855, the family moved to New Orleans but maintained ownership of Myrtle Grove. The momentousness of being a Southern slave owner on the cusp of the Civil War is communicated by Caroline Merrick's extraordinary memoirs. A passionate leader of the women's suffrage movement in Louisiana and a friend of Susan B. Anthony who decried "the great evil of slavery" while also expressing doubts about the capacity of African Americans to thoughtfully execute their status as freedmen, Caroline fled New Orleans in advance of its imminent capture, which, she wrote, "caused me to spend the whole period of the war with my family on the Atchafalaya river" at Myrtle Grove. Throughout the war's duration, she lived on the plantation with her two daughters, her young son, the family servants, and the Union soldiers who took up occupation on their front lawn as a staging ground for the Siege of Port Hudson while her husband remained in New Orleans and her eldest son, David, was on the battlefield. As Confederate defeat became inevitable, Caroline recognized a major concern for slave owners: how to protect their investment by persuading freed slaves to stay and work the land instead "stealing away" to follow the Union army north. In 1900, she recalled her advice to fellow plantation owners that, rather than force, a dose of reason, good faith, and treatment of the freedmen as consenting adults was the most effective strategy.

> [S]tate to them that they might be free just where they were—that it was not necessary they should leave their homes, their little children, their household effects, tools and other "belongings" which could not be carried on the march (to say nothing of the hogshead of sugar nearly all of them had in their cabins), their poultry, dogs, cows and horses. If it were candidly explained to them that their freedom was to be a certainty, and that they might be hired to work by their old owners, doubtless many would be convinced of the wisdom of remaining at home and taking their chances—all would depend on the confidence the negro had in the master—but they

should, in all cases, be left to make their own decision—whether to go or stay. . . .[O]ur slaves remained on the place, and many of them and their descendants are yet in the employ of the family.[4]

It is unclear whether Captain David Merrick took on his parents' ex-slaves as paid workers when he purchased a farm in the unincorporated village of Legonier, or if he hired his own. But the 1880 U.S. census indicates that among the many field hands working on David Merrick's plantation, nicknamed "Gumstump," were twenty-five-year-old Paul Clark, his twenty-two-year-old wife Celia and two of their children, a three-year-old son named Boston and an infant daughter named Isabelle. If it is the case that the Clarks were legally owned by Edwin and Caroline Merrick before working as freedpersons for their son David, then Mahalia Jackson's grandparents were born into enslavement by the chief justice of the Louisiana Supreme Court.

The Clark family called Gumstump home for more than a half-century. Blues musician Buddy Guy (b. 1936), born and raised until the age of fifteen six miles down the road in Lettsworth, remembered the area still in the 1940s feeling like a land beyond time.

> I didn't know it at the time, but we were living and farming like people lived and farmed a hundred years before. When I got my little flour sack and went out in the field, I was doing something my people had been doing ever since we were herded up like cattle in Africa, sent out on slave boats, and forced to work the land of the southern states of America.[5]

Visiting Legonier even today, it is difficult to not to feel the crushing remoteness of its location. Legonier (pronounced leh-GOH-nyuh) is twelve miles due west of Angola State Prison, opened in 1901 on land bought with profits from the slave trade. In the late nineteenth century, Legonier would have been accessible either by ferry across the Atchafalaya from Simmesport in neighboring Avoyelles parish or by wagon from the train station ten miles away in the town of Torras, since wiped off the map by flooding. To Rosa Williams, who knew the Clarks both in Pointe Coupée and in New Orleans, Legonier "wasn't a town. It was pure country."[6] Because of its isolation and Reconstruction Era social organization, Gumstump developed into a relatively self-contained, predominantly black community, one that included a long street of houses, called "the Quarters," where field workers lived with their families and the white wooden St. John Baptist Church, which during the week was converted into a school organized by the Freedman's Bureau. With a post office, a general store, a church, and a school right on the Gumstump plantation, Legonier was a place of visitation for black residents on plantations within walking distance.

Highly respected within his community, Paul Clark was a powerful presence in his family. Born *c.* 1855, he would have been a young child when Abraham Lincoln issued the Emancipation Proclamation in 1863. Our only knowledge about Clark's parents is Goreau's account that "his father [was] the family coachman and his mother the prized cook" for the Merricks.[7] Thomas King, a black Legonier native who worked for David Merrick's daughter Caroline (the mother of Joseph Merrick Jones), is the principal source of information on Gumstump when the Clarks lived there. King remembers Clark as a child attending the school set up at St. John, originally run by white teachers "to educate the black people sufficiently until they could take over and run the school themselves," and learning how to read there. Clark's favorite book was said to be the Bible and he earned a reputation as a man of upright dignity with deep knowledge of scripture who was consulted by young ministers and would himself "take over the pulpit from time to time" and preach at St. John in relief of regular pastor Reuben Hunter. Clark farmed land rented from the Merricks, assisted by his children who, like Buddy Guy years later, worked in the fields picking cotton, the youngest ones cleaning stems, though they also attended school, scheduled around the cotton crop. Overseen by Captain Merrick's son Edwin, Clark was given the additional responsibility of running the cotton gin on the Belair property, an engine that seeded and baled cotton for transport down the river and ground corn into grain during the off-season. When he got up in years, Clark opened a barbershop on the Gumstump plantation and took it up as his main profession. The name of Paul Clark's wife appears in the 1880 and 1900 U.S. censuses, respectively, as "Ophelia" and "Felia." Goreau, however, reports that Bell named her daughter Cecile after her mother, so the discrepancy could be attributable to a mishearing by the census takers, though the same mistake twenty years apart is curious. I will refer to her, somewhat as a compromise, as "Celia Clark." Paul and Celia had their first child around 1877 and over the next twenty-five years she bore as many as thirteen children. She died in Legonier sometime before 1910, never making it out of the country.[8]

The Merricks lived on in Clark family lore, and we get differing accounts of them as employers. Jackson's as-told-to autobiography recounted stories about life in Gumstump attributed to her Uncle Porterfield, said to believe that God would "put a curse on that part of the South" for the way his family was treated by the Merricks. King had a more favorable impression and offered an explanation for why the Clarks remained on the property: "The Merricks were very fine people to work for. Everybody will tell you that. People would stay on from one generation to the next. If the Merricks wasn't good to work for, why would they have stayed? No, the Merricks were fine people to work for, and kind. People stay into the third generation with them." Both perspectives may be true. Working for the Merricks was perhaps the best among the limited, suboptimal choices for a poor, disempowered black family scratching out a living in the Jim Crow South during the collapse of

Reconstruction and the "nadir" of American race relations.[9] Regardless, the Clark children began leaving Legonier around the turn of the century and moved to New Orleans. Paul Clark, by then widowed, finally "went to New Orleans during World War I, like so many of the men did," remembered King. But it is worth underscoring how long the Clarks lived in Pointe Coupée before their migration to New Orleans initiated the next chapter of the family story.

A Child of New Orleans

I came from New Orleans, Louisiana. Way down near the tracks,
as I always like to let people know. I've said that so many times.[10]

Of Paul and Celia Clark's thirteen children, their daughters were the dominant presence in the life of Mahalia Jackson. The "seven sisters" identified by Goreau were Mahala or "Duke" (born *c.* 1878), Isabelle or "Bell" (1879), Charity (1891), Hannah (1896), Alice (1897), Rhoda (1898), and Bessie (1902). There were also two surviving sons, Boston (1877) and Porterfield (n.d.). At least four Clark offspring appeared to have died as small children on the Merrick plantation: sons Cleveland (n.d.) and Harrison (n.d.) and daughters Sarah (1893) and Ollie (1899).[11] As Bessie remembered, "We just come one by one to New Orleans after my mother died," Porterfield being the first to leave Legonier to become a riverboat cook, followed by his intrepid teenaged sister Hannah. Hannah returned to Gumstump in 1910 to retrieve Duke, Bessie, Bell's children Allen and Cecile (known as "Celie"), and Charity and her two-year-old son Roosevelt "Peter" Hunter, shepherding them all to New Orleans by train. According to Allen, Hannah's real motivation was concern for her sister Charity, who had been chronically ill throughout her life and was brought to New Orleans to have access to a fully equipped hospital.[12] This core of four Clark sisters—Hannah, Duke, Charity, and Bessie—became the nucleus of a new family base in New Orleans, joined within a few years by those still remaining up north in the country.

Like Legonier, New Orleans is surrounded by water, encased by Lake Pontchartrain to the north, by a system of human-built inland canals linking up with the Gulf of Mexico to the east, and by the snaking path of the Mississippi River in its southernmost region (Figure 2.1). The city is divided into seventeen districts known as wards, which have been fixed since 1880. A report to the British Board of Trade published the year of Jackson's birth found the upriver part of the city west of the French Quarter, which locals call Uptown, to be notable for its socioeconomic and demographic composition.

There are areas of some magnitude in which no coloured people live, and some districts which are almost exclusively occupied by them. It is only in this inland district that the two races are separated to any considerable

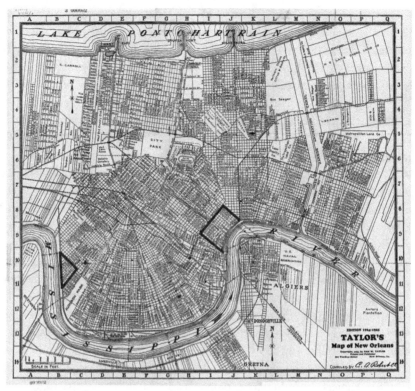

FIG. 2.1 Map of New Orleans, Louisiana, in 1924. The French Quarter is the rectangular area outlined in the center and the "Black Pearl," the neighborhood where Mahalia Jackson was born, is the triangular area outlined to the left. Louisiana Division/City Archives, New Orleans Public Library.

extent. All along the belt between Magazine Street and the river bank, white and coloured people live in close proximity.[13]

The waterfront area where the Clarks settled in New Orleans exhibited similar features but lay even further upriver, four miles from the French Quarter. The family and their neighbors predominantly traversed a geographic space that spanned three socially interconnected wards of the city: the strip adjacent to Audubon Park in the 14th Ward, known as Greenville, that funneled residents and workers toward the bustling Walnut Street wharf; the "Pigeon Town" neighborhood on the Uptown side of Carrollton Avenue in the 17th Ward that hugged the bend of the Mississippi River; and, wedged in between, a triangular enclave in the 16th Ward that some residents still refer to as "Nigger Town." The latter neighborhood, which city planners in the 1970s euphemistically dubbed "Black Pearl," is bordered by Lowerline Street to the southeast, by St. Charles Avenue to the northeast, and to the west by the Mississippi River, along which run the levee, railroad tracks, and the highway road on Leake Street. As late as 1978, this area, pinned against the riverfront by Audubon Park and the grand mansions of St. Charles, was still considered to be a part of the city that existed in "comparative isolation," one to which "no one travels unless his destination is within the neighborhood."[14]

The Clarks lived deep in the heart of this Greenville–Black Pearl nexus, sharing a house on Water Street (now Constance) directly adjacent to Leake Street and the levee that protected the neighborhood from the Mississippi River. According to urban geographer Richard Campanella, the Clark's two-story "shotgun double" on Water Street, though less prevalent than the single-floor double shotgun houses seen throughout the city, was not uncommon in the working-class neighborhoods of turn-of-the century New Orleans and surrounding areas. The photo of the house taken by Bill Russell in 1954 (Figure 2.2) records its extraordinary proximity to passing trains—"way down near the tracks," as Jackson recounted—and, in the left background, the tiny and even more remote batture houses on the other side of the levee, "the abode of transients, homeless, and people living on the margins of society." Jackson vividly remembered the men, women, and children occupying this area of extreme precarity, literally at river's edge, where "the levee banked the Mississippi River, and there used to be people that used to live back there and they used to catch fish back there."[15]

Like most black women in the neighborhood, the Clark sisters worked primarily as domestic help in white homes. Charity and her older sister Bell, who

FIG. 2.2 Mahalia Jackson's birth home at 7015 Water Street (now Constance Street) in New Orleans. Photograph by Bill Russell. The William Russell Jazz Collection at the Historic New Orleans Collection, acquisition made possible by the Clarisse Claiborne Grima Fund, acc. no. 92-48-L.331.786.

according to Bell's son Allen came to New Orleans by boat as a refugee from the flood that devastated Pointe Coupée in 1912, worked for the family of Henry and Ella Rightor and their four children and became members of the household. At various points in time, three other Clarks, Rhoda, Alice, and Bessie, worked for the Rightors, who were described by the sisters as "the best white people I ever knew in my life" and "just the same as our family and we loved them just like they loved us." Rightor family members spoke with particular affection about Bell, at whose funeral they remembered being the only white people.[16]

This complicated rub of rigid racial hierarchy and interpersonal intimacy is a feature of New Orleans and of the Jim Crow South more broadly, but it was especially characteristic of the Clarks' densely populated and ethnically diverse neighborhood (which I will hereafter refer to anachronistically as the "Black Pearl"). There were just under 2,500 Black Pearl residents reported in the 1920 census, 55 percent identifying as white and 45 percent as black or creole. A full third of its white residents were either foreign-born or American-born children of at least one immigrant parent.[17] Clark family members interviewed by Goreau repeatedly referred to their interactions with owners of family businesses that contributed to the bustle around the intersection of Magazine and Walnut Streets: Jung's Grocery, owned by a first-generation Bavarian American; Casserta's Drugstore, run by the son of an Italian father and Irish mother; and the Bisso Towboat Company, operating out of the Walnut Street wharf, run by the prominent Italian family that controlled most of the Greenville waterfront and employed Jackson's Aunt Alice as a housekeeper. The neighborhood, as Jackson herself described it, was both isolated—one in which "under all of its segregation . . . the Negro stayed by himself"—and notably integrated, "a mixed-up neighborhood, with Negroes, French, Creoles, and Italians all trying to scratch out a living." This doubleness of segregation and aggregation was in part a result of the common local neighborhood structure sociologists call "superblocks," where elite whites lived in large homes surrounded by the much humbler dwellings of black service workers.[18] The pervasive commingling was also, however, attributable to the fact that the Walnut Street wharf was a primary source of livelihood for a cross-ethnic assemblage of working-class men employed at the local docks.

One of these men, John A. Jackson Sr., exemplified the proximity of many black residents to activity near the riverfront. Born around 1849, Jackson came from a family that made its living as truck farmers in the town of Kenner, ten miles west of New Orleans. By 1900, he had settled in Greenville, where he secured steady employment as a stevedore, identifying himself as a "longshoreman" who handled cotton shipments. Jackson Sr. lived in a double shotgun house on Walnut just blocks away from the wharf, right next door to the Bissos, with his wife Annie, his daughter Hannah, and his twenty-four-year-old son, John Jr., who worked as a day laborer. In 1910, John Jackson Jr. was living with his own wife and children in Pigeon Town, though within a year he had met the recently arrived Charity Clark (Figure 2.3), who shortly thereafter gave birth to their child, Mahala. Mahala, nicknamed "Halie" and who became "Mahalia" when she moved to Chicago, was named after her Aunt Duke, though the name was taken from the Bible, derived from "Mahalath," granddaughter of King David. John Jackson Jr. and Charity Clark neither married nor lived together and he was essentially an absent parent— "He was no kind of father, I know that," said Allen Clark—so Charity raised her now four-year-old son Peter and her newborn daughter with the support of her sisters. "Mahalia's father seem like he was a kind of man [who] would always pretend that he was going to marry" then "disappear from you," Allen's sister Celie remembered. "That's the kind of man he seemed to be because he had several children by different women." As she grew into childhood, Mahala made considerable efforts to cultivate a relationship with her father, though Rosa Williams was blunt in her recollection that John Jackson Jr. and his family kept her at arm's distance until years later when her singing began to earn her acclaim.

FIG. 2.3 Charity Clark, Mahalia Jackson's mother. Laurraine Goreau Photograph Collection, Hogan Jazz Archive, Tulane University. By permission of the Mahalia Jackson Family Estate.

I'm going to tell you the whole shoot about this. They didn't care nothing at all about Halie until Halie left here and started singing and [was] trying to make her living and she got to Chicago. . . .Them people just started to pay attention to Halie *then*, after she got up there, started to singing, come back here, singing around here, wanted to visit. . . .Because her daddy didn't do nothing for her, no more than when he'd meet her he'd call her "Chocolate." She say that's the sweetest name she ever got from him, from any of them. None of them Jacksons didn't pay that child no mind.[19]

Being born into the Jackson family meant, however, that Mahalia symbolically represented family ties that bridged Legonier and New Orleans. Since black dockworkers like John Jackson Sr. received cargo on steamboats arriving from upriver, Mahalia Jackson had a maternal grandfather who baled cotton in Pointe Coupée that was perhaps unloaded by her paternal grandfather in New Orleans (Figure 2.4).[20]

FIG. 2.4 Paul Clark, Mahalia Jackson's maternal grandfather. Laurraine Goreau Photograph Collection, Hogan Jazz Archive, Tulane University. By permission of the Mahalia Jackson Family Estate.

A lingering discrepancy in writing on Jackson involves one of the most fundamental of biographical facts: the year of her birth. Her birth certificate indicates that she was born on October 26, 1911, but Goreau came to the firm conclusion that Jackson was in fact born a year later after speaking to family members in the early 1970s, and in particular to three of Jackson's maternal aunts, Bessie Kimble, Alice Stamps Lawson, and Hannah Robinson. The three women communicated that the family had always believed that their niece was born in 1912 until Jackson had to apply for a passport for her first European tour in 1952 and needed a copy of her birth certificate. "That's the first we knew of that," said Aunt Alice referring to the official 1911 birthdate, "but we just went along with it after that."[21] Privately, the family maintained their convictions. For Goreau, the clinching perspective came from Aunt Bessie, who insisted that Jackson was born in 1912 based on her memory of other births in the family but primarily because of her recollection that Jackson was born in the same year as a historically catastrophic multiple-state flood, "high water" resulting from an overflow of the Mississippi River and its branches, including the Atchafalaya.[22] Goreau's exchange with Kimble in her April 1972 interview in New Orleans is important because it reveals both the reasoning behind and the irreversible momentum toward the biographer's final verdict about Jackson's birth year.

BK: My sister's child was born the same month [. . .] she born in 1912, in the country; the child was born in the country . . . and Mahalia was born here [in New Orleans], in the same month, in the year of the high water, 1912. . . . Mahalia was born in 1912.

LG: Everything figures out right from 1912, but if you figure from 1911, it doesn't add up.

BK: That's wrong then, that birth certificate was wrong. . . .

LG: You figure that birth certificate is wrong?

BK: That's right.

LG: It has to be 1912?

BK: Yes. That's right.

LG: OK. We're going with that; it has to be 1912.

BK: Yes, 1912.

LG: All right. You know it for a fact by the year of the high water, and Celie [Taylor, Jackson's first cousin] knows it by the date of her brother's birth.

BK: That's right.

LG: And Alice and Hannah must figure the same way, because they put 1912 on the Chicago [funeral program].

BK: Yes, that's right.

LG: Okay, that's clear then. Because 1911 was throwing everything off, her baptism and everything, because [neighborhood friend] Annise Jackson is positive that

Mahalia was no older than about 14 when she was baptized, and that comes
out right to 1912.

BK: That's right.[23]

This moment in Goreau's interviews provides the basis of all subsequent claims
that Jackson was born in 1912. From a certain perspective, Goreau seems admirably determined to crosscheck her facts, value the memories of flesh-and-blood
people, and not fetishize the authority of official documents. She does, however,
seem to be operating from a premise that oral historical accounts will eventually
"figure out right" and her frustration with any recollection that "doesn't add up"
or "throws everything off" is palpable in many of her interviews. Goreau made a
note to herself that she explained to Aunt Alice her "theory" that the "error in recording" Jackson's birth year came from the "recopying of ledgers and shift of this
wrong one into the 1911 file, where it is now."[24]

For more than a half-century, 1911 was the accepted year of Jackson's birth. As
gospel scholarship has regained its footing in recent years, however, dedicated
historians writing about Jackson have rolled up their sleeves and taken on the not
easy work of hacking their way through Goreau's tortuous faux-colloquial prose.
Doing so has produced a perceptible tilt toward 1912 as the likely alternative. In his
2004 *New History of Black Gospel Music*, Robert Darden writes of Jackson: "The
circumstances of her impoverished childhood in New Orleans were well known,
even to noninitiates, although the exact year of her birth is still uncertain (probably
1912)."[25] Marovich explained the uncertainty in slightly more detail: "According to
Jackson's birth certificate, Jackson was born on October 26, 1911, but her aunts
insisted the actual date was October 26, 1912, recollecting that Charity was preg-
nant with Mahalia during the May 1912 flood of the Atchafalaya River."[26] In the
liner notes to his recent compilation of rare, unreleased Jackson recordings,
Anthony Heilbut, popularly considered to be the dean of gospel historians, is un-
equivocal, stating matter-of-factly that Jackson "was born in 1912, not the more
commonly reported 1911," a conclusion he reached having confidently accepted
Goreau's determination. Heilbut expressed his frustration that "you still see 1911"
in current writing due to Jackson's erroneous birth certificate.[27]

What about that birth certificate? Goreau drew on her interviews to illuminate
how births, not infrequently to unmarried couples like Jackson's parents, were
commonly documented in early twentieth-century New Orleans.

Births by law must be recorded, but City Hall custom casually went along
with the "open" arrangement: leave the Negroes to themselves. "In the
old days," says Elliott Beal, "City Hall let the child take the name of the
father even though there was no marriage. The mother's statement was
just accepted, without any checking, when she went down to register the

birth—or when the midwife went, which was more the custom; like a doctor would file it today."

So Charity made no issue of her newborn, nor any embarrassment in church. She told [midwife] Granny Lee to register the birth Mahala Jackson, lawful; and she kept her peace.

As Beal explained, in the Clarks' New Orleans community, the delivery of babies at home by midwives meant that registry of the birth was not triggered automatically by hospital bureaucracy but by a witness physically going to the office of the Recorder of Births, Deaths, and Marriages, sometimes weeks or months after the fact, and having an official document drawn up based on their testimony. Jackson's Aunt Hannah also asserted that common practice was for the midwife to provide City Hall with documentation of a birth: "No, not Charity. The midwife goes down, just like the pastor and a marriage."[28] With this understanding of the customary procedure, Goreau offers a straightforward narrative: Charity Clark had her baby delivered by midwife "Granny Lee," then let Lee take care of the paperwork and forgot about "City Hall."

Jackson's birth certificate tells another story. The document reads as follows, with the information entered in the blanks on the form by the clerk indicated by underlining and italics.

Be it Remembered, that on this day to wit: the *fifteenth of January* in the year of our Lord One Thousand Nine Hundred and *twelve* and the One Hundred and 36 of the independence of the United States of America, before me, WM. T. O'REILLY, M.D., Chairman Board of Health and Ex-Officio Recorder of Births, Deaths and Marriages, in and for the Parish and City of New Orleans, personally appeared *Charity Clark*, native of *this city* residing *at no. 7015 Water Street* who hereby declares, that on *the twenty sixth of October last year (26 Oct 1911) at her residence* was born a *female* child, named *Mahala Jackson (Colored) lawful* issue of *John Jackson* a native of *this city* aged 33 years, occupation *carpenter* and *Charity Clark* a native of this city, aged *21* years.

Thus done at New Orleans, in the presence of the aforesaid *Charity Clark* as also in that of *P. H. Lanauze and P. J.* [illegible last name] both of this City witnesses by me requested so to be, who have hereunto set their hands, together with me, after due reading hereof, the day, month and year first above written.

Charity Clark [signature]

P. Henry Lanauze [signature]

P J [?] [signature]

W. T. O'Reilly M.D. [signature stamp]
Chairman Board of Health and Ex-Officio Recorder,
Sworn to and subscribed before me this 15 day
of *January* 1912
P. Henry Lanauze [signature]

The story told by this document is quite specific, largely because it is *not* a conventional birth certificate. It reports that on January 15, 1912, Jackson's twenty-one-year-old mother, not her midwife, went downtown to the Recorder of Births, Deaths, and Marriages and told the clerk—apparently, judging from the handwriting, the person with the illegible last name—that the previous October 26 she had given birth to a daughter named Mahala at her home on Water Street and that the father of her child was thirty-three-year-old local carpenter John Jackson. The clerk inscribed the information and Clark signed the document, along with the official Recorder P. Henry Lanauze and the office clerk as required witnesses to her affidavit, "after due reading hereof, the day, month, and year." Lanauze, on behalf of W. T. O'Reilly, the Chairman of the Board of Health, then signed off on the document a second time.

Bureaucratic error is a daily occurrence, yet we must acknowledge what must be true in order for Jackson's birth certificate to be incorrect. The document would had to have been dated a year too early—not unheard of in early January—but this misdating would have occurred in four separate places: the day Clark came to the office, the 136 years after U.S. independence in 1776, the actual date of Jackson's birth, and the date at the bottom of the document. These errors would have been missed by at least three sets of eyes. Because the original signatures appear, there was no error introduced by recopying the document, as Goreau speculates. Moreover, since these certificates of birth were filled out chronologically, were paginated consecutively, and remain archived together in the original booklet of forms, it is easy to confirm that the surrounding certificates—recording the births registered by the persons who came into the office before and after Charity Clark—have the same year, meaning all of them are wrong, or none. If we are to resist blind faith in the unshakable veracity of official documents—and we should—we must also be willing to accept the greater frailty of even the most confident human memory, which is why we write things down. The certitude of her aunts notwithstanding, barring an extraordinarily unlikely and inexplicable set of circumstances, Jackson was born on October 26, 1911, as her birth certificate indicates, not a year later.

It would be understandable to read this discussion and come away with the impression that the question "Was Mahalia Jackson born in 1911 or 1912?" is mostly a matter of fussy historical hairsplitting, but it in fact points to larger issues. Goreau's determination to get the story right, by whatever means necessary, reflects her seriousness and very good intentions, and her decision to correct the official record demonstrates a deep and admirable respect for her human sources. She communicated her guiding principle explicitly to Aunt Alice: "Clerks can make errors in records, so take the family recollection that is accepted as the best evidence." Goreau did, however, have a copy of the birth certificate in hand—notice that she drops in the word "lawful," plucked from the document—and even with conventional documentary evidence staring her in the face she went with the aunts' story. In her defense, Goreau was a deadline-pressed writer having to make a difficult call on the fly with conflicting evidence and personal relationships with her sources. That more recent writers have chosen to leave the discrepancy uninterrogated is more telling. There will always be leaps of faith, whatever source one uses, and gospel literature has by necessity been built on oral history and shared anecdotes passed on to writers from eye- and ear-witnesses. These have been and to a certain extent will always be the bedrock of gospel historiography. But the recurring tendency to too willingly settle for such evidence, reiterated in one secondary source after another, has limited the development of a more robust, dialogically dynamic, and usable body of gospel scholarship. In this sense, the rhetorical and symbolic gap between the birth certificate's exordium "Be it Remembered" that Jackson was born in 1911 and Goreau's more off-the-cuff "We're going to go with" 1912 is meaningful. In black music studies more broadly, the romance of *mythos* and a penchant for intuitive interpretation has often outrun the work of culling both oral *and* written (and sonic) evidence more assiduously and evaluating it more rigorously so that lives and careers can be assessed more critically and artists can be situated more historically.

But the question of Jackson's birth year is also consequential because it presents an instance when historians can in fact have it both ways and reap considerable benefits from doing so. My position here is that Jackson's aunts, not her birth certificate, were "wrong" about the year of Jackson's birth. It is fair to wonder how women so close to Jackson could misremember their own sister bearing her only daughter the year of a colossal flood. In the larger scheme of things, however, the difference between remembering Jackson being born six months before the flood struck as opposed to six months afterwards is negligible. Had Charity not died in her mid-twenties, she may have been able to correct her sisters about when her child was born and prevent an honest mistake from developing a life of its own over the next forty years and acquiring the comfortable certainty of an iterative family story. Whatever the circumstances, the error is rather illuminating. The vagaries and ostensible "failures" of oral history, those moments when, oral historian Sandy Polishuk observes, "the story we recorded disagrees with the written historical record," can be uniquely productive. Many times, conflicting accounts or outright mistakes are "actively and creatively generated by memory and imagination in an effort to make sense of crucial events." More importantly, "often the discrepancies tell us more than facts."[29]

In this case, for Aunt Bessie, Aunt Alice, and Aunt Hannah, "1912" was not an arbitrary year; it was the year of a flood that devastated the area in Pointe Coupée where Jackson's entire family was born. For early twentieth-century New Orleanians, natural catastrophes were markers of time: the deadly 1915 hurricane that crippled Jackson's brother when he was electrocuted by a downed power line; the 1918 influenza pandemic during which, Aunt Bessie remembered, "People

[were] dying like flies, all around the neighborhood"; and the 1927 Mississippi River flood, the most destructive in U.S. history, that left New Orleans under four feet of water and inspired blues songs by Blind Lemon Jefferson, Lonnie Johnson, and Charley Patton.[30] When the 1912 flood hit, Clark family connections to Gumstump were very much alive. As recently as April 1910, Charity Clark was still living in Pointe Coupée with her father and infant son. Two years later, the flood drove the final Clark family members still living in Legonier to New Orleans.

In other words, Jackson was a child of New Orleans but her infancy marked a kaleidoscopic period when the Clarks were in the midst of migrating from country to city. She was, in fact, the very first Clark born in New Orleans. With this context, we gain a broader perspective on Jackson's place in American history, registering that her birth was closer in time to her grandparents' emancipation from slavery by Abraham Lincoln than to her own participation in the March on Washington on the steps of the Lincoln Memorial. The conjoining of Jackson's birth and the 1912 flood through an act of mismemory—or, perhaps better, meaningful forgetting—tells us what sober legal documents never could: that wherever and whenever Jackson was officially born, her aunts recognized her as part of a family story that extended back in time to antebellum enslavement, took shape amid the isolation of Gumstump, and gained significance with Jackson's subsequent triumphs. If a birth certificate gives us access to facts that may help us set the record straight, memories, even incorrect ones, can open the door to deeper emotional truths. Both matter. The Clarks' Pointe Coupée roots help explicate why Jackson's deep historical consciousness, manifest in her persistent self-presentation as a vessel for musical sensibilities forever rooted in the legacy of a family of black Americans, remained so front and center over the course of her career as a gospel singer.

Coming of Age

A strongly French cultural influence made Louisiana a predominantly Catholic state, with the United States' highest concentration of black Catholics living in New Orleans. Jackson remembered the city as "dominated" by Catholics.[31] But the Clarks were staunch Baptists and the church was the focal point of their life in the Black Pearl. "We had to go every time the church door opened," remembered Celie. "Three times a week, and then on Sunday . . . we go to 6 a.m. prayer service, then Sunday School, then 11 o'clock church, then we go home and get our dinner, and then back for BTU [Baptist Training Union, the youth department], then from BTU, had to stay for night service."[32]

Going to church meant continuous interaction among a closely interwoven cluster of four black Baptist congregations in the neighborhood, all established in the nineteenth century and still in existence today: Plymouth Rock Baptist Church, Zion Travelers First Baptist Church, Mount Moriah Missionary Baptist

Church, and Broadway Mission Baptist Church. Separated by only six blocks, the four churches stretched along a geographic band that never strayed more than two blocks from the Mississippi River, yet another reminder of where the African American population in the neighborhood primarily lived. The Clarks were scattered across these churches: Aunt Bessie and Aunt Alice were baptized at Zion Travelers, "but my family's church . . . was Plymouth Rock," said Allen. "That's where Hannah and all of them belonged to." The rest, including Duke, Bell, Charity, and Mahalia went to Mount Moriah (Figure 2.5). Aunt Bessie remembered that Paul Clark "loved Mount Moriah. He used to preach there all the time," and as he did "back home" in Pointe Coupée her father would impart his wisdom by hosting theological discussions. "All the young preachers used to come by my daddy. Sit on the porch and my daddy have the Bible, teaching them different things."[33] Mahalia's biological father, John Jackson Jr., was a member of Broadway, which also organized a kindergarten in the church basement and a night school for adults who wanted to improve their literacy.[34] In later years, Jackson liked to suggest in interviews that her father was more of a presence in her life than he probably was in actuality, particularly by identifying herself, some-what misleadingly, as the daughter of "a preacher in a small church." There is no reason to doubt that John Jackson Jr. filled in to deliver a Sunday sermon every now and then, a common practice at many churches, though from all indications it would be a stretch to claim he was *the* "preacher" at Broadway, pastored from at least 1926 by Reverend James S. Morgan.

FIG. 2.5 Mount Moriah Missionary Baptist Church on Millaudon Street, Jackson's home church in New Orleans, 1954. Photograph by Bill Russell. The William Russell Jazz Collection at the Historic New Orleans Collection, acquisition made possible by the Clarisse Claiborne Grima Fund, acc. no. 92-48-L.331.810.

Church walls were fluid and members of these four congregations constantly intermingled by "visiting around." The all-day commitment described by Celie and the close cooperation among these four Baptist churches is vividly documented by a newspaper report on Sunday services at Plymouth Rock on September 14, 1925. We cannot, of course, know for sure whether Jackson was there, but it is hard to imagine that 13-year-old Mahalia, a member of Mount Moriah, would not have been in attendance for at least some of the proceedings.

> The Sunday School opened at 9:30 a.m. with the pastor [Reverend C. W. Brooks] presiding. . . .
> The 11 o'clock service was conducted by the pastor, Bro. A. S. Jamerson, from the Zion Travelers B.C., [who] preached a spiritual sermon. . . .
> Night service began at 8 p.m. Devotional exercises were conducted by the pastor. . . .
> The B.Y.P.U. [the earlier name for the BTU] opened at 6:30 p.m. . . .The following named Baptist Young People's Unions and their presidents were present and took an active part on the program: Mount Moriah Baptist Young People's Union and Broadway Mission Baptist Union. . . .Both unions had a large attendance and raised a large amount of collections. All who were present enjoyed the splendid program put over by the young people.[35]

Meanwhile, there was work. At the Rightors, Charity Clark's household responsibilities were to be a housecleaner, a cook specializing in "New Orleans creole" food, a chaperone for the older children, and a nursemaid for the family's infant son. Charity's son Peter, who could manage some Jelly Roll Morton–style piano and had a knack for extemporaneous song making, and daughter Mahalia, who even as a small child would entertain the Rightors by singing songs like "Ballin' the Jack," accompanied their mother to work, occupying the Rightor children as playmates.[36] Eventually, however, Charity's poor health caught up to her and she died sometime before Mahalia's seventh birthday. Jackson believed that she was four years old when her mother died, which would have been sometime in 1916. Her older cousin Allen, however, remembered saying goodbye to a gravely ill Charity just before he enlisted in the Navy in 1918: "She didn't live very long afterwards. I left here on I think the thirteenth of May and somewhere around the latter part of June she passed." According to Goreau, the Clark family, with Mahalia in tow, took Charity's body by train back to Gumstump, where she was buried in the graveyard behind St. John's. Allen explained that in the Clark family, the aunts "claimed" each other's children when the mother was absent: "Hannah always claimed me" after he was brought from Legonier to New Orleans and Aunt Duke, in turn, adopted Mahalia and Peter when their mother died.[37]

It was with her mother dead and her father largely out of the picture, that Jackson entered her childhood and adolescence in New Orleans. Jackson was born with physical challenges, including eye trouble that made her oversensitive to light as an infant and severely bowed legs—"very, very extremely bow-legged. Extremely," Allen hammered home—that along with her poverty and parentlessness made her a sympathetic figure in the neighborhood. Despite bowed legs that earned her the nickname "Hooks," Jackson was known as "a regular tomboy" who excelled at sports, especially baseball, which she played in a Sunday School league, and was nimble enough to clamber up onto the train when it slowed down to scrounge lumps of stone coal that the family could cook and warm the house with. But several of Goreau's interviewees, including family members and white and black members of the community, also characterized Jackson as "a poor, raggedy, bare-foot girl" who "didn't have nobody but her aunts," as "the black sheep of the family" who "was darker than the others," and as a "very thin, very homely child," if possessing "a lot of personality." According to one of her closest childhood friends, Annise Jackson (no relation), parents in the neighborhood "would tell their children how fortunate they was and how unfortunate Mahalia was. Not to scorn her, not to make fun of her. She just didn't have a mother or a father." Jackson was not, therefore, just another poor black kid in the neighborhood. Those who knew Jackson considered her to be living under particularly difficult circumstances.[38]

Jackson's youth in New Orleans was shaped by a highly local sense of place. Walking the Black Pearl today, the class stratification that organized the neighborhood spatially is still clearly legible in its architecture, with the opulent dwellings on St. Charles and Lowerline becoming incrementally smaller, and their original inhabitants progressively poorer, as you move toward the river, until they eventually become mostly cramped double shotgun houses adjacent to Leake Street. It is no coincidence, then, that throughout her life in New Orleans, Jackson lived exclusively within blocks of the levee, first on Water Street and then with her Aunt Duke several blocks north on Pitt Street. As her Aunt Bessie noted, such movement was perpetual, as residents relocated often, if within a restricted radius: "People used to move around when they felt like it, didn't live no place for years and years."[39] Living with Aunt Duke meant being a stone's throw from Mount Moriah Baptist Church, right around the corner on Millaudon Street, and even closer to a small Pentecostal church that, according to Aunt Bessie, Jackson also liked to visit because of its more ecstatic style of worship.

> It was right in the same block as Duke. Sanctified. Oh, they had a joyful time. Yes, indeed. They used to have a time in there, honey. We used to go. But I didn't do what they do, because I didn't know how to shout like they do. Them people has a good time. I like it, though. Mahalia liked it, too. Mahalia liked Sanctified.[40]

Jackson was christened at Plymouth Rock but she was baptized in the river as a member of Mount Moriah. Like her peers, Jackson sang at church, often leading them in a particularly popular song of her youth, the spiritual "Hand Me Down My Silver Trumpet, Gabriel," which Annise said was one "that we used to really love to sing 'til they told us they was tired of hearing us sing that." Mount Moriah had a senior choir that sang anthems and spirituals and a junior choir Jackson joined that rendered "jubilee selections." Mahalia recalled that it was "a very, very fine junior choir and we went from church to church singing the Lord's praises." To Celie, her cousin's "voice was beyond all other voices" in the junior choir, "so she went into the big choir when she was about twelve years old." According to Pearl Robinson, the piano accompanist for the youth choir, it was her brother Fletcher Robinson, a member of Jackson's Sunday School class, who really "started her with the singing" by encouraging her as a soloist in church. Annise remembered that Jackson "set that church on fire" singing lined-out Baptist hymns, also known as "Dr. Watts" or "long-meter" hymns, like "Jesus, My God, I Know Your Name."[41]

Jackson's home church was the place for both spiritual and perhaps surprisingly secular social activity. Mount Moriah hired trucks for monthly crosstown excursions for church picnics at Seabrook Harbor near Lake Pontchartrain.[42] Otherwise, "the only recreation that we kids would have would be in church," Jackson recalled. "The church was the center for all of us children to meet there and play, and we used to be in the back of the church, which was called the community house of the church. We children would meet there and sing and what little games that we created ourselves we would play."[43] The Mount Moriah community house was a large hall where the BYPU leaders "would give concerts, fish fries, and movies"—"mostly cowboy pictures," Jackson's cousin Isabella added, except at Easter—and set up a stage for concerts where Jackson would sing such popular songs as "My Blue Heaven," "Swanee River," and "Old Black Joe." Her childhood idol, vaudeville blues diva Bessie Smith, recorded W. C. Handy's "St. Louis Blues" for Columbia Records in January 1925 with hometown hero Louis Armstrong on trumpet, and according to Annise the tune became Jackson's calling card at Mount Moriah socials: "Mahalia was very big on singing 'St. Louis Blues.' That was her song."[44] These accounts of youth activity at Mount Moriah do not so much affirm familiar claims that the music of the Saturday night club and the Sunday morning sanctuary are stylistic kin as they indicate something more striking and noteworthy: that there was an actual and seemingly unproblematic co-presence of music-making identified by Jackson and others as religious and popular, respectively, right on the church premises. In Chapter 7, I will discuss in more detail how Jackson's diverse early musical influences shaped her practice of voice.

To a notable degree, Jackson's reminiscences of New Orleans communicate a keen awareness of socioeconomic disadvantage but also a striver's mentality. She recalled in particular detail police brutality in the New Orleans of a century ago in terms that sound hauntingly familiar.

> I know that there was a very bad police system there that were hard. They would run the colored people in if they just saw them standing in their own community, run them in and put them in jail. And a lot of them were put in jail and a lot of them were beat up bad and a lot of them were killed that even resisted an officer. . . .Maybe the police would beat them up because they would call them a "bad Negro" and all like that, and then maybe he would kill up one of them because they'd make out the Negro was trying to shoot him or something. And those things made us feel that we didn't have any protection.

Jackson highlighted the limited employment possibilities for local black men in her neighborhood in the 1920s: the Public Belt switch train, the Government Fleet, the whiskey distillery, the sugar refinery, Bisso's docks, or ad hoc work as barbers, fruit sellers, small restaurateurs, or caddies at the Audubon golf course. Opportunities were even more limited for women, who primarily "worked for the white people, where they did days' work on the place, or they took washing and ironing at their home, where the children would go to the white people's house and get the clothes on top of their head or on their shoulders and bring it home." Other than schoolteachers or the rare doctor or lawyer, "there wasn't many professional people that I know of," yet she acknowledged "as a child, my greatest ambition was to be a schoolteacher or a nurse." Jackson's nearness to the train tracks and the Mississippi was an omnipresent part of her memoryscape, as she recalled hustling coal from passing railroad cars, gathering, drying, and chopping driftwood from the river, bumming free rides on the ferry to Westwego, and catching fish, crab, and crawfish. "A lot of times we were able to eat the type of food we want because we were close to the river and we could catch this kind of food which made us eat pretty good food because we lived close to the levee front," Jackson said. "Those that lived downtown in the French Quarter and other parts didn't quite live that way."[45]

Socially, the neighborhood action was down on Magazine Street, where men would gather on payday to shoot dice on the sidewalk, and slightly further uptown where most of the music venues were located. "We never heard the jazz much around Magazine Street because it was more numerous with white families than it was colored," Jackson's first cousin Celie remembered, "but we heard a lot of jazz in the Uptown section, the Carrollton section. We would hear it from the clubs when they would have their lawn parties." Jackson and her peers recalled hearing music coming from local haunts like the Buffalo Club, the Merry-Go-Round, Johnny Flowers's Lounge, the Bumblebee, and the Pride of Carrollton

Aid and Pleasure Club, and from Kid Foster, King Oliver, Bunk Johnson, and the Original Tuxedo Band (the top dance band in town) playing from trucks that drove through the neighborhood to advertise their shows downtown. At the same time, Carrollton and St. Charles Avenues also marked intra-'hood boundaries that separated youth in Jackson's 16th Ward from their cross-street rivals in "P-Town" in the 17th Ward. Locals still disagree on what the "P" stands for: Pigeon? Pidgin? Pension? Goreau referred to it as "Pinching Town," but misapplied the nickname to Jackson's own neighborhood. Her interviewees clarified that "up in the 17th Ward [we] call that Pinching Town" and that one had to know the distinction. "They didn't allow our boys on this side of the avenue on the other side of the avenue and our boys didn't allow them on this side," remembered Annise Jackson, who was backed up by others who agreed "we couldn't go up to Pinching Town, and they couldn't come by us," even during second-line processions, at the risk of street fights.[46]

Despite the territoriality, Jackson was inspired by the *Laissez les bon temps rouler* attitude of her black community: "There's a lot of people down there in the early days never did worry about getting rich. They believed in enjoying life. And that was a wonderful part of life to see in New Orleans. Though people didn't have nothing, they certainly did have a wonderful spirit." For herself, though, Jackson claimed an acute consciousness of poverty that was also mixed with social aspiration.

> Way back in those days, when I was a girl, the houses were pretty shabby, and many of them are the same way, and the rent was no more than about six or eight dollars a month. And things was pretty lean. And, I don't know, I was born into this condition, but it was kind of a sad feeling I'd have, cause there weren't many of us that lived too well. But I had this feeling that I could live better, and I used to dream of living better. . . . I've always been a child that thought way in the beyond of the future. . . .
>
> I had to be the secretary to all of the benevolent societies, which kept me away from a lot of the young people. That's why I was always more mature thinking than the other young people at the time. That's why I always had this sad feeling, because I had to be with the old people to be the secretary and, of course, it gave me a little deeper mind than the average kid.

Jackson confessed that she "never did like Mardi Gras" because of her discomfort with the sometimes fatal clashes between Mardi Gras Indian tribes and the seemingly recrimination-free violence by anonymous maskers among "my race of people" during the celebrations Uptown, while "the white people would have theirs with the big floats down the main part of Canal Street, which were very beautiful and high-class."[47] Attention to the details of Jackson's childhood is essential for understanding how her lifelong acute sensitivity to social status was a product of her upbringing amid the class and ethnic mixture of her segregated city and neighborhood, and how this background shaped how she articulated her biographical narrative, thought about her practice of voice, and pursued her ambitions.

By the mid-1920s, the New Orleans public school system for African Americans comprised twenty-one elementary schools and one high school for 14,000 students. For the years that she was enrolled in school, Jackson attended the all-black, coed McDonogh 24, one of over thirty New Orleans schools created through the bequest of millionaire merchant and former slave owner John McDonogh for the "education of the poor of all castes and races." One member of the McDonogh 24 faculty when Jackson was a student was Orlando Capitola Ward (O. C. W.) Taylor (1891–1979), a Texas native who came to the school fresh out of Wiley College and became its only male teacher, hired at a salary of $45 a month. Taylor was immediately struck by New Orleans's peculiar equilibrium between racial and ethnic mélange and segregation. "New Orleans was an interracial town. If Gabriel blew his saxophone now, he couldn't unmix the races," said Taylor. "But there was a line you couldn't cross. . . .There was always a line of demarcation."[48] Despite belonging to possibly the largest black education system in the country, schools like McDonogh 24 were largely left to themselves. "In those days, there was very little supervision of the Negro schools. They let you do anything you wanted to do," remembered Taylor, who also taught at McDonogh 35, then the city's only black high school. "They really weren't interested in Negro education. They just suffered it." Taylor described the majority of his fellow teachers as exceedingly strict "spinsters" who freely meted out discipline with a strap. At McDonogh 24, it was a cardinal sin for boys and girls to socialize too closely, even in the yard during recess, and Taylor remembered Jackson being punished for excessive humming at school.

But the college-educated Taylor is also a study in the complexities and contradictions of class status for the black intelligentsia in the Jim Crow South. When Jackson was at McDonogh 24, he "was just at the beginning of my teaching career. I taught for prestige and worked as assistant head waiter at New Orleans Country Club for a living," said Taylor. "I wasn't Mahalia's teacher, but I had a good bit to do with Mahalia." Jackson also worked as a housekeeper at the Jewish New Orleans Country Club and bonded with Taylor on after-school streetcar rides to work that blurred hierarchies as they transitioned from a faculty-student relationship to fellow service workers: "We had long talks. She seemed to confide in me a bit. Not only was I a teacher, I was in the nature of a domestic." Meanwhile, Taylor's best paying job was as a butler for New Orleans's "Banana King" Samuel Zemurray, president of the United Fruit Company, and he strategically benefited from the cheek-by-jowl intimacy and paternalism: "There was a lot of money in that and they would help you: if you were sick they would pay doctor bills, put out for rent. They took care of their help. Still fathers from old slavery days."

Though he remained deeply involved with the New Orleans school system for decades, Taylor left classroom teaching in 1925 to cofound the *Louisiana Weekly*, the city's first African American newspaper, with successful insurance businessman Constant C. Dejoie. For its first issues, Dejoie and Taylor called their paper the *New Orleans Herald*, after which the name was changed to the *Louisiana Weekly*, reflecting their ambitions to more broadly serve "the Negro people of Louisiana." During the mid-to-late 1920s, which overlapped with Jackson's teenage years, the *Louisiana Weekly* insistently emphasized the importance of black business initiatives, education, urbanization, social uplift, and protest of racial injustice. "We believe that editorially, in matters pertaining to the race, a paper should not straddle," Dejoie and Taylor wrote in an editorial that appeared the paper's inaugural issue. "There is only one course for a Negro paper to take in matters pertaining to Negro life, and that is the right side. Any attempt to sidestep and to 'pussyfoot' is more harmful to the race than anything else."[49] The *Louisiana Weekly*'s expansive political vision accommodated both its strong advocacy of the integrationist agenda of the National Association for the Advancement of Colored People (NAACP) and its enduring support for the black nationalist vision of Marcus Garvey's United Negro Improvement Association (UNIA). As an educator and as a journalist for an explicitly activist newspaper, Taylor's career as an intellectual leader in black New Orleans reminds us what the geographic specification of the "Harlem Renaissance" often conceals about what was in fact a national movement.[50] Taylor's close one-on-one contact and "long talks" with the young Jackson, as well as the likely second- and third-hand, on-the-street circulation of *Louisiana Weekly* discourse across black social classes, invite us to consider more intently the early exposure to philosophies of black liberation by a woman who went on to become a tireless civil rights activist.

Yet Taylor and others close to Jackson also recognized that her formal education was doomed by her home responsibilities. "She had to really take care of herself because the family was poor. She was almost self-sustaining from the very beginning," Taylor remembered. Unable to pursue a passion for sports that rivaled her love for music, the athletic Jackson was heartbroken when she was prohibited from participating when Taylor started baseball and basketball teams for black youth because she was expected to be home immediately after school to complete her household chores. According to Annise Jackson, fulfilling Aunt Duke's expectations was not just a barrier for extracurricular activities.

Mahalia had to miss a lot of school at McDonogh 24. She'd go one day, some weeks no days. . . .I don't think Mahalia put in a straight week at McDonough 24. She had to go to her aunt's place when she was working and then she had to stay home and nurse those two kids, Isabella and Brisko. I think she went to night school when they started it . . . [but] she missed so much, she was held back and couldn't keep up with her real class. The last grade she finished was fourth. She wasn't with us in fifth.[51]

Staying at home meant that Jackson was under the firm hand of Mahala Paul, her Aunt Duke, the oldest Clark sister who "ruled the clan," according to Celie. "Whatever she said, they all listened to her." From a previous marriage to Nathan Duskin, Aunt Duke bore a son on the Gumstump plantation named Fred, who the family called "Atchafalaya." She remarried around 1904 to Foster Hill and then a third and final time to Manuel Paul. Atchafalaya produced two children of his own, a son named Manuel (who went by the nickname "Brisko") and a daughter named Isabella. But he was a free spirit who enjoyed the sporting life—untenable under his mother's non-negotiable rules—and he departed New Orleans when his children were infants, leaving them with his mother, who had already taken in Mahalia and her brother.

The Pauls' "half a double" (Figure 2.6)—one side of a double shotgun house—had a wood-burning stove, a backyard garden, and even a Columbia Grafonola, but no indoor plumbing, so the family had to use an outdoor sanitary toilet, bathe in a tin tub, and wash clothes with boiled water on a washboard. Aunt Duke worked

FIG. 2.6 The home of Mahala Paul, Mahalia Jackson's Aunt Duke, at 7567 Pitt Street, where Jackson lived from the time of her mother's death until in 1931, when she moved to Chicago, 1954. Photograph by Bill Russell. The William Russell Jazz Collection at the Historic New Orleans Collection, acquisition made possible by the Clarisse Claiborne Grima Fund, acc. no. 92-48-L.331.798.

as a domestic, laundering clothes for a private family. As the second-oldest female under her roof, Jackson's responsibilities were to take care of the house and her infant cousins, Brisko and Isabella. Jackson's "biggest hangup was she had those two children," said childhood friend Tom Castine. "She have to stay with them, keep them within because they was too small to be without. And the other children were having their fun. That kept her kind of close to the house." Aunt Duke's strictly enforced work demands eventually made school impossible. "Mahalia better get hers done. Wash, iron, scrub. She had to keep that house spotless," her Aunt Bessie recalled. "Mahalia had to bend over that washboard. She washed for the whole family, and she wasn't nothing but a youngster. She's been washing and ironing since she was about eleven years old." Mahalia "was like a slave. She has to do everything and [Aunt Duke] never could be pleased," in the view of Jackson's older cousin Allen. "She just kept raising children and do cleaning [and] she had to do coal and the wood and everything. . . .The whole time she was there she had to stay home and watch the children and do those things first."[52]

By all accounts, Aunt Duke, the rock of the family cast in interviews as both uncommonly generous and uncomfortably harsh, took her role as Jackson's care-taker with the utmost seriousness. She undoubtedly wanted to keep her name-sake niece on the narrow path and she did so through draconian punishment that attained legendary status. Jackson's aunts remembered that their sister "didn't let Mahalie get out her sight" and continually admonished Jackson "about playing out in the streets, and she should be home on time and never let her go out to dances and things." The consequences for any perceived infraction could be severe. "She had a strap, but most of the time it was that broom," Annise Jackson remembered of Aunt Duke's beatings. "She tried to break the broom on the girl." Celie also witnessed her Aunt Duke being "very strict on Mahalia," claiming she made Jackson kneel on brick while she whipped her with a cat-o-nine-tails. While acknowledging that the level of Aunt Duke's discipline could be "very, very foolish," Allen Clark suggested in her defense that she was simply following the approach to parenting modeled by the no-nonsense Paul Clark: "She came up under a hard father. He was rough on children. Guess she got some of that from him." Bessie acknowledged that her sister "had her old folk ways," but the more extreme behavior tended to obscure the fundamental nature of "about the sweetest person you ever seen. You could get her last nickel, and she'd give you her last piece of bread in the house. She'd feed you. And she'd give you a place to stay if you didn't have nowhere to stay. And that wasn't a mean-hearted person."[53]

Yet it was difficult for the Clark sisters and many in the neighborhood to watch Aunt Duke's dominion over Jackson. Out of concern for her well-being, they tried to intervene, sometimes directly by pleading for leniency, other times through back channels. In 1907, seven-year-old Walter Lamana was kidnapped, murdered, and dismembered in an act of attempted extortion by New Orleans Mafia operating under the control of mob boss Charles Matranga, known as the "Black Hand." For decades afterward, the "Black Hand" became a sort of local bogeyman, "the terror of our neighborhood," Marguerite Rightor remembered. The Rightors responded to an appeal from Aunt Bell with a scare tactic on Jackson's behalf.

> Bell came: "Oh, Mama, they just treating that poor little girl so bad! Can't you do something about it?" So mama, who had quite a sense of humor, sat down and wrote a letter . . . this was the time of the Black Hand . . . and she wrote: "We have learned how badly you are treating little Mahala. If you don't do something about it, we're going to come and get you." She put a big Black Hand on it, signed it, scared her to death. Bell said they really started treating her good after that.[54]

Beyond the physical abuse, there was the nagging worry that "Mahalia could not enjoy her young life" because of the continuous work and Aunt Hannah, who had since moved to Chicago, began to receive urgent requests from New Orleans to come get Jackson. As her Aunt Bessie explained, Jackson was more than ready.

> You not a child all the time. You get tired of that sometime. A dog get tired if you mistreat him, he'll walk off. You gets tired, you get a certain age that you don't want to be beaten and dogged around, you go on about your business. . . .
> After my sister came, she wanted Celie, but my sister Bell wasn't going to let Celie go with nobody. So I told her to take Mahalia. . . ."Hannah, if you want to take anybody, why don't you take Mahalia?" Cause we was all grieving for her, all the time, from one house to another. So she agreed to ask Mahalia. She asked Mahalia did she want to go. She said yes, she would go. Hannah said: "Yeah, I'm going to pack you up. You going with me." I was so glad when she went up there. Sometime, by changing [you] might do better. And it did. It brought her from a long ways.[55]

Jackson apparently told Goreau that she left New Orleans in 1927, though, in fact, two years for Jackson's departure from New Orleans have circulated in the literature. Those relying on Goreau have cited 1927, but in her autobiography with Wylie, Jackson claims she left in 1928 and authors consulting this source have repeated this date.[56] When Goreau interviewed Isabella Duskin in 1972, she asked specifically when Jackson moved to Chicago.

LG: How old do you think you were when Mahalia left? Were you in school yet?
ID: Oh, yes indeed, Lord! I was about the third grade, something like that.

LG: Then you can't be twelve years younger than Mahalia, if she left at sixteen!

ID: I'm 48 and Mahalia was 60 when she died [three months earlier].[57]

Goreau seemed perplexed that Lazard's memory did not square with her accepted story that Jackson left New Orleans in 1927. Having decided that 1912 was her year of birth, Goreau wrote that Jackson was "a scared 15-year-old" when she moved north.[58] But if Jackson's younger cousin was indeed in "about the third grade" when Jackson left New Orleans, this would have made Isabella around eight years old and Jackson around nineteen or twenty, with her year of departure 1930 or 1931.

Another of Goreau's interviewees, Ethel Adams, corroborated Lazard's time-line. A family friend of the Clarks, Adams moved to Chicago but returned to New Orleans with Jackson's Aunt Hannah for Thanksgiving in 1931 and decided to stay. Adams recounted how she was the one who assisted Jackson with the logistics of getting to Chicago.

You see, when Mahalia first went to Chicago, I was up there in Chicago with my little son Charles. He was small then. And so Hannah came down and I came home for Thanksgiving, the same train. Hannah and I came together. Well, you see, Mahalia was still there. She had never been to Chicago. . . . So she came by my house that night . . . and she said "Ethel, Aunt Hannah told me if I could get a ticket back to Chicago she would take me back." . . . Cause I wasn't going back. . . . So I told her, I said "Oh Mahalia, I'm sorry. Had I known this I would have saved my ticket, but I sold my ticket at the station for four dollars to one of the red caps." So I said, "Now, I'll tell you what to do. You go down to the station and find out from some of the red caps, see if they have a ticket." You know, they was selling to people that was going back there. And I said, "You see if you can find a ticket at one of them, but if you can't . . . go to the Page Hotel and you ask for Mr. Allen cause he has the excursions. . . . I'm sure he will get you back." Now that's how Mahalia went to Chicago. . . . And that was in 1931.[59]

Goreau took Adams's account seriously; she wrote "1931 definitely" prominently in her notes. After speaking to Adams, Goreau even confessed her agnosticism to Pearl Robinson, the accompanist for the Mount Moriah youth choir, during an interview later that same day.

Let me tell you, I thought I had it settled in my mind it was positively after Thanksgiving of 1927 [that Jackson went to Chicago]. But today when I spoke to Mrs. Ethel Adams, she said she came down the train with Hannah and it was Thanksgiving of 1931. So that really throws all my calculations off completely. So now I've got a little problem to try to resolve that year right, you know. . . .So now I'm puzzled . . . because that makes Mahalia a lot older when she left.[60]

Aunt Hannah herself had also told Goreau "That was 1930 when we went up." But in her book, despite noting that Jackson moved shortly after Thanksgiving, Goreau did not mention the discrepancy and affirms Jackson's repeated assertions that she migrated to Chicago in 1927. As in her interview with Isabella, Goreau's commitment to building the story around 1927 meant disputing the memories of interviewees like Jackson's Aunt Alice (Alice Stamps Lawson) when they did not fit her narrative.

LG: Now, tell me this. What was the year that you went up to Chicago?
ASL: I came here in '29. Twenty-nine.
LG: No, no, no. Oh, no, no. Well, it can't be '29 because Mahalia came up in Thanksgiving in 1927.
ASL: Well, I was up here before Mahalia was.
LG: Well, that means you came sometime in 1927.[61]

A final piece of evidence points to the likely conclusion that 1931, or 1930 at the earliest, was the year of Jackson's move to Chicago. The 1920 U.S. Census shows that Jackson and her older brother Peter were living on Pitt Street with Aunt Duke and Manuel Paul as adopted children. The census taken a decade later—recording "each person whose place of abode on April 1, 1930, was in this family"—indicates that the Paul household had added Duke's grandchildren Brisko and Isabella and her father Paul Clark, and that her eigtheen-year-old niece "Mahaly" was also still an occupant.[62] Again, it is useful to account for what must be true if Jackson did indeed move to Chicago in 1927: Aunt Duke had to have told the census taker that Jackson was still living with her nearly three years after she left New Orleans. This is not impossible—perhaps it was wishful thinking that her niece would come back home. But in light of Isabella's memory, Aunt Alice's and Aunt Hannah's recollections, and especially Adams's meticulous account, all corroborated by the 1930 census, it seems highly probable that Jackson was still in New Orleans in 1930 and then, just after Thanksgiving 1931, moved to Chicago with her Aunt Hannah. In the following chapter, I will discuss why her later arrival in Chicago is significant with regard to gospel historiography. For now, it will suffice to note that with her move, Jackson, having just turned twenty the previous month, was herself now a participant in the second leg of the Clark family's migration away from Pointe Coupée.

"It's hard for me sometimes to believe I came from the back streets of New Orleans and now I have people sitting in the aisles and listening to my gospel songs."

THE LOUISIANA WEEKLY

THE OLD NEGRO AND THE NEW

FIG. 2.7 "The Old Negro and the New," cartoon in the *Louisiana Weekly*, February 19, 1927. By permission of the *Louisiana Weekly*.

So Jackson opened her 1966 autobiography, as recorded by Evan McLeod Wylie. Jackson's identity as a daughter of New Orleans was always a cornerstone of her self-narrative, but her earlier family history, a quintessentially African American story of enslavement, emancipation, and hopeful migration from country to city and from South to North, was profoundly formative as well. During her final years in New Orleans, Jackson shared Aunt Duke's home with her grandfather, the family patriarch, and it is no coincidence that she and Wylie included an extended discussion of the origins of the Clark family "on a white man's cotton plantation on the Chafalaya River."[63] But Jackson's two decades in New Orleans also invite a reassessment of her hometown. Long overdue focus on the Uptown community in which Jackson was born and raised broadens our geographic sense of black New Orleans beyond the French Quarter, Storyville, Central City, and Tremé. Jackson's experience illuminates the multiple ways in which the citizens of this singular city were "mixed-up," continuously shuffled and reshuffled along the axes of race, class, gender, labor, education, sociality, intra-community boundaries, and religious practice.

Moreover, Jackson's upbringing resonates with uniquely African American configurations of class politics. When in later years we hear Jackson describing her early appreciation of recitalists Marian Anderson and Roland Hayes, see her subsequent business initiatives in Chicago, and admire the devoted activism of her adulthood, we might discern and acknowledge, perhaps for the first time, that whatever her socioeconomic marginalization from elite black New Orleans, the cultural politics and political philosophy of the 1920s Negro Renaissance, promoted resolutely on the pages of the *Louisiana Weekly*, were a pillar of her intellectual development. A cartoon in a February 1927 issue of the *Louisiana Weekly*, depicting "The Old Negro and the New" (Figure 2.7) seems to prophesy and neatly summarize the century-long family journey from Paul Clark's field labor on the Merrick plantation to Jackson's future prosperity as the "Queen of Gospel." This more historically situated Jackson emerges from her place in the story of the Clarks of Louisiana. But with her move to Chicago in 1931, Jackson was adopted by new families: a national body of black Baptists through which she built her reputation and a gospel singing movement that welcomed her and offered the promise of a burgeoning new field.

3

Family Affairs, Part II

BLACK BAPTISTS AND CHICAGO GOSPEL

Introduction: New Home Chicago

Like many Southern participants in the Great Migration of the 1920s and 1930s that remapped black America, Mahalia Jackson arrived in Depression-era Chicago trying to survive but hoping to flourish.[1] Jackson's Aunt Hannah brought her to Chicago shortly after Thanksgiving 1931 and Jackson moved into Hannah's South Side apartment with another aunt, Alice, and her daughter, also named Alice. The latter two were distinguished as "Big Alice" and "Little Alice." Soon, a third Clark sister, Aunt Bessie, joined them, though Jackson remained in close communication with her family back in New Orleans, for which she felt a predictable homesickness. Jackson was in Chicago when her beloved grandfather Paul Clark suffered a stroke during a sweltering summer visit; shortly thereafter, he returned to New Orleans where he died around 1937. Hannah and Alice did domestic work for white families in Chicago, but Jackson arrived with her dreams of becoming a professional of some sort still intact. She hoped to become a teacher, then a nurse, and she tried to pick up her schooling from where she left off at McDonogh 24 only to have it disrupted yet again by responsibilities at home, where she had to take care of Little Alice and her three aunts when they became sick. Eventually, Jackson herself picked up service work, first part-time for a family in Hyde Park, for a time at a date factory, and finally full-time, earning $12 a week as a housekeeper at the Edgewater Beach Hotel.

The deeply devout Jackson was quickly involved with black religious communities on the South Side and was active as a church singer. She became a member of stately Greater Salem Baptist Church (Figure 3.1), where she sang in the choir and joined an ensemble based there called the Johnson Singers. Initially made up of three brothers, Robert, Wilbur, and Prince Johnson, and Louise Lemon, the Johnson Singers added Jackson and gained popularity at Greater

FIG. 3.1 Greater Salem Baptist Church at 3300 South La Salle Street, Jackson's home church in Chicago. Photo by Bill Russell. The William Russell Jazz Collection at the Historic New Orleans Collection, acquisition made possible by the Clarisse Claiborne Grima Fund, acc. no. 92-48-L.331.875.

Salem and eventually at other black Chicago churches. The group performed in a manner conveying the influence of the dynamic modern gospel sound, "rocking them everywhere they went," according to gospel songwriter Thomas A. Dorsey. Despite the number of singers and the mixed personnel, many who remembered the group, like gospel singers Eugene Smith and Brother John Sellers, considered them a quartet, typically indicated stylistically by the presence of one singer providing a bass line.

In addition to her work with the Johnson Singers, Jackson also sang as a soloist in black churches, though her reception was mixed. On the one hand, some found her manner of performance, particularly her bodily involvement as she sang, contrary to the spirit of reverent worship. "At that time she had a beautiful shape and with her style of singing she was more or less a sexy singer," said Jackson's friend Robert Anderson, also a noted gospel singer, pianist, and composer. "Mahalia would move her body and this was the thing [that] actually intrigued the people." What was intriguing to some prompted resistance from others, said another friend and fellow singer, Ernestine Washington, who remembered "the biggest objection was the movements. She sang with her whole body." According to Sallie Martin, because of Jackson's uninhibited stage manner "some churches didn't receive her too well" and certain singers were unwilling to appear on programs with her, including the Roberta Martin Singers, who "wouldn't seemly get with her in any way." Sallie Martin offered practical advice to the rough-around-the-edges Jackson, who in her view had not yet habituated herself to the expected repertoire of respectable woman's decorum, like crossing her legs on an elevated platform. "Now listen, Mahalia, you must get a robe," Martin lectured. "I just can't be on the pulpit and you sitting there and your dress all up because you just *sit* and that's *it*."[2]

On the other hand, response to Jackson as a performer was enthusiastic enough that she was asked to assist some black clergy as a singing evangelist. These included Reverend Junius Caesar (J. C.) Austin, pastor of Pilgrim Baptist Church, and Reverend (later Bishop) Alvin Alexander (A. A.) Childs, who held street corner tent revivals, to which Jackson helped draw large crowds through her ministry in song, her "first church money," according to Goreau.[3] (Throughout much of the twentieth century, it was conventional for many black ministers, particularly in the South, to identify themselves by their first two initials—e.g., Reverend J. C. Austin and Bishop A. A. Childs. Some have explained this as a means of conveying authority and status to their congregation though others have claimed that it also increased their likelihood of being referred to by their last name, ideally prefaced by "Reverend" or "Mister," and thereby guard against ritual disrespect from white Southerners who might call them either by their first name or by a disrespectful nickname.[4]) Dorsey remembered that Jackson would help publicize his newly written gospel songs by singing them on South Side street corners. She also earned pocket change as an on-call singer for local funeral parlors where she was paid $2.00 per service. Following one funeral at Ebenezer Baptist Church, she was introduced to African American record executive J. Mayo "Ink" Williams, for whom she cut her first four commercial recordings on May 21, 1937. These were released on two 78 RPM singles by Decca Records: "God's Gonna Separate the Wheat from the Tares" b/w "Keep Me Every Day" and "God Shall Wipe All Tears Away" b/w "Oh, My Lord." ("B/w" is a common discographical abbreviation for "backed with," indicating the flip side of a record release.) Though the commercial response was minimal, Jackson's cousins Celie Taylor and Allen Clark remembered that these records, especially "God Shall Wipe All Tears Away," created an uproar back in the old neighborhood. Her New Orleans family huddled at Johnny Flowers's lounge in the Black Pearl to hear her debut sides while others gathered "out in the street, like Carnival" listening to the sound of the records pouring out of bars and music shops. In barrooms where the record was played, "people would stop dancing and just listen," remembered New Orleans native Elliott Beal, and "give it perfect reverence."[5]

Jackson was also invited to add her singing voice to political causes in Chicago. Goreau passed on Jackson's recollections of how the first opportunities came from elected aldermen representing Chicago's South Side.

Politics. She wasn't old enough to vote, but black Democrat Louie B. Anderson had seen Halie mesmerize a tentful and sought her for his meeting. . . .Halie had seen that the Second Ward had its black policemen, black firemen, black owned stores. Now she realized it had its own government too: a black alderman who sat in with the mayor and had precinct captains and such. Halie, who never did anything halfway, became a fervent voice for Louie B. Anderson. He won. Hallelujah. It was a big thing. . . .

Alderman Wm. L. Dawson was running hard for Congress from District 1—1st and 2nd Wards—that summer of '32, and Halie Jackson was running right along with him. "Not only for the big meetings; for all the precinct-captain meetings too—I sang for I don't know how many of those different meetings a night. . . .And baby, all those politicians would go crazy!"[6]

Fine-tuning the details and clarifying the historical context makes the full significance of Jackson's initial years of political involvement more discernible. In 1917, Anderson followed Oscar De Priest as alderman of Chicago's Second Ward, replacing De Priest as the city's only black city council member. Anderson served eight consecutive two-year terms until his retirement in 1933, when he was succeeded by William L. Dawson. With the strong encouragement of his constituents, Anderson challenged De Priest for his seat as the only black member of the U.S. Congress, but lost in an April 1932 primary. The defeat effectively marked the beginning of the end of Anderson's life as an elected official; he made a comeback bid in 1938, but lost again in another congressional primary race, this time against Dawson. It is not clear, then, which Anderson campaign Jackson was a part of. If it was for alderman, the Second Ward would have been reelecting a shoo-in warhorse incumbent, hardly a "big thing," though it might have been for Jackson. If it was for Congress, then it was a losing campaign.

Regardless, the transition in South Side leadership from Anderson to Dawson situates Jackson at a key period of political transformation for the African American electorate nationwide. Importantly, Anderson was in fact a Republican, as were Dawson and most black Americans until the reelection of Franklin Delano Roosevelt in 1936, when the black vote switched decisively from the "party of Lincoln" to the Democratic Party. "You know, the Second Ward used to be dead Republican, and Dawson started out Republican too," Jackson explained, "but he must have seen the way the thing was going, because he switched to Democrat and turned the whole thing around." Dawson, who maintained a close relationship with Jackson over the years, changed his affiliation to Democrat in 1939, so Jackson herself apparently identified as a Republican in the early 1930s but was singing for the Democrats by the end of the decade. Jackson told Goreau that she also sang in support of Roosevelt's first presidential campaign in 1932, though it could have also been, and perhaps more likely was, in connection with his later reelection bids.

In Sallie Martin's view, Jackson was to an unusual degree open to making herself available for progressive political events. Martin specifically recalled but could not remember the name of a "white fellow here downtown" who "was a political fellow" that called on Jackson on a regular basis and reciprocated by becoming an influential figure in her career. "They'd have their political meetings and she'd go down and sing for them," said Martin. "By getting with them, that was the thing that helped her get with Apollo. And then getting with Apollo, of course, he helped sell her over to Columbia." Martin is almost certainly recalling John Hammond, a record producer and an activist for black social causes as a board member of the NAACP, who had strong connections to Chicago through his work for Mercury Records in the late 1940s. Hammond was probably minimally involved with Jackson's Apollo signing in 1946, though he was instrumental in her making the jump to Columbia in 1954. But Martin's comments call our attention to the fact, or at least her perception, that alongside Jackson's black church base, such influential white male liberals as Hammond, Studs Terkel, Marshall Stearns, and Mitch Miller, all believers in the political salience of black vernacular musical performance, played a crucial role in advancing her career along previously untrodden paths.

In Chicago, Jackson cultivated a rich social life that brought together her professional aspirations, her church community, her musical activities, and her family of fellow gospel singers. By 1937, Jackson met her first husband, Arkansas-native Isaac "Ike" Hockenhull (1901–1973), who was ten years her senior and previously married. A newspaper notice suggests that Jackson and Hockenhull married in late 1941 and perhaps very briefly lived in St. Louis.[7] Though his strong predilection for the racetrack precipitated the marriage's demise, Hockenhull partnered with Jackson on her first business endeavor: selling her mother-in-law's line of cosmetics out of their small apartment. Jackson proved to be as inveterate an entrepreneur as Hockenhull was a gambler. Around 1940, she obtained her beautician's license and saved up enough money to purchase the requisite equipment and a vacant storefront on South Indiana Avenue, where she opened a shop, Mahalia's Beauty Salon, that made her a self-employed businesswoman. After living in cramped quarters in the back of the salon, Jackson moved into a much larger apartment four blocks away at 3726 South Prairie Avenue. When an opportunity arose to purchase her four-unit apartment building, Jackson took it, using her earnings to become a property owner and landlord. Sallie Martin saw in the young Jackson an ambition that occasionally made her "over anxious" and even competitive. "Mahalia was very determined" and clear-minded about "what she desired in life," said Martin, though Jackson also appeared constantly "afraid that the other fellow is trying to outdo me or trying to beat me out of something."[8]

On the other hand, Jackson's apartment and beauty shop became gathering places for a bustling circle of friends and gospel singers that included locals Emma Jackson, Robert Anderson, and Brother John Sellers, to whom she became a surrogate mother, and out-of-towners like Sister Rosetta Tharpe, Ernestine Washington, and the Ward Singers. The black gospel field grew steadily in the 1930s and 1940s, as did recognition of Jackson's name and voice. Even as she tried to manage her business and real estate interests, her work with the Johnson Singers and as a soloist made her an in demand singer on an expanding circuit of black Chicago churches and she added to her workload by accepting a position as director of the St. Luke Baptist Church choir. By the early 1940s, Jackson was an entrenched part of the Chicago gospel community while approaching the cusp of wider renown in her own right.

But we should also bear in mind that Jackson arrived in Chicago precisely when a black gospel singing movement was rippling outward with notable efficiency. Dorsey, Theodore Frye, and Magnolia Lewis Butts established gospel choruses for their own congregations, spurred the creation of gospel choruses at other local churches, networked these Chicago singers into a choral union, supported the organization of gospel-friendly choral unions in other cities and states, and aggregated these unions as the National Convention of Gospel Choirs and Choruses (NCGCC). By the time Jackson began to work on a consistent basis with Dorsey in the late 1930s and early 1940s, Dorsey's name and the NCGCC had staked out ground in a black gospel field that enabled her to take her own distinctive place. As a Baptist, Jackson was also forging ties with the National Baptist Convention, the governing body of black Baptist congregations across the country. Baptist Young People's Union programs at Mount Moriah, Zion Travelers, and Plymouth Rock and Sunday School Congresses held in New Orleans had already introduced Jackson to this institutional side of the Baptist church. But Jackson's personal initiatives and the increasingly rapturous reception of her singing operated both alongside and eventually in direct complementarity with these two families, the Baptists and the Chicago-based gospel pioneers. This chapter seeks to distinguish the work of Jackson, the National Baptist Convention, and the Dorsey-led NCGCC, highlighting the distinctive contributions of each, then put them back together, illustrating how the relationships among these parties contributed to the creation and subsequent reshaping of the black gospel field.

The National Baptist Convention, U.S.A., Incorporated

Jackson's connections to her Baptist church family in Chicago were cultivated through her membership at Greater Salem but were deepened through her navigation of the music programs of the National Baptist Convention, the largest black Christian organization in the world and a principal influence on the musical worship in black churches. The National Baptist Convention was founded through the merger of three separate black Baptist groups in 1895: the National Baptist Convention of America, which undertook missionary work in the United States; the Baptist Foreign Mission Convention, which focused on Christian ministry in West Africa; and the National Baptist Education Convention, which developed curricula and job training opportunities for students enrolled in church schools.[9] Reverend Elias Camp (E. C.) Morris (1855–1922) of Little Rock, Arkansas, born into slavery, was elected founding president, serving for the first twenty-eight years of the organization's existence. The core purpose of the National Baptist Convention was to coordinate the activities of black Baptist congregations across the country and to spearhead Christian education initiatives consistent with Baptist beliefs. This mission was pursued through a number of departments and auxiliary groups created to carry out specific charges. Principal among these were the National Baptist Laymen and Women's Auxiliary (the men's and women's departments, respectively), the Baptist Foreign Mission, the Sunday School Congress and Baptist Young People's Union (BYPU), and the National Baptist Publishing Board. The BYPU was subsequently renamed the Baptist Training Union (BTU).

The National Baptist Publishing Board had special significance. Initially, all published materials used by black Baptists were provided by the white-run Home Mission Society and American Baptist Publication Society, which were resistant to contributions by black writers. As a result, in its second year of existence, the National Baptist Convention supported the creation of an autonomous publishing board to produce its books and periodicals, educational materials for Sunday Schools, and songbooks from a black Baptist perspective. Within years, the Publishing Board, operating in Nashville under the direction of Dr. Richard Henry (R. H.) Boyd, became an enormously influential and lucrative operation, described by W. E. B. Du Bois as the "greatest single accomplishment of the National Baptist Convention." It also became the most prolific source of religious music by African American composers and spearheaded the circulation of new songs of worship within the black Baptist Church. The activity of the National Baptist Publishing Board, including its music offerings, was closely linked to the ideals of black uplift. The preface to an important early collection, the 1906 *National Anthem Series*, delineated its intent to offer a selection of songs "best suited or adapted to both the intellectual and spiritual awakening of our people" and "to encourage the use of such anthems as are doctrinally sound, of high-class music and spiritually inspiring."[10] The increasingly powerful Publishing Board was not, however, legally a part of the National Baptist Convention. A climactic struggle for control in 1915 resulted in a split into two separate organizations: the National Baptist Convention of America, which maintained affiliation with the Sunday School Congress and

Boyd's Publishing Board (and whose members were thus sometimes referred to colloquially as the "Boyd Baptists"), and the National Baptist Convention, U.S.A., Incorporated. Both are still active today, though the latter organization eventually became the predominating institution.

At the time, however, the National Baptist Convention, U.S.A., was left without an educational arm or a publishing operation. These were both reconstituted after the split, with Lucie E. Campbell (1885–1963) of Memphis appointed music director of the new Sunday School Congress and BYPU in 1916. Luvenia George has written that in this key position, Campbell, in collaboration with fellow Tennessean Reverend Edmund Walter David (E. W. D.) Isaac Jr. (c. 1886–1955), "became one of the most influential women in the history of Afro-American music." Campbell was born in Duck Hill, Mississippi, and as a small child moved with her family to Memphis where she lived the rest of her life as a self-taught musician, earning a reputation as a contralto soloist, a respected public school teacher, and writer of religious songs. Campbell's musical sensibilities were attuned with the National Baptist Convention's deeply rooted respectability politics. In 1904, in coordination with the National Federation of Colored Women Musicians, the teenaged Campbell organized the Music Club, which presented local concerts under the motto "Finer Music."

Campbell (Figure 3.2) contributed to the musical practices of Baptists nationwide by pursuing multiple, overlapping domains of activity. As head of youth music at the National Baptist Convention, she produced pageants—staged historical allegories involving drama and music—for the Sunday School Congress, which met annually but separately from the parent body, and assembled groups of young vocalists, most notably the Goodwill Singers, that toured nationally and sang as the de facto "house" ensemble at the convention. Campbell was also an important and productive songwriter who did not receive the same acclaim as many of her male counterparts, likely because she wrote specifically for the National Baptist Convention and not for commercial profit. Several of her compositions were not copyrighted until decades after they were originally introduced. But many Campbell songs—"Something Within," "He Understands, He'll Say 'Well Done,'" and "Footprints of Jesus," among others—remain touchstones of black musical worship across denominations. Responding to the times and shifting tastes in the 1940s and 1950s, Campbell also adapted her style and composed gospel songs recorded by many singers, including "Touch Me, Lord Jesus," an enormously popular hit in 1949 for Philadelphia's Angelic Gospel Singers; "Jesus Gave Me Water," which Sam Cooke recorded at his first session with the Soul Stirrers in 1950, scoring his first breakthrough with the group; and "In the Upper Room," a signature record for Jackson, who recorded it as a double-sided single for Apollo in 1952. When the National Baptist Convention, U.S.A., established its new publishing board in 1920 with Dr. Arthur Melvin (A. M.) Townsend as president,

FIG. 3.2 Lucie Campbell, influential music director at the National Baptist Convention, at the piano, May 1947. By permission of the Preservation and Special Collections Department, University Libraries, University of Memphis.

Campbell was involved in the compilation of important songbooks in the 1920s, most notably the landmark *Gospel Pearls* in 1921, but also *Inspirational Melodies*, a collection of gospel songs that she co-edited with Isaac in 1929.

Campbell's most influential role, however, was as talent adjudicator for the annual convention, a responsibility that she exercised for nearly a half century. The "National Baptist Convention" refers both to the organization and to the multiple-day gathering held each September in a different host city, with daily morning, afternoon, and evening sessions for the parent body and separately scheduled meetings for committees, boards, and auxiliaries. Sessions blended devotional services, sermons, and speeches and presentations on various topics, though the convention was also where black Baptist churches conducted official business. Attendees heard departmental reports, financial updates, new resolutions, proposals for the next year's host city, special tributes to individuals, and the president's annual address. Delegates also voted, some years amid aggressive campaigning and rancorous debate, to elect church leadership.

To an extraordinary degree, music was a centerpiece at the convention. An account of the 1950 gathering in Philadelphia conveys the meeting's atmosphere and the omnipresence of music as it circulated in various forms.

There's nothing to compare with the super-active, teeming National Baptist Convention. . . .

The main auditorium, with all of the fervid activity of a political convention, yet wearing the subdued atmosphere of a church, resounds to the speeches, reports, motions, suggestions and calls of the Baptist large and small, minister and layman.

Music from renowned religious-gospel singers fills the great hall to punctuate the speeches and talks which tend to tire the listeners. From the famous and non-famous churches in America, women singers step before the microphones during the lulls and render the songs which have aged in the church and the memory of the members. . . .

In the basement, the scene bears on the carnival side with booths and more booths selling or exhibiting wares of the various trade schools, record publishing houses' products by way of sheet music and wax recordings.[11]

Gospel singer and historian Pearl Williams-Jones called the National Baptist Convention "the primary vehicle for spreading Black sacred music repertoire." Within Baptist circles in particular, composers relied upon the convention to introduce a national audience to their compositions, sold as sheet music to soloists, ensemble leaders, and choir directors eager to learn the latest songs. Dorsey's breakthrough as a gospel writer came with the positive response to his song "If You See My Savior" at the 1930 convention. "The Baptists were really the ones who pushed the music," said composer and arranger Kenneth Morris of the gathering's reputation-making potential. "If you didn't go to the National Baptist Convention, you could just forget it."[12]

Beyond the immediate prestige of performing for the large gathering, the annual convention was also a crucial mechanism through which soloists, quartets, and gospel groups pitched themselves to church communities across the country in hope of securing future engagements. "At a convention, it's dog-eat-dog, everybody trying to make a quarter," said Jackson's frequent musical collaborator James Lee. But "you usually get quite a few engagements by being at the convention because if you're heard, . . . ministers and promoters and sponsors usually want to contact you for the aftermath."[13] In this sense, Campbell became a gatekeeper of sorts for aspirant singers, earning a reputation as the "Great Presenter." According to Boyer, "Campbell was so important and powerful in the National Baptist Convention that anyone who wanted to sing on the program had to audition for her, singing the same song he or she planned to sing on the program." Jackson enjoyed sharing the story of how Campbell barked "Stand up straight, young woman!" during her own audition for the convention, though at the Music Inn in 1951 she also identified Campbell as "one of our fine [gospel song] writers that lives today . . . and one of our national workers at our National Baptist

Convention."[14] Campbell screened the talent for the large concerts that kicked off both the annual Sunday School Congress and the national convention. This positioned her as an important mentor to young singers. At the 1919 convention in Newark, New Jersey, Campbell introduced twenty-two-year-old Marian Anderson to the Baptist gathering, accompanying the contralto on piano. Perhaps her most intimate protégé was J. Robert Bradley, who became so closely associated with the convention that he earned the nickname "Mr. Baptist." Campbell enlisted the impoverished Bradley into the Goodwill Singers and later paved the way for him to get formal vocal training in New York and Europe, underwritten by the National Baptist Convention. Bradley enjoyed an esteemed career as a singer with equal comfort on a sanctuary pulpit or a concert stage, though he also expressed pride at becoming "the first gospel singer to really hold an office" in the organization when he succeeded Campbell as music director for the Sunday School Publishing Board following her death.[15]

Singing by the convention chorus, smaller ensembles, soloists, or gathered attendees was interspersed with nearly every item on the agenda at the national meeting. Whether in vaudeville or on a gospel program, where in the lineup one was scheduled to perform communicated status and accrued prestige, and according to Goreau, Jackson believed she was given a less visible time slot in her earliest appearances because Campbell was lukewarm toward her style of music.

> [T]his was a time when the leaders' respect went to those in music who had studied in the white studios in the Loop. It showed in the National Baptist Convention, when President L. K. Williams would say, "Mahalia, you can sing, but—" And Miss Lucie Campbell, real power of the music there, wanted culture put up, didn't want Mahalia in the big programs; pushed her off to the early morning.[16]

The published minutes for the 1940 National Baptist Convention in Birmingham, Alabama, providing blow-by-blow documentation of the meeting, help illustrate the place of music on the convention floor. Reverend Lacey Kirk (L. K.) Williams, pastor of Olivet Baptist Church in Chicago, became the second president of the National Baptist Convention following Morris's death in 1922 and he presided over the Birmingham meeting. Each session began with singing, either by the convention chorus or in a song service led most often by Isaac. Folded into the official proceedings, which included comments by Martin Luther King Sr., were numerous selections, mostly by the chorus (Campbell conducted the choir for several numbers, including the anthem "All Hail the National Baptist Convention" and Dorsey's "Take My Hand, Precious Lord") and by the congregation singing such familiar hymns and church songs as "Must Jesus Bear This Cross Alone," "Leaning on the Everlasting Arms," and "Just a Little Talk with Jesus." Campbell also programmed additional performances by guest singers that diversified the offerings. At the Friday morning session, the choir from historically black Leland College near Baton Rouge, Louisiana, performed "Inflammatus" from Gioacchino Rossini's *Stabat Mater*, a work of art music that remains a staple at many black mainline churches. Not all performers were specified in the published minutes for the Birmingham convention. Friday evening, designated "Booker T. Washington Night" for the convention's yearly tribute to the African American statesman and founder of Tuskegee College in Alabama, "a song fest was given by Prof. Isaac and various singers, which kept the audience in good cheer." An extended set of music was also programmed for the Sunday afternoon session, at which "various singers rendered selections. This musical period lasted for thirty minutes and gave artists opportunity for a display of rare talent in that line."[17]

We cannot know exactly who were these "various singers" who generated "good cheer" with "rare talent" in their "line" of music, though perhaps a clue comes from a postmortem of the 1940 convention written by Reverend Porter W. Phillips and published in the *Pittsburgh Courier*. The commentary by Phillips, whose bachelor's and master's degrees were included in his byline, highlights the intra-racial politics of representation that were contested as black gospel music steadily broadened its popularity in the 1930s and 1940s. The previous year, Phillips attended the convention of the racially mixed Baptist World Alliance in Atlanta, where he felt immense pride listening to a "fine group of Negro singers" who "sang to the honor and credit of themselves, their respective churches, [and] of the race" for thousands assembled "who listened with rapt attention and deep emotion to the sweet melodies of the 'Soul of Black Folk.'" At the 1940 National Baptist Convention in Birmingham, however, Phillips was shocked to encounter the "local and imported 'gospel whooping and jazz swinging singers' that swooped down upon the convention like Hitler's blitzkrieg." Phillips made further use of military metaphors to communicate his alarm at what he perceived as a distressing lapse of dignity.

> These high-powered, extraordinary, evangelistic gospel whooping, star singers, tried to turn the convention into an old fashion revival but they almost turned it into a minstrel show. They skipped and hopped and wrung and swung and whooped and jazzed themselves into a mad frenzy....Then, in a vain attempt to "move" the convention, a more violent "singing air raid" was turned on, as different ones at certain intervals hugged and kissed the "mike" and yelled with all the lung power at their command. Just what effect this animal-like discordant and discourteous note in the harmony of music was supposed to have upon intelligent human beings I do not know. But to me it sounded like a "bellowing bull" or a "braying ass."

Judging from the minutes, singing by the official convention chorus and by the congregation dominated the proceedings in Birmingham, so the unidentified "various singers" may have been the performers that affronted Phillips's sensibilities. We might with good reason dismiss his perspective as one coming from a prude cultural elitist or a conservative curmudgeon. But his observation that the presentation of gospel singing in Birmingham was in effect promotional, "introduced to the pastors at the convention as being available for evangelistic services," resonates with the recollections of Lee while also registering the sense of black gospel singing as not just a musical style but also as a purposeful, if ambivalently received, movement.[18]

As many writers have observed, the proliferation of black gospel singing and performance practices sparked controversy that still crackled well into the 1940s, though the "conservative" point of view is rarely taken seriously.[19] Gospel singing was frequently represented as a direct threat to the authority of the concert spiritual. Esteemed Tuskegee Institute choir director and spiritual arranger William L. Dawson, who harbored deep skepticism toward the growing popularity of gospel music, devoted his career to shaping a public reception of the spiritual that affirmed its artistic seriousness and cultural significance.[20] Grievances about new styles of musical worship in black churches were aired openly in the black press by such commentators as Wilson King of Newport News, Virginia. Highly respected in Virginia's Tidewater region, King was a former organ and choral conducting student of British master organist Norman Coke-Jephcott at St. John the Divine Cathedral in New York who became a local high school music teacher, the owner of a private music studio, and minister of music at Queen Street Baptist Church. "With all due respect to the type of Gospel song now the vogue—and they do have their place in religious music—it is my opinion that our pastors emphasize these songs at the sacrifice of good accepted hymn singing," Wilson told the *Norfolk New Journal and Guide* in 1944. Though resonant with the discourses of uplift, respectability, and racial affirmation evident in Phillips's comments, King's perspective, expressed in a series of articles, was undoubtedly shaped as well by his personal investment in professional training.[21]

Orrin Suthern, also a classically trained black musician as well as a professor of music at Florida State A & M University, shared this outlook. Much as King was skeptical of "ministers who have been known to urge their choir and pianists to 'whoop' it up," Suthern perceived that pastors "championing the cause of 'whoop-it-up' kind of singing" were "in the ascendancy," in part because "the gospel chorus is a financial success, which accounts for its favor with the average pastor." The fact was, King and Suthern were convinced, gospel singers came cheap. Both men linked gospel's florescence to a political economy of style within the black church, fostered, King argued, by "churches that don't or won't pay for the higher type of

sacred music and musicians that are trained and devoted to their work." As a result, job opportunities in musical ministry were increasingly determined less by
formal training than by "musicians' ability to swing it." This perception that gospel
singing posed the threat of an unruly amateurism is apparent as well in Phillips's
review of the 1940 National Baptist Convention. The musical preferences of black
congregations increasingly attracted to gospel singing had material, generational,
and cross-denominational consequences for professional church musicians. In
1942, sixty-eight-year-old Lizzie Ward Johnson, after over forty years as organist at
Baltimore's John Wesley Methodist Church, agreed to retire, faced with pressure
from "younger choir members [who] wanted to get more zip into their music."[22]

Working on a Building

The person most closely associated with the production and proliferation of "the
type of Gospel song now the vogue" was Thomas Andrew Dorsey (1899–1993).
Dorsey's journey during the interwar years from preacher's kid in Atlanta to blues
pianist "Georgia Tom" to prolific gospel songwriter has been well documented.
The most comprehensive scholarship on Dorsey, a 2018 Blues Hall of Fame in-
ductee, remains Michael Harris's monograph *The Rise of Gospel Blues: Thomas
Andrew Dorsey and the Urban Church.*[23] Harris structures his narrative of Dorsey's
life and career and of "the rise of gospel blues" around tensions arising from
interwoven sets of "dualities": sacred and secular, the preacher and the bluesman,
"old-lineism" and vernacular worship, the mainstream and downhome blackness, assimilationist and traditionalist social orientations. Particularly suggestive
of such a reading is Dorsey's career in the 1920s, when he was a working blues
musician, backing vaudeville singer Gertrude "Ma" Rainey and partnering with
guitarist Hudson "Tampa Red" Whittaker, while writing gospel songs on the side.
His first published gospel song, "If I Don't Get There," appeared in 1922, in the
second edition of *Gospel Pearls*. Just two years after recording his biggest hit with
Tampa Red, "It's Tight Like That," for Vocalion, he was introduced by Campbell at
the 1930 National Baptist Convention in Chicago to great acclaim, on the strength
of his well-received song "If You See My Savior." By the early 1930s, Dorsey, who
moved permanently to Chicago in 1921 and became a member of the prestigious Pilgrim Baptist Church, was fully committed to writing and selling gospel
songs, disseminating them through his publishing company Dorsey's House of
Music. Boyer claims "there are more extant compositions by Thomas Andrew
Dorsey than by any other gospel music composer." His best known numbers,
including "Peace in the Valley," "The Lord Will Make a Way Somehow," "Search
Me, Lord," "If We Never Needed the Lord Before, We Sure Do Need Him Now,"
and the internationally famous "Take My Hand, Precious Lord," have achieved
canonic status. The latter, which adapts of the melody of the nineteenth-century

hymn "Must Jesus Bear the Cross Alone" (sometimes known as "Maitland") with original text penned by Dorsey, was written following the death of Dorsey's wife during childbirth and is surely one of the best known religious songs the United States has produced. Dorsey promoted his songs aggressively, setting up a booth each year at the National Baptist Convention, taking out advertisements in black newspapers, and touring with singers whom he believed could best demonstrate the effectiveness of his compositions and their lyrics. Like Wilson and Suthern, Dorsey recognized that the gradual embrace of gospel singing by established black churches was both spiritual and economic: "gospel songs helped people get through the Depression. And when a church got into hard luck, *then* it was glad to get the singer to fill the collection box."[24]

In growing his business, Dorsey worked closely with a close circle of like-minded associates. Throughout much of the 1930s, Dorsey's main collaborator on these song-promoting tours was Sallie Martin (1895–1988), an effective singer who had even greater impact on the emerging field through her immense organizational prowess. Martin remembered beginning her work with Dorsey in 1929, first singing in the small ensemble that he directed then touring with him as a featured soloist until 1939, when she branched out and formed an ensemble of her own—"the nation's first all-woman, touring black gospel group"—and a year later opened an important music shop, the Martin and Morris Music Studio, with composer and arranger Kenneth Morris.[25] Martin's application of her entrepreneurial savvy to ordering and boosting the business side of Dorsey's work as a religious song composer in the 1930s was a catalyst for his subsequent success. Another musical colleague was Theodore Frye (1899–1963), who came to Chicago from Fayette, Mississippi, and in whom Dorsey had recognized a potential comrade when he paired his songs with Frye's charismatic performance style. "We teamed up and traveled through the South, East, and Midwest making the national meetings and winning the acclaim of every audience we sang and played to," said Dorsey, remembering Frye's trademark "strut" while he sang. "He didn't have the right material to walk to 'til he found me."[26]

Closely tied to the growing circulation of Dorsey's songs through sheet music and performance was the institution building that began in Chicago and helped create the conditions for the formation of the black gospel field. Harris describes Dorsey's frustration with the marginalization of gospel singers at many mainline churches by their relegation to midweek services or, if they did sing on Sunday, to the back of the sanctuary. This changed, virtually all histories of black gospel music concur, with the formation of the city's first gospel chorus under Frye at Ebenezer Baptist Church in January 1932 and under Dorsey at Pilgrim months later.[27] Both created a sensation. But a third Dorsey collaborator, Magnolia Lewis Butts (1880–1949), in fact predated both Frye and Dorsey in putting together a choral ensemble carrying the spirit of the movement. A member of Metropolitan

Community Church, a classically trained soprano, and assistant director under Metropolitan's esteemed choral conductor J. Wesley Jones, Butts, a native of Tipton, Missouri, was charged with organizing a gospel chorus at Metropolitan for the purpose of providing a stylistic alternative to Jones's senior choir.

Hewing to the conventional Dorsey-centric narrative of the "birth" and "rise" of gospel in Chicago, one that situates the formation of the Ebenezer and Pilgrim gospel choruses in early 1932 as a watershed moment, both Harris and Marovich mention yet take somewhat odd pains to moderate the potential significance of Butts's seminal and even groundbreaking role in the organization of a bona fide "gospel" choir as early as the late 1920s.[28] But other sources have in fact credited Butts's group, the W. D. Cooke Singers, as being the first gospel chorus in Chicago. Reverend Esther Greer, who according to Harris had a "first-hand" view of musical activity at Metropolitan in the 1920s, remembered that the group "began to sing according to the dictates of Magnolia's heart and mind" and "moved into the gospel area."[29] In the absence of recordings, questions of stylistic breakthroughs are difficult to address with full confidence. As Lynn Abbott and Doug Seroff have shown, there are references to ensembles in Chicago called "gospel choirs" as early as 1910.[30] What distinguishes the work of Dorsey and his cohort in the early 1930s, however, is the purposeful institutionalizing of black gospel singing and the extension of this organization nationally, launching a movement that in effect built gospel singing into a new field of cultural production.

Witnessing the response to their respective choirs, Dorsey, Butts, and Frye met in the spring of 1932 to formalize "the gospel chorus movement," mounting "a drive advocating a renaissance of gospel singing in the churches of Chicago" by forming a gospel choral union. "Within two months," the *Chicago Defender* reported, "20 churches responded with organizations dedicated to the singing of gospel songs only." This was quickly followed by promotional tours by "Professor Dorsey and his executive committee," resulting in "the formation of Gospel chorus groups in 24 states" that in turn organized into new unions. To celebrate a year of spectacular growth, and "to further consolidate the choruses throughout the country," a new organization, initially called Gospel Choruses of America, hosted a convention at Pilgrim Baptist Church for the various gospel chorus unions from August 29 to September 1, 1933. The gathering featured solo, choral, and congregational singing, a dedicatory sermon by Pilgrim pastor J. C. Austin, an address by Dorsey, and the election of officers, including Dorsey as president, Butts as vice president, and Frye as treasurer. By its second meeting in St. Louis the following year, the group had adopted a new name, the National Convention of Gospel Choirs and Choruses.[31]

Placing Jackson's arrival in Chicago in late November 1931, not 1927 or 1928 as is commonly accepted, helps us better understand her place in the early history of the black gospel field. The dating of Jackson's arrival in Chicago may seem a

trivial and pedantic matter until we recognize that what would have been her actual first full year in Chicago, 1932, overlapped precisely with this feverish and
highly systematic mobilization of black gospel singing nationwide. The specific
nature of Jackson's relationship to the black gospel field becomes obscured when
we take Jackson at her word that she was a child who "came to Chicago when I was
in my early teens," as she told Studs Terkel in 1954, and fail to register that she
was in fact a twenty-year-old adult woman poised to be a beneficiary of a newly
innovated landscape presented to her by the organization and growth of gospel
singing within months of her arrival in the city. This is not to say that Jackson
did not "stand on a street corner and demonstrate" Dorsey's songs throughout
much of the 1930s, but rather to argue that this was not in 1929, as Goreau writes,
which would have been before Dorsey started touring with Sallie Martin, before
the establishment of the gospel choirs at Metropolitan, Ebenezer, and Pilgrim, and
before the creation of the NCGCC.[32] Jackson was able to hit the ground running
so quickly because these institutional structures were, through hard work, already
being put in place when she arrived. In other words, she was joining a program
already in progress.

Jackson's own recollections in later years suggest that she was at ground zero
of the movement. Addressing a group of gospel-curious jazz aficionados at the
Music Inn in Lenox, Massachusetts, in the fall of 1951, Jackson recounted working
alongside a fledgling Dorsey to help launch the gospel movement.

> And a long way back in the thirties come a professor, Thomas Dorsey, one
> of our finest gospel writers. . . .He had about two, three little songs. But
> I was singing back that time and Mr. Dorsey, I used to sing some of his
> songs, and I still do today. Out of his songs it seems to create an interest
> in the church. Looked like the young people liked that type of songs, and
> way back in 1930 we organized what was known as a gospel chorus at the
> Ebenezer Baptist Church, the first gospel chorus in the United States.
> And next at the Pilgrim Baptist Church. And next at the Olivet Baptist
> Church . . . And then, after we had that first chorus, many choruses were
> organized. And then there were young choruses, junior choirs, junior
> gospel choruses. So therefore, it spreaded all over the United States, into
> New York, way down in Georgia and Mississippi and Louisiana.

Interpretation of these comments is tricky. Jackson gets the basic story right, about
the churches involved and about the dramatic growth of the movement. But if her
use of "we" is taken at face value—and if the judgment that she arrived in late 1931
is correct—it does leave us with the choice of either revising history as it has come
down to us and crediting the fresh-off-the-train Jackson with helping to establish
Chicago's very first gospel choirs; calling out Jackson on her misrepresentation

of facts; or giving her the benefit of the doubt and assuming that by "we" Jackson meant members of her gospel family in Chicago. Goreau, shifting the dates of significant gospel movement events to fit her timeline for Jackson, clearly chooses the first option, writing: "In 1930 she helped [Dorsey] form Pilgrim Baptist's first gospel chorus."[33] It is perhaps most accurate and clarifying to understand Jackson's "we" as the Chicago gospel family of which she became an indispensible part, maybe not as an organizer per se—her name is never mentioned in the voluminous newspaper coverage of the NCGCC—but as a comrade, a colleague, a collaborator, and very soon, through her performances as a Johnson Singer and as a spectacular soloist, a catalytic force that garnered even more illustrious exposure for black gospel. Still, a subplot of this story of Dorsey, the NCGCC, and his affiliations with charismatic artists like Jackson involves the ways in which Jackson, throughout her career, subtly tailored her self-narrative to her audience in order to shape understandings of her art and her place in gospel music and African American history.

From its very first years of existence, the NCGCC pursued an ambitious agenda, reflected in its operations, promotion, and discipline in rearticulating the organization's mission. The NCGCC was the beachhead from which Dorsey, Butts, Frye, Sallie Martin, and other leaders sought to build a gospel singing movement predicated on a vision encompassing a range of remarkably well-coordinated axes of operation: repertory, musical practice, institutional structure, interdenominational cooperation, interorganizational collaboration, spiritual fortification, mobilization of racial pride, and commitment to social relevance. Following the model of the National Baptist Convention, the NCGCC board gathered at a midwinter meeting early in the year to discuss official business and plan the national convention in August. Even if Dorsey was its most recognizable public face, the NCGCC relied heavily on a coterie of coworkers in official positions, many of them prominent women gospel singers, who were not "helpmates" but rather were instrumental and integral to the organization's growth and stability. Besides Butts, whom NCGCC historian Loreta Garrett called "the brains behind the operation," these included Roberta Martin (National Supervisor of the Youth Department), Artelia Hutchins from Detroit (second vice-president), Willie Mae Ford Smith from St. Louis (national supervisor of the Soloist Bureau), and above all Sallie Martin (national organizer), thanks to whom "many new groups have been added" to the NCGCC fold.[34] On a practical level, marshaling the explosion of gospel choruses in the early 1930s benefited Dorsey by building a national network of customers for his increasingly popular songs. Though founded by three Baptists, the organization broadened its reach through an interdenominational openness that from the first convention purposefully included Methodists, and particularly Colored Methodist Episcopal (CME) choirs. The 1937 and 1938 conventions in Indianapolis and Dayton, Ohio, respectively, were the first though hardly the last hosted by

Methodist churches. Ministers and "gospel enthusiasts of all denominations" were welcomed and present at NCGCC gatherings. From early on, therefore, modern gospel was explicitly positioned as a denominationally mobile practice of singing.[35]

Early coverage of the NCGCC reveals other noteworthy features of the organization. There was considerable early resistance to gospel-style singing from music directors at major black churches, including Dorsey's own congregation. "I felt it was degrading. How can something that's jazzy give a religious feeling?" wondered conservatory-trained vocalist, composer, and director of the senior choir at Pilgrim Baptist Church Edward Boatner, remembering his opposition to folding a gospel choir into his church's musical ministry. "The only people who think it isn't a desecration are the people who haven't had . . . any musical training." Harris, encapsulating his book's core argument, characterizes the rise and spread of the black gospel chorus—which he describes as "organized indigenous singing" that was "anchored to downhome blues"—as a final repudiation of such views and a reconciliation of binaries woven through black church music culture and made manifest in Dorsey's own musical life.[36] Yet whatever resonances of "downhome blues" one might hear in Dorsey's songs, it is nonetheless striking to note the degree to which the NCGCC made as its mission a regulation and conventional professionalization of gospel practice, promising to impart the very training that critics insisted gospel singers lacked.

At his very first convention in 1933, Dorsey told delegates that his ultimate goal was "a home or headquarters with departments to study, rehearse, and develop the highest type of gospel singing with the very best interpretation of the spirituals and heart songs." The following year, the NCGCC instituted an annual adjudicated competition, with expert coaches, to award a $150 scholarship to a worthy young singer. Shadowed by the class-based skepticism toward gospel singing expressed by figures like Phillips, King, Suthern, and Boatner, the NCGCC immediately and continuously highlighted its focus on quality control. The organization formalized its enforcement of musical standards at its 1935 board meeting through

> the establishing of an examining board composed of recognized musicians, one in each section where there is a gospel choir or chorus and before anyone can be admitted into the National Convention of Gospel Choirs and Choruses as a director, he must be prepared by having a course of study and pass an examination set up by the board of examiners. Gospel singers who would be known as Gospel soloists must also come before this board of examiners.

Accordingly, annual conventions featured instruction in "the proper technique of singing gospel songs," a daily "amateur hour" during which prospective singers were "tutored by trained vocalists," breakout sessions to address best practices for gospel choir accompanists, and seminars led by Butts on "Requisites of a Choral Director and How to Attain Them." This educational thrust remains a centerpiece of NCGCC activity today, most notably through its Artelia Hutchins Training Institute. A corollary to this emphasis on training was a downplaying—at least officially—of gratuitous flamboyance as a requisite element of gospel performance. Some reports on convention gatherings noted "shouting as never before seen here" and "people shouting never before seen doing thus." Nonetheless, "This Convention is not given to show or showmanship," read a 1940 story in the Dorsey-friendly *Atlanta Daily World* that sounded like a NCGCC press release. "It does not aim to set forth striking personalities or individuals, with single pet ideas, but it does attempt to give a sound, comprehensive program of study, lectures, demonstration, etc., on problems pertinent to the ministry of Gospel music in the church." Mobilized through the NCGCC, this discourse of regulated gospel practice continued into the following decade. A 1941 issue of the *Pittsburgh Courier* displayed a photograph of Virginia Heath Williams under the bold headline "Accredited Gospel Singer." Williams, the caption read, "received her certificate as a member of the National Convention of Gospel Choirs recently in a competitive examination at New York City. The certificate was signed by Thomas A. Dorsey and another official of the national group. This certificate says that Mrs. Williams is an accredited soloist." Eventually, Dorsey did get a home and headquarters for the movement in 1945, when the NCGCC purchased property and opened a "Gospel Singers College" at 4048 South Lake Park Avenue in Chicago to train aspiring vocalists, provide accommodations for traveling gospel musicians, and shelter retired singers in need of caretaking.[37]

Another component of the NCGCC's legitimizing strategy were alliances with other established black institutions. The active music program of the National Baptist Convention, which Dorsey, Frye, Butts, and Martin attended regularly, was a natural ally and there was surely some cross-promotion. The NCGCC also curated a "mammoth songfest" as part of the 1940 American Negro Exposition in Chicago and assisted the New York Gospel Chorus Union's collaboration with the *New York Amsterdam News* in presenting a Jubilee and Gospel Song Festival in Brooklyn and Manhattan in 1945. A particularly important partner that helped the NCGCC build credibility was the Chicago-based National Association of Negro Musicians (NANM), founded in 1919 by J. Wesley Jones. Chicago was a radial point for classically trained African American musicians, and the NANM and the Chicago Music Association represented two of the most influential organizations in the country supporting black classical musicians.[38] There was already a connection to the NANM through Butts, who was member, and Jones spoke at the NCGCC meeting in its first year, delivering remarks "profuse in his congratulations upon the work the singers had already done" and offering his recommendations for correcting "their defects." The two organizations exhibited more concrete ties when the executive committee of NANM officially invited the NCGCC to participate in its "giant song-fest" at Metropolitan Community Church in March 1940.[39]

The NCGCC heavily underscored the continuity of modern gospel music with African American musical heritage in its early years. At the inaugural convention, Butts welcomed attendees with remarks on "the origin of the spirituals and what heart songs mean to us." Assisted by the black press, the organization sustained this particular music-historical and pedagogical emphasis, repeatedly calling on its members to memorialize "the songs of our forefathers and mothers." At its 1936 Winter meeting, the NCGCC formed "a board to research work with reference to Negro music" so "that boys and girls of our racial group may have authentic knowledge of Negro music." Gospel songster Sister Rosetta Tharpe created a sensation but also a stir when she cut sides with the big band of Lucky Millender in 1938, including swing versions of such church songs as "Down by the Riverside" and "Rock Daniel." In March 1939, Reverend George W. Harvey, pastor of New Hope Baptist Church in Braddock, Pennsylvania, wrote a two-part denunciation of the practice of "swinging spirituals," fuming that such "sacrilegious desecration of Spirituals, the only real American music, as it is swung in gin shops, dance halls, over the radio and on records at various non-descript amusement places is a disgrace to the whole race." Lest his work legitimizing the gospel singing movement be undermined through guilt by association, Dorsey was quick to offer up an "Amen" on behalf of the NCGCC. "[K]eeping sacred the songs of our forefathers and mothers is a thing I've been fighting for and preaching for the last five years as President of the National Convention of Gospel Singers, Inc.," Dorsey responded in a letter to Harvey published in the *Courier*. "I have spent untold sums to keep my songs from being desecrated by the worldly musicians." Dorsey cited his injunction against Tharpe following her swing-adapted performance of his song "Hide Me in Your Bosom" at the Cotton Club over live radio that sparked "heavy protest from the church choirs who had been singing the number."[40]

Dorsey, Butts, and Frye would have been well aware of seminal commentary on spirituals, sometimes referred to in the 1910s and 1920s as "heart songs," that resonated broadly within the black public sphere. Most influentially, W. E. B. Du Bois's exegesis of the "sorrow songs" in *The Souls of Black Folk* (1903), James Weldon Johnson's poem "O Black and Unknown Bards" (1922) and introduction to *The Book of American Negro Spirituals* (1925), and Alain Locke's essay on "Negro Spirituals" in *The New Negro* anthology (1925) imparted to a generation of African Americans a hermeneutics of this sacralized repertory.[41] It is likely in this context that the NCGCC claimed as its mission "to promote greater appreciation for race music" through commemoration of black musical ancestors. In this sense, we might consider the formation of the NCGCC, and thus the organizational arm of the gospel singing movement, as a capstone project fostered in part by the 1920s Negro Renaissance.

Extending from these commemorative impulses were narratives that bridged the history of the spiritual and the production of modern gospel songs. The NCGCC sought "to preserve Negro jubilee, folk songs, and introduce new ones" by encouraging "young musicians to write and teach others to write new folk songs and spirituals." As "the Race's greatest song writer," Dorsey himself became singularly situated as an heir, upholder, and continuation of this legacy. At a pomp-filled "Founder's Day" ceremony in 1935 to honor Dorsey's, Butts's, and Frye's leadership of the organization, Pilgrim's assistant pastor Reverend R. C. Keller praised Dorsey for "the perpetuation of the songs of the fathers" through his latter-day sorrow songs.

> Monuments over the graves of departed heroes cannot equal the tangible abiding merit in appreciative hearts for the solace, in times of sorrow, the courage in moments of despair, and edification during the worship hour, brought in these songs written by Dorsey and used for the inspiration of countless millions of lives.[42]

Over the next several years, Dorsey's personal stature was boosted further, right alongside the growth of the NCGCC. At the convention, his annual address became one of the marquee events, often directly engaging such political topics as desegregation, anti-lynching legislation, police brutality against black citizens, anti-Semitism, the Italo-Ethiopian wars, and "what gospel singers can do to help in the post-war world."[43] In the late 1930s, the *Atlanta Daily World* and other black newspapers printed guest columns written by Dorsey, featuring his wide ranging, ruminating commentary on gospel music practice, religious belief, and African American culture. By the height of his fame around 1940, "Dorsey" had become a brand name in religious music, inspiring frenzy at his National Baptist Convention booth, books on his accomplishments (including one self-written), study of his "life and works" on black college campuses, and "Dorsey Days" at churches dedicated to the singing of his latest music. Photos of "America's foremost gospel songwriter" with such major cultural figures as Arna Bontemps and Paul Robeson and details of his social life appeared in African American newspapers. Meanwhile, the popularity of Dorsey and the musical movement with which he was associated continued to cause consternation among some observers forced to grapple with the rapid expansion of the black gospel field. In 1940, columnist Gamewell Valentine observed: "The wide circulation of Thomas A. Dorsey's gospel songs has caused young students of music, as well as many ministers, musicians, and educators, to ask, 'Is the gospel song most appropriate, or appropriate at all, for religious worship?'"

Dorsey was touring primarily with Sallie Martin until 1939. His most meaningful work with Jackson came very shortly afterward, by which time Dorsey was
one of the most respected African American musicians in the country (Figure
3.3). A sense of Dorsey's standing at the time is suggested by descriptions of
how he "blazed the trail, pioneered the field, made a new market and brought to
the churches throughout America new life and spirit through his gospel songs."
Jackson and Dorsey appeared together in a newspaper photo taken at the 1939
National Baptist Convention in Philadelphia, showing them "demonstrating one
of the dramatic poses which punctuate their singing." Sallie Martin believed that
the Dorsey-Jackson collaboration "didn't last long. I don't know whether they traveled together for a year," though in fact, their joint appearances were more extensive, much to Jackson's benefit. The period of closest association were the war
years of 1941–1944, when their programs in the Midwest, on the East Coast, and
in Dorsey's native Atlanta were hyped in black newspapers. Dorothy Love Coates,
who would later become lead singer of the Original Gospel Harmonettes, saw

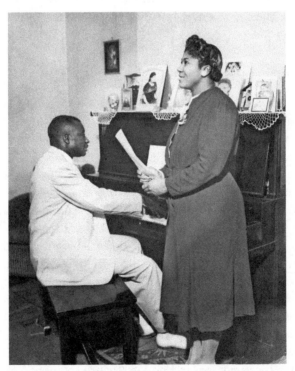

FIG. 3.3 Thomas A. Dorsey and Mahalia Jackson rehearse at Dorsey's apartment,
probably late 1930s or early 1940s. A photo of National Convention of Gospel
Choirs and Choruses co-founder Magnolia Lewis Butts sits on the piano between
Dorsey and Jackson. GTN Pictures.

Jackson and Dorsey team up in her hometown of Birmingham, Alabama: "Mr. Dorsey would just keep handing Mahalia these ballads and she'd stand there reading the words while she sang. She'd do fifteen, twenty songs a night like that." According to Brother John Sellers, it was Dorsey who spontaneously called Jackson "the Empress" while accompanying her at a 1940 gospel program at Morning Star Baptist in Chicago; shortly thereafter we see the honorific appear in promotion for such programs as one at Bethel Baptist Church in Brooklyn in 1941 that advertised "Professor Thomas A. Dorsey, America's foremost gospel song writer, and Mahalia Jackson, Empress of Gospel Singers." On June 2, 1943, Jackson performed at a major program at DuSable High School in Chicago celebrating Dorsey's twenty-first anniversary as a gospel songwriter, a concert that featured a stellar lineup of singers that also included Butts, Frye, Sallie Martin, Willie Mae Ford Smith, Myrtle Jackson, and Roberta Martin.[44] But as Dorsey's fame as a celebrity black gospel songwriter reached its peak, Jackson's own star was beginning to rise as her dynamic performances gained notice beyond the Midwest. This expansion of her national profile was facilitated in part through her association with Dorsey but was perhaps most consequentially impacted by her building a reputation on the biggest stage of all, at the National Baptist Convention.

Breaking Out with the Baptists

At a gospel program in Chicago in June 1955, Jackson acknowledged Reverend John L. Branham Sr., L. K. Williams's right-hand man at Olivet, for having given her "the chance to make herself known through the National Baptist Convention" when she was a young singer. Williams was killed in a plane crash less than two months after the 1940 convention in Birmingham and was succeeded as president by Reverend David Vivian (D. V.) Jemison of Selma, Alabama, so Jackson had probably already been given a coveted opportunity to perform at the convention by the late 1930s. Her appearances in the 1940s, however, indicate a clear upward trajectory of prominence as her national reputation grew. At the Atlanta convention in 1946, the featured performers at a "National Artists Night Concert" during the Friday evening session—the Goodwill Singers, the Martin and Morris Singers, the Theodore Frye Singers, the Thomas Dorsey Singers, and the Roberta Martin Singers—indicated the prominence of the NGCCC gospel pioneers, though it also suggested that Jackson was still just one singer among many: Jackson, Bradley, and Clara Ward were among a group of "others" who also performed at the concert. Two years later, the convention was in Houston. Though chorus and congregational singing still predominated, the dramatic shift in the presence of gospel music in the six years since Phillips's scathing attack was made evident the Tuesday night before the opening of the convention. A "special preconvention musical featuring

leading gospel singers from all over the nation" at Sam Houston Coliseum included a 500-voice chorus conducted by Frye and appearances by guest artists that
included Jackson, Martha Bass, the Ward Singers, the Sallie Martin Singers, and
the Roberta Martin Singers. Like James Lee, Jackson used the convention to so-
licit engagements. "I would attend the National Baptist Convention and we'd have
from thirty to forty thousand people there, the national body, and I would always
be the singer there," she recalled to Terkel in a radio interview. "When I'd leave the
convention, I'd be booked up for a whole year. So that's how my name got around
nationally among my people."[45]

To this day, one of the most often accentuated highlights of Jackson's early
resume was her designation as the "official soloist" of the National Baptist
Convention. As 1948 dawned, Goreau narrated, success "swept over Halie like a
flood of gold. 'Move On Up a Little Higher' slid onto the market, and streaked like
greased lightning. Nothing remotely like this had ever hit the gospel field." Then
came the news from the Baptists: "Dr. D. V. Jemison. Baptist Convention president, topped them all: 'Mahalia, I am making you official soloist of the National
Baptist Convention.' Never *been* such a thing before!"[46] When J. Robert Bradley
was asked about the circumstances of Jackson's honor, however, he resisted the
suggestion that her status at the convention was "official" in any meaningful
sense, as if to gently set the record straight.

> Now, I'm afraid I'm going to be a little contradictory about this. Now,
> Mahalia sang at the National Baptist Convention I guess for years. But
> this goes back to when she was selling music. You know, they'd have little
> booths and she'd have her booth and she'd come in there . . . because eve-
> rybody loved her. But you see, . . . I'm the longest one that's been with them
> and the Convention has never had what you call an "official soloist." . . . But
> I guess if you want to call it "official," it's all right.[47]

Bradley came close to insinuating that if anybody would have been named official soloist, it would have been "Mr. Baptist" himself. His doubts aside, there is
in fact no record that Jackson that was named "official soloist" in the published
proceedings of the convention. This does not mean that Jackson did *not* receive
such an honor, only that there is to my knowledge no documentation of the organization singling out Jackson in this way, other than anecdotal claims. The fact of
her being "official soloist" of the National Baptist Convention seems to have been
established through its sheer repetition.

Yet despite the lack of concrete evidence, faithful reiteration of the "official soloist" accolade since the 1940s, by the press and by friends in oral histories, does make
one wonder if Jackson was acknowledged in some manner by the National Baptist
Convention. Jackson's long-time piano accompanist Mildred Falls offers a clue

of how this might have unfolded. Falls remembered being with Jackson when she was named official soloist: "If I'm not mistaken, it was 1948. 'Cause I can remember in 1948, in February, we went to New Orleans for the Congress—not the whole convention, the Congress." The National Baptist Convention Sunday School and BTU Congress held its midwinter board meetings annually in February to plan the Congress Convention in June, and the winter meeting in February 1948 was indeed in New Orleans. According to Falls, Jackson's father, John Jackson Jr., surprised his daughter by showing up unannounced at one of the Congress sessions: "That's the year she was made official soloist, 1948."[48] The clarification offered by Falls—that Jackson was made official soloist by the Congress, "not the whole convention"—would explain why there is no indication of such an honor in the parent body's convention minutes. The president of the National Baptist Convention was typically present when the Congress met and one can imagine Jemison making the proclamation, however symbolic, giving Jackson extravagant public plaudits in her hometown.

But the timeline adds another layer of complication. In newspaper reports announcing her signing with Apollo Records, Jackson was already referred to as the "official soloist" of the National Baptist Convention as early as December 1946, more than a year before the New Orleans Congress.[49] One hypothesis that would reconcile Falls's memory that Jackson was honored by the Congress and her identification as "official soloist" before 1948 is that Jackson actually received the commendation at the June 1946 Sunday School Congress in Chicago, a very high profile gathering attended by the president of the World Baptist Alliance and Chicago Mayor Edward Kelly. As always, Campbell and Isaac were in charge of the musical proceedings, but considerable influence was wielded by Chicago's gospel power brokers, including Frye, Pilgrim Baptist Church musical director George Gullat, and Jackson's close friend and community leader Willa Saunders Jones. We might then speculate that Jackson could have been given special recognition at this major Baptist event in her new hometown.[50] Reports that December of her being "official soloist" of the National Baptist Convention would have been relatively recent, if somewhat misleadingly reported, news. The "official soloist" acclamation did circulate with increasing frequency after Jackson became more widely known from 1948 on, but bearing in mind the timing of the institution's recognition, in however fuzzy a form it might have come, shifts the moral of the familiar story. If the National Baptist Convention, through its Sunday School and BTU Congress, honored Jackson in 1946, it would have been purely on the basis of her work as a church singer, not as a recording star, as Goreau suggests. That is, the National Baptist Convention would not have been honoring an Apollo artist; rather, Apollo Records would have been signing the woman recognized as the most eminent black Baptist singer in the country.

The 1948 meeting of the parent body in Houston was an important year for Jackson because of the debut of the National Baptist Music Convention, a new auxiliary that arguably represented her most concrete and legitimizing role with the organization to date. The Music Convention was created on February 5 of that year with its founder, Frye, named as president, Georgiana Rose as secretary, and Jackson as treasurer and eventually local president in Chicago. In April, Frye organized a fundraising "All-Star Musical," billed as a "Singing Bowl," at Monumental Baptist Church in Chicago, but the Music Convention's official coming out was in Houston, where Frye, Rose, and Jackson submitted its first annual report. Placed into the record was a nine-article constitution declaring the new auxiliary to be "desirous of giving to the churches of the denomination training in better church music." Highlighting quality as a principal objective, the constitution spelled out the Music Convention's commitment to "the elevation of the standard of church music in the Baptist churches throughout America for a broader understanding of, and training in, better church music" and "to establish departments for the training of directors choirs, choruses, ensembles, individuals, and the church in its entirety in hymnology, spirituals—and gospel music."[51]

The Music Convention's report included data indicating that first-year membership represented seventy-two churches in thirty-two cities in eighteen states and that of the $1,500 in income taken in during its inaugural year, $300 came from a personal donation by Jackson, who Falls attested "would do anything" out of her unshakable devotion to her close friend Frye. As an officer, Jackson—or as Frye liked to call her, "Sister Treasurer"—attended the auxiliary's first board meeting in Memphis in June 1949 to make plans for that year's convention in Los Angeles. Weeks before the meeting, the group took out a full-page newspaper advertisement in the *Los Angeles Sentinel* listing its full leadership, publicizing its upcoming session, and inviting prospective members to "Help Save the World Through Better Music" (Figure 3.4). Jackson and other officers represented the Music Convention at the July 1950 Baptist World Alliance in Cleveland. At the National Baptist Convention in Philadelphia that September, Jackson was in charge of organizing a "mammoth musical program" at Tindley Temple on behalf of the auxiliary.[52]

In founding the Music Convention, Frye carried forward NCGCC foundational ideals for gospel-centered "training in better church music." Sallie Martin did the same through her music shop. In 1949, Martin and Morris Music Studio published a short book, *Improving the Music in the Church*, with Martin's business partner Kenneth Morris as lead author.[53] Officially endorsed by both the National Baptist Convention and the NCGCC, and including a chapter on "Ministry of Music in the Church" contributed by Dorsey, *Improving the Music in the Church* offered crash courses on Western European music history and theory as part of a primer on the craft of a church musician. While he delineated the duties and qualifications of successful choral directors, accompanists, and organizational officers, Morris strongly emphasized the importance of apt repertory. He

FIG. 3.4 Advertisement for the second convening of the Music Convention at the 1949 National Baptist Convention in Los Angeles, *Los Angeles Sentinel*, September 1, 1949. Mahalia Jackson is identified as treasurer.

identified six types of religious songs that a minister of music should know: instrumental music played during "transitory intervals"; anthems "generally sung by a trained group of singers"; chants and responses; solos; hymns, "the backbone of all religious services"; and "gospel or evangelistic songs," which required more explanation because their more recent vintage.

Although this type of music is relatively new, already it has made a place for itself in our modern church services. Because of the newness of this type of music, the music leader has to be very careful when selecting songs of this type. . . .

If the leader of music will carefully plan an *intelligent* rendition of the selections, nothing but success will be his; for no type of music can give the spiritual flavor to a service like the *intelligent* rendition of GOSPEL and EVANGELISTIC SONGS. (Emphasis in the original)

Morris included a chapter focusing specifically on "The Evangelistic or Gospel Singer," which he defined, rather cagily, as "a singer of songs true to scriptural texts, or songs that contain a message for the soul or heart, or songs that are applicable to every day life and experiences." Morris's chapter on gospel singing, which opened with a debt of thanks to Sallie Martin, without whom "this chapter could never have been written," outlined "nine main qualifications necessary for an Evangelistic or gospel singer," only one of which directly pertained to singing. Even this prerequisite set the bar rather low in warning against enlisting any singer who "is tone-deaf or has a shrill, harsh or nasal voice." The other requirements grouped into issues of religious integrity (being a Christian and belonging to a church), stage presence (leadership, an "enthusiastic and radiant personality," and sensitivity to an audience), and above all a careful selection of repertory dependent upon interpretation of the text, good musical taste, and a broad knowledge of appropriate songs. The reticence to address questions of performance style and the pains taken to define gospel singing as the singing of certain kinds of songs is striking though perhaps predictable coming from the likes of Morris, Martin, and Dorsey, none of whom approached Jackson's capabilities as a singer but rather made their money selling newly written and arranged songs in the form of sheet music.

Indeed, the late 1940s mark a pivot point in the black gospel field that shadowed the popular music industry more broadly. In these years, the NCGCC-cultivated economy of gospel *songs* commodified as sheet music marketed to black Christians ceded ground to gospel *singing* commodified as recordings by charismatic performers like Jackson that were available to a less predictable body of music fans. Concurrently, as Jackson's Apollo recordings earned her national visibility beyond her church family, she fully transitioned from an eager participant standing in the wings to a headlining Baptist celebrity. Her appearance at the 1949 National Baptist Convention in Los Angeles was anticipated by the newspaper headline "Top Gospel Singer Attends Bapt. Meet." On Booker T. Washington Night, the published proceedings read, the "Mahalia Jackson musical group from Chicago gave several selections to the delight of the delegates." In a roundup of the Los Angeles convention in the *Courier*, Jackson was now touted as a major player in the black gospel field, appearing with Campbell, Frye, and Detroit singer and organizer Sallie Jones in a photograph captioned "Musical Bosses." By the 1952 National Baptist Convention on her home turf in Chicago, eight months after her appearance on Ed Sullivan's *Toast of the Town* and a month before her third date at Carnegie Hall, she was an event in and of herself. The convention "began on Monday evening when Mahalia Jackson, 'Empress' of gospel music, sang to an audience packed to the rafters at Tabernacle Baptist church."[54]

As her career took off, Jackson's direct involvement with Music Convention operations apparently shrank, but the auxiliary continued to grow. Approaching the stature of other larger departments like the Laymen and the Women's Convention in just its fifth year of existence, the Music Convention was given its own eight-day slate of services, musical programs, and official business at the 1952 convention in Chicago, highlighted by an address by President Jemison at the Friday afternoon session. Jemison's address hit predictable notes about the importance of singing "in the time of crisis, when all is dark," the salience of the auxiliary's Baptist foundation, and the core objectives of the Music Convention: "better knowledge of church music" throughout Baptist congregations, more harmonious cooperation between ministers of music and church pastors, and a commitment to "elevate and raise the standard of music in our churches" through more rigorous training of singers, directors, and accompanists. Other emphases, however, revealed his clear recognition that gospel singing was no longer an interloping country cousin among more established sacred repertories, like anthems and concert-arranged spirituals. Though he did not call gospel music by name, Jemison offered a caution that emerging practices of black religious singing risked embracing the prestige of charismatic artistry at the expense of devout integrity. "There are too many singers and groups singing in our churches who neither serve nor belong to anyone's church," said Jemison, who observed with concern "one of the greatest evils in our church life today": the misuse of gospel music by a number of "great artists [who] have become so conceited that they think the Holy Spirit has chosen them."

But there was also an unmistakable element of diplomacy in Jemison's address to a Music Convention founded by Chicago gospel pioneers Frye and Jackson. Even as he expressed his "fervent conviction that services in the house of God should be of the very highest type," he encouraged Baptists to embrace popular acclaim as an asset, calling for "a full realization of the importance of the appeal which music has to the Christian layman." Jemison's major recommendation to the Music Convention was to build a big tent under which a range of tastes could be accommodated and where both tradition and innovation could fully thrive.

In order that this purpose be accomplished, I believe that the following music departments should be organized as elements of the National Baptist Music Convention; the Senior Choir Department which will deal with the training in the interpretation of anthems, oratorios and various other religious classics; the Gospel Chorus Department for training in the heart songs and Negro spirituals; a department for the instruction of directors of all types of church music; and a department for the training and development of accompanists. . . .A songwriters and composers department would be of infinite value to this organization, for we must always have something new to offer in our churches.[55]

Jemison's address, advocating a productive balance between consistently high standards and a catholicity of musical tastes, came at a key transitional moment for the black gospel field. Tensions in the 1920s and 1930s between African Americans firmly based in the North and new arrivals from the South, and between more venerable repertories—"the spirituals and old-time hymns" preferred by Lizzie Ward Johnson—and newer-styled gospel songs, were real. Some have explained the initial resistance to gospel's acceptance as a matter of discrepant class politics driven by reactionary presumptions of respectability. But an analysis of the National Baptist Convention and the NCGCC complicates a story of dissidence between moldy fig mainliners and gospel singers, each doing battle for the hearts, minds, and souls of black folk. Together, the NCGCC, Frye's Music Convention, Martin and Morris's *Improving the Music in the Church*, and Jemison's address illustrate how modern gospel's trailblazers consciously and continuously adopted prevailing cultural-political discourse recognizable to many black churchgoers, emphasizing proper training, a self-consciousness of practice, elevation of taste toward "intelligent" singing, and an enforcement of musical standards. It is in part due to these strategies, alongside the spiritual persuasion, widespread popularity, and economic potential of gospel singing, that the way was prepared for the mainstreaming of black gospel during the post-war years. The institutional history of black gospel in the late 1940s reveals a determined rebranding of "whoop-it-up" singing as "good music," though, importantly, this followed a consciously formulated game plan put into play with great discipline nearly two decades earlier by Dorsey, Frye, and Butts in South Side Chicago.

From this alternative perspective, we can see that the initial phase of the mainstreaming of black gospel music exemplified the durability of respectability politics, not a game-changing triumph over them. Furthermore, the overlap of the mid-century consensus that affirmed gospel music institutionally with Jackson's popular breakthrough is more indicative of reciprocity than cause-and-effect. Jackson's escalating stature among Baptists and as a public figure in the late 1940s indicated multiplying forms of prestige that increasingly included charismatic artistry and recognition, such as Jackson had begun to accrue through her recordings and her appearances on television and at major venues. Yet coverage of Jackson proceeded from the premise that the integrity of her music, though also the terms for her crossover to new audiences, were predicated on her ongoing intimacy and legitimacy with the black church. "Today, Mahalia is welcomed into almost any American community," read a feature story in the *New York Amsterdam News* publicizing her 1952 Carnegie Hall appearance. "For she is official soloist for the four million Negro Baptists in the United States."[56]

Sociologist Priscilla Ferguson has asked: "At what point do structures and sensibilities, institutions and ideologies, practices and practitioners cohere to 'make' the configuration that we designate a cultural field?"[57] Beginning in earnest in the early 1930s and reaching a point of decisive climax in the late 1940s, complementary interaction among the gospel movement built by Dorsey, Frye, and Butts, the gradual acceptance of gospel singing by the National Baptist Convention, and Jackson's rise to fame shaped this configuration for black gospel music. If Harris seeks to chart "the rise of gospel blues," my hope is to illuminate the "making" of the black gospel field during these years. However much gospel singing was cast as a "renaissance" in 1932–1933, the proliferation of gospel choirs in conjunction with the NCGCC and the popularizing of gospel singing though Jackson and groups like the Johnson Singers undoubtedly represented something recognizably novel for many black church congregations, though, frustratingly, we are left with few recordings documenting these 1930s singers. One benefit of field analysis, however, is to reorient the usual focus on musical style toward sensibilities, ideologies, and practices that were perhaps even more instrumental in positioning the NCGCC as a field-making catalyst: purposeful organization and institutionalization around a specific cultural product, implementation and oversight of field-specific standards, a conscious national networking of the local, and the production of discourse seeking to shift the perception of gospel singers from undisciplined, whoop-it-up singers teetering toward minstrelsy to impeccably trained musicians guided by evangelical intention. Fully recognizing the production of this foundational discourse, clearly drawing on the politics of uplift and respectability, does not come easy, but it potentially refines our present-day understanding of how the modern black gospel field emerged and unfolded over time. The unmistakable centering of regulation, protocol, and training in the early 1930s has largely been overlooked in stories about "the rise of gospel blues" through Dorsey and the NCGCC, and yet this rhetoric was preserved and ultimately reabsorbed at mid-century within the National Baptist Convention itself. At the same time, in its explicit interdenominational thrust, the NCGCC, though dominated by Baptists, situated the black gospel field as bound to, but also to a discernible degree autonomous from, the institutional structures of the black Baptist church.

Despite seeking to build a national gospel song movement, Dorsey's organizational ambitions were founded upon a core desire to increase the body of consumers for his sheet music, emphasizing the product by downplaying "showmanship" and "striking personalities or individuals," except as a vehicle for selling a song—"a marketing plan involving live performances," as Kay Norton has described it.[58] With his days as "Georgia Tom" well behind him, Dorsey was content to put a firewall between the gospel movement and popular culture. But gospel singing as charismatic performance took on new significance in the 1940s, nudging the music and its consumption toward the realm of popular culture. Gospel singing as a mobile commodity and as an end unto itself destabilized the institutional moorings put in place by Dorsey and his associates and became manifest in an increasingly in-vogue pop-cultural phenomenon: the gospel song battle.

4

Gospel Singing as Black Popular Culture

PUBLICITY FOR A Sunday afternoon gospel program at Harlem's Golden Gate Auditorium on April 11, 1948, may well have left readers uncertain which promotional pitch was intended to be the most appetizing lure (Figure 4.1). In the 1940s, the Golden Gate, a five-thousand-seat ballroom at the corner of 142nd Street and Lenox Avenue, became known among New York City gospel singers and their fans as a venue for large concerts of black religious music produced by African American promoter Johnny Myers, founder and president of the Religious Concert Followers Club (RCFC). The April 11 program featured two women who were much-admired gospel soloists and personal friends, Mahalia Jackson and Ernestine Washington. It was a bill with expected appeal in black communities throughout the area, judging from tickets available for purchase not only through Myers, but also at music shops, newsstands, beauty salons, pharmacies, clothing stores, and hotels in Harlem, Brooklyn, Queens, and New Jersey. Myers's cluttered ad bristles with enticements: an exclusive "one performance only" Manhattan event, an "East vs. West" regional showdown, the crowning of "America's Gospel Singing Queen" as determined by the audience, and even the "Johnny Myers Presents" brand itself. Yet it is Jackson who tops the marquee. With the Brooklyn-based Washington, "Gospel Songbird of the East," and opening acts from Baltimore (the Ivory Gospel Singers) and Richmond, Virginia (the Bright Light Sextette), Jackson the Chicagoan brought four-city representation to the program, though her billing as "Gospel Songbird of the Nation" also accorded her status boosted by translocal eminence.

A recording artist for Apollo Records since October 1946, Jackson would have likely been the main draw based on the timing of the concert alone. At her second Apollo session seven months before the Golden Gate program, Jackson, accompanied by pianist James Lee and organist Herbert Francis, recorded four

JOHNNY MYERS PRESENTS
ONE PERFORMANCE ONLY — NO OTHER
METROPOLITAN APPEARANCE

WHO IS AMERICA'S GOSPEL SINGING QUEEN?

You Are the Judge
EAST vs. WEST

GOSPEL SONGBIRD OF THE NATION

MAHALIA JACKSON
of Chicago

JOHNNY MYERS
World's Foremost
Religious Concert
Producer-Promoter

GOSPEL SONGBIRD OF THE EAST

Mme. Ernestine B. Washington

— PLUS —

IVORY GOSPEL SINGERS
of Baltimore

NO OTHER ARTISTS APPEARING
FAMOUS GEORGIA PEACH, M. C.

Sensational

BRIGHT LIGHT SEXTETTE of Richmond, Va.

GOLDEN GATE AUDITORIUM
142nd STREET and LENOX AVENUE

Advance $1.50 — At Door $1.85 (Tax Included)
RCFC Members and Children $1.20 At Door
ONE PERFORMANCE ONLY

SUNDAY, APRIL 11

Afternoons 3 To 6 P. M. — Doors Open 1:30 P. M.

FOR TICKETS AND INFORMATION Call Johnny Myers, Riverside 9-3690, 222 West
129 Street, N. Y.; Rainbow, Harvard & Lehman Music Stores, 125th Street,
Near Lenox Ave.; Bells Newsstand, 140th Street & 8th Ave.; Amsterdam News,
2340 8th Ave., N. Y. C.; Gottesman's Pharmacy, Fulton & Albany Aves.; Kennedy
Clothing Stores, Fulton & Marcy Aves. and Fulton and Claver Place; Birdell's
Music Shop, Fulton and Throop Aves., Brooklyn, N. Y.; Mr. M. Mason, 49
Church Street, Inwood, L. I.; Pea Wee's Parlor, Barclay and Spruce Streets;
Hotel Coleman, 59 Court Street, Newark, N. J.; Leola's Beauty Salon, 573
Jackson Ave., Jersey City.

FIG. 4.1 Advertisement for a gospel program presented by Johnny Myers on April 11, 1948, at the Golden Gate Auditorium in Harlem. *New York Amsterdam News*, April 3, 1948. By permission of the *New York Amsterdam News*.

songs, "What Could I Do," "Even Me," "I Have a Friend," and an extended version of W. Herbert Brewster's "Move On Up a Little Higher." The latter, released in December, became a singular phenomenon. By the early months of 1948, "Move On Up a Little Higher" had reportedly already sold tens of thousands of copies in Chicago alone and was receiving heavy radio airplay. "The greatest thrill of my life after I had made this record [was that] you could just hear it all over, every place I'd go," said Jackson, remembering her arrival in Harlem that spring. "When I came to New York after I had made this, I was standing at 125th Street and they must [have] had about six music shops, and I could hear this song [coming from] all of them, all the shops with the same thing going at once."[1] Jackson arrived at the Golden Gate for her song battle with Washington—re-staged five days later at Greater Zion Baptist Church in Harrison, Pennsylvania—with a reputation that had already been built steadily and solidly through her appearances at the National Baptist Convention and on gospel programs while on tour, but her star power was augmented dramatically by the meteoric success of her double-sided hit single.

The April 1948 concert and Jackson's return to the Golden Gate in January 1949 as the unquestioned headliner represented her New York coming-out. But we should also take stock of the packaging of a Jackson-Washington gospel program for consumption as a competition, however friendly, with explicit individual and territorial stakes, however symbolic, and an active, if imaginary, role for audience members, who by purchasing a ticket to the concert were authorized to be "the Judge." What kind of gospel singing event was this? Where might it be positioned within the black gospel field? What kinds of prestige and authority derived from a concert to crown "America's Gospel Singing Queen" as determined by New York gospel fans? If Jackson and Washington were church singers, what is the place and role of the church at such an event? And who was Johnny Myers, self-proclaimed as "America's foremost quartette and religious concert promoter?"

Jackson's 1948 appearance at the Golden Gate introduces two influential post-war developments in the black gospel field that were separable from the activity of the NCGCC and the National Baptist Convention: the "battle of song" that emerged during and following World War II and the high-profile religious concerts presented by Myers in New York from 1943 to 1949. Publicity and commentary in major African American newspapers help us understand how the song battle enabled black gospel singing to circulate as a form of popular culture. Assessing more fully black gospel as popular culture accentuates the extra-religious meanings and reciprocity between gospel's performers and fans.

We know very little about Myers, but his dogged promotion of his concerts left a paper trail that brings into focus a discernible picture of the strategic goals of his gospel programs. Myers created a symbiotic "syndicate" of singers, independent record labels, and media outlets into which Jackson was introduced in fairly routine fashion, though this network precipitated her watershed success as an Apollo artist. Together, the song battle and Myers's concerts foreground a story of gospel singers and presenters with highly diversified motivations, interests, desires, and visibility and gospel audiences with shifting roles as church goers, radio listeners, record buyers, and popular music fans.

Camaraderie and Competition on the Programs

Like many music scenes, the post-war black gospel field was often energized by a productive tension between camaraderie and competition among performers. The basic terrain for both was the gospel program. For in-demand singers like Jackson, it was not unusual to be called upon to sing any day or night of the weekend or during the week (referred to by some singers as "off nights"), and even multiple times in a single day. Some Sundays, Jackson remembered, she sang a number for a service at one Chicago church, then hustled to another to perform again or sing on a more extended program in the afternoon or evening. Bill Russell, who documented Jackson's day-to-day activity in Chicago in the mid-1950s, described her "running all over town singing on Sunday."[2] Earnings in these contexts were unpredictable at best. "In those days, I was still singing . . . but I wasn't getting nothing. Purely for the glory of the Lord," Jackson reminisced in 1954 about her early career in Chicago. "From every storefront on State Street and all through the country to the great Olivet Baptist Church."[3] Selections sung by soloists or groups during the course of the regular church service—my childhood church in San Francisco called these musical offerings "special music" to distinguish them from songs rendered by the choir—were typically limited to one or at most two numbers, but independent musical programs scheduled separately from the "11 o'clock hour" were typically presented around 4:00 p.m. after the post-service meal, or that evening. Brother John Sellers, a frequent collaborator with Jackson in Chicago during the late 1930s and early 1940s, explained that performances during church services sometimes functioned as same-day advance publicity called "demonstrations," meaning "you had to sing in the Sunday morning where the big crowd was at, to let them know what they was going to have, a sample of what was coming" at the more extended program later in the day.[4]

Concerts of religious music hosted or sponsored by African American churches could feature full-length European concert works, especially at Baptist and Methodist churches; more stylistically diverse "musicales" that mixed concert spirituals, anthems, gospel songs, and classical music, along with spoken presentations; or, especially since the 1940s, gospel music exclusively. In an ethnographic study of gospel quartets in New York City conducted during the late 1980s, Ray Allen observed how gospel programs involved multiple social actors that included sponsors (i.e., church groups, individuals, or local ensembles who acted essentially as producers), pastors, bookers, managers, promoters, emcees, singers, and audiences, and served various functions, ranging from fundraising and membership recruitment for the church to prestige, publicity, and merchandise sales for the performers. Allen emphasized that all parties steadfastly worked "to maintain the spiritual integrity" of gospel programs, though he also observed continuous negotiation of the status of these "singing events" as a form of religious worship and as entertainment. Ultimately, he concluded, "the situation is best viewed as a continuum in which age, commercial aspiration, artistic concerns, level of performance stylization, degree of interpersonal communication, perceived sincerity of spiritual commitment, and audience size, nature, and location serve as the primary variables."[5]

In matching local and touring performers, presenting amateur and professional groups, and operating via flexible (and at larger programs not infrequently exploitative) financial arrangements set by the promoter, gospel programs cultivated what Allen calls "cooperative networks" among singers and their home churches. Singer, pianist, choir director, songwriter, and publisher Robert Anderson (1919–1995) acknowledged this social function of gospel programs. As a child, Anderson migrated from Anguilla, Mississippi to Chicago, where he became a widely admired soloist and was instrumental in the establishment of two of black gospel's most influential groups. After becoming an original member of the Roberta Martin Singers in 1933, Anderson started an ensemble of his own with female backing singers who in 1952 broke off to form an independent group, the Caravans, under the leadership of Albertina Walker. Anderson frequently performed with and worked as a piano accompanist for his close friend Mahalia Jackson in the 1940s and he spoke of how the brother- and sisterhood of gospel singers relaxed interdenominational rivalries.

> Back in those days the gospel singers were more closer to each other. We were more as a family. I mean, it wasn't no strangers with us, you know, when we were finished singing. Now, [when] we would have programs and go to various churches, we would all go together. Just like if Mahalia was going to have a concert, all the singers were there. When we have a concert, Mahalia was there. You understand? We were just like a family. And then that which brought us together actually brought the different denominations of churches together, because at one time the churches was actually segregated. I mean, the Methodists didn't go to the Baptist church and things like that.[6]

One particular type of gospel program that drew upon this support system was the anniversary program, which many groups, soloists, promoters, and ministers held annually to mark each year of their career in gospel music or pastorship of a church. Variants of the anniversary program were birthday and "appreciation" programs honoring the significance of a particular individual to the community, such as that celebrating the birthday of Lucille Henderson in 1945. Henderson was an original member of Chicago's best-known women's gospel quartet, the Golden Harp Gospel Singers, and later founder and president of a new group, the Southern Echoes, with whom she performed at her birthday program. Identified as a "baritone" in a publicity flyer for the Golden Harps, Henderson was part of a community-based quartet singing movement stimulated in Depression-era Chicago by the migration of singers from the quartet hotbed of Birmingham, Alabama, most notably Norman McQueen, who founded the Chicago Progressive Quartet Association in 1931. Gospel historians Lynn Abbott and Doug Seroff have documented how McQueen was "especially effective in establishing and training female quartets in the four-part harmony style" with the bass line that distinguishes quartet singing. Henderson cited McQueen as a trainer for her groups in the 1930s. Though she was immersed in quartet culture, Henderson's birthday program also brought together other popular local ensembles, including the Beatrice Lux Singers, a fixture of the 1940s Chicago gospel scene, and a group directed by songwriter and publisher Kenneth Morris, with "noted gospel singer" Mahalia Jackson serving as mistress of ceremonies.[7]

The somewhat unusual listing of Jackson the emcee above the featured performers in the *Chicago Defender* story on the Henderson birthday program reveals textures of prestige that were even more pronounced at other types of programs. Almost a year to the day after Japan's surrender to the United States ended World War II, fans of gospel music in black Chicago were invited to a Sunday afternoon "Battle of Songs" between Jackson and Roberta Martin at Tabernacle Baptist Church. As a child, Martin (1907–1969) migrated with her family from Helena, Arkansas, to Chicago where she became a pivotal figure in the development of modern gospel music through her innovations as a pianist and as the architect of the sound of the Roberta Martin Singers, one of the earliest mixed modern gospel ensembles. Trained as a classical pianist, Martin confessed having knowledge only of "church hymns, anthems, choir music and secular songs" until her first encounter with gospel singing in the early 1930s inspired her to form her own group in 1933, comprised of Anderson, Eugene Smith, James Lawrence, Willie Webb, and Norsalus McKissick. Martin subsequently added Bessie Folk and DeLois Barrett Campbell.[8] Through live performances, recordings, sheet music distribution, and disciplined vertical integration of Martin's work as a soloist, piano accompanist, musical director, songwriter, arranger, and publisher, the Roberta Martin Singers exerted enormous nationwide influence on black gospel well into the 1950s and 1960s. We might think of the Roberta Martin Singers as black gospel's equivalent of Art Blakey and the Jazz Messengers, the band that for thirty years was a springboard for a steady stream of up-and-coming jazz stars. Pearl Williams-Jones and Horace Clarence Boyer have written that the deep roster of talent identified, nurtured, graduated, and replenished by Martin "created and left a dynasty of gospel singers" who produced an ensemble sound so pervasive at mid-century that "it is necessary to look at the Roberta Martin choral style to understand classic gospel singing."[9]

Both Jackson and Martin, known by many as "Berta," were migrants from the South who were in the vanguard of the modern gospel movement and had by war's end built their reputations on church circuits both within and beyond Chicago. As of their August 1946 battle in song, however, their respective work as commercial recording artists was negligible; the Roberta Martin Singers had appeared only on a self-made vanity record from around 1945, and Jackson had not been in the studio at all since cutting four relatively unnoticed sides for Decca in 1937. Yet even without recordings in circulation, their shared program was "long awaited," publicity flyers announced, and performances by "openers" Anderson, Sallie Martin, and future Roberta Martin Singer Myrtle Scott set the stage for the Jackson-Martin song battle.[10] Pastoring the host Tabernacle Baptist Church was Reverend Louis Rawls, foster father of twelve-year-old Lou Rawls, who sang in the church choir, made his first recordings at eighteen with the Chosen Gospel Singers, and would go on to enjoy an illustrious career as a soul crooner.

Two perceptions of the relationship between Mahalia Jackson and Roberta Martin suggest the complexities of gospel family dynamics. Anderson's recollection of the two artists highlights their distinctive talents, considerable eminence, and occasional collaboration. Martin, he claims, was the piano accompanist that Jackson "felt" most naturally when she sang and Jackson was quick to honor Martin publicly.

> Roberta Martin was one of the greatest musicians in the gospel field and she had a style that coincided with Mahalia. . . .A lot of musicians . . . would come to hear her play because with the style that Roberta had and the type that Mahalia had, it was really outstanding. . . .For funerals, a lot of times she played for Mahalia. . . .That's right, there were several occasions when Roberta asked to play for Mahalia. . . .Mahalia, she always felt that Roberta Martin was a soul searching musician. . . .And they blended so well together. . . .When Mahalia would make her appearances, she would have her own musicians [i.e., accompanists], but there are some occasions that Mahalia would come in places and Miss Martin would be there. Then she would play and Mahalia would always give Roberta a beautiful accommodation or tribute to the gospel field. So they both were outstanding people. The only thing [was that] Roberta was classified as an accompanist and . . . Mahalia [as] a singer, although Roberta was a great singer too.

A very differently focused point of view comes from a singer who was also close to Jackson, John Sellers (1924–1999), popularly known, following the example of Sister Rosetta Tharpe, as "Brother John." As a young child, Sellers migrated from Clarksdale, Mississippi, to Chicago where, orphaned and living with an aunt, he became a fan of Jackson through her work with the Johnson Singers. Sellers remembers being about eight years old when he was taken in by Jackson and her then-husband Ike Hockenhull and became deeply entrenched in their home life. In effect, Jackson became Sellers's surrogate mother as well as a forma-tive musical mentor. Through his intimacy with Jackson—"I was right there," he remembered. "Sometimes I'd sleep between them in the bed"—Sellers developed a gospel singing style that he acknowledged was closely modeled on Jackson's and he performed with her as a backing singer in Chicago and on tour in the 1940s. The first known recorded version of "Move On Up a Little Higher" is not Jackson's but a performance by Sellers, recorded in 1946 for the small independent Chicago label Miracle Records and undoubtedly plucked from Jackson's repertory.[11] Sellers went on to attain his greatest success in the 1960s, reinventing himself as a folk singer and as the singing voice in multiple works by African American dancer-choreographer Alvin Ailey, most notably the groundbreaking *Revelations*.

In light of his closeness to Jackson, one might forgive Sellers's bias when comparisons of Jackson and other singers cropped up among friends and family members with whom he "used to always get in fights over Mahalia."

> My aunt used to say, "I like Roberta Martin's singing." I say, "I don't care what you say, Mahalia Jackson can *sing*!" She say, "You don't think nobody can sing but Mahalia!"
>
> "Well, I *know* she can sing. Berta and all them all right, but they will never outlast Mahalia Jackson." "Oh, I don't believe that." "Well, you'll see."

Bucking up Jackson when her confidence flagged by telling her, almost like a boxing cornerman, "Can't nobody beat you singing," Sellers remembered similar conversations with Anderson and other members of the Roberta Martin Singers—"cause *they* all was with Berta!"—as well as the cool reaction toward Jackson by Reverend Clarence Cobbs, influential pastor of First Church of Deliverance, one of Chicago's main hubs for modern gospel, "cause he was crazy about Berta and Sallie Martin."[12]

Sellers put his money on Jackson, surely out of loyalty and recognition of her gifts as a singer. But his memory of these exchanges also betrays an investment in distinct personal favorites and a sense of rivalry with the favorites of others that can only be characterized as fandom. As a former musical colleague of both Jackson and Martin, Anderson seemed to savor most his recognition and appreciation of the artistic, spiritual, and professional affinity between the two gospel artists. Sellers, on the other hand, a master storyteller who cherished his role as an on-the-ground source for Jackson's two principal biographers, Laurraine Goreau and Jules

Schwerin—"I'm giving you some information, girl, you couldn't get *nowhere!*" he crowed to Goreau—laid bare his intrigue with the catty partisanship and gossipy insider details that were part of the gospel scene as he liked to remember it.[13]

Sellers, who observed "a clique among gospel singers, everyone trying to outdo each other," asserted that gospel audiences would sometimes respond enthusiastically to their favorite singers while deliberately withholding affirmation of others, a practice that he called "sitting on" singers. According to Sellers's vivid account of a program at Ebenezer Baptist Church in Chicago, Jackson, with the help of a small but persistent band of sympathetic supporters, gradually won over a skeptical congregation initially partial to Sallie Martin and Roberta Martin. Based on Sellers's recollection that Dorsey was accompanying Sallie Martin and the Helen Green was Jackson's pianist, the incident likely took place sometime in the late 1930s. Sellers's highly performative recounting of events, worth quoting at length, suggests how listeners brought their preferences to a gospel program, made them known, and negotiated these preferences in dialogue with the performances on the floor.

Way back [then], they used to make fun of her . . . Sit in the back of the church, say she couldn't sing. . . .I never shall forget at Ebenezer one time, Sallie Martin and Roberta—Ebenezer was presenting them—Roberta Martin, big program, packed *out!* Give Berta a beautiful robe and everything. So Mahalia had a black dress with a cape. . . .And she came in that night and she was singing, and the people—you know, people used to sit on you in those days, when you were singing. . . .So one woman in the back say, "Come on, Mahalia, you can make it." She was singing [Sellers sings]:

After while, it will all be over

After while, the sun going to shine

It going to shine, hallelujah, after while

And one woman in the back say: "*Come* on, Mahalia, you can make it!" They were just sitting on her, because they wanted Sallie and Roberta to go over! They were sitting there, wouldn't do nothing but sit. Wasn't reacting to her singing. So when this woman say, "Come on, Mahalia, you can make it!" another woman say, "Yeah, honey, come on. You can make it!" Then the crowd began to say, "Come on, Mahalia! Come on!" Cause everybody was pulling for Roberta and Sallie! They couldn't see Mahalia! And Dorsey was playing for Sallie there on the program. Helen Green was playing for Mahalia. "Come on, Mahalia!" And Mahalia broke up that church. When she got through, everybody was in an uproar.

After while, it all be over

After while, the sun going to shine

Clouds will pass over, after while.[14]

The scene at Ebenezer as recreated by Sellers may provide partial context for the claim on publicity posters that the 1946 Jackson-Martin "Battle of Songs" at Tabernacle was "long awaited" by black Chicago. Above all, we can imagine how this battle may well have accommodated the distinct sources of pleasure for Anderson, who enjoyed those special occasions when Martin and Jackson could combine their artistry, and for Sellers, the protégée who relished seeing Jackson out-sing her competition.

Battles of Song

Notwithstanding the promotional functions of staged showdowns between Jackson and Martin in 1946 and between Jackson and Washington in 1948, such contests, real and imagined, have constituted an extraordinarily rich component of post-war gospel music history. Whether presented operatically in Richard Wagner's *Die Meistersinger* or televised as the Eurovision Song Contest, whether pitting Wolfgang Amadeus Mozart versus Muzio Clementi or James P. Johnson versus Willie "the Lion" Smith, competitive musical performance has long fascinated music scholars. Writers have explored the historical, cultural, and political significance of the Swing Era battle of the bands and hip-hop battles, old-time fiddling contests and high school choral and band competitions, the Metropolitan Opera auditions and Trinidad and Tobago's epic steel band competition during Carnaval known as Panorama, among an array of other examples.[15] As Seroff has noted, "quartet singers claim that anytime two quartets appeared on the same program, there was *automatically* a contest, each group intent upon stealing the house from the other." But black sacred song has a venerable tradition of more formally structured competition with roots that extend back to at least the late nineteenth century.[16] Closely intertwined with this history are the explosion of black male one-on-a-part vocal groups singing four-part harmony in the decades after Reconstruction and the contemporaneous cultivation of what historian Evelyn Higginbotham has influentially termed a "politics of respectability."

In perhaps the earliest reference to the tradition of black small-group vocal harmony contests, James Weldon Johnson (1871–1938) recalled quartet singing being an inescapable part of his soundscape as a small child growing up in Jacksonville, Florida; at fifteen, he and his brother Rosamond "were singing in a quartet which competed with other quartets." By the turn of the century, Abbott writes, quartet singing had become "nothing less than the black national pastime." African American newspapers were documenting quartet contests as early as January 1894, when the *Indianapolis Freeman* announced the upcoming "national Contest between the Tennessee Warblers, the Chicago Quartette and the Hoosier Quartette" at the local YMCA, to be attended by "a great many white people." The song contest, often with official judges, cash prizes, and detailed scoring systems, was a core component of quartet culture, which was itself part of a broader vision for black self-definition. Higginbotham has described how in response to the representational violence that flourished during the darkest days of postbellum U.S. race relations, when African Americans were ritually lampooned in word, imagery, and sound, black Baptist women spearheaded a movement to counter racist propaganda with reform of individual manners, morals, behavior, and attitudes among African Americans across a range of discursive arenas. A mode of strategic conformity, "respectability" became an ideology—or as Higginbotham puts it, a "bridge discourse"—conditioning African Americans to transcend social and economic circumstances psychologically. Sanctioned by advocates of education, family, and the church as a respectable activity and taught at many black schools and colleges as part of a "voice culture" curriculum, male four-part singing—two tenors, baritone, and bass—became folded into a repertory of symbolic behavior, and by the 1920s the quartet contest became a vehicle for demonstrating mastery of that behavior.[17]

Along with diction, singers cited "time, harmony, and articulation" as the principal criteria of judgment. Reverend Alton Griffin migrated from North Carolina to New York where he sang with the Golden Stars in the 1930s and 1940s. At quartet contests, the "judges were usually people who knew music, maybe the organist of the church, or someone who was well trained and familiar with vocal singing," Griffin remembered. "They judged in the techniques of the voices and how close the voices could blend. That's the way they did it—on your English, and closeness of voices. They were judging everything, even the way you stand. We stood straight, we didn't move on those songs." A story on a 1943 contest in Lynchburg, Virginia, indicates that in some places the format of earlier quartet contests and desires for vocal harmony to function as a bridge discourse between blacks and whites were still in operation at midcentury.

> First prize in the annual quartet contest went Monday night to the Gospel Four with the Excelsior Quartet only four points behind the winner. The Melody Four was third. Close to 500 persons including many whites spectators [sic], were in the Court Street Baptist Church for the event. . . .Cash prizes were awarded three leaders. Judges were Mrs. S. Boyd Owen, Mrs. R. R. Leftwich, and S. D. Perkins, all white.[18]

In April 1939, the Soul Stirrers traveled from their home base in Houston to Detroit for a contest at Ebenezer Baptist Church pitting them against the hometown Flying Clouds quartet. The syndicated report on the event by the black national news service the Associated Negro Press (ANP) is notable, however, for registering the presence—and disagreement—of multiple sources of authority: the institutionally ratified knowledge of the expert adjudicators and the taste preferences of the gospel fans in attendance.

The Five Soul Stirrers who had recently defeated the Flying Cloud group in Cleveland accepted another challenge and came back to Detroit only to go down in defeat themselves according to the three white judges from the Detroit Conservatory. The plaudits and some boos went up at the judges' decision but the singing of the local lads so far surpassed that of their opponents, in the judges' estimation, that the Flying Cloud was handed the decision by a wide margin.[19]

In this mixture of approbation and dissent voiced by the "more than 2,000 music lovers" at the Detroit contest we can detect new dynamics. Beginning in the late 1930s, quartet contests grounded in the "behavioral self-regulation" of respectability politics shaded toward what was more frequently billed as a "battle of song." Competitive religious singing was already widespread. In Chicago, contests between black church choirs were noted as early as 1910, and amateur glee clubs assembled in workplaces competed in spiritual-singing competitions for "the right to be called the best industrial singing organization in the city." Chicago's two most respected choir directors, James Mundy and J. Wesley Jones, "both friends and enemies" by virtue of their complementary work, engaged in a "battle of the choirs" featuring spirituals and classical repertory in 1930. Jones described these battles as "a purely friendly demonstration of the points the audience found to its liking."[20] But some singers specifically identified developments in performance practice ushered in during the late 1930s and early 1940s with the song battle, including a tempering of the emphasis on tight harmonizing, ensemble cohesion, and stage decorum in favor of a new interest in stylish, charismatic, extroverted performance and, accordingly, a shift from "well trained," official judges to winners determined by enthusiastic audience response.[21]

Certain functions of the earlier song contest were preserved in the battle of song that emerged during World War II. Song battles continued to further the work of black churches, providing spiritual entertainment that was often an extension of worship—"the more singing is heard the better we understand the preaching," advised an advance story on a 1943 quartet battle—and a fundraising mechanism to help support church schools, building improvements, and other operations. Some took for granted that that these two objectives were interconnected. In February 1950, two Georgia quartets, the Humble Gospel Singers and the Ever Ready Singers, "engaged in a song battle this week closing out a very successful time, both spiritually and financially." The skepticism of some church members toward the propriety of song battles was acknowledged and countered by longtime *Atlanta Daily World* columnist I. P. Reynolds, who came to the defense of competitive gospel singing. Reynolds argued that a recent program offered "great wholesome entertainment for the many who attended," citing ministers who believed that song battles fit squarely within a church's mission and regular activities.

As one Pastor said "Reynolds, I would like to see a crowd of the Masses get together at some church every night if possible and listen to singing and in other words make them feel at home in the church. As the contact with the church is good and wholesome entertainment." [sic]

Another pastor adds just as church sponsors baby contests, popularity contests to aid the church, why object to those young men matching wits in gospel singing which financially helps the church.

Like musicales and gospel programs, quartet contests and song battles were opportunities for fellowship among congregations and ensembles, who by trading off sponsoring duties were introduced to new audiences in host cities. Black newspapers in the 1940s publicized and recounted battles of gospel song at Baptist, Methodist, Church of God in Christ (COGIC), Spiritualist, Presbyterian, and Seventh-Day Adventist churches, among other denominations. At the same time, battles were advertised as friendly crosstown, intercity, and regional rivalries, with the hometowns of participating quartets almost unfailingly identified. Stories are legion about such musical events as the "song battle between the Royal Gospel Singers of Fairmont, West Virginia, and the Dennis Four Quartet of Pittsburgh" or "the great musical song battle between the Birdetts Singers of Aliquippa, Pa., the Kings of Harmony of Alabama, [and] the Sallie Smith Singers of Cleveland." The specific capital of the gospel field was always at stake. On hand at Chicago's Pilgrim Baptist Church in 1947 for the "coronation" of that year's "Gospel Song Queen" was "Mayor of Bronzeville" Benjamin Younge (the unofficial but community-elected leader of black Chicago), shown in the *Chicago Defender* ceremoniously placing a crown on the head of Ora Harville as Dorsey, Pilgrim pastor J. C. Austin, and the runners-up looked on. Whether declared the "winner" on a judge's score-card or by acclamation, a well-received set in friendly competition with one's peers offered spiritual uplift for audiences but also accrued the prestige of recognition and charismatic artistry for singers.[22]

Despite continuities with earlier quartet contests, the battles of song that grew in popularity in the black gospel field during and immediately following World War II—one wonders whether the notion of a "battle" was perhaps itself a product of wartime rhetoric—took on recognizably new features and dynamics. Some newspaper accounts of gospel programs publicized as competitive encounters note the novelty of the format, suggesting that the practice was more common in some places than others. The 1938 gospel singing contest in New Orleans be-tween Sallie Martin and local singer Equilla White, with Dorsey also appearing, was called "one of the most unique affairs held in the Crescent City." Modern gospel was itself a relatively late arrival in some cities. Jacqueline DjeDje's docu-mentation of the emergence of St. Paul Baptist Church as a gospel center in Los Angeles is a reminder of how nascent gospel music still was in many parts of the country as late as midcentury. It had only been in 1946 that Reverend John L. Branham, formerly of Chicago, took over the pastorship of St. Paul, immediately and aggressively transplanting the Chicago gospel sound to his church, most decisively by hiring J. Earle Hines as his minister of music and bringing to Los Angeles pianist Gwendolyn Lightner, who remembered gospel still being "in its young stages at the time." With Los Angeles's gospel scene still coalescing, a "battle of songs" in 1948 at Canaan Baptist Church between Emily Mae Braham and Mary Collier marked "the first time these two singers have met in a program of this kind." Description of some events as "a musical program *in the form of a great song battle*" (emphasis added) indicates that battles of song were a particular structural format, we might even say packaging, for the production, performance, and consumption of black gospel music.[23]

Pastors made purposeful use of battles of song to enhance the visibility and electricity of their churches and ministry. Broadcasts of black church services, pioneered in 1930s Chicago by Elder Lucy Smith of All Nations Pentecostal Church and by Reverend Clarence Cobbs of the First Church of Deliverance, successfully brought together the popular and youth appeal of gospel music, the growing demand by black Southern migrants for charismatic preaching, and the extended, intimate reach of live radio. Smith's broadcast of her worship services, *The Glorious Church of the Air*, prominently featured gospel music from its beginnings in 1933. Twenty years later, a news report claimed that many of the program's Chicago listeners still "kept up with the latest song hits from Sister Lucy's church just as they did with juke box favorites." While many churches and their ministers hung their hat on the draw of gospel songs, some placed particular faith in the gospel song battle. In another Midwest gospel center, Bishop Sumter E. Looper, pastor of First Unity Church of God, became an active presenter of gospel music in Cleveland. The city earned the nickname "AlabamaNorth" for its extraordinary number of Southern migrants from Alabama and especially from the Birmingham area in Jefferson County, a cradle of black quartet singing. The Birmingham-to-Cleveland pipeline produced one of the most active quartet scenes anywhere. "You couldn't find quartets, particularly gospel quartets, in Detroit," remembered singer and promoter Arthur Turner, who moved to Cleveland in 1929 with one of Birmingham's signature groups, the Dunham Jubilee Singers, "but Cleveland, now there was a quartet on every street corner, just like Birmingham."[24]

Looper catered to Cleveland's apparently hearty appetite for gospel programs in the form of a great song battle. A graduate of Lane Seminary in Cincinnati, Looper delivered sermons and directed the First Unity Gospel Chorus during on-location midnight services aired live on the second and fourth Sunday of each month over radio stations WHK and WSRS. The thirty-minute broadcasts also featured numbers by Cleveland's top quartets and gospel groups—including the Eley Sisters, the Voices of Love, the Deep River Song Birds, and the Shield Brothers (with Turner)—that Looper also presented on programs at his church. The central place of gospel music in Looper's ministry is clear from a 1945 display ad urging readers to support a drive to raise $12,000 for "our future home," a new church building designed to house "gospel singers, recreation center, day nursery, and missionary house." Sure enough, that same year, the regularity of First Unity gospel programs picked up and increasingly featured fundraising face-offs between quartets that Looper began aggressively publicizing as "song battles." As these battles expanded to include touring groups from other parts of the country, including the May 1947 contests at First Unity between two national heavyweights, the Pilgrim Travelers and the Soul Stirrers, so too did the intensity of the promotional rhetoric in black Cleveland's flagship newspaper, the *Call and Post*. News "stories" that appear to be deceptively formatted ad copy, took on the tone of a carnival barker, promising in steady escalation "the greatest song battle ever held in Cleveland," "the greatest song battle of all times," and "the greatest song battle in the history of gospel singing."[25]

Taking part in many battles of song at First Unity Church was one of the most popular quartets in Cleveland, the Live Wire Singers, formed in 1929 and still in their heyday in the post-war years. One of the many local quartets influenced by the influx of Birmingham-style quartet singers, the Live Wires appeared regularly on Looper's WHK broadcasts and had a weekly Sunday morning radio show of their own on WCLE, but they never recorded. Yet throughout the 1940s, the Live Wires were considered worthy competitors in quartet battles, hyped during some tours as "Ohio's best quartette," and were frequently embraced as representatives of Cleveland in showdowns with big-name visiting groups. Some of these clashes lived on in local lore. Years later, ex–Live Wire singer and *Call and Post* writer Clarence Simmons kept alive the memory of the day in 1937 when Richard Ford, the group's late lead singer, "sang down the radio and well-liked Flying Clouds Quartet of Detroit, Mich., before more than 2,000 persons." The flexible narratives about Live Wire battles reveal the range of meanings that press coverage offered readers who were fans of the music. In 1946, a series of programs at local churches presented "a battle between the killers of the North and the killers of the South. The famous Live Wire Singers, radio artists of WHK vs. the Dixie Humming Birds, CBS radio, recording and concert artists of Greenville, S.C. . . .People come from miles around to hear these boys put their numbers down." Two years later, the formidable Swan Silvertones, starring tenor Claude Jeter, "known as having one of the sweetest voices this side of Heaven," came to town.

The country's number 1 gospel singing group will be in Cleveland Sunday. You have [heard] them on radio and on record—now you have a chance to hear them when they make their first Cleveland appearance. The Swan Silvertone Singers of Knoxville, Tenn., and now from Pittsburgh, will be in

a battle of song with our own Live Wire Singers. . . . The Live Wire Gospel
Singers have not lost a song battle in the past two years.[26]

In black press reporting on gospel music during and in the years following World
War II, particularly in "battle of song" coverage, it is difficult to ignore the remarkably pervasive references to winners and losers, national stars and local heroes,
liveness and mediation, singers who responded perceptively to their audiences,
and fans who kept close tabs on the ebb and flow of status. Moreover, the music's
diversifying performance venues, the increasing financial benefits for performers,
the expanding role of fandom, and the repeatedly pitched opportunity to see "in
person" gospel artists previously experienced only through mass mediation only
ramped up the pop-cultural energies that enlivened black gospel throughout the
1940s and facilitated its mobility beyond the black church.

Spiritual Entertainment

Larger gospel programs held at high school or city auditoriums to accommodate
audiences that exceeded the capacity of church sanctuaries were already common
during the war, though other contexts explicitly offered the experience of gospel
music as popular entertainment. In January 1945, "a great battle of songs, featuring
five famous male quartettes," the Soul Stirrers, the National Independent Gospel
Singers of Atlanta, the Flying Clouds of Detroit, the Shield Brothers of Cleveland,
and the Bay State Gospel Singers of Philadelphia, was held at Cleveland's only
black-owned skating rink, the Pla-Mor, which with its in-house Hammond organ
often doubled as a music and dance venue. In some cases, the financial reward
of a contest victory created extra enticement for singers and fans. Usually the
bounty was symbolic—Thermon Ruth Sr. remembered his group winning "a
big 50 pound cake"—but cash prizes for first, second, and third place winners
even in early quartet contests were not uncommon, if nominal, often $5 or less.
But a markedly different sense of production and spectacle is evident in 1950 at
the 2,300-seat Soldier and Sailors Hall in Pittsburgh, where, days after their appearance at the Melody Skating Rink, the Swan Silvertones vied with the South
Winds of Macon, Georgia, the Nightingales of Philadelphia, and the Soul Stirrers
on an "All-Star" Father's Day program, sponsored by the *Pittsburgh Courier*, with a
$1,000 cash prize in the balance for the winner.[27]

We might reasonably conjecture that quartet fans were captivated not only
by charismatic singing but also by the perception of extra-religious benefit for
the performers, whether they were earning monetary reward or, in such cases as
the Live Wires, extending their winning streaks and reputations. This investment
on the part of audience members could be even more direct. A particularly intriguing example is the "Pastor's Singing Contest" in 1946 at Zion Baptist Church

in Newport News, Virginia, pastored by Reverend J. B. Reid. Reid was one of eleven ministers from nine local churches—six Baptist, two Episcopal, and one Methodist, with two unaffiliated pastors also in the running—who were listed as contestants. There is no specific mention of gospel singing, though some of the longstanding functions of song battles—fellowship among denominations and financial support for the host church—are evident in advance publicity. The specifically prescribed role for the audience is, however, striking:

> Congregations of all the churches represented are expected to be present, the Reverend Reid stated. The purpose of the contest is to raise funds for the rally being sponsored by the church, which closes on May 26. The response from the audience will determine the winner of the contest, the pastor said.[28]

Black newspaper accounts of quartet contest judges in the 1920s and 1930s retiring to the pastor's study and, after sober deliberation, reemerging to announce the winner to an expectant audience are a far cry from the sense of a more unmediated populism at Zion Baptist Church, with congregations showing up en masse to exuberantly cheer their pastor on to victory. The determination of song contest winners by audience response was a practice that according to Thermon Ruth Sr. first became noticeable at gospel programs in the late 1930s, timing that was in synch with national pop culture. "Letting the crowd decide" would have been anathema to caretakers of the ethos that voice culture was intended to inculcate. But honoring the expressed preferences of the audience and reorienting perceptions of cultural authority would have been entirely in alignment with the fad of adjudication by audience response that emerged as part of wartime popular culture.

Entertainment trade magazines in the mid-1930s noted a general "trend toward informality" and "public participation" that spawned multiple developments, including a "new gadget," the applause meter, designed to give a decibel reading of audience response. After its commercial rollout in 1936, the applause meter was almost immediately taken up within popular culture, from beauty pageants to live and radio-broadcasted amateur talent contests. By 1947, crowd response as a measure of a compelling performance was on network television, most notably on CBS's popular television variety show *Arthur Godfrey's Talent Scouts*, which made the applause meter a central feature. There is unmistakable resonance between Reverend Reid's explanation of operating procedures for the 1946 singing contest in Virginia ("the response from the audience will determine the winner") and a 1947 *Billboard* review of the Godfrey program describing how "the winner of each show is decided by the applause which is registered on a meter." At a "mammoth songfest" in Chicago in August 1954, billed as the Mahalia Jackson Gospel Song

Festival, this connection was explicit. Besides Jackson, "Famous gospel singers from Detroit, New York, Los Angeles and other metropolitan cities will appear on the giant program which promises to be one of the greatest in Chicago's history. Another feature will be a song contest between the various Chicago churches; the winner to be chosen by applause meter."[29]

It is undoubtedly true that for some members of black congregations gospel music was strictly religious entertainment, delivered by singers with devout integrity. But newspaper coverage indicates that for other fans of the music, battles of gospel song increasingly became pop-cultural happenings, documented in many cases as if they were sporting events. As Robert Marovich writes, "gospel music aficionados demonstrated as much loyalty to their favorite singers and groups as sports enthusiasts did to professional athletes."[30] But the specific rhetoric of athletic competition began to permeate quartet contest culture. In the 1940s, followers of the black press read more and more frequently about quartets like the Sunlight Four Quartet of Aliquippa, Pennsylvania, issuing "a challenge to every quartet in Western Pennsylvania to participate in a contest," others like the Kings of Harmony from Birmingham, Alabama, that went into some battles as "favorites," and week-long series of quartet contests structured in the manner of a round-robin tournament. Some battles, like the Jackson-Martin and Jackson-Washington programs, were hyped as particularly mouthwatering matchups. "Can the Famous Harmonizing 4 of Richmond, VA Stop the Sensational 5 Blind Boys of Jackson, Miss.?" an ad for a Myers-produced "Interboro War in Songs" asked breathlessly in November 1947, starkly pitching the program as something resembling a gridiron clash or a no-nonsense, back alley throwdown: "Each group guaranteed to sing 10 to 15 selections. You are the judges! No preliminaries. No other artists appearing. No M.C.—No announcements."[31]

In 1988, Ruth looked back on the rivalry between his Selah Jubilee Singers, regulars on the song battle circuit despite being predominantly a jubilee group, and the Dixie Hummingbirds. The losses to their nemesis hurt: "The worst whipping the Selahs ever taken was from the Hummingbirds." Ruth also recalled gentleman's bets between the groups' avid followers in the parking lot before their battles. "Men used to just sit on the front seat there and just almost bet money on the Selahs or Dixie Hummingbirds," said Ruth. "You know, it wasn't a public thing, but it was a known thing as far as we were concerned." The rhetoric of competitive sport could be remarkably explicit: a notice in the *New York Amsterdam News* publicized a "North vs. South" quartet contest in Harlem at which the Sunset Jubilee Singers "will take the mound for the North." Though the stakes were largely symbolic, the press called attention to them in ways indicating that they were nonetheless meaningful. In Florida during the summer of 1944, an outdoor "city-wide musical extravaganza" brought together "all of the quartets of Jacksonville in a mammoth contest for the city championship." Quartets sometimes represented not their hometown but their affiliated media outlets. With

"Quartet War Declared!" in 1942 between the Dixie Hummingbirds of radio station WCAU and the Royal Harmony Singers of station KYW, the two groups engaged in a heavily publicized song battle at Mother Bethel AME Church in Philadelphia "for the city radio championship."[32]

A singular cultural event in black Chicago, the Bud Billiken parade and picnic, offers a final example of how the packaging of gospel singing in the "battle of song" format by churches, by promoters, and by the singers themselves mobilized black gospel as a type of popular culture. *Defender* founder Robert Abbott and managing editor Lucious Harper started the Bud Billiken Club as a social networking mechanism for black Chicago youth. The club's success encouraged Abbott to inaugurate a Bud Billiken Day in 1929 featuring a parade that culminated with a picnic in Washington Park. The Bud Billiken Parade, held the second Saturday in August, is the oldest African American parade in the country and continues to draw spectators in the millions. For the twentieth-anniversary parade and picnic in 1949, the club planned the biggest blowout ever, with "20 different events—all going on at the same time." The *Defender's* advance publicity for this "20-ring circus" promised something for everybody.

> Listed for your entertainment are:
> Block dancing
> Tennis games
> Horse shoe pitching
> Volley ball
> Casting
> Fishing
> Boating
> Water show
> Canoe tilting
> Soft ball games
> Hard ball games
> Croquet
> Disc jockey show
> Gospel song battle
> Battle of swing bands
> Track and field games
> Progressive games
> Puppet show
> Red Cross first aid exhibit
> Climbing the greasy pole
>
> Now you have it! Just take your pick and be a part of this "circus."

Two weeks later, with Bud Billiken Day fast approaching, the paper followed up with a clarification that the gospel song battle was not simply another activity among a motley assortment of family-friendly recreation. It was the main event.

> Who are the best gospel singers in Chicago, men or women? Well, you'll find the answer at the *Chicago Defender* Bud Billiken Club's 20th anniversary picnic in Washington Park on Saturday afternoon, August 6.
>
> Miss Evelyn Gay, general chairman of the Gospel Music Committee, announced that a "Battle of the Gospel Singers" would be the biggest feature of the picnic.
>
> The contest will be between male and female and mixed choral groups, with the huge picnic audiences acting as judges. There is no charge for entry. For more details about the gospel song battle, jus' write or call ol' Bud Billiken at the *Chicago Defender*.[33]

Battle plans were in good hands. Evelyn Gay (1923–1984) came from one of Chicago's most formidable gospel clans, the oldest daughter of migrants from Georgia who moved to Chicago's West Side and became members first of Elder Lucy Smith's All Nations Pentecostal Church and later a COGIC church on the West Side. With the Dorsey movement and the Swing Era gathering momentum side by side, the five Gay children grew up in a household where gospel and jazz lived under the same roof. Their mother, Fannie Gay, known to all as "Mother Gay," directed the COGIC church choir and the oldest daughters, Evelyn and Mildred, sang in the choir and eventually formed a popular duo called the Gay Sisters. The sisters had already built reputations performing on Elder Lucy's radio broadcasts and their Sanctified roots are on full display with the prominent tambourine and vocal exhortations on their 1951 recording "I'm a Soldier." Their brother, Robert Gay, a trumpeter and flutist more inclined toward jazz, later played with Dizzy Gillespie and Sonny Rollins. Evelyn was also a gifted pianist who gained musical literacy through formal lessons, but her sister Geraldine learned to play by ear and developed a unique personal style heavily seasoned with adventurous jazz harmonies. Geraldine and baby brother Donald, a child prodigy evangelist who by the age of five was sermonizing as "Preacher Gay," eventually joined Evelyn and Mildred to expand the family group, renamed the Gay Singers, with Evelyn as the principal songwriter and arranger. The Gays had close ties to Jackson, for whom Evelyn was an accompanist in the early 1940s. Young Preacher Gay appeared at Jackson's Carnegie Hall debut in 1950 and the Gay Singers performed at her 1954 Carnegie concert. Jackson also regularly consulted Mother Gay for faith healing. At the time of the Billiken blowout in 1949, however, the Gay Sisters had yet to record—their biggest hit for Savoy, "God Will Take Care of You," was still two years away—but they were already touring as a group and twenty-five-year-old Evelyn was a respected choral director in Chicago, likely reasons for her appointment as chairperson of the Billiken Day Gospel Music Committee.[34]

The fact that gospel singing was so prominently featured at a major cultural event is indicative of the extent and nature of the music's popularity in Chicago at the time. Though the male groups surely included quartets, the promised participation of "male and female and mixed choral groups" and winners who could be "men or women" indicates a consciously inclusive competition, but also a battle that was a test of *gospel singing*, whatever the makeup of the ensemble. The Billiken Day gospel song battle overseen by Gay, the centerpiece of a day of entertainment that included baseball, horseshoes, croquet, puppetry, and deejays, also vividly illustrates how the song battle format was not incidental to the field but rather was instrumental in making gospel a highly mobile and thus more readily consumable musical practice. The available prestige—bragging rights as "the best gospel singers in Chicago"—are stated in particularly forthright terms, and the dual role of audience members, who were circus spectators while also "acting as judges," dangles what would have been a familiar and fashionable pop-cultural hook.

Furthermore, the peculiarity of this particular instance, in some ways the extreme case of gospel music as black popular culture, raises numerous questions that suggest fresh ways future scholars might interrogate the locales and forms of gospel singing in the post-war years: How would the religious content and expressive function of gospel songs have figured amid the "circus" atmosphere of such a battle? What did it mean to be publicly acclaimed as the "the best gospel singer in Chicago" in the eyes of an audience fully aware that Chicago's own Mahalia Jackson was already widely recognized as black gospel's preeminent national star? What economies of prestige were at play? Where did singers who participated in gospel song battles, and those who did not, position themselves within gospel as a field of cultural production, and as religious persons? Tracking the myriad places, forms, and meanings toward which the song battle led, a field analysis perspective on black gospel music forces us to account for gospel singing wherever and however it might appear, before determining in advance what should or should not count as "the real thing."

"Johnny Myers Presents"

With a picture of how and why the battle of song emerged, flourished, and functioned as it did in the black gospel field in the 1940s, we can circle back to the Jackson-Washington program at the Golden Gate. Myers brought Jackson to New York a total of four times to perform on his Golden Gate extravaganzas. The promoter first became familiar with Jackson when he heard her at a concert in Detroit and he brought her to New York to appear on a January 13, 1946, program that included Georgia Peach and the Two Gospel Keys, a popular female duo. According to Sellers, Jackson was paid $1,000 for the appearance, her biggest payday to date.[35] The program also included a sermon by the "world's wonder radio preacher" Elder Benjamin H. Broadie, charismatic pastor of the COGIC church in Newark, New Jersey. This book's cover image, a photograph by Skippy Alderman that shows Broadie, Myers (shadowed in the center background), Georgia Peach, and Jackson at the Golden Gate, was likely taken at this concert. Highlights from this Myers program were broadcast on the radio, including Jackson's rendition of "Beams of Heaven." Known alternately as "Some Day," "Beams of Heaven" was published in 1905 by Charles Albert Tindley (1851–1933), the songwriter whom Boyer speculates was not musically literate yet came to be regarded by many as the progenitor of African American gospel music for his influence on a number of gospel song composers, including W. Herbert Brewster, Lucie Campbell, and Thomas A. Dorsey. Such early twentieth-century Tindley songs as "We'll Understand It Better By and By," "Stand by Me," and "Take Your Burden to the Lord and Leave It There" remain widely familiar and actively performed church standards. Born to a family of free blacks in Berlin, Maryland, Tindley made as profound an impact as a Methodist minister, renowned for erudite sermons reinforced by the message of his songs. For thirty years, Tindley served as pastor of a landmark church in Philadelphia that in 1924 was renamed Tindley Temple.[36]

The recording of "Beams of Heaven" from the Golden Gate, the only known documentation of Jackson singing between her 1937 Decca session and her first recordings for Apollo in 1946, is useful for comparing her style with that of the best known black religious soloist of the mid-1940s, Sister Rosetta Tharpe, who recorded the song for Decca seven years earlier in January 1939. In an all-too-familiar practice, Tindley's song was copyrighted three months later identifying "Rosetta Thorpe" as having written the words and music.

Verse
> Beams of heaven as I go
> Through this wilderness below
> Guide my feet in peaceful ways
> Turn my darkness into days;
> When in the darkness I would grope
> Faith always sees a star of hope
> And soon from all life's grief and danger
> I shall be free one day.

Chorus
> I do not know how long 'twill be
> Nor what the future holds for me
> But this I know, if Jesus leads me
> I shall get home some day.

As was the case with each of the fourteen songs she recorded in her first three sessions for Decca—all in the identical key, B-flat—Tharpe sang "Beams of Heaven"
self-accompanied on guitar. Tharpe transforms the triple-meter hymn by taking
it in an up-tempo $\frac{4}{4}$, phrasing the words elastically over the gentle swing of her
supporting guitar. Though she adds little elaboration to the syllabic and predominantly pentatonic melody, Tharpe's technique of applying slight punch to words
placed just off the beat gives the tune subtly dynamic life through the tug-of-war
between a strongly articulated pulse and a syncopated delivery that is the essence
of swing. Tharpe sings through two verses of Tindley's text, each followed by the
chorus. In 1947, Tharpe re-recorded "Beams of Heaven" in a thrilling duet with
Marie Knight accompanied by the Sam Price Trio.[37]

Jackson takes a dramatically different approach from Tharpe.[38] Disregarding
steady meter altogether, she draws out the melody from the opening phrase with
her breathy entry on "Beams" at a sustained *sotto voce*, the delicate scoop on "of,"
and melismatic flourishes on "heaven." Jackson repeats the chorus but only
sings one verse, yet her performance takes four and a half minutes, compared to
Tharpe's, which is just over three. Several idiosyncrasies of her style that would
soon be heard on her Apollo sides—the rolled "R" in "free," the chopping of words,
and the repetition and interpolation of text—are in evidence in this performance,
particularly in her effusive delivery of the final chorus, which turns Tindley's compact message of hope into ecstatic personal testimony:

> *Well, I do not know, Lord, how long, how long, how long it will be*
> *Oh, nor what the fu–, oh Lord, really holds for poor me*
> *Oh, but one thing I do know, if my Jesus doth lead me*
> *Then I, I, I shall get home, oh, one of these mornings I shall get home*
>   *some day.*

"Beams of Heaven," is one example of the many hymns in triple meter that
Jackson performed with a "free" feel influenced by black Baptist lined-out-
hymnody, disregarding metronomic time and strictly measured rhythms and liberally elaborating the melody with moment-to-moment ornamentation. We might
in fact characterize Tharpe's and Jackson's approach to the song as "Sanctified"
and "Baptist," respectively. As I discuss in Chapter 6, Jackson recorded several of
these free triple-meter hymns for Apollo, with whom she signed later that year.

As Sellers remembers it, when Jackson made her next appearance at the
Golden Gate in the face-off with Washington in 1948, "Ernestine kind of stole the
program," not so much by outperforming Jackson as by running out the clock.
After sets by the opening groups and by Washington, and especially Washington's
extended rendition of "I Thank You, Lord," perhaps a plug for her recording
of the song released the previous fall, the time was short for Jackson and her

backing ensemble, which included her former paperboy in Chicago, sixteen-year-old James Cleveland. In the end, "they put the lights out on her when they were singing 'Move On Up a Little Higher.' "[39]

As the "home team" in the contest, Washington's indulgence was perhaps permissible. A soloist since her childhood in Little Rock, Arkansas, Ernestine Beatrice Thomas married Holiness minister Frederick Douglas Washington in 1934 at the age of nineteen and shortly thereafter moved with him to New Jersey to establish Trinity Temple Church of God in Christ in Montclair. Both "marital and religious partners," the Washingtons relocated to Brooklyn in 1951 where Reverend Washington was a tent evangelist with an enormous following that eventually led him to purchase the building that became Washington Temple Church of God in Christ, still in operation today. Washington Temple was the childhood church of Reverend Al Sharpton (*b.* 1954), who preached his first sermon there at the age of four and was licensed as a minister and closely mentored by Reverend (later Bishop) Washington, among the most powerful black ministers in the COGIC denomination. Jackson and Ernestine Washington met in Chicago and were friends well before their Golden Gate concert (Figure 4.2). Washington believed that Jackson's first-ever appearance in the New York region was at a program sponsored by Trinity Temple, and she stayed with Jackson whenever she made appearances in Chicago, getting her hair done at Jackson's beauty salon.[40]

Washington's career as a gospel performer was complex. She sang to support her husband's ministry, became, according to Boyer, "official soloist" of the Church of God in Christ, and in the 1940s and 1950s cultivated a substantial career as a religious recording artist. Boyer observed that Washington's distinctive nasal timbre with rapid vibrato, characteristic of many Sanctified singers and reminiscent of Tharpe, was deeply indebted to Texas-born pianist and singer Juanita "Arizona" Dranes (1891–1963). Washington first recorded in 1943 and was unusually productive on record for a gospel soloist at the time, cutting sides with piano accompaniment and with the backing of male quartets. She also sang on commercial recordings of her husband's sermons. In the 1940s, Washington was one of the most visible figures in the relatively underdeveloped New York gospel scene, though in the years leading up to her Golden Gate program with Jackson, she also seemed to be crossing over into secular contexts. In January 1946, Washington agreed to record four religious songs backed by the jazz band of trumpeter Bunk Johnson, an offer that, according to Russell, was extended to Jackson as well following her 1946 appearance at the Golden Gate, "but Mahalia refused to record with a dance band."

In 1948, Washington, identified as a "gospel singer," sang at a New Year's Day memorial jazz concert at New York's Town Hall, "Blues for Bessie," marking the tenth anniversary of the death of vaudeville blues singer Bessie Smith and celebrating the first public showing of the newly rediscovered short film *St. Louis*

FIG. 4.2 Sister Rosetta Tharpe, Ernestine Washington, and Mahalia Jackson. Photo by Lloyd Yearwood. Courtesy of Anthony Heilbut. By permission of the Lloyd Yearwood Estate.

Blues, the only known footage of Smith. More provocative is a furtive comment from *Baltimore Afro-American* columnist E. B. Rea in 1947: "Ernestine Washington, recorder of spirituals for Disc Records, divides her time between singing in nightclubs and in her husband's church." Pentecostal denominations, which often worshipped with tambourines, drums, and brass instruments, were traditionally more open to secular music influences than Baptists and Methodists, so

Washington may have felt more latitude to experiment, particularly with her influential husband as a safeguard of her reputation. While her sound may have struck some ears as slightly dated by the 1950s, she was a fixture in New York gospel music circles from the 1940s until her death in 1983. Washington can be heard singing in her home church *c.* 1958 on the album *Gospel Singing in Washington Temple* and was an occasional host and performer on the early-1960s syndicated television program *TV Gospel Time*.[41]

More than simply being a local favorite, Washington was a regular feature of Myers's gospel programming in the New York City region. Myers's name often comes up in passing in literature on black gospel music, though his brief but highly impactful role within the New York gospel scene has been nebulous. Despite his face appearing in virtually all of his ads, one gospel encyclopedia identifies the African American Myers as a "white music promoter" who "began to exploit gospel's commercial possibilities."[42] This invisibility of Myers (*c.* 1906–1966) has in part been due to virtually nonexistent biographical information. What exists is sketchy: census records indicate that he was born in South Carolina and was living in Harlem by 1930, but an obituary in the *New York Amsterdam News* claims he was an Ohio native with eleven siblings.[43] Yet even his body of work as a concert promoter in the 1940s, and particularly its place within the commercial structures of the still-emerging black gospel field, has hovered beneath the radar. Working closely with a syndicate of singers, ministers, independent record producers, broadcast media, and pop cultural figures, Myers was at the center of a symbiotic operation involving live performance, radio, recording, and the power of promotion. He was an important catalyst for much of what was to come in postwar gospel, including the launch of Jackson's career as a national figure through her association with Apollo Records and the later and better-known ventures of black promoters Joe Bostic, who brought gospel "downtown" with his concerts at Carnegie Hall and Madison Square Garden, and Thermon Ruth Sr. and Doc Wheeler, who both produced major gospel programs at Harlem's Apollo Theater. It was the Jackson-Apollo nexus, mediated and facilitated by Myers, that brokered a union of the musical innovations of the Chicago gospel scene and the production capacity of New York's independent record industry.

One of Myers's not-so-secret weapons as a promoter was his heavy investment in publicity. Despite Sellers's disappointment over Jackson being crowded out by Washington, he believed that she nonetheless benefitted from the concert from a pure public relations standpoint: Myers "was the man that really put Mahalia over, 'cause he really spent money on promoting that program."[44] Myers's relentless, attention-grabbing advertising in the *New York Amsterdam News* enables us to reconstruct a reasonably coherent picture of his concerts. Myers appears to have begun his career as a producer of religious concerts in earnest in the fall of 1943, with a "farewell concert" for the Golden Gate Quartet. The influential "Gates," a jubilee quartet at the peak of their fame on the strength of their appearance at John Hammond's 1938 "From Spirituals to Swing Concert," their residency at Café Society, and their White House performances for Franklin and Eleanor Roosevelt, were headed for Hollywood to fulfill a two-year movie deal with Paramount Pictures. In many ways, this concert already exhibited many of the recurring ingredients that became such a successful combination for Myers: a strong predilection toward quartets, the "battle in song" format, a blend of national and local talent, heavy reliance on a stable of recurring performers, the promise to present mass-mediated artists live and in person, and the familiar confines of the Golden Gate.

The Golden Gate Ballroom was a main feature of the "Johnny Myers Presents" operation. Promised during its construction to be the "most magnificent ballroom on the face of the earth," the Golden Gate opened on October 19, 1939, as part of an ambitious attempt by entrepreneur Jay Faggen to break the monopoly held by Harlem's Savoy Ballroom, run by his former business partner Moe Gale. Lavishly designed by the country's preeminent builder of theaters and ballrooms, architect Thomas Lamb, the Golden Gate's 25,000-square-foot space with 40-foot-high ceilings boasted a dance floor with a capacity of 5,000, with room for thousands more as spectators, earning the nickname the "Madison Square Garden of Harlem." Yet less than five months after its smash debut, the Golden Gate lost its beer license due to purported violation of liquor regulations and was in foreclosure, eventually taken over, rather suspiciously, by the Savoy.[45] The conversion of the Golden Gate from a dance ballroom to a "social ballroom" did, however, lay the ground for Myers's gospel concerts. In the early 1940s, the Golden Gate became a diverse community-use space, hosting dry dances, but also amateur boxing matches, pageants, recitals by Paul Robeson and Roland Hayes, and a slate of civil rights rallies and addresses by progressive figures that included Republican presidential candidate Wendell Willkie, Adam Clayton Powell, Eleanor Roosevelt, Mary McLeod Bethune, Walter White of the NAACP, and Richard Wright, discussing his new novel Native Son. The winning formula of Myers's religious concerts, which precluded the sale of alcohol, delivered reliably packed and well-behaved houses, and bore relatively miniscule artist fees compared to those commanded by top dance bands, made his programs another fixture at the venue.[46]

The dominance of quartet singing at the farewell concert for the Golden Gate Quartet was typical of "Johnny Myers Presents" programs. Publicity for the event highlighted not only the group of honor, but also the Harmonaires, Georgia Peach with backing singers (almost certainly a male quartet), and undisclosed "other radio quartets." It was not uncommon for Myers's advertisements to list the names of two or three groups followed by the promise of "25 Other Outstanding Quartettes" or "50 Special Invited Quartettes" that were to also appear. Myers was clearly an advocate for quartet singing. Receiving much press attention was the National Quartet Convention at St. Peter Claver Auditorium in Brooklyn in September 1944, which touted the expected participation of "more than 100 quartets." Myers was identified as "Vice President" of the convention. With quartet singing as a focus, it is not surprising that the song battle format, framed as a regional faceoff, was a frequently exploited device in Myers's offerings. A mid-summer "North Battles South" program featured two New York–based groups, the Southern Sons and the Harmonaires, versus the Harmonizing Four of Virginia and the Dixie Hummingbirds of South Carolina. In 1946, the Soul Stirrers made their New York debut going head-to-head with the Reliable Jubilee Singers of Atlanta. As part of a pair of cross-borough concerts to celebrate the "triumphant return to New York" by "America's Sensational Gospel Singing Favorite" Sister Rosetta Tharpe—in the afternoon in Queens and that same evening in Brooklyn—the Dixie Hummingbirds, the "Champion of Champions," took on the National Clouds of Joy from Jacksonville, Florida. The "East vs. West" Jackson-Washington contest in 1948 was simply a continuation of this promotional theme.[47]

The recurring presence of the Harmonaires, a local group that Myers managed and perhaps sang with as well, indicates another essential feature of Myers's concerts. The promoter did often build programs around special appearances by nationally known groups: jubilee-style quartets that were widely familiar through appearances on major network broadcasts (the Golden Gate Quartet, the Trumpeteers, and the Jubalaires); quartets inclined toward more contemporary, lead singer–dominated performances (the Soul Stirrers, the Pilgrim Travelers, and the Five Blind Boys of Mississippi); and highly reputed soloists like Jackson, Washington, Tharpe, and Ethel Davenport. But Myers's bread and butter were a stable of regulars, many of them professional mid-level quartets of high quality but with a less elevated profile. Some, like the Sunset Jubilee Singers, the Jubilee Stars, the Sky Light Jubilee Singers, and the Harmonaires, were based in the New York City area; others, like the Southern Sons from Memphis, the Reliable Jubilee Singers from Atlanta, the Ivory Gospel Singers from Baltimore, or the Chicago Crusaders, were quartets making extended stays in New York or that had regular access or solid ties to the area.

A border-straddling case is the Dixie Hummingbirds, whose rise from an aspiring quartet still making a name for itself to bona fide stars in the gospel field overlaps directly with their years of association with Myers. Formed in Greenville, South Carolina, the Dixie Hummingbirds followed their professional opportunities to Philadelphia, from where they established a network of New York contacts during their engagement at Café Society Downtown (opposite the Golden Gate Quartet in residence at Café Society Uptown) from November 1942 to January 1943. The Birds were back in New York the following summer, making perhaps their first of at least six appearances at Myers's concerts over a period of three years. Over the span of these engagements, the group, fronted by the dynamic and influential Ira Tucker, became one of the best-known quartets in the country and a New York favorite. On November 10, 1947, Myers presented a massive afternoon-evening concert doubleheader at the Golden Gate and Holy Trinity Baptist Church in Brooklyn in celebration the twelfth anniversary of "your famous Dixie Hummingbirds."

In addition to quartets, the "house" talent at Golden Gate and affiliated programs included gospel groups and soloists, above all the Two Gospel Keys, the Thrasher Wonders, Georgia Peach, and Ernestine Washington. Washington appeared well over a dozen times at Myers's concerts as a performer and/or an emcee, but she was just one of his go-to artists. The Two Gospel Keys were a vocal harmony duo originating at a COGIC church in Augusta, Georgia, made up of guitarist Emma Daniel and Sally Jones playing tambourine. Daniels was in her late fifties and Jones in her late sixties, and "great-grandmothers both," when they first recorded and began singing on Myers's programs in the mid-1940s, by which time they reportedly had been performing together for more than forty years. Sellers described them as "two old ladies [who] wore bonnets" and had "sixty-nine grandchildren" but who "were famous then making records" that enjoyed considerable popularity in the late 1940s. [48]

The Thrasher Wonders became Myers's pet project. They were a family gospel group that began in the 1930s as a trio of small children out of Zion Methodist Church in Wetumpka, Alabama: Gerhart Thrasher and younger sisters Berenice and Duaine. They subsequently added two more members, younger brother Andrew and schoolmate Homer Jones, becoming a quintet. The first major publicity for the Thrasher Wonders came in May 1941, when they performed in a widely reported concert of "non-concert music" at the New York Museum of Modern Art called "Jubilee," structured as a stylized revival meeting. Myers was programming the popular and crowd-pleasing Thrasher Wonders regularly on his concerts by 1944 and, judging from a reference the following year to "Johnny Myers and his Thrasher Wonders," he seemed to take on some sort of managerial role as well. In 1953, Gerhart and Andrew Thrasher, still in their early twenties, crossed over from gospel to join the rhythm and blues vocal harmony group the Drifters, fronted by former gospel singer Clyde McPhatter. The rough-hewn "rootsy" sound of the Two Gospel Keys and the Thrasher Wonders, both of which appeared numerous times at the Golden Gate, was somewhat unique among the artists who worked with Myers. Their recordings were packaged together for a 1950 album released and marketed by Moses Asch, eventual founder of Folkways Records, on his Disc label. In his liner notes for the album, Frederic Ramsey, deploying a persistent rhetorical framework that would shadow Jackson as well when she was compared to Marian Anderson, pitted the "real voice" of artists like the Two Gospel Keys, "people who sing and live spirituals" against the "musical hoax" of "gelded" versions offered by "conservatory-taught arrangers who have 'harmonized' the spiritual for concert presentation."[49]

Within black gospel music history, Georgia Peach (*c.* 1904–1964) is a bridge between South and North and between an earlier era of black religious music recording and the age of post-war gospel. One of six siblings, she was born Clara Hudmon to C. V. and Clara Hudmon in the unincorporated town of Chipley, Georgia, where her grandfather had been freed from slavery at age sixteen following the Civil War.[50] Sometime after 1910, the family moved eighty miles north to Atlanta where they joined the newly founded Mount Moriah Baptist Church. Mount Moriah was also the home church of the highly reputed congregational song leader Reverend C. J. Johnson (1913–1990), who recalled the popularity of Hudmon's rendition of "Daniel in the Lion's Den" throughout black Atlanta in the 1920s.[51] Hudmon was a childhood friend of fellow Atlantan Thomas Dorsey, who after he moved to Chicago "gave me his ballads" to sing. She also sang in support of Reverend J. M. Gates, who pastored Mount Calvary Baptist Church in Atlanta and became nationally famous through his more than two hundred commercially recorded sermons for a number of labels between 1926 and 1941. Hudmon can be heard singing on several Gates recordings made in 1934 for Bluebird, including the Dorsey song "There's Something About the Lord Mighty Sweet."

Hudmon's recording history prior to her association with Myers captures the contours and sound of black religious commercial records before the dawn of modern gospel. In 1930, she made her first known recordings as Sister Clara Hudmon, cutting four sides in Atlanta for Okeh assisted by Deacon Leon Davis, Sister Jordan, Sister Norman, and other anonymous voices offering exhortations behind her. Shortly thereafter she married Mount Moriah's pastor Reverend T. T. Gholston, a controversial union because of their age difference. In 1931, the newlywed Gholstons began singing for a radio show on Atlanta's CBS affiliate WGST starring John and Mary Dodgen, the regionally popular white husband-and-wife blackface comedy team. Known as Sunshine and Snowball, the Dodgens were CBS's answer to NBC's Amos 'n' Andy.[52] The Dodgens invited the Gholstons to New York to record with them for Columbia and the resulting side, though nominally a Snowball and Sunshine release, featured Clara singing the Charles Tindley song "Take Your Burden to the Lord and Leave It There" backed by a thirteen-voice choir, with Snowball interjecting remarks to the "congregation" in black dialect. The Gholstons were eventually banished from Mount Moriah by its scandalized congregation and moved first to Detroit and then to New York, where they divorced. It was in New York where Clara Gholston, having acquired a local reputation singing on the radio and performing with a group of male backing singers at the 1939 World's Fair, was given the name "Georgia Peach" by Harlem's Bishop R. C. Lawson. Singing lead while fronting male quartets appeared to be her preferred ensemble configuration. In 1942, she recorded a pair of sides for Decca as "Clara Belle Gholston, the Georgia Peach and Her Gospel Singers," including what was to become one of her signature numbers, "Do Lord, Send Me."

The subtle contrasts among Georgia Peach's early recordings are an illuminating reminder of the range of black religious singing and her own flexible vocality. Her 1930 Okeh sides are in the universe of Gates's popular records, conceived almost as stylized field recordings that summon a service through black church folk in-studio giving enthusiastic responses to the preaching and singing. Deacon Davis and the two Sisters, who stoked Hudmon on her songs with shouts of "Praise God," "Well, well," and Sing it," were apparently "expert witnesses," so to speak, since they are regulars on Gates's recordings as well. "Leave It There" also simulates a black church atmosphere with Reverend Snowball presiding over the imaginary worshippers, if more satirically. Whereas for Okeh—especially on "Now Is the Needy Time" and "I Want to See Jesus"—Hudmon sang in a forceful chest voice with punched, halting cadences supported by the minimalist "boom-chuck" piano accompaniment, on the 1931 Snowball and Sunshine record she is backed by a solemn organ and harmonized choir and approaches the song with a rounded tone colored by controlled vibrato, employing more lyrical phrasing and crisper diction with rolled Rs. The multiple faces of performed blackness are brought into focus when one recognizes that the Okeh and the Snowball and Sunshine sides, though complemented by the sound of purportedly "real" black singing, all sought to produce highly constructed representations of black musical worship, the former insinuating *in situ* authenticity and the latter, along with Reverend Snowball's comedic sermon "Moses and the Bull Rush" from the same session, maintaining one foot in vaudeville minstrelsy. Yet it is easy to overlook the distinctly different vocal practices Georgia Peach herself employs even on the Tindley songs she recorded for Okeh and Columbia, respectively, "Stand by Me" and "Leave It There," a function of their variably performative contexts.[53] Hudmon recalled her pride in being "raised to be a young lady" at her Baptist church in Atlanta and in her further study in New York with African American concert recitalist and respected voice culture pedagogue Cora Mann.[54] But her work with blackface comedians indicates the continual interface of black respectability with professional opportunities that some black elites surely perceived to be in tension with idealized social identities and values.

A useful conjuncture for comparison of the voices and singing styles of Georgia Peach, Washington, and Jackson at the time of Myers's Golden Gate concerts are their recordings of gospel songs of a similar type made within a nine-month-span in 1946–1947: Jackson's "I'm Going to Tell God" and Georgia Peach's "Just One Moment," both for Apollo, and Washington's "The Lord Will Make a Way" for Manor. The three songs' sixteen-bar harmonic progressions and melodic arcs share a basic resemblance, most conspicuously, the move to the dominant at the end of the second four-bar phrase setting up the singers' dramatic arrival on the upper tonic to begin the concluding half of each verse. Both Georgia Peach and Washington are accompanied by a male quartet. But whereas Georgia Peach's deft interplay with her chanting backing singers and her chopped phrasing seem closer in approach to quartet singing, Washington sounds closer to Jackson stylistically in their employment of blues-rooted pitch ambiguity, more active embellishment, and long, fluid lines that, together, produce a greater sense of forward-pressing aesthetic urgency.

Like Washington, Georgia Peach was a centerpiece of Myers's concerts and she became a matron figure in black New York church circles while remaining beloved in Atlanta as one of the city's "favorite daughters of music." Known in later life as Clara Gholston Brock after marrying another minister, Reverend Haywood Brock, she identified most strongly as an in-demand revival singer and was buoyed by the prestige of devout integrity and venerable status. "My inspiration comes strictly from the hymns," she told Mura Dehn, a devoted champion, who perceived in her comments an implicit swipe at Jackson: "My inspiration comes from no blues." Georgia Peach died on New Year's Eve 1964. At the time of her packed funeral at Faith Temple COGIC in Harlem, she was living in poverty. Despite her insistence that "Clara [Ward] is greater than Mahalia," she was nonetheless eulogized as "the woman to introduce the unsurpassable Mahalia Jackson to New York audiences" at Johnny Myers's concerts in the late 1940s.[55]

Beyond gospel singing, Myers enhanced the spiritual and entertainment value of his programs through appearances by charismatic ministers, unorthodox religious figures, and even sports stars. With his wife a being focal point of Myers's concerts, it is not a surprise that Reverend Washington was a regular as well, both preaching and serving as emcee. Another local celebrity minister closely associated with the Myers concerts was Elder Benjamin Broadie, a COGIC pastor known for his popular Sunday night radio broadcast on Newark's WHBI, the "gospel station" with an unusual policy of transmitting only on Sundays, with most of its live church programs targeting black listeners. Washington and Broadie, who occasionally worked in tandem for Myers, also made commercial recordings of their sermons with members of their respective congregations. They can be heard to good effect on Reverend Washington's "The Wildest Creature," supported by a singing group led by Ernestine, and on Elder Broadie's artful retelling of the parable of the prodigal son, "Come On Back Home, Baby, Papa Ain't Mad at You" with the backing of another Myers group, the Ivory Gospel Singers. Also participating in Myers programming was the pastor of Harlem's Abyssinian Baptist Church and soon-to-be congressman Adam Clayton Powell, who was guest of honor at a large quartet program in 1944.[56]

Myers attempted to expand the appeal of his programs by featuring more unconventional figures, such as divine healer Prophetess Dolly Lewis, "the God-sent Miracle Woman of Detroit," and four-year-old preacher from Tifton, Georgia, Reverend Samuel Theophilus Holmes. Holmes was the "wondrous child disciple whose adult knowledge of Holy scripture from Genesis to Revelation has confounded world religious experts and divinity students" and Myers booked the prodigy for a two-week revival in March 1948 highlighted by preaching, quartets, and an "old fashioned camp meetin' song feast." "Johnny Myers Presents" religious concerts also dipped into the world of popular culture, with prominent appearances by heavyweight champ Joe Louis and middleweight title holder Sugar Ray Robinson, as well as Brooklyn Dodgers All-Star catcher Roy Campanella. Joe Bostic, who would soon surpass Myers as New York's preeminent black gospel promoter, particularly by presenting Jackson annually at Carnegie Hall beginning in 1950, cut his teeth at Myers's programs. A sports reporter, WLIB disk jockey, and writer for *People's Voice*, the leftist black newspaper founded by Powell, Bostic gained exposure to the gospel field as Myers's "assistant" and occasional master of ceremonies at the Golden Gate.[57]

The Myers Syndicate

The aspect of "Johnny Myers Presents" that is less easily discernible, but that appears to be the engine that made the entire operation work, is a dialectic of liveness and mediation that was strategically manipulated for the benefit of both the performers and their audiences. The heyday of Myers's Golden Gate religious concerts during and following the second World War coincided directly with the extraordinary proliferation of independent recording companies focusing their efforts on lesser-known talent, in many cases African American jazz, rhythm and blues, and folk musicians. This was not an arbitrary overlap. Many of the artists on Myers's programs, especially his regulars, were systematically recorded by a constellation of small, New York–based independent record companies run by some of the leading figures in the business: Irving Berman's Regis, Manor, and Arco labels; Apollo Records, run by the husband-and-wife team of Ike and Bess Berman; brothers Bob and Morty Shad's Haven Records; Herb Abramson's Jubilee Records; Moe Asch's folk-leaning Disc, Asch, and Solo imprints; Elliot "Eli" Oberstein's Varsity Records; Bob Thiele's Signature Records; and Hub Records, owned by future James Brown manager Ben Bart, assisted by future Mahalia Jackson manager Harry Lenetska (both ex–Moe Gale employees). Also to be included among this group of record producers, though in a notably distinct capacity, are the Coleman Brothers, a successful black family quartet that pooled its resources to open the Coleman Hotel in Newark, catering to African American patrons, particularly musicians who had difficulty finding places to stay on the road with their options limited by Jim Crow. Anticipating Sam Cooke's SAR Records by a decade, the Colemans, partly out of frustration with the handling of their sides recorded for Manor, set up a studio in the hotel basement from where, beginning in 1948, they cut and released records on the Coleman label.[58]

Table 4.1 delineates the correlation between appearances at Johnny Myers concerts and recording opportunities just described. Two immediate observations

Table 4.1 Concerts and Recording Dates for Johnny Myers Artists

Performer	Known Appearances on Johnny Myers Programs (at the Golden Gate Auditorium [GG] unless otherwise indicated)	Labels Recorded for (Date)
Quartets		
Harmonaires	August 1, 1943	Apollo (Feb. 1946, with Georgia Peach)
	April 9, 1944	Varsity (c. Dec. 1947)
	July 16, 1944	
	August 21, 1944 (Salem Methodist Church, Harlem)	
	September 10–17, 1944 (St. Peter Claver Auditorium, Brooklyn)	
	September 24, 1944	
	December 24–25, 1944	
	April 1, 1945	
	April 15, 1945 (Third Separate Battalion Armory, Brooklyn)	
	December 9, 1945	
	December 8, 1946	
Sunset Jubilee Singers (aka Sunset Four)	April 9, 1944	Hub (c. early 1946)
	September 24, 1944	Duke (c. early 1946)
	October 29, 1944	Haven (April 1946)
	December 24–25, 1944	
	April 1, 1945 (Jamaica Arena, Long Island)	
	November 18, 1945	
	December 9, 1945	
	November 10, 1946	
	December 8, 1946	
	January 12, 1947	
	September 28, 1947	
	March 14–28, 1948	

(continued)

Table 4.1 Continued

Performer	Known Appearances on Johnny Myers Programs (at the Golden Gate Auditorium [GG] unless otherwise indicated)	Labels Recorded for (Date)
Jubilee Stars	September 10–17, 1944 (St. Peter Claver Auditorium, Brooklyn) September 24, 1944 October 15, 1944 December 24–25, 1944 April 1, 1945 (Jamaica Arena, Long Island) April 15, 1945 (Third Separate Battalion Armory, Brooklyn) May 6, 1945 November 10, 1946 (GG and Holy Trinity Baptist Church, Brooklyn)	Haven (c. Oct. 1946)
Dixie Hummingbirds	July 16, 1944 September 24, 1944 October 29, 1944 (GG and Laurel Gardens, Newark, NJ) December 9, 1945 November 10, 1946 June 29, 1947 (Jamaica Arena, Long Island and Holy Trinity Baptist Church, Brooklyn)	Regis/Manor (July 1944) Apollo (July 1946–Jan. 1949)
Coleman Brothers	September 10–17, 1944 (St. Peter Claver Auditorium, Brooklyn) September 24, 1944 October 15, 1944	Manor (Oct. 1943; Feb. 1947) Coleman (c. 1948)
Kings of Harmony	November 12, 1944 May 6, 1945 (Jamaica Arena, Long Island) November 24, 1946 (GG and Trinity Baptist Church, Brooklyn)	Manor/Arco (Sept. and Dec. 1944)

Harmonizing Four	July 16, 1944 October 29, 1944 (GG and Laurel Gardens, Newark, NJ) September 28, 1947 November 9, 1947 (GG and Holy Trinity Baptist Church, Brooklyn)	Coleman (c. Aug. 1948)
Selah Jubilee Singers	November 12, 1944	Manor (1944)
Southern Sons	April 9, 1944 August 13, 1944 September 24, 1944	Haven (c. Oct. 1946)
Heavenly Gospel Singers	November 18, 1945 December 9, 1945	Manor (c. Oct. 1945, c. Dec. 1945; c. mid 1948)
Sky Light Singers	September 24, 1944 December 24–25, 1944 April 13, 1947	Regis (c. Dec. 1944) Manor (Feb. 1945 [with Georgia Peach], c. Oct. 1945)
Reliable Jubilee Singers	October 24, 1946 November 24, 1946 (GG and Holy Trinity Baptist Church, Brooklyn) December 8, 1946 June 22, 1947	Apollo (c. Oct. 1946, Dec, 1946 [with Georgia Peach], c. Feb. 1947)
Silver Echo Quartet	September 24, 1944 November 18, 1945	Regis/Manor/Arco (Jan 1943, Feb. 1944, c. March/April 1944, Dec. 1944)

(continued)

Table 4.1 Continued

Performer	Known Appearances on Johnny Myers Programs (at the Golden Gate Auditorium [GG] unless otherwise indicated)	Labels Recorded for (Date)
Chicago Crusaders	January 12, 1947 April 13, 1947 September 28, 1947 December 14, 1947 March 14–28, 1948 April 26–27, 1948 (Salem Methodist Church and Mt. Morris Presbyterian Church, Harlem)	Coleman (c. 1948)
National Clouds of Joy	April 13, 1947 June 22, 1947 June 29, 1947 (Jamaica Arena, Long Island and Holy Trinity Baptist Church, Brooklyn) September 28, 1947	Coleman (c. 1948)
Bright Light Sextet	April 11, 1948	Apollo (July 1948)
Silvertone Gospel Singers	January 11, 1948 December 26, 1948 January 9, 1949	Solo (c. Jan. 1949) Coleman (c. June 1949)
Ivory Gospel Singers	March 14–28, 1948 April 11, 1948 April 26–27, 1948 (Salem Methodist Church and Mt. Morris Presbyterian Church, Harlem) January 9, 1949	Coleman (c. 1948, 1949) Apollo (May 1949)

Groups

Thrasher Wonders	April 9, 1944	Disc/Asch (Jan. 1946)
	September 24, 1944	
	November 12, 1944	
	December 24–25, 1944	
	April 1, 1945 (Jamaica Arena, Long Island)	
	November 18, 1945	
	December 9, 1945	
	November 10, 1946 (GG and Holy Trinity Baptist Church, Brooklyn)	
	December 8, 1946	
	September 29, 1947	
	December 14, 1947	
	March 14–28, 1948	
Two Gospel Keys	January 13, 1946	Jubilee (c. Jan. 1946)
	November 10, 1946 (GG and Holy Trinity Baptist Church, Brooklyn)	Solo (late 1946)
	November 24, 1946 (GG and Holy Trinity Baptist Church, Brooklyn)	Apollo (Feb. 1947, Apr. 1947,
	December 8, 1946	July 1948)
	June 29, 1947 (Jamaica Arena, Long Island and Holy Trinity Baptist Church, Brooklyn)	
	September 28, 1947	

(continued)

Table 4.1 Continued

Performer	Known Appearances on Johnny Myers Programs (at the Golden Gate Auditorium [GG] unless otherwise indicated)	Labels Recorded for (Date)
	December 14, 1947	
	January 11, 1948	
	March 14–28, 1948	
	April 26–27, 1948 (Salem Methodist Church and Mt. Morris Presbyterian Church, Harlem)	
	December 26, 1948	
	November 18, 1945	
Johnson Brothers Soloists	December 9, 1945	Manor (Dec. 1945)
Georgia Peach	August 1, 1943	Manor (Feb. 1945, Dec. 1957)
	April 9, 1944	Apollo (Feb. and Dec. 1946)
	October 15, 1944	Candy (c. 1946–1947)
	October 29, 1944 (GG and Laurel Gardens, Newark, NJ)—also Emcee	Shelton/Signature (c. 1946–1947)
	December 24–25, 1944	
	April 1, 1945 (Jamaica Arena, Long Island)—Emcee	
	April 15, 1945 (Third Separate Battalion Armory, Brooklyn)	
	November 18, 1945	
	December 9, 1945	
	January 13, 1946	
	October 24, 1946	
	November 10, 1946 (GG and Holy Trinity Baptist Church, Brooklyn)	
	December 8, 1946	

	September 28, 1947	
	March 14–28, 1948	
	April 11, 1948—Emcee	
	December 26, 1948—Emcee	
Ernestine Washington	April 9, 1944	Regis/Manor/Arco (Jan. 1943, c. 1943, July 1944)
	August 21, 1944 (Salem Methodist Church, Harlem)—Emcee	Jubilee/Disc (Jan. 1946)
	September 24, 1944	
	October 29, 1944 (GG and Laurel Gardens, Newark, NJ)	
	December 24–25, 1944	
	April 15, 1945 (Third Separate Battalion Armory, Brooklyn)	
	May 6, 1945 (Jamaica Arena, Long Island)—Emcee	
	November 18, 1945	
	December 9, 1945	
	November 10, 1946 (GG and Holy Trinity Baptist Church, Brooklyn)	
	September 28, 1947	
	December 14, 1947	
	March 14–28, 1948	
	March 28, 1948	
	April 11, 1948	
Mahalia Jackson	January 13, 1946	Apollo (Oct. 1946–June 1954)
	April 11, 1948	
	January 9, 1949	
	May 14, 1950	

(continued)

Table 4.1 Continued

Performer	Known Appearances on Johnny Myers Programs (at the Golden Gate Auditorium [GG] unless otherwise indicated)	Labels Recorded for (Date)
Marie Knight	June 22, 1947	Haven/Candy (Apr. 1946,
	June 29, 1947 (Jamaica Arena, Long Island, and Holy Trinity Baptist Church, Brooklyn)	c. Oct. 1946) Decca (Nov. 1947)
Preachers		
Elder Benjamin H. Broadie	January 13, 1946	Coleman (c. 1948–49)
	March 28, 1948	
	March 29, 1948	
	April 26–27, 1948 (Salem Methodist Church and Mt. Morris Presbyterian Church, Harlem)	
Rev. Frederick D. Washington	September 24, 1944	Manor (Aug. 1947)
	October 29, 1944 (GG and Laurel Gardens, Newark, NJ)—Emcee	
	March 28, 1948	

can be made. First, the table provides a snapshot of the quartets, groups, soloists, and pastors that became the bedrock of Myers's concerts from the fall of 1943 to their oddly abrupt end in January 1949. But also apparent is the consistent mating of these artists with the cluster of independent labels identified above. In cases like Varsity, Hub, Signature, Jubilee, and Asch, the recordings seemed to be isolated ventures; the one or two sessions recording Myers artists constituted these labels' only involvement in black gospel music. But other companies, in particular Regis/Manor/Arco, Haven, Apollo, and (less surprisingly) Coleman, made a more significant commitment to recording "spiritual" artists. But all of these gospel-curious New York indies—and this is the important point—were recording, almost without exception, performers appearing on Myers's programs. As with the many independent labels that came and went in the mid-1940s, artists were sometimes impulsively recorded regardless of the intent to release the results; if circumstances changed, the masters could be sold to another label. This was the case with Abramson at Jubilee, who recorded Ernestine Washington with Bunk Johnson's band and the Two Gospel Keys and sold these masters to Asch, who released them on his Disc label, packaged with his own recordings of the Thrasher Wonders. A glimpse of the record-first-and-ask-questions-later practices of some independent record labels is communicated in a letter from the Two Gospel Keys via their manager Fred Jones to Asch, who was preparing a release of their recordings.

> We have been notified that you have announced that you are releasing certain records by the Two Gospel Keys. Upon learning of this, we now notify you that we object most strenuously to any such release.
>
> We at no time recorded for you for the purpose of producing phonograph records to be sold. We were never paid for our recording services. When we appeared at your studio, we were told that we were making test records only, and were given the sum of $10.00 each as expenses for our time and trouble in making the tests. We at no time authorized release of these test records, and never authorized you to use our name or pictures in connection with these test records.
>
> If these records are released we will have suffered damages and will be forced to take steps to protect our rights, and stop and enjoin you from issuing and selling these records.[59]

A different case was Irving Berman, owner of the G & R Record Shop in Newark, who went into the record business when he started Regis Records in 1942 with the intent to "specialize in colored spirituals" then later branched into jazz and rhythm and blues by launching the companion labels Manor and Arco. In a May 1946 *Billboard* advertisement publicizing the Manor catalog, the label's religious offerings—by the Silver Echo Quartet, the Kings of Harmony, the Heavenly Gospel Singers, the Coleman Brothers, Georgia Peach with Sky Light Singers, and Ernestine Washington—exclusively feature Myers artists. Beyond their live performances, the Dixie Hummingbirds made their name through their recordings for Regis, cut the same month as their debut at a Myers concert, and to an even greater extent for Apollo. After appearing on a Myers program, Marie Knight, publicized as having been "discovered by Sister Rosetta Tharpe," made a similar debut as a solo artist by recording a series of singles for Haven, owned by the Shads, also former Brooklyn record store owners. Even groups like the Selah Jubilee Singers and the Harmonizing Four, who had active careers and recorded for Decca, indulged Manor and Coleman, respectively, for one session.

It is tricky to pinpoint the specifics of this enterprising business relationship among ambitious entrepreneurs—an African American impresario who hailed himself as "America's Foremost Quartette and Religious Concert Promoter" and a group of largely Jewish-American independent record producers—though we might hazard some speculative conclusions. At some point in the process, Myers seemed to function as the middleman between these independent labels and the artists that he programmed. One can imagine Myers parading a considerable array of battle-tested talent available for record labels owners at what amounted to free auditions at his Harlem, Brooklyn, Newark, and Queens programs, while at the same time gaining the musicians' loyalty through his proven ability to deliver on the promise that they would have a precious opportunity to record if they appeared on his programs. Perhaps Myers even paid his artists in recording opportunities. The relationship would have been both flexible and mutually beneficial, with more locally known groups pursuing a possible break to get ahead by cutting a record or two, and startup labels having a chance to record artists walking into the studio with well-rehearsed repertory and a fan base. The fact that so many of the quartets on Myers's programs were able to record whereas an esteemed Midwest quartet like the Live Wires of Cleveland never cut a single side is telling, revealing the role of geographical region in the historiography of the black gospel field. Though the pattern is not consistent, in many cases the close timing of a performer's appearance at a Myers gospel extravaganza and their recording session suggest a possibility that the two opportunities may have been part of a coordinated package deal for the performers. Myers's efforts to, if necessary, establish his performers as recording artists through his matchmaking with local independents sweetened the deal for the singers, but it also boosted their marketing potential for his own concerts. We might also conjecture in reverse: the Matchless Love Gospel Singers, a mixed group from Detroit led by Mae Gooch, recorded for Manor both as backing singers for Georgia Peach in 1947 and on their own the following year. Though their name never appears in a Myers advertisement, these recordings suggest a likelihood that they would have at some point performed as one of the many "other" groups that appeared on his programs.

This reciprocal leverage of live and mediated performance is also apparent in Myers's promotion, which highlighted opportunities to see performers like the Coleman Brothers, "New Jersey's No. 1 Quintet" and "Radio and Recording Artists" in the flesh. Mediation endowed a prestige of recognition that boosted the perception of immediacy when audiences experienced artists "in person," as Myers's ads frequently tempted. Singers were regularly identified with their cities of origin, but also with an affiliated radio outlet, for instance the "Sunset Jubilees of WINS," the "Afro Jubilees of WHBI," the interracial Coast Guard Quartet "heard every Sunday morning on *Navy Goes to Church* on WOR," and the "CBS Popular Jubalaires" headlining a concert with Ernestine Washington, "gospel Songbird of WAAT," as emcee. Some coverage of the concerts seemed to acknowledge that Myers was consciously cultivating a nexus of live performance, recordings, and radio appearances. "Johnny Myers, quartet promoter and sponsor of Religious Concerts, goes on apace as he chalks up one success after another," observed an *Amsterdam News* columnist following Myers's ambitious "Interstate Quartet Contest" in Newark and the Golden Gate. "This energetic young man is developing top network material in these unique harmonisers."[60]

There is evidence to suggest that Myers's intention was to operate almost as a booking agency, packaging the artists on his roster even for events that were not his own. As early as 1945, Myers advertised a benefit concert in Brooklyn with the Harmonaires, the Jubilee Stars, Georgia Peach, and Ernestine Washington as "His All Star Quartette Attraction." In subsequent years, we see his artists appearing on the programs of others. Reflecting the Popular Front–era interest of the American Left in black gospel music evident at "From Spirituals to Swing" and Café Society, the folk music collective People's Songs presented a concert at New York's Town Hall on March 15, 1947 called "Spirituals at Midnight" exclusively featuring Myers artists, making it probable that there was some communication between the event's organizers and Myers, or at the very least familiarity with his concerts. Following the model of "Johnny Myers Presents," the People's Songs' Town Hall concert presented the Two Gospel Keys as an opening act preceding a "battle of music" between the Coleman Brothers, the Reliable Jubilee Singers, and the Chicago Crusaders. This would have been a high-profile appearance, and for a group like the Reliables it represented one of the ways in which they garnered visibility through their association with Myers. The quartet, which performed at Myers concerts in 1946 and 1947, returned to their hometown of Atlanta "in a great blaze of glory" after spending a year in New York where, the local black newspaper boasted, "they won nation-wide acclaim and chalked up the most enviable record of any religious group from the Deep South." Cited were successfully exploited opportunities, all generated by the Myers syndicate. The story offers a tidy summary of the ways Myers's various operational components worked together.

> While in New York, these boys landed some of the best contracts in the singing business there. They are now Apollo Recording Artists and now have in the various music stores in the country some fine recordings. They appeared in concert with the Champion of the World, Joe Louis [i.e., their October 24, 1946 song battle with the Soul Stirrers at the Golden Gate]. They appeared in Brooklyn Academy of Music and in the downtown hall in New York City [i.e., the People's Songs Town Hall concert]. On numerous occasions they have appeared at the Golden Gate Ballroom in New York City and many others.

This story in the *Atlanta Daily World* publicized the group's "home-coming" concert at Wheat Street Baptist Church, which featured the Pilgrim Travelers and several lesser-known local favorites. But also present at the program was Myers himself, who brought with him from New York the Two Gospel Keys to complete the package and served as a guest speaker, surely elucidating the narrative of the Reliables' success through "Johnny Myers Presents."[61]

THE RECEPTION OF "Move On Up a Little Higher" in early 1948 stands on its own merits, though bringing into the picture Jackson's head-to-head battle with her comrade and competitor Ernestine Washington at the Golden Gate that spring suggests a story more expansive, consequential, and meaningful than the sensational success of a single record. Situating Jackson's breakthrough in 1948 in the context of "Johnny Myers Presents," an interlocking ecosystem of national and local talent, entrepreneurial record companies, mass media, and charismatic church figures spanning the Greater New York City region, it becomes clear that she represented a fairly typical example, if a singularly spectacular outcome, of Myers's work with gospel artists. Myers heard Jackson at a program in Detroit, invited her to New York to sing on one of his radio-broadcasted programs in January 1946, after which Abramson, who likely heard her at this program, made an offer for her to record with Bunk Johnson's band for his Jubilee label, just as Washington had done weeks before. Jackson declined, unwilling to work with jazz musicians; unlike Washington, she had not had an opportunity to record for nine years and may have had understandable discomfort with returning to the studio as a gospel artist in such a context. But groups performing at Myers's concerts had been actively recording for other local independent labels for well over a year. In fact, two of his key artists, Georgia Peach and the Dixie Hummingbirds, recorded for Apollo Records in February. "So," Sellers remembers, "Johnny Myers got Bess Berman to record with Mahalia," an arrangement documented by a 1946 newspaper photo showing Jackson seated with Apollo president Hy Siegel as she signed a two-year contract, with "her manager, Johnny Myers" standing between them. As the program for Jackson's twenty-fifth anniversary concert at the Chicago Coliseum in October 1951 reported—inaccurately from a chronological standpoint, but conveying the underlying truth—Jackson's second Johnny Myers concert in 1948 was part of "a ten-day, city-wide revival" presided over by Elder Broadie, and "from this engagement, she received an Apollo Recording Contract."[62]

Jackson returned to the Golden Gate a third time in January 1949, this time as a star, headlining a pair of sold-out concerts, and several additional local concerts were scheduled to meet the overwhelming demand. Sellers remembered Jackson earning "a thousand to twelve hundred, sometimes fifteen hundred a night . . . from the halls and things" in New York during this visit. Jackson's name was still largely unknown among white audiences, but the enthusiasm generated by her Apollo recordings and her New York triumphs brought her unequaled national acclaim as a soloist among black gospel fans. "Mahalia Jackson, famed as the nation's Queen of Gospel Singers, arrived in New York this last week on tour and has smashed local attendance records in churches and auditoriums, winning new laurels and thousands of new followers for the magnetic young spiritual singer," according to one southern African American newspaper. "Jamming in New York's Golden Gate auditorium to capacity twice in one day, Miss Jackson, sang many numbers that are loved by hundreds of thousands as she sings them on Apollo records, including 'Move On Up a Little Higher,' her recent 'Dig a Little Deeper' and her new rendition of 'I'm Tired.' "[63] Her fourth and final Golden Gate Auditorium appearance under the auspices of Myers was at a 1950 Mother's Day concert, for which block-long lines of fans queued up hours in advance to get a seat. The concert, which also featured Jackson's friend, the classically trained J. Robert Bradley, and upstaged a show by Sister Rosetta Tharpe and Marie Knight at the Golden Gate earlier in the day, kicked off Jackson's multi-state tour of the South and Midwest.[64]

Soon thereafter, according to Sellers, Jackson had a falling out with Myers over a financial disagreement that ended their concert work together.[65] Waiting in the wings, however, was Myers's protégée Joe Bostic. Myers and Bostic were just two of several African American promoters of black gospel music to emerge in the area, including Edna Mae Crenshaw, Doc Wheeler, and Thermon Ruth Sr. in the New York boroughs, and Ronnie Williams in Newark, New Jersey. But it was Bostic who went on to become the preeminent gospel promoter in New York City in the 1950s, making his name through his association with Jackson, though in looking back in the 1980s, Bostic remembered the situation in reverse.

Mahalia Jackson was my creation. She was singing gospel on the Apollo label. When she came to town, I heard her at the Golden Gate—a huge dance hall and auditorium just north of the Savoy Ballroom on Lenox

Avenue—with Johnny Myers. I got an idea—a Mahalia Jackson concert at
Carnegie Hall.[66]

Jackson's "grand debut" at Carnegie on October 1, 1950, an event that Bostic billed
as the first annual Negro Gospel Music Festival, also featured the Ward Singers,
the Landfordaires, the Gospel Clefs, Chicago's child-preacher Reverend Donald
Gay, and others. Whatever Bostic's self-congratulatory excesses, the Carnegie
appearances bolstered Jackson's resume like nothing before. The presentation of
black gospel music at the prestigious venue elicited considerable press coverage,
including a write-up in the *New York Times*, but nowhere more so than in the
black press. The *Amsterdam News*'s extensive review of the concert emphasized
Jackson's status as "truly a great artist," meriting an appearance at Carnegie, the
"Milky Way of music." Jackson "was even more electrifying than her fame, spread
by thousands of her aficionados who practically swoon under the spell of her soul-
stirring voice and emotional appeal. There was no need to wonder about her vocal

FIG. 4.3 Mahalia Jackson handing the winning ticket to a raffle contestant at
Harlem-based radio station WLIB, with *Kiss Me Kate* cast member and on-air host
Lorenzo Fuller (far left) and unknown others. This may have a promotional event
publicizing Jackson's Carnegie Hall debut on October 1, 1950, at which Fuller also
performed. Photo by Frank Donato, Impact Photo, Inc. Schomburg Center for
Research in Black Culture, Photographs and Prints Division.

training or ability to project her songs right into the hearts of listeners" for she possessed "as much passion and rapture as any prima donna who ever graced the stage." As a measure of the perceived significance of the event for Jackson and for black gospel, a headline in the *Chicago Defender* blared "8,000 Witness First Negro Gospel Concert at Carnegie Hall," despite a Carnegie capacity of under 3,000.[67]

A concert at Carnegie Hall with Jackson topping the bill was Bostic's brain-child and perhaps even a watershed moment of sorts. Coming just five months after her final "Johnny Myers Presents" concert at the Golden Gate, however, it might be more profitably understood as the capstone of her New York City expo-sure through Myers. As Jackson's career unfolded in subsequent years, writers repeatedly pointed to her appearances at Carnegie Hall as a guage of her growing fame. But the perceived elite distinction of gospel making it "downtown" should be calibrated against an altogether different kind of prestige: the immense ca-chet that Jackson accrued as the "Gospel Songbird of the Nation" performing year after year uptown at the Golden Gate in front of packed houses of African Americans who consumed gospel music both as spiritual entertainment and as black popular culture (Figure 4.3). Myers cannot be fully credited either with Jackson's breakthrough or with putting Apollo Records on the map. But the labo-riously constructed mechanisms of curatorial vision, professional relationships, and economic exchange maneuvered by Myers, aided by the leverage of pop-cul-tural hooks like the song battle, kept gospel singers in New York and beyond in the public's eye and ear and facilitated one exceptional case that reshaped the black gospel field.

Apollo Records and the Birth of Religious Pop

THE LAUNCH OF Decca Records in 1934 had consequence for black gospel music when shortly thereafter the label initiated a 7000 series for "race recordings" exclusively featuring black artists. Decca's 7000 series offered disks by such sacred vocal harmony groups as the Mound City Jubilee Quartet, the Golden Eagle Gospel Singers, and the Norfolk Jubilee Quartet that documented the late-1930s stylistic transition from jubilee to gospel quartet singing.[1] Bob Miller, a funeral home owner in Chicago who acted as Jackson's unofficial manager in the 1930s, claimed that he was with Jackson at a small South Side studio when she made a self-produced recording of "You Better Run, Run, Run" to sell at the National Baptist Convention, though no copies of this record are known to have survived.[2] Instead, it was Decca's "race" catalog, overseen by pioneering black record executive J. Mayo Williams, that offered Jackson's first commercially available recordings. On May 21, 1937, the twenty-four-year-old Jackson, accompanied by Estelle Allen on piano and organ, recorded four sides that were released as the singles "God Shall Wipe All Tears Away" b/w "Oh, My Lord" and "God's Gonna Separate the Wheat from the Tares" b/w "Keep Me Every Day."

The modest attention these disks received, and Jackson's rejection of Williams's recommendation that she broaden her target audience by recording secular repertory, resulted in her being dropped by Decca. "When I made those Decca records they promised me great things if I would make some blues records," Jackson told Bucklin Moon. "I wouldn't, and they cut me off and took on Sister Rosetta Tharpe instead. Even if I had been willing to compromise a little they would have built me up, but I didn't want that."[3] Jackson would not record again for nine years. Tharpe, on the other hand, enjoyed sustained success at Decca, along with the Selah Jubilee Singers, both of whom began recording for the label in 1938.

Until the late 1940s, male quartets dominated commercial recordings of black sacred music, representing over half of the black religious performers known to have recorded in-studio between 1943 and 1948. Documented to a lesser extent were variously accompanied male and female soloists and a very small handful of female or mixed gospel groups and choirs.[4] For most gospel singers, live performances at programs and in conjunction with the National Baptist Convention remained the principal vehicle for making one's name well into the 1940s. Several factors conspired to shift the culture surrounding gospel recording and make records "the predominant measuring stick for success" for black gospel singers after World War II.[5] The 1940 founding of the performing rights organization Broadcast Music Incorporated (BMI), which became a counterweight to the American Society of Composers, Authors and Publishers (ASCAP), provided fresh stimulus for composers beyond Tin Pan Alley, offered new professional vistas for gospel songwriters, and placed a new body of repertory into media circulation.[6] Meanwhile, entrepreneurs launched hundreds of independent labels in the mid-1940s devoted in varying degrees to the production of rhythm and blues, with "spiritual" records often folded into the category.

Complementing this development was a growth of black-targeted radio and the increasing curatorial power of the disk jockey, which together significantly boosted the supply and accessibility of black gospel music. In New York, Johnny Myers became an influential agent, weaving together this nexus of live performance, recording, and radio play of gospel music. Myers often functioned as a middleman between singers and labels, as was the case when Apollo signed Jackson in the fall of 1946. And though the tide was already turning, Jackson's work for Apollo was itself a watershed. In particular, the popularity of "Move On Up a Little Higher," which broke nationally in early 1948, coaxed many more gospel singers to relax their ambivalence toward recording. Jackson herself was convinced that "Move On Up a Little Higher" was the song that "opened the doors for me many places," teaching gospel singers and the music industry that "you could take religious songs and sing them just like you sing in the church, put them on records, and people would buy them."[7]

Jackson's first session for Apollo was on October 3, 1946, and she remained with the label for nearly eight years. Her career with Apollo is closely yoked to the woman who ran production matters at the label virtually single-handedly, Bess Berman. Like Myers, Berman has been both an omnipresent and shadowy figure in the literature on Jackson, but while information about her is limited, a partial picture of Berman and her impact on Jackson's career can be sketched through study of available sources. Both women, each in their own right, were trailblazers in the music industry and were joined at the hip at Apollo. Chapters 5 and 6 offer a historical and critical assessment of Jackson's career as an Apollo recording artist. The current chapter considers the various ways in which Jackson and Berman were mutually reliant, if contentious, partners and how Apollo strategized success for Jackson in response to significant transformations within the music industry and across the national public sphere, particularly the emergence of religious pop around 1950. The chapter that follows offers a stylistic analysis of Jackson's Apollo recordings.

Bess Berman and the Business of Apollo Records

If writers have been fond of representing Jackson as the devout, charismatic, ample-figured black church lady, Bess Berman has invariably been cast as the flinty Jewish broad. "Apollo Records was owned by a woman, Bess Berman," recalled singer and songwriter Doc Pomus, who recorded for Apollo. "She was a very tough kind of lady, and everybody was terrified of being in a room with her because she seemed a very strong aggressive woman." Through passing references and the occasional anecdote, Berman (1902–1968) emerges as the "stocky, jowelled Jewess" who ran Apollo Records as the "imperious," "formidable," "domineering," and "notoriously difficult wife" of Ike Berman, the label's founder. Gospel singer Thermon Ruth Sr., leader of a male vocal harmony group that backed Jackson on several Apollo sides, also remembered her: "Bess Berman from Apollo. Everybody was scared of her because she was a mean woman."[8] Her reputation notwithstanding, the controversial and historically elusive Berman managed to put her stamp on a transitioning post-war popular music industry and on Jackson's life and career in ways that have yet to be meaningfully illuminated.

Bessie Merenstein was the fourth of seven children, born on July 14, 1902, to immigrants living in a densely packed Yiddish-speaking enclave in Lower East Side Manhattan.[9] The birthplaces of her parents, Louis and Emma Merenstein, are not entirely clear. A likely scenario is that Bessie's father and mother were both born in Russia in the 1870s, fled with their families to Germany and Austria, respectively, amid the outbreak of pogroms and aggressively anti-Semitic policies that followed Alexander III's ascension to the Russian imperial throne in 1881, then, along with many other Russian Jews, immigrated in the early 1890s to the United States, where they met and married. Emma was a housewife and Louis drove a beer truck then worked as a hat maker until his death in 1930. Bessie found employment as an office clerk and as a manicurist before marrying Isaac "Ike" Berman in 1926 (Figure 5.1). Ike had a son and a daughter from a prior marriage, but Bess never bore children. Ties between the Merensteins and the Bermans were deepened and knotted when Bess's youngest brother Charles and Ike's daughter Harriet married in 1936. Ike Berman, the son of a German-Jewish immigrant father, got into the music industry in the early 1930s when he started Economy Supply Company, a business based in New York and Baltimore that sold parts and supplies for coin-operated "amusement machines," specializing in jukeboxes, and employed both his son Jack and another of Bess's brothers, Sidney Merenstein.[10]

FIG. 5.1 Bess and Ike Berman with Bess's mother Emma Merenstein, September 25, 1948. By permission of Ronald Merenstein.

Partnering with Herman "Hy" Siegel and Sam Schneider, Ike started Apollo Records in 1943 as a bicoastal production and distribution company operating initially out of Teddy Gottlieb's Rainbow Music Shop in Harlem.[11] Apollo was part of the wave of startup independent labels launched in what Marovich has aptly described as a mid-1940s "explosion of entrepreneurship" in the music industry.[12] Like many indies, Apollo advertised a catalog that was "first with hits by popular colored artists," making its principal focus black jazz and rhythm and blues. The company broke into the business cutting sides by an impressive roster that included Coleman Hawkins, Dizzy Gillespie, Illinois Jacquet, Wynonie Harris, Josh White, and a twenty-one-year-old Dinah Washington backed by Lucky Thompson, Milt Jackson, and Charles Mingus. But the label cast its net widely, also recording calypsonians Duke of Iron and King Houdini, such country and western bands as Curt Barrett and the Trailsmen and Bob Gregory and the Cactus Cowboys, and a striking array of "ethnic" musical acts that indicated the actual diversity of a postwar pop mainstream habitually depicted as "white." Record buyers could purchase early Apollo disks featuring polkas by Joe Meresco, sentimental Irish numbers by Frank Saunders, "gypsy" drinking songs by the Russian Yar Tzigany, Italian folk melodies sung by Tony Bari, Latin American ballads by crooner Chucho Martinez, and Jewish parodic songs and comedy routines by Abe Schwartz, Cantor Wagoner, and Sam Levinson. Sellers remembered that within a year of its launch, Apollo had become a "big label, but they just didn't have no gospel singers" yet.[13] It was not until 1946 that Apollo began recording "spiritual" artists—a catch-all for black performers of religious repertory—the first cohort of which were all part of the Johnny Myers syndicate: Georgia Peach and the Dixie Hummingbirds in February, followed by the Reliable Jubilee Singers and Jackson in October. Apollo recordings by another Myers mainstay, the Two Gospel Keys, ensued the following year, and the label continued to record black religious singing by the Golden Tones, sisters Dorothy Mae and Georgia Lee Willet, and Reverend B. C. Campbell and his congregation and Prophet Powell's Holy Mount Singers, the latter two in on-location church performances.

Ike Berman embraced his wife as an integral part of conducting the family business. Upon his death, *Billboard* eulogized Ike as "a pioneer in the coin machine business, [who] was active in the field for 26 years," while also indicating that from early on Bess, "well known in the trade for activity in the juke box field," was involved in a robust way. When Jackson signed her first two-year contract with Apollo in 1946, a newspaper photo showed her with Myers and Siegel, the former identified as Jackson's manager and the latter as the label's president. But in "a major executive and financial face-lifting," Apollo restructured its operations in May 1948 and Bess Berman purchased the holdings of Siegel and Schneider outright and was named president of Apollo Records by its board of directors. "Contrary to earlier reports," *Billboard* reported, her husband "did not acquire any portion and will not be directly connected with the Apollo organization." Ronald Merenstein, son of Charles Merenstein and Harriet Berman (thus Bess's nephew *and* step-grandson), remembered Ike Berman as a "visionary" always thinking of the next big thing. To him, it made sense for his grandfather to have relinquished day-to-day operations of Apollo to Bess, which freed him to turn his attention to his thriving jukebox business and other projects, including the acquisition of radio stations. Still, to many outside observers, Ike's decision to put his wife in complete charge of Apollo was remarkable. In 1954, *Cash Box* acknowledged Bess Berman for having "built the label" as "the only woman ever to break through with outstanding success in the male-dominated recording industry."[14]

The timing of Bess Berman's takeover, coming directly on the heels of the company being blindsided by the overwhelming response to "Move On Up a Little Higher," leads one to suspect that Apollo was gearing up to fully capitalize on the commercial impact of a record that has come to represent the "Big Bang" of post-war black gospel recording. The fact that Jackson's 1946 Apollo signing was deemed worthy of coverage in the black press suggests that the singer had, to at least some degree, already attained a translocal profile even without any recordings to speak of. Jackson repeatedly acknowledged that it was her work for Apollo, and above all "Move On Up a Little Higher," that elevated her career to unprecedented heights, though she also maintained a personal belief, rooted in sales figures that over the years took on a life of their own, that Apollo was the house that Mahalia built.

> You know, that company was a very small company when I started with them. Not large as Decca or the other companies. . . .[W]hen the record hit in New York, it hit so fast, they didn't even have a truck to deliver the records to the different places. . . .And it got so popular here in Chicago, the shipping would come in every day, four to five thousand records a day would be sold. . . .And I'd have to take my car and go down there and pick them up, and help to distribute. . . .Yeah, they got a big building and a hundred and ten people. Pretty big company now.[15]

A key development at Apollo during its association with Jackson was the modernizing of the label's gospel offerings. Myers's Golden Gate concerts were undoubtedly the highest profile gospel programs in late-1940s New York, but the promoter's predilection for quartets was conservative. With few exceptions, the groups he steered toward New York independents were quartets in a more traditional and stylistically derivative vein. Even Washington, Georgia Peach, and the Two Gospel Keys were not representative of developments taking place in Chicago or Philadelphia, modern gospel centers that were producing dynamic groups like the Roberta Martin Singers, the Ward Singers, and the Davis Sisters that were electrifying audiences with more contemporary repertory and performance styles. Jackson's success at Apollo catalyzed a merger of the New York independent record industry and the Chicago gospel scene. From 1949, there was a discernible shift in Apollo's gospel tastes as many of the more old-fashioned and "rootsy" musicians and jubilee-oriented quartets were phased out as the label began recording popular contemporary gospel performers like the Martin Singers, Alex Bradford, Robert Anderson, Maceo Woods, the Gospel All-Stars (led by James Cleveland), and the Gospelaires, a trio of Cleveland, Bessie Folk, and Norsalus McKissick.[16] Jackson's close friend J. Robert Bradley also recorded a pair of sides for Apollo. The introduction to modern gospel provided by Jackson and her Chicago associates may have also encouraged Apollo to record the outstanding Daniel Singers from New York. The Ward Singers submitted a demo recording to Apollo as an audition, "but at that time no one was interested," Willa Ward remembered.[17]

Jackson and Berman had a complicated relationship, perhaps because of their similarities. Both were strong-willed women from hardscrabble backgrounds who did not bite their tongue and kept an eagle eye on the bottom line. Jackson's musical collaborators saw the two butt heads frequently over artistic and financial matters, though in recalling the label boss, these African American observers made their perception of Berman's Jewishness a conspicuously immediate point of emphasis. Berman was only in her mid-forties when Jackson began working at Apollo, yet as James Francis, the organist on "Move On Up a Little Higher," remembered it: "Bess was an old eccentric Jew. She and Mahalia was always having run-ins. Mahalia wanted to do one way, Bess wanted to do another. . . .[Mahalia] didn't choose her words. . . .Bess wasn't no aristocrat [and] didn't choose her words either." Sellers trafficked coarsely in predictable physical stereotypes: "Bess Berman was a short, stocky woman. She was a typical Jewish woman with heavy voice and big features. . . .Big nose, big mouth." Robert Anderson had the opportunity to record for Apollo through Jackson's intervention on his behalf. When asked "what kind of person" Berman was, Anderson responded: "She was a Jew. Very precise . . . very dominant. . . .Her and Mahalia . . . had their differences."[18]

The two women apparently had their differences early and often. According to an unattributed anecdote relayed by Goreau, Jackson was determined to record the nineteenth-century hymn "Even Me" (also known as "Lord, I Hear of Showers of Blessing") but was met with resistance from Berman. Berman eventually relented and let Jackson record the song, but made it the B-side of "What Could I Do" (Apollo 178). "Even Me," Goreau concluded in surely hyperbolic vindication of Jackson, "sold more than a million records."[19] The timing and circumstances that Goreau attributes to the conflict do not entirely add up. It occurred, she says, when there was "a new contract under discussion." But "Even Me" was recorded at Jackson's second session, the same session that produced "Move On Up a Little Higher," meaning Jackson was still a newly-signed Apollo artist with nothing more than a couple of tepidly received initial singles to her credit. Still, Francis's recollection that "Mahalia wanted to do one way, Bess wanted to do another" suggests that production and repertory choices were a subject of debate. Anderson said that in early 1954, after Jackson "spoke to Bess Berman about me" and "got me on Apollo," Jackson "came down to direct my session" to make sure that he was produced properly.[20] To Berman's credit, however, throughout her eight-year partnership with Jackson, Apollo allowed the singer to regularly record material drawn directly from her church repertory. Columbia Records, on the other hand, "got ideas of what's commercial. Some of the songs they pick for me I don't understand, and those I couldn't put myself into," said Jackson in 1957. "At least at Apollo I picked what I wanted."[21]

Another issue, an omnipresent one in the industry and especially at independent labels, was the question of mechanical royalties, the earnings due a performer or songwriter based on a contractually determined percentage of net receipts from the sale of recordings. Many black performers perceived the issue to be inevitably bound up with racial politics. In 1948, Berman lent hearty public support to an aggressive campaign led by *Pittsburgh Courier* writer George F. Brown to banish the industry's distasteful "race," "sepia," and "ebony" designations for recordings by black musicians. "Apollo Records never has used these terms," Berman told the paper, "and disapproves of the practice strongly."[22] Yet jazz drummer David "Panama" Francis, who recorded four sides for Apollo in January 1952, insisted that where the rubber hit the road, Berman exemplified the intersection of entrenched racial ideologies and fundamentally exploitative business practices.

> White people, especially intellectuals, felt that black people had to be led by hand like children, so a lot of the contracts that the[y] drew up were so ridiculous that even a child could see through them. They had all the authority for anything that you did. . . .These people were ruthlessly taking advantage of black artists, and never thought twice about changing one word of a song by a black composer so they could put their name on it as a co-writer. Bess Berman recorded almost everybody including Mahalia Jackson, and she had one of those contracts where she took care of all the business. There was a lot of wrongdoing in those contracts.[23]

Sellers claimed that Apollo A&R staffer Art Freeman was a consistent advocate for Jackson, to his own detriment. Freeman "was the one telling Mahalia how many records she had sold, because Mahalia didn't know. Bess was not giving the right counting and Bess fired him on that account."[24] On May 5, 1953, her tenth Apollo date, Jackson recorded the songs "I'm Going Down to the River" and "One Day." *Jet* magazine reported that during the "violent session" Jackson "walked out in the middle of a number. She temporarily forgot her religion long enough to 'bless' out Bess Berman, prexy of the firm. Mahalia told Bess she had a 'plantation attitude' toward Negroes."[25]

In other contexts, Jackson and Berman appeared to have also shared moments of relative intimacy that imply Berman's recognition of Jackson's special place at the company. In fall 1951, Berman accompanied Jackson to the "Definitions in Jazz" roundtable of scholars and aficionados at the Music Inn in Lenox, Massachusetts, where the two women bunked together in a converted horse stall. "I finally made it into the white folks' world and look where it landed me," Jackson cracked in her autobiography.[26] Before singing "Jesus (He's My King)," Jackson told the roundtable audience of bonding with her roommate by sharing her faith.

> I've been talking to Mrs. Bess Berman. I asked her one time. . . "Do you ever pray?" She says, "No, I don't have anything to pray for." I couldn't understand a person not having nothing to pray for. So last night, I was reading the Bible to her and I prayed . . . and finally she woke up this

morning and she said: "You know, I feel so good. I kind of prayed a prayer last night."[27]

Jackson made reference to Berman multiple times in her commentaries to her Lenox audience. "Those type of songs you sing them from your throat and your throat get tired quick," Jackson said after a driving version of Dorsey's "Search Me Lord" that left her winded. "Miss Berman's kind of afraid. She still want me to croon." We cannot know to what degree Berman's concern for Jackson was motivated by a personal connection and to what extent she simply viewed Jackson as Apollo's prized thoroughbred. Berman and Jackson's manager Harry Lenetska traveled with Jackson during her first European tour in fall 1952. Jackson was seriously ill with sarcoidosis and uterine fibroids during the tremendously successful tour, which, despite a full schedule of bookings, eventually had to be cut short when Jackson, who reportedly lost 90 pounds, was forced to return to the United States for a hysterectomy.[28] Bradley, Jackson's friend since the 1930s through Baptist circles, was studying voice in London and attended to her closely at her hotel. Told privately by doctors that Jackson's life was at risk, Bradley urged Jackson to insist that Berman and Lenetska abort the tour even earlier.

> I was conscious of them pushing her. Because she said, "Well, I got to do it, baby," she told me. I said, "Well, why don't you just stop?" She said: "I got to do it, you know. And the contract." I didn't know that Bess Berman was staying right next door to us. So when we would leave, Bess and them would come in and rub her and alcohol her down and just try to get her straight to make those appearances. . . . Bess did anything for her.

Asked if Berman and Jackson battled, Bradley said: "Well, they probably did because Mahalia would fight with anybody, baby. Now, let's face it. . . . [But] they had a great affection."[29] According to Berman's nephew Lewis Merenstein, when Jackson and Berman came to Baltimore for appearances, Jackson stayed at their family home.[30] As a measure of her status at the company, when Jackson renewed her Apollo contract in the summer of 1952, Berman honored her with a luncheon at the Hotel Theresa in New York attended by specially invited disc jockeys and members of the press. In celebration of her twenty-five years in the gospel field, Jackson was presented with an inscribed gold plaque by emcee and "Mayor of Harlem" Willie Bryant "in appreciation and gratitude on behalf of millions of record buyers whose lives and spirits are enriched with the music you give from your heart and soul."[31]

But the relationship between the two women was further entangled by Berman's demonstrably bad habit of evading royalty payments to gospel song composers. Kenneth Morris acknowledged that when he and Sallie Martin first went into business and launched the Martin and Morris Music Studio in 1940, they "knew nothing about copyrighting or any of that end of it." For a song that sold as sheet music for ten cents a copy, "the expense of copyrighting was about two dollars, so it wasn't even worthwhile. . . .After 1944, we started copyrighting all of our music." But as Marovich observes, even when "gospel songwriters such as Dorsey were profiting on sheet music sales, they were missing out on royalties from public performances of their songs or placement on phonograph records."[32] It is easy to imagine that black gospel writers—and undoubtedly many of the largely disempowered musicians and songwriters across the music industry—lacked the tenacity, will, wherewithal, or time to take on record labels and executives who profited disproportionately from their copyrighted work. Dorsey was somewhat of an anomaly, both because he had become a brand name within the black gospel field and because many of his songs were known among both African American and white performers and audiences, but he was nonetheless a frequent victim of musical plagiarism.

Dorsey took steps to protect his intellectual property in 1947 when he was granted an injunction in U.S. District Court against Detroit minister Lee A. Greer, who had been publishing and selling songbooks containing several of Dorsey's copyrighted songs without attribution. In his essay for Martin and Morris's *Improving the Music in the Church*, a fed-up Dorsey vented: "I think it is very low to take another man's song over which he has worked hard, publish it, leave his name off the copy and place another's name there who never wrote a note."[33] It is perhaps out of this frustration that in 1951 Dorsey struck a deal with Hill and Range Songs, the publishing company that dominated the post-war country music field. Hill and Range began administering the copyrights of several Dorsey songs, first on a limited and then on a more expanded basis. Country singer Red Foley's 1951 recording of Dorsey's "There Will Be Peace in the Valley for Me," originally copyrighted in 1939, became a best-seller for Decca, which initially asserted that the song was in the public domain before being alerted to its provenance by Hill and Range on Dorsey's behalf.[34]

Hill and Range's opportunistic control of songs written and copyrighted by Dorsey and other black gospel writers became a thorn in Apollo's side, with Jackson's actively selling recordings as a repeated target. To bypass the legal obligation of royalty payments, many independent labels established publishing arms and exclusively recorded their own songs. In early 1952, Apollo created a publishing affiliate, Bess Music, as a copyright holding company and the following year launched Lloyds Records, a subsidiary label specializing in Apollo's more pop-leaning sides.[35] Jackson released two of the first singles on the Lloyds imprint, "Consider Me" b/w "I Believe" (Lloyds 103) and "No Matter How You Pray" b/w "My Cathedral" (Lloyds 105). Backed by a male vocal harmony group called the Melody Echoes, Jackson recorded "Consider Me" on August 8, 1953, and five days later Berman registered a copyright for the song, claiming that it had been written by Jackson and was the property of Bess Music. In fact, "Consider Me" was a new song that Dorsey self-published in early 1953 as "Consideration" and subsequently assigned to Hill and Range. In November, Hill and Range filed a copyright infringement suit against Lloyds Records and Bess Music for not acquiring a license to record "Consideration" and for "also threatening to publish the version of the plaintiff's copyrighted tune." The suit further sought "an accounting of the profits derived from the alleged infringement." The two sides of Lloyds 103 offer a telling contrast indicating that Berman knew how to pick her battles. Whereas one side of the record lists Jackson as the composer of Dorsey's "Consideration," the flip side accurately identifies the white songwriters of "I Believe," Ervin Drake, Jimmy Shirl, Al Stillman, and Irving Graham. One is left to conclude that to Berman, black songwriters were easier pickings. Less than a year after the "Consideration" suit, Alberta Hunter, a star during the 1920s heyday of black vaudeville blues divas, independently challenged Apollo for recording Jackson singing her song "I Wonder If I Will Ever Rest" under the title "Will the Day Ever Come" without attributing proper credit. Threatened with a Hunter lawsuit, Berman quickly capitulated and settled out of court when she "admitted that the song is the same one" written by Hunter and "agreed to correct the label copy and render a retroactive accounting and royalty payments for the popular recording by the gospel singer."[36]

But it was Hill and Range, which continued to acquire the copyrights of newer black gospel songs, that most aggressively held Apollo's feet to the fire. In April 1955, Berman and Bess Music were named as defendants in a suit filed in New York Federal Court by Hill and Range over eighteen songs under its copyright that were recorded and distributed since 1951 "without having served notice of use or payment of royalties." The 80-page complaint, as described in *Variety* and *Billboard*, specifically cited "sacred songs that had been recorded by gospel singer Mahalia Jackson for Apollo Records," many by Dorsey but also others by W. Herbert Brewster, Kenneth Morris, Alex Bradford, Virginia Davis, and J. W. Alexander.

> According to H. & R., the diskery had claimed these tunes for its affiliated publishing firm, Bess Music, while actually all of the works have established authorship and belong to Hill & Range. In one specific case, involving the tune "What Then," H. & R. charges that the diskery listed Bess Berman and Miss Jackson as writers, while the actual writer is the well-known gospel cleffer, Thomas A. Dorsey. Further, the plaintiff claims to have in its possession a signed statement from Jackson in which she denies authorship of the number.[37]

Berman's disregard for respecting copyrighted gospel material was so brazen and so systematically reliant on Jackson's name as cover that it must be highlighted as an important, if heretofore unacknowledged, subplot of Jackson's Apollo career. It is a story that raises many questions, some perhaps unanswerable, not least: What did Jackson know and when did she know it? According to the Library of Congress Catalog of Copyright Entries, between March 1952 and June 1954, Berman attributed at least twenty-seven songs to Jackson as a songwriter, claiming all as under the ownership of Bess Music (Table 5.1). In eleven of the first twelve instances, either "Bobby Smith" or "Bess Reles"—surely fictitious aliases—are identified as having composed the music to Jackson's lyrics. In every other case, Jackson is credited as having written both the words and music. The overwhelming majority, and perhaps all, are identifiable as tunes written by black songwriters, many of them people Jackson would have known well, including Lucie Campbell, Theodore Frye, Kenneth Morris, Lucy Matthews Collier, Doris Akers, and W. Herbert Brewster. Berman even claimed Jackson's authorship of established hymns like "It's Real," "The Last Mile of the Way," "Come to Jesus," and "Amazing Grace," as well as African American spirituals like "I'm On My Way to Canaan Land" and "Nobody Knows the Trouble I've Seen," despite these being public domain. The fact that Jackson is credited with both words and music indicates that it was not simply an "As sung by" arrangement that was being copyrighted. We may never know whether or how much Jackson was aware of Berman illegally copyrighting dozens of songs in her name—whether, for instance, there was a backroom agreement of some sort between her and Berman. We are left to wonder if her gospel-writing friends questioned her about their royalties for her recordings—about Berman, to put it bluntly, using Jackson's name to rip them off. Jackson's "signed statement" denying songwriting credit for "What Then" is an indication of her forthrightness once Hill and Range pressed the issue. It is entirely possible that she had no knowledge whatsoever of Berman's practices. Whatever the case, it is certainly discouraging that it was only through the self-profiting intervention of a powerful white-owned publishing company playing the heavy that black gospel songwriters were able to garner their just reward for songs that had already been legally copyrighted.

Within the story of black gospel music, the question of authorial attribution emerges not simply as a legal matter. Jackson's frequent presentation of some of her material as vaguely primordial tended to reproduce ideas about "culture" as its own self-generator. The disparate stories about the source of her breakout hit, Brewster's "Move On Up a Little Higher," provides one example. When Goreau suggested to Jackson's pianist and fellow New Orleans native James Lee that "Move On Up a Little Higher" was "a song that Mahalia had heard way back from the time she was a child," Lee replied diplomatically: "Well, now *she* says this . . . so now maybe it was, but I know Reverend Brewster in Memphis was the first one to put it out." Sellers, who recorded the song a year before Jackson, remembered him and Jackson hearing Brewster's song at a revival at Elder Lucy

Table 5.1 Bess Music Copyrights of Songs Recorded by Mahalia Jackson, 1952–1954

Song	Songwriter	Bess Music Attribution	Copyright Date
I'm Glad Salvation Is Free	Isaac Watts/ J. W. Dadmun	Mahalia Jackson (w), Bobby Smith (m)	March 20, 1952
He's the One	Lucy Matthews Collier	Mahalia Jackson (w), Bobby Smith (m)	March 31, 1952
In the Upper Room	Lucie Campbell	Mahalia Jackson (w), Bobby Smith (m)	May 12, 1952
Said He Would	Unknown	Mahalia Jackson (w), Bobby Smith (m)	January 28, 1953
God Spoke to Me	Doris Akers	Mahalia Jackson (w), Bobby Smith (m)	January 28, 1953
Even Me	Elizabeth Codner and William Bradbury	Mahalia Jackson (w), Bobby Smith (m)	March 25, 1953
Let the Power of the Holy Ghost Fall on Me	Kenneth Morris	Mahalia Jackson (w), Bess Reles (m)	April 20, 1953
I Can Put My Trust in Jesus	Kenneth Morris	Mahalia Jackson (w), Bess Reles (m)	April 20, 1953
Tired	John Walter Davis	Mahalia Jackson (w & m)	May 4, 1953
Do You Know Him	Mary Lou Parker Coleman	Mahalia Jackson (w), Bobby Smith (m)	May 4, 1953
One Day	Kenneth Morris	Mahalia Jackson (w), Bobby Smith (m)	June 2, 1953
Consider Me (Consideration)	Thomas A. Dorsey	Mahalia Jackson (w & m)	August 13, 1953
Move On Up a Little Higher, Part 1	W. Herbert Brewster	Mahalia Jackson (w & m)	August 28, 1953
I Want to Rest	Unknown	Mahalia Jackson (w & m)	August 28, 1953
I'm Going to Tell God	Traditional	Mahalia Jackson (w & m)	August 28, 1953
He Knows My Heart	Theodore Frye	Mahalia Jackson (w & m)	September 2, 1953
Move On Up a Little Higher, Part 2	W. Herbert Brewster	Mahalia Jackson (w & m)	September 4, 1953
Dig a Little Deeper	Kenneth Morris	Mahalia Jackson (w & m)	September 4, 1953

Table 5.1 Continued

Song	Songwriter	Bess Music Attribution	Copyright Date
Amazing Grace	John Newton	Mahalia Jackson (w & m)	September 4, 1953
Come to Jesus	Edward Payson Hammond	Mahalia Jackson (w & m)	October 23, 1953
I Wonder If I Will Ever Rest	Alberta Hunter	Mahalia Jackson (w & m)	October 23, 1953
It's Real	Homer Cox	Mahalia Jackson (w & m)	October 26, 1953
Walkin' to Jerusalem	Unknown	Mahalia Jackson (w & m)	October 26, 1953
Hand of God	Unknown	Mahalia Jackson (w & m)	October 26, 1953
I'm on My Way (to Canaan Land)	Traditional	Mahalia Jackson (w & m)	June 16, 1954
My Story	Unknown	Mahalia Jackson (w & m)	June 16, 1954
Run All the Way	I. C. Rector	Mahalia Jackson (w & m)	June 25, 1954
Nobody Knows (the Trouble I've Seen)	Traditional	Mahalia Jackson (w & m)	June 25, 1954
The Last Mile of the Way	Oatman/Marks	Bobby Smith (w & m)	December 30, 1954

Source: Library of Congress Catalog of Copyright Entries.

Smith's All Nations Pentecostal Church in Chicago—"That's where we heard it at first. . . .That's where we got the song from." Jackson herself may have given conflicting accounts. Jules Schwerin relayed Jackson's identification of "Move On Up a Little Higher" as a song written by Brewster that, having heard it performed by Queen C. Anderson at the National Baptist Convention and by her organist Herbert Francis, she was "certain she could add her unique swing style to." Jackson also copyrighted her own arrangement of the song in 1948, fully crediting Brewster as the songwriter. But in her autobiography, as communicated through Evan McLeod Wylie, Jackson recalled it as "an old spiritual song that I had known since I was a child. . . .Don't anybody know who wrote it, honey. I've always sung it since I was a little child down in New Orleans."[38]

Jackson expressed aggravation with Wylie's unreliable representation of her life story, but her identification of repertory that was from "way back" and simply in the air during her childhood in New Orleans was a recurring rhetorical gesture that served multiple purposes. The move situated Jackson as a vessel of black folk culture but also, as she increasingly began performing for and speaking to audiences beyond the black church, satisfied white desires, extending back to the first iterations of the Fisk Jubilee Singers, to hear "old, traditional Negro spirituals" sung by authenticated black subjects. In other contexts, Jackson readily credited black gospel songwriters, especially Dorsey, though she also embraced her role as mediating for white audiences venerable black folkways that purportedly sprung spontaneously from the people, fetishizing both her personal biography and southern African American culture. The music industry's persistent identification of black gospel songs with concrete and verifiable authorship as "traditional" or "public domain" is a byproduct of this ideological dynamic. Jackson was not alone. In 1947, Martin and Morris published an arrangement of "I'm Going to Move On Up a Little Higher" by Kenneth Morris, "as sung by the Famous Five Soul Stirrers of Chicago," but did not credit Brewster, instead identifying the song as "A Spiritual Arrangement." The specifics of Jackson's encounter with "Move On Up a Little Higher" are less important than the ways in which the various accounts of her biggest Apollo hit exemplify a politics of origins in the study African American music, the challenge of "gospel truth" in a field of scholarship so reliant on oral history, and how Jackson strategically negotiated her representation of black cultural production, black gospel music, and herself as a public figure.

Jackson and the AFM Recording Bans

When Jackson entered the Apollo studio at 457 West 45th Street in New York for her first session with the label on October 3, 1946, she was a highly acclaimed church singer who had not cut a record in nearly a decade and black gospel music recorded for commercial release was still a highly speculative venture. By her final session for Apollo on June 10, 1954, Jackson was a highly coveted recording artist and "spiritual music" was a booming field in the popular music industry. Over this span, Jackson, working closely with Berman, was recorded in at least fourteen sessions for Apollo in New York and Chicago. The timing, production choices, and repertory of Jackson's Apollo sessions reflect the label's strategic efforts to both guide and be responsive to the rapidly unfolding career of their unexpected star.

Jackson came into her first three Apollo sessions at a time when she was still building her reputation. The four sides that Jackson recorded at her initial Apollo session with Buffalo-born piano accompanist Rosalie McKinney, who roomed at Jackson's apartment building, produced the singles "Wait Until My Change Comes" b/w "I'm Going to Tell God" (Apollo 110), released in January 1947, and "He Knows My Heart" b/w "I Want to Rest" (Apollo 145), released in May. Both records were listed as new religious releases in *Billboard*, though neither was reviewed nor drew extensive attention, not an uncommon fate for a gospel release at the time. According to Sellers, Jackson's Apollo career was in jeopardy because her first records were slow sellers, but Freeman "begged Bess to record 'Move on Up a Little Higher' because Bess was getting ready to drop Mahalia" and as a result a second date was scheduled.[39] At this next session, on September 12, 1947, in Chicago, Jackson again recorded four songs, though the date was most notable for producing the double-sided recording of "Move On Up a Little Higher" (Apollo 164) with pianist James Lee and organist Herbert "Blind" Francis. The record generated her first critical notice in a music trade publication, a review in the December 6 issue of *Billboard*: "There's beaucoup of religion and rhythm in the Negro spiritual singing of (Miss) Mahalia Jackson as she shouts out for both sides of the platter. Unfortunately, her rhythmic contagion isn't caught by the organ and piano providing a solemn accompaniment. For race buyers." The need for clarification that "Mahalia" was a woman and the recommendation that vendors push the record as race music is indicative of the place of Jackson and gospel singing within the industry at the time. It would not be surprising, however, if the *Billboard* notice affirmed Apollo's decision to arrange yet another Jackson session just days after the review appeared.

If the Johnny Myers syndicate offers one way of understanding Jackson's debut as an Apollo recording artist, significant changes in the music industry help account for the strength of the label's commitment to Jackson at her third session. A chain of developments in 1947 that began in American politics rippled outward to impact Jackson's career. After fifteen years of dominance by New Deal Democrats, both houses of the U.S. Congress were retaken in the 1946 midterm election by a momentarily resurgent Republican party determined to roll back the enhanced power and prestige of organized labor. Republican sights were particularly set on powerful and provocative labor bosses like James Caesar Petrillo, president of the American Federation of Musicians (AFM). A conquering lion to many AFM union members, Petrillo became notorious within the music industry and among pro-business members of Congress when in the middle of World War II he called for a ban on all recordings by AFM members. The ban lasted from August 1942 until November 1944. Petrillo's driving concern was how new uses of recordings—in jukeboxes, on radio, and eventually on television—would adversely impact the employment of working musicians. Petrillo's terms for settling the 1942 recording ban were the establishment of a Recording and Transcription Fund, created through a royalty paid by record companies to the union for every record sold. Republicans specifically targeted this disbursement of a fund for out-of-work AFM musicians by their own union, and made it illegal through the watershed Labor Management Relations Act, better known as the Taft-Hartley Act, passed by Congress in June 1947 over President Truman's veto. Taft-Hartley was also a document of the early Cold War that sought to purge communist influence from organized labor by requiring of each union officer an affidavit "that he is not a member of the Communist Party" nor "supports any organization that believes in or teaches, the overthrow of the United States government."[40]

In response to Taft-Hartley restrictions, Petrillo announced at the union's October 16 meeting in Detroit that the AFM executive board "unanimously voted to stop making recordings and transcriptions, once and for all PERIOD, and never again to make them, because eventually records and transcriptions will destroy" professional musicians. "We know of no business that makes an instrument to destroy itself." From a present-day perspective, Petrillo's suspicion of recordings is perhaps quaint, but reasonable. On the one hand, his pronouncements that musicians were self-destructively "making their own competition" by cutting records seem shrill and shortsighted. At the same time, Petrillo's position, like "The Ballad of John Henry," simply re-iterated a recurrent anxiety throughout labor history: the fear of dis-employment that shadows technological innovation. The music industry economy and the status of live performance were indeed undergoing metamorphosis in response to the new preeminence of recordings, in ways that were difficult to predict from the standpoint of the musicians represented by the AFM, the majority of whom were not recording artists.

Petrillo's announcement of the second recording ban created a frenzy. Music trade magazines reported that throughout the fall of 1947 "the diskeries are piling up master records against the imminent December 31 stoppage," with record labels frantically "invading every available recording studio in an effort to pile up masters for anywhere from six months to five years." With modest encouragement from the *Billboard* review of "Move On Up a Little Higher" and with a looming recording ban, Apollo doubled down on Jackson, bringing her in for an extended session on December 10, 1947 at which she recorded seven songs. These masters, along with those recorded at the previous session in September, gave Apollo enough material to be able to release five Jackson singles over the course of the work stoppage.[41] A year later, on December 14, 1948, the AFM and the recording industry came to terms on a musicians' welfare fund that satisfied Taft-Hartley provisions, ending the year-long strike, and Jackson returned to the studio for her first post-ban session on July 15, 1949. One of the paradoxes of Jackson's career is that her breakthrough as a recording artist came in a year when the making of records essentially came to a halt. But as Scott DeVeaux has argued, AFM tactics helped to precipitate the rise of independent record companies that served as a balance of power against the dominance of major labels. Together, unprecedented demand by record buyers and the "unsettled conditions" in the music industry brought about by the staggered settlement of the 1942–1944 record ban fostered a mid-1940s explosion in startup indies focusing on "marginal specialty markets."[42]

The black gospel field was a beneficiary of these conditions. Virtually all of the New York independent labels recording Myers's Golden Gate artists, including Apollo, were established and began recording gospel in the years following the first AFM ban. Jackson's Apollo output became the capstone of this growth in the recording of black gospel singers. By the summer of 1949, Jackson, on the strength of "Move On Up a Little Higher" and her subsequent singles released during the ban, had become the principal face of gospel among many black audiences and especially white connoisseurs. Beginning with the July 1949 date, Apollo enthusiastically resumed recording Jackson in four sessions over the course of the next fifteen months. Berman then continued to document Jackson with single sessions in 1951 and 1952 and another four sessions in 1953. Jackson's final Apollo session was on June 10, 1954, shortly after which she was signed away from an irate Berman by Columbia Records. Jackson recorded "Closer to Me" and "Didn't It Rain" (Apollo 313) at undated sessions that perhaps took place in 1950 and 1953–1954, respectively.[43]

If Jackson's recording of gospel songs, spirituals, and Baptist hymns was a continuity throughout her Apollo career, the conspicuous addition of popular religious songs to her repertory drew a clear dividing line separating her first six sessions from her final eight. To whatever extent Jackson consented, Berman extended Jackson's Apollo repertory beginning with her seventh session on October 17, 1950, two weeks after her Carnegie Hall debut. Following up a five-song session on September 11 at which she recorded four gospel songs and a traditional hymn, Jackson returned to the studio a month later and recorded two Christmas-themed selections, the carol "Silent Night" and the spiritual "Go Tell It on the Mountain," and three popular religious songs, "I Walked Into the Garden," "Bless This House," and "The Lord's Prayer." These selections, and the latter three songs in particular, indicate Apollo's intent to expand Jackson's repertory to cultivate a broader audience beyond her African American church base. The black press noticed the shift, observing that Jackson "for the first time is singing standard religious music," reinterpreting traditional seasonal favorites "with a new soul and a new intimacy." In later years, Jackson expressed disdain toward some of the newer material. " 'I Walked into the Garden' . . . is not a gospel song; it's sort of a ballad," she said in 1967. "I got tired of putting out that mess."[44] But the timing of this re-orientation is part of a larger story that continued to unfold over the course of the decade, one that foregrounds Jackson's ambivalent positioning as a recording artist. The midpoint of the century and of Jackson's Apollo career, 1950 proved to be a pivotal year in the relationship between international politics, American religiosity, and the economies of popular song.

Religious Pop

Coming out of the nearly year-long AFM recording ban that ended in December 1948, there was no recognized category of "religious pop" in the sense that there would be just two years later. Religious material was actively recorded, though primarily by "folk" and "spiritual" specialists, categories conventionally raced within the industry as white and black, respectively. As 1949 dawned, *Billboard* reviews and advance notices of new religious releases listed records cut almost exclusively by a cross-racial assortment of groups known primarily as performers of Christian material. Though they may have been promoted and merchandised differently by record companies, deejays, and juke box operators, *Billboard* categorized recordings by country acts like the Chuck Wagon Gang, the Speer Family, and the John Daniel Quartet alongside those by black quartets, gospel groups, choirs, and soloists like the Dixie Hummingbirds, Wings Over Jordan, and Mahalia Jackson, with sporadic entries by prominent concert choruses like the Mormon Tabernacle Choir. These listings represented, however, a small fraction of available religious recordings, a field dominated, as in the case of most specialty markets, by independent labels. Major labels did occasional dip their toe in the water: in addition to the Selah Jubilee Singers and Sister Rosetta Tharpe at Decca, Los Angeles's St. Paul Baptist Church Choir, heard weekly on the church's Sunday night "Echoes of Eden" radio broadcast, became perhaps the first black gospel choir with commercial recordings, cut live on location for Capitol Records in 1947.

In July 1949, Capitol sowed the seeds for a new orientation of the religious field when the label released a recording of "Whispering Hope," sung as a duet by Jo Stafford and Gordon MacRae. The sound of the record was all pop: Stafford and MacRae harmonized sweetly in thirds supported by strings, woodwinds, and celesta with waltz time marked gently by a standup bass and brushes on a snare. Despite referring in its final verse to "the Master" entering the despondent soul to instill the "blest hope of glory," the song was at best an ambiguously religious number, perhaps most accurately characterized as "inspirational." But this fact was of less significance to commentators than the record's brisk sales and the implications of Capitol having scored a hit by drawing from a bottomless well of public domain material. To the music press, the success of "Whispering Hope," a song written by nineteenth-century American composer Septimus Winner, was noteworthy for having disaggregated the hand-in-glove relationship between commercial recording and the commodification of newly copyrighted songs as sheet music, a nexus that had long been the lifeblood of the music industry. In the fall, another major label, RCA Victor, released a single by crooner Perry Como, backed by organ and New York's Church of the Incarnation choir, that coupled Franz Schubert's "Ave Maria" and Albert Hay Malotte's well-known setting of "The Lord's Prayer." The October 29 issue of *Billboard* listed the Como release as a popular record (there were no new religious releases promoted that week), and again the religious nature of the record was a mere subplot. Trade publications considered it more consequential that RCA was using the Como recording, which sold well, as part of its strategy to promote its new 45 RPM single, weaning record buyers off of the older 78 RPM format.[45]

It was not until the spring of the following year that industry observers, particularly those at major labels, began to put the pieces together, sensing and actively seeking to exploit a possible new trend. In March 1950, Decca announced that it was launching its "Faith Series," a new line of recordings of religious material by its top pop stars. Decca executives were surely inspired by the success of recent releases by its marquee artist, Bing Crosby. In his first session after the recording ban was lifted, Crosby entered the studio in early May 1949 for a five-day recording marathon that included "a group of 16 religious sides, covering hymns of all religious denominations" backed by the Ken Darby choir. The new Decca series, which besides Crosby featured recordings by Red Foley, the Andrews Sisters, the Mills Brothers, Ernest Tubb, and Bill Kenny of the Ink Spots, signaled a recognition of the growing appeal of traditional religious favorites recorded with more burnished production than that typically given "folk" or "spiritual" sides. As both *Variety* and *Billboard* reported, the Faith Series was a consciously conceived alternative to the artists conventionally associated with religious releases. The religious field "in the wax business has primarily been concentrated away from popular artists and focused for the most part on sacred music specialists," but Decca now recognized "that a large market for religious recordings sliced by top-line pop artists exists," a development that "will shed a new light—musically and commercially—on old religious favorites." With polls showing that religious music had begun to surpass other recorded styles in popularity, Columbia followed suit a month later, announcing that it too would initiate recordings of "standard hymns by name artists." Columbia was clearly inspired by Stafford and MacRae's "Whispering Hope," which was still selling strongly, and launched its series by teaming up Dinah Shore and Gene Autry for "The Old Rugged Cross" and "In the Garden," following it up with sacred albums by semi-classical soprano Jessica Dragonette and folk singer Burl Ives.[46]

A key observation for apprehending the trajectory of Jackson's career in the 1950s is not so much the emerging vogue of "church music by pop artists" as the growing interest by major labels in a domain of the popular music industry that had largely been ceded to independents. RCA was next to get in on the action, launching a religious line in May 1950, but with a decidedly different tack. Instead of pop artists, the label focused on the more conventional purveyors of commercial religious records, white country and black gospel musicians. For the country market, Victor offered releases by the Harmoneers Quartet, Johnnie and Jack, the Blue Sky Boys, the Carter Family, and Charlie Monroe, older brother of bluegrass pioneer Bill Monroe. On the gospel side, the series included disks recorded by black artists shortly after the lifting of recording ban, including the Freddie Evans Gospel Trio, jubilee quartet the Five Trumpets, and the popular crossover vocal harmony group the Deep River Boys. Most notably, Victor made the first recordings of the Original Gospel Harmonettes, founded by Evelyn Starks Hardy, all cut in June 1949 by the pre–Dorothy Love Coates iteration of the group.[47] The eight Harmonettes sides were packaged as four singles, two released in 1949 and two in June 1950 as part of the new RCA religious series. Two of the songs that the group recorded for RCA, both led by Mildred Miller, were part of Jackson's Apollo repertory: "Move On Up a Little Higher," perhaps to piggy-back on the Jackson hit, and "In the Upper Room," recorded two years before Jackson's double-sided version. The Harmonettes were one of the earliest, if not the first, all-women black gospel groups to be recorded by a major label.

By the spring of 1950, "Whispering Hope" was recognized, retroactively, as having been a bellwether of things to come, and Capitol went back to the well to cut another religious-themed duet for the Easter season, recording Margaret Whiting and Jimmy Wakely singing "Let's Go to Church Next Sunday Morning." The marketing of this otherwise innocuous song vividly illustrates the rapid accumulation of meanings activated by religious subject matter circulating in a pop music economy. Written by twenty-eight-year-old Los Angeles radio personality and future piano-playing television talk show host Steve Allen, "Let's Go to Church Next Sunday Morning" slickly wove together assertions of faith in God and the promise of heteronormative bliss within closely bonded social communities, expressed through the lighthearted pop sound and lyric of a conventional love song.

> Let's go to church next Sunday morning
> We'll see our friends on the way
> We'll stand and sing on Sunday morning
> And I'll hold your hand as we pray
> Through the years we'll always be together
> You'll be mine and we won't fear the stormy weather
> Let's go to church next Sunday morning
> Let's go through life side by side

The song's title and sentiment represented a slight but significant deviation from other contemporaneous religious recordings, which, whether rendered by "popular artists" or "sacred music specialists," largely relied upon familiar church-associated repertory. "Let's Go to Church Next Sunday Morning" openly endorsed the cultivation of religious habits, reflective of ambitious efforts by the Protestant Radio Commission, the Gospel Broadcasting Association, and other organizations to promote church culture and to project religious values within the entertainment industries, including radio, recordings, film, and the new medium of television. Capitol aggressively marketed the song by printing 20,000 "Let's go to church" promotional posters that were distributed to churches and religious groups in cooperation with the National Federation of Churches. The record label also sent deejays nationwide a copy of the record in a "blanket radio campaign" that unmistakably conveys how the transformation of the religious music field was closely linked to the national political climate. Promotional copies of the Whiting-Wakely record arrived with a memo from Capitol's vice president of sales Floyd Bittaker urging deejays to push the disk, since "current world conditions call for a return to religion" and "church org[anizations] would appreciate airing of this platter for the assist it may give in getting people to attend their various churches, regardless of faith or creed."[48]

In a lengthy feature article published in the *New York Times Magazine* in November 1950 with a title asking "Is There a Revival of Religion?," theologian Reinhold Neibuhr pondered "the coincidence between religious faith and historic crises." More recently, some scholars of the post-war U.S., most notably Lisle Rose and Robert Ellwood, have spotlighted 1950 as a critical year of events that amplified calls for a return to religion. In particular, Rose and Ellwood argue, the rise of McCarthyism, the escalation of thermonuclear weapons development, and the outbreak of the Korean War powerfully shaped domestic understandings of the Cold War and galvanized advocates for a renewed emphasis on religion in public life. From the very moment of his entrance on the national stage, Wisconsin Senator Joseph McCarthy placed religious belief at the heart of the Cold War struggle. In a speech on February 9, 1950, in Wheeling, West Virginia, that first thrust him into public prominence, McCarthy described a world "split into two vast, increasingly hostile camps." Throwing down the gauntlet, McCarthy announced: "this is the time for the show-down between the democratic Christian world and the communistic atheistic world." McCarthyism is most closely identified with the cultivation of a rabidly obsessive national suspicion of communist infiltration, but the parallel theme of a planet partitioned into a Judeo-Christian democratic West and an axis of "godless communism" became one of the definitive discursive tropes of Cold War America. In the pulpit and in political discourse, the formulation "godless Communism" came to neatly encapsulate the moral crux of the Cold War and, more importantly, pinpoint an essential and easily digestible ideological distinction between the United States and the Soviet Union. By 1954, a U.S. poll indicated that what Americans knew about communism, above all else, was that it was "against religion."[49]

For many, the stakes of heightening rhetoric between the United States and the Soviet Union had been raised days before McCarthy's Wheeling speech when news broke that Klaus Fuchs, a German-born British scientist working for the U.S. government, had shared secret hydrogen bomb research with Russia. *New York Times* journalist William S. White surely expressed the view of many when he wrote in the aftermath of the Fuchs revelation that the incomprehensible visions of annihilation summoned by the atomic age had "thrust into the ordinary way of life a clutching mass fear of death not even fully understood." The invasion of South Korea by the North Korean People's Army in June, just five years after a hard-won peace at the end of World War II, further destabilized the national confidence and optimism of the late 1940s amid fears of a third world war between "two vast, increasingly hostile camps," both armed this time for mutual obliteration.

Rose has argued that the shock of this trio of psychically crushing Cold War anxieties in 1950—mass anticommunist paranoia, fear of "the bomb," and the outbreak of the Korean War—produced a sense of national distrust and an "expectation of impending calamity" that marked the onset of a recognizably new political era in the United States. Ellwood has further suggested that the aggressive promotion and growing popularity of religion, stoked by the events of 1950, were at once an instrument for anticommunist national unity and a response by a U.S. population that, faced with a seemingly apocalyptic modernity, became increasingly receptive to faith and the nostalgic notion that "somewhere within age-old traditions, not in anything newly minted today, was to be found a power and vision equal to the desperate times."[50] The abrupt surge in the production and consumption of religious pop in 1950 is a conspicuous outcrop of this political landscape. Allen's lyric for "Let's Go to Church," voicing a couple's affirmation that "If we have the Lord as our guide . . . we won't fear the stormy weather," was a pop-cultural reinforcement of the "back to church" mandate delivered by religious leaders and Capitol Records in light of "current world conditions."

Beyond promoting religion and registering anxieties about current events, "Let's Go to Church Next Sunday" was also an early indication of the most consequential development in the religious music field in 1950: the sudden multiplication of newly composed religious pop songs. The breakthrough came rather inauspiciously during the summer. In June, Gladys Gollahon, a forty-two-year-old Cincinnati housewife, wrote "Our Lady of Fatima," a prayer of "intercession for peace and unity," and sent a home-recorded acetate of her singing the song to local deejay and Sunday School teacher Bill Dawes, who played the record on air to astonishingly enthusiastic response. The song was picked up by New York music publisher Robbins Music and in turn by multiple record labels. "Our Lady of Fatima" was an unlikely sensation and recordings of the song appeared on the market in rapid succession, in versions by Richard Hayes and Kitty Kallen for Mercury, Tony Bennett for Columbia, and separate recordings by Red Foley and Bill Kenny for Decca, among many others. If Gollahon's song was initially dismissed as a fluke— "one of those amateur things that caught on," *Variety* harrumphed—by the fall there was no mistaking that new "religioso tunes" couldn't be written fast enough.

Leading the way was Stuart Hamblen, a Columbia Records artist and bornagain singing cowboy working closely with the organization Youth for Christ and its charismatic public face, thirty-one-year-old evangelist Billy Graham. Much as faith-based youth groups have done for contemporary Christian music today, Youth for Christ provided a robust market for the growing body of popular religious recordings in 1950. In early October, Hamblen debuted his pop-country song "It Is No Secret (What God Can Do)," which forged an even more spectacular path than "Our Lady of Fatima." The song was covered by numerous singers and—rare for a pop song—continued to appear on new records well into the following year, including Jackson's Apollo recording in July 1951. "It Is No Secret" has become a religious pop standard that is still performed and recorded today.

Verse
> The chimes of time ring out the news
> Another day is through
> Someone slipped and fell
> Was that someone you?
> You may have longed for added strength
> Your courage to renew
> Do not be disheartened
> For I have news for you

Chorus
> It is no secret what God can do
> What he's done for others, he'll do for you
> With arms wide open, he'll pardon you
> It is no secret what God can do

Country artists like Red Foley and Ernest Tubb regularly performed and scored hits with familiar religious songs. Foley's recording of "Just a Closer Walk with Thee" with the Jordanaires for Decca's Faith series was one of the year's best selling country and western disks. But Hamblen, who later wrote "This Ole House" and "Open Up Your Heart and Let the Sunshine In," became a specialist as a religious pop songwriter and his tunes, along with others like Albert von Tilzer's "I'm Praying to Saint Christopher," Meredith Willson's "May the Good Lord Bless You and Keep You," and Ken Carson's "Wondrous Word," were snapped up one by one by publishers and eagerly recorded by major and independent labels. As *Variety* reported in November 1950:

> Tin Pan Alley has gotten religion—but good. What was noticeable as a mild trend a month ago has developed into a fullscale scramble by publishers to secure and exploit religious songs. Record company officials report they are swamped with religious tunes, and the likelihood is that the first of the year will witness wholesale release of dozens of the tunes.
> Since Robbins Music's "Our Lady of Fatima" broke into the pop market as a hit, top writers have been submitting religious items to publishers.

The latter have not only grabbed them up but have been on the search for
more, with a number of them having purchased and revived old songs for
immediate exploitation.

Though whetted by Gollahon's and Hamblen's surprise hits, the music industry's
insatiable appetite for original pop-flavored religious repertory was also repeatedly
tied to a worrying political climate that made sectarian divisions less important
than religiosity as a national ethos: "Current feeling is that with current taut international situation, the public is experiencing a genuine religious feeling that
overrides differences in religions but is a desire for peace and security." As the
second verse of "It Is No Secret" reminded unsettled listeners girding themselves
for a Soviet communist takeover: "There is no power can conquer you while God
is on your side." Particularly noticeable was the fact that in a Protestant-dominated
nation, explicitly Catholic songs like "Our Lady of Fatima" and "I'm Praying to
St. Christopher" found resonance across denominations. On Jackson's radio
show, which debuted in 1954, listeners heard the born and bred Baptist perform
Ethelbert Nevin's sentimental Gilded Age song "The Rosary."[51]

Berman was clearly aware of the emergent trend. Beginning with Jackson's
seventh session on October 17, 1950, undertaken precisely when the wave of religious material for pop consumption was cresting, Apollo recorded Jackson
singing three songs that can be characterized as popular religious fare. Of these,
the most widely known, and the closest to Jackson's regular repertory, was "The
Lord's Prayer," written in 1935 by organist and Hollywood film music composer
Albert Hay Malotte. It was quickly adopted by concert recitalists and popularized
through a best-selling RCA Victor recording by baritone John Charles Thomas.
The song's cross-racial presence was immediate and lasting. Already in 1936,
the *New York Amsterdam News* reported a performance of "The Lord's Prayer"
by African American baritone Edward Matthews, who created the role of Jake
the fisherman in Gershwin's *Porgy and Bess*, at a recital in Harlem.[52] Over time,
the song's broad familiarity gave it classical-to-pop crossover mobility, evident
in recordings by doo-wop group Sonny Til and the Orioles in 1950 and Dinah
Washington in 1953. A more obscure choice for Jackson was "I Walked into the
Garden," a waltz-like religious ballad written by Marion Weaver and published
in 1947. In 1950, Bibletone Records began using its choral recording of "I Walked
into the Garden," perhaps the first, as a demonstration disk to promote it as material suitable for church choirs.[53] "Bless This House," with words that are also a
prayer, was an example of one of the "revived old songs" that took on a second life
amid the clamoring for religious material. Written by English lyricist Helen Taylor
and Australian composer May Brahe 1927, "Bless This House" received its most
notable early recording by Irish tenor John McCormack and broader exposure
during World War II through morale-boosting performances by British singer

Vera Lynn. It largely remained a continental item until 1946, when it was adopted as the theme song performed weekly on CBS radio's *Prudential Family Hour* by co-host and Metropolitan Opera mezzo-soprano Risë Stevens. As a result of this new exposure in the United States, "Bless This House" received a surge of popularity and was recorded extensively from 1947 on, including performances by Kate Smith for MGM in 1947 and by Perry Como for RCA, Rosemary Clooney for Columbia, and Jackson for Apollo, all in 1950.

The vogue for religious pop continued into 1951 and after a lull it was reignited by Frankie Laine's recording of "I Believe," released in January 1953. Jackson's sessions for Berman continued to track the fluctuation of this trend. At her very next session, in July 1951, Jackson recorded Hamblen's "It Is No Secret," which Apollo released in October immediately after "Bless This House" and the "Lord's Prayer," coupled with another popular cross-cutting religious standard that appears in *Gospel Pearls*, "His Eye Is on the Sparrow." Otherwise, for the next two years, Apollo returned to recording Jackson singing almost exclusively gospel songs. But in the wake of the success of the Laine recording and the widely recorded hit "Crying in the Chapel," and with reports that "Faith-flavored songs are again hitting a money-making disk and sheet sales stride," Jackson was coaxed even more strongly toward popular religious songs.[54] In back-to-back sessions in August and October 1953, Jackson recorded a small flurry of religious pop tunes, including "I Believe" and three other recently written songs, "Hands of God," "No Matter How You Pray," and "My Cathedral." At the August session, Jackson also recorded "I'm Going Down to the River," a new song conceived in the spirit of pseudo–black vernacular, pop-folk songs like "Old Man River," "The Lonesome Road," and "That Lucky Old Sun."

When Jackson began her career as an Apollo recording artist in 1946, she entered a Wild West of maverick independent record label proprietors like Bess Berman seeking to capitalize on "marginal" musics like black religious singing, marketed largely to black Christians as sacred music and to white connoisseurs as a black roots music. Jackson's releases alternated with those by other Apollo religious specialists like Georgia Peach, the Dixie Hummingbirds, the Two Gospel Keys, and Prophet Powell. By the time she left Apollo in 1954, the music industry had been transformed considerably by a burgeoning field of religious pop in which major labels were arguably becoming the most influential players. Berman sought to stay apace with the shifting tide. Even as Jackson continued to be acclaimed as the "Queen of the Gospel Singers," the modification of her repertory that began in October 1950 was an overture to her eventual position as a Columbia artist with peers constituting a distinctly different band of "sacred music specialists" that included such hymn and inspirational singers as George Beverly Shea and Tennessee Ernie Ford, and other album artists recording religious repertory for adult pop consumption.

The emergence and dramatic expansion of the religious popular music field signaled several developments in the 1950s popular music industry and also altered the parameters of Jackson's career. With such songs as "The Lord's Prayer," "It Is No Secret," "I Believe," and "Go Tell It on the Mountain" and such artists as Perry Como, Risë Stevens, Red Foley, and Mahalia Jackson all part of a coalescing phenomenon, the religious market gave the proximity of singers and vocal styles conventionally distinguished as "pop," "hillbilly," "race," and "classical" new coherence for record buyers. As *Boston Globe* music critic John Riley mused in a review of religious albums by Como and by Roy Rodgers and Dale Evans, "it seems strange to find one faction of the music world leaning over into the boundaries of another."[55] As a child, I remember my initial surprise and confusion over my Panamanian grandmother owning an Elvis Presley LP, until I realized that it was *How Great Thou Art*.

With many independent labels focusing less on producing sheet music than on securing copyrights for their publishing arms, as did Apollo with Bess Music, the religious pop market also rebooted alliances between the publishing and recording industries. Sheet music sales declined after World War II and as stereophonic listening gradually displaced musicking in the home, the recorded performance steadily became the commodity many consumers prized over the song. Church services and religious events, however, continued to be, and still remain, an active bastion of amateur performance, and thus helped preserve a market for new religious songs. The rising tide of religious pop in the early 1950s thus uniquely lifted all boats, scoring hits for record companies that in turn cultivated a market for sheet music. The situation was more complicated and the economy rather separate for black gospel writers, who, despite the active market for gospel sheet music, had their songs recorded less frequently and, even when they were, found themselves much less protected from authorial erasure and royalty infringement.

These developments could, however, put performers, often variably devout Christians recording for variably agnostic record producers, in an ambiguous position. The situation was especially complicated for Jackson, pointing to the ambivalent status of black gospel performance in the 1950s, with Jackson as the nonpareil instantiation: Did listeners draw conceptual boundaries between, or did they conflate, gospel singing as "black culture" and gospel as an expression of the religious faith identified by President Truman as "the heart of America's greatness?" What was the relationship between Jackson's position within the gospel field and the place of black gospel music within the popular music industry? No doubt, depending on the listener, Jackson's Apollo output was simultaneously available for consumption as black gospel, as race music more broadly, or as religious pop, though as the following chapter will show even her "gospel" material can be disaggregated stylistically.

6

Mahalia Jackson's Apollo Recordings

"TO HEAR MAHALIA Jackson for the first time is a memorable experience," jazz critic Max Jones testified in the London-based music magazine *Melody Maker* in June 1951. The previous month, recently launched Vogue Records made Jackson's recordings available in Europe for the first time. Created by the Parisian Societé Jazz-Disques in coordination with trumpeter Doug Whitton and discophile Colin Pomroy, the British label sought to share the wealth of "traditionalist and modern" African American music by offering "the cream" of U.S. independent record labels like Blue Note, King, and Apollo. Through fellow connoisseurs, Jones had already become acquainted with Jackson's recordings even before they hit Europe and in his review of "In My Home Over There" b/w "Since the Fire Started Burning in My Soul" he recommended her reissued Apollo sides, "attaining a rapturous quality unparalleled so far as I know on records," with a near breathless sense of urgency.

> I was introduced to her Apollo Records about 18 months ago. . . .At once the magnificence of her voice and style struck home; afterwards I began to doubt if her voice could be as wonderful as I remembered it. Finally I bought an Apollo—"Tired" and "Amazing Grace"—and found out that it was. . . .
>
> I am at a loss to explain the characteristics that make Mahalia's singing so exceptional. I can only entreat you to hear . . . her formidable technique and thrilling voice.[1]

Already creating ripples in the United States, in part because of their surprising appeal to record buyers, Jackson's Apollo sides became the foundation of her continental reputation. Co-members of the prestigious Hot Club de France (and eventual rivals) Hughes Panassié and Charles Delaunay learned about Jackson independently during visits to New York and spearheaded the circulation of her recordings in their home country. In March 1951, through the promotion of Panassié, Jackson received a Grand Prix du Disque for her 1950 single "I Can Put My Trust in Jesus" b/w "Let the Power of the Holy Ghost Fall on Me."[2] If Jackson's church base had gotten to know her voice through her appearances on gospel programs and at the National Baptist Convention, many others, like Jones, became devoted fans and continually renewed their admiration through listening to her records.

Collectively, Jackson's Apollo recordings have come to occupy a special place in gospel music history and in the study of black vernacular music. Among fans and record collectors, they are frequently held up as exemplars of a period of relative gospel purity preceding the re-routing and overproduction of Columbia Records crossover efforts. There is some truth to this narrative. In subsequent years at Columbia, parallel projects of producing Jackson at Columbia, by George Avakian and by Mitch Miller, sought to present the gospel singer as a jazz-leaning album artist, showcasing her gospel voice as a vehicle for various forms of religious pop, though many of these same stylistic negotiations were underway even at Apollo. Yet, somewhat paradoxically, the lavish praise for and revered status of "Mahalia Jackson's Apollo Sessions" has largely bypassed sustained consideration of the actual body of recordings.[3] Following a preliminary discussion of trajectories of production, instrumental backing, and sources of Jackson's sacred repertory, this chapter considers how the sixty-eight songs that Jackson recorded for Bess Berman reveal distinguishable stylistic approaches and performance choices, even within her gospel repertory.

I hear Jackson's Apollo recordings as falling into four categories. One of these is the religious popular music that emerged around 1950, as discussed in the previous chapter. Jackson's other recordings, comprising those rooted in her gospel repertory, can be sorted according to what I call distinct "feels." Though a "feel" may seem an ambiguous music-analytical rubric, each of these feels is established by determinable factors that include tempo, metrical organization, rhythmic impulse, expressive strategies, vocal approach, and even repertory. By "feel" I mean something different from what Ingrid Monson suggests when she refers to "the achievement of a groove or feeling" in a jazz performance. A "feel" as I conceive of it here is not something that is attained (or not) in the act of performance. It is, rather, something closer to what Albert Murray, in his analysis of the idiomatic and procedural expertise required for "playing the blues," characterizes as "a very specific technology of stylization."[4] A feel is something gospel musicians bring to their performance of songs, based on their knowledge of prior performances, or, to adapt Murray, the gospel-idiom tradition of stylization. My discernment of three feels on Jackson's Apollo recordings—a "swing" feel, a "gospel" feel, and a "free" feel reserved primarily for hymns—is based on my study of this body of work and

I am not proposing an all-encompassing taxonomy for all black gospel recordings made in the 1940s and 1950s. There are other types of gospel numbers that Jackson tended not record, despite her obvious awareness of them, for instance, the very up-tempo, driving numbers sung by many post-war women's and mixed gospel groups, or songs with extended vamps over which charismatic quartet leads liked to preach-sing. But approaching gospel recordings of the 1940s and 1950s with my ears attuned toward listening for these three feels, I have found that they recur to a consistent degree, and even those recordings that resist easy categorization do so precisely because of how they blur distinctions between swing and gospel feels especially. My hope is that the analysis in this chapter will open up, not foreclose, discussion of these and other gospel recordings.

A word of encouragement to general readers: Many who consider themselves to be musical novices can often find themselves intimidated by analytical discussions of musical sound. My discussion of Jackson's Apollo recordings is deeply grounded in my experience as a listener, not as a musicologist. I have tried to keep music-analytic jargon to a minimum, though when musical terms are used, they are almost always a convenient stand-in for aspects of the recordings that most sensitive listeners, musically trained or not, are likely detecting with their own ears when they pay close attention to what they are hearing. The rewards of listening, considering the analysis, and then listening again (and again) will, I believe, be well worth the time spent and will hopefully stimulate further study and discussion of this historically important body of work and other contemporaneous gospel recordings.

Jackson's Apollo Sessions

The instrumental accompaniment on Jackson's Apollo recordings exhibits a clear trajectory that was already apparent in her first three sessions (Table 6.1). After a first session at which she was heard only with piano and a second that added organ, Jackson's backing was expanded further on four of the seven tracks that she recorded at her third session just before the AFM recording ban with the addition of guitarist Samuel Patterson. These first three sessions also indicate that Jackson was still searching for a regular accompanist since a different pianist supports her at each session: first Rosalie McKinney, then James Lee, and finally Mildred Falls (1921–1974), who played piano for all of Jackson's subsequent Apollo sides (Figure 6.1). Like Jackson, Falls was part of the interwar Great Migration. Two-year-old Mildred moved with her parents, George and Carrie Carter, from Magnolia, Mississippi, to South Side Chicago, where she learned to play on the upright piano her parents bought for her, and she later studied at a small local music school. Falls first came to admire Jackson as a child when she heard her with the Johnson Singers. In her teens, Falls directed church choirs in Chicago before moving to

Table 6.1 Mahalia Jackson's Apollo Records Sessions

Session	Date	Song	Composer	Accompaniment
1	October 3, 1946	I Want to Rest	Ruth Burks	Rosalie McKinney (piano)
		He Knows My Heart	"Harris"	Rosalie McKinney (piano)
		Wait Until My Change Comes	Thomas Dorsey	Rosalie McKinney (piano)
		I'm Going to Tell God	Traditional	Rosalie McKinney (piano)
2	September 12, 1947	What Could I Do?	Thomas Dorsey	James Lee (piano)
				Herbert "Blind" Francis (organ)
		Move On Up a Little Higher, Pts. 1 & 2	W. Herbert Brewster	James Lee (piano)
				Herbert "Blind" Francis (organ)
		Even Me	Elizabeth Codner (w)	James Lee (piano)
			William Bradbury (m)	Herbert "Blind" Francis (organ)
		I Have a Friend Above All Others	Lucie Campbell	James Lee (piano)
				Herbert "Blind" Francis (organ)
3	December 10, 1947	Dig a Little Deeper	Kenneth Morris	Mildred Falls (piano)
				Herbert "Blind" Francis (organ)
				Samuel Patterson (guitar)
		Tired	John Walter Davis	Mildred Falls (piano)
				Herbert "Blind" Francis (organ)

	Date	Title	Composer	Performers
		If You See My Savior	Thomas Dorsey	Samuel Patterson (guitar)
				Mildred Falls (piano)
				Herbert "Blind" Francis (organ)
		In My Home Over There	Herman James Ford	Herbert "Blind" Francis (organ)
				Mildred Falls (piano)
		There's Not a Friend Like Jesus (No! Not One)	Johnson Oatman Jr. (w) George Crawford Hugg (m)	Herbert "Blind" Francis (organ)
				Samuel Patterson (guitar)
		Amazing Grace	John Newton	Herbert "Blind" Francis (organ)
				Mildred Falls (piano)
		Since the Fire Started Burning in My Soul	Aaron Bash Windom	Herbert "Blind" Francis (organ)
				Samuel Patterson (guitar)
4	July 15, 1949	I Can Put My Trust in Jesus	Kenneth Morris	Mildred Falls (piano)
				Herbert "Blind" Francis (organ)
				Unknown (guitar)
		Let the Power of the Holy Ghost Fall on Me	Kenneth Morris	Mildred Falls (piano)
				Herbert "Blind" Francis (organ)
				Unknown (guitar)

(continued)

Table 6.1 Continued

Session	Date	Song	Composer	Accompaniment
		A Child of the King	Harriet Buell (w) John Sumner (m)	Mildred Falls (piano) Herbert "Blind" Francis (organ) Unknown (guitar)
		Get Away, Jordan	Traditional	Mildred Falls (piano) Herbert "Blind" Francis (organ) Unknown (guitar)
		Walk with Me	Traditional	Mildred Falls (piano) Herbert "Blind" Francis (organ) Unknown (guitar)
		Prayer Changes Things	Robert Anderson	Mildred Falls (piano) Herbert "Blind" Francis (organ) Unknown (guitar)
5	January 12, 1950	Shall I Meet You Over Yonder	Charles Bridges	Mildred Falls (piano) Herbert "Blind" Francis (organ)
		The Last Mile of the Way	Johnson Oatman Jr. (w) William Marks (m)	Herbert "Blind" Francis (organ)
		Just Over the Hill	W. Herbert Brewster	Mildred Falls (piano)

	I Do, Don't You	Melville Miller (w) / Edwin Excell (m)	Herbert "Blind" Francis (organ) / Unknown (guitar) / Herbert "Blind" Francis (organ)
	God Answers Prayers	Unknown	Mildred Falls (piano) / Herbert "Blind" Francis (organ)
	I'm Glad Salvation Is Free	Traditional	Mildred Falls (piano) / Herbert "Blind" Francis (organ) / Unknown (guitar)
	Do You Know Him	Mary Lou Parker	Mildred Falls (piano) / Herbert "Blind" Francis (organ) / Unknown (guitar)
6 September 11, 1950	I'm Getting Nearer My Home	W. Herbert Brewster	Mildred Falls (piano) / Herbert "Blind" Francis (organ)
	I Gave Up Everything to Follow Him	Isaac Watts (w) / J. W. Dadmun (m)	Mildred Falls (piano) / Herbert "Blind" Francis (organ)
	It Pays to Serve Jesus	Frank Huston	Louise Overall Weaver (organ)
	These Are They	W. Herbert Brewster	Mildred Falls (piano) / Herbert "Blind" Francis (organ)
	He's the One	Lucy Matthews Collier	Mildred Falls (piano)

(continued)

Table 6.1 Continued

Session	Date	Song	Composer	Accompaniment
7	October 17, 1950	I Walked into the Garden	Marion Weaver	Louise Overall Weaver (organ)
				Mildred Falls (piano)
		Bless This House	Helen Taylor (w)	Louise Overall Weaver (organ)
			May Brahe (m)	Mildred Falls (piano)
		Go Tell It on the Mountain	Traditional	Louise Overall Weaver (organ)
				Mildred Falls (piano)
		Silent Night	Joseph Mohr (w)	Louise Overall Weaver (organ)
			Franz Xaver Gruber (m)	Louise Overall Weaver (organ)
		The Lord's Prayer	Albert Hay Malotte	Louise Overall Weaver (organ)
8	July 7, 1951	How I Got Over	Clarence Cobbs	Mildred Falls (piano)
				Herbert "Blind" Francis (organ)
				Unknown (backing vocalists)
		Just as I Am	Charlotte Elliott (w)	Mildred Falls (piano)
			William Bradbury (m)	Herbert "Blind" Francis (organ)
		Jesus Is with Me	Kenneth Morris	Mildred Falls (piano)
				Herbert "Blind" Francis (organ)
				Unknown (backing vocalists)

		Song	Composer	Personnel
		I Bowed on My Knees and Cried Holy	Nettie Dudley Washington (w) / E. M. Dudley Cantwell (m)	Mildred Falls (piano), Herbert "Blind" Francis (organ), Unknown (backing vocalists)
		A City Called Heaven	Charles Albert Tindley	Mildred Falls (piano), Kenneth Morris (organ)
		It Is No Secret What God Can Do	Stuart Hamblen	Mildred Falls (piano), Herbert "Blind" Francis (organ)
		His Eye Is on the Sparrow	Civilla Martin (w) / Charles Gabriel (m)	Mildred Falls (piano), Herbert "Blind" Francis (organ)
9	March 21, 1952	God Spoke to Me	Doris Akers	Mildred Falls (piano), Herbert "Blind" Francis (organ)
		In the Upper Room Parts 1 & 2	Lucie Campbell	Mildred Falls (piano), Herbert "Blind" Francis (organ), Unknown (bass), Unknown (drums), Southern Harmonaires (vocals)
		Said He Would	Unknown	Mildred Falls (piano)

(continued)

Table 6.1 Continued

Session	Date	Song	Composer	Accompaniment
		He's My Light	Lucy Matthews Collier	Unknown (bass)
				Unknown (drums)
				Southern Harmonaires vocals)
				Mildred Falls (piano)
				Herbert "Blind" Francis (organ)
				Unknown (bass)
				Unknown (drums)
		If You Just Keep Still	Willie Mae Ford Smith	Southern Harmonaires (vocals)
				Mildred Falls (piano)
				Herbert "Blind" Francis (organ)
				Unknown (bass)
				Unknown (drums)
10	May 5, 1953	I'm Going Down to the River	Traditional	Mildred Falls (piano)
				Unknown (organ)
				Unknown (guitar)
				Unknown (bass)

		One Day	Kenneth Morris	Unknown (drums)
				Melody Echoes (vocals)
				Mildred Falls (piano)
				Unknown (organ)
				Unknown (guitar)
				Unknown (bass)
				Unknown (drums)
				Melody Echoes (vocals)
11	August 8, 1953	I Believe	Ervin Drake	Mildred Falls (piano)
			Irving Graham	Unknown (organ)
			Jimmy Shirl	Unknown (guitar)
			Al Stillman	Melody Echoes (vocals)
		Beautiful Tomorrow	Thomas Dorsey	Mildred Falls (piano)
				Unknown (organ)
				Unknown (guitar)
				Unknown (bass)
				Unknown (drums)
				Melody Echoes (vocals)

(continued)

Table 6.1 Continued

Session	Date	Song	Composer	Accompaniment
		Beautiful Tomorrow (Alternate Version)	Thomas Dorsey	Mildred Falls (piano)
				Unknown (organ)
				Unknown (guitar)
				Unknown (bass)
				Unknown (drums)
				Melody Echoes (vocals)
		Consider Me	Thomas Dorsey	Mildred Falls (piano)
				Unknown (organ)
				Unknown (guitar)
				Unknown (bass)
				Unknown (drums)
				Melody Echoes (vocals)
		What Then?	J. W. Green (w)	Mildred Falls (piano)
			Thomas Dorsey (m)	Unknown (organ)
				Unknown (guitar)
				Unknown (bass)
				Unknown (drums)
				Melody Echoes (vocals)

12	October 9, 1953	Hands of God	Unknown	Mildred Falls (piano)
				Unknown (organ)
				Belleville Choir
		It's Real	Homer Cox	Mildred Falls (piano)
				Unknown (organ)
				Belleville Choir
		No Matter How You Pray	Blanche Allen (w)	Mildred Falls (piano)
			Ben Machan (m)	Unknown (organ)
				Belleville Choir
		My Cathedral (The Home I Love)	Hal Eddy (w)	Mildred Falls (piano)
			Mabel Wayne (m)	Unknown (organ)
				Belleville Choir
13	October 12, 1953	Walking to Jerusalem	Unknown	Mildred Falls (piano)
				Unknown (organ)
				Unknown (guitar)
				Unknown (drums)
				Melody Echoes (backing vocals)
		I Wonder If I Will Ever Rest	Alberta Hunter	Mildred Falls (piano)
				Unknown (organ)

(continued)

Table 6.1 Continued

Session	Date	Song	Composer	Accompaniment
				Unknown (guitar)
				Unknown (bass)
				Unknown (drums)
				Melody Echoes (backing vocals)
		Come to Jesus	Edward Payson Hammond	Mildred Falls (piano)
				Unknown (organ)
				Unknown (guitar)
				Unknown (drums)
				Melody Echoes (backing vocals)
14	June 10, 1954	I'm on My Way to Canaan Land	Traditional; Mahalia Jackson, arr.	Mildred Falls (piano)
				Unknown (organ)
				Unknown (bongos)
				Unknown (maracas)
				Melody Echoes (backing vocals)
		I'm on My Way to Canaan Land (Alt. Version)	Traditional; Mahalia Jackson, arr.	Mildred Falls (piano)
				Unknown (organ)

Title	Composer	Personnel
My Story	Unknown	Unknown (bongos) Unknown (maracas) Unknown (organ)
I'm Willing to Run All the Way	Traditional	Unknown (bongos) Unknown (maracas) Mildred Falls (piano) Unknown (organ) Unknown (tenor saxophone) Unknown (bass) Unknown (drums)
Nobody Knows the Trouble I've Seen	Traditional	Mildred Falls (piano) Unknown (organ) Unknown (bass) Unknown (drums)
Nobody Knows the Trouble I've Seen (Alternate Version)	Traditional	Mildred Falls (piano) Unknown (organ)

(continued)

Table 6.1 Continued

Session	Date	Song	Composer	Accompaniment
				Unknown (bass)
				Unknown (drums)
X	Unknown	Didn't It Rain	Traditional	Mildred Falls (piano)
				Unknown (organ)
X	Unknown	Closer to Me	Doris Akers	Mildred Falls (piano)
				Herbert Francis? (organ)

California to work as the pianist for a gospel group led by Emma Jackson. After an ill-fated relationship with a minister she "married too young," Falls moved back to Chicago in 1947 and became reacquainted with Jackson, now a soloist, at a gospel program at St. Paul Church of God in Christ. By the end of the year, Jackson, who up to that point worked with a rotating stable of accompanists, had asked Falls to be her regular pianist, a position Falls maintained for most of the next twenty-five years.[5]

Varying combinations of piano, organ, and guitar held until Jackson's eighth Apollo session on July 7, 1951, at which she recorded with the addition of vocal harmony. Backing singers were a part of every subsequent Jackson Apollo session, though not on every song. The particular vocal ensembles varied, though worth singling out is the group identified as the Southern Harmonaires, a spinoff of one of the most accomplished pre-war male quartets, the Selah Jubilee Singers, led by Thermon Ruth Sr. Ruth's career as a quartet singer represents his unique positioning in the gospel field.[6] Born in 1914 in Pomaria, South Carolina, Ruth formed the Selah Jubilee Singers as a teenager after his family relocated to Brooklyn, New York. The Selahs developed their reputation singing Sunday mornings on the radio and Sunday evenings at Ruth's home church, the Pentecostal St. Marks's Holy Church, pastored by one of their most stalwart supporters Bishop (Mother) Eva Lambert. Their prestige traveled beyond the New York City region when they relocated to Raleigh, North Carolina, and engaged in frequent head-to-head

FIG. 6.1 Mildred Falls, Mahalia Jackson's longtime piano accompanist, November 22 or 23, 1954. Photo by Guy Gillette. Sony Music Entertainment Photograph Archive.

battles with other quartets, including their long-time friendly rivals the Dixie Hummingbirds. Modeling their sound on the harmonic blend of the Golden Gate Quartet, the Selahs cut sides for Decca's race record series from 1939 to 1944. These were transitional years for quartet singing, during which the cohesive ensemble approach of jubilee quartets, close in sound to many pop-oriented vocal harmony groups, began to yield to arrangements featuring dynamic lead soloists supported by backing singers in modern gospel quartets. "We were looked on as jubilee or spiritual," said Ruth, who remembered gospel music and its recognizably distinct performance practice emerging noticeably in the 1940s. "I wasn't even used to it. We were entertainers, let's put it that way. We didn't try to get the folks to shout all that much, we entertained the folks, we had a lot of novelties and stuff." The Selahs can be counted among the many well received and highly skilled but not exactly cutting-edge jubilee quartets at Myers's gospel concerts at the Golden Gate Auditorium in Harlem. When Ruth took the Selahs to Chicago, it was a stark reminder that times were changing in other cities.

> The Selahs went to Chicago one time—our first trip to Chicago—and we were tight with the jubilee, but Chicago was a gospel town with Mahalia Jackson and James Cleveland and Thomas A. Dorsey. They was doing gospel and they actually laughed at us with our jubilee. We went out to Dorsey's anniversary, they had us out there, and we were great with that jubilee and, man, it just didn't go out there. It was something different, but it wasn't nothing that they could get happy and shout off of. As I said, we were more entertainers and Chicago was just a gospel town.[7]

In navigating the longevity of his group's popularity and the changing styles of quartet singing, Ruth periodically replenished the ensemble with younger singers, who also had the inclination and freedom to travel.

As self-acknowledged "entertainers," the Selahs' opportunities to record secular music presented another stylistic fault line. Around 1950, Ruth teamed with Eugene "Gene" Mumford to form a new group that marked a decisive transition, culminating in one of the most remarkable single days for any recording artist or ensemble. On October 5, 1951, Ruth's quintet, hoping to land a recording contract, recorded under four different names for four separate independent record labels: as the Selah Jubilee Singers for Jubilee, as the Jubilators for Regal, as the Four Barons for Savoy, and as the Southern Harmonaires for Apollo. Straddling the sacred and the profane, the group recorded "I Got Heaven on My Mind" for Regal then raced to Savoy to cut "Lemon Squeezer" ("The way I squeeze your lemons is a low-down dirty shame"). Impressed with Ruth's group, Berman signed them to an Apollo contract though she insisted that they record pop and rename themselves the Larks to capitalize on the popularity of such black vocal harmony "bird groups"

as the Orioles, the Ravens, and the Flamingos. Berman launched the Apollo subsidiary Lloyds Records as a "pop label" to showcase her new find. The Larks went
on to success as a doo-wop group—the sumptuous Mumford delivers wonderful
performances on "My Reverie" and "If It's a Crime"—opening a phase of Ruth's
career that was both ancillary and complementary to his ongoing participation in
the gospel field as a radio host and as the promoter of wildly popular and field-
broadening gospel shows at Harlem's Apollo Theater.[8]

Despite their awkward initial encounter with Chicago gospel, on March 21,
1952, the Larks, identified as the Southern Harmonaires, backed Jackson at a
session that produced her second double-sided hit, "In the Upper Room," and
supported her on four other songs. From her July 7, 1951 session on, Jackson was
regularly heard with backing singers. At that date, an unidentified mixed gospel
group—with some excellent voices—accompanied Jackson on "How I Got Over,"
"Jesus Is with Me," and "I Bowed on My Knees (And Cried Holy)." After her
recordings with the Larks/Southern Harmonaires, another male quartet identified
as the Melody Echoes, which also recorded independently for Apollo, appeared
on four separate sessions. We might think of these dates with the Southern
Harmonaires and Melody Echoes as Jackson's "doo-wop sessions." Jackson's collaboration with Ruth's group undoubtedly led to or proceeded from the inclusion
of the Selah Jubilee Singers in the "Gospel Train" package, headlined by Jackson
and Clara Ward, that was touring the East Coast and South in February and March
1952 (Figure 6.2).[9] At a four-song session on October 9, 1953, Jackson is backed
by the Belleville Choir, an African American chorus from Portsmouth, Virginia,
producing a sound, particularly on "Hands of God," "No Matter How You Pray,"
and "My Cathedral," leaning closer to religious pop than gospel.

Meanwhile, Apollo took steps toward more ear-catching production of Jackson
by recording her with new instruments. Beginning with Jackson's ninth session
on March 21, 1952, Berman added bass and drums to Jackson's core piano-organ
accompaniment, and the session that followed on May 5, 1953, brought back the
guitar, beefing up the rhythm section further. Sessions ten through thirteen feature her fullest accompaniment at Apollo, with the five-piece rhythm section
(piano, organ, guitar, bass, and drums) and the backing vocals of the Melody
Echoes giving her the equivalent of a full band to work with. The arc of Apollo's
production vision for Jackson is audible when listening to songs that have similar
tempos and "feels" but are recorded with different backing ensembles. Compare,
for instance, Jackson's recording of Robert Anderson's "Prayer Changes Things"
at session three or of the spiritual "Get Away, Jordan" from session four, which
share more spare piano, organ, and guitar backing, with her reading of Kenneth
Morris's "One Day" at session ten or Dorsey's "Beautiful Tomorrow" from session eleven, both of which include the full instrumentation. Jackson's accompaniment helped shape her vocal performances. The walking bass line of "Beautiful

FIG. 6.2 Mahalia Jackson performing with the Selah Jubilee Singers, probably in February or March 1952 as part of the "Gospel Train" touring package. Laurraine Goreau Photograph Collection, Hogan Jazz Archive, Tulane University.

Tomorrow" in particular locks in the tempo from beginning to end much more than is typical with Jackson's recordings, on which the pace can fluctuate considerably, usually speeding up over the course of the song.

A final stage can be heard in Jackson's last Apollo session, which is the most experimental from the standpoint of accompaniment. Two of the four songs recorded, "I'm on My Way to Canaan Land" and the enigmatic "My Story," include bongos and maracas, giving them a Latin feel inspired by mid-1950s "mambo mania" fueled by such popular U.S.-based Spanish Caribbean bandleaders as Perez Prado, Xavier Cugat, and Tito Puente. After Jackson performed "I'm on My Way to Canaan Land" on her radio show three months later, Jack Halloran, the leader of her backing vocal quartet, asked her on-air in scripted dialogue: "What was that beat in the background anyway? Sounded kind of like a mambo." Jackson, credited by Halloran as the song's arranger, responded: "Well, that's Cuban, Jack, mixed with African." A third song at Jackson's final Apollo session, "I'm Willing to Run All the Way," added, for the only time, a tenor saxophone playing fills as a complement to a rhythm section of piano, organ, bass, and drum, producing an after-hours rhythm and blues vibe that likely raised eyebrows among her church base. The beginning and end points of the transformation of Jackson's performance setting at Apollo through graduated instrumentation is evident hearing side-by-side two similar type songs recorded eight years apart, the intimate "I'm

Going to Tell God" from her first session and the more fulsome "I'm Willing to Run All the Way" from her last.

Church Songs

Over the course her first six sessions for the label, Jackson performed exclusively gospel songs, traditional African American spirituals, and Baptist hymns. In fact, two-thirds of Jackson's repertory prior to fall 1950 were published gospel songs. Nearly half of these were by Brewster, Dorsey, or Morris, though throughout her Apollo years Jackson continued to record songs written by a number of other respected gospel songwriters, including Charles Albert Tindley, Lucie Campbell, Doris Akers, Robert Anderson, Lucy Matthews Collier, Mary Lou Parker Coleman, and Theodore Frye. The three spirituals from Jackson's late-1940s sessions were ones regularly heard in black churches and on the concert stage. "I'm Going to Tell God" from her first session is a gospel-blues variant of "I'm Going to Tell God All My Troubles (When I Get Home)." Black recitalists ranging from bass-baritone Paul Robeson to contemporary countertenor John Holiday Jr. have performed the brooding "I'm Going to Tell God All My Troubles," sometimes worded "I'm Going to Tell God How You Treated Me." Also performed as an art song is "I Want Jesus to Walk with Me," alternately known as "Pilgrim's Journey," which Jackson renders with a gently propulsive swing complemented by single-string guitar fills, transforming what is often performed as a portentous aria into something closer to rhythm and blues. The more rousing spiritual "Get Away, Jordan" first appeared in print during Reconstruction, identified as a "cabin and plantation song," and subsequently became a gospel standard through a spate of postwar recordings by gospel luminaries. Jackson's recording was but one of many recordings of "Get Away, Jordan" between 1944 and 1951, including sides by the Sallie Martin Singers, the Trumpeteers, J. Earle Hines and His Goodwill Singers, the Ward Singers, the Davis Sisters, Ethel Davenport, the Dixie Hummingbirds, and the Gospel Harmonettes, among others. From 1950 on, Jackson continued to record spirituals for Apollo, many of them popular favorites like "Go Tell It on the Mountain," "Nobody Knows the Trouble I've Seen," "Didn't It Rain," and "I'm on My Way to Canaan Land."

Jackson also recorded hymns on an ongoing basis as an Apollo artist. Hymns are Christian songs, typically set to multiple stanzas of rhymed poetry and sung congregationally. Twelve of the fourteen hymns that Jackson recorded for Berman came from two seminal Baptist hymnals produced by the National Baptist Convention in the 1920s, *Gospel Pearls* and *The Baptist Standard Hymnal*. Eileen Southern has called the 1921 publication of *Gospel Pearls*, an anthology of 164 songs popular among black Christian congregations, "a milestone in the history of Black hymnody."[10] Compiled by the music committee of the National Baptist

Convention Sunday School Publishing Board, headed by Willa A. Townsend, the Convention's first official songbook sought "to supply the present day needs of the Sunday School, Church, Conventions and other religious gatherings." The contents offer an institutional account of church music commonly used by black Baptists, encompassing venerable eighteenth-century English Protestant hymns setting texts by Isaac Watts and Charles Wesley; songs by prolific nineteenth- and early twentieth-century American hymn writers like Johnson Oatman Jr., Fanny Crosby, Charles Gabriel, and Ira Sankey; spiritual arrangements, including nearly a dozen by brothers John and Frederick Work of Fisk University; and more recent compositions by black sacred songwriters, most notably the influential Tindley, who is represented by six songs, and Campbell and Dorsey, who each contributed one number. In 1924, Townsend's sixteen-member Music Committee, which included six women, published the more expansive *Baptist Standard Hymnal*, a 745-song collection of "good old soul-stirring hymns" designed to counter what "seems now to be a tendency to get away from that fervency of spirit and song that characterized the church and altar worship of other days." *The Baptist Standard Hymnal* remained the standard source among black Baptist congregations until it was updated in 1961 and eventually superseded in 1977 by *The New National Baptist Hymnal*.[11]

Meeting the needs of both the home and the church, of both informal fellowship and liturgical proceedings, *Gospel Pearls*, or "*GP*," as it was often called, gained tremendous popularity among black Christians, but it was also a resource for singers. *Gospel Pearls*, the editors promised, was "a boon to Gospel singers" that indexed notable early-twentieth century black Baptist soloists through familiar songs associated with them. Horace Boyer underscored the significance of the explicit reference to "Gospel" in the title. Those who first encountered *Gospel Pearls* in the 1920s would have understood its contents not only in relation to songs and singers, but also in terms of a distinctive vocal practice—"gospel singing"— that, Boyer claims, slightly "tempered" the more ecstatic vocality heard in COGIC churches, resulting in an approach that was influenced by Pentecostalism yet suited black Baptist tastes. "This *GP* style of singing," he observes, "leaned heavily on the nineteenth-century Baptist lining hymn tradition of singing songs in a slow tempo and elaborating each syllable with three to five embellishment tones."[12]

In this sense, published Baptist hymns had a double life: as songs that could be sung more or less as written by congregations and as repertory that could be rendered in a more freely expressive manner by soloists. Widely admired soloist Hattie Parker, who appeared on programs with Jackson and the Johnson Singers, recorded at least nine numbers from *Gospel Pearls* with the Chicago-based Pace Jubilee Singers in the 1920s. *GP* was a go-to-source for Jackson as well. In 1938, Jackson, persuaded by then-husband Ike Hockenhull, reluctantly auditioned for the Chicago production of *The Swing Mikado*, an all-black cast adaptation of the

Gilbert and Sullivan operetta presented by the WPA's Federal Theatre Project. Jackson remembered that when she was met by the audition coordinator who had instructed her in advance to "Bring your own music" to the tryout, "I pulled my little *Gospel Pearls* out of my pocketbook to show her." Told this would not serve the purpose, Jackson ran to a nearby music store and bought the sheet music for "Sometimes I Feel Like a Motherless Child." Recalling his touring days with Jackson, Dorsey recalled that when Jackson was not plugging his own songs "she was singing out of her little *Gospel Pearls*." As I discuss below, Jackson's drawn out, ornamented delivery of hymns from *Gospel Pearls* and the *Baptist Standard Hymnal* is captured on several Apollo recordings.[13]

Jackson's Apollo recordings not categorizable as religious pop exemplify three basic feels: a "swing" feel, a "gospel" feel, and a "free" feel, the latter reserved primarily for her approach to Baptist hymns. Though this does not, of course, represent the only way to think about Jackson's Apollo recordings or about gospel singing, this taxonomy does help us zero in on some of the musical details and performance choices as she put her voice into action. Being attentive to the feel of a recording has also drawn my own ears toward nuances in the individual styles of standout gospel piano accompanists like Falls, Roberta Martin, Willie Webb, Clara Ward, Curtis Dublin of the Davis Sisters, Herbert "Pee-Wee" Pickard of the Original Gospel Harmonettes, James Cleveland with the Caravans, and others, as represented on post-war black gospel recordings. The latter is a topic that is ripe for more focused music-historical investigation.[14] There is, of course, no substitute for close listening, and, as I proposed above, readers will undoubtedly benefit the most from the musical discussion that follows by spending time as a listener with Jackson's Apollo recordings, all of which are readily available.[15]

"Bounce" and the Swing Feel

In mid-1950s interviews, Jackson often characterized her more energetic gospel numbers as having an added "bounce," both rhythmically and in their manner of performance. In a 1957 interview with Nat Hentoff, Jackson observed that there was "more bounce in gospel singing in recent years," adding: "I think I'm the cause of a lot of that bounce." As if handed a gift, members of the media that covered Jackson, like Larry Wolters of the *Chicago Tribune*, eagerly identified her as "the gospel singer with a bounce." The press increasingly leaned upon this branding as Jackson began to cross over to non-black audiences. Asked repeatedly to explain her style of music for gospel initiates, Jackson continued to reinforce this depiction of her vocal approach, particularly in the promotional flurry leading up to her CBS radio program, *The Mahalia Jackson Show*, which debuted in September 1954. "I don't know if you'd call it a style," she told a national gathering of CBS radio network affiliates being pitched the program. "I just sing the way I feel and the bounce in my singing is just sort of making a joyful noise unto the Lord, as David said." If Jackson grounded bounce in scripture, some stories dabbled in double entendre that linked the "bounce" of Jackson's singing to her physical body, summoning the recurring visual trope of the animated, buxom black woman. In December, the weekly 15¢ newsstand magazine *People Today* praised Jackson's "vibrant, powerful contralto & ultra-emotional delivery" while also providing her Tale of the Tape—"She's 43 and 5'7", weighs 225"—in a short feature titled "Mahalia: More Ounce to Her Bounce."[16]

Chicago's omnipresent media figure Studs Terkel, Jackson's most ardent early champion, hosted the singer on his radio show, *Studs Terkel Almanac,* and asked her for clarification.

TERKEL: Now, you call your up-tempo spirituals music with a "bounce." What do you mean by that?

JACKSON: Oh, you know, put a little pep in it, a little joyfulness in it. Like "Upper Room" or "Move Up," or something like that.[17]

Jackson never forgot early criticism from conservative black Baptists that the pep she put into her performance of gospel songs crossed the line and veered toward sacrilege. On an episode of her radio program, Jackson set up her performance of "Just a Closer Walk with Thee," a song closely associated with traditional jazz funerals in New Orleans, by again validating "gospel bounce songs" in more specifically religious terms.

People say: "Oooh, they're singing jazz in the church!" David said: "Make a joyful noise unto the Lord. Clap your hands and come before his presence with singing." The Lord don't like us to be dead. Be alive! If you feel like it, pat your feet. Sometime I don't only pat my feet. I dance to the glory of God, because he said so. So that's why we like these songs that got a bounce.[18]

The tendency of some commentators to focus on shared features between gospel and jazz as Jackson came to prominence betrayed a cultural-political investment in holistic views of black culture and aesthetics, though these often came at the expense of attention to other features of gospel practice.[19] In this particular case, however, Jackson's reference to "singing jazz in the church" is closer to the point because what Jackson's performances of "bounce" songs often share is an unmistakable sense of swing. When Dorsey laid groundwork for the modern gospel movement in the early 1930s by establishing a gospel chorus at Chicago's Pilgrim Baptist Church, he faced strong resistance from Pilgrim's senior choir director Edward Boatner who found it "degrading" to hear "the rhythm of jazz" in church.

Dorsey himself admitted that unlike the "solemn type" of performance then preferred by many mainline black Baptists, "gospel chorus music has a swing to it." Dorothy Austin, the classically-trained daughter of Pilgrim pastor J. C. Austin, struggled to fill the role of piano accompanist for Dorsey's gospel chorus, finding herself unequipped to deal with this feature of the music: "I didn't play by ear and I had never practiced any sort of swing. I didn't feel at ease doing it.[20]

As a musical concept, swing is most closely associated with jazz and is frequently cited, music theorist Matthew Butterfield notes, as "the central rhythmic quality native to jazz." Typically identified with an uneven long-short subdivision of principal beats, it is tempting to think of swing in its most basic sense as close kin to "compound" meter—the division of the principal note values into triplets as opposed to the bipartite subdivision of "simple" meter. In practice, however, for both performers and listeners, swing is a distinct and more difficult to explain sensation, much more a feel than a rhythmic specification. In jazz, swing is rarely, if ever, notated; it is either implicit in performance practice or communicated with an instruction on the printed page to swing the "straight" eighth note subdivisions. Boyer has written that in the early decades of modern gospel music "gospel meter," which he equates with compound meter (i.e., dividing each beat into triplets, giving a ₄ bar 12 subunits) was a matter of performance practice as well.

> Since 1950, the so-called gospel meter has been ⅛. . . .This is the basic gospel beat. . . .[But] it is interesting to note that in [his] 158 songs, Dorsey did not use ⅛ once, even though he helped create it. The ⅛ did not appear in published music until 1970. . . .If the performer is *inside* the tradition, he or she knows the tradition and automatically plays it this way. So Dorsey wrote his music in ₄, but it was played in ⅛. When he taught his music to the choir, although the score before them was in ₄, he would play it in ⅛, and it would sound like a gospel waltz.[21]

In her autobiography, Jackson remembered being perplexed by the gap between ways of perceiving "gospel meter" when she appeared at the Music Inn in 1951.

> One young professor kept insisting that I didn't even know my own meter. "You keep telling us you're singing four-four time," he said, "but I tell you you're not. You're singing in twelve time."
>
> "You're telling me wrong," I shouted. I stand up here tapping my own foot with a four-four-beat and you tell me I'm tapping twelve-twelve. One of us is crazy.[22]

As Dorothy Austin confessed, having learned the hard way trying to interpret Dorsey's sheet music, "Just because it's ₄ time, you don't play it that way." Yet, as

I explain below, Boyer's explanation somewhat collapses a significant distinction between swing and compound meter that in Jackson's Apollo output plays out quite differently from recording to recording at the level of "feel."

Commentators on the feel of swing sometimes explain its visceral impact in terms of what Charles Keil has called "engendered feeling," an intangible human quality that supplements what notation and music theory can only weakly imply. Jazz critics André Hodeir and Gunther Schuller, respectively, have attributed to swing the "vital drive" and "forward propelling directionality" in jazz rhythm. Butterfield helpfully captures the way in which swing might best be thought of as at once a matter of individual technique, ensemble cooperation, and an almost involuntary attitude.

> The term "swing" designates the use of uneven eighth notes, to be sure, but it also refers to a lilting rhythmic groove emerging from the interaction of bass and drums as they maintain the beat. More importantly, however, swing designates a general rhythmic ethos—a mysterious quality purport-edly transcending representation in musical notation—prompting active listener engagement, often expressed through spontaneous foot-tapping, head-bobbing, hand-clapping, finger-snapping, or even dancing.[23]

In the parlance of blues musicians, the feeling of swing is often indicated through the related concept of a "shuffle," but the latter lacks the full symbolic and aes-thetic affirmation conferred upon music that "swings." I have never heard a lis-tener exclaim with approval: "Man, that band really *shuffles!*"

Nearly all of Jackson's Apollo recordings with a steady pulse exhibit either the "rhythmic ethos" of swing or a more sharply chiseled compound meter. Her only recordings for the label with "straight" eighths are "I'm on My Way to Canaan Land," "My Story," and the slightly ambiguous "Walking to Jerusalem." But in addition to the eighth-note subdivision, the recordings that I am specifically identifying as conveying a "swing *feel*" (Example 6.1) also share four relatively equally accented beats to a bar and faster tempos. One can easily capture the feel of Jackson's "swing" recordings by speaking the following phrase with its natural accentuation:

Yes, I want to see my Je-sus, Yes, I want to see my Je-sus . . .
  1   2   3   4   /1   2   3   4 . . .

Jackson's swing tunes for Apollo are never slower than 75–80 beats per mi-nute (bpm) (e.g., "There's Not a Friend") and extend to songs taken at 145–150 bpm (e.g., "Said He Would"). Topping out at around 175 bpm is the breakneck-paced "Didn't It Rain," Jackson's fastest tune of this type. It is this combination of

---

EXAMPLE 6.1

Mahalia Jackson Songs Recorded for Apollo with "Swing" Feel

I Want to Rest
Wait Until My Change Comes
What Could I Do?
Move On Up a Little Higher
Dig a Little Deeper
Tired
There's Not a Friend Like Jesus
Let the Power of the Holy Ghost Fall on Me
Get Away, Jordan
Walk with Me
Prayer Changes Things
Shall I Meet You Over Yonder
Do You Know Him
How I Got Over
Jesus Is with Me
Said He Would
If You Just Keep Still
I'm Going Down to the River
One Day
Beautiful Tomorrow
Walking to Jerusalem
Didn't It Rain

---

four-beats-to-a-bar articulation, swung eighth notes, and fast tempo that defines Jackson's songs with a swing feel. This feel is provided by the accompaniment regardless of Jackson's vocal line. Songs with the "gospel feel," which I discuss in the following section, exhibit functionally differentiated beats in a bar, slower tempos, subdivisions that are closer to strict compound meter, and, in several cases, triple meter.

Though all are brisk, the range of tempos among Jackson's swing numbers creates considerable variety. The strength of the swing feel can also be emphasized differently by the instrumental backing, Jackson's own energy, and even a song's text. Whereas on "Prayer Changes Things" Jackson is accompanied by piano, organ, and guitar, "One Day" adds bass, drums, and the Melody Echoes as background singers. Though the two songs both have a swing feel and are taken at essentially the same tempo, a listener might perceive that the on-the-beat walking bass in "One Day" helps the performance, and even Jackson herself, swing "harder," especially in the lead up to and arrival of the chorus. A similarly noticeable impact of the backing ensemble can be heard by comparing the piano-accompanied "I Want to Rest" and the driving "Said He Would," which Jackson sings at the same tempo but with a full rhythm section and backing singers. In "I Want to Rest," it is interesting to hear Jackson's insinuation of voice culture with the conspicuously rolled Rs on "breast" and "oppressed," a gesture we also hear in recordings by older singers Arizona Dranes, Georgia Peach, and Mary Johnson Davis, though they are a peculiar one-off for Jackson. Her pianists also shaped the strength of the swing feel. The left hands of McKinney, who takes an almost stride piano approach on "I Want to Rest," and of Falls, stomping out a boogie woogie–leaning left hand on "Shall I Meet You Over Yonder," guide roughly similar songs toward very different sounding performances.

Even without a rhythm section, Jackson took matters into her own hands on some songs, riding the swing feel with notable force. At her eighth session, her first with backing singers, Jackson sounds particularly inspired—and more effectively miked—doing some of her fiercest singing on record on the swing numbers "How I Got Over" and "Jesus Is with Me." A song's words could also boost Jackson's inclination to swing harder: the short-long iambic feet of many hymn texts—for instance, "A *charge* to *keep* I *have*" or "A*maz*ing *grace,* how *sweet* the *sound*"—are less amenable to be swung than the long-short trochaic accentuation of gospel lines like "*Dig* a *little deep*er" or "*Let* the *po-wer of* the *ho-*ly *ghost.*" In other cases, Jackson deliberately foregrounded a song's swing feel by pulsing vowels in a manner that anticipates soul singer Mavis Staples, singing "*Get* a-*way*-ay-*ay, Jo*-o-*or*-dan" or "*Ti*-i-i-ired *Lo*-ord, *so*-oul *is*-a *res*-ted." Notably, Jackson sings all four of these songs—"Dig a Little Deeper," "Let the Power of the Holy Ghost," "Get Away, Jordan," and "Tired"—in B-flat. This is a key that she seemed to reserve for tunes in which she wanted to complement the hard swinging feel with strong blues inflection by belting the blue third above the upper tonic (D-flat) with maximum power at climactic moments in the song. Two other "B-flat swing tunes," as I call them, are "Move On Up a Little Higher" and "Walk with Me." D-flat was right at the ceiling of Jackson's range, adding a touch of dramatic urgency, though on a select number of Apollo recordings she briefly extended to a D-natural ("I Can Put My Trust" and "Shall I Meet You Over Yonder") and in one instance to E-flat ("How I Got Over"). If the tape speed or acetate transfer did not distort the pitch, Jackson reached an E-natural in her live performance of "Beams of Heaven" at the Golden Gate Auditorium in January 1946.

Jackson could achieve a range of effects within a swing feel. One of Jackson's most outstanding Apollo sides, Dorsey's "Wait Until My Change Comes," recorded at her very first session, begins with a move to the subdominant and four bars of rhythmic unison at the top of the chorus ("I'm gonna wait . . . right here . . . all day long"). The latter functions almost like stop time, momentarily coiling energy that is then gently released by the continuation of McKinney's lightly swinging piano accompaniment. On "If You Just Keep Still," Fall's hammered piano triplets, the brushes on the snare, and Jackson's deliberately behind-the-beat delivery— "Well, he never *lost a battle*"—results in a performance that proceeds with an un-apologetically lazy blues shuffle. "If You Just Keep Still" is one of several Jackson recordings, including "Walk with Me" and "There's Not a Friend," that are less notable for Jackson doubling down rhythmically on the swing feel than for her elastic phrasing over it. "I'm Glad Salvation is Free" is a brooding transformation of an Isaac Watts hymn, Jackson's only swing tune in a minor key.

"Move On Up a Little Higher" swings—Ralph Ellison heard "a riff straight out of early Ellington"—though its atmosphere is marked less by propulsive drive than by a stubbornly relaxed pace established through the deliberate saunter of Lee and Francis's piano-organ accompaniment.[24] Very little "happens" in "Move On Up a Little Higher," a record that feels both hypnotic and insistent, intensifying the impact of the vocal line. The form is articulated by the recurrence of an eight-bar cadential formula, worded differently each time, with a concluding four-measure circle-of-fifths–based progression (I–VI–II–V–I–IV–I). The progression doubles as the introduction, leading to two opening statements of the full cadential refrain:

> One (of) these morning
> One (of) these morning
> I'm gonna lay down my cross, get my crown.
>
> One of these evening, oh Lord
> Late one evening, my Lord
> Late one evening I'm going home, live on high.

Jackson's delivery of the words is typical for her; she only implies "of," ghosting the word in the manner of a jazz musician, and dropping the final "s" to trans-form the original "One of these mornings" into something closer to "One these mornin'," which concentrates the swing feel by emphasizing the on-the-beat accents. Between the varied statements of the cadential formula—"I'm going to live up in glory after while," "It will be always howdy-howdy and never goodbye," "I'll be waiting at the beautiful golden gate," etc.—Jackson sings rhymed couplets over the harmonic stasis of Lee and Francis's vamp:

> Just as soon as my feet strike Zion
> Lay down my heavy burden
> Put on my robe, Lord, in glory, Lord
> Sing, Lord, tell my story
> Come over hills and mountains, Lord

Up to the Christian fountain
All of God's sons and daughter, Lord
Drinking that old healing water

It is not unheard of for Jackson to sing a song built around strung-together couplets over static harmony—the verses in "Walking in Jerusalem" are another example—but it is not common, or at least less common than one might encounter in other gospel contexts. Much as early blues singers borrowed familiar couplets that migrated from song to song, gospel singers, and especially lead singers in male quartets, often recycle "gospel couplets" heard in dozens of performances, especially in "drive" sections when the harmonic progression pauses to accommodate an open-ended loop. Some of the most frequently deployed gospel couplets heard during such vamps are:

If you don't believe I've been redeemed
Follow me down to the Jordan stream . . .

The Jordan River was chilly and cold
It chilled my body but not my soul . . .

I looked at my hands, my hands looked new
Looked at my feet and my feet did too . . .

I went to the valley, didn't go to stay
My soul got happy and I stayed all day

One of these mornings, and it won't be long
You'll look for me and I'll be gone . . .

If you get to heaven before I do
Tell all my friends I'm coming too . . .

When I get to Heaven, gonna sit right down
I'll ask King Jesus for my starry crown . . .

When I get to Heaven, gonna sing and shout
Won't be no one there to put me out . . .

Male jubilee groups—most influentially, the Golden Gate Quartet—specialized in songs built from a refrain that alternates with the syncopated, proto-rap delivery of extended strings of newly-written rhymed couplets used as a storytelling mechanism, whether for folksy recounting of biblical tales (e.g., "Jonah," "What a Time," and "John the Revelator"), commenting on current events ("Why I Like Roosevelt" and "Jesus Hits Like an Atom Bomb"), or rendering lighter, comic novelty numbers ("The Preacher and the Bear").

In "Move On Up a Little Higher," following the drawn out cadential refrain at the end of side one ("Oh Lord, and never falter"), Jackson switches from rhymed couplets and adopts a univocal call-and-response structure at the beginning of part two, singing of fellowship awaiting "up in glory after while." Her one-woman dialogue heightens the record's mesmeric groove.

> Move on up a little higher, Lord
> Meet with old man Daniel
> Move on up a little higher, Lord
> Meet with the Hebrew children
> Move on up a little higher, Lord
> Meet with Paul and Silas
> Move on up a little higher, Lord
> Meet my loving mother
> Move on up a little higher, Lord
> Meet that lily of the valley, yeah

The smooth glide of Jackson's adamant incantation—"*Mooove* on up a little higher"—executed with the stylishness of a Temptations side step, hailed listeners as they flipped the disk and became the record's defining gesture. Though the *Billboard* review of "Move On Up a Little Higher" expressed disappointment that Jackson's "rhythmic contagion isn't caught by the organ and piano providing a solemn accompaniment," pianist Lee recalled that after the record came out, "critics all seemed to feel that I was the main support of the record being a hit, of giving her the type of background she really needed."[25] Regardless, what is so striking, and in many ways novel, about "Move On Up a Little Higher" as a commercial recording was how the forward momentum that we might associate with the "bounce" of Jackson's singing and with the swing feel established by the instrumental backing deliberately and paradoxically works against itself, creating simultaneous tension and release through a perpetual motion that manages to stand still, as if listening to Jackson testify for not one but two sides.

The "Gospel Seesaw"

Jackson recorded a distinct group of songs for Apollo that she performed with a "gospel" feel distinguishable from her swing numbers (Example 6.2). The definitive characteristic of the gospel feel is a metric and rhythmic aspect, rooted in the dialogue heard in many quartet and gospel group performances, which I refer to as the "gospel seesaw." Jackson's swing recordings maintain four solid beats per bar and thus a continuous pulse that could be reinforced by a walking bass. In contrast, a common practice in post-war gospel performances

EXAMPLE 6.2

Mahalia Jackson Songs Recorded for Apollo with
"Gospel" Feel (in $\frac{4}{4}$)

I'm Going to Tell God
I Have a Friend
Since the Fire Started Burning in My Soul
I Can Put My Trust in Jesus
God Answers Prayer
I Gave Up Everything to Follow Him
Go Tell It on the Mountain
He's My Light
Consider Me
I Wonder If I Will Ever Rest
Run All the Way

is a volleying back-and-forth between a soloist and a backing group structured such that the lead sings phrases centered on or around the pickup and downbeat of a $\frac{4}{4}$ bar—beats four and one—leaving space for the supporting vocalists to fill out the middle two beats of the bar (two and three), or vice versa. Though this phrasing is not always consistent from beginning to end of a performance and usually involves some overlap, this structure of solo-group exchange can be heard on countless gospel recordings. Examples include the Sallie Martin Singers' "God Is a Battle Axe," the Pilgrim Travelers' "Straight Street," the Original Gospel Harmonettes' "Sometimes," the Five Blind Boys of Alabama's "You Got to Move," and the Roberta Martin Singers' "I Can Make It." The subdivision of the beat is also crucial to this gospel feel, which, differently than swing, emphasizes all three triplets of compound meter, particularly on the second and fourth beats of the bar. Together, these elements divide a four-beat bar into two two-beat segments: triplet upbeats that prepare arrivals on the accented first and third beats in the bar. These subunits are felt as "up-and-a DOWN, up-and-a DOWN" and more specifically in $\frac{4}{4}$ time as "four-and-a ONE, two-and-a THREE."

This complementary phrasing—the continuous alternation of what we might identify as the "4-1" and "2-3" ends of the seesaw—is a signature feature of Jackson's "gospel" recordings. In this sense, Jackson and Falls were co-partners in producing this feel. Jackson's accompanist took on the structural role of the backing singers, bridging her sung phrases with the triplet-plus-quarter note rhythmic motive that is the basic building block of the gospel seesaw: ♫♩.

EXAMPLE 6.3

Phrasing of Lyrics in "Gospel Seesaw" Songs

4-and-a ONE	2-and-a THREE	4-and-a ONE	2-and-a THREE	4-and-a ONE	2-and-a THREE	4-and-a ONE
	(Piano)		(Piano)		(Piano)	
I'm gonna tell God		all about it,		One of these days		oh Lord, one of these days
Somebody knows		when I am tempted,		Somebody cares, Lord		when things go wrong
There are those		who will deceive you,		No matter what		your trust may be
When		I sought the Lord,		And I heard		his blessed word
Use me, Lord		in thy service,		Draw me nearer, Lord		every day

On all but one of her Apollo gospel feel recordings in ⁴⁄₄, Jackson sings during the "4-1" part of the bar with Falls playing "2-3" fills that sound almost like an assent; Example 6.3 illustrates how this phrasing of the words works in a handful of Jackson recordings. Lucy Matthews Collier's shimmering "He's My Light" is a slight departure in that Jackson reverses the phrasing during the verse, largely singing on "2-3," then, as if by an imperceptible sleight-of-hand, switches to "4-1" during the chorus. This reversibility of roles on the gospel seesaw is in some ways analogous to the invertible 3-2 and 2-3 clave rhythms in Afro-Cuban music, each offering different phrasing opportunities within a consistent feel.[26]

Some gospel songs, like Dorsey's "Consideration" (recorded by Jackson as "Consider Me"), were published with the melody already phrased in this manner. Though it is not specified in the published sheet music, a piano accompanist would know that her or his job was to fill in the "2-3" end of the seesaw. Thus it is not a coincidence that of the sixteen songs that Jackson recorded with a gospel feel, eleven were published gospel songs, though she also adapts the spirituals "I'm Going to Tell God" and "Go Tell It on the Mountain" in this manner as well. The text itself often accommodates gospel seesaw phrasing, with the natural accentuation of phrases like "one of these days," "somebody knows," "no matter what," and "I sought the Lord" already articulating the "*ta-ta-ta Ta*" gospel seesaw rhythmic cell (Example 6.3). Another identifying factor in Jackson's particular approach to gospel feel Apollo recordings is tempo: her songs rendered with a gospel feel were invariably taken slower than those with a swing feel. All but two were performed under 60 bpm, with the majority recorded between 40–50 bpm. Not every instance is clear cut: "God Answers Prayers" has the tempo and four-to-a-bar regularity of the swing feel even as the rhythmic organization of Fall's piano accompaniment offers hints of a gospel feel throughout. Conversely, on "Go Tell It on the Mountain," Falls emphasizes the gospel feel clearly but without the support of Jackson's vocal line, which eschews the more customary gapped phrasing and brings out the on-the-beat accentuation and natural swing rhythm of the text. The fastest of Jackson's gospel feel songs by a considerable margin, "Go Tell It on the Mountain" is also taken at a tempo (70 bpm) that makes it a borderline case, blurring the boundary between swing and gospel. It is important to note that the gospel seesaw is not simply an instance of call and response, since its feel is produced not only by the back-and-forth dialogue but also by tempo, rhythm, and specific orientation within the bar.

Though they are typically more up-tempo than Jackson's performances in this vein, numerous rhythm and blues and soul recordings project their gospel-influenced sound precisely through some insinuation of the gospel seesaw. An explicit case is the chorus of Marvin Gaye's "Pride and Joy," during which Gaye ("4-1") and his female backing singers ("2-3") trade off, dividing the bar in a manner straight out of gospel. Other secular recordings built upon gospel seesaw phrasing accentuate the steady triplets of compound meter, to establish a distinct feel, if for only parts of the song. Sam Cooke's "Nothing Can Change This Love" and "Bring It On Home to Me," William Bell's "You Don't Miss Your Water," Wilson Pickett's "If You Need Me," Etta James's "I'm Gonna Take What He's Got," and Aretha Franklin's "Dr. Feelgood (Love is a Serious Business)" are examples of such recordings, the latter two featuring James and Franklin taking the "2-3" part of the bar. Cooke's "Bring It On Home" builds the device into the arrangement by introducing a new violin fill in the third verse ("I'll give you jewelry / and money too") that sounds the gospel seesaw rhythmic motive. During the stop time verses of the blues song "Hoochie Coochie Man," the alternation of the famous harmonica riff ("4-1") with Muddy Waters's singing ("2-3") also exhibits a trading-off identical to the gospel seesaw, despite the record sounding nothing like gospel.

Delving a bit deeper, one of the more compelling features of the gospel feel is that there is in fact a double seesaw at work that creates a subtle but dynamic metric ambiguity. On the one hand, each pair of beats, "4-1" and "2-3," has an upbeat—which music theorists, borrowing from the terminology of poetic meter, call an "anacrusis"—followed by a downbeat. Beats four and two are pickups to the landing beats one and three, respectively, producing two up-down "seesaws" in each four-beat cycle. But we can also feel the "4-1" and "2-3" subunits of each measure as having a more slowly moving upbeat and downbeat relationship with respect to each other, with the first beat of the bar functioning as a downbeat answered by the pickup of the third beat of the bar. As a result, we get "mixed messages" on beats two and three, which can be perceived in contradictory ways. As part of the faster moving seesaw, beat two is a pickup to the arrival on the third beat:

4 -and-a   1,   2 -and-a   3   / 4 -and-a   1,   2 -and-a   3
up-and-a **DOWN**, up-and-a **down** / up-and-a **DOWN**, up-and-a **down**

But if the third beat is heard as part of the slower moving seesaw, with beat one as the downbeat and beat three as its upbeat, beat two is a prolongation of this larger structural downbeat and beat three becomes an anticipation of the strong anacrusis on beat four:

4 -and-a   1,   2 -and-a   3   / 4 -and-a   1,   2 -and-a   3
UP-and-a **DOWN**, **down**-and-a up / UP-and-a **DOWN**, **down**-and-a up

Put another way, in the first context, the third beat is a more weakly accented downbeat compared to beat one, and in the second, it is a weaker upbeat compared to beat four. The latter metrical frame, both complementary to and competing with the first, also makes us hear the two sets of triplets differently: on beat four as part of a pickup and on beat two as a prolongation of an arrival. Because of the metrical ambivalence of the middle of the bar, the "2-3" end of the seesaw, especially at a slow tempo, can often feel slightly "busier" than, or at least qualitatively different from, the relative clarity and consistency of the "4-1" part of the bar.

Ambiguities abound in the gospel feel, and these subtleties can only be perceived through close attention to the singer and accompanist. Listening to certain recordings, like "I Gave Up Everything to Follow Him," my ears sometimes switch involuntarily back and forth between feeling the bar divided as "4-1" + "2-3" and, if I am drawn to the sense of a double downbeat and double upbeat of the slower seesaw, hearing it as a slow two-beat bar, "1-2" + "3-4." Either way, I believe the "handoffs" between Jackson and Falls, riding and expressively manipulating their respect ends of the gospel seesaw, and the meditative tempo that enables listeners to savor the distinctive metric tension and rhythmic animation virtually within each beat, partially account for a "feelingful" quality of this group of Apollo recordings. "I Wonder If I Will Ever Rest," which opens with an unaccompanied tom-tom playing the gospel seesaw motive as a rhythmic ostinato, achieves a unique effect as the only such Apollo such tune in minor mode, which banishes much of its gospel feel.

EXAMPLE 6.4

Mahalia Jackson Songs Recorded for Apollo
with "Gospel" Feel (in ¾)

He Knows My Heart
He's the One
Closer to Me
I Bowed on My Knees and Cried Holy
What Then?
Come to Jesus

A different though in certain respects more straightforward version of the gospel seesaw occurs in Jackson's gospel feel songs in triple meter (Example 6.4). In these cases, there is only a single unbalanced seesaw: the feeling of two variably weighted downbeats on beats one and two and a pickup on beat three, articulated, as is typical in gospel feel songs, with a triplet (one, two, three-and-a). Unlike her songs in four, there is not the reliably structured alternation between Jackson and her accompanist in these triple meter numbers, which often achieve their feel from Falls gently deemphasizing the downbeat and accentuating the second beat slightly with increased rhythmic activity, to build momentum toward the strong upbeat on beat three.

The triple-meter gospel feel and an elegantly balanced dialogue between singer and pianist are in evidence in "Closer to Me," written by the important Los Angeles–based gospel singer, pianist, and composer Doris Akers (1923–1995). Akers occupied yet another complex position within the post-war gospel field that was beyond category in multiple ways. One of gospel's most prolific composers, said to have written over 500 songs, Akers was born in Brookfield, Missouri, where she learned piano by ear and as a teenager led the jazz band Dot Akers and the Swingsters. She moved to Los Angeles in 1945, just before the modern gospel movement there took full root two years later with the arrival of Branham, Hines, and Lightner at St. Paul Baptist Church. Making her name initially as a pianist and choir director, Akers served as accompanist for the Sallie Martin Singers and as music director at Opportunity Baptist Church. But she was continuously active as a songwriter and formed a nationally popular group with Dorothy Simmons, the Simmons-Akers Singers, in part to perform and record her rapidly growing catalog of songs. Some of her songs, including "You Can't Beat God Giving," "Sweet, Sweet Spirit," and "Lead Me, Guide Me" remain rock-solid standards in black Christian repertories. Akers also kept an occasional foot in popular music. She wrote "Pink Champagne" for rhythm and blues singer and bandleader Joe Liggins, whose recording of the song eventually was awarded a gold record for selling over a million copies, prompting Liggins to claim authorship.

Akers's achievements are disproportionate with her customary place in gospel historical narratives. Though in Los Angeles by early 1960s she had earned the nickname "Miss Gospel Music," she goes virtually unacknowledged in either Heilbut's *The Gospel Sound* or Darden's more recent *People Get Ready!*. Some speculate that this is due to gospel's cultural politics. Akers's work as a gospel musician, in compositional style and in performance, actively reached across racial boundaries. Like Dorsey's compositions, Akers's songs were performed by both black and white religious singers—Elvis Presley scored a success in 1972 with "Lead Me, Guide Me"—though, in contrast with Dorsey's reception, some writers have characterized her songs as "not overly black in tone," sometimes highlighting that her best known recordings were made with the interracial Sky Pilot Choir. Significantly, Akers performed and even recorded with popular white gospel quartets like the Statesmen, associations that, Opal Louis Nations believes, account for his sense that Akers was "never fully accepted by the greater body of the black church." Jacqueline DjeDje is perhaps closer to the point in describing her as "the first to bridge the gap between black and white gospel music," a fact that makes it easy for Akers to slip through the cracks that separate the literature on black gospel and Southern gospel music. Regardless, Akers remains an extraordinarily accomplished figure whose multifaceted musical career and complicated reception call for long overdue scholarly research.[27]

When Jackson recorded Akers's "Grow Closer" (as "Closer to Me"), the song was a recent contribution to gospel repertory that exhibited its composer's affinity for popular music with its AABA structure and lyrical "hook."

A There's a still small voice saying to me
   "Closer, closer. Grow closer to me"
A In a whispered tone never leaves me alone
   "Closer, closer. Grow closer to me"
B I want to hear every message clear
   Yes, I want every word to come through
A For if I make it in, I will walk close to him
   Closer, closer, grow closer to him

Akers published the song as "Grow Closer" in 1952 and recorded it with the Simmons-Akers Trio in 1953. The exact date of Jackson's recording of "Closer to Me" is not certain; one estimate places the date in September or October 1950, which seems too early in light of the dates of the sheet music and the Simmons-Akers recording, though not impossible if the song was debuted at the National Baptist Convention. Jackson's sparsely phrased words leave ample space for Falls, who is more prominent in the mix than usual. Francis also supports Jackson with subdued chords on the organ. But despite this bed of sustained harmony and the slowness of the tempo—at 37–38 bpm the slowest, in fact, that Jackson took in any of her Apollo recordings with a steady pulse—there is deceptively dynamic rhythmic life, provided entirely by Falls. The unhurried pace enables the compound triple meter ($\frac{9}{8}$) to accommodate even a swung subdivision of the eighth note. Falls, who sympathetically responds to and sets up Jackson, uses the swing of these smaller note values to slingshot herself into the anacrustic (upbeat) energy of the triplet on the final beat of the bar, often played staccato, as if to soften the landing on the downbeat. Whenever it took place, Jackson was in superb voice at this session, sounding powerful, confident, and without a hint of strain as she extends into the upper part of her range for the repeated B-flats and Cs in the bridge (i.e., the "B" section). Her performance is also striking for how un-bluesy it is; other than passing ornamental blue thirds in the melismatic tails appended to the ends of phrases in the bridge, Jackson sticks almost exclusively to the song's E-flat pentatonic scale (E-flat–F–G–B-flat–C). The symbiosis of Jackson's and Falls's performances and the distinctive energy flow of the triple-meter gospel seesaw—a gradual build to the small jolt of exertion on the lift of the third-beat pickup and relaxation on the downbeat—make the magnificent "Closer to Me" one of the hidden gems among Jackson's Apollo records.

The same characteristic triple-meter gospel feel is evident in another outstanding recording that captures Jackson in top form, "I Bowed on My Knees and Cried Holy." The song was published in 1924 by white hymn writers E. M. Dudley Cantwell and Nettie Dudley Washington and recorded by Jackson at the same session that produced the hard-swinging "How I Got Over" and "Jesus Is with Me." It is at the other end of the tempo spectrum, clocking in at 61–68 bpm, nearly her fastest gospel feel performance, though still slower than any of her swing numbers. The unidentified group of singers that join Falls and Francis in accompanying Jackson are especially integral to the sound of the record, "oohing" and "aahing" softly during the verse but opening up to words and full voice during the chorus. Falls's largely chordal accompaniment is more understated and conservative than in "Closer to Me," exhibiting an almost processional, even plodding, time-keeping regularly. Yet as the record unfolds, the solid foundation of the more equally emphasized beats in the bar feels necessary to support the husky muscularity of Jackson's vocal performance, as if Falls, Francis, and the backing singers are bracing themselves for the forceful impact of Jackson's entry at the chorus, repeated twice. Whether in four or in three, the persistent feeling of pickup and landing—in the case of "I Bowed on My Knees and Cried Holy," the "up-and-a down, down" (three-and-a, 1, 2 . . .) rhythmic-metric motive heard from the outset of the record—is essential to the particular kinetic feel of the gospel seesaw, which, as "Closer to Me" and "I Bowed on My Knees and Cried Holy" vividly demonstrate, can provide the means to quite different sonic ends.

EXAMPLE 6.5

Mahalia Jackson "Free" Triple-Meter Hymns Recorded for Apollo

Even Me (aka Lord, I Hear of Showers of Blessings)
In My Home Over There
Amazing Grace
A Child of the King
The Last Mile of the Way
I Do, Don't You
It Pays to Serve Jesus
I Walked into the Garden
Silent Night
City Called Heaven
His Eye Is on the Sparrow
Just as I Am
God Spoke to Me
It's Real*

* Published in ⁴⁄₄.

"Free" Triple-Meter Hymns

The third feel on Jackson's Apollo recordings is most closely linked to her performance of hymns. Jackson recorded fourteen hymns for Apollo, a dozen of which had become standard among black Baptists by their inclusion in *Gospel Pearls* and the *Baptist Standard Hymnal*. Just as notable, eleven of the fourteen were in triple meter, a fact made more significant by the specific and consistent manner in which Jackson performed these "waltz" hymns. Jackson invariably took these numbers at the exaggeratedly slow tempo that Boyer identified as characteristic of *GP* performance practice, though her hymn performances are perhaps better described as "free" in their general non-adherence to either a steady beat or strictly measured rhythms, making room for her liquid intonation and expressive use of vocal runs. Some of these hymns, like "The Last Mile of the Way," were originally published in ⁶⁄₈, but at a slow tempo each measure is essentially felt as two three-beat bars. Jackson's flexible approach to these "free" triple-meter hymns (Example 6.5) ranges from some, like "Just as I Am" or "The Last Mile of the Way," in which the gestalt of the three-beat bar, however opaque, is still perceptible, to others, like "It Pays to Serve Jesus" or "Amazing Grace," in which a relevant sense of an organized pulse essentially evaporates. Up through her seventh session for Apollo, all of Jackson's free hymns were accompanied solely by organ, which, unlike piano, could more easily sustain pitches and accommodate the liberty she took when singing these songs. From her eighth session on, Jackson's hymns in this style added piano to the organ, with her final free hymn for Apollo, "It's Real," the only instance in $\frac{4}{4}$, also adding a backing choir.

As some gospel historians have observed, Jackson's style of performing hymns reflects the influence of a venerable type of congregational singing known among black Baptists as lined-out or "Dr. Watts" hymnody. Perhaps the first to make this claim in print was William Tallmadge, a historian of Baptist hymnody who in 1961 wrote that black gospel singing is "derived from 'lining-out'" insofar as "familiar hymn tunes are sung in a very slow and ornamented manner." Later, Heilbut also observed that even at her session for Decca in 1937, Jackson recorded "Keep Me Every Day" (also known as "Lord, I Want to Live for Thee"), a turn-of-the-century hymn by Franklin Eiland and Emmett Dean included in the *Baptist Standard Hymnal*, "adapting the old Dr. Watts manner to a more recent composition." Jackson cut "God Shall Wipe All Tears Away," the record that took the Black Pearl by storm, at the same Decca session taking a similar approach, and her rendition of "Beams of Heaven" at the Golden Gate in January 1946 also falls into this category of performance. Boyer has argued that Jackson, who claimed "the Sanctified or Holiness churches we had in the South" as a formative influence, was not in the purest sense a "Baptist singer," except in the case of hymns like "Even Me," "Amazing Grace," and "In My Home Over There" that she interpreted "in the Baptist lining hymn tradition." These performances, Boyer wrote, "show the kind of treatment of the melody line, restrained improvisation, and most of all the legacy of the older styles of African American religious music that the Baptists treasured."[28]

"Lining-out" refers to an oral-traditional performance practice of singing eighteenth-century hymn texts, predominantly among Southern Baptist congregations. Hymns are lined-out in the sense that a song leader introduces one individual line or one couplet of text at a time, sometimes spoken. It is then sung in a more elaborately drawn out variant by the congregation, which by convention usually stands on its feet. Since many of the more famous of these hymn texts were written by English theologian Isaac Watts (1674–1748), black Missionary and Primitive Baptist congregations frequently refer to the practice as "Dr. Watts" hymn singing, even when the text being sung is not by Watts. The practice spread as a result of the First Great Awakening, a mid-eighteenth-century revitalization of religious piety that gave rise to Congregationalist, Methodist, and Baptist churches in the United States. Evangelicals in the 1730s and 1740s proselytized and introduced hymns texts to poor whites and enslaved African Americans who adapted European lining-out practices to accommodate hymn singing within Christian communities comprising persons with varying degrees of literacy.

Lined-out hymn singing flourished most strongly in the late nineteenth- and early twentieth-centuries, when it was widely prevalent among Southern black Baptists and Methodists, and through migration spread to the North between 1880 and 1950. Today, it is preserved almost exclusively among Regular Baptist, Missionary Baptist, and Primitive Baptist congregations. In present-day black churches where it has lapsed from regular practice as other kinds of music, including gospel, took central place in worship, Dr. Watts hymn singing is often introduced with its rhetorical framing as a back-to-the-roots act of cultural memory and preservation: "Some of you younger children probably don't remember this" or "I remember when I was a little boy and grandfather would strike out on a song" or "Can we go back for a little while?"[29]

The repertory, sometimes referred to as "long meters" or the "old one hundreds," is not huge. In his study of Dr. Watts hymn singing, William Dargan documented that black Missionary Baptist hymn repertory in most regional traditions contains fewer than ten texts, sung to a limited number of tunes. In practice, lined-out hymns, some published in Baptist hymnals, others not, are rendered during the opening part of a Baptist worship service known as devotions, during which deacons, deaconesses, or other laypersons lead a sequence of songs, scripture reading, and prayer before the clergy take their place on the pulpit. Dr. Watts texts are metered poetry traditionally sung in a cappella unison or in heterophony with highly melismatic, largely pentatonic melodies that Dargan describes as "winding and deliberate" and drawn out by "extreme slowness and rhythmic license." In one recorded version of a lined-out hymn, "My Work on Earth Will Soon Be Done" from a meeting of southeastern Primitive Baptists, the singing of a single four-line verse lasts over three minutes. This manner of singing also manifests a distinct attitude toward the integrity of individual words. In lined-out hymns, individual syllables are in many instances broken up into multiple-note clusters and the completion of words is even interrupted with "licks of repetitive melisma" sung on "whoa," "yeah," or a moaning hum.

Jackson's close childhood friend in New Orleans, Annise Jackson, sang with her in the Mount Moriah Baptist Church youth choir and remembered Jackson singing "an old Dr. Watts" as a solo for her baptismal service: "Mahalia set that church on fire when she came through with that long meter."[30] On one occasion during his period of association with Jackson decades later, Bill Russell tape recorded Jackson singing three well known Dr. Watts "chants" at her home in Chicago: "Father, I Stretch My Hand to Thee," "Before This Time Another Year," and "Dark Was the Night and Cold Was the Ground." Russell described the experience in a letter to Columbia producer George Avakian.

Then, sort of to educate Mildred (not to mention me) she got off on the subject of the old *unaccompanied* chants, such as those of Dr. Watts (real old time stuff) and sang these for over an hour. Really beautiful and un-usual stuff that white people practically never get to hear. In all my years of going to hear Mahalia in Negro churches I never heard these until six months ago. In the churches they're always done by the old timers in the congregation (with a leader).[31]

Russell's recordings of these three Dr. Watts hymns are a treasure for students of American vernacular music, offering an extraordinarily rare opportunity to hear a singer of Jackson's power and eminence demonstrate this repertory as she learned it in the pews. The rendering of these hymns would likely vary from region to re-gion and congregation to congregation, and it is not clear whether Jackson learned these particular versions in New Orleans or in Chicago. In one of these Dr. Watts demonstrations, "Before This Time Another Year," Jackson modeled the leader-group division of labor by first singing a line and then repeating it in a much more drawn out fashion. Despite having a steady pulse, the gospel quartet ar-rangement of "Before This Time Another Year" recorded in 1952 by the Chosen Gospel Singers, led by tenor E. J. Brumfield, still manages to capture some of the freedom of Dr. Watts singing.[32]

Jackson's free triple-meter hymns do not reproduce Dr. Watts singing per se. They are, however, guided by a performance practice influenced by lined-out hym-nody, and Jackson brought aspects of this vocal style to her performances of the hymns that she recorded for Apollo. One of these, the Christmas carol "Silent Night," captured the imagination of audiences beyond black church communities. Jackson's recording of "Silent Night," a song published in the *Baptist Standard Hymnal*, made a deep impression on Marshall Stearns, who featured Jackson at his "Definitions in Jazz" roundtable at the Music Inn in Lenox, Massachusetts, in the fall of 1951. In the opening pages of his jazz history text *The Story of Jazz*, Stearns offered readers a description of Jackson's vocal style—and the corroborating testi-mony of an anonymous black vernacular voice—as documentation of one of "the qualities that make jazz a little different and immediately recognizable" as African American music.

> At her annual concert at Carnegie Hall, Mahalia Jackson, "Queen of the Gospel Singers," creates an almost solid wall of blue tonality. It's not a matter of tempo. She'll sing a slow tune that we all know by heart, "Silent Night," for example—adding embellishments that take your breath away. As a member of a Sanctified Church in Mount Vernon once told me: "Mahalia, she add more flowers and feathers than anybody, and they all is exactly right." She breaks every rule of concert singing, taking breaths in the middle of a word and sometimes garbling the words altogether, but the full-throated feeling and expression are seraphic.[33]

A year after "Definitions in Jazz," Jackson recorded an interview for Danish State Radio that was broadcast throughout Scandinavia as advance promotion for her first European tour in fall 1952. Following the broadcast, Jackson's recording of "Silent Night," recently released in Europe on Vogue, reportedly sold 20,000 copies. According to Jackson, "Silent Night" was also the recording that piqued the interest of Mitch Miller enough for him to recruit Jackson away from Apollo and sign her at Columbia. In an interview on an unidentified television show, Jackson said that Stearns turned Miller onto her music around the time of his Music Inn roundtable: "They were studying this type of music and they had me, and that's how Mitch heard me. I made 'Silent Night.' He brought it to Mitch['s] attention."[34]

The "embellishments" and "flowers and feathers" that Stearns found so breathtaking in "Silent Night" refer to Jackson's ornamentation of the tune with vocal gestures indebted to Dr. Watts hymnody, though gospel novices likely enthused so strongly over the record because of the familiarity of the tune and the unfamiliarity of the approach. Novel or updated readings of "oldies" were in vogue in the 1950s popular music industry, as demonstrated by the flood of traditional religious songs recorded by pop stars. But "Silent Night" was in fact one of the more conservatively elaborated hymns that Jackson recorded for Apollo. A particularly dramatic approach is taken on Tindley's "A City Called Heaven," also known as "Pilgrim of Sorrow," a showpiece for Marian Anderson, the Hall Johnson Choir, and numerous male quartets in the 1940s, and 1950s and a fixture of Jackson's repertory in years to come. Jackson is also more deliberate and sounds particularly connected emotionally on her recordings of "Even Me" from the *Baptist Standard Hymnal* or "A Child of the King" and "I Do, Don't You?" from *Gospel Pearls*. Dorsey, at the time pursuing a career as a blues musician, claimed that hearing the "turns and trills" and "touch of the blue note" that singing evangelist W. M. Nix brought to his thrilling rendition of "I Do, Don't You?" at the 1921 National Baptist Convention in Chicago, in part to promote the newly published *Gospel Pearls*, induced in him "a deluge of divine rapture" through which he was "inspired to become a great singer" and gospel songwriter. "The thing that sold the song," remembered Dorsey, "was the personal pronoun, *I*."[35] Likewise, from the controlled filigree of the opening phrase to the rhetorical gesture of juxtaposing a surprising blue third to begin the penultimate line ("I love and adore him") with the ensuing major third, the deeply expressive "I Do, Don't You?," which Jackson approaches with the intimacy of personal testimony, is one of her most outstanding free hymn performances.

A song on which Jackson takes even more extraordinary liberty is "Amazing Grace," the popularity of which is suggested by the fact that it is the only hymn recorded by Jackson that appears in both *Gospel Pearls* and the *Baptist Standard Hymnal*. Jackson's disk belongs to a long lineage of performances of "Amazing Grace," commonly sung employing a performance practice that tends toward a Dr. Watts–style approach. In white Regular and Primitive Baptist churches,

"Amazing Grace" is still in fact often sung congregationally as a lined-out hymn. The slow tempo and metrical freedom that black gospel singers bring to "Amazing Grace" is exemplified on recordings of the song by quartet leads like Ira Tucker with the Dixie Hummingbirds (1946) and Claude Jeter with the Swan Silvertones (1962), by women's gospel groups like the Caravans (1962), and by soloists like Sister Rosetta Tharpe (1951) and J. Robert Bradley (c. 1960). Reportedly, Jackson was particularly awed by Bradley's interpretation of the song: "Nobody need mess with 'Amazing Grace' after Bradley gets through with it."[36] Jeter's gripping performance with the Swans blends sustained backing harmonies and an insinuation of lining-out practice through forceful spoken interjections by Louis Johnson. A similar approach is taken by the Spirit of Memphis Quartet on their recording of another Dr. Watts hymn, "The Day is Passed and Gone." As recently as March 2014, Aretha Franklin, who is closely associated with "Amazing Grace," sang the song in this free manner for the PBS-televised "Women in Soul" tribute concert hosted by President Barack and First Lady Michelle Obama in the East Room of the White House. More dramatically, Obama himself sang "Amazing Grace" in his best simulation of this style at the June 29, 2015, memorial service following the murders of nine worshippers at Emanuel AME Church in Charleston, South Carolina. Within the structure of Baptist devotionals, Dr. Watts hymns immediately precede a prayer, and at the end of a hymn members of the congregation often continue intoning the song on a hum or a moan behind the leader as he or she prays. Jackson's recording of "Amazing Grace" perhaps invokes this convention when she sings through the verse and then hums the first half of the tune. More idiosyncratically, the syllabic fracture of individual words in Dr. Watts texts when lined out by black Baptist congregations might be a partial explanation for Jackson's occasional treatment of lyrics as abstract vehicles for melodic content, as, for instance, when she opens the song by singing: "Amay ahn grace."[37]

Hybrids

Finally, a handful of Jackson recordings for Apollo were variously combined hybrids of these three types of songs (Example 6.6). Each of the three feels discussed above can be situated along a continuum from slower to faster tempo—extending from free to gospel to swing—and, not surprisingly, in her hybrid recordings Jackson always uses a slower feel to set up a mid-song shift to a faster one. In an interview with dance historian Mura Dehn in 1952, an African American "coach-arranger and composer" in Harlem identified only as "Mr. Johnson" claimed that the use of accelerated tempo in certain songs was a novel device at mid-century, indeed "the only thing that is new in gospel singing."[38] On the double-sided "Just Over the Hill" and in "Nobody Knows the Trouble I've Seen," the transition is from a free-tempoed, unmetered opening verse to swing for the chorus. Part of

---

EXAMPLE 6.6

Mahalia Jackson "Hybrid" Feel Songs Recorded for Apollo

If You See My Savior	Free	—> Gospel
Just Over the Hill	Free	—> Swing
These Are They	Gospel ($\frac{3}{4}$)	—> Swing
I'm Getting Nearer My Home	Gospel	—> Swing
In the Upper Room, Parts 1 and 2	Free	—> Gospel
Nobody Knows the Trouble I've Seen	Free	—> Swing

---

the effect of these records is the emergence of a solid pulse from the metrical "void" of the opening. Part two (i.e., the B-side) of "Just Over the Hill" features some of Jackson's most in-the-pocket swinging on record. "If You See My Savior" and "In the Upper Room" begin free and move to a gospel feel, making for a gentler transition. "In the Upper Room" is singularly unique because of Jackson's multiple roles. The Melody Echoes, whose gospel quartet–style chanting ("*In the upper room . . . In the upper room . . .* ") sits on the "2-3" end of the seesaw, are particularly prominent and forward in the mix. Midway through the flipside, Jackson switches to the chant and becomes a backing vocalist in a duet with the bass singer who, in a stock device from 1950s doo-wop, takes the lead. The reversal of the seesaw roles thus becomes part of the song's arrangement. It is the only instance I know of on a Jackson record when another singer carries the lead, though it does not last long: in a wonderful and even stagey effect, Jackson's increasingly exuberant singing of the backing part gradually percolates to the surface and midway through the chorus is transfigured into a new lead that fully eclipses the bass.

A third hybrid type is represented by "I'm Getting Nearer My Home" and "These Are They," which begin with a gospel feel and modulate to swing. "I'm Getting Nearer" is an illuminating example that, on top of the change in tempo, vividly illustrates the differently accentuated beats of the quadruple-meter seesaw versus the "four-to-the-floor" emphasis of swing that make these two feels recognizably distinct. "These Are They," discussed in Chapter 1, features the double contrast of a switch in feel and in meter, moving from a triple-meter gospel seesaw to $\frac{4}{4}$ swing. Notably, three of these hybrid records, "Just Over the Hill," "I'm Getting Nearer," and "These Are They," are songs by Brewster, who specified the mid-song shift in the published sheet music. A hybrid of a different sort and one of Jackson most deliciously rollicking records is "Walking to Jerusalem," which stubbornly maintains a tension between straight and swung eighths that goes "back home" to

EXAMPLE 6.7

Mahalia Jackson Religious Pop/Popular Religious Songs Recorded for Apollo

I Walked into the Garden

Bless This House

The Lord's Prayer

It Is No Secret

I Believe

Hands of God

No Matter How You Pray

My Cathedral

capture a swampy New Orleans rhythm and blues groove in the spirit of Professor Longhair. The extended stretch of verse couplets from 1:26–2:34 is a magnificent minute of music, again, to my ears, offering a foretaste of what we would later hear from Mavis Staples and perhaps even a tantalizing glimpse of what Jackson the soul singer might have sounded like.

Religious Popular Songs

At Apollo, Berman encouraged Jackson toward religious music that was more broadly familiar or in a more popular vein (Example 6.7) beginning with her seventh session in October 1950, which included "I Walked into the Garden," "Bless This House," and "The Lord's Prayer." Each of these three songs presented Jackson with distinctive technical challenges and interpretive opportunities. The gradual escalation in dramatic intensity and in register over the course of "The Lord's Prayer" puts a singer on a flattering pedestal—part of its lasting appeal—though potentially out on a limb. This does however, allow us to experience the full ambit of Jackson's voice. As with the equally treacherous "Land of the *free* . . . " in "Star Spangled Banner," the song has a large range that spans an octave and a fifth and eventually reaches a climactic sustained fifth above the upper tonic on "for-*ev*-er." On Jackson's Apollo recording of "The Lord's Prayer," Jackson, accompanied only by organ, takes the song in F, placing the melodic climax at a C, near the very top of her range. Other parts of the song dip to her lowest register; the cadence on "in heaven" takes her down to a husky-sounding F below middle C, which she struggles to project. With the sustained G before this cadence, she has to break "heaven" in the middle of the word to support the low F. Idiosyncratic handling of the phrasing and pronunciation of words is an inescapable feature of Jackson's style—she sings what sounds like "All Father" instead of "Our Father" to begin the song and indulges her Southern "brogue" by pronouncing "earth" as "oyth"—though such liberties feel particularly exposed to the ear in a song as familiar to many listeners as "The Lord's Prayer." When Jackson elevates from the bottom of her range to sing "For thine is the kingdom" in the upper octave (C–F–E–F–A–G), she moves into her vocal wheelhouse, progressing from her precariously breathy bottom to her confident chest voice. After the ascent to the high C on "forever"—which, despite possessing an almost operatic power, she shies away, hurrying to and away from the slightly strained pitch—the song ends back in her comfortable midrange.

Jackson would have undoubtedly heard "The Lord's Prayer" often at services and musicales in Chicago and it remained an important number in her repertory throughout her career. Evidence of the song's possible significance to her and its reception by audiences is the fact that four years later she performed the song on the debut episodes of both her national radio show and her local television show in Chicago. In many respects, her radio performance with the Jack Halloran Quartet surpasses the more tentative Apollo recording in confidence and refinement. On her television show, *Mahalia Jackson Sings*, Jackson, in set-up dialogue with host Jim Conway, introduced the song in an unexpected way.

CONWAY: Can you remember the first spiritual that you ever sang?

JACKSON: Oh, well, I been singing so many spirituals, but I can remember this particular song, "The Lord's Prayer."

CONWAY: You think that you'd like to sing that? This is Sunday, this is your first television show.

JACKSON: Yes, and this is my first television show of my own and I'm so thankful and grateful 'til I think that this song would be quite appropriate, "The Lord's Prayer," thanking him for this wonderful opportunity to be on CBS.[39]

Surely Jackson did not mean to insinuate that "The Lord's Prayer" was a spiritual, and since it was only written in 1935 she could not have known the song until after she moved to Chicago. But Jackson seemed to want to communicate to her audience that "The Lord's Prayer" existed alongside spirituals and other church songs in the regular musical worship of mainline black Baptists.

Jackson's incremental mastery of "The Lord's Prayer" suggests how in 1950 she was still finding her way toward interpreting songs with more sculpted melodic profiles. Other than the *ad libitum* tempo, approaching the feel of a free triple-meter hymn, and scattered ornamental flourishes, Jackson delivers "I Walked into the Garden" with a conspicuously conservative approach to the melody,. She also sings the melody of "Bless This House" relatively strictly, though she sounds less expressively straitjacketed by the tune. This is partially due to the respective melodies. The tunesmith's hand feels heavier in the deliberately crafted melodic contour of "I Walked into the Garden"—for instance, in the athletic opening octave leap and the chromatic coloring—than in "Bless This House," in which the triadic and stepwise movement, affecting the artless innocence of a children's song, is designed to express a humble prayer. "Bless This House" shares the same on-the-beat rhythmic regularity (and remarkably similar opening melodies) with the "Alphabet Song" song, which seems to give Jackson more freedom to phrase according to her will than did the insistent two-bar syncopated rhythmic motive of "I Walked into the Garden."

Both songs, sung at a loose tempo, are representative of Jackson's leisurely approach to more lyrical non-gospel numbers. Because Jackson takes "Bless This House" so slowly, most of the second verse is cut, and after the piano interlude Jackson moves directly to the final line to fit the three-minute record. "I Walked into the Garden" only reaches as high as an A above middle C, right in the meaty part of Jackson's range, so in certain respects she sounds more vocally relaxed than in "Bless This House." In the latter, as in "The Lord's Prayer," a high C on "dwell" is the melodic and dramatic peak of the tune and Jackson again sounds like she is at the upper limits of her comfort zone; in fact, this time, trying to sustain the C, she peters out on the pitch. Still, judging from the two Apollo recordings, it is clear that Jackson felt more expressive freedom reading "Bless This House" than "I Walked into the Garden," and the song remained a part of her repertory in subsequent years. Berman, too, must have considered the former a superior record. "Bless This House," backed with "The Lord's Prayer," was released in September 1951, but "I Walked into the Garden" was withheld until 1955, well after Jackson had already left Apollo to sign with Columbia.

Jackson's other Apollo date with a heavy dose of inspirational pop came almost exactly three years later: an October 1953 session at which she recorded "Hands of God," "No Matter How You Pray," and "My Cathedral," backed by the African American Belleview Choir of Portsmouth, Virginia. All three were new songs copyrighted in 1953, the latter two by veteran songwriters Ben Machan ("No Matter How You Pray," with words by Blanche Allen) and Mabel Wayne ("My Cathedral," with words by Hal Eddy). In light of Berman's track record and the neat AABA structure straight out of Tin Pan Alley, the third song, copyrighted as "Hand of God" with Jackson credited as the sole songwriter, was likely written by an undetermined composer. Jackson tries to breathe life in "No Matter How You Pray" with occasional falsetto flights, but her approach on these inspirational songs for the most part tends toward deliberate and unadventurous reserve, again with notable fidelity to the melody and a minimum of the ornamentation heard in her free hymns. Together, the three songs communicate recurring themes in 1950s inspirational pop songs penned in an era of Cold War religiosity: the power of prayer, the balm of faith in a menacing world, God's omnipresent benevolence, and the unassailable sanctity of the Christian home. Standing alone in type is the slightly bizarre and experimental sounding "My Story," a minor-mode song recorded at Jackson's final session, on which she sings rhymed couplets over austere and slightly "out" jazzy organ, bongos, and maracas.

Two religious pop songs recorded earlier by Jackson were perhaps the genre's most paradigmatic hits: "It Is No Secret," from July 1951, and "I Believe," cut in August 1953. On many of these records, there is a sense of Berman, Jackson, and Falls trying to figure out the most comfortable approach to the repertory. The Belleville Choir's high soprano voices, sounding almost theremin-like, tilt the arrangement of "Hands of God" more in the direction of pop production, and "My Cathedral" is performed in an oddly low key, A-flat, which takes Jackson down to a nearly unmanageable E-flat below middle C. More successful is Jackson's recording of Hamblen's "It Is No Secret," a country-leaning song given touches of a $\frac{4}{4}$ gospel feel, especially during the chorus. The considerably slower tempo permitted time only for a single verse, but the reading of the song resulted in a more comfortable-sounding singer. Jackson's inspirational pop sides for Apollo are a precursor of her Columbia recordings in the years to come, which seem to pull off this repertory in a more commercially attractive manner because of the major label budget that enabled Jackson's voice to be captured by better technology and fuller backing.

The reception of Jackson's Apollo output marked a turning point in her career. Not only did her fame grow dramatically among black churchgoers and record buyers across the country, but the admiration of influential white jazz afficionados helped to broaden her visibility within the entertainment industries. An outcome of this transitional moment was Jackson being given a nationally broadcast radio show, a Chicago-based television program, and a high-profile contract with Columbia Records that moved her from an independent to a major label. At the center of it all, however, was Jackson's singing voice, rooted in influences from her youth in New Orleans and heard, even by Jackson herself, against the backdrop of social meanings that shaped her self-identity as an artist.

7

Hearing Voices

MAHALIA JACKSON: THE woman who took Bessie's Smith's blues voice to church, the stylist whose vocal approach some heard as "spiritualized bebop," the black gospel diva whom Ed Sullivan believed "should be in opera." Cross-cutting Jackson's career, reception, and self-identity are a cluster of questions pertaining to the status of her voice, virtually all inflected by issues of race, place, and class. A recurring narrative hook during Jackson's emergence as a pop-cultural celebrity was the presumed incongruity of her illustrious achievements as a singer and her lack of vocal training. Press coverage seemed transfixed by a story of the "Queen of the Gospel Singers," born in a shotgun shack bordering the levee in New Orleans, somehow reaching Carnegie Hall and the concert stages of Europe despite being a completely natural talent untouched by conventional methods of musical cultivation. "Last week untrained but talented Mahalia was rehearsing in Chicago for her own radio show," a 1954 *Time* magazine feature read. "Her arranger, Jack Halloran, suggested that she start singing on the eighth bar of 'I Believe.' Said Mahalia: 'Jack, don't talk to me about bars. What word do you want me to start on?'" The nub of many news stories was the encounter between savvy pros and the "untrained contralto voice" of an "offbeat songstress" too rapt with unmediated self-expression to be distracted by musical formalities.

> When Mahalia Jackson occasionally runs into a new accompanist who, accustomed to orthodox singers, asks her in which key she wants to sing a song, she'll calmly reply: "Don't worry about that, honey. Just play it nice."
>
> "I don't know nothing about that music, I just sing it. . . .I just sing them the way I feel them. It's a natural way of singing like I've been hearing since I was a child going to church."[1]

In such cases, one cannot help but wonder how much of this was either a simple case of misunderstanding or a bit of a put on, an interview subject knowing the juicy quote a reporter wanted to hear. A professional singer utterly indifferent to key is in itself a nonsense. Moreover, as the pianist who knew her best, Mildred Falls, remembered years later, playing for Jackson meant being all "eyes, ears, and fingers," a task, recordings of her home rehearsals reveal, that hardly amounted to just playing nice with the demanding Jackson. "I don't care how hard you worked," said Falls, "it was something else that needed to be done, where she was concerned, to push her a little farther because she *had* more." Robert Anderson claimed that it was he that "trained Mildred to Mahalia's style" since "everybody just couldn't play for Mahalia."[2] Whether she understood her own singing voice as hewed out of the mountain or as one that benefited from the complement of sympathetic accompaniment, it is clear that throughout her career Jackson thought deeply about her voice in relation to voices that she heard around her. Vocal models for Jackson were everywhere—at church, in the streets, on recordings, over radio and television—and she spoke frequently about the expressive impact and social meaning of singing voices. Whatever Jackson may have known or not known about "that music," she had much to say about perceived distinctions between "natural" and "trained" singing voices.

Comments over the course of many years communicate Jackson's considerable ambivalence about her relationship to what American musicologist H. Wiley Hitchcock characterized as "vernacular" and "cultivated" traditions in American musical culture. Hitchcock's distinction is derived from the work of cultural historian and public intellectual John Kouwenhoven, whose 1948 book *Made in America: The Arts in Modern Civilization* influentially argued for extending the common connotations of "vernacular" from language to culture in the United States. Kouwenhoven's project was to persuade Americans to resituate art conceptually from the museum to everyday life, and indeed to broaden the notion of "art" itself, in order to embrace the distinctiveness of a national aesthetic, "a quality in the total sum of our painting, our architecture, our music, or our literature which is distinct from . . . Europe." It was this uniquely homegrown and democratic quality, "the unself-conscious efforts of common people to create satisfying patterns out of elements of their environment," that Kouwenhoven termed "vernacular." In a chapter titled "Two Traditions in Conflict," he delineated how the vernacular crystalized through prolonged reciprocal interaction "with the tradition of cultivated taste which flowed into our national life from the reservoirs of western European culture."[3] Two decades later, in what was to become a widely used textbook, Hitchcock adopted Kouwenhoven's framework to outline "two major traditions in American music."

I mean by the term *cultivated tradition* a body of music that America had to cultivate consciously, music faintly exotic, to be approached with some effort, and to be appreciated for its edification—its moral, spiritual, or

aesthetic values. By *vernacular tradition* I mean a body of music more ple-
beian, native, not approached self-consciously but simply grown into as
one grows into one's vernacular tongue, music understood and appreciated
simply for its utilitarian or entertainment value.

Like Kouwenhoven, Hitchcock perceived the American vernacular to have
emerged in agonistic relation to cultivated aesthetics. If the distinction between
the two was "hardly visible" at the end of the eighteenth century, he argued, "as the
nineteenth century unfolded we can distinguish with increasing clarity two bodies
of American music, two attitudes toward music" at which point "an eventually profound schism in American musical culture begins to open up."[4]

The cultivated-vernacular model is not without its critics and drawbacks. At the
time of its publication, one conservative reviewer of *Made in America* accused the
author of "cultural isolationism" for not acknowledging "meaningful continuity
between west European and American culture" and moreover questioned an un-
bridled celebration of the vernacular that imperiled "an order of esthetic values, an
order of quality which Mr. Kouwenhoven now proposes that we scrap." Hitchcock's
contrast of the "moral, spiritual, or aesthetic values" of cultivated music traditions
with music "appreciated *simply* for its utilitarian or entertainment value" already
carries idealist biases and assumptions that make the duality problematic as a reliable rubric for analysis. More relevant, black musical worship itself calls into question the utility of rigid distinctions and oversimplifying dichotomies. Instructive
in this regard is the reminder from African American theologian Charles Adams
that black church music is in fact "splendidly various as it runs the gamut from
classical hymns and anthems to the sophisticated arranged spirituals to the raw,
unadulterated spirituals, to the Black metered hymn to the jazz, improvised gos-
pels. . . .The Black churches which I know do not force the worshipper to choose
between J. S. Bach and James Cleveland." In 1949, Dorsey explicitly prescribed
this splendid variety in musical ministry: "A well balanced worship service should
consist of a processional hymn, chant of the Lord's Prayer, a hymn that can be
sung by the congregation, two spirituals, two gospel songs, a meditation hymn for
the period of silence, a soul stirring solo (if you have a soloist)."[5]

But if we understand the distinction of "cultivated" and "vernacular" musics
as a recurring *discourse*, without becoming distracted by the separable question of
its truth or actuality in practice, we can recognize the ways in which a socially and
historically situated Mahalia Jackson operated from the premise and implications
of what Hitchcock describes as a "dualistic musical culture" in trying to make
sense of her own practice of voice. To be clear: my objective is neither to reinforce
nor refute the objective validity of this dualism. Instead, I hope to highlight how
greater attentiveness to Jackson's repeated references to this framework for the
purpose of projecting her own sense of herself as a singer makes her thinking

about her personal practice of voice more legible. Moreover, critically interpreting Jackson's comparative assessment of her singing voice both particularizes and extends beyond the Kouwenhoven-Hitchcock model. Judging from her own not always consistent commentary on how singing voices communicate social meanings, Jackson's thoughts on the subject are far more multilayered than have been acknowledged. There can be no question that Jackson was thoughtful about and nuanced in her craft. As the analysis of her Apollo recordings in the previous chapter showed, and as the discussion of her radio show in Chapter 9 will consider further, Jackson had a formidable toolkit of vocal strategies, which is precisely why it is intriguing to register how often she herself contributed to the impression that her singing style was utterly "natural" and instinctive, that, like Topsy, she "jes' sang."[6] In short, the present chapter asks: To what use did Jackson put this discursively constructed distinction between "vernacular" and "cultivated" singing, both personally and professionally?

IN INTERVIEWS, JACKSON regularly credited her expressiveness as a singer to the vernacular traditions of black New Orleans, citing a wide range of influences. Like many Baptists, she maintained an affinity, whether open or covert, for Pentecostal musical worship. "I know now that the great influence in my life was the Sanctified or Holiness Churches we had in the South," Jackson remembered. "We Baptists sang sweet" but singers at the Sanctified church down the street from her home "came out with real jubilation."[7] The sermons she heard in church presented her with another model for vocal performance.

> I would always find myself drawn to the church and it's because I liked the songs and I liked the way that the preacher, the old preacher, would preach in his method. He weren't educated like some of our ministers today, but there was a way that he would preach [that] would have a singing tone in his voice that was sad and it does something to me. Really, it is the way that I sing today, from hearing the way the preacher would preach in a cry, in a moan, would shout sort of like in a chant way, a groaning sound, which would penetrate to my heart.

Jackson also claimed sources beyond the church. She noted her appreciation for the musical sound and affect of black produce vendors in a neighborhood where you could "hear a man coming down the street selling bananas in a tone that was very sad. Or vegetables. A very sad song."[8] Living a stone's throw away from the Mississippi River levee and the train that ran alongside it, Jackson also remembered learning from "the men that used to work on the railroad tracks [and] used to sing" as they laid down ties. In his journal, Bill Russell recorded a visit to Chicago by a "man from the New Orleans levee" whom Jackson's Aunt

Alice claimed "definitely taught Mahalia to sing." Singing to herself as a child, Jackson told the *Chicago Tribune*, "I put in the sadness I heard in the men's voices as they worked on the railroad tracks nearby, and the trains themselves." To a striking degree, Jackson emphasized the quality of sadness in the "back home" voices that she was drawn to—"I still like songs with the 'cry' in them," she told an interviewer—though often for the purposes of communicating the process of spiritual overcoming of material circumstances that for her was the essence of singing gospel songs. "There is a sadness, but always there is the hope and the faith in the Lord and the forgetting of sadness and trouble in praising Him." On another occasion, she linked this quality to black historical experience and a blues hermeneutics. "I have a type of voice I hear people talk about that has a blue note in it," Jackson told another interviewer, "In other words, it has the cry in it. It's sort of hardened, you know."[9]

Jackson recalled hearing the city's top jazz musicians at lawn parties and dances, as well as brass bands, playing syncopated versions of hymns like "Nearer My God to Thee" or "What a Friend We Have in Jesus," in funeral processions returning from Green Street Cemetery in Carrollton or another burial ground "close to the community."

> A lot of our songs that I sing today have that type of beat, because it's an inheritance, things that I've been doing, the things that I was born and raised up and seen that went on in New Orleans. In coming up North, a lot of people have questioned me about the way I sing these religious songs. But I've heard them being rendered this way from a child. So that's why maybe a lot of the songs that I sing they might think it sounds jazzy because the jazz musicians played it, but it was something that I heard from a little bitty girl on up to this day.[10]

Jackson came of age during the rage for the great vaudeville blues divas of the 1920s who appeared in regular succession at the Lyric Theatre in the French Quarter at the corner of Iberville and Burgundy, billed as "America's Largest and Finest Colored Playhouse." The *Louisiana Weekly* ran prominent ads for week-long runs at the Lyric by Mamie Smith, Ida Cox, Clara Smith, Ethel Waters, and Bessie Smith as well as top vaudeville teams like Butterbeans and Susie. "I remember when Bessie Smith used to come to the Iberville Theater [i.e., the Lyric] I always went to hear her," Jackson said. But it was not always possible to find the time or money for trips to the French Quarter to hear these singers live, so their recordings, blaring from nearby black homes, became yet another part of her early musical education. "Everybody was buying phonographs . . . and everybody had records of all the Negro blues singers," said Jackson. "You couldn't help but hear blues." Foremost among these singers for her was Bessie Smith. In perhaps the earliest feature story on Jackson, a 1949 article by Bucklin Moon in the jazz collector's magazine *The Record Changer*, Jackson readily admitted that Smith was the singer that "meant the most" to her growing up and that she "learned to sing by listening to Bessie Smith records."[11] In particular, Jackson admired Smith's "quality of voice. I would listen to the way she would make a tone when she'd sing 'Love, oh careless love.'" In a radio interview, Jackson and Studs Terkel fell out laughing when, in an affected posh voice, she impersonated the lady who approached her at a press junket. "'Oh, tell me dear. Where *did* you get your training?' I said I never had a teacher," Jackson recounted. "The only teacher I know of . . . was the records of Bessie Smith."[12]

For Jackson, the social proximity of sacred and secular songs, even at Mount Moriah youth socials, was a product of relationships with childhood peers who as both churchgoers and fans of popular music would gather at the train tracks at night, "make a fire and sit around and sing songs. Some of them would be spiritual and some of them would be some of the songs that we had heard on some of the records." It was this diverse New Orleans soundscape, Jackson asserted—"songs that I'd hear in the church, songs on the records, songs I would hear on the railroad tracks," along with early jazz played by brass bands in second-line processions—that most profoundly shaped her sense of a vernacularly acquired practice of voice: "This type of singing and this type of doing in the olden days is just me. It's a part of New Orleans people, the things that they do. It's just like eating red beans and rice."[13]

Yet even as a young child "sitting around the altar" at the circuit of churches in the Black Pearl, Jackson perceived a stylistic and experiential distinction between singing by the senior choir and a more individually charismatic vocality through which "the whole church would catch the spirit of the song." When Terkel asked Jackson if there was "some particular person back in your childhood days who first led you onto the road of gospel singing and spirituals," she recalled "a missionary, a woman named Sister Burke." Jackson "liked the way she sang because she didn't sing like the people sang in the choir," but also because of the deeply cathartic, participatory response Burke's singing elicited from the "old sisters" in the congregation.

> That's the way I like. I don't like all the time be listening to soloists. I think if the people would sing in the church—anyplace you are, get the people to sing and they'll forget about their trouble. Cause a lot of times they're listening at your voice and trying to hear how pretty it sounds and if you're making the right notes. But if they forget about all the technical parts about singing and just relax and sing, everybody would feel better.[14]

The pleasure Jackson took in congregational singing derived specifically from its having "a different tone quality than what the choir would have."[15] The persistent references to the "tone" she heard in her various New Orleans influences—in a preacher's moan, in Smith's crooning, in a street vendor's cry, in the sincerity of a congregation's vocalized devotion—highlights her keen perception of and discrimination between musical sounds and the importance she placed on maximally expressive sonic ideals, however untutored. Jackson strongly self-identified as an embodiment of a black vernacular ethos. In a 1962 feature in *Jet* magazine, she stated bluntly and provocatively: "I'm America's most primitive singer."[16] At the same time, these values also indicated her awareness that other qualities of tone were available—for instance, the "pretty" or more "technical" sound of featured soloists and well-rehearsed choirs—and in other contexts she betrayed her sensitivity about a lack of training in this vein.

Even in New Orleans, Jackson had an equivocal intrigue with classically trained voices. Beyond studying the recordings of Smith and other blues singers, she claimed less predictable models from the world of concert music: "I saved all my money to buy records. I bought the records of Roland Hayes, and especially Grace Moore and Lawrence Tibbett. It was from them that I learned diction, the correct way to breathe, and what little I know of technique."[17] A product of Fisk University, Hayes was likely the most acclaimed African American concert tenor in the first half of the twentieth century, popularizing the performance of spirituals on vocal recital programs, along with contralto Marian Anderson and bass-baritone Paul Robeson. Jackson kept pictures of Anderson and Robeson in a hinged double frame on the piano at her Chicago home.[18] Soprano Grace Moore and baritone Lawrence Tibbett were white American singers who performed at the Metropolitan Opera from the 1920s to the 1940s, while gaining pop-cultural currency through appearances in Hollywood films and Broadway musicals. A taste for such voices was also a product of Jackson's upbringing in New Orleans, where opera and light classics were another inescapable part of the city's soundscape. Her reference to such singers is reminiscent of similar comments by fellow New Orleans native Louis Armstrong, who cited analogous influences: "I had Caruso records too, and [pop crooner] Henry Burr, [Amelita] Galli-Curci, [Luisa] Tetrazzini—they were all my favorites. Then there was the Irish tenor, John McCormack—beautiful phrasing."[19]

Registering Jackson's interest in classically trained voices prods us to consider the breadth of her vocal ambitions but also situates her historically. The times in which Jackson lived instilled in her a class politics of voice that she carried with her in the years to come. During the late nineteenth and early twentieth centuries, particularly as music came to occupy a unique role in education initiatives for African Americans, formally trained singing voices were endowed with special value through what was known as "voice culture." Taught at colleges and conservatories, through private instruction, in public demonstrations, and via recorded lectures, voice culture sought to develop a range of techniques identified with concert singing, among them proper breathing, burnished tone, sculpted phrasing, controlled dynamics, clear diction, and refined stage comportment. Georgia Peach called specific attention to her voice culture credentials and their place within a politics of respectability in her 1960 interview with Mura Dehn, pointing to her study with respected black vocal pedagogue Cora Mann in New York as an example of how she was "raised to be a young lady."[20]

Some historical accounts of the early years of gospel in Chicago, resonant with Kouwenbroven's representation of American-style modernism, emphasize an agonistic struggle between cultivated and vernacular traditions. These writers highlight the encounter between the musical values of Northern old-line churches, featuring performances of "dicty" anthems and European concert music, and the preferences of newly arriving Southern black migrants seeking to hold on to familiar styles of worship less beholden to the sonic and behavioral ideals of voice culture. This position is articulated unequivocally and polemically by Dorsey biographer Michael Harris, who argues that the repertory and performance styles featured in many of Chicago's larger established churches were indicative of a "mimicry of white music standards" that set in motion "the deculturative process of old-lineism."

> [T]he cultural mission of old-line churches was based on a weak supposition: black progress was to be undertaken without regard for black cultural heritage. Progress, therefore, was measured in terms of virtual annihilation of as many vestiges of black worship customs as possible. . . .
>
> It is unlikely that any minister, choir director, or anyone else advocating or implementing the new worship standards stated publicly that his goal was to imitate white churches. The imitation, however, was implicit and inevitably occurred. . . .The ethos of white churches was undoubtedly, therefore, the standard.

Though he does not call voice culture by name, Harris sets musical differences observed by Jackson at Mount Moriah Baptist Church into more forceful opposition, describing the existential threat posed by the "replacement of indigenous music practices (such as congregational singing, hand-clapping, foot-patting, and other demonstrative behavior) by choirs directed by trained musicians" until the vernacular was revivified and vindicated by the rise of Dorsey's gospel movement.[21]

Scott Carter has extended an invitation to understand voice culture in a broader context, that is, as not simply a marker of class and regional identities within black communities but as also part of a national project that sought to internally manage the United States' growing imperial stature. Carter considers how racial and ethnic diversification of the American public sphere and the growing influence of the popular culture industries amplified the voices of African Americans and

European and Asian immigrants, creating anxieties among turn-of-the-century cultural elites over how the voice—"more than anything else, the revealer of the presence or absence of culture," in the words of one voice culture pedagogue— should represent the nation-state. The voice culture movement that flourished and peaked between 1880 and 1920, producing over 150 singing manuals nation-wide, represented a discourse of purity mobilized to discipline individual bodies into appropriate national subjects. In conceptualizing the sound and staging of the voice as a means of linking public display of the body and the enactment of appropriate citizenship, voice culture represented an "attempt by the nation's cultural elites to secure their continuing monopoly over the conditions of national, racial, and class belonging."[22]

Recognizing its intrinsic discourse of whiteness, Carter underscores "the racial basis of voice culture" in a national context. Yet these ideals took on distinctly inflected meanings within black communities. Most influentially, voice culture was promoted among African Americans in the early decades of the twentieth century through the tireless advocacy of such black musical pedagogues as Emma Azalia Hackley and Harriet Gibbs Marshall. The overlap of initiatives to produce ideal national subjects described by Carter with the more focused objectives of black "musical social uplift" is clear in a brochure for the Washington Conservatory of Music, founded by Marshall in 1903: "Music—a great factor in race development. Why? It cultures, refines and educates those emotions which make for higher citizenship." But whereas the national voice culture movement sought to address a deficiency by *producing* and *establishing* "standard vocal expressions representative of the nation's cultural, economic, and political achievements," black missionaries of voice culture sought to unlock existing but untapped "art-capabilities of the colored race." Thus we see the remarkable Hackley, who abandoned her career as a concert soprano to travel coast-to-coast giving innovatively hybrid "voice demonstration" recitals, attempting to educate tens of thousands of African Americans in the basic principles of trained singing in free mass voice classes.

Significantly, both Hackley and Marshall eventually incorporated African American spirituals and works written by black composers into the study of voice culture, melding the goals of national citizenship, social refinement, and black cultural pride. With African Americans pressed to prove not just social cultivation but a more fundamental collective capacity and worthiness for citizenship, Hackley argued that the voicing of "fitness" held "great possibilities for racial good" by demonstrating black musical aptitude while also eliciting "an immediate exaltation of race consciousness" through the study of black repertory. Though learning European concert works and singing techniques was an inescapable facet of voice culture, this additional and easily effaced element of *African American* voice culture—that is, situating and appreciating emblems of black cultural achievement directly alongside study of what Jackson called "the technical parts about singing"—complicates easy interpretations of formal vocal training by African Americans as simply a cultural-genocidal aping of "white" manners. When Jackson invoked the symbolic capital of "training" and "musical education," she indexed not only the questions of the technique interwoven with voice culture, but also the multiple meanings activated by listeners when a black voice sounded these values both within African American communities and for white audiences.[23]

"People who heard me sing were always complimenting me on my voice and telling me I should be taking lessons," Jackson said, according to her autobiography. One senses that she was genuinely of two minds, of conflicting attitudes, when it came to the question of "vernacular" and "cultivated" singing.[24] "When you begin to get famous, all sorts of people come and begin to analyze you and ask so many questions," she explained to an interviewer in 1965. "So many kept saying, 'But you've never been to music school!' My goodness, people don't go to music school to sing. You sing what you feel inside you."[25] Perhaps because of her complex positioning within the black gospel field, Jackson mused with striking openness, if inconsistency, about the issue of vocal appropriateness. At the Music Inn in 1951, she deflected elite Baptist criticism of her blues-tinged vocality, casting gospel aesthetics as evidence of contemporaneity, not backsliding: "I'm what you call . . . the *modern* gospel singer. I suppose the one that they claim that has brought a lot of sin in the church—the blues. It wasn't my intention. I just wanted to sing, and I sing with what God gave me. If I had a blues voice and wanted to give it to the glory of God, that's what I tried to do." Jackson explained singing gospel songs with "a little bounce on it" as, in part, an intentional choice made to accommodate "the way folks like music" in "the modern day."[26] In a 1952 interview with Jules Schwerin, Jackson, with signifying inflection on the word "art," defended black vernacular vocality against those who devalued its aesthetic validity.

> Some people, I think, was a little 'shamed of folk songs and gospel songs because it didn't take a lot of long studying. It was a simple song of people's heart and sometimes folks didn't even think that was *art*—what they called *art*—something that is complicated and goes through a period of study. But something that came from the heart was I suppose a matter of too simple to be accepted.[27]

The tension between freedom and self-consciousness spanned speech and song. Jackson's diction became an issue when she was touring with Dorsey, who Sallie Martin claimed "tried to check her on some of her ways of saying her words." Martin believed that it was Jackson's erratic pronunciation that brought her collaboration with the songwriter to an end in the early 1940s, causing "trouble with Mr. Dorsey . . . so they stopped traveling together." Jackson believed that this complication was also a matter of training. "Because I was uneducated," she told Goreau in a 1967, "I had to even learn to speak so that people could understand me. When I come from New Orleans, I had that brogue, you know, and I still have it, but even in singing it was hard sometimes to understand." Back home, "people sang like they felt. They didn't worry about their diction, or their words. They just went on and sang."[28]

From Dorsey's perspective, however, Jackson's commitment to gospel singing brought with it the requisite of proper training that was already part of the NCGCC's foundational mission in the 1930s. Jackson apparently approached Dorsey and asked him to be her vocal coach, after which he "took two months out to train her." Dorsey characterized his work with Jackson in terms that are resonant with core concerns in classical training, even if they are tailored to the specific practice of gospel singing: vocal production (teaching her how "to breathe correctly, and to use her voice with ease . . . and to smooth the roughness out of her singing"); effective pacing, timing, and taste (how to "shake at the right time; shout at the right time"); ornamentation (how to execute "trills and turns and the moans of expression"); and even repertory choice and concert design. "I taught her a number of slow, gentle, sentimental types of songs, so that her full program would not be all of the fast shouting types of songs," said Dorsey. Far from representing incidental or experiential training, these recollections of what Harris describes as Dorsey's "pedagogical sculpting of Jackson" indicate a highly self-conscious inculcation of technique, suggesting that the social meanings attached to certain types and contexts of training were at least as significant as the fact of "training" itself.[29]

Despite her self-study of recordings and work with Dorsey, Jackson found it "very unfortunate not to be educated the way I had always desired to," both in school and vocally. Before a gospel program in Detroit in September 1953, she granted an interview to Robert Nolan of the African American newspaper the *Detroit Chronicle*. Again, Jackson seemed to know her audience, or at least the pedigree of her interviewer. Besides being a music critic, Nolan, a graduate of Howard University and "a pianist and accompanist of national repute," was one of Detroit's elite music teachers, Dean of the Robert Nolan School of Music and the National Association of Negro Musicians' organizer for the state of Michigan. Jackson told Nolan of her regret that she had not been given the opportunity by her "parents" to study voice culture and cautioned aspiring black singers to steer clear of rugged gospel belting, however inspired, and learn to produce proper vocal tone.

> Years ago when I had a youthful voice, my parents could not afford to pay a teacher to train me. My only means of learning anything vocally, was by sitting and listening to phonograph records by Lawrence Tibbett, Bessie Smith, the blues singer, Marian Anderson, and Grace Moore. . . .I don't

advise our present generation of young singers to resort to this kind of shouting—but rather, get a good musical education.

At one point during their close association, Jackson asked Bill Russell to teach her how to read music, primarily to help her learn the new songs suggested by CBS and Columbia more efficiently. During their first lesson, Russell recalled, the phone rang, Jackson talked for a half hour, and never did resume the lesson—"and that ended it."[30]

If Jackson offered conflicting opinions about vocal training, many white observers—including Russell, who was wary of Jackson learning music formally—savored Jackson's voice precisely for striking their ears as untutored. In 1950, Jackson's early Apollo sides were released in Europe for the first time, drawing the attention of jazz discophiles. These recordings were praised lavishly by British music critic Max Jones, who in a review for *Melody Maker* wrote that Jackson and Bessie Smith both possessed "great 'natural' voices, untaught from the academic viewpoint (luckily for us)," further noting that Jackson's singing "leaves you unprepared to listen afterwards to any but the greatest musicians."[31] Other writers introduced Jackson to their readers as a more appropriately vernacular alternative to concert spirituals as rendered by cultivated black recitalists. In 1951, a reviewer for the Italian magazine *Musica Jazz* positioned Jackson in relative terms.

> One should not think that she has something in common with the celebrated Marian Anderson, who, though black, comes closer to the tradition of European singing. Jackson, who was born in New Orleans forty years ago, has, on the contrary, remained faithful to the traditions of her race; her singing has preserved all of the brute expressivity of Negro musical folklore, the same expressivity that is essentially characteristic of blues singing.[32]

Correlation of the voices of Jackson and Bessie Smith became a staple of the gospel singer's reception. Perhaps more surprising is Anderson's recurrence as a point of reference. In December 1938, Jackson and her accompanist Estelle Allen embarked on an evangelistic tour of the Cleveland area. Advance publicity billed her appearance as a preview of Anderson's upcoming recital: "Though the celebrated Marian Anderson does not come . . . until February, many Clevelanders who have heard Miss Mahalia Jackson, young contralto solo evangelist of Chicago, say she is a foreshadow of what is to be expected in the early part of next year." Desite being likened to Anderson in Cleveland, Jackson remembered that in those days she was also "criticized by a lot of my own folks" who were skeptical of gospel singing and "didn't think any music was anything but the great Marian Anderson."

Overseas, however, the tenor of Jackson-Anderson comparisons in the early 1950s consistently invoked a cultivated-vernacular distinction to praise Jackson at Anderson's expense, as in the *Musica Jazz* review. In May 1952, *Pittsburgh Courier* columnist Izzy Rowe received a letter from a reader in Tel Aviv, Israel, invoking the cultivated-vernacular distinction to describe how listening to such "folksingers as Leadbelly and Leroy Car" was his gateway to Jackson.

> That's how I discovered there was, among so many others, a Mahalia Jackson. And don't be surprised to read Mahalia Jackson instead of Marian Anderson for I like best those spirituals which are sung in the spirit in which the people sing in the churches. And that spirit is more gen-uine in the ecstatic singing of Mahalia Jackson than in the more refined interpretations of Marian Anderson. Concert-type interpretations of folk songs are not very much to my liking. I like the music of the people.

That November, *Baltimore Afro-American* columnist Ollie Stewart reported on Jackson's first European tour: "Mahalia is just about the hottest thing to hit Paris in a long, long time. French newspapers, comparing her to Marian Anderson, said she was more 'moving' than the great contralto." When "pop gospel" be-came the rage in the early 1960s, performed at gospel-only cabarets like the Sweet Chariot in New York's Times Square, Jackson disapproved and seemed vindicated by success on her own terms, though the yardstick remained Anderson. "They say everybody else is making it, going into night clubs," she told Leonard Feather. "I don't have to. I go into all the big concert halls Miss Marian Anderson goes into." The triangulation of Mahalia Jackson, Bessie Smith, and Marian Anderson—and more specifically the counter-positioning of Anderson and the concert spiritual vis-à-vis Jackson and gospel singing—indicates more nuanced and more histor-ically situated ways of hearing voices than the go-to Jackson-Smith homology that yoked Jackson to the blues and sequestered her from more formally trained voices.[33]

A different perspective was offered by Moon. In some ways, Moon followed a predictable script when he told Jackson that "hers was the greatest untrained voice, with the possible exception of Bessie's, that I had ever heard." But Moon's reflection upon Jackson's aspirations and self-assessment as a singer, and not merely in his own phenomenal experience of her voice, made his *Record Changer* feature one of the more circumspect pieces of writing about Jackson at any point in her career.

> When she got to Chicago she had wanted to become a classical singer, but there was no money for lessons and no one to provide the means. It was almost, she told me, as though she had two voices. Her outer voice, the one

that she used the most, was the lower register; the other voice, the one that she hoped to develop, was at the upper end of her vocal range.

From one perspective, Moon mused, Jackson was "lucky" that she never received formal training that might have compromised her natural style: "Had she gotten a teacher who did not know his business this ease might have gotten lost." But, not knowing the future heights of Jackson's career as a gospel singer, he was ultimately able to create distance from his own pleasure, considering her voice and accomplishments with a rare self-reflexivity: "Sitting there I wondered what might have happened if she had found the proper teacher, how far she would really have gone."[34]

A key takeaway from Jackson's comments over the years is her clear understanding of vocal training as inseparable from socioeconomic advantage. She remembered saving her pennies to buy classical records, being unable to afford a voice teacher as a child in New Orleans despite her recognized talent, and having "no money for lessons" when she moved to Chicago. But Jackson's calculation of the value of a "good musical education" maps out a more complex terrain of meaning. Jackson liked to share the story of her "one and only singing lesson," though the narrative details varied from one telling to the next. In one version, as reported by Russell, she shared with the audience at a church program in Chicago her reminiscence of spending a portion of her first-ever earnings as a gospel singer—$4.00 from a program at Pilgrim Baptist Church—on a lesson in black voice culture with Pilgrim's minister of music, George A. Gullatt.

> She took out $1.50 from the $4 and went to Professor Gullatt to have her voice trained, and that meant a *big* job she said. Professor Gullat could teach both anthems and the "Negro Spirituals" (that were born in slavery she said). The first song he "taught" her was "It's Me Oh Lord—Standin' in the Need of Prayer." But he didn't really have to *teach* it to her because she had sung it ever since she was a little girl in Louisiana.[35]

In a story from her autobiography, likely massaged somewhat through Wylie's literary license, Jackson recalled the painful episode of a lesson with Professor DuBois, "a great Negro tenor" who "didn't think much of my way of singing a song," particularly the "hollering" that DuBois told her was "not a credit to the Negro race." Jackson came away "hurt and angry" from this head-to-head confrontation with a black politics of respectability, an experience that she reportedly characterized as a crisis of artistic conscience and a personal turning point.

> I felt all mixed up. How could I sing the songs for white people to understand when I was colored myself? It didn't seem to make any sense. It was

a battle within me to sing a song in a formal way. It felt too polished and I didn't feel good about it. I handed over my four dollars to the Professor and left. . . .It turned out to be my one and only singing lesson. I haven't had one since.[36]

A third and more detailed version of "The Voice Lesson," one that seems to blend the Gullatt and DuBois encounters, appears in *Just Mahalia, Baby*. It offers a taste of Goreau's voice as a biographer while also suggesting how the features of the story, like Jackson's performance of a gospel song, morphed in expressive strategy and meaning through each iteration. Jackson's reputation as a house wrecker in Chicago's black churches was undeniable, Goreau writes.

> But no getting around it, she wasn't educated. Then one of the girls from Salem said she was going up to audition for Professor Kendricks, see if he'd give her some lessons, Halie went along: $4 each—big money. It was still the South Side, his studio, but she'd never been face to face with so grand a man: the tall, light-skinned tenor holding himself as if he were still on the concert stage. Bolder than her friend, Halie tried it first—a spiritual. But the professor's pianist started so slow, Halie had to pull on up, pick up the beat. The great man stopped her. He demonstrated how it should be sung: with dignity—stage presence. Halie started again: the rhythm wouldn't hold back. Prof Kendricks had enough. . . . "Young woman, you've got to stop that hollering. That's no way to develop a voice, and it's no credit to the Negro race. White people would never understand you. If you want a career, you'll have to be prepared to work a long time, to build a voice."
>   . . . When they hit the street, Halie gripped the ground. "I'm not studying his high-class stuff! I'm not singing for white people! I'm singing in the church, for myself!"[37]

The shape-shifting "Professors" and plot points in the narrative of Jackson's voice lesson, as relayed through her three documentarians, surely indicate each writer's personal investments and their interpretation of what "the story," with all its vagaries, meant to Jackson. Russell's version emphasized questions of epistemological authority: What did it mean to "know" the spirituals when Jackson through vernacular exposure had already learned the knowledge to be dispensed through Gullatt's cultivation? In Wylie's telling, DuBois brought to a head Jackson's "battle within," pitting "my way of singing a song" and the "formal way," and the cultural-political imperative of averting discredit to the race by acquiring sufficient cultivation for white listeners to "understand" black vocal performances. Goreau echoed themes from the DuBois version while introducing still other issues: Jackson's rejection of the prolonged labor of voice culture in favor of the instant gratification of her own irrepressible rhythmic instincts, and the class dynamics of the "uneducated" Jackson standing face-to-face with the "grand" and "light-skinned" Kendricks, force-feeding her his "high class stuff."

But the various re-tellings of the story—perhaps cobbled together from multiple incidents—ultimately point back to Jackson herself. In the final analysis, Jackson's "one and only singing lesson" is less important as a factually airtight narrative than for capturing the unstable mix of conviction and uncertainty, defiance and accommodation, that fine-tunes the personal significance of the cultivated-vernacular framework as a discursive trope. "The Voice Lesson" is in fact a story within a story: a ritually recounted autobiographical anecdote that Jackson used strategically to represent the moment in her life and career when she cast her lot with the vernacular and renounced the class politics of voice articulated by black elite uplift ideology. That Jackson repeatedly recalled the popular triumph of gospel music despite earlier criticism of her "suggestive" and "undignified" style indicates that her dramatizing of the choice of the black vernacular tradition over the cultivated tradition was an important vehicle of self-representation for a woman who was constantly in the public eye. But the neat moral of the story, as it has come down through Jackson's biographers, masks the full range of Jackson's feelings about her lack of "education," both in school and as a singer. These feelings, it would appear, emerged less as a rejection of crass deference to potential white audiences than within a more textured history of cultural hierarchies, pedagogical values, and politics of style among African Americans that in music studies is still only beginning to be fully explored.[38]

As Jackson's growing fame carried her to performance settings beyond predominantly black communities, her class politics of voice generated both anxiety and wry humor, particularly in high-profile appearances. Recalling the pressure of her 1950 Carnegie Hall debut, Jackson told Terkel: "I was so afraid to know I'd be standing in the same spot where the great singers [stood], like this great tenor Caruso! And Roland Hayes and Madame [Ernestine] Schumann-Heink and all those big people. Oh, honest to God, I was so afraid!"[39] In May 1955, Russell noted Jackson's thin-skinned defensiveness following her nationally televised appearance on *Arthur Godfrey and His Friends*. In a review of Jackson's performance, *Chicago Daily News* columnist Ethel Daccardo wrote that the singer would have been better served by her local Chicago television production staff than by Godfrey's CBS network crew in New York.

> She evidently misunderstood it as a criticism of herself. She said she didn't know anything about music (fancy singing—words to that effect) and maybe she didn't sing right, etc., and they might find fault with some things, but she *knew* she could tell the story of the gospel and she could sing about that and no one could take that away from her.[40]

One strategy for dealing with her mixed feelings when hearing her own voice in relation to trained singers was playful mockery. A frequent target was her friend J. Robert
Bradley (1919–2007). Jackson and Bradley were close friends, though the class politics of voice created a rub. Bradley (Figure 7.1) was born in poverty in Memphis,
Tennessee, and his unusual musical career was shaped by influential mentors. After
coming to the attention of Lucie Campbell, Bradley, still a teenager, toured for several
years with the Goodwill Singers, a gospel group "singing and preaching" under the
banner of the National Baptist Convention. "When I was singing with them, we were
just whooping it up," Bradley remembered, but he eventually was taken under the
wing of Thomas Shelby, the pianist and music director at his church in Memphis,
who broadened his repertory beyond gospel songs. Bradley's description of his study
with Shelby squares with the ideals of voice culture and offers a telling contrast with
Jackson's self-conscious assessment of her own obtrusive "brogue."

> He started teaching me the hymns of the church, gospel music, and some
> classics. He started me in all this. He made me bite a hook that I could

FIG. 7.1 J. Robert Bradley in London in 1954. Courtesy of E. Christopher Jackson,
J. Robert Bradley Estate.

never turn aloose. One of the great classics he first taught me first was "Where'er You Walk" by Handel. . . .Beautiful. He taught me to stand still and sing, keep my chest up and say your words clear. Speak clearly that you could be understood. And that's one of the things that the critics of the world have given me credit for. They said that I spoke well and you could understand what I was singing all the time.[41]

While touring the South as a soloist with Shelby as his accompanist, Bradley was heard at a church program by white composer, folklorist, and Peabody College professor Charles Bryan, who persuaded Bradley to study voice privately with him. Too poor to pay for lessons, though by now well connected within the black Baptist establishment, Bradley, at the recommendation of Campbell, was sponsored financially by Sunday School Board director Dr. A. M. Townsend. Bradley's work with Bryan eventually led to further study in New York and eventually in London at Trinity College, where for three years he pursued advanced work with tenor Frank Titterton, baritone Roy Henderson, and composer Roger Quilter. As a singer, Bradley, who earned the nickname "Mr. Baptist" for his lifelong dedication to the convention, represented yet another distinct positioning within the gospel field, a church and concert artist who, Boyer writes, was able "to sing a gospel song with all the fire of a sanctified preacher and delivered with all the care and cunning of an opera singer." Campbell, who preferred her songs "sung in a classical style," frequently called upon Bradley to debut her latest compositions at the National Baptist Convention.[42]

While living in Chicago in the late 1930s and 1940s, Bradley developed an intimate friendship with Jackson, seven years his senior. Their disparate paths as singers were not lost on Jackson, who enjoyed facetiously calling Bradley "the great artist" and, after having been hurt by the thorny reception from some Baptists, teased him about his coziness with the National Baptist Convention. "She'd always speak of me being 'with the Baptists,'" Bradley remembered. For his part, Bradley was reportedly stung by the news of Jackson's Carnegie Hall debut in 1950, certain that an appearance at the hallowed venue was his own destiny.[43] Jackson was quick to acknowledge her great admiration for Bradley as a singer, though on multiple occasions she also cast his pursuit of a career as a concert artist as a disowning of his gospel roots. "We attended the Baptist Convention together, and he is one great singer," Jackson told Goreau. "But he didn't want to be no gospel singer; he felt that was inferior." Goreau confronted Bradley with Jackson's accusation, telling him "Mahalia said that you initially looked down your nose on this gospel music." Bradley disagreed, reminding Goreau of his years with the Goodwill Singers: "I left Memphis singing gospel music. . . .I didn't get the training until after." In May 1955, Russell watched television at Jackson's home and heard her again raise the cultivated-vernacular question in the context of an admonishment and burlesque of Bradley.

When Mahalia watched the T.V. story of girl who had operatic ambitions, Mahalia talked again about Robert J. Bradley [sic]. He was the best singer, and the best gospel singer she ever heard. Came from hills of Memphis, last saw him in London in '52. It looked like he was ashamed or wanted to get away from the music of his own people. Mahalia told him that as a result God took the power away from him and gave more to her. All he wanted to sing was operatic stuff and she imitated him as she had in Cleveland (repeating "Victorio" over and over up high).[44]

Whether for the purpose of playful sport or curious exploration, Jackson liked to put on a classical voice in private. In home rehearsals for her radio show, it is fascinating to hear her consciously experimenting with a notably different, more concertizing voice on the songs "Danny Boy" and "Going Home." Particularly in her run through of "Going Home," Jackson sings in a highly mannered, quasi-operatic voice with exaggerated vibrato, reduced throatiness, and pseudo-British pronunciation, including conspicuously rounded vowels and rolled Rs.[45]

Other times, Jackson wondered why trained voices were so fetishized in the first place. Russell related an incident that also occurred while watching a television program with Jackson, "a sort of musical, about a girl who had operatic ambitions but had to sing some other type of stuff and dance." The show was an episode of the CBS program *Shower of Stars* entitled "High Pitch," starring singers Marguerite Piazza and Tony Martin, but Russell got the plot only half right. Piazza, who in real life took an unprecedented path to the Metropolitan Opera stage through her appearances on network television, plays opera singer and baseball diehard Dorothy Meadows, who woos the star of a rival team to her beloved Hooligans.[46] In the episode, Piazza, who like Jackson hailed from New Orleans, sings arias from Verdi's *La Traviata*, Puccini's *La Bohème*, and Bizet's *Carmen* as well as "I Hate Men" from Cole Porter's *Kiss Me Kate*. But the big production number—after Martin's character confesses "I don't go for that longhaired stuff"—was Piazza's performance of the rhythm and blues song "Dance with Me, Henry," first recorded by Etta James and at the time a top ten hit as a "whitewashed" cover by Georgia Gibbs.[47] The scene's comedic payoff is reliant upon the viewer's recognition of a cultivated-vernacular divide: the perceived mismatch of an opera diva hip to the latest chart-topping pop. But Piazza's performance of "Dance with Me, Henry," though spirited and liberally seasoned with handclaps and knee bends, is agonizingly square. According to Russell, Jackson found Piazza's effort hysterically goofy, though she also noted its irony: "She got a big kick out of the show when they made the girl do a dance to some late rhythm and blues number (like 'Sha-boom'). Mahalia asked why it is that people talk like the opera music is so wonderful yet everybody *likes* the other stuff (popular-rhythm, etc.)."[48]

Jackson's casual question about the rationale for cultural hierarchies seems appropriate coming from a singer who faced questions about the orientation of her vocal style and repertory throughout her career. If the pleasure taken in "the other stuff" made its value self-evident, what was the source of value for the cultivated tradition? Proponents of voice culture might count edification, uplift, and management of national and cultural subjecthood among these values, but it is easy to dismiss the pleasures of the sound of trained voices and the gratification of the physical comportment of concert performance for singers and their audiences. As Jackson's catholic record buying habits, the co-presence of Sister Burke and the church choir, and the multiple practices of voice embodied by Bradley indicate, the "schism" between vernacular and cultivated traditions described by Hitchcock is more discursive than lived. Nonetheless, as a black Chicago-based church singer who increasingly began to perform for a demographically diversified audience, Jackson's comments and cues in a range of contexts suggest an ongoing calibration of the sound of singing voices with the social values ascribed to them.

It is important to identify and disaggregate these two tracks—biography and sound—in the reception of Jackson's voice in the early 1950s. The story through which audiences were introduced to Jackson, one in which Jackson herself played a central role in crafting, emphasized her humble origins and eclectic vernacularism as she drew on voices heard in the streets, in the pews, and in the grooves of popular recordings, influences seemingly at a far remove from conventional forms of musical training. In 1954, the *Chicago Sun-Times* introduced Jackson as the woman with the "exciting contralto voice" who "is held in esteem by critics and fellow performers," and yet "has never taken a music lesson." A decade later, in 1963, her musical illiteracy remained a set piece: "I never had a music lesson and I still can't read music. I don't know anything about chord structure—I just sing it." Two years before her death, she reminded Goreau, "I don't look at the notes. I can't read a note big as a boxcar."[49] Jackson's lack of formal training and inability to read music notation bears little significance in and of itself, but the ways in which she used musical literacy and the cultivated tradition as a foil against which she could deploy her self-identity as a natural woman is an important subplot of her career. Jackson's positioning as a singer bred in the bosom of vernacular purity was shaped not by her obliviousness to "musical training" but rather by her intimate familiarity with it, through the ideologies and prestige of voice culture that circulated freely and were understood fully within interwar African American communities.

The underlying appeal of this "natural woman" narrative, of course, is the curious delight long taken in essentialist perceptions of black performers possessing innate musical abilities. But the fact that the question of training arose again and again as a talking point in connection with Jackson—almost as expressions of disbelief that a Southern black woman could produce a voice of such magisterial power, projection, and resonance without a "musical education"—offers hints that help us detect how *un*naturally impactful many listeners perceived the sound of her voice to be. As Moon testified, it was, to his ears, "the greatest untrained voice, with the possible exception of Bessie's, that I had ever heard." This cognitive dissonance—between the experience of sound and deeply entrenched ideological expectations—was paralleled by another originating with Jackson herself: the mismatch of the stories she told about her singing and her deeply self-reflective ruminations on the relative prestige of vernacular and cultivated practices of voice. Both perspectives highlight a class politics of voice as a continuous point of reference for Jackson and her listeners. If Jackson's place in the gospel field is singular, it is precisely for how over time Jackson, singing Dorsey songs in the world's most prestigious concert halls, blurred the very cultural hierarchies that preoccupied her since her childhood. We gain some sense of what this process meant for some of her admiring fans when we hear the Los Angeles–based gospel pianist Eddie Kendrix extol Jackson as "the concertizer" who became "sort of like the Pavarottis and the Leontyne Prices of the gospel community."[50] At times defensively though more often with a sense defiant advocacy, Jackson constructed a personal narrative for public consumption reliant upon a historically and culturally distinctive understanding of the vernacular-cultivated divide, even as her vocal performances unsettled it.

8

Gospel According to Bill Russell

SATURDAY NIGHT, APRIL 28, 1951, Jackson was part of an unusual concert at the Wendell Phillips High School auditorium, a regular locale for black gospel programs in Chicago. That evening it was the venue for "'Lift Every Voice and Sing': A Program of People's Music," sponsored by an organization called the South Side Cultural Association and "co-starring" Jackson and folk singer Betty Sanders, with Bernie Asbell and "Others" also on the bill. It had been a rugged week for Jackson, who was returning from a southern tour and recovering from a cold. The previous Sunday afternoon she headlined the "season's biggest gospel sing" at Atlanta's City Auditorium, presented by local gospel promoter Howard Nash, with the Original Gospel Harmonettes and a group led by Roberta Martin Singer Norsalus McKissick. Jackson was also scheduled to appear in concert at the City Auditorium in Texarkana, Texas, presented in conjunction with a meeting of the Southwestern regional chapter of the National Baptist Convention. As it turned out, she did not perform, as rumors circulated among angry audience members, some of whom demanded and received a refund, that Jackson refused to go on when she did not receive the $500 up front that she had been guaranteed.[1]

Jackson hustled back from Texas and arrived at Wendell Phillips just in time for a different type program. Sanders was known as a singer of folksongs in nearly two dozen languages and for her overseas tours for the United Service Organizations (USO) during World War II. Asbell, who in subsequent years became a prolific author and a writing professor at Yale and Penn State, was valued in folk circles as a talented songwriter. At the time of the concert, both were stalwarts of a folk song movement that was closely, and with increasing risk, associated with the politics of the Left. On December 31, 1945, a group of folk singers, union educators, and progressive-minded choral directors met in the basement of Pete Seeger's Greenwich Village apartment and founded People's Songs. Determined "to spread [folk songs] around, to bring to as many people as possible, the true democratic message that came out of this music," the members of People's Songs, including Woody Guthrie, Alan Lomax, and Sanders, collected folk songs, published songbooks and a monthly bulletin edited by Asbell, led classes on the use of music for political action, and performed at labor rallies and at live, participatory variety shows called hootenannies. Morale on the Left was severely undercut by fierce anticommunist reaction to a tide-turning series of events in 1949: Paul Robeson's comments in support of the Soviet Union in Paris, a benefit concert starring Robeson halted by a violent riot by conservative locals in Peekskill, New York, and the polarizing Waldorf Peace Conference in Manhattan. People's Songs folded that year, its dispersed members taking cover from the gathering tsunami of McCarthyism. It regrouped institutionally a year later as People's Artists, with Asbell continuing to be its point person for folk singing activity in Chicago. Historian Richard Reuss has noted that despite Seeger's official leadership, throughout People's Artists' brief existence Sanders "was chairwoman and took a leading role in policy decisions."[2]

"Lift Every Voice and Sing" was thus presented at a precarious, transitional time for the American Left and the folk song movement, though it also came at a moment when the parameters of Jackson's own political calculus were shifting. The Wendell Phillips concert was not the first time that she lent her talent to progressive causes. In April 1947, Jackson, Robert Anderson, Elyse Yancey, R. L. Knowles, the Soul Stirrers, and other gospel singers performed in a program at the Lake County Music Festival at Washington High School in East Chicago, Indiana, sponsored by the black Communist Young Men's Progressive League. A year later, Jackson and bluesman Big Bill Broonzy provided the entertainment at a campaign party in support of Progressive Party presidential candidate Henry Wallace's "program for peace, progress, and prosperity," an event that featured addresses by representatives of the Congress of Industrial Organizations (CIO) and Progressive Citizens of America. By 1952, Jackson proceeded with much more caution. Thomas Doherty has described how during the early Cold War even "a favorable review or a tangential mention" in the American communist newspaper the *Daily Worker* "tarred the recipient with subversive residue" that more often than not led to blacklisting. After a story in the *Daily Worker* publicized a Jackson appearance at a "Peace Rally" on Randall's Island sponsored by the New York Peace Institute, Jackson, through Bess Berman, released a statement denying her participation. Jackson authorized her lawyer to file suit against the *Daily Worker* and the New York Peace Institute "both for improper use of my name and possible danger to my career." Jackson's management team was undoubtedly wary of anything resembling the devastation of Robeson befalling Jackson just as her own star was on the rise. In subsequent comments, Jackson, tapped into rhetoric about "godless communism" and anxieties about perfidy that were common coin during the Red Scare: "I believe in peace, but I also believe in God. You can't truly believe in one without believing in the other. People who talk of peace and cry out against God are false and disloyal. I will never lend my name to their cause."[3] The "Program of People's Music" at Wendell Phillips during the early years of the Cold War might then be read as Jackson's last hurrah with the American Left.

Whatever the presenters' intention for the Wendell Phillips program, Jackson's between-song comments, perhaps directed toward the agnostic People's Artists crowd in attendance, emphasized the personal and Christian meanings of the six numbers that she performed at the concert. "Until we come back to God, we won't be able to accomplish anything," Jackson sermonized before singing "Lord It's Me," speaking as Falls set her up at the piano. "Let us not fool ourself. All things are possible with God." Before Eugene Smith's "I Know the Lord Will Make a Way (Yes, He Will)," Jackson remarked, again over Falls's introduction: "He said: 'I'm the way, the truth, and light' and I'm dependent on God to make my way." Then after a pause, she added, almost to herself: "I love this song." Jackson rounded out the rest of her set with "Pilgrim of Sorrow," the nineteenth-century hymn "Savior, More Than Life to Me," "I'm Glad Salvation Is Free," and Brewster's "Move On Up a Little Higher," which she introduced, with some factual license, as "the first real spiritual out of the church . . . that was put on record [and] that sold more than three million. This is the song that introduced me." Though she never made a commercial recording of the song, "Savior More Than Life to Me" (known alternately as "Every Day and Every Hour") has all the markings of the hymns that were her bread-and-butter—a triple-meter number from *Gospel Pearls*—and thus, based on her recordings, one might expect her to interpret it with a free feel or at a conspicuously slow tempo with interpolated embellishments. But here, in a wonderful performance, she followed the black gospel practice of performing the song in four with a swing feel, a convention that can be heard in recordings of the song by Alex Bradford, Princess Stewart, and Doris Akers.[4]

Documentation of this "Program of People's Music" survives because of one member of the audience who was captivated by Jackson and her voice: lanky forty-six-year-old William "Bill" Russell, a concert violinist, experimental modernist composer, trailblazing historian of New Orleans jazz, music critic, record producer, and avid fan of Mahalia Jackson, whom he was hearing in person for the first time. Like many mid-century jazz experts, Russell assiduously collected and deeply admired Jackson's Apollo recordings, though he already knew of her as early as January 1946, when he heard her sing "Beams of Heaven" on the radio broadcast of a Johnny Myers program at the Golden Gate. Having for a decade recorded living masters of early jazz for his American Music label, Russell hauled his reel-to-reel tape recorder to Wendell Phillips specifically to preserve Jackson's performance. It was a transformative experience. "After I heard her in person," Russell wrote to a friend three weeks later, "I never wanted to hear her records again."

Over the next four years, Russell came to occupy a singular place in Jackson's professional life, voluntarily becoming her unlikely personal assistant and documentarian during a crucial period in her career, comprising the end of her association with Apollo and her signing by CBS and Columbia Records. Fortunately, Russell's hoarding tendencies and obsession with capturing musical sound produced one of the most extraordinary chronicles of any American musician. Russell taped Jackson's public appearances, preserved scripts and recordings of her radio and television shows, and captured her home rehearsals with Falls, occasionally with Russell himself on violin. Most remarkably, Russell, who at one point planned to write Jackson's biography, maintained a journal of her day-to-day activity. He had kept similar diaries of his interactions with musicians since at least the early 1940s. The Jackson log is riveting for how it captures some of the fine-grain texture of her daily life: Russell, a man whom even his closest friends and collaborators characterized as genuinely, if endearingly, eccentric, provides nitty-gritty details about everything from meals, home repairs, and Jackson's steady stream of visitors, to recording sessions, conversations among Jackson and her musicians during road trips, and Russell's own critical assessment of Jackson's performances. In the early-to-mid-1950s, Jackson was still singing actively on a Chicago church circuit etched in often-vivid detail in Russell's journal. Russell describes Jackson's contributions to church programs but also the ministers, worship styles, and physical spaces of Chicago's black sanctuaries. Russell's surviving notes are most concentrated and detailed between the spring of 1954 and the fall of 1955, the period during which Jackson prepared for and executed her transition to CBS and Columbia.

Through close examination of Russell's journal, homemade recordings, and correspondence, this chapter introduces a fresh perspective on Jackson and black gospel in 1950s Chicago. Russell's journal entries—which are illuminating to quote at length—uniquely enable us to assess the reciprocal relationship between what were essentially Jackson's two simultaneous careers: as a constantly-in-demand church singer in Chicago and as a radio, television, and recording star for a major network and recording label. What emerges is the unacknowledged but pivotal role that Russell, one of the more remarkable figures in U.S. musical life during the 1930s, played in facilitating the coexistence of these two spheres of professional activity, which redrew the boundaries of and sources of prestige within the black gospel field. Jackson's identity as the "Queen of the Gospel Singers," both nationally and in the gospel world, relied upon her calibration of the "street cred" garnered through intimate local appearances and the pop-cultural cachet crystalized through performances newly mediated for a broader public.

A Missouri-Born Student of Music

Despite their disparate musical backgrounds, Russell (Figure 8.1) was from childhood already linked to Jackson by the Mississippi River that connected New Orleans and his birth city of Canton, Missouri.[5] Russell was born Russell William

FIG. **8.1** Bill Russell in Chicago, January 1956. Photo by Anatie "Natty" Dominique. The William Russell Jazz Collection at the Historic New Orleans Collection, acquisition made possible by the Clarisse Claiborne Grima Fund, acc. no. 92-48-L.331.862.

Wagner in 1905, the grandson of German immigrants who fought in the Civil War and the son of parents who introduced him to the violin at the age of ten, against his preference to play the drums. He first studied violin with an aunt, then eventually took lessons weekly in a nearby town, "traveling on a Mississippi steamboat the greater part of the year." At the time, a career in music was not in his plans. Russell maintained a practical career strategy, graduating from Quincy Conservatory of Music in Illinois in 1923, the only boy in a class of five, before enrolling in Culver-Stockton College in Canton as a chemistry major. During his first three years at Culver-Stockton, Russell earned a local reputation as a talented violin soloist. He also won fourth prize for a "symphonic caprice" he submitted to a national contest for young American composers sponsored by the *Chicago Daily News*, despite, he confessed, "never having the opportunity to even hear a symphony orchestra" until he was twenty-two years old. Russell received his teacher's certificate in 1926 and for a year taught music and science at a high school in nearby Ewing, Missouri, before deciding that it was time to leave the Midwest and explore bigger opportunities in New York City.

Carol Oja has documented how during the 1920s New York became established as "an energetic force in modern music, offering "unprecedented charm and unlimited potential" to aspiring young composers and performers.[6] Arriving in New York in the summer of 1929, Russell began to pursue his multiplying areas of musical interest, both formally and through self-guided study. He enrolled in the music education program at Teachers College at Columbia University and continued to hone his chops as a player. For a year and a half, Russell took private violin lessons with Maximilian Pilzer, a student of Brahms's close associate Joseph Joachim, and studied conducting with Leon Barzun, while also becoming an active orchestral string player. Russell supported himself in the 1920s and early 1930s by catching work as a music teacher on Staten Island and Long Island and in New Rochelle, where he directed the band and gave lessons while also coaching tennis and his other great love, theater, on the side. Around 1930, he took his first steps toward immersing himself in ethnomusicology. Russell enrolled in courses on "Oriental and African Music" taught by composer Henry Cowell at the New School for Social Research, studied Chinese music privately with Chan Kai Ping, and took a two-month trip to Haiti in the summer of 1932 to familiarize himself with its "native music" and to collect Afro-Caribbean instruments. In 1939, Russell claimed membership in the American Society for Comparative Musicology, the institutional precursor of the Society for Ethnomusicology, founded by Charles Seeger.

Most pivotal in the expansion of Russell's musical horizons was his discovery of jazz. As it had been for Jackson, the sound of jazz was inescapable for Russell during his youth due to its proximity. He heard black dance bands playing during his regular rides on riverboats but paid little notice, and admitted sometimes racing home after disembarking to cleanse his ears of the cacophony heard on the steamboats by furiously practicing violin. But he was able to pinpoint the moment of epiphany: discovering a 78 RPM recording of "Shoe Shiner's Drag" by Jelly Roll Morton's Red Hot Peppers left behind in the Staten Island Academy classroom where he was an orchestra and band teacher. The record only caught Russell's eye because of the bizarre names of the band and the song. Russell took the record home, played it repeatedly, and, fascinated by its sound, began his voracious collecting of interwar recordings of black vernacular music. By the late 1930s, Russell was still on the job market as a music teacher, and on his resume, under the category "Special Musical Training," he boasted: "Owner of probably the world's best record collection (about 2,500 records) of Negro blues." Russell came to be recognized nationally as a preeminent authority on small group New Orleans jazz—big bands struck him as "overweight"—and his research led to his contribution of three cornerstone chapters to *Jazzmen*, the 1939 anthology edited by Frederic Ramsey and Charles Edward Smith. The book had considerable and lasting influence on the reception and study of jazz, recrafting historical narratives by situating New Orleans as the music's originary source.[7] Russell's legend among record collectors grew when during his work for *Jazzmen* he located the previously incommunicado Bunk Johnson (1879–1949) in New Iberia, Louisiana. Johnson was the trumpeter identified by of several of Russell's interviewees, including Louis Armstrong, as one of New Orleans's seminal early jazz figures.

Russell's diversifying interests began to merge and feed each other. Having studied Chinese instruments with Chan, in 1933 he became music director and "a one-man orchestra" for the Red Gate Shadow Players, a pioneering Chinese shadow theater company directed by Pauline Benton. Russell gained proficiency on the *yangqin* (hammered dulcimer), *erhu* (bowed lute), *yueqin* (plucked "moon lute), and several other traditional Chinese instruments. One reviewer wrote that for Benton's productions Russell composed and played "special music, arranged to carry out the Chinese atmosphere in terms we can all appreciate." By 1935, he cultivated enough expertise in traditional Chinese music that he was giving lecture-recitals at which he performed on as many as ten different string, wind, and percussion instruments, including one event described, due either to a typo or a pun, as a program of "Authentic Confusion Temple Music." Russell toured nationally with Benton's group until 1940, making his first trip to New Orleans in 1937, but increasingly the group's various concert stops became opportunities for Russell to scrounge fresh stockpiles of jazz records. In 1936, the Red Gate Shadow Players performed at the White House as entertainment for a Christmas party for Franklin and Eleanor Roosevelt's granddaughter. A breathless Russell arrived late, nearly missing the gig, when he lost track of the time while record shopping at Washington's Quality Music Store.[8]

Meanwhile, Russell continued to compose concert scores, and his works from the 1930s quickly moved him into the vanguard of modern percussion music. It was as a composer working in what he described as an "ultra experimental vein" that Russell William Wagner, believing that there was room for only one Wagner, adopted the *nom de plume* William Russell. Cowell, described by Michael Hicks as a "patron saint of the self-taught," became an advocate of Russell's music and opened doors that enabled it to be heard.[9] Russell's Fugue for Eight Percussion Instruments was published by Cowell's New Music Editions and was programmed at a historic and highly publicized concert at Carnegie Chapter Hall on March 6, 1933. Sponsored by the Pan-American Association of Composers (founded by Cowell) and conducted by Nicolas Slonimsky, the concert was highlighted by the debut of Edgard Varèse's landmark percussion work *Ionisation*. Throughout the rest of the decade, Russell's music—particularly his *Three Dance Movements, March Suite*, and *Studies in Cuban Rhythm*—were programmed with some frequency on modern music programs in New York and especially at experimental percussion concerts, at which Russell was an occasional performer. Russell's compositions were included in a series of percussion music concerts in the late 1930s and early 1940s curated by composer John Cage, then teaching at the Cornish College of the Arts in Seattle, Washington. These Cage-produced programs were de facto showcases for the Cowell circle, featuring the percussion music of Russell, Cage, Lou Harrison, Johanna Beyer, Ray Green, and Cuban composer Amadeo Roldán, all Cowell protégées.

Russell and Cage, seven years Russell's junior, followed remarkably similar paths in these years. Both shared interests in music from the African continent and in experimental techniques, nurtured while they were Cowell students at New School, and they co-authored an article for a contemporary dance journal. Cage hoped to study composition with Arnold Schoenberg, who joined the music faculty at the University of California at Los Angeles in 1936, but Cowell recommended he do so only after first doing some preparatory study in New York with Adolph Weiss, the principal exponent of Schoenberg's technique in the United States. Weiss specialized in "students who, through lack of training, were not ready to study" with Schoenberg. Cowell must have given Russell similar advice because in 1939 the thirty-four-year-old Russell moved from New York to San Francisco to take remedial intersession and summer courses in analysis, composition, and harmony at U.C. Berkeley, before enrolling in UCLA's master's program in music for the 1939–1940 academic year. Russell took three courses with Schoenberg— "Composition," "Harmonic Construction," and "Double Counterpoint, Canon, and Fugue"—supplemented by classes in music history (with Walter Rubsamen) and instrumentation. Russell apparently held Schoenberg in enormous esteem. He saved an article on the composer from the UCLA student newspaper that characterized Schoenberg as a "modern Bach" and toward the end of his year of study with him, Russell published an article entitled "Schoenberg the Teacher" in the Los Angeles–based music education magazine *Tempo*, calling his professor "the greatest living master of composition." It was during his time at UCLA that he composed the jazz-influenced *Chicago Sketches*, which premiered in 1940 in San Francisco with Russell percussively playing the suitcase. Cage was skeptical of "serious music" derived from jazz, which in his estimation too often "becomes rather silly." However, "one must make an exception in the case of William Russell," who may have "lacked the academic skills which would have enabled him to extend and develop his ideas," but produced works that were "short, epigrammatic, original, and entirely interesting."[10]

It was not always easy for writers to capture the breadth and depth of the activities of "William Russell, Missouri-born student of music, composer, authority on hot jazz and the native music of Africa, islands of the Caribbean and the Pacific, and extraordinary performer on percussion instruments." One gets a sense of Russell's reception in 1940 from the San Francisco music critic who identified him simply as having "the largest vocabulary of sound possessed by any musician of the day." Yet with the outbreak of World War II, Russell abruptly moved to Pittsburgh in 1940, took a job working in electronics, and turned his focus to producing jazz records. This was perhaps precipitated by the revered Schoenberg's apparent skepticism of Russell's abilities as a composer: "I cannot help you this time," an exasperated Schoenberg wrote on one assignment. "This cannot be improved by corrections." His career decisively reoriented, Russell began making important recordings of New Orleans jazz musicians for his American Music Records label, especially the series of records featuring Johnson that revived the trumpeter's career. Russell's renewed focus streamlined his reputation and sense of vocation and defined him once and for all as perhaps the world's preeminent expert on early jazz.[11]

"A Person with Her Heart and Body Completely Full of Music"

In the years after Russell tracked down and started recording Bunk Johnson, he followed Johnson from city to city as the trumpeter made his mid-1940s comeback. Once again living in Canton, Russell visited New York for four months to assist with an extended engagement by Johnson's band at the Stuyvesant Casino that opened on September 28, 1945. During his stay, Russell conducted business and socialized with a group of influential white male hot jazz enthusiasts that included Eugene "Gene" Williams, Ralph de Toledano, Ralph Gleason, Rudi Blesh, Barry Ulanov, Herb Abramson, Gus Statiras, and John Cieferskor, all of whom were recording or reissuing older sides by traditional jazz musicians whose careers had been given a boost through the reception of *Jazzmen*. Williams, Gleason, and Russell were all Columbia men and Williams's apartment on Washington Square in Greenwich Village became "a jazz salon for the Columbia crowd," especially after Williams brought Johnson from New Iberia to New York and hosted a gathering for him in the summer of 1942. In the introduction to his 1947 edited collection *Frontiers of Jazz*, which included an essay by Russell on boogie-woogie, de Toledano characterized his circle as "that rare breed of men who thrive on the dust of Salvation Army depots, hock shops, thrift shops, and the backwaters of the record trade, who live for the pleasure of turning up an unknown master, a well-known soloist on a forgotten label, who feel that of such is the kingdom of heaven if they unearth a cache of Claxtonolas or a King Oliver Gennett."[12] They were, in other words, Russell's tribe.

At least since the early 1940s, Russell documented his interactions with musicians and his discophile colleagues in a meticulous journal. On New Year's Day 1946, the Greenwich Village chapter of the American Committee for Yugoslav Relief presented the concert "A Night in New Orleans—A Tribute to the Cradle of Jazz" at New York's Town Hall, co-produced by Abramson and Bernard Katz and emceed by actor and director Orson Welles. Johnson's band was featured, but to Russell the highlight was Ernestine Washington, who, backed by Johnson's ensemble, sang "Just a Closer Walk with Thee," "Where Could I Go But to the Lord," and "Precious Lord, Take My Hand"—"in the camp-meeting 'shouting' manner," the *New York Times* reported. Immediately following the concert, Washington and the Johnson band, accompanied by a small posse of observers that included members of Russell's New York circle, headed to the East Side for an after-hours recording session at Empire Studios overseen by Abramson and his soon-to-be Atlantic Records co-founder Ahmet Ertegun. Russell wrote in his journal that the Washington-Johnson recordings in fact represented Abramson's first efforts "to go into the record biz." Originally cut for Abramson's Jubilee label, the masters were shortly thereafter purchased by Moe Asch for his Disc label and released as "Sister Ernestine B. Washington, acc. by Bunk Johnson Jazz Band," a septet rounded out by Jim Robinson (trombone), George Lewis (clarinet), Alton Purnell (piano), Lawrence Marrero (banjo), Alcide "Slow Drag" Pavegeau (bass), and Warren "Baby" Dodds (drums).[13]

Chapter 4 described how Irving Berman (no relation to Ike and Bess) recorded several black gospel quartets for his Manor, Regis, and Arco labels as early as 1943, becoming the first among the New York independent record makers to tap into Johnny Myers's pool of talent. Abramson's recordings of Washington and other members of the Myers syndicate indicate that early on he was also in the loop and was perhaps the connective tissue between the New York circle of hot jazz collectors and the gospel scene at the Golden Gate Auditorium. Russell's journal indicates that two weeks after recording Washington, Abramson, Williams, and Gleason's wife Jean, attended the Myers concert on January 13, 1946 at which Jackson made her Golden Gate debut.

> Early in January 1946 Mahalia first came to N.Y. and sang over a broadcast from the Golden Gate Auditorium (Ballroom) on Sunday afternoon (Jan [13]) at about 4 pm. She sang only one song, "I Do Not Know" [i.e., "Beams of Heaven"], which Gene [Williams] had [John] Cieferskor to take off the air. Gene went up to hear the program. The Two Gospel Keys were also on the program.[14]

Afterwards, Abramson, on the hunt for more gospel singers, approached Jackson with an offer to record her along the lines of the Washington-Johnson session. "Herb Abramson saw her after the concert and wanted her to record with Bunk's band," Russell wrote, "but Mahalia refused to record with a dance band and a day or two later I heard that she signed with Apollo. Herb then recorded the Two Keys that week."[15]

Russell had been invited to the Golden Gate program, but he was on a self-imposed "economy budget" and decided against spending the $1.50 for a ticket after learning that he could hear a condensed half-hour broadcast of the "singing festival" later that afternoon on the radio. Russell listened to the concert highlights, including Jackson's performance of Brewster's "Beams of Heaven," at Ralph Gleason's apartment.

I got to Gleason's just as program was starting. Mahalia Jackson sounded wonderful, especially in quality, although Ralph said her voice was a little rough and hoarse after a week's singing, although she says a real gospel singer doesn't have to shout (a la Ernestine Washington?). The Georgia Peach also sang but she didn't impress me much.[16]

Jackson had not been in the recording studio since her four Decca sides cut a decade earlier, so the only way to have experienced what she sounded like at this point in her career was to hear her either in person or on the radio. Fortunately, Williams had Cieferskor tape record the Golden Gate broadcast and thus survives Jackson's performance of "Beams of Heaven," preserved on an acetate recording. Like other jazz enthusiasts in the period just after the war, Russell was impressed enough by Jackson's Apollo recordings that he began to collect them all, becoming increasingly enthralled by her voice. Bucklin Moon, author of perhaps the earliest feature story on Jackson, was one of the many jazz writers for whom Jackson's recordings summoned the memory of Bessie Smith. "I'm not so sure that I wouldn't go you one better and say Mahalia has a better voice than Bessie," Russell wrote to Moon in 1949. "Of course I've never heard M. in person, so it's difficult to compare her with Bessie, whom I've heard several times."[17]

The main preoccupations of many early jazz and blues record collectors were re-releasing material that had been recorded in the 1920s and 1930s and cutting new recordings by older musicians considered to be paragons of the style. A major player in this field was John Steiner, a friend of Russell living in Chicago who purchased the massive back catalogue of Paramount Records, the leading producer of inter-war "race records." In 1948, Steiner revived the label, which had dissolved during the Depression. Russell, deciding that a partnership between American Records and Steiner would be "an advantageous arrangement for business purposes," moved to Chicago in June 1950 and took up residence in Steiner's apartment at 1637 North Ashland Avenue in the Bucktown neighborhood, where the two worked in tandem but maintained separate companies. During his six years in Chicago, all spent living with Steiner, Russell worked closely with New Orleans–born musicians who had migrated there, particularly drummer Warren "Baby" Dodds and trumpeter Anatie "Natty" Dominique. But for Russell being in Chicago also meant more frequent opportunities to hear Jackson in person.[18]

His first occasion to do so was the "Program of People's Music" at Wendell Phillips on April 28, 1951, and it is around this time that he began documenting his encounters with Jackson. In a letter to a friend identified only as "C" drafted a few days after the concert, Russell gushed about having spoken to Jackson on the telephone. Jackson had apparently gotten word that he had recorded her and Russell wanted information about an upcoming gospel program at Wayman AME Church.

Right after your most enjoyable letter came I talked with Mahalia Jackson on the phone. She wanted copies of her part of Saturday's program and I had to find out where the church in which she will sing Friday is located. . . . Mahalia asked me suddenly how bad she sounded Saturday night, and before I know it, I was telling her how marvelous she sang, [but] I told her also that I knew her voice wasn't "right" that evening, and I asked if she had been singing too much lately. She said no, that she had a very bad cold Saturday [and] also [that she] was so tired from just returning from Texas that day, that she hadn't known if she could make it. Yet she made the audience shout with joy. Anyway, I was so overjoyed/excited at the thought of possibly hearing her at her best this Friday, and also relieved to learn that her marvelous voice wasn't really starting to wear out after all (as I halfway feared when I heard her Saturday) and also just so happy in general to hear that great warm friendly voice again, even for just a few minutes on the phone that I began thinking *everybody* must hear her.

Russell, still kicking himself for declining the invitation to the Myers program at the Golden Gate five years earlier, tried to persuade his friend that he "should hear Mahalia as soon as possible."

One time I traveled over 5,000 miles (road trip) just to hear Bunk play one afternoon, and I've never regretted it. But for five long years I did regret missing my first opportunity to hear Mahalia in person (in New York 1945–46) and it really took me a long time to catch up with her. In New York one Sunday, she sang up in Harlem at some . . . spiritual "festival" and I decided that I couldn't afford $1.50 to go. . . . I stupidly decided I had to economize, and besides a part of the program was to be broadcast. As soon as Mahalia started her song on the broadcast I knew what a terrible mistake I'd made. I[t] still sends chills up and down my spine just remembering that song. I still had my dollar and a half (for another day or so at least) but what a thrilling experience I could have traded it for. So don't make the same mistake I did. Maybe you'll have 100 opportunities to hear Mahalia, let's hope you and Mahalia both live 100 more years, but who knows what the future holds.[19]

Two weeks later, Russell sent "C" some jazz recordings along with a copy of Jackson's performance at the People's Artists concert. Russell elaborated on his growing infatuation with Jackson's voice, though the follow-up letter, which reads almost like a Credo, also reveals his quirky particularity, phonographic obsessions, and almost guileless passion for the sound and spirit of the music and musicians that he loved, above all his idol Johnson, who died in 1949.

Then there's a home made acetate from Mahalia's April 28th program, although it's rather unfair to her to let out any copies when her voice wasn't in form. But her Apollo records don't do her justice either. I once had all of them but after I heard her in person I never wanted to hear her records again so [I] sold them all at ½ the price (also most of my Bessies). So remember this record represents about 25% of what Mahalia is like. However, even if Mahalia's voice "isn't there," when anyone has as much music in her as that woman has they just can't do anything wrong or bad. So I hope this record will give you a little faint idea of Mahalia's greatness that I wrote so ineffectively about before. I'm sorry to keep harping on Mahalia and music when you no doubt have many other interests and activities, and I'll admit I have a one-track mind, but Bunk taught me that music can be the most important thing in the world and that if a person really has the right kind of music in their mind, heart, and body they are likely to think and act right, will move, dance, and walk right, and will be happy, love everyone, and hate no one. Music could even prevent wars if it helped everyone get together and be happy. If all this sounds like a religion I'm sorry, but until these ideas can be proven wrong I'll go on believing Bunk was right, and as long as there's a living demonstration around like Mahalia, it's going to be difficult to believe I'm wrong. For there's a person with her heart and body completely full of music. Just listen to her talk, such as the introduction to "Every Day" [i.e., "Savior More than Life to Me"], and tell me where the talk stops and the music and song begins. Every word and movement, everything she does is . . . musical and rhythmical. She's in St. Louis this week but will soon be back in Chicago and promised to let me know when her next Chicago appearance will be.

Try to find a *large* speaker if possible to hear Mahalia's record so that some of the lower frequencies can be brought out, to restore a little of the natural mellowness to her voice. All I had was some old blank discs that Bunk gave me over two years ago and the acetate is so hard that it also accentuates the high frequencies and makes her voice sound even worse than it was, so if there is a tone control turn down the highs a little. Any needles (if good) will do, but . . . it will be well to use the . . . needles I sent.[20]

These letters offer some insight into why a man with Russell's reputation and accomplishments would eventually devote himself so tirelessly to following and attending to Jackson's day-to-day career for nearly two years. For Russell, Jackson offered links to two of his most admired musical idols: to Smith through her voice, and to Johnson through her Louisiana roots. Less than two years removed from being shaken by Johnson's death—"If he could only come back now for just one more night I'd gladly pawn everything I have and give it to him," he told

"C"—Russell may have appreciated Jackson as much for being a New Orleans musician as for being a gospel singer. His anxieties over whether Jackson's instrument was "starting to wear out" and the priority he placed on "hearing her at her best" were perhaps the flipside of his work as a revivalist. Since the late 1930s, Russell had been locating and documenting older jazz musicians, master practitioners still, but in many cases players who had seen their heyday two decades earlier. In Jackson, he had found a New Orleans singer of the highest caliber who was still in her prime, and moreover one he perceived to be "a living demonstration" of Johnson's philosophical outlook, "a person with her heart and body completely full of music" whom he could embrace as an apostle of the "religion" preached by Bunk.

Over the next three years, Russell surely noted Jackson's rapid accumulation of prominent and newsworthy achievements: return engagements at Carnegie Hall, rapturous acclaim at the Music Inn, winning the Grand Prix du Disque, her performance on Ed Sullivan's *Toast of the Town*, a triumphant European tour, an appearance on the cover of *Ebony* magazine, a feature story in *Newsweek*, and several more sessions as an Apollo artist that produced some of her most outstanding sides. But Russell also began to follow Jackson's career on the ground. He attended Jackson's program at Wayman AME Church—he was still learning, mishearing it as "Wayman AB," his notes show—and saw her at least three more times during the summer of 1951, at a "Gospel Musical" presented by Liberty Baptist Church at Du Sable High School and on programs at Tabernacle Baptist Church and Gammon Memorial Methodist Church, where former Johnson Singer Robert Johnson directed the gospel chorus.[21]

At this stage, Russell's notes were sketchy, noting only dates and locations of the Jackson programs he attended, but his curiosity led him to encounter gospel scenes known almost exclusively within black Chicago church circles, such as the Easter 1952 program at an unnamed South Side church featuring Jackson and much-admired local singer Ozella Weber, and multiple programs sponsored by Mount Eagle Baptist Church, the home church of the Staple Singers, pastored by one of Chicago's most prominent Baptist ministers, Reverend Charles James (C. J.) Rodgers.[22] Russell also attended Jackson's twenty-fifth anniversary concert at the Chicago Coliseum on October 19, 1951. Bernice Bass's effusive and detailed tribute to the "Louisiana Cinderella" in the concert program hailed the ascent of "the Magnificent Mahalia" as a story "that could happen only in America": a singer "born to an underprivileged family way down in Louisiana," raised as a "young woman who never had a doll to play with," and who achieved a string of breakthrough achievements on "her tortuous climb up the ladder of success" in Chicago. Jackson herself was quoted voicing the crux of the "Louisiana Cinderella" narrative, charting her rise from the humble origins with which she would continuously identify: "Who would have thought that a little barefooted girl from Louisiana who played ball along the levees by the Mississippi River would someday stand on the stage at Carnegie?"[23]

Beginning in the spring of 1954, Russell's interactions with Jackson became much more regular and personal. On March 18, Russell's first surviving journal entry on Jackson records his and friend LaVonne Tagge's visit to the singer's recently remodeled apartment. "Some walls were in red. In one corner was a grand piano with all her trophies on top. She had a nice new and large TV set," on which he, Tagge, and Jackson watched *This Is Your Life*.[24] His investment in documenting Jackson's life and career deepened in May when he traveled south with her entourage, first to Memphis for a large Mother's Day program at Ellis Auditorium—Russell was unable to enter the hall because local Jim Crow laws barred whites from attending—and then to visit Jackson's family in New Orleans, where he took photographs of her childhood homes, school, and churches.[25] Russell claimed that he had trained his memory to recall events in detail as much as a year later and it is often evident that he is filling in some journal entries a day or more after the fact. Over the summer of 1954, as Jackson's signing with CBS and Columbia seemed inevitable, Russell's entries became more and more frequent, lengthy, and detailed. By June, he had apparently decided to write a biography on Jackson, with material gathered through close observation and oral interviews. Jackson, wanting to make sure he got the story straight, made Russell put in writing "all copyrights of the story of your life, to be tape-recorded by me, shall remain your property. None of the material shall be used for publication without your approval." Russell also told friends of his intentions. "The news of your doing a book about Mahalia Jackson is wonderful indeed," *Jazzmen* co-editor Frederic Ramsey wrote to Russell on September 28. "As you may guess, my enthusiasm for her is 'undiluted.'" As with many of Russell's writing projects, the Jackson biography never came to fruition, in this case, Russell claims, because he could never get Jackson to find the time to tell her story on tape.[26]

Singer Alice McClarity, who was living with Jackson in 1955, described Russell as a groupie who was "captivated by Mahalia" and understood his presence simply as a case of someone who "would do anything to be around a star, be in their presence, be in their house. And that's all it was with him." The demure and self-effacing Russell never disclosed his background, so McClarity, who is mentioned several times in his journal, knew nothing about his prior accomplishments; sixty years after the fact, she was shocked when I described them to her during an interview. Jackson would occasionally introduce Russell during church programs. Russell wrote in his journal that during a program at Greater Salem, Jackson announced to the audience that he "followed her around everyplace and was helpful, that I was 'from the other race but you wouldn't know it.'"[27] Russell clearly never told Jackson much if anything about himself. During Jackson's radio interview on *The Studs Terkel Almanac* in September 1954, Terkel mentioned on-air that

Russell was in-studio with her, identifying him as "one of the eminent jazz critics of the country," co-author of "a Bible of jazz." Jackson responded with obvious surprise: "Oh, is that so? He never tells me about it. I didn't know that." Russell's self-designated purpose during his close association with Jackson appeared to be to listen and observe, to record action and sound, and he set as his task to assist Jackson's career any way he could while registering an eyewitness account of her day-to-day life and her place within a Chicago church community that was a driving force in the post-war black gospel field.[28]

Church Activity

When Terkel asked Jackson in 1954 where she sang during her early years in Chicago, she laughed and answered: "from every storefront on State Street . . . to the great Olivet Baptist Church" (Figure 8.2). Her response was intended to convey a continuum of institutional pedigree, but it also offered a sense of South Side geography, spanning the area between the stately edifice of Olivet, Chicago's oldest black Baptist church at 31st and South Parkway Boulevard (now Martin Luther King Jr. Drive), and the bustling commercial stretch of State Street to the west known as "the Stroll" that stretched south to 47th Street. Russell's journal represents a far from complete picture of Jackson's Chicago, already at the time her home for over twenty years, though it does offer a rough sketch of the urban space that she traversed in the mid-1950s.

Most of the events that Russell attended at churches, school auditoriums, ballrooms, and other venues took place primarily in a plot of the South Side extending from 31st Street to a few blocks beyond the southern end of Washington Park and from Dearborn Avenue eastward to Cottage Grove Avenue. This geographic space corresponds with the "Black Belt" that was the focus of sociologists St. Clair Drake and Horace Cayton's landmark 1945 volume *Black Metropolis*. It was an area that continued to grow in the decade immediately after World War II through a fresh wave of black Southern migrants. This new expansion transformed the Black Belt to such an extent that historian Arnold Hirsch, in another important study of Chicago, perceived the creation of a "second ghetto" distinguishable from the pre-war black South Side documented by Drake and Cayton.[29] Jackson's apartment building and her home church, Greater Salem, were located in this area, but she also made many appearances at churches in Chicago's other predominantly black enclave, the West Side, particularly around Douglas Park, and on a handful of occasions at white churches on the North Side. Her performances in the greater Chicago area also took her as far west as Downers Grove and as far south as East Chicago, just across the Indiana border, a trip she recalled making numerous times back in the days of her "5¢ and 10¢ concerts."[30]

FIG. 8.2 Mahalia Jackson and Mildred Falls arriving at a gospel program at Greater Mount Sinai Baptist Church in Chicago, August 26, 1954, the night before Jackson taped the debut episode of her radio program *The Mahalia Jackson Show*. Photo by Rosenberg. The William Russell Jazz Collection at the Historic New Orleans Collection, acquisition made possible by the Clarisse Claiborne Grima Fund, acc. no. 92-48-L.20.

Jackson was an active participant in Chicago's black church communities, in more ways than one. The continuous Sunday-to-Sunday church services and gospel programs, and the value of her presence at these events, brought Jackson to church multiple times per week. Whether or not she sang, Jackson was an enthusiastic participant, "very active in responses (vocal and action) to the sermon," Russell observed.[31] At a Monday evening service at Elder Lucy Smith's All Nations Pentecostal Church, Jackson arrived nearly 90 minutes late but immediately took a seat in the front row and "her voice and fan were soon in evidence as she shouted 'Yes, Lord,' the usual 'Amens,' and 'Sho-nuff.'"[32] Two decades later, Russell recalled witnessing Jackson "get happy" and "lose control" only twice: once at a program where she was scheduled to sing but was so overcome with excitement from the music and preaching that she couldn't perform and was dragged out of the church repeatedly shouting "Thank you, Jesus!"; and another occasion when she got filled with the spirit and began banging her heavy handbag on the head of the woman sitting in front of her.[33]

Jackson was called upon to contribute more directly at key moments in the service. Singers are commonly asked to render an appropriate selection during the altar call, when the minister invites those who are not already church members to come forward and publicly accept Christ following the sermon. "Come to Jesus" and "By and By" were among the numbers Jackson sang during these calls. On the closing evening of a three-night revival on the West Side at Adams Street Baptist Church, as guest speaker Reverend Clay Evans (b. 1925), pastor of Fellowship Baptist Church, reached the climax of his sermon, Jackson was an integral part of the proceedings both as a soloist and as an evangelist. Russell was in attendance and described the scene.

As usual, for the last five minutes or so of the sermon the preacher went into his rhythmic chanting and the tension began mounting; Mahalia was singing and shouting and answering the preacher as loud as he was "singing" and soon the preacher began asking for converts and for a show of hands as to church membership. When they located a woman who was a non-member on [the] next to last row, both preachers and Mahalia rushed back and the pressure was really on, with pleading, praying, and singing for the next 15 minutes. Finally they got her to stand up and soon she walked by degrees up front and then the rejoicing really started. Mahalia led "When the Saints Go Marching In" and sang probably seven or eight different verses. This was a very slow (comparatively) tempo, even a shade slower than the bands march to it in New Orleans. They voted on accepting the woman's (Monette) membership, also on the baptism of a boy, and had speeches by three women on the committee thanking Mahalia. After the collection and speeches Mahalia sang a final solo—"[Just] Over the Hill," in very good form with full voice.[34]

Never shy about ensuring that concert promoters coughed up what they owed her in performance fees, Jackson was a particularly potent presence during the collection of the offering. Typically, Jackson would sing to set the mood as the ushers took their places and would in some instances deliver what Russell called the "collection speech," encouraging the congregation to be generous as the offering plates passed through the pews. On one occasion, she counted the collection on the spot and insisted that the $87 wouldn't do and that they try to make a hundred. Jackson's fervor in urging the congregation to open up their wallets and pocketbooks made her, it seems, something of an offertory specialist. Midweek evening church gatherings often have a comparatively casual tone in comparison with the more liturgically ordered Sunday morning services, and certain scenes illustrated the theatricality and at times burlesque comedy that could complement the ritual. During the taking of the offering at a Thursday night evangelistic meeting at Greater Mount Sinai Baptist Church, also on the near West Side, Jackson teamed up with Reverend Louis H. Boddie (1878–1965), the esteemed Greater Harvest Baptist Church pastor known among black Chicagoans as "The Rock" for his signature affirmation "Jesus is my rock." Boddie encouraged the congregation to give as much as they could because the Lord would always provide more: "Where did he get his money?" Boddie asked with characteristic flair. "He didn't know except that as fast as he'd hand it out, all he had to do was hold his hands up to God and more would drop in it."

Then he worked into a plea for the collection and Mrs. Jones or someone, asked that another table be brought in from the back room, so that Mahalia could be at one and Prof. [Theodore] Frye at the other. When the tables were in place the Rock took out his roll of bills, peeled off slowly five and threw them over on one table, then five more for the other table, a couple landed on the floor.

About that time Mahalia who was sitting quietly way over by West wall yelled out loudly, "What kind of money is that Rev. Boddie's putting down there?" Then as she jumped up and hurried across the front of the church she added, "That ain't no money, I thought those were $20 and $10 bills etc., they ain't nothing but dollar bills." Boddie was perhaps slightly startled but recovered quickly as the congregation roared with laughter, and entered into the comedy. He offered to put down a $5 bill on each table if Mahalia would match his offering. She began fishing in her brazere [*sic*] and drew out a few $1 bills but wouldn't put them down at once. Then began a lot of rapid exchanges, which no one could keep up with, as first Boddie then Mahalia would grab up the money they'd just put down, with Mahalia getting the bigger laughs. Once she challenged him to put down some 20s saying, "You always say the Lord is my shepherd, I shall not want; so go ahead and put some real money down on the table." First she'd put some of her money on the table, then grab it back. Once she said, "It sure does my soul good to show up Rev. Boddie this way." Finally she said she couldn't match his money because Rev. B had a big congregation and she didn't have anybody. Finally everything quieted down suddenly and Rev. Boddie left the pulpit and went out the side door.[35]

Beyond the kinetic energy, personal charisma, and celebrity buzz that she contributed to church events, Jackson was also active in the frequency of her attendance. Church ministers repeatedly called upon Jackson to assist revivals, some lasting the entire week, and to show up for radio broadcasts. As a fan of the music and a friend of fellow gospel musicians, she was also a regular supporter of programs, especially anniversaries and special concerts featuring prominent out-of-town singers. One of the fundamental observations we might make on the basis of Russell's journal is the sheer number and variety of events connected to the Chicago gospel music scene in the early 1950s. Among the many programs Russell attended with Jackson were Willie Webb's annual late-summer anniversary programs at Tabernacle Baptist Church. Webb's anniversaries were blowout events that always offered an all-star lineup; an advertisement for his fourth anniversary concert in 1951 announced an appearance by Dinah Washington, who was "coming back to church that night." His August 1955 program featured the Raymond Rasberry Singers from Cleveland along with Chicago-based Princess Stewart, Bessie Griffin, the Caravans, and the Soul Stirrers with lead singer Sam Cooke. Webb's spectacular 1955 anniversary concert has additional significance for gospel fans and historians because it came just five weeks after a now-famous program at the Shrine Auditorium in Los Angeles on July 22. "The Great Shrine Concert," as it has come to be known, which included both the Caravans and the Soul Stirrers, was recorded and released commercially and would presumably give a sense of some of the music Jackson and Russell heard at Tabernacle on August 29.[36]

Sometimes Jackson would sing at these programs (Figure 8.3), sometimes she would not, though by the mid-1950s even when she did not perform she was invariably acknowledged by the emcee and was frequently asked to make comments. Jackson herself occasionally presented concerts with other singers, such as the program at Fellowship Baptist Church in August 1955 featuring Emily Bram, visiting from New York where she was a member of Bishop Frederick and Ernestine Washington's Holiness church in Brooklyn. At Fellowship, Bram sang several songs, during which "Mahalia was shouting her 'Yes, Lords,' etc., and waving her hand plenty sitting on [the] pulpit back of Emily. At times she had to stand up and finally got up beside Emily and helped her sing one song." Jackson gave Bram a breather by making a compelling ten-minute speech about how singers "wanted

FIG. **8.3** Mahalia Jackson, Princess Stewart, and Theodore Frye singing, accompanied by Mildred Falls on piano, at a gospel program at Greater Mount Sinai Baptist Church, August 26, 1954. Photo by Rosenberg. The William Russell Jazz Collection at the Historic New Orleans Collection, acquisition made possible by the Clarisse Claiborne Grima Fund, acc. no. 92-48-L.163.

to get out on the road, when there ain't nothing but hard times out there," then, despite not intending to sing that night, was inspired to perform "I'm Willing to Run All the Way."[37]

It was not unusual for Jackson to take in "doubleheaders," attending more than one event in a single night. On Wednesday, May 18, 1955, Jackson, just back from a road trip to Youngstown, Ohio, where she performed at an NAACP benefit at Stambough Auditorium two days before, was scheduled to sing at a program organized by one of black Chicago's mainstay church organists, Louise Overall Weaver. The concert commemorated the opening of the Madden Park Fieldhouse, a new recreation center adjacent to the Ida B. Wells housing projects on the South Side. Jackson, citing laryngitis, did not perform, but she showed up to express her support for the project and stuck around to hear the other featured group, a jazz trio led by pianist Ahmad Jamal, despite being "disgusted" with the unacceptably poor sound equipment. Later in the evening, Jackson, with Russell in tow, went straight from Weaver's event to a program at First Church of Deliverance, pastored by Reverend Clarence H. Cobbs, to hear the Caravans. The Caravans "broke up the meeting" singing a hypnotically slow, fifteen-minute-long rendition of "The Solid Rock" that included James Cleveland's interpolated sermonizing recitation of the text. The group had just recorded the song in March for the local independent States label, and their performance of "The Solid Rock" that evening induced one young woman to pass out. Afterwards, Cleveland "had Mahalia make a speech and she talked at least ten minutes [about] how happy she was to be there (she had stood up before to shout). She stressed that gospel singers were nothing unless they centered their activities around the church." Jackson spoke with pride about knowing and watching Caravans Albertina Walker, Gloria Griffin, and Cleveland "ever since they were kids."[38]

At times, Russell's fastidious, quasi-ethnographic descriptions of musical worship among Chicago's black Baptists preserves an almost cinematic picture of the church events that Jackson frequented in the mid-1950s. Russell's recorded descriptions include commentary on neighborhoods, church edifices and sanctuaries, choirs, preaching and vocal styles, attendance, audience participation, what pastors, choirs, and Jackson wore, and even his bus and "L" rides to the programs. Russell took photographs of several church facades, showing particular interest in small storefront churches on the South Side. One representative example of his attention to minute details and his critical ear is his description of the radio broadcast of a Sunday afternoon service at Fellowship Baptist Church. Having already seen Jackson that morning at Adams Street Baptist Church, Russell was attending the Fellowship broadcast on his own without her—or so he thought.

Sunday afternoon I arrived a few minutes before the 4 o'clock broadcast, was greeted by Rev. Evans at the door. The church is only half or quarter finished from a very large rather low garage room. The 40- to 50-piece choir was seated on the three-foot platform, behind pulpit. A Hammond organ was going full blast and a grand piano was at opposite end of platform. I sat about halfway up near north side, and half a minute after I sat down someone gave me a hard poke on left arm. It was Mahalia, as she walked by. . . .She still had on her dark blue dress with sort of white collar and trimmage. I was really surprised that she showed up. She went up (was escorted by men ushers) and sat in first row by center aisle. Almost immediately the broadcast began, with a girl in sort of silk blue robe (or dress) reading the announcements, etc., then three or four songs, with the choir and soloists. One man soloist, under Billy Eckstein influence [sic], but not too bad, had fairly powerful voice and went over fairly well. They also had a P.A. system with probably eight to ten medium-size speakers scattered through church, near ceiling.

Then a woman choir member with good quality high notes but bad quality medium register sang, rather loudly, and got a good response. Then another younger girl sang "Does Anybody Here Know My Jesus," which was very good. It was sung at a fairly fast tempo, and used a tune quite similar to some fast blues number I've heard. It was a sort of break number and/or stop time in the style of the old preaching blues. This was a very good audience and the response to this song was very enthusiastic. . . .

The sermon was not very long, although the entire broadcast took an hour. . . .When the broadcast program was over, Rev. Evans announced that Miss Jackson was there but that she wasn't able to sing since she wasn't feeling well (she really had been in bed all day Saturday). However he said Mahalia agreed to sing a couple of verses of a song for them. She got up on the platform rather slowly, and said a few words to their regular pianist and then took her place behind one of the two mikes, on the pulpit. . . .Mahalia's song [was one] which I'd never heard, and possibly was largely improvised.[39]

In the early 1950s, Jackson was a highly visible star within the black gospel field and by the end of 1955 she had become an increasingly visible national media presence as well. Less conspicuous is her long and deep involvement with the daily work of black Christian churches in Chicago and around the country, activity that enables us to appreciate her management of dual positions as a church singer and as a performer and public figure in the 1950s. Russell's documentation also reveals another axis of identity: Jackson as the "Queen" in a city overflowing with gospel singers.

Singers and Preachers

Musicians love to hang out with other musicians. The centrally located Martin and Morris Music Studio in the 4300 block of Indiana Avenue was one of the most trafficked social spaces for gospel musicians in Chicago in the 1940s and 1950s.[40] Another regular haven was Mahalia Jackson's apartment at 3728 South Prairie Avenue, which saw a steady stream of houseguests coming and going. Many of her visitors were singers, and Jackson cultivated a welcoming household both for locals and for gospel musicians on the road who were passing through Chicago. A *Chicago Tribune* article reported that her apartment was "a gathering place for visiting gospel singers and teams, ministers of the gospel, church workers, recording executives, and 'just friends.' "[41]

Nineteen-year-old Alice McClarity (b. 1935), already a reputed gospel singer in New Orleans, moved to Chicago in 1955 to "get from under my mother's rules and regulations" and start her adult life. In New Orleans, McClarity had been a soloist and pianist with the gospel choir at Second Baptist Church and also led a women's trio that sang at the funeral of John Jackson Jr., Mahalia's father, in July 1953. As a teenager, McClarity pursued a formal musical education at Xavier University, getting "voice trained" and studying piano, until she was met with her voice teacher's convictions about irreconcilably different practices of voice. "I was being trained to be an opera star by my teacher in school, but she would not train me once she saw that I wouldn't get out of my church choir," McClarity recalled. "She was going to train me to sing for the New Orleans Symphony Orchestra, but I wouldn't get out of my choir, and she could hear me on Sunday nights because we had a very popular broadcast, and since I wouldn't get out, she stopped training me."

When she arrived in Chicago, McClarity moved into the YWCA and planned to stay there until she got on her feet, but Jackson, remembering her from her father's funeral, insisted that the teenager live in her brownstone apartment, a gesture McClarity considered both "a New Orleans thing" and typical of Jackson. "When I was coming up, people from New Orleans were always committed to New Orleans, and if you went anywhere and you call somebody and say 'I'm from New Orleans,' they took you in as if you had never left New Orleans," said McClarity. "That was the culture of the city." But McClarity also remembered that it was Jackson's nature to be "motherly to everybody," especially fellow gospel singers.[42] In the early 1940s, Jackson's hair salon was also a place to regularly congregate and the small apartment where she lived with then-husband Ike Hockenhull became known to young, cash-poor singers like J. Robert Bradley as "a place you could get a good solid meal" prepared on a portable double-burner stove by "one of the greatest cooks that ever lived." The portly, classically trained Bradley remembered that on occasion Jackson even volunteered to do his laundry to spare him the expense—"You need that money," she reassured him. "Halie gonna wash and iron 'em"—but then "put the coals on" him by needling him in front of others about the extra work: "Honey, I'm so tired. You know 'the artist' is in my house, J. Robert Bradley, and I'm washing and ironing his clothes. His shirts are as big as sheets, you know."[43]

From time to time, Jackson might grumble to Russell how "she didn't like the way all the gospel singers expect to come and sponge off of her and eat. She never does that when she's on the road." One evening, Jackson tutted that Robert Anderson "now owes her $200 and yet can buy a new car." Before Russell took a brief trip home to Canton, Jackson warned him not to bring his family's pet cats back to Chicago: "I got enough mouths eatin' off me now."[44] But McClarity described how in the mid-1950s Jackson nonetheless continued to be a strong mentorial presence, offering her "all types of advice, musically and social . . . just like a mother would talk to her own daughter," and because, despite her complaints, "Mahalia always liked a lot of company," her home was a thriving social hub for gospel singers. The piano in Jackson's apartment enabled her to practice with an accompanist—usually Falls, but occasionally drop-ins like Dorsey or Webb—but it also drew other singers seeking a place for rehearsal, jam sessions, and fellowship.

All the musicians would come around and they would sing and play and sing and play. And musicians were very close-knitted at that time, and so they would all come to the house. She loved to cook and feed people. So everybody would come eat and sing, eat and sing. That's what they did. So I met a lot of the people there. Of course, nobody was known at the time, but all of the upcoming singers would come to her house and sing and play, and I met all of them there.[45]

Pastors were another omnipresence in Jackson's life and in the black gospel field. The powerful authority of ministers in the black community, particularly pastors of "big churches" in Chicago like Boddie, Cobbs, or Evans, could alternately be enhanced or tempered by Jackson's popularity and renown. Performing as often as she did in churches—at services, during revivals, on programs, and over radio broadcasts—Jackson worked in constant tandem with preachers. Favorite subjects during her mid-program "talks" (as Russell called them) were her long association with certain pastors and her reminiscences of how far both she and they had come since she arrived in Chicago. In August 1954, Russell found his way to a program on the West Side at the New Macedonia Baptist Church, pastored by Reverend William M. Austin. Russell arrived with proceedings already in progress, to the sound of lined-out Dr. Watts hymns.

It was down a small dark street, and when I got there I couldn't tell which was the main door. . . . I went up front steps and a lady asked if I'd bought a ticket. They were $1 and [she] called the event a *concert* "by our friend Mahalia Jackson."

They were praying when I arrived, and then began one of the slow African ornamental-like, unaccompanied chants, led by a deacon (sort of response, etc.). After the first song I heard, they led Mahalia and Mildred up in front. They had just come in I suppose. This was also an old neighborhood synagogue, but rather plain and with few decorations. It probably seated 200+ and about 150+ people were there.

Rev. Austin immediately introduced Mahalia, telling that she was an old friend and came over every time they called on her. They had just moved recently but needed money to fix up the church. Mahalia later mentioned how their old storefront church was one of first places she sang.[46]

Black clergymen hitched their wagons to Jackson's rising star in 1954–1955. In a story heavily reported in the black press, Reverend James Lofton argued that in a time of Cold War the U.S. government would be well advised to do the same. Jackson and Lofton, the young, dynamic pastor of Detroit's 6,000-member Church of Our Prayer, had great mutual admiration. One night during a week-long revival at Greater Salem in June 1955, Jackson spotted the visiting Lofton in the audience and after giving him "a great build up," marveling at the enormous success of his church, she invited him to the pulpit to make brief comments that quickly developed into a fiery sermon. "In thirty seconds he had the church in an uproar," Russell observed, with "everybody up and yelling including Mahalia."[47] That month, Vee Jay Records released a double-sided single featuring Lofton and his 250-voice Church of Our Prayer choir singing "Great Day."[48]

Jackson was beginning to be recognized by some as an agent of cross-cultural understanding. In February, the Chicago Conference for Brotherhood awarded Jackson with their top award for having "contributed her time and talent to further the cause of Brotherhood and strengthen democracy."[49] Lofton believed that Jackson's cross-cutting popularity and her "sincere demonstration of faith, hope, love, and triumph over mere material obstacles like race or color" presented a unique opportunity for overseas diplomacy. In the summer of 1955, President Dwight Eisenhower delivered a speech expressing interest in goodwill cultural ambassadors who could alleviate Cold War tensions. Shortly thereafter, in a letter to Secretary of State John Foster Dulles, Lofton cited Jackson's path from humble beginnings to international artistic acclaim in recommending that the U.S. government enlist her as a peace envoy to Russia as a representative of Christian faith and as "a symbol of opportunity offered under the American system." Jackson's "winning personality, her magnificent gift of song, and other numerous and powerful qualities of character, persuasion and inspiration," Lofton argued, would be "a 'tremendous hit' with peoples all over the world" and "contribute a great deal toward cementing relations and building bridges of understanding between our nation, the entire Free World, and peoples who now find themselves on the other side of the Iron Curtains [sic]." The proposal received the backing of clergy in Chicago and Detroit, was formally adopted in a resolution issued by the Baptist Youth Fellowship, and according to Lofton was supported as well by international Mahalia Jackson fan clubs composed of American and overseas college students. Howard Cook, chief of the State Department's Public Services Division, responded to Lofton, thanking him for "the spirit which prompted you to write" and letting him know that Dulles would take his suggestion under advisement. The savvy recognition by one of the country's most prominent black ministers of the relationship between race and religion in official U.S. foreign policy discourse is the most explicit early evidence of the intersection of political vectors effected by Jackson's emergence as a national figure.[50]

Yet as she admitted while playing the dozens with Boddie during the collection at Greater Mount Sinai, Jackson also took pleasure in showing up a preacher from time to time. At the Caravans' program at First Church of Deliverance, Russell heard Jackson rib Cobbs by telling the audience an anecdote about the days when he was living high on the hog while she had to settle for second-class status.

She talked awhile about Rev. Cobb [*sic*], and that she doesn't get to see him much lately. She told about one time a couple years ago when she saw him on a train to Florida. Of course he was up in front with a whole coach to himself . . . and Mahalia was in back next to the caboose with baggage piled all around her, babies squealing and yelling and flies swattin' at you all around.[51]

Like singers, local and out-of-town pastors were Jackson's friends and regular houseguests, and they too were on the receiving end of both her generosity and her sharp tongue. In September 1955, Russell overheard Jackson's telephone conversation with a minister identified only by the last name "Lewis."

She told Lewis she'd been worn out the last day and night with preachers visiting her, that they are the worst people in world to entertain, they all expect to be treated like little gods and waited on every minute. She said, "None of them are any good and that goes for you too." They kept talking for about 30-plus minutes, I believe. Evidently he told her she should try him as a husband for six months (or weeks) and she said she didn't want or need a husband and she laid him out good (but really just for fun), said he didn't have a pot to pee in, and yet wanted to get married.[52]

Ernestine Washington was one of many women singers who became a pastor's wife, a common arrangement because of the practical benefits of a preaching and singing team. A topic of frequent speculation in the black press was Jackson's romantic life. This interest may give a sense that, despite her fame, Jackson represented an unstable model of femininity, falling short of fulfilling conventional markers of black respectability and domestic ideals for women: finding and keeping a husband and having children. Jackson married and divorced twice, decades apart, but it was the handsome, debonair Reverend Russell Roberts, pastor of Shiloh Baptist Church in Atlantic City, New Jersey—and shadowed by the reputation of being a slick operating ladies man—for whom she held a flame even after he died of cancer in 1959, still promising Jackson that he was holding on "to carry you across the stoop."

Also a singer, Roberts was in Chicago during the summer of 1954 to team with ex-heavyweight boxing champion Jersey Joe Wolcott, who had momentarily taken up the ministry, in a series of widely publicized revival meetings with Roberts, his former sparring partner and now "spiritual advisor." Jackson sang for packed Roberts-Wolcott appearances at Reverend Joseph Branham's South Shore Baptist Church, Elder Lucy Smith's All Nations Pentecostal Church, Reverend George Williams's Greater Mount Sinai Baptist Church (Figure 8.4), and a "mammoth songfest" and benefit concert for the South Side Boys Club at the Trianon Ballroom.

FIG. 8.4 Mahalia Jackson following a gospel program at Greater Mount Sinai Baptist Church with (standing from left to right) Rev. Russell Roberts, unknown man, unknown girl, Willa Saunders Jones, ex-heavyweight boxing champion turned evangelist Jersey Joe Walcott, and unknown man, August 26, 1954. Photo by Rosenberg. The William Russell Jazz Collection at the Historic New Orleans Collection, acquisition made possible by the Clarisse Claiborne Grima Fund, Mss. 520, fol. 3284.

In January 1955, Jackson traveled east to sing for an audience of 1,500 in a recital at Atlantic City High School Auditorium presented by Roberts' church. In November, she stayed at the Liberty Hotel in Atlantic City, where Roberts lived, while in town to attend a dinner in his honor. Black newspapers whispered about possible involvement of the "young, suave and immaculately dressed" Roberts with Clara Ward when the pastor "profitably linked" his weeklong non-sectarian "Faith Crusade" with the Ward Singers' box office–busting tours in 1954. "They are always marrying me to every woman with whom I appear on a religious program," Roberts shrugged at his Casanova reputation.

Jackson reportedly confessed that there was "something going" with the Massachusetts-born Roberts—"a Southern girl with a Yankee," she told a friend giddily—but her accompanist perceived a more complicated relationship. Falls respected Roberts for being "very well educated" and a "very fine preacher" and she even recognized the chemistry between Roberts and Jackson during services. However, Falls also believed that the tension between qualitatively different fonts of charisma flowing from Jackson the down-home church singer and Roberts, eulogized by *Jet* as the "cafe society minister," produced class-rooted power dynamics that made them a bad match. In the end, Jackson's self-consciousness about her lack of formal education led the woman Falls so deeply admired to over-accommodate Roberts's pretentious, masculine authority.

> After Russell would get through preaching . . . he would come out of the pulpit and the man part of Russell would come out. . . .When he would get ready to preach and she would know just what to sing, they were a *beautiful* team. Beautiful team. But when he would get through preaching and she'd get through singing they weren't coordinated, as my way of thinking. . . .Because Mahalia was a simple and down-to-earth type. I don't mean stupid when I say simple. Down-to-earth type person. Reverend Russell Roberts was not. He was not. He wasn't a simple, down-to-earth man. He was a man that lived in his mind very high. And she didn't. . . .And if I could say Russell Roberts was a simple, down-to-earth man, I would say they were perfect for each other. See, but he had all this education. He knew it. . . .[Mahalia] could be sophisticated, all right. It wasn't that. . . .She could fit in anywhere. But the fact that he had more education than she did was a thing that sort of, to me, would make her not live up to the great Mahalia that she was. To me, she would bend a little too much. Understand? She felt inferior to him and she shouldn't have. She was superior.[53]

Jackson occupied multiple roles within the Chicago gospel community—performer, audience member, critic, role model, matron, material supporter—and as her publicist Al Duckett wrote in the *Defender*, Jackson's "close connection with ministers and churches all over the country has made her repository of choice bits of information on many of their activities."[54] The hive of activity around Jackson as her career began to take off in the mid-1950s also exhibits a heterogeneous and generationally differentiated black gospel music scene in post-war Chicago. One of the paradoxes of this period in Jackson's career is that despite the goal of keeping young people involved in the church through modern gospel music, precisely when Jackson's pioneering successes opened doors for a new generation of gospel artists, she increasingly identified with Chicago's old guard.

At programs in the mid-1950s, Jackson regularly recounted "back in the day" anecdotes about her early work putting gospel on the map during the 1930s and 1940s, referencing on many occasions her musical and personal connections to the older Dorsey, Frye, and fellow Johnson Singers Robert Johnson and Louise Lemon, all born around the turn of the century. At a revival at Greater Salem, Jackson sang a duet with Johnson, after which she told the audience "how they organized the Johnson singers and how gospel music started in Chicago that way."[55] Russell noted that Jackson liked to tell audiences at programs an anecdote about "how after her first paid concert with the Johnson Singers she got $4 and quit her job working for the white folks."[56] Jackson also seemed bonded with slightly junior peers like Ernestine Washington, Robert Anderson, and Willie Webb, musicians who, like herself, were born before 1920 and whom she interacted with regularly, both socially and on programs. Jackson lent support more in a mentoring or collegial vein to a younger cohort of gospel musicians living in Chicago at the time, including Princess Stewart (1922–1967), Bessie Griffin (1922–1989), Alex Bradford (1927–1978), Albertina Walker (1929–2010), Gloria Griffin (1931–1995), James Cleveland (1931–1991), and Maceo Woods (b. 1932). A newspaper notice publicizing a Stewart concert in Jacksonville, Florida, cited her pedigree, indicating that Stewart "studied at the Chicago Conservatory of Music and under Mahalia Jackson, noted gospel singer."[57]

Gospel musicians who crossed paths with Jackson covered a broad continuum. Russell's recordings and notes of performances at Jackson's apartment captured a husband and wife duo singing old-time Dorsey-style gospel songs, piano soloists, a visit by CBS radio's nationally popular jubilee quartet the Trumpeteers, and younger groups performing in the latest styles. Jackson was conscious of stylistic changes in the black gospel field in the 1950s and expressed some skepticism about directions the music was taking. If Jackson was occasionally equivocal about a more classical, concertizing approach, she was also a bit leery when it came to a more extroverted "shouting" style. After delivering an up-tempo rendition of Dorsey's "Search Me Lord" at the Music Inn in 1951, Jackson acknowledged the physical toll of the fast, driving numbers preferred by Pentecostal churches.

> And sometimes I sing those kind of songs when I get to different congregations. All of my folks don't like those type of songs, but to please my public I have to learn to sing them and of course it kind of works me a little hard. Now when I go to the Holy Rollers' church that's what they like . . . but, oh, when I get through I'll be there working for my money. I'm going to try to sing one that's not quite so fast because those type of songs you sing them from your throat and your throat get tired quick, you know. You don't have time to get your breath when you stumble so therefore you go to hollering from right here [presumably pointing to her throat].[58]

However much songs demanding a more forceful delivery were intended "to please my public," Jackson also clearly relished performing these numbers. Her point was that a singer could not realistically rely on "shouting" every number to move an audience, at least not for long. Jackson's object lesson in this regard was fellow New Orleans native and longtime musical colleague James Lee. In the car on the way home from a program at Mount Joy Baptist Church in the far South Side neighborhood of Morgan Park, Jackson "laughed about how bad James Lee's voice has been in recent years," claiming that "she sang with him because of old times' sake." Jackson reportedly blamed Lee's singing style for the decline: "With all his yelling . . . it's no wonder he lost his voice." On another occasion at Jackson's home, Russell tape-recorded a few groups rehearsing as Jackson listened, including a young gospel group led by a wailing female lead singing "Come into My Heart." Afterwards, Jackson can be heard praising the group but also cautioning them about over-singing, warning: "You gonna sound like James Lee."

If "whooping it up" was met with criticism from skeptics of gospel singing in the early 1940s, perceived vocal excess in the form of "hollering" was suspect in the view of some in the early 1950s, revealing aesthetic preferences and emerging generational divides within the black gospel field. "What most gospel singing groups need to learn is close harmony and less hollering," advised B. H. Logan of the *Pittsburgh Courier* in 1953. "Even lovers of gospel music are growing tired of the groups who feature the who-can-holler-the-loudest style of singing." Logan could have been speaking for Jackson. As much as Jackson was known for her ability to create an uproar through the power of her voice, as far back as 1945 Russell remembered Jackson's dictum: "a real gospel singer doesn't have to shout." A decade later, Jackson herself told Russell "there were a lot of Negro groups that yelled loud and were no good anyway."[59]

Persistent "hollering," or singing "from the throat," threatened vocal wear and tear that could shorten a career, and fast songs, Jackson also felt, risked diminishing a song's communicative possibilities. She observed how in live performance certain audiences rapturously received her hard swinging songs, despite the fact that "she said she always liked the slow ones."[60] At the Music Inn, she whipped the eager roundtable participants into a hooting, hand-clapping frenzy with several fast bounce numbers, then requested that they tamp down their enthusiasm for her performance of "Move On Up a Little Higher," which for her carried personal testimonial meaning: "Now, you needn't clap for this one 'cause this is my heart. Now, when you clap, you don't hear me." Jackson's criticism of some younger gospel singers emerging in the mid-1950s was that they relied too heavily on the sensory stimulus of hard singing at fast tempos with repetitive drive sections. For this reason, among the up-and-coming groups, she expressed particular appreciation for the Caravans, whom Jackson invited to sing on her Mother's Day program at Carnegie Hall on May 8, 1955. Weeks later, Russell was at Jackson's apartment recording members of the Princess Stewart Singers rehearsing for a program at St. Stephens AME Church on the West Side that evening. Jackson was out running errands.

> They'd just started rehearsing good when Mahalia came home. . . .The trio got sounding pretty bad when they got into a riff number that all the groups sing and Mahalia came back and remarked also that it was the way all the young gospel singers sang today. I thought they should have been there to

hear Mahalia give her speech the Tuesday night before at Rev. Cobb's [sic] church. She congratulated the Caravans on singing songs slow enough that people could hear and understand the words and get their message.[61]

As one might expect, Jackson commented frequently on musicians, both publicly and in private. At the Emily Bram program, Jackson performed with Webb accompanying on organ, then praised the self-taught Webb effusively for a sensitivity to gospel aesthetics that he had shown "ever since they had to put him on a box on the piano stool" and that surpassed cultivated musicians "who had gone to schools." Calling out pianists who claimed they had a personal style untouched by Webb's influence, Jackson barked "in great disgust" to the congregation: "You ain't gonna get *nothin'* in 'your own style' by yourself."[62] At the same time, on one occasion Russell overheard Jackson express skepticism about Webb's singing group, the Willie Webb Singers, rejecting them as possible guests on her television program "because they yelled too much and didn't sing in parts enough."[63] Russell found appeal in the playing of Edward Robinson (1933–2014), the young Birmingham-born pianist for Boddie's Greater Harvest Baptist Church, who had also learned by ear. Jackson was less impressed: "Mahalia said he wasn't a good musician, that he couldn't play for her, he couldn't read and he couldn't transpose, etc. He was just a good (equivalent word of 'stomp') pianist. When I mentioned they called him 'King of the Ivories' over radio, she said of course they'd say anything. Willie Webb is a better *pianist* than Edward."[64] As it turned out, Robinson became a regular accompanist for Jackson in the late 1950s, touring with her for several years.

Russell's assessment of gospel performances he heard during his association with Jackson extended to Jackson herself. Hearing Jackson sing so frequently, on a near daily basis in a range of contexts, he acquired an acute sensitivity to her voice that was far more reflective than impressionistic and he regularly commented on the state of Jackson's voice on a given day, the suitability of specific song for her range, or the effectiveness of a particular performance. For her radio and television shows, Russell often wrote out song lyrics for Jackson on large cue cards that he held them in front of her as she sang. He did so when Jackson sang "Search Me Lord" on an episode of her television show: "At the last rehearsal when I held the sheet right in front of her it sounded wonderful. She changed a few of the lines, always simplifying them, leaving out a word or syllable here and there, giving the lines more punch." Jackson took a liberal approach to the lyrics she sung, which some have interpreted as casual disregard. But here, Russell heard this tendency as a matter of an intuitively idiosyncratic technique that heightened the rhythmic energy of her performance.[65]

For Russell, the distinct qualities he perceived in black vernacular music were the source of his appreciation, though he was not without his own race-based biases. One evening, he and Jackson watched the Jack Halloran Quartet win first place on *Arthur Godfrey's Talent Scouts*, beating out Louise Parker, "a colored girl from Philadelphia, who sang [the] Habanera song from *Carmen*." Parker (1926–1986), the first African American graduate of the Curtis Institute of Music in 1950, went on to become an internationally respected concert contralto, singing the role of Monisha in the 1972 world premiere of Scott Joplin's *Treemonisha*. "Although she had a good voice," Russell wrote in his journal, Parker "deserved to lose for singing that kind of stuff in place of something natural." As she often did to parody classical singers, Jackson also "imitated her after the program."[66] Often, Russell was also skeptical of the repertory recommended to Jackson by Columbia producer Mitch Miller, much of which he considered lightweight and "cheap" and not suited to Jackson's artistry or voice. Jackson tested some of the newer inspirational pop tunes in rehearsal or on her radio and television programs before putting them on record for Columbia. After recording Jackson's demo of "His Hands" in April 1955, Russell wrote in his journal that the song "really made her voice sound bad, especially on the high notes."[67]

The word that Russell reserved for what he heard as Jackson's best singing was "mellow." In his letter to "C," he gave explicit recommendations for how to highlight the "natural mellowness" when listening to her recorded voice. But he was clearly convinced that Jackson's voice was most compelling when it was not mediated by recording. In his journal, Russell, referring yet again to "His Hands," recorded an extensive and uncharacteristically personal entry after hearing his favorite Jackson performance, an impromptu selection at the program featuring Bram at Fellowship Baptist Church in August 1955. Russell's resistance to some of the Columbia repertory was surely informed by the fact that his point of reference in listening to Jackson was not pop but the blues.

After about six songs Mahalia got up to talk a minute to give Emily a rest. She hadn't intended to sing at all that night, but soon she started a real old number (she said later it felt good to get back to some of those old time numbers). Title was possibly "I'm Willing to Run All the Way."

Just as she started I heard her say or half sing "lower" to Willie Webb, but I never heard him change keys and in any case it was perfect in her range. Every note was perfect quality and it was probably the most beautiful singing job I ever heard Mahalia do.

Even with the poor speaker system the sound was wonderful. The first few notes real soft, but full and round and so beautiful.

Soon I was wondering just where I'd heard the song and what it was. It was in a minor key and the most bluesy thing I can remember her singing. Then I thought that's really like Bessie Smith, or is it just one of her songs. Then I realized it was the same general style and theme of the various "calamity" blues such as "Shipwreck Blues," "Stormy Sea," "Back Water Blues," etc. Mahalia started each phrase rather high on a repeated note (the key note for instance) then after repeating it several times she made a rather fast run down on the minor chord to an octave below.

It was a medium slow bounce tempo (just like the slow blues) and the church (and organ) really rocked with her.

When Mahalia finished and sat down Willie kept on playing and the church kept on rocking with hand claps and foot stomps, and Mahalia got up and sang parts of the song two more times. No excited demonstration, but just a wonderful mellow feeling and the wonderful tone . . . And just the week before (after all the "His Hands," etc.), I had told someone she really didn't have such a good voice, it was the way she sang that made you forget how bad her voice was at times. But here she was the most mellow singer I ever heard. Never had she been that good on radio, TV, or records.[68]

Russell seemed to have not known that Jackson had recorded the song as "Run All the Way" in her final session for Apollo fourteen months earlier, and judging from the record, his detection of an unusually bluesy performance is apt. "Run All the Way" featured Jackson backed by the usual piano and organ accompaniment but augmented by bass, drums, and tenor saxophone, producing her most explicitly blues-influenced recording. The tempo, feel, and descending arpeggios that Russell describes (more blue than minor), are all in evidence on the Apollo side as well, suggesting, even without the sax fills, a fluidity between the blues-leaning feel on the record and her performance in church.

Working for Mahalia

When he was interviewed by Goreau in the early 1970s, Russell said that he "went to work for Mahalia" in the mid-1950s when his employment options in Chicago had dried up.[69] Russell's journal indicates that at times this verged on becoming a full-time unpaid job. McClarity recalled that Russell came by Jackson's home nearly every day, typically arriving in the early evening and, especially when they rehearsed together, often staying until well after midnight. On those rare occasions when things were slow, he would simply lounge with Jackson. "During the first part of week," he wrote, "after TV Sunday night she likes to relax and do different things before she gets busy the last part of week." Eventually, Russell became an indispensable aid to Jackson as she made her transition to radio, television, and the Columbia label and he was determined to help her out any way he could. However little Jackson's circle may have known about Russell, McClarity is surely correct when she remembered that Russell was increasingly—and, as he had been for Bunk Johnson, willingly—at Jackson's "beck and call."

Russell expressed no complaints, at least in his journal, but it is difficult not to perceive that over time Jackson took Russell for granted and even to an extent began to take advantage of him. He helped out with secretarial and public relations–type duties, assisting with correspondence and other communications, wrote program notes, and when necessary answered the phone to screen calls. Jackson relied on him especially to keep her press notices up to date. On one occasion in June 1955, Russell wrote that doing so "meant an all night job for me, pasting in clippings ever since last of December '54." The next day, he managed to make it to a program at Greater Salem, though he admitted that he "was plenty tired too, having worked for 12 hours Monday night and Tuesday (on 3½ hours sleep) to fix up the scrapbook."[70] Russell also edited together tapes of Jackson's local and national television appearances so she could scrutinize them later. By the latter stages of his association with Jackson, Russell was running errands, satisfying her seemingly insatiable appetite for fruit by bringing grapes, bananas, cherries, plums, strawberries, watermelon, and oranges (which he juiced for her), and doing household chores. Russell matter-of-factly described visits during which he "emptied the mouse trap," "worked on dining room drape," "repaired plastic cover on south sofa," "open[ed] storm sash and fix[ed] screen door in her bedroom window," "put out the gladeolis [sic] bulbs out (4 to 6" deep—6" apart) along south fence by neighbor's shed and watered the plants in front room." When he arrived on May 13, 1955, "She'd left word for me to fix the kitchen light switch (three-way). Also Saturday I fixed the light in hall closet." When Russell lent a hand to blind and disabled gospel singer Princess Stewart, taking her fruit and sawing off her crutches, Jackson affected jealousy: "Alright, you've found someone else you like."[71] Russell kept an extraordinarily detailed log of Jackson-related expenses, documenting every penny that he spent or that she borrowed, also recording that Jackson, to her credit, unfailingly reimbursed him. He told a correspondent a few years later that he had no regrets about his work for Jackson: "I had the time of my life and really stayed in Chicago over a year after I planned to move [to New Orleans], just so I could get to know her and hear her sing almost every day it seems."[72]

Russell's total immersion in Jackson's life coincided with, and was perhaps directly motivated by, a decisive development in her career: her signing with CBS, which resulted in a national radio program, a local television show, and heightened visibility and status as a Columbia Records artist. The new set of responsibilities that came with these ventures were a formidable challenge for Jackson, and it is difficult to overstate the contribution made by Russell at this crucial juncture in Jackson's career. Russell did the grunt work of selling tickets for tapings, posting publicity flyers, making cue cards, looking after the copyrights for Jackson's arrangements, and going on food and coffee runs for Jackson and her accompanists while they were working in the studio. In a letter to George Avakian, he described Mitch Miller's visit to the taping of an episode of Jackson's radio show: "He doesn't know my name, of course, but no doubt saw me in my usual capacity of hamburger, Coke, and grape rusher around the studio."[73] But with extensive experience as a musician and knowledge of the music industry, he was also able to uniquely support Jackson by helping her learn new repertory at home rehearsals, making trips to Chicago's Lyon & Healy music store to find sheet music for potential songs (transposing them, if necessary), recording demo tapes, and functioning as an intermediary between her and the CBS and Columbia production teams. Scripts, recordings, journal entries, and the extensive press coverage of Jackson's new media presence bring into focus the scope and historical significance of *The Mahalia Jackson Show*, its competing projects, and the meanings of a nationally broadcast radio show starring an African American gospel singer, "the first in her race to have a sustaining program on the CBS nation-wide chain."[74]

9

"Singing Comes as Natural as Breathing"

THE MAHALIA JACKSON SHOW

AMONG THE MOST historically significant music news items in the United States during 1954—*the* story of the year in entertainment for African Americans, according to some black newspapers—was the signing of contralto Marian Anderson by New York's Metropolitan Opera, making her the first African American soloist to appear with the illustrious company since its founding in 1883.[1] On October 7, Met General Manager Rudolf Bing contracted Anderson to sing the role of the sorceress Ulrica in an upcoming production of Giuseppe Verdi's *Un ballo in maschera* to be conducted by Dimitri Mitropoulos, also making his Met debut. Anderson was already established as a recitalist of international renown before becoming a *cause célèbre* when she performed on the steps of the Lincoln Memorial on Easter Sunday 1939, having been barred from Constitution Hall in Washington, DC, by racial segregation policies enacted by the Daughters of the American Revolution. But being signed by the Met for her first-ever operatic role made the forty-seven-year old singer "feel like a high school girl again, with her dream come true."[2]

The Anderson-Met pact was a national story, eliciting reportage and celebratory editorial comment in major newspapers across the country, but nowhere more enthusiastically, even emotionally, than in the black press. Because Anderson had been among the most admired and beloved figures among African Americans for nearly three decades, recognition by the institution that represented the pinnacle of the profession, however unjustly belated, carried powerful import. A year-in-review rundown in the *Chicago Defender* placed the Anderson story at the top of a list of notable achievements by black artists in 1954.

Certainly there was joy in Sepialand when bias was replaced with a contract that makes Marian Anderson a member in good standing at the

Metropolitan Opera Company. Even those few who lament the fact that Miss Anderson's break came in the "fall season" of her illustrious career are screaming from the house tops the old tune "better late than never."

Cleverly signifying on the incongruity of an artist of Anderson's stature making her opera debut as she approached middle age, Earl Brown of the *New York Amsterdam News* wrote sardonically that in signing Anderson, "the Met at long last will have arrived." But the blow struck against the color barrier at the Met was only the high point of a banner year for African Americans in the music industry, one that included the release of *Carmen Jones*, Otto Preminger's all–black cast film adaptation of Georges Bizet's famous opera, starring Dorothy Dandridge and Harry Belafonte. Black woman vocalists in particular made important strides, as Sarah Vaughan, Leontyne Price, and Eartha Kitt also enjoyed noteworthy professional successes. Among these achievements in black entertainment, the *Defender* observed, was a first for black gospel music: "Mahalia Jackson, long a favorite of the concert circuit with her singing of spirituals, hit the top late in 1954 when she was signed for a regular singing spot on CBS radio."[3]

More than a "singing spot," *The Mahalia Jackson Show* was a 25-minute "semi-religious" program that aired Sunday evenings on CBS affiliates nationwide. Premiering on September 26, 1954, eleven days before Anderson's signing, and canceled just a month after her January 7, 1955, Met debut, the show featured Jackson singing a mix of repertory that included spirituals, religious-themed popular music, sentimental "oldies," and the occasional gospel song for a live studio audience. The program's run unfolded in discernible stages as CBS experimented with how to ensure the success of a show that many black Americans embraced as a collective achievement. Studs Terkel's scripts for the show, recordings of programs and rehearsals, newspaper coverage, and Bill Russell's journal reveal how Jackson was entrusted with the responsibilities of creditably representing her faith, her race, and herself.[4] But the show was also a turning point for Jackson as an artist and as a public figure, as she negotiated a newly diverse repertory and an at times ambiguous performance context. More broadly, *The Mahalia Jackson Show* spoke to its historical moment, highlighting the interdependence of Cold War and civil rights discourse voiced by the performances of a gospel singer asked to broker the often conflicting meanings of black religious song for a national audience.

A "Pet Project" in Production

Jackson's recording of "Silent Night" was yet again a catalyst for new opportunities. Independent radio producer Louis Cowan heard jazz scholar Marshall Stearns play the record in an on-air interview with actress and radio host Faye Emerson and pitched the idea of a show starring Jackson to CBS executives. According to Emerson, hearing Jackson "interested Lou Cowan so much that he went out to Chicago to meet Mahalia, signed her to a contract and took an audition of hers to Bill Paley, boss man at CBS. By now, you know the end of the story. Mahalia Jackson has her own program on the CBS-Radio network." In other accounts, it is Mitch Miller who charged Cowan with coming up with radio programming to showcase Jackson. Either way, the news had already begun to trickle out in the summer of 1954. Though the show did not premiere until the fall, there was talk about the network's interest in a *Mahalia Jackson Show* as early as June, when Jackson admitted to the *Pittsburgh Courier* "that she will be starred in a coast to coast television and radio show in September." The next month, Jackson met in Chicago with CBS vice president of radio programming Lester Gottlieb to hammer out details that included her $1,500 a week salary. Official word came in an August 12 press release announcing Jackson's signing by Columbia Records and the launch of a weekly 25-minute Sunday evening program on the CBS radio network, a partnership that would "bring her universal appeal and superb talent to a larger public than she has reached even with highly successful tours."[5]

The production team for *The Mahalia Jackson Show*, originating out of Chicago's CBS radio affiliate WBBM, were all Chicagoans who participated in the transition from radio to television as the country's dominant entertainment medium. Working as a volunteer consultant and director of domestic affairs for the U.S. Office of War Information during World War II, Cowan maneuvered to create positive portrayals of African Americans in radio programming at a time when the armed forces were still racially segregated. Among his initiatives was persuading soap opera producers to fold black characters into their scripts. As the president of his own production agency after the war, Cowan achieved success creating the hit TV quiz show *The $64,000 Question*, but in late 1954 the *Mahalia Jackson Show* was his "pet project." In 1940, Cowan had collaborated with John Lewellen to launch the long-running hit NBC radio and television show *The Quiz Kids*—Chicago's six-year-old gospel singing and preaching prodigy Donald Gay became the show's first black contestant in 1952—and Lewellen and *Quiz Kids* producer Jay Sheridan became producer and director, respectively, of Jackson's radio program. Despite the network's nervousness about McCarthy-era scrutiny of Terkel's political sympathies, Jackson successfully lobbied for Terkel to be the show's scriptwriter. Musically, Jackson was to be backed on the program by the Jack Halloran Quartet, a white male vocal harmony group, and her own accompanist team of Falls on piano and newly hired organist Ralph Jones from Detroit. Hal Stark, a familiar host and anchorman on WBBM radio and television programs, was the show's narrator.[6]

Production picked up momentum in the months leading up to the airing of the first episode. Preliminary rehearsals for the show had already begun by at least

August 2 at the Wrigley Building at 400 North Michigan Avenue, where the show was mostly recorded. Final rehearsals were on Wednesdays and shows were taped Friday evenings. Perhaps because of her inexperience with the medium, several of the set piece performances featuring Jackson and the quartet were recorded in advance at Universal Studio and edited into the live components taped at the Wrigley Building for a ticketed audience of about 200. As *Chicago Sun-Times* columnist Lucia Carter described, the unusually casual manner of taping the program was calculated to ensure that the energy of engaged observers would be one of its signature features.

> The recording sessions are unorthodox. Spectators are asked to wander in at 8 p.m. or so, while rehearsal is still in progress.
>
> After a while, director Jay Sheridan decides that it's time to start recording. So he does—but not all in one piece. There are frequent interruptions and decisions to backtrack. And during all this the various people involved in the show talk to the spectators and share little jokes with them.
>
> In some strange way, this sense of being in on the production adds a new warmth to the audience response. This, in turn, becomes a part of the show.

Jackson reportedly told Goreau that the audience was predominantly white ("the blacks were streaks here and there"), but with enough familiar faces, a *Chicago Defender* columnist observed, for Jackson to feel at home.

> Definitely the place to be on Fridays is WBBM radio station in the Wrigley Building where the "party of the week" is being thrown by Mahalia Jackson of the golden voice and magnetic personality. Flanked by old friends and new, she holds forth in a recording session for her new radio series which starts on Sunday, September 26th.
>
> Her "Yes, darlin'" to director Jay Sheridan's orders from the control room and waves to friends out front set a new style in workouts and give the e[n]gineers a real problem trying to record the full sweep of her wide range of volume and tone.[7]

Four complete shows were taped before the debut episode aired on September 26. Meanwhile Jackson was learning repertory for the show in home rehearsals with Falls and Russell. Russell brought his violin to Jackson's house to play along and help her get the tunes in her ear and also documented rehearsals on his Magnavox tape recorder, which he stored behind Jackson's couch for two years (Figure 9.1).

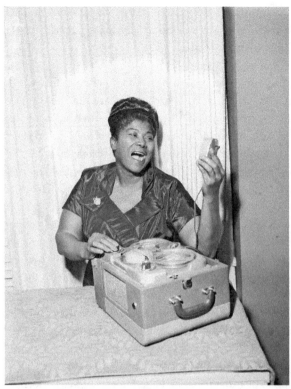

FIG. 9.1 Mahalia Jackson at home singing into a tape recorder, probably belonging to Bill Russell, February 12, 1954. DN-Q-0699, *Chicago Daily News* Negatives Collection, Chicago History Museum.

Russell's recordings of two rehearsals leading up to the show's debut help us assess Jackson as a singer at this point in her career. At a rehearsal on Labor Day, Jackson, accompanied by Falls on piano and Russell on violin, labored to master Stephen Adams's "The Holy City," the chorus of which was the inspiration for the opening theme of Duke Ellington's "Black and Tan Fantasy."[8] Russell later described the rehearsal in his journal.

Mahalia was informally dressed, as usual, and had the air conditioner on, and TV going, which I turned off after trying to play the "Holy City" on violin for her. Soon Mildred came and we decided that A-flat (or F) was too high for her and put it in D-flat (an octave lower than the highest published solo). . . . Her piano was fairly well up to pitch but not very well in tune. Mildred also had an old copy of "Holy City," in lowest published key, so Mahalia used one copy for the words as she sat on sofa by north wall. She had considerable trouble with the rhythm (or time value), wanted to double

up on some measures, and questioned the way Mildred and I played ♫ ♫
and ♫ ♪ (in which we *weren't* accurate). Once she stopped and asked me to
explain the note values of ♪ . . .

Russell's tape recording documents Jackson grappling to find a feel for the song. Transposing "The Holy City" in D-flat would have put the song's climactic fifth above the tonic at a manageable A-flat, as opposed to what would have been an C or E-flat in the keys of F and A-flat, respectively. The C was certainly within her range, but Jackson appeared to feel more comfortable taking on the uppermost end of her register when the pitch was a blue note that she could "sing from her throat," as in the "B-flat swing tunes" that took her up to a D-flat, than when she needed to execute a pitch with a more rounded, controlled tone. Here is an instance where she perhaps bumped up against the limits of not having received formal vocal training. Russell's tape also shows Jackson trying to find a feel for the song, especially in the bridge and in the transition from the shorter note values in the beginning of the verse to the broadening of the rhythm in the approach to the chorus. As it turned out, she never performed the song on the show. Listening to the rehearsal, it is hard to imagine how Halloran's quartet would have been able to cleanly follow her unpredictable lengthening and shortening of bars. Yet the recording is illuminating in retrospect: noting her difficulties getting a grip on the song in 1954 demystifies and humanizes the act of performance, making it all the more inspiring to hear the command and majesty of her performance when she eventually did record "The Holy City" backed by Percy Faith on the 1960 Columbia album *The Power and the Glory*.[9]

Russell documented another Jackson home rehearsal on September 18, a marathon session lasting from 8:30 p.m. until 2:00 a.m. Like "The Holy City," two songs from this rehearsal, the traditional spiritual "Jacob's Ladder" and R&B singer Chuck Willis's message song "Peace and Love," wound up on the cutting room floor. The latter is an instance of repertory being tested for commercial recording. Willis recorded "Peace and Love" in 1954 for Columbia subsidiary Okeh Records, but it was unreleased. Miller apparently saw something in the song because he sent Willis's recording along with other possible material to Jackson for her consideration. Again, we hear Jackson initially struggle to find a compelling take until Falls, in a second run-through, brings the somewhat languorous tune to life with "gospel-feel" triplets and ear-catching augmented harmonies that seemed to set a more appetizing table for Jackson. Jackson never did record "Peace and Love," but another song at this rehearsal, the newly written inspirational pop song "One God," was cut at her first session for Columbia. That evening Jackson also worked on four other songs that were undoubtedly new repertory for her and did end up on the show: "Danny Boy," Johannes Brahms's famous "Lullaby" (his "Cradle Song," op. 49, no. 5), "How Are Things in Glocca Morra?" from the musical *Finian's Rainbow,* and "Goin' Home," the opening theme from the slow movement of Antonin Dvořák's "New World" Symphony as set to text in 1922 by William Arms Fisher. Fisher added the words, in stylized black vernacular, having discerned "the form of a negro spiritual" in Dvořák's melody, and over time "Goin' Home" accrued status as an "honorary" spiritual.[10] These rehearsals illustrate the challenges and compromises that emerged from the interface of orality and notation as Jackson, who readily acknowledged her inability to read music, prepared for her show. But they also illuminate the cooperative roles that Falls and Russell played in making the demands of the endeavor workable, exemplifying what David Chevan has described as a "circle of musical literacy."[11]

The studio setting and Jackson's own working methods took some mutual accommodation. If Falls and Jones provided Jackson with a sense of familiarity, Halloran, the show's musical director, was cut from slightly different cloth, though the assignment was a big break for him as well. After graduating from a small college in his home state of Iowa, Halloran (1916–1997) moved to Chicago and pursued advanced music study at Northwestern while working in a department store, teaching music at a public high school, dabbling in acting, and taking on singing and choral directing jobs for Chicago radio productions. At Northwestern, Halloran formed a male close harmony group called the Cadets that he eventually renamed the Jack Halloran Quartet. In the early 1950s, the group began to provide backing vocals for pop records by Vic Damone, Joni James, Xavier Cugat, and many others, but Halloran's group did most of their work in commercial recording for Chicago-based Mercury Records, whose jazz division was overseen at the time by John Hammond. Hammond was perhaps the link between Mercury and Columbia that helped Halloran land the *Mahalia Jackson Show* job, undoubtedly the most lustrous of his career to date.

Halloran was a key figure in making *The Mahalia Jackson Show* work. On Jackson's program, the Jack Halloran Quartet—comprised of Halloran with Bill Kanady, Bob Tebow, and Bill Cole—sang backing harmonies behind Jackson on most of her selections (Figure 9.2). Halloran was tasked with creating these arrangements, performing change-of-pace numbers with the quartet, and engaging with Jackson in scripted between-song transitional banter. To assist Halloran, Russell recorded Jackson singing through repertory for future shows to give him a sense of her feel, phrasing, and potential idiosyncrasies in each song. Other times, it was Halloran who helped Sheridan understand how some of the repertory that Jackson performed worked. In a rehearsal of "Nobody Knows the Trouble I've Seen" for Show #4, Sheridan, trying to work out the timing, threw Jackson a curve ball by suggesting that she shorten her performance by ending at a point in the song that did not make musical sense. Halloran helped explain that the song worked "sandwich style," with the verses ("Sometimes I'm up, sometimes I'm down . . . ," "If you get there before I do . . . ," etc.) sung between

FIG. 9.2 Mahalia Jackson rehearsing with Mildred Falls and the Jack Halloran Quartet for her CBS radio program *The Mahalia Jackson Show*, 1954. Halloran is third from the right, holding the sheet music. Photo by Myron Davis. Laurraine Goreau Photograph Collection, Hogan Jazz Archive, Tulane University.

statements of the chorus ("Nobody knows . . . ").[12] As Russell's account of the rehearsal for Show #2 makes clear, regular translation—of music terminology, of musical style, and from extemporaneity to more tightly arranged performance— was one of the biggest initial challenges in crafting the show.

> The Friday night before they . . . remade some of the first broadcast, I believe. Mahalia said a couple of numbers with the quartet didn't go quite right. She thought the engineers at Universal had been better, but couldn't say anything to the CBS men.
>
> After trying "My Friend" two or three times they finally got it very good. Mahalia was especially good, and when the engineer or Sheridan (the boss from the agency producing the show) mentioned that they really got it that time, Mahalia said "You can't do a song unless you feel it; the Goast just came." [*sic*]
>
> She complained occasionally to Mildred that everything was "too flat," meaning the music (and singing of quartet, etc.) was without spirit, and possibly that the tempo was too slow. Her use of other musical terms at other times was a little confusing. Once they worked up to the "climax" (a word she used effectively a few times), she wanted them to come "up the scale."

The other numbers on the second program were "Trees," and "Joshua Fit the Battle of Jerico" [sic] and finally "Summertime." . . . At the end of "Joshua" Mahalia put a little humming coda starting up in the falsetto and running down and they decided to leave it in. At first it was an afterthought, rather late, but next time she started it a little sooner, so as to finish before the quartet ended their last long chord.[13]

In an interview on *The Studs Terkel Almanac* two weeks before the first episode, Jackson expressed her gratitude for the opportunity as well as a sense of her personal aspirations: "I'm glad to get this break . . . [to] start singing on CBS. I think it's the most wonderful thing in the world that's going to happen to me. It really is an answer to my prayer."[14] But working to get a feel for her own voice rendering new repertory, for the tone and timing of semi-live radio, and for Halloran and the quartet, Jackson seemed to have also recognized that the added investment in production raised the stakes of her career.

CBS was also heavily invested in *The Mahalia Jackson Show*, rolling out an aggressive fall promotional blitz. The network publicly introduced Jackson and pitched the show at a national meeting of radio affiliates at the Edgewater Beach Hotel in Chicago, where Jackson had for a time worked a $12-a-week job as a maid in the 1930s. Jackson appeared with talent from other CBS programs, including ventriloquist Edgar Bergan with his sidekick Charlie McCarthy and the McGuire Sisters of the *Arthur Godfrey Show*. In the view of *Chicago Sun-Times* columnist Ben Stegner, Jackson, though yet unknown to many in attendance, "stole the show" as the celebrities, the seen-it-all radio managers, and "even the elevator operators cheered as her bouncing contralto carried through the ballroom doors." Her success, Stegner gloated, was also a feather in the cap of a city desperately clinging to its reputation a major media center: "Who says Chicago is dead as an origination center for radio programs?" In her conversation with emcee Robert Q. Lewis, Jackson described her style to the spirited crowd: "I don't know if you'd call it a style. I just sing the way I feel and 'the bounce' in my singing is just sort of making a joyful noise unto the Lord, as David said."[15]

Cowan and CBS radio executives also hosted a party for Jackson in New York days after the show's debut, for which they distributed a glitzy twenty-two-page press packet detailing her life and career and selling the program to broadcasters for the "gross weekly talent cost of $4,210." The booklet noted that Jackson was "deeply religious" and that the show would be "spiced with Mahalia's personal philosophy." But CBS also promoted *The Mahalia Jackson Show* and its star, whose "singing appeals to all types of music lovers," with language projecting a mood-music vibe that made the narrow context of faith optional for listeners.

You are listening to CBS radio at 10:05 pm on Sunday. You hear a slow and easy rhythm with the instruments muted in the background. An amazing contralto voice that's by turn sweet and low, powerful and clear, takes up the intro melody.

You are listening to *The Mahalia Jackson Show*. It's an exciting addition to radio programming, presenting a compelling personality singing from the heart.

Toward the end of her relentless string of New York events, Cowan told Jackson that her final responsibility was to be filmed for a newsreel. "Newsreels?" she marveled. "How fabulous can I get?"[16]

Jackson proudly recounted her promotional trip to New York during a large gospel program at Pilgrim Baptist Church, attended by Russell: "She told of singing at the party on Park Ave. . . .with all the New York people sitting on the floor to hear Mahalia Jackson, the girl who came up from the back sticks of Louisiana, how the *president* not vice president of CBS was there, etc., and she sang for them just the same way she does on CBS and in all her churches."[17] Jackson's sense of her emerging role as a musical performer bearing cultural-political significance that stirred the waters was not gratuitous. In a profoundly introspective column, pioneering *Pittsburgh Courier* journalist Evelyn Cunningham described her unexpected feelings of racial pride when she heard the homespun Jackson at the swank New York event, "a Park Avenue reception for her, attended by lots of big names and big brains, mostly white." Though she admired Jackson's talent, the Long Island University graduate initially felt that black gospel singing "seemed far, far removed from my life and environs" and even "on occasion made me ashamed of my heritage." But hearing Jackson sing at the CBS fête "made me choke up and feel wondrously proud of my people and my heritage. She made me drop my bonds and become really emancipated." Jackson, Cunningham confessed, is "one of the few human beings who has made me ashamed of being ashamed."[18]

Al Monroe of the *Chicago Defender* noted this massive publicity push, observing "CBS has gone all out in promoting Mahalia Jackson's debut on radio." These efforts resulted in a slew of features throughout the fall, with advance coverage of the show in every major black newspaper. In the first installment of his two-part story on Jackson for the jazz magazine *Down Beat*, Mason Sargent described her as a "classicist of the spiritual" and employed the stock rhetorical gesture of comparing Jackson with the reigning black diva: whereas Marian Anderson and other concert singers "have translated it, so to speak, into the language of European song writing," Jackson sings "the spiritual as it was, and still is, sung in its home, the church." In this coverage of Jackson, perhaps the most pronounced storyline was her rags-to-riches story: "Mahalia Jackson was born in a Negro shack in New Orleans in 1911 and went to work as a washerwoman at 13," read *Time* magazine.

Cumulatively, publicity recounted the "Louisiana Cinderella" narrative arc: hard-scrabble beginnings in sub-Dickensian poverty in New Orleans, deep religious faith, a powerful voice that had never received formal training, unglamorous work in several service jobs, a catalog of commercially successful recordings for Apollo that "revolutionized the gospel singing field," and eventual lucrative success through the CBS/Columbia imprimatur. "Mahalia Jackson, the Negro gospel singing star will be a CBS (radio) feature starting the 26th," widely syndicated gossip columnist Walter Winchell told his readers. "She was once a laundress."[19]

The capstone of the PR offensive was a feature story in the November 29 issue of *Life* magazine, titled "Gospel Queen Mahalia—She Makes Hymn Singing Pay," a spread that included images of Jackson performing at Pilgrim Baptist Church and of Duke Ellington having dinner and playing piano at Jackson's home (Figure 9.3). In 1958, Ellington would collaborate with Jackson both in the studio and at the Newport Jazz Festival in the "Come Sunday" movement of his extended work *Black, Brown, and Beige*, though by the early 1950s he had already developed a personal relationship with his soon-to-be fellow Columbia artist. Before they had even met, Ellington sent Jackson a large get-well bouquet of fruit when she was recovering

FIG. 9.3 Dinner party hosted by Mahalia Jackson with guests (from l to r) Alfred Duckett, Duke Ellington, Marshall Stearns, and Theodore Frye, October 13, 1954. Photo by Myron Davis. Laurraine Goreau Photograph Collection, Hogan Jazz Archive, Tulane University.

from her December 1952 hysterectomy following her European tour, and they soon became fast friends and mutual admirers. On September 15, 1953, Ellington called a press conference at the Sutherland Hotel in Chicago to announce the formation of the Artists Society of America (ASA), a non-profit organization created to "offer help and hope to the many fine, aspiring performers—both in the popular and serious fields—who need and deserve encouragement and inspiration." The black self-help organization's purpose was twofold: "To encourage the careers of aspiring performers in all phases of show business and entertainment and to promote the equitable integration of the talented artists in the fields of radio, television, screen, and stage." Ellington introduced himself as founder and advisory chairman, singer Billy Eckstine as president, and Jackson as vice-president, with Nat "King" Cole and bandleader Illinois Jacquet as board members. Indicating her desire to "aid unknowns in the gospel and spiritual field," Jackson praised Ellington's initiative and discussed the distinct needs of gospel singers within the entertainment industry. "Gospel singing is not as highly organized as the blues and other popular fields," Jackson told a gathering of ASA leadership, "However it is just as influential." The greatest problem facing gospel singers, she believed, was "the need for hard-working managers, top-flight booking agents, sincere legal advice—and of course, financial backing."[20] As Ellington recalled with characteristically dry wit in his memoir *Music is My Mistress*, he was an enthusiast not only of Jackson's musical gifts and leadership potential but also her culinary talents.

> Bill Putnam, founder, builder, recording engineer, and President of Universal Recording Studios in Chicago, was having a party on a yacht one evening out on Lake Michigan. There were a lot of bigwigs from the Loop there, and a representative of Columbia Records came up to me, all glowing.
>
> "Say, you must hear this new girl we've got signed up!" he said.
> "Who's that?"
> "Mahalia Jackson."
> "Oh, yeah, she's a good cook."
> "No, she's a singer."
> "I know," I said, "but she's a good cook, too."
> She's the best, a great cook. I had been to her house several times before ever she signed with Columbia, and she always had fine soul food out there.[21]

Many African Americans closely followed the voluminous Jackson coverage and read it with a critical eye. Jimmy Brown commented on the *Life* feature in his column for the *Philadelphia Tribune*, registering his frustration that "the article did not show the gentle touch that *Life* writers usually reserve for matters of a religious nature." He specifically objected on the basis of the piece's "tongue-in-cheek" tone and photo captions that were "cruel." In ignoring the fact that Jackson "once turned down a $10,000-a-week offer to sing in a New York nightclub," the story, Brown believed, was overly focused on her material gain from a breakout success.[22]

Jackson did her part getting the word out by rallying her base at gospel programs, where she and the sponsoring churches urged black congregations to support the show by listening faithfully on the radio or calling WBBM for tickets to be a part of the studio audience. "When the show goes on the air'" the *Defender*'s Arnold de Mille reminded his readers, "it will become the only Negro radio program on a national network." But as with Jackson's appearance on Ed Sullivan's *Toast of the Town* two and a half years earlier, many also welcomed the show as an emblem of recognition for black gospel communities. A remarkable account of a recital turned mass listening party suggests the significance of *The Mahalia Jackson Show* for African Americans who could only marvel at how far the singer and black gospel had come since the dawning days of the Dorsey movement. On the night of the show's debut, Jackson's organist, Ralph Jones, was giving a concert attended by "an overflow crowd of more than 3,000 people" at Alpha and Omega Missionary Baptist Church in his hometown of Detroit.

> As the recital progressed, Mr. Jones appeared to grow more and more apprehensive about something. When the Rev. Zolia Robinson, pastor of the church, asked what was disturbing him, he told her he wanted to listen to the radio, because that was the night of the premiere broadcast of the "Mahalia Jackson Show."
>
> A radio was brought into the auditorium and hooked up to the public address system for those in the hall to hear.
>
> Word quickly passed out to the street and those who couldn't get into the church turned on their automobile radios.
>
> The crowds that had gathered about the Alpha and Omega Church to hear Ralph Jones' recital gravitated into groups of twenty or more crowding around the automobiles parked about the church, listening, with approval, to the first broadcast of the woman who had sung at that church 18 years ago—for an audience that paid an admission price of 15 cents.[23]

Shows #1–4: "We're Not in Church—We're on CBS"

Throughout the twenty-episode run of *The Mahalia Jackson Show*, Lewellen and Sheridan tinkered with the program to maximize its appeal and manage its most immediate challenges. The show's development took place in four stages, progressing from a straightforwardly scripted show (#1–4), to one with greater informality (#5–9), to a turn back toward an even tighter structure (#10–16), and finally to a shortened program (#17–20). In the first four shows, the format was consistent: the theme song sung by Jackson accompanied by Stark's spoken introduction, four musical selections by Jackson interwoven with two by the Jack Halloran Quartet, scripted remarks by Jackson and Halloran between songs, and a farewell by Jackson and Stark to conclude each program.

The show's theme song was a point of substantial discussion. At one point Brahms's lullaby was briefly considered, but Lewellen and Sheridan decided against it. "His Eye Is on the Sparrow" was another possibility. Within years of its initial publication in 1905 by composer Charles Gabriel and lyricist Civilla Martin, both white, "His Eye Is on the Sparrow" quickly became, and still remains, an important staple of black church repertory. Ethel Waters popularized the song in *The Member of the Wedding*, a stage adaptation of the Carson McCullers novel that ran on Broadway for over a year, and in the 1952 movie version of the play. Because the song was "identified too much with Ethel Waters," Russell wrote, "it was vetoed." A conspicuous melodic feature of "His Eye Is on the Sparrow" is the octave descent on the word "sparrow" toward the end of the chorus, which Jackson, who first recorded the song for Apollo in 1951, always rendered with a slow descending glissando, one of her favorite vocal gestures. Instead of using the song, Russell reported, "Mahalia worked out her own little theme on 'I Keep Singing' using the octave downward slide at end as it was in 'Sparrow.' "[24] Sheridan and Terkel penned the throwaway words for the short jingle, copyrighted as "Mahalia Theme" with Jackson and Halloran credited as composers.

The show thus began with Jackson, backed by the quartet and the Falls-Jones ensemble singing:

> *I keep singing as I go*
> *Feeling high, feeling low*

The "octave downward slide," transplanted to "*loooow*," cued Starks's introduction of Jackson, which highlighted her vocal charisma and widespread fame though without recognizing her identity as church singer:

> That's Mahalia singing. Mahalia Jackson of Chicago, New Orleans, of London, Paris, of *everywhere*. To Mahalia singing comes as natural as breathing. This is the first of a series of programs on the CBS radio network presenting our new singing star, Mahalia Jackson. The CBS radio network takes pleasure in presenting one of the most exciting voices of our time, Mahalia Jackson![25]

The "singing comes as natural as breathing" line was Terkel's conscious adaptation of a Jackson remark in at least one interview with him. "Studs, I just love to sing. If you take singing from me you also take my breath away because I'm dead," Jackson told Terkel in an interview weeks before the first episode aired, to which Terkel alertly responded, as if prepping listeners for the show's opening: "Singing comes as natural to you as breathing."[26] Jackson finished singing the theme—"*I keep singing along the way*"—to studio audience applause and Stark's acknowledgment of the Halloran Quartet and the "Falls-Jones instrumental group." The structure of the first four shows was nearly identical: two songs by Jackson followed by performances featuring the quartet and Jackson in alternation. The lone departure from this format was show #4 when the Halloran's group sang only one song instead of two. The Halloran group predominantly sang jaunty close harmony numbers, including the Irish ditty "Back to Donegan," a cover of the recent Rosemary Clooney hit "This Old House," and the barbershop quartet standard "Camptown Races." These were in deliberate stylistic contrast with Jackson's selections on shows #1–4, a body of repertory that can be read in multiple ways.

On the one hand, Jackson sang no recent gospel songs, with the exception of "Jesus Met the Woman at the Well." She did perform five traditional spirituals: "Joshua Fit the Battle of Jericho," "Sometimes I Feel Like a Motherless Child," "Didn't It Rain," "Nobody Knows the Trouble I've Seen," and "I'm on My Way to Canaan Land." Jackson had recorded the latter three songs in her final session for Apollo just three months before. Halloran credited Jackson on-air with writing "I'm on My Way to Canaan Land," but the song is in fact an old camp meeting revival number shared by black and white congregations. Jackson's—and surely Falls's—contribution was the stylish reimagining of the song in a brooding minor key with a *tresillo*-driven, Spanish-Caribbean rhythmic foundation that Jackson (via Terkel's script) identified as "Cuban, mixed with African." Two other songs Jackson performed on the early shows, "His Eye Is on the Sparrow" and "The Lord's Prayer," though neither gospel nor spirituals, would have also been well familiar to many black congregations.

Perhaps to the disappointment of many fans drawn to Jackson's singing through her gospel songs recorded for Apollo, more than half of Jackson's repertory on these first four shows fell into the category of recently written religious pop ("I Believe," "My Friend," and "Have You Talked to the Man Upstairs"), sentimental oldies ("Because," "Trees" and "Danny Boy"), and show tunes ("Summertime" and "You'll Never Walk Alone"). Of these, "I Believe" was the only song Jackson had yet recorded. Brahms's lullaby, a curious one-off, might be interpreted as a sentimental oldie or simply as an attempt to take a stab at a popular classic recorded just the year before by Clooney, also a Columbia artist.[27] Though at face value we might disassociate many of these songs from Jackson's base gospel repertory, it is instructive to read Willa Ward's recollections that she and her younger sister Clara learned wistful parlor songs like "Trees," "Danny Boy," "Beautiful Dreamer," and "The Last Rose of Summer" in junior high school music classes growing up in North Philadelphia: "It was as a soloist singing these songs in school assemblies that I first started holding the high note—a precursor to what became known as 'the high who.'"[28] Listening to Jackson's performances of sentimental oldies on the radio program, we also experience her voice in a different light, one that at times illuminates technical shortcomings but also hints provocatively at what Columbia executives might have heard as untapped potential.

What are we to make of Sullivan's recollection that when he first heard Jackson on *Toast of the Town* his "personal reaction was that she should be in opera"; Lucia Carter's absence of stylistic qualification when she wrote that "Miss Jackson's voice is one of the greatest I've ever encountered"; and, more mysteriously, the far-fetched rumor reported in *Jet* magazine, surely sparked by Anderson's debut, about "Heavy pressure being exerted to land a title role at the Metropolitan Opera for gospel singer Mahalia Jackson"?[29] What were these listeners hearing? As CBS stated in its press release, Columbia's hope was that Jackson would cross over to a broader market, a hope presumably rooted in the perception of a unique quality of her voice. If we are to judge from some of the repertory on *The Mahalia Jackson Show*, network producers seemed to believe that Jackson's singing held a capacity to deliver the impact of operatic singing, even if her technical training was grounded in the vernacular influences she herself claimed. It shifts our perspective to note, for instance, the surprising number of Jackson's radio songs that were in the repertory of one of the most popular singers of the early 1950s, American tenor and film star Mario Lanza (1921–1959).

Lanza's career was both singular and meteoric, hitting its peak in 1951 when he was a box office idol, invaded the pop charts, earned unprecedented receipts on the concert stage, and appeared on the cover of *Time* magazine. Like Jackson, he was a unique crossover figure blending popular and "specialist" repertory, accomplishing the notable achievement of scoring Top 20 hits with both sentimental pop songs like the million-selling "Be My Love" and, more notably, the famous *Pagliacci* aria "Vesti la giubba." Critics in the classical music establishment dismissed Lanza as "not so much an opera singer as a lot of people's conception of what an opera singer sounds like." But as with Jackson, the narrative of a singer with a lack of formal training became part of Lanza's immense appeal and promotional strategy. In striking consonance with Jackson's own childhood recollections, Lanza, a former prizefighter and piano mover who sought "to bring opera to the people," described learning to sing while growing up poor in South Philadelphia's tough Little Italy, acknowledging that until the age of twenty "I really didn't study at all. I picked up everything myself." In the process, Italian tenor Enrico Caruso became Lanza's Bessie Smith.

We didn't have a lot of money, but when Dad could afford it, he would always buy a new Caruso record for us. . . .Later, when it was thought that
I might have a voice, my parents and friends urged me to sing like Caruso,
so I would try to sing note-for-note with the records. . . .You could say in
fact that I was raised on Caruso.[30]

We might speculate that, despite rising to fame contemporaneously with radically
different sounds and repertories, Jackson, the "Bessie Smith of the spirituals,"
and Lanza, "the American Caruso," were improbably resonant figures in the early
1950s.[31] Marketed to a public primed by religious revivial to be receptive to the
pleasures of God-given gifts, both singers were celebrated as possessors of powerful, deeply affecting, "natural" voices bearing unmediated emotional authenticity. This is not to say that the CBS radio show was modeling Jackson on Lanza,
as much as it is to register the matchmaking of Jackson's voice with such songs
as "Trees," "Because," "The Rosary," "Danny Boy," "Without a Song," "The Lord's
Prayer," "You'll Never Walk Alone," and "Somebody Bigger Than You and I," all
sweeping bravura numbers recorded by Lanza that featured soaring climaxes and
profited from big, dramatic voices.

In print and in oral histories, and even in the words of Jackson herself, one
occasionally encounters the view that as a black church singer Jackson was less
exceptional than the magnitude of her international fame would suggest. It is a
perspective meant less to detract from her reputation or to begrudge Jackson her
success than to encourage appreciation of the quality and quantity of singers in
black gospel churches. Therman Ruth Jr. articulated this view candidly in his discussion of Jackson during my interview with him in 2009.

My aunt and daddy was a Mahalia Jackson fan because he was her road
manager for a while. . . .Last time I saw her in full concert was at the Met
in Philly and the place was jam-packed. They billed her as "The World's
Greatest Gospel Singer." But every church had a Mahalia Jackson in it.
Every black church had their own Mahalia Jackson that could sing just as
good. They might not sing as good, but when it came to, I'd say, relaying
the spirit of the song, every church had one. So I wasn't all that gaga over
Mahalia Jackson too much.[32]

Whereas his father, Thermon Ruth Sr., knew Jackson from her Apollo years,
having recorded with her as a backing singer, Ruth Jr., born in 1936, is of a slightly
younger generation that got to know the "ultra conservative" Jackson when she
was a mainstream public figure and a Columbia album artist. There is an essential truth in Ruth Jr.'s remarks, which in distinguishing between "good singing"
and "relaying the spirit of the song" capture the broad spectrum of expectations

that church singers attempted to meet. Heilbut has asserted that "gospel voices are easily the most phenomenal outside of opera," noting how the black gospel field has offered perhaps the deepest and most widely influential pool of vocal talent. The specific techniques of gospel singing, carried into popular music in the 1950s and 1960s by church-reared singers, became the cornerstone of an ethos and enactment of charismatic vocal performance that emerged in the post-war decades and in many ways remains a lingua franca of popular singing to this day.

Yet casual claims about the bevy of voices "just as good" or better than Jackson's in black churches, which will in any event be inescapably subjective, can veer dangerously toward over-naturalizing her talent, underappreciating, even masking, the particular musical labor she was asked to execute. It is not self-evident that other great post-war gospel divas—Clara Ward, Dorothy Love Coates, Bessie Griffin, Marion Williams, Edna Gallmon Cooke, Cora Martin, Ruth Davis, Ernestine Washington, Georgia Peach, Sister Rosetta Tharpe, among many, many others—could have successfully pulled off the range of repertory we hear Jackson, whatever her stumbles, performing on her radio show. Or, as gospel pianist Eddie Kendrix observed at a Jackson concert, delivering a solo recital of twenty-eight songs in a large auditorium, on top of singing throughout the week at church programs and touring widely. It is not that other gospel singers could not have taken full advantage of the opportunities that Jackson was fortunate enough to have been given. But no gospel singer to that point had been extended such opportunities, which came with the not insignificant task of managing a multi-faceted career and the considerable responsibility of representing the field even as she transformed it. In this sense, Jackson's positioning within the gospel field in 1954, which extended beyond the category "gospel singer," *was* exceptional, even though—and this is one of the book's core claims—she remained fully operative within the field even when she was performing in contexts ostensibly apart from it. Jackson was engaged in flows of dialogue with many tributaries that unfolded differently in private, in the media, and face-to-face with her black public.

Jackson's maneuvering around questions of voice, repertory, and self-identification as a church singer crops up again and again in Russell's journal. In rehearsal, we hear Jackson honing her delivery of the long lyrical lines of "Danny Boy," and even going further to explore what she herself might sound like singing a song "in a formal way" in "Going Home."[33] We also see Jackson's ironclad pledge to only sing "God's music" in "God's places" occasionally stretched thin. Whatever the passing references to Gabriel's horn in "The Lonesome Road," to the Jordan River in "Without a Song," or to Heaven and "the good Lord above" in "That Lucky Old Sun," these songs—and others that she performed on *The Mahalia Jackson Show* like "Summertime," "Lullaby" "Juanita," or "How Are Things in Glocca Morra"—are not plausibly religious or devotional in content. Russell recalled a conversation with a skeptical Falls who "wasn't sure either if '[My] Rosary' was a real 'Catholic' song or a love song."[34] In a *Time* magazine feature, Jackson explained her choice to perform "Danny Boy" on the show, grasping, it seems, for the protective cover of Du Boisian "sorrow song" hermeneutics: "That's a sad song. It tells the experience of one who has grieved, so I can sing it. I love to sing songs with a sorrow aspect."[35] The very fact of Jackson's self-permission to perform certain songs—predicated in the latter case on rather tenuous rationalization—indicates that she was in fact fighting yet another "battle within": upholding her sense of responsibility to not abandon any sense of being a church singer while faced with the crossover repertory that she was asked to deliver on her radio show.

Also in play were the inescapable politics of representation through Jackson's early career. Jackson seemed aware that some listeners purchased her records and tuned into her show for tantalizing glimpses of what Curtis Evans has called the "cultural images of black religion."[36] In a 1954 interview for *Down Beat*, Sargent asked Jackson whether she might ever make a live recording in the context of an actual service. Jackson's response communicated her concerns about the risk that cultural voyeurism would overshadow the religious content of black worship and represent the race poorly: "Sometimes our churches become highly emotional, and if a record of that were released to people who didn't understand, that record might look like it was making a mockery of religion. I wouldn't want that to happen."[37] *Time's* report on *The Mahalia Jackson Show* concluded with a description of its star trying to keep a lid on the response of her studio guests: "When the audience began cheering and stamping, Mahalia warned them: 'Don't you start that or we'd tear this place apart. You got to remember, we're not in church—we're on CBS.' "[38]

But on other occasions, Jackson deftly played the fluctuating expectations off of each other, calling attention to the compromises of a "semi-inspirational" show and the awkward limitations that the controlled environment of radio broadcasting placed on a church-based gospel singer. These issues emerged vividly at the taping of Show #4 on September 24. Russell's expansive journal entry provides a snapshot of Jackson in-studio that conveys both the playfulness that seduced commentators and the dynamics cultivated by the unorthodox informality of the show's taping sessions. The scene also makes concrete Jackson's ambivalent positioning as a gospel singer, by spiritual calling and by almost accidental profession.

> Twice after about 15 seconds of ["I'm on My Way to Canaan Land"] Jay stopped her, which started Mahalia on a series of lectures to the audience. She told how the man upstairs destroyed all the spirit by his "Stop" every time they started going good. Then Mahalia would poke her face out toward the audience and say "See." Then she said something like "Someday I'm going to mess up CBS like they've never been messed up before." The next time they stopped her, she stood there as though dejected for a few

seconds, then turned to audience and said "Now, if anyone ever had a desire to sing, it sure would have been gone now, wouldn't it?"

In a minute, she said "I'm used to singing in churches where we sing until the Lord comes."

Once when Jay asked, "Are you ready Miss Jackson?" Mahalia replied "Yes, Mr. Cecil B. DeMille."

On "Way" Jay once stopped them and asked if Mildred could play a little lighter, that the "piano was rocking" (meaning it actually was shaking). Mahalia sort of mumbled to herself but really to the audience, that that was the way she liked it, that it helped her a lot. Then she made a joke about how they were going to make everything rock.

A little later in a rather religious speech she told how when they got "in" good with CBS they'd be able to use all the good old numbers, such as "Upper Room" etc., and that they'd turn the place into a church meeting, and said "We'll *rock* this place."

Almost as soon as she started this program she stated again that CBS put her on "cold storage" . . . [and that she] wanted to make this a real church service someday.

Before that she had told how CBS had first heard her and of course then she was singing her regular gospel songs etc., but now she implied they're trying to change her and make her something she isn't and said "Now they're having me sing "Danny Boy" and did a lot of funny and high satirical warbling on the words "Danny Boy" for a few seconds.[39]

In such a moment, the challenges Jackson faced in balancing practicality and principles amid such an artificial and experimental context are plain to see. We can recognize and even take pleasure in the unmistakable element of gamesmanship in Jackson's performance-within-a-performance for the audience as she took jabs at a network "trying to change her and make her something she isn't." We do, however, in the end, have to acknowledge as well that Jackson is trying to have it both ways: holding onto the capital of devout integrity by claiming, as she did four months later to a Swedish interviewer, "I sacrifice myself and don't use my voice for anything else but singing religious songs" even as she pursued the prestige of recognition by singing love songs on a radio show.[40] Recording for Berman at Apollo, Jackson could lean on the familiarity of "the good old numbers"; on *The Mahalia Jackson Show*, the excitement and flattery of the opportunity had to have been mitigated somewhat by the anxiety-producing unfamiliarity of repertory, production, and musical backing, and by the suppression of her impulse to "have church," all of which called upon Jackson to continually recalibrate what now constituted "gospel truth" in a field of cultural production under transformation.

Shows #5–9: Being Natural

On the next five episodes of *The Mahalia Jackson Show*, the ratio of songs that might be heard in black churches to songs in a more popular vein remained about 50-50. Jackson performed several traditional African American religious songs ("Ezekiel Saw the Wheel," "Just a Closer Walk with Thee," "In that Great Getting Up Morning," and "When the Saints Go Marching In"), two of Dorsey's gospel compositions ("If We Ever Needed the Lord Before" and "I'm Going to Live the Life I Sing About"), and Tindley's "A City Called Heaven." She also sang two songs originally written by white nineteenth-century hymnodists that had since been adopted by black congregations ("My Faith Looks Up to Thee" and "When They Ring the Golden Bells"). In addition, Jackson interpreted recent inspirational pop songs ("Somebody Bigger Than You or I" and "Bless This House") and Gilded Age–era sentimental oldies ("The Rosary," "Juanita," and "A Perfect Day"), though the increased number of Tin Pan Alley numbers is striking. Not coincidentally, in four of these ("The Lonesome Road," "Without a Song," "That Lucky Old Sun," and a by-popular-demand repeat of "Summertime") the vernacular tint of the lyrics suggests that the singer is African American. A fifth show tune, "How Are Things in Glocca Morra," is another "ethnic" song from *Finian's Rainbow*, the Broadway musical about an Irish immigrant living in a racially mixed tobacco farming community in the American South.

Commentators responded positively to Jackson's voice but also to her personal charisma. The spontaneous interactivity between the performers and the enthusiastic audience, especially off-mic, played to the strengths of Jackson, whose charm, CBS staffers said, made rehearsals feel "like a Sunday-school picnic." In the opinion of the *Variety* writer who reviewed the debut episode, "Miss Jackson's between-tunes palaver with Halloran, scripted by Studs Terkel, neatly captured the gal's infectious personality."[41] The dialogue was unavoidably mechanical because of its function of moving the show forward, but Jackson was perhaps more comfortable with it than she might have otherwise been. Because the script was adapted directly from her many conversations with Terkel, the provenance of the anecdotes was at least familiar. Still, Jackson never seemed entirely at ease speaking her lines fluidly, sounding halting in her phrasing of sentences, particularly in juxtaposition with the experienced Halloran's polished delivery. Surely to Halloran's chagrin on a national radio broadcast, it took several weeks for the star of the show to figure out how to pronounce his name correctly, as Jackson repeatedly called him "Jack Halloree." A representative example of the show's script is the following transitional dialogue bridging Jackson's performances of the 1920s ballad "Trees" and the spiritual "Joshua Fit the Battle of Jericho," transcribed from Show #2.

HALLORAN: Mahalia, may I ask you something?
JACKSON: Jack Halloree, you may say what's ever on your mind.

HALLORAN: I was thinking how nice it would have been if the man who wrote those words could have heard you sing them just the way you did.

JACKSON: I was only singing about a tree the way I remember them. In New Orleans, we lived in a small house near the railroad tracks. And, oh, those beautiful oak trees and the perfume of the magnolia trees! I remember looking up at them. They were taller than my father. And he was a very tall man.

HALLORAN: I'm beginning to see what you mean, that gentle thoughts lead to gentle songs.

JACKSON: You got it, Jack. It's the way you feel at a certain time that leads you to sing a certain kind of song. Now, if I feel joyful I want to sing something with a beat, with a bounce, with all kinds of strength.

HALLORAN: And how strong might that be?

JACKSON: As strong as Joshua. He blew them ram horns seven days. He walked all around the town of Jericho. And on the seventh day—oh, how those walls came tumblin' down.

If off-mic—though, rather cheekily, under the network's own roof—Jackson protested to her audience that CBS was trying to "make her something she isn't," Terkel's scripts, whatever the song, regularly cast Jackson as a singer whose every vocal utterance was a transparent expression of how she felt at that moment, as a woman "who speaks her thoughts in song" and for whom "singing is as natural as breathing." These characterizations must have only reinforced for some listeners how Jackson's delivery of her spoken lines sounded anything but inborn.

It appears that CBS took a similar view because after the fourth show, perhaps in response to listener feedback, the production team addressed these flaws by moving toward greater informality and letting Mahalia be Mahalia. One hypothesis is that Russell himself, who was present for most rehearsals and tapings—preparing cue cards, making coffee and food runs for Jackson, Falls, and Jones, and occasionally debriefing with Lewellen afterward—made the suggestion, having seen Jackson extemporize at length during her church programs. Beginning with Show #5, Terkel's scripts were amended considerably, in some cases with entire segments of written text replaced by casual conversation. For the fifth show, after Jackson sung "Summertime," Terkel wrote an extended reverie for Jackson that had her reminiscing on her train ride to Chicago about songs she sang back in New Orleans, how she would pass the time working in "a big house of a very rich woman" by singing a song like "Down by the River" as "I'd scrub away on that washtub." Instead, what aired was a quick, candid exchange that offered listeners a behind-the-scenes glimpse and elicited mischievous chuckles from Jackson and roars of laughter from the studio audience.

JACKSON: Come on, Jack. You want to do "Down by the River?"

HALLORAN: All right. Be a pleasure.

JACKSON: This is a very beautiful song, and we don't know it so well. So, I hope you like what we *do* know. All right, let's start it out.

The cathartic release that greeted this moment of stepping out of radio character seemed to allow Jackson to exhale. She and the quartet received energetic applause after finishing "Down by the River"—recorded for Apollo as "I'm Going Down to the River"—then immediately launched into a reprise of the song during which Jackson kicked into gear, delivering perhaps her most inspired and swinging performance of the entire run of the show. Jackson can be heard periodically inserting an emphatic backbeat handclap, always a sign that she was feeling a song. CBS recognized that they had captured some of Jackson's best singing because they rebroadcast just this short reprise on Show #10. Catching her breath after the song, Jackson confessed on-air that loosening the straightjacket and letting a song stretch out was more her style.

> You know, I kind of liked that one a little bit. I kind of felt like myself (*audi-ence laughter*). I was just getting ready to sing. I get so tired of these notes, you know. I just used to singing the way I feel and let it come out. Well, you got to stop and worry about the notes and that takes my spirit away.

Part of the revised strategy was to make the interplay of performers and audience more explicitly a part of the show. On the same episode, Jackson's spirits were revived when the quartet surprised her by leading the audience in singing "Happy Birthday" for her forty-third birthday, which fell two days after the scheduled airdate. "Well, I didn't think anybody remembered my birthday since I was twenty-one," Jackson said, clearly moved. "Well, let us get into the 'Ezekiel Saw the Wheel,' before I start crying."[42] On the following show, Terkel's script set up Jackson's mostly unscripted acknowledgment of "my good friend Thomas Dorsey," who was in the studio audience to hear Jackson's performance of one of his songs, accompanied, unusually, only by the Falls-Jones ensemble with the quartet sitting out. "Tommy Dorsey, the trombone player?" Halloran asked to cue her up.

> No, Jack. It was written by our own Thomas A. Dorsey, one of the world's greatest gospel songwriters. And he's here tonight. I think Mr. Dorsey ought to stand. You give him a big hand. Thomas A. Dorsey. (*applause*) Mr. Dorsey have wrote more gospel songs than I believe than anybody in the world. He used to play the blues way back there in the early days. Used to play for Ma Rainey and now he's writing all these fine gospel songs. So we're happy to have him here tonight and I called him and told him that we

was going to sing it. So here we go with one of Dorsey's fine gospel bounce songs, "If We Ever Needed the Lord Before."

In Shows #5–9, Jackson's awkwardness on the earlier episodes was subtly but unmistakably reframed as simply a matter of a natural woman chafing against the artificiality of the medium. "It's the funniest thing," Jackson said in an aside that drew loud guffaws during her introduction of "That Lucky Old Sun," also on Show #6. "When someone want me to say something, I can't do it. But you come to my house and I just runs all over people."[43]

As these transcribed remarks indicate, giving Jackson the latitude to go off-script meant broadcasting to the nation the down-to-earth Jackson in the raw, colloquial warts and all. Whatever this meant to CBS producers, the tactic introduced new stakes for black listeners. Russell's most provocative journal entry is his record of a visit to Jackson's home on October 14.

> I stopped by Mahalia's at 6:00 for a few minutes on the way to Cylestine's. She was in her white bathrobe lying on north sofa watching TV. I left some grapes, which she began to eat at once. I also had the *Courier*, but no notices in it. Mahalia showed me a note she'd received that day and seemed much discouraged about [it]. . . .
>
> The note, she said, was from some colored person who knew her and went something like this:

A Note to You

Mahalia: Please don't be a Beulah, you are a great gospel singer and should talk as intelligently as you sing. Don't try to be a comedian and a nigger. For God's sake and the sake of the race cut out the dis and dat. Be natural, and as intelligent as you are.

Thanks

> It was neatly written, but unsigned and I believe had one grammatical error.
>
> Mahalia said the note was from someone who knew her, possibly a jealous gospel singer, or maybe, she said later to Mildred (aside and softly), someone from Sister Lucy's church, possibly who could be the one who called her up about same thing one night. She had me call up Studs about it. As Mahalia said, the Jewish and Irish people don't object, but the Negroes, because they are uneducated etc., worry so much.
>
> She wondered if they should have her talk at all, if they'd cut out some of the talking there would be room for another song, or perhaps all they need have her talk would be to read some Bible verses or something.

Cylestine said she'd talk to her later and explain that she should pay no attention to an unsigned letter, etc.[44]

If the sense of collective triumph elicited by Marian Anderson's Met signing offers one vantage point on *The Mahalia Jackson Show*, the demise of the popular radio and television character Beulah is another and perhaps even more immediate backdrop. From Harriet Beecher Stowe's Aunt Chloe to *The Help*, the female African American house servant has been among the best-known stock characters in U.S. popular culture, at once an object of nostalgic memory and a centerpiece of the menagerie of black stereotypes in a white American *commedia dell'arte*. A northern derivative of the Mammy figure from the antebellum South, the African American maid is identifiable as a persistent trope both through her appearance—heavy set, dark complected, speaking in dialect marked as black and Southern, and perpetually attired in service clothes—and through her behavior. The black maid is valued by her white employers for being a skillful cook and an affable, sexless, faithfully devoted member of the extended family, with an inexhaustible reservoir of patience and mother wit to manage their children and the vagaries of their home life.

A direct descendent of this lineage, Beulah debuted in 1939 as a recurring character on NBC radio programs before becoming the star of a show of her own, a CBS spinoff, in 1945. In 1950, with *The Beulah Show* still running on radio, ABC turned the program into a 30-minute television sitcom, on which Beulah worked for Harry and Alice Henderson and their young son Donny. Spanning three national media networks, Beulah was also notable for being performed by multiple actors. The first Beulah betrayed the character's roots in blackface minstrelsy in being played by white male performer Marlin Hurt speaking in stylized black dialect. When Hurt died of a sudden heart attack in 1946, another white actor, Bob Corley, briefly took on the role before it was given to black movie actress Hattie McDaniel in 1947. By that time, McDaniel (1895–1952) had become firmly established as a black maid specialist, having played versions of the role in a slew of films, most famously Queenie in *Show Boat* (1936), Mammy in *Gone with the Wind* (1939), and Aunt Tempy in *Song of the South* (1946). In mastering the character, McDaniel earned unprecedented acclaim: in 1940 she became the first black actor to win an Academy Award when she received the Oscar for Best Supporting Actress for her performance as Mammy. But she also faced a painfully conflicted reception linked to backlash against pejorative black stereotypes on early network television.

The principal lightning rod for reaction was the long-running comedy show *Amos 'n' Andy*, which made its own transition from radio to television and from white dialect-speaking actors to an all-black cast of performers just a year after *The Beulah Show*. As situation comedies, *Beulah* and *Amos 'n' Andy* differed in important ways. *Beulah* was built around the interracial interaction of a selfless, save-the-day maid with her benevolent employers, and, other than the comic relief of

Beulah's shiftless, non-committal boyfriend Bill and ditzy sidekick Oriole, played things relatively straight. In contrast, *Amos 'n' Andy* was immersed totally in black life and relied upon outlandish characters and plots for its humorous effect. What they shared was the distinction of being the only two series on television at the time prominently featuring African Americans. With "no other show on nation-wide television that shows Negroes in a favorable light," the NAACP argued, the two programs represented the race to the viewing public with Andy the credu-lous simpleton, Kingfish the bombastic rogue, Sapphire the implacable shrew, Calhoun the incompetent shyster, and Beulah the lovable but tirelessly deferential maid. At its 1951 convention in Atlanta, just days after *Amos 'n' Andy*'s television premiere, the NAACP unanimously passed a resolution that launched an aggres-sive campaign to force the show, widely popular since its creation in 1928, off of the air. *Beulah* was guilty by association.

> Radio and television programs, such as the *Amos 'n' Andy* and *Beulah* shows, which depict the Negro and other minority groups in a stereotyped and derogatory manner, definitely tend to strengthen the conclusion among uninformed or prejudiced peoples that Negroes and other minorities are inferior, lazy, dumb and dishonest.[45]

McDaniel had a history with NAACP disapproval, having witnessed organized protests of *Gone with the Wind* on similar grounds. The NAACP's anti–*Amos 'n' Andy* campaign dominated headlines in 1951, then lost some steam when it turned out that many African Americans took the view that something was better than nothing, trusted whites to see the caricatures for what they were, or, much to the organization's dismay, simply enjoyed watching the shows. In the case of *Amos 'n' Andy*, the significance for some African Americans of the unprecedented image of black television characters, however contrived, interacting beyond the gaze of white characters, should not be underestimated. In the end, however, partly from political pressure on sponsors, though also because of dipping ratings and changing directions in television programming, *The Beulah Show* was canceled in December 1952 after three seasons; *Amos 'n' Andy* followed shortly thereafter in April 1953, though it lived a robust afterlife through syndicated reruns.[46] The down-fall of these two shows is a reminder of the limited African American presence in post-war networked media and thus the avid interest in *The Mahalia Jackson Show*. *Beulah* was the first nationally broadcast weekly television series with a black actor in a lead role. After *Beulah* and *Amos 'n' Andy* were canceled in a four-month span in 1952–1953, there was not another black lead on a television show until 1965 when Bill Cosby was featured in *I Spy*, with Diahann Carroll following three years later as the star of *Julia*.

In more ways than one, the letter writer admonishing Jackson to clean up her radio act and desist from being "a comedian and a nigger" was revealing in telling her not to be *a* Beulah. Though the role is most closely associated with McDaniel—opposition to *Beulah* occasionally morphed into ad hominem "Hattie McDaniel Must Go" slogans[47]—it was a character-prescription filled by a sequence of black actresses. The first television Beulah was played not by McDaniel but by Ethel Waters, a role that some felt was beneath her in light of her esteemed career, her starring role on Broadway in *The Member of the Wedding* (in which Waters played Southern maid Berenice Sadie Brown), and her well-received, recently published autobiography *His Eye Is on the Sparrow*. Waters, needing the money but disillusioned by charges that she was giving "succor and aid to those who advocate second-class citizenship," stepped away from the show after one season and was briefly replaced by an ill McDaniel, who was in turn succeeded by Louise Beavers when McDaniel died of breast cancer in 1952.[48] The radio show continued until 1954; following McDaniel's death, the role was taken up in turn by Lillian Randolph and her sister Amanda Randolph. Counted with the two white men who inaugurated the role, these black women bring the total number of Beulahs in the eight-year lifespan of its radio and television iterations to seven.

In this sense, the anonymous, sharply worded advice to Jackson—echoed, Russell relates, by another church member "who called her up about [the] same thing one night"—was a specific warning to resist a ready-made template that black actresses were repeatedly asked and, in part because of scarce opportunities, chose to fill.[49] As McDaniel, so often stung by her critics, often liked to retort: "Hell, I'd rather play a maid than be one."[50] Some writers have implicitly, and in some cases explicitly, shoehorned Jackson into this role. In feature stories, the repeated praise of Jackson's excellence as a cook affirmed both her exalted culinary skills and her gendered domestic bona fides, though these plaudits occasionally flirted with stereotypes of a buxom, Southern black woman's acumen in the kitchen. More inescapably egregious is Jules Schwerin's mischaracterization of Jackson's appearance in Douglas Sirk's 1958 remake of *Imitation of Life*, discussed in the introductory chapter. Schwerin's erroneous and irresponsible claim that Jackson plays "a segregation-era caricature of the happy 'colored' servant" in the film is so deeply offensive precisely because of the highly charged history of what it meant to play or not to play, or even suggest, these characters. As late as 1959, Barbara Coopersmith sent a discreet letter to NAACP Executive Secretary Roy Wilkins letting him know "Several people noted that Mahalia Jackson referred to Dinah Shore as 'Miss Dinah'" during an appearance on Shore's television show, "with some negative reactions." As Farah Griffin has observed, the work of the Mammy figure and its associations can be enacted even more potently when linked to African American women's voices, as mobilization of the "figure of the singing black woman is often similar to the use of black women's bodies as nurturing, healing, life and love giving for the majority culture."[51] Beyond conjuring a specific character, "Please don't be a Beulah" was a container for sensitivities about a constellation of issues, concerns, and, in the view of some, self-inflicted wounds. This stark caution indexed the venerable disciplinary regimes of respectability politics but also very recent, highly publicized controversy within the African American public sphere over the elevated stakes of black representation in a rapidly changing media landscape.

The frustrating and disorienting predicament for Jackson, however, what likely left her so "discouraged," was that the counsel to "cut out the dis and dat" and "be natural" was in effect advice to *not* be herself. Another African American commentator on the relationship between Jackson's on-air persona and questions of black representation raised by *The Mahalia Jackson Show* was Edward "Sonny" Murrain, owner of the Elks Rendezvous nightclub in Harlem and an entertainment reporter for the *New York Age*. Over the period of three weeks in early January 1955, Murrain commented on Jackson's radio program in his "Front and Center" column. In a year-in-review rundown on New Year's Day, Murrain wrote that the show, "considered a venture of stature to offset the 'Amos and Andy' type of programming," left him "bitterly disappointed."[52] Murrain admitted in more extended remarks the following week that while he had "never been a fan of Mahalia, the truth remains that she is undoubtedly the greatest gospel soloist in the country." He was far less impressed with Jackson's versatility as a singer. "We expected to hear the peer of gospel singers at the pinnacle of expression in this medium. Instead, we hear an artist trying her darndest to be everything in creation except a gospel singer," Murrain wrote of her program's wide-ranging repertory, "and it is obvious, to everyone but her, that this is stretching talent a little thin. We acknowledge the fact that she is a topflight exponent of religious tomes, but must candidly opine that Miss Jackson should harness her efforts in any other direction." Murrain was faulting Jackson for repertory choices that were largely out of her hands. But as a staunch critic of "that Iron Curtain which has been the bane of the Negro entertainers seeking a regular radio or television slot," Murrain had deeper concerns resonant with the NAACP's campaign against pernicious black stereotypes. Noting "there could be no mistaking Miss Jackson for anything else but a Negro," Murrain perceived that her breakthrough had a dark underbelly. Black performers "who don't sound 'colored,'" he regretted in astute analysis, were not adequately promoted by record labels and media outlets, not because they lacked talent but because they did not exemplify the "right sound," resulting in "discrimination in reverse."

> So it would seem that CBS wasn't suddenly overcome with compassion for Negro talent, and tempered by a realization of the abundance thereof, when they welcomed Mahalia into the fold. They wanted a "Negro" program, not

just another CBS network show, and they have succeeded admirably. The Iron Curtain is still there; but only a few are perceptive enough to recognize it—least of all the Negro listeners, who feel that their lengthy cries for shows showcasing Negro stars have been answered.

Not attempting to take anything away from Mahalia Jackson (or alienate any of her fans), we can't help but wonder at the reticence of CBS and other major networks to sign the likes of Nat "King" Cole, Lena Horne, Billy Eckstine, Eartha Kitt or Billy Daniels to network shows. . . .

[I]t would seem that the garlands of praise handed out to CBS radio may have been a little premature, and the network's "democratic" move a little tainted. We say, in all honesty, that the Mahalia Jackson show alone is no indicative of the Negro's contribution to the entertainment world, or even to the sphere of religious music. It should be complemented by Negro-participant shows of equal stature, on a regular program basis. Then, and only then, will we believe the major networks are sincere in their wish to integrate.[53]

This calling out of the CBS network represents a rare and perhaps even singular skeptical assessment of *The Mahalia Jackson Show* to appear in print, and Murrain admitted receiving "a flood of protests." Yet he harbored no regrets about being a gadfly: "The difference in opinion did give us something to muse about, and opened up a heretofore unexplored terrain of thought in the field of performing arts, the 'yardstick' by which Yours Truly and other heralds and critics must eventually judge the efforts of those gifted persons in the race."[54]

Still, as indicated by the anonymous letter Jackson received and the sharp debate about *Beulah* and *Amos 'n' Andy* that were a prelude to her radio show, the CBS opportunity thrust the "down-to-earth" Jackson onto terrain that proved treacherous to negotiate. As a performer, Jackson was asked to execute repertory and work within mass-mediated entertainment formats that challenged her musically and highlighted both her potential abilities and her limitations in new ways. But these challenges may have been exceeded by a more specific dilemma. One begins to comprehend the tightrope that Jackson walked by recognizing how she had to maneuver among competing claims about her "naturalness." Jackson was the star of a show that extolled her for being perfectly natural, while facing accusations from members of her community that her behavior was not natural enough—that she was putting on a Beulah act—and the disappointment of others like Murrain who believed that she was too natural, to the point of crude, and lobbied for the presentation of black performers exhibiting more conventional markers of refinement.

Hovering over *The Mahalia Jackson Show*, and Jackson herself, was the unsettled question of preferred black culture and the bind faced so often by black performers who are perpetually asked both to transparently exemplify black culture and, as representatives of a "people," to transcend common expectations. In response to the controversy over *Beulah*, McDaniel told a reporter: "True we have our Marian Andersons, but most of our people are artisans, who add to the comfort of the world but extract very little pay."[55] Whatever one may think of Murrain's assessment, he was certainly correct that for many white American radio listeners the Mahalia Jackson of Shows #5–9 offered a comfortably familiar black persona, though any associations of Jackson with "a Beulah" had to have been blunted by the quality and breadth of her vocal performances. Still, as black reception of *Amos 'n' Andy* suggests, Murrain may have underestimated the pleasure numerous black Americans in the early 1950s, many of them residents in or migrants from the South, took in seeing images and hearing sounds resonant with their drylongso lived selves in network media.

Shows #10–17: Managing the Message

The producers of *The Mahalia Jackson Show* shifted strategy yet again beginning with Show #10, a makeover even more conspicuous than that undertaken in the fifth show. These changes were undoubtedly motivated by multiple factors, some speculative—perhaps dissatisfaction with the results of the informality of shows #5–9—but others highly concrete, most notably the introduction of Jackson as a Columbia recording artist. The more consequential results of the new tack were a dramatically expanded role for the show's narrator and a diminished presence of Halloran and the quartet. Together, these streamlined the show and shone a brighter spotlight on Jackson the artist than on Mahalia the affable personality.

The airing of shows #10–17 coincided with the holidays, and CBS presented special episodes for the two Sunday programs preceding Christmas Day. For these, Jackson sang "Joy to the World," "O Come, All Ye Faithful," "Go Tell It on the Mountain," "White Christmas," and of course "Silent Night," which was heard on both shows. She also performed two Nativity-themed songs with black vernacular lyrics, "Children, Go Where I Will Send Thee" and "There Wasn't No Room at the Inn." New repertory on this narrator-driven version of the show followed the pattern of earlier episodes, mixing several spirituals ("It's Me, Oh Lord, Standing in the Need of Prayer," "Hold On," "Deep River," "Go Down, Moses," and "Down by the Riverside"); a pair of Dorsey gospel songs ("I'm Going to Live the Life I Sing About in My Song" and "How Many Times"); and contemporary inspirational pop ("Crying in the Chapel" and "I'm Grateful"). On these shows, Jackson finally performed the Dvořák-Fisher stylized spiritual "Going Home" that she rehearsed three months earlier, as well as "Battle Hymn of the Republic" and "The House I Live In," a song that originated as a wartime plea for religious and racial tolerance.

In the tenth episode, Hal Stark, previously relegated to the program's introduction and closing credits, became the voice of *The Mahalia Jackson Show*. Jackson's speaking was limited to one short monologue per show and a canned farewell. Her opening and closing theme song was also changed from "I Keep Singing" to the chorus of "His Eye Is on the Sparrow," accompanied by piano, bass, and drums.

I sing because I'm happy
I sing because I'm free
His eye is on the sparrow
And I know he watches me.

The switch to a more substantial theme song and the shortening of Stark's prior effusively worded show opening—now simply: "That's Mahalia singing. Mahalia Jackson"—thrust Jackson the song artist front and center from the start. Halloran never spoke again on-air after Show #9. Stark's scripted remarks between each song, spoken over the musicians quietly playing or humming the next number in the background, gave the show a much tighter feel. Sacrificed to this more carefully directed version of the show was the energy of the live studio audience; in many places, the script reads: "Dub in applause." A few of these shows retained the same structure as earlier episodes, with four or five songs by Jackson and one or two by the quartet. But on others, the producers experimented with varying formats. Show #14 was an "all-request program," with Jackson "singing again the numbers most requested in your letters" and no independent contribution from the Jack Halloran Quartet.

At Jackson's first recording sessions for Columbia on November 22–23, 1954, she cut a whopping seventeen songs. This investment gave the show a new purpose and function that shaped its content. The first evidence of this was Show #11, which aired twelve days after these sessions and was used to give advance publicity to Jackson's forthcoming Columbia releases. This was the first episode with no music recorded specifically for the show. Instead, Stark's commentary was interspersed with a sampling of the Columbia recordings: "Didn't It Rain," "One God," "Jesus Met the Woman at the Well," a new version of "Move On Up a Little Higher," and a Dorsey arrangement of the spiritual "I've Got Shoes," retitled "Walk All Over God's Heaven." Starks opened Show #16, which aired on January 9, with the announcement: "Yesterday, the first four songs Mahalia has recorded for Columbia Records became available in record shops throughout the country. She will sing the same four songs for you tonight." These were the singles "Walk All Over God's Heaven" b/w "Jesus Met the Woman at the Well" and "A Rusty Old Halo" b/w "The Treasures of Love." Jackson's Columbia recording of "You'll Never Walk Alone" was played as well. The show heavily plugged the A-sides of these records: "Walk All Over God's Heaven" was played twice on Show #11 and again on

Shows #16, #17, and #19, and "A Rusty Old Halo" was heard twice on both Shows #16 and #18.

Curiously, other than passing extemporaneous remarks by Jackson on two of the more informal episodes, there is no mention at all during the entire run of the show that Jackson's specialization was gospel music. By comparison, the title of Jackson's first Columbia LP, released in March 1955, proclaimed her *The World's Greatest Gospel Singer*. As much as Jackson wanted to sing "her regular gospel songs" on the radio show, the strategy seemed to have been to rebrand her as a less stylistically typecast singer. Learning new songs, many of them with lyrics confronting her with a different lexicon and more of a mouthful and than she was accustomed to, meant that getting a song's words on the tip of her tongue could be as tricky for Jackson as reading her spoken lines. In a performance of the verbose "Battle Hymn of the Republic" on Show #10, for instance, Jackson sang: "With a glory in his bosom drafts frat trigger you and me."[56] If on *The Mahalia Jackson Show* CBS was striving to present Jackson delivering a broadly appealing diversity of repertory, Show #15 may have been the most successful of the entire run, according to these standards. The episode merits some attention for how it showcases Jackson's artistic range and on-the-job growth as a vocalist.[57]

Jackson opened Show #15 with "Because," a performance that was notable for a few reasons. "Because" is unambiguously a love song, exemplifying yet again Jackson's moving goalposts and occasional compromise. The only insinuation of religious faith comes in the final lines:

> Because God made thee mine I'll cherish thee
> Through light and darkness, through all time to be
> And pray his love may make our love divine
> Because God made thee mine.

For some, Jackson's unevenly fulfilled pledge to only sing religious repertory was leavened by her ability to render a secular song so that it *felt* religious, or, as music critic Nat Hentoff observed, to "convert a pseudo-religious popular song like 'I Believe' into honesty."[58] "Because" is also the only example I know of Jackson singing an art song firmly rooted in European concert music repertory; by the 1950s, Brahms's *Wiegenlied*, which Jackson also sang on the program, was more likely recognized in the United States as a popular lullaby than a classical composition. The song was written by French pianist and vocal instructor Helen Guy Rhodes, who composed under her better-known pen name Guy d'Hardelot. As a teenage student at the Paris Conservatoire in the 1870s, d'Hardelot was championed by composers Charles Gounod and Jules Massenet and celebrated soprano Emma Calvé (an influential early Carmen) and after settling in London she wrote hundreds of dramatically-sculpted sentimental songs, the most lasting of which is *Parce que*, set in English as "Because" in 1902 by Edward Teschemacher. "Because" has been a staple of the tenor repertory for over a century, recorded as early as 1913 by Caruso (in French), in the 1930s and 1940s by noted American Met tenors Richard Crooks, Jan Peerce, and Eugene Conley, and revived in the 1950s by Lanza and Richard Tucker. With its tripartite structure, "Because" was tailor-made for the "Three Tenors," Luciano Pavarotti, Placido Domingo, and José Carreras, who performed it regularly in concert. The song crossed over momentarily into the pop field in 1948 via a hit recording by Perry Como for RCA Victor and a subsequent version by the Four Coins in 1959 (reworded as "One Love, One Heart), and it remained among the most popular wedding songs through much of the twentieth century.[59] It is nonetheless exceptional to encounter this showpiece for concert tenor in Jackson's radio repertory.

Jackson's rendition of "Because" on Show #15 is particularly noteworthy because it was a second, entirely new performance of the song on her radio program. She sang the song on the third episode of *The Mahalia Jackson Show*, but her performance three months later surpasses the earlier version, indicating a singer gaining in confidence and in interpretive skill. Jackson's reading of "Because" takes the asymmetrical phrasing of d'Hardelot's melody, typically given even more elasticity by bel canto tenors through rubato, and transmutes one form of rhythmic freedom into another by rendering the song in a manner approaching the feel of her free Baptist hymns. But Jackson is in particularly strong voice on this episode and the high B-flats at the central climax and the final cadence are powerful, crystal clear, and fully supported, though in both cases instead of holding the note she opts for her much-beloved descending glissando. "Because" is a remarkably, even unexpectedly, effective performance that calls to mind Aretha Franklin's memorable rendition of Puccini's "Nessun dorma" as Pavarotti's surprise replacement at the 1998 Grammy Awards. Bringing two vocal practices into compelling conversation, Jackson transforms the song through moments of delicate, localized expression while somehow preserving its imposing sweep, in the process presenting the listener with what almost feels like a novel style, one we might call "gospera."

Jackson's next three numbers on the episode—a modern gospel composition, a stylized folksong, and a "real" spiritual—were all in different respects "African American," though they exhibit the diverse provenance of black song. Gospel songs performed on *The Mahalia Jackson Show* are few in number, but the rollicking "How Many Times" is one of four Dorsey compositions or arrangements heard during the program's run, and for this performance Jackson, sounding utterly at ease, goes "back home" and sings accompanied only by the Falls-Jones ensemble (Figure 9.4). Like many gospel songs, the chorus of "How Many Times" is written so that a backing ensemble enters on the chorus to sing antiphonally with the lead singer, but here Jackson handles both duties, toggling back and forth, barely finishing words, to capture the interplay of the two parts.

FIG. 9.4 Mahalia Jackson with her regular accompanists, organist Ralph Jones and pianist Mildred Falls (here on organ), often identified as the Falls-Jones Ensemble, November 22 or 23, 1954. Photo by Guy Gillette. Sony Music Entertainment Photograph Archive.

The arrangement of the next song, "Going Home," opens with the quartet, backed by piano, organ, and celesta, singing the distinctive four-chord progression that opens Dvořák's Largo, acknowledging the neo-spiritual's source. Again, Jackson sings in the slow, unmetered manner heard on her triple-meter hymns recorded for Apollo, less through improvised elaboration of the melody than with carefully manicured vibrato, subtly shaded dynamics, and occasional gospel-blues inflection. Her fourth number, "Hold On," sometimes known as "Keep Your Hand on the Plow" or "Gospel Plow," is a traditional song in the minor mode that Marian Anderson sang often as a concertized spiritual but that Jackson performed with a swing feel, complemented by Fall's modified "Salt Peanuts" riff in the piano accompaniment.[60] Jackson recorded the song at her first Columbia sessions, singing it in the key of G, which sat too low in her range and prevented her from drawing on the energy of her upper register. On the radio broadcast a month later, she took it up to B-flat, enabling her to use her prime "belting" range (B-flat–D-flat), and the performance has much more vitality than the Columbia record. "Hold On" became a fixture of Jackson's repertory in years to come and in subsequent performances—at the 1957 and 1958 Newport Jazz Festivals, for instance—she sang it in the higher key.

Jackson's final selection on the show was of an entirely different stripe. If "Because" was a product of early Edwardian-era sentimentality and "Going

Home" sounded like late Romantic folk nationalism, "The House I Live In" was spawned by the cultural politics of the Popular Front. The politically progressive co-songwriters of "The House I Live In," Abel Meeropol (aka Lewis Allen) and Earl Robinson, composed, respectively, perhaps the two most famous musical testaments of the period: "Strange Fruit," a song inextricably linked to Billie Holiday, and the Paul Robeson vehicle *Ballad for Americans*, both recorded in 1939. A plea for pluralism, "The House I Live In" debuted in the 1942 musical *Let Freedom Sing* and became best known through recordings by Paul Robeson and especially Frank Sinatra, who sang it in the 1945 ten-minute short film named after the song. Jackson's opportunities to ornament the melody seem limited and she sings the tune about as straightforwardly as one would ever hear from her, though as in "Going Home" she shapes its sound through timbral shading in her chest range. If "How Many Times" was a glance back to Jackson's Apollo singles of the late 1940s and early 1950s, "The House I Live In" is a look forward to the singer that would be featured on Jackson's Columbia LPs in the late 1950s and early 1960s. In all, Show #15 was notable for its range of repertory, offering a concert aria, black vernacular song, and didactic message music, but also for how it indicated Jackson's coming to terms with an expanding vocal arsenal.

The representation of Jackson's vocal style in the show's scripts was also closely bound up with the multiple meanings derived from African American spirituals, which through their framing on the show became an emblem of time, place, cultural history, political philosophy, and Jackson's personal biography. The work of the spiritual on *The Mahalia Jackson Show* was activated primarily through the program's spoken dialogue, which cast the spiritual both as a concrete artifact of black historical experience—coming "from the days of the galley ships" and "from the Southland, from the cotton fields of Georgia, South Carolina, and Mississippi" where, Jackson told listeners, "my people have sung it at camp meetings, at picnics, and all kinds of gatherings"—and somehow beyond history, articulating their message "from time out of mind." Jackson claimed the spiritual's omnipresence in her upbringing, while also, in being always-already there songs she had "heard all my life," hovering at the distant, frayed edges of individual memory: "When They Ring the Golden Bells" was "one of the earliest songs I can remember" and "A City Called Heaven" was "a spiritual I've heard ever since I can't remember." Through the written scripts for Shows #10–17—which sound less like Terkel's work—and through Jackson's voice, the show sought to reinforce narratives about African American history and about Jackson's personal authenticity, as well the indissoluble bond between of the two.

Religious content became particularly germane to the spiritual's evolving role on the program. As Russell reported, Jackson confessed to her audience how she hoped to "turn the place into a church meeting" and "make this a real church service someday." But even in the weeks leading up to the show's premiere, Jackson, via her press agent and ghost-writer Al Duckett, told *Chicago Defender* readers "what I want you to know when you hear me singing on your radio." Duckett quoted Jackson delineating her personal evangelical goals for the program.

> When the Columbia Broadcasting System asked me to do a regular Sunday night broadcast from coast to coast, I saw this as an opportunity—not only for myself—but also to expand the advertising campaign which Christians must wage to publicize God's message. To be able to go into thousands of homes and tell a story of faith in song and words is a magnificent challenge. I have accepted that challenge with absolute humility.[61]

Notwithstanding Jackson's intentions to assist the "advertising campaign" for religion that was cresting nationwide, the program's mix of repertory and spoken commentary suggest a more Gordian message. CBS publicity characterized the show as "semi-religious," and as Stark's introduction of "One God" on Show #11 suggests, references to faith tended to be generic endorsements of monotheism, not Christianity per se: "There are more than two and one half billion people on this earth. Hundreds of languages, thousands of dialects. People of many colors, opinions, ways of worship. But no matter what language, no matter what way we follow, we all serve one god."[62] Such an appeal reverberated with an early Cold War geopolitical outlook in the U.S. that celebrated religious pluralism yet also, as Wisconsin Senator Joseph McCarthy blared, emphasized a unifying dichotomy articulated by the "great difference between our Western Christian world and the Communist atheistic world."[63]

Complementing the show's reinforcement of the highly politicized meanings of "religion" within mass-mediated Cold War–era popular culture was its repeated advocacy of "freedom." Some of the scripted iterations of this theme were given to Jackson, who on her eighth show explained "In that Great Getting Up Morning" as a cry for deliverance: "That's called a song of jubilee, of joyfulness. Looking forward to that day when everybody will be free. It is one of the oldest of spirituals."[64] In the setup of "A City Called Heaven" on Show #10, Jackson's lines read: "Every song has got its own meaning, its own thoughts. Here's a spiritual I've heard ever since I can't remember. It has its own meaning, and one thought: freedom."[65] Such calls for liberation easily strike the ear as reaffirmations of the black freedom struggle, particularly when linked to the spiritual and articulated by an African American gospel singer whose voice, Robert Anderson provocatively asserted, "took the people back to slavery times."[66] Cowan's track record of using radio to broadcast positive representations of African Americans suggests that making *The Mahalia Jackson Show* his "pet project" had, at least to some extent, progressive motivations.

At the same time, in the climate of 1950s red-baiting, the dangers of aligning oneself too openly with the civil rights movement were real, though this threat could in certain contexts be mitigated through recourse to religion. In 1957, Martin Luther King Jr., whose civil rights organization was originally called the Southern Negro Leaders Conference, successfully lobbied fellow organizers for a name change to the Southern Christian Leadership Conference (SCLC), specifically to deflect any charge of Communist leanings. SCLC co-founder Ella Baker recalled: "part of the thought that was developed was that, well, if you're confronting the power structure, you might be less suspect being called Christian. And you would, perhaps, avoid being tagged as 'Red' by being called Christian."[67] The rhetoric of double entendre often attributed to the Negro spiritual made it a prime vehicle for the deployment of multiple meanings. "Everybody dreams," said Stark introducing "When the Saints Go Marching In" on Show #14. "He dreams of the great day of Jubilee. No more heavy burden to tote from day to day. Everybody dreams of freedom time, of belonging to that number."[68] Freely substituting "freedom," "jubilee," and "Heaven" softened the endorsement of full citizenship for black Americans by blurring distinctions between civic freedom for African Americans with divine deliverance available to all.

The connotative ambiguities on *The Mahalia Jackson Show* were further complicated by the fact that "freedom" was one of the most resonant buzzwords of the early Cold War era, a favored theme within popular discourse that pitted democracy's promise of political, economic, and personal liberty against the coercive "slavery" of the communist system. The sense of "freedom" as a political philosophy materializing in the act of choice by an atomized democratic citizen was suggested most strongly on Show #15. The scripted set-up of "Because" had Stark explain Jackson's performance as exemplifying the abdication of fealty to pre-determined practice in favor of an individually guided abandon.

> A song can be interpreted in so many different ways. In the traditional concert manner, crossing every "T" and dotting every "I," following the score note for note. It can also be sung out in the free spirit too, following only the singer's inner feeling. Like this:

In his introduction of the next song, "How Many Times," Stark's lines directly linked individual autonomy, expressed through personal style, to the spiritual, while slyly contrasting Jackson's freedom to be "natural" with the watchful eye of a compulsory system, an easily digestible political parable insinuating a national ethos for a 1950s U.S. audience.

In the world of singing it's the spiritual that cries out most for deep-felt natural singing. No barriers are permitted here. There is no one to say: "This
must be sung in such-and-such a way." Each singer must be free to follow
his own road. This is Mahalia's road.

Close analysis of *The Mahalia Jackson Show* reveals that Jackson was not simply a
church singer who "crossed over," one who, depending on one's perspective, either endeavored to spread the word of God to a broader audience or succumbed
to the lure of financial gain. Acknowledging Jackson's presence within U.S. popular culture enables us to understand her as a Cold War figure, while also
recognizing performances of black culture in the early Cold War United States
as embedded within widely circulating public discourse that cast entirely separable beliefs about civil rights, religious belief, citizenship, global politics, and
individual subjecthood as mutually reliant.[69] As the show's producers balanced
a desire to present Jackson's voice to the nation in transformative ways and the
more pragmatic need to find sponsorship that would enable the program to survive, it was important to get the message right. Tightening the show's production
and communicating to audiences through the controlled counterpoint of Stark's
narrating voice and Jackson's sung performances made this delicate dance more
manageable.

Shows #18–20: Supporting Your Own

Despite good reviews and solid ratings, by the New Year *The Mahalia Jackson Show*
was in peril, and the program was abruptly shortened from twenty-five minutes to
ten. Lucia Carter of the *Chicago Sun-Times*, an admirer of Jackson who was rooting
for her success, registered her disappointment with the latest developments in her
television and radio column.

> In what I think is a pretty shortsighted move, the CBS radio network
> is going to cut gospel singer Mahalia Jackson's excellent program to 10
> minutes. A sponsor hasn't been found, it seems.
>
> In routine instances, I won't fight these business office moves. But
> there are exceptions where, because of program content and quality, art
> ought to take precedence over commerce. This is one.
>
> Ironically, the program cut coincides with the release of Miss Jackson's
> first major commercial record album which probably will add a lot to
> her fame.

Another of Jackson's devoted champions in the Chicago press, Herb Lyon of the
Tribune, praised Jackson as "merely the most magnificent singing talent to come

along this millennium" and echoed Carter's view of the awkward timing of CBS's cutback: "No sponsor. The irony of it is that Mahalia's waxings are just beginning to whirl in all the record shoppes and she's getting TV offers on all sides. Mitch Miller, the Columbia record boss, is fit to be tied—it's a body blow to her big build-up and CBS oughta cringe."[70]

In its abbreviated version, the show featured three numbers by Jackson alternating with scripted dialogue by Stark. The opening selection doubled as the show's opening; Stark momentarily interrupted the song to introduce Jackson, who then finished the number. Show #18 was noteworthy for offering two songs by black gospel songwriters, Dorsey's "Beautiful Tomorrow" and Akers's "God Spoke to Me," sandwiched around "A Rusty Old Halo." Shows #19 and #20 were structurally identical, featuring a Columbia recording ("Walk Over God's Heaven" and "Jesus Met the Woman at the Well," respectively,) bracketed by a spiritual ("Joshua Fit the Battle of Jericho" and "Every Time I Feel the Spirit") and an inspirational song ("One Step Toward the Lord," recorded by the Blackwood Brothers in 1953, and the sentimental oldie "My Task," published in 1903 and revived by Johnny Hartman in 1948 for RCA Victor). "His Eye Is on the Sparrow" continued to be the theme song heard in tandem with the final farewell and closing credits.

The ten-minute version of *The Mahalia Jackson Show* lasted for just three episodes, all recorded in a batch on January 14, and the program was canceled following the airing of Show #20 on February 6. "After a razzle-dazzle buildup, CBS radio has dropped gospel shouter Mahalia Jackson," a short notice in the *Washington Post* read. *Variety* also observed a failure of the massive marketing offensive to coax advertisers to put money behind the program: "The Lou Cowan–fronted gospel singer was launched on the web [i.e., networked media] last fall with lotsa fanfare but failed to make the sponsor grade." Some black listeners already saw the writing on the wall when the show was shortened in length. One steadfast but irritated fan of the program urged African Americans to feel a sense of collective ownership and responsibility for the show's survival. *Pittsburgh Courier* theater columnist Izzy Rowe reprinted a "curt note from a Southerner" chastising commentators who bemoaned the absence of African Americans on radio and television but failed to take matters into their own hands by putting black capital to effective use.

> You're always beefing about no Negro commercials without doing anything about one. The Mahalia Jackson radio show is a great one, you never forget it once you've heard it, so why don't some of the rich Negroes you're always writing about sponsor her? Better yet, some of the bigger churches could pick up the tab. Already down from a half-hour to fifteen minutes, the show may go off the air and that would be a shame.

Rowe was receptive and, if only as a diplomatic gesture, she seconded the correspondent's call for black self-help: "Think this writer has got something there, so come on, let's do a bit of sponsoring ourselves."[71]

But Jackson's career was moving into a phase in which the question of black folks supporting their own had less and less relevance as CBS and Columbia were now deeply invested in the success of their artist. Despite the disappointment of the cancellation of her radio program, five weeks later Jackson made her own transition to a television series when Chicago station WBBM-TV inaugurated the local show *Mahalia Jackson Sings*. In fact, 1955 was a year that saw multiple developments of major consequence for Jackson. Now fully within the fold of Columbia Records, she was introduced to the public as an album artist and, heavily promoted by Columbia, she made increasingly high profile appearances that moved her into more regular proximity with well-known personages from the world of entertainment. At the same time, Jackson was becoming a major star herself, and her growing prominence as a public figure meant that she was now negotiating two distinct yet intertwined careers: as a pop-cultural celebrity and as the most illustrious member of Chicago's African American church circles. The final chapters assess the implications of Jackson becoming a Columbia recording artist, underscoring the meanings of a black church singer, and the black gospel field, achieving unprecedented visibility and prestige.

"The World's Greatest Gospel Singer"

"MAHALIA JACKSON, WHO is billed as 'the world's greatest gospel singer,' sings neither jazz nor blues," began John Wilson of the *New York Times* in his review of Jackson's 1955 debut LP for Columbia Records.

> But the jazz singer and the gospel singer are products of a common root, the spiritual, and the qualities that make a great jazz singer also produce a great gospel singer. The difference is in the sentiments expressed.
>
> Miss Jackson has a big, ranging voice, an ease of projection and a swinging attack that would be the envy of any jazz singer. On *Mahalia Jackson* (Columbia), a collection of her gospel songs, these attributes are supplemented by her obviously deep sincerity.[1]

For Wilson, ruminating on black musical roots and fruits, Jackson ratified conventional understanding about a holism that aggregated spirituals, the blues, jazz, and gospel as branches of a single family tree. Other commentators seemed to agree that she was a jazz singer in all but name. Jackson, some argued, instantiated in voice and in temperament the marriage of Saturday night and Sunday morning encapsulated in a quality that *Variety*, echoing Wilson, described as "the right kind of swinging sincerity."[2]

In a contested maneuver, Columbia signed Jackson away from Apollo Records in the summer of 1954, then began recording her in the fall, releasing her first recordings, as singles and on LP, in the early months of 1955. Later that year, additional singles and a Christmas album followed. Columbia pursued Jackson with the hope that she would become a star by branching out even further, bringing her gospel voice to a greater range of repertory. After all, *Billboard* pointed out to readers, long-standing racialized boundaries between the rhythm and blues and pop charts were slowly but surely dissolving with "the emergence of the Negro as a pop artist." Black vocalists as diverse as Sammy Davis Jr. on Decca, Roy Hamilton on Epic, LaVern Baker on Atlantic, and Harry Belafonte on RCA were not only making inroads on the hit parade of singles but were also showing promise as pop album artists. "Columbia, too, is exploring such pop and album potential with Mahalia Jackson, the great gospel singer."[3]

To an even greater extent than in her work for Apollo, Jackson's early years as a Columbia recording artist saw continuous negotiation of repertory, musical style, accompaniment, and working methods, along with the distinguishable expectations of singles and albums. The latter was particularly significant. The attempt to reconcile gospel performance as understood by Jackson and production and marketing possibilities envisioned by Columbia played out through recordings produced for and released in different formats. Jackson's Columbia sessions in 1954 and 1955 generated their share of both fruitful collaboration and questionable experiments. Still, whatever Jackson's ambivalence, the crossover moment also became an opportunity for her to explore and assess the breadth of her vocal practice. Becoming a Columbia artist brought with it new and increasingly multilayered discourse on Jackson as a singer. The rhetorical shift, as the "Empress" and "Queen" of gospel, as she was popularly honored by her black fan base in the 1940s, was pitched by the biggest record company in the industry as "the world's greatest" in the mid-1950s, was subtle but not without significance. These revisions were further complicated by Columbia's simultaneous efforts to market Jackson performing religious pop and to laud her as possessing the stylistic touch of a jazz singer, all the while according her the status of a master vocalist beyond stylistic category. If Jackson earned a reputation as a "spiritual" singer at Apollo and as a natural woman on the radio, her work for Columbia Records rebranded her as a genre-defining singer and a world-class artist.

Recruitment

Jackson's departure from Apollo Records involved an opportunistic courtship and extended deliberation that began as a prelude to her CBS radio show. In the early 1950s, independent record labels may have led the way in producing "specialty" musics like modern jazz, rhythm and blues, country, and "ethnic" recordings, but the pop market was dominated by a group of major labels known in the industry as the "big five": Columbia, RCA Victor, and Decca in New York, Mercury in Chicago, and Capitol in Los Angeles, with M-G-M often considered a sixth major. Though the category was somewhat fluid, a "major" label generally indicated a company that was able to record, manufacture, and distribute its music internationally. Independent labels typically had to outsource the pressing and distribution of their disks, often relying upon major labels to handle the tasks. The oldest continuous brand in the recording industry, Columbia entered the 1950s not only with its venerable status but also with the distinction of having introduced the

33⅓ RPM long-playing album in 1948, primarily to accommodate extended works of classical music. In 1951, Columbia also adopted the 45 RPM single invented by RCA, which eventually replaced the more cumbersome and fragile 78 RPM single. Jackson's recordings would be released on all three formats in her early career as a Columbia artist.

At the heart of Columbia's popular music operations was Mitch Miller (1911–2010). A classical oboist from Rochester, New York, turned intrepid pop producer, the Mephistophelean-bearded and irrepressibly impish Miller left his position as head of Artists and Repertory (A&R) at Mercury in 1950 to accept the same job at Columbia where he quickly built a reputation as a no-holds-barred hit-maker with a roster of stars that included Frankie Laine, Rosemary Clooney, Judy Garland, Tony Bennett, Doris Day, and Jackson's beloved Liberace. "Before Mitch came along, pop music was vestigial," said Atlantic Records head Jerry Wexler. "He changed all that. He threw out the 32-bar song form; he used bastard instruments. He was the first great record producer in history."[4] Miller's fellow producer at Columbia was George Avakian (1919–2017). Born in Armavir, Russia, Avakian immigrated with his Armenian parents to the United States in 1923 in the wake of the Bolshevik Revolution and fell in love with the music of Duke Ellington, Fletcher Henderson, and Louis Armstrong listening to the radio as a teenager. Avakian enrolled at Yale, where he befriended fellow English major and jazz enthusiast Marshall Stearns and produced what many call the first jazz album, *Chicago Jazz*, for Decca during his sophomore and junior years. After serving in World War II, Avakian was hired by Columbia in 1946 and eventually worked alongside Miller, transforming the image of jazz by improving recording quality, releasing LPs with substantive liner notes, and marketing the music from within the pop department. The career of one of Avakian's most important signings, trumpeter Miles Davis, was considerably impacted by the producer's efforts to remodel the commodified face of jazz in the 1950s. When Columbia approached Jackson in 1954, the label was in the midst of the most successful year in its history, with record sales up 25%, and sought to strengthen its industry position further by upping its production and promotion of hi-fidelity classical "masterworks," Broadway musical soundtracks, modern jazz, and country-western music. The pursuit of Jackson as the label's first gospel artist was likely part of the refueled ambition of Columbia's mid-1950s vision.[5]

With a hunch that Bess Berman had neglected to exercise her option to extend Jackson's Apollo contract when it expired on June 13, Miller moved fast in wooing Jackson that summer. The key figure facilitating these efforts was John Hammond (1910–1987), who became an intermediary between Jackson and Miller. Born in New York into tremendous wealth as a member of the Vanderbilt clan, Hammond expressed an early interest in music, writing, and social justice, and to his parents' dismay dropped out of Yale in 1931 to pursue a career in the record industry as a producer and music critic. Hammond claims that he "was already enthusiastic about gospel in the 1920s" and knew of Jackson's first sides for Decca when they were released shortly before he presented Mitchell's Christian Singers, the Golden Gate Quartet, and Sister Rosetta Tharpe at his first "From Spirituals to Swing" concert at Carnegie Hall on December 23, 1938. "When I really got enthusiastic about Mahalia, though, was when she made those wonderful Apollo records," said Hammond, who in New York "went to as many gospel things as I could. I was crazy about it." According to Sallie Martin, Hammond enlisted Jackson to sing at political events in Chicago when he was a Mercury Records executive. In the 1940s, he had a further series of encounters with Jackson in New York through gospel promoter Joe Bostic and through Brother John Sellers, who remembered Hammond coming by his apartment to visit with Jackson when she was in town for her 1948 song battle with Ernestine Washington at the Golden Gate. Hammond also attended Stearns's 1951 "Definitions in Jazz" roundtable at the Music Inn, where Jackson was the featured performer (Figure 10.1).[6]

As an influential producer and impresario, Hammond's relationship with African American musicians was long and complicated, crisscrossing the line between a fierce, career-making advocate with a track record of devoted civil rights activism and a paternalistic gatekeeper who self-righteously policed what he believed to be appropriate stylistic bounds of black cultural politics. In 1935, Hammond eviscerated Ellington's "un-Negroid" extended work *Reminiscing in Tempo* for what he viewed as a pretentious dabbling in the musical language of Western European art music. *Reminiscing in Tempo* offered conclusive evidence that its composer "shuts his eyes to the abuses being heaped upon his race."[7] Recalling the 1930s and 1940s, Hammond described himself to Goreau as "the only white critic who got the so-called race records" and he situated the acuity of his taste as even ahead of the black middle class.

> In 1947, I was on the NAACP Legal Advisory Board, and to raise some money I suggested to Thurgood Marshall that we give a concert by Mahalia Jackson. He looked at me sort of stonily and said, "All that shouting and carrying on?" I said, to kid him, "What are you, some kind of Episcopalian?" And it turned out he was! Later on, though, of course, they got to be very good friends. But at that time, the Negro bourgeoisie weren't for gospel at all.[8]

Miller, who had worked with Hammond at Mercury, also knew Jackson's Apollo recordings and had "been an admirer" from afar, but made strategic use of Hammond's more personal familiarity when he proposed that she make the leap to Columbia. Hammond remembered that "Mitch used my name freely in talking with Mahalia" and Miller himself confessed that Hammond "helped me get her," unsure how things would have played out "if it weren't for John." Miller invited

FIG. 10.1 Participants at the "Definitions in Jazz" roundtable held at the Music Inn, Lenox, Massachusetts, August 1951. From left to right: accompanist Mildred Falls, Mahalia Jackson, drummer Dennis Strong, pianist John Mehegan, anthropologist Richard Waterman, English literature and jazz scholar Marshall Stearns, record producer John Hammond, and musicologist and folklorist Willis James. Photograph by Clemens Kalischer. Image Photos/Clemens Kalischer.

Jackson to his Central Park West apartment in New York and took Jackson and Hammond to lunch to discuss her contract situation and make a formal offer. Jackson's cogitation over Miller's invitation was deep and equivocal; she carried the contract in her purse for weeks, reading and re-reading the terms before finally agreeing to sign.[9] According to Hammond, Jackson consulted him about the matter. His recollection of his advice, surely shaded retrospectively by his disapproval of the direction of Jackson's post-Apollo career, is consistent with his long-standing idealization of hermetically sealed black musical expression.

> As I remember it, Mahalia called me from Mitch's office, where Mahalia was at the time, and said, "Mr. Hammond"—she wouldn't call me John— "Mr. Hammond, what about this?" I told her, "Mahalia, if you want to make a lot of money, they'll promote you and take out page ads in things like *Life* magazine because Mitch believes in promotion. But if you go with

Columbia, they don't know anything about your kind of music and you'll lose your own people." And that proved to be correct.[10]

On August 12, Columbia's PR department issued a press release announcing that the label had signed Jackson as a recording artist in conjunction with the launch of *The Mahalia Jackson Show*. Miller explained the advantages of the union: "Columbia's advanced engineering facilities and extensive distribution system will bring her universal appeal and superb talent to a larger public than she has reached even with highly successful tours."[11] Berman, however, insisting that Apollo had indeed picked up Jackson's option and that there was another year remaining on her contract—or perhaps determined, as a matter of pride, that her star would not be poached by a major label without some restitution—contested the legitimacy of the Columbia deal. The music trade press recognized the stakes of the battle for Apollo—*Variety* called Jackson "the backbone of its roster"—but reported Columbia's counterclaim that Apollo, perhaps unaware of the bigger label's aggressive behind-the-scenes recruitment, had simply forgotten to renew Jackson's contract. This may have been the case because the next month Berman relented and Jackson became a Columbia artist through a negotiated buyout. On September 20, Columbia attorney Alfred Lorber sent a memo to Miller, copied to label president James Conkling and executive vice president Goddard Lieberson, letting them know that the dust had finally cleared: "If nothing blows up, the settlement in the Mahalia Jackson matter will be signed with Apollo Wednesday, September 22nd."[12]

Lorber's memo detailed the terms of agreement. The contract, backdated to July 1, guaranteed Jackson $50,000 over a five-year and three-month period for recording eight sides in the first nine months and eight more every six months thereafter. The sum due Jackson was scheduled to be paid out evenly at a rate of $833.33 per month. Miller believed that the reliability of a paycheck earned from making records was a lynchpin in getting Jackson to accept his offer: "She had been treated so badly before by Apollo, and she had to have trust in somebody. And the first thing we gave her was a good guarantee."[13] In addition, Jackson would receive a 5 percent royalty on 90 percent of all records sold. Columbia was prohibited from releasing recordings of Jackson singing any song that she had recorded for Apollo within the prior five-year period. Apollo also received cash compensation from Columbia in the amount of $5,220. One third of this ($1,740) came out of Columbia's own pocket, but Jackson essentially reimbursed Columbia the remainder, with one-third treated as an advance against her royalties, and the final third deducted from her guarantee during the first two years of her contract, reducing her monthly salary over this period to $760.83 per month. Jackson also had to return to her former label all paychecks that she had received since June 13, the expiration date of her Apollo contract. Columbia reimbursed Jackson $600 of this, but this too was counted against her royalties, as were any Columbia expenses for accompanists, arrangements, and copying. By comparison, when RCA Victor purchased Elvis Presley's contract and masters from independent Sun Records a year later in November 1955, Sun owner Sam Phillips exacted a $35,000 buyout plus $5,000 in back royalties, the largest such sum to date. RCA gave Presley the identical royalty of "5% of 90" that Jackson received from Columbia, though he also received a $4,500 signing bonus not deductible from future earnings.[14] With terms in place, Jackson was now contracted by the label for whom she would work exclusively for the rest of her life. "If you do not hear from me by next Monday," Lorber wrote Miller, "you can promptly begin to record Mahalia."

First Sessions

Jackson's CBS radio show, already in the works, did begin promptly, debuting just six days after Lorber's go-ahead, but she did not enter the Columbia recording studio until two months later, for a two-day session in New York on November 22–23. Jackson had two producers at Columbia, each with separate responsibilities: Miller, who crafted Jackson's pop-oriented singles, and Avakian, who oversaw the production of her albums (Figure 10.2). Having been given assurance from Avakian that

FIG. 10.2 Mahalia Jackson at her first recording session for Columbia Records, with (from l to r) Bill Russell, George Avakian, and Mitch Miller, November 22, 1954. Avakian surprised Jackson with a gift: the recently released album package by pianist Liberace, of whom Jackson was an avid fan. Photo by Guy Gillette. Sony Music Entertainment Photograph Archive.

"she should record what she wants to record" for her first LP, Jackson decided that it "would be a collection of true gospel songs."[15] Five days before the first session, Russell informed Avakian that Jackson was doing her best to prepare—even working on "a *new* song she's trying to compose, which she might try to surprise you all with"—but managing her accumulating responsibilities, on top of daily life, was a challenge. "There are a lot of distractions," Russell wrote, "such as photos for the *Defender*, two check-ups at hospital (just 'routine') and a big cooking of gumbo (a 3 gallon pot) yesterday—the best I ever tasted incidentally."[16]

Rehearsing material for two Christmas episodes of her radio program that week was another distraction, but *The Mahalia Jackson Show* also played an intrinsic role in Jackson's career as a Columbia recording artist in multiple ways. Throughout the fall, Miller was sending Jackson songs to try out, some of which were performed on the show, recorded for Columbia, or both. Russell's reel-to-reel recorder captured Jackson rehearsing songs that she did not sing on air but did record for Columbia, including the inspirational pop song "One God" and two gospel songs, Thelma Gross's "Out of the Depths" and Robert Anderson's "Oh Lord, Is It I?" Four songs that she recorded at her first session had, however, been given test runs on the radio show beforehand, two in a popular vein—"You'll Never Walk Alone" (Show #1) and "Somebody Bigger Than You or I" (Show #5)— and two gospel songs surely chosen by Jackson, "Jesus Met the Woman at the Well" (Show #3) and Dorsey's "I'm Going to Live the Life I Sing About in My Song" (Show #7). The radio show also helped promote her releases. On Show #11, which aired two weeks after she cut her first Columbia sides, the program's format was altered and instead of live performances with the Jack Halloran Quartet, five forthcoming sides were previewed. Years later, *The Mahalia Jackson Show* was in effect commemorated with the 1962 release of Jackson's Grammy Award–winning Columbia album *Great Songs of Love and Faith*, on which nine of the twelve tracks, arranged by Johnny Williams, were newly recorded versions of sentimental parlor songs that she sang on her radio show eight years earlier.[17]

As on the radio show, Jackson's backing group for her initial pair of Columbia sessions was billed as the "Falls-Jones Ensemble," which Avakian originally hoped to supplement with the sound of New Orleans brass by adding trumpeter Natty Dominique and trombonist Turk Murphy. In the end, Falls and Jones were joined by a three-man rhythm section of veteran players. In Art Ryerson, Jackson had one of the most respected studio guitarists of his day. With a remarkably expansive five-decade career that witnessed the achievement of playing with Paul Whiteman in the 1930s and Elvis Presley in the 1950s, Ryerson arrived at the Jackson session having backed a multitude of major vocalists, including Frank Sinatra and Ella Fitzgerald, and played on records by artists running the gamut from Charlie Parker to Bill Haley and the Comets. Responding to Jackson's in-the-moment flights during performance was a task even for Falls, and Ryerson's stylistic breadth had at least prepared him for the challenge. As he remembered it, however, there was still a learning curve. Jackson "didn't care for my playing," Ryerson believed. "She just wanted me to do something that I just couldn't do, or that she just couldn't communicate. It was nothing significant, but she was a great singer."[18]

Avakian rounded out the backing band with players who also brought a wealth of experience: double bassist Frank Carroll, a Columbia studio regular who years later wrote a method book for electric bass, and drummer Norris "Bunny" Shawker, who in his career backed singers ranging from Billie Holiday to Sam Cooke. A principal hurdle for the session was melding and balancing what were essentially two discrete ensembles—Falls-Jones and Ryerson-Carroll-Shawker— and two styles, particularly the gospel feel of Falls and the jazz dialect of Ryerson, in a manner that maximized Jackson's comfort. Jackson did, however, admit that she enjoyed singing backed with the addition of guitar, bass, and drums "as on Columbia records" because "it was easier to sing that way."[19]

Jackson cut her Columbia sides at an abandoned Armenian church in New York located at 207 East 30th Street, near Third Avenue. In 1949, Avakian helped to scout out the space, which became known as the 30th Street Studio, or simply "The Church." Miller was so smitten by the sound captured by the room's wood flooring, drape-covered plaster walls, and 100-foot high ceilings that he prohibited janitors from mopping out of a fear that the acoustics might be altered. It quickly acquired a reputation as one of Manhattan's elite recording studios, producing many of Miller's signature pop vocal recordings as well as a body of era-defining albums in the 1950s, extending from Glenn Gould's metamorphic *Goldberg Variations* to Davis's *Kind of Blue*.[20] During her two-day November sessions at the Church, Jackson recorded seventeen songs, of which twelve were self-selected church songs (Example 10.1). Of these twelve, three—"Didn't It Rain," "Amazing Grace," and "Move On Up a Little Higher"—were songs that she had previously re-corded early in her Apollo career. These re-recorded songs give us an opportunity to assess the recalibration of approach and Jackson's development as an artist over a period of time. On Jackson's new version of her breakthrough hit "Move On Up a Little Higher," the faster tempo (100 bpm) and prominent walking bass give the song a notably different personality, with more forward momentum but without the deliberate pace and with less space for the searing scoop on the titular hook, which, together, made the Apollo record so distinctive. Revealing in a different way is her performance of "Amazing Grace," which Jackson described as "one of the old meters of the church."[21] Recorded seven years after her Apollo side cut in December 1947, Jackson's Columbia version of "Amazing Grace" is delivered with considerably more authority, breath control, and purposeful phrasing, exhibiting a matured mastery over her instrument and greater certainty of what she wanted to do with the song on record. Falls's more expressive accompaniment and the

EXAMPLE 10.1

Mahalia Jackson's Columbia Record Sessions, 1954–1955

Session Date	Song
November 22, 1954	
	The Treasures of Love
	One God
	A Rusty Old Halo
	Jesus Met the Woman at the Well
	I'm Going to Live the Life I Sing About in My Song
	Walk Over God's Heaven
	You'll Never Walk Alone
	Didn't It Rain
	When the Saints Go Marching In
	Somebody Bigger Than You or I
	When I Wake in Glory
	Out of the Depths
	Oh Lord, Is It I?
	Amazing Grace
November 23, 1954	
	Jesus
	Move On Up a Little Higher
	Keep Your Hand on the Plow
May 31, 1955	
	Silent Night, Holy Night
	O Little Town of Bethlehem
	Go Tell It on the Mountain
	White Christmas
	I Wonder as I Wander
June 1, 1955	
	I See God
	His Hands
	You're Not Living in Vain
June 2, 1955	
	Sweet Little Jesus Boy
	The Holy Babe

EXAMPLE IO.I

Continued

Session Date	Song
	No Room at the Inn
	Joy to the World
	O Come, All Ye Faithful
August 4, 1955	
	A Satisfied Mind
	The Bible Tells Me So
	The Lord's Prayer
November 3, 1955	
	The Lord Is a Busy Man
	I Asked the Lord
	I'm Grateful
	Down by the Riverside
	Trouble in My Way
	Without a Song
	Joshua Fit de Battle of Jericho
	Summertime/Sometimes I Feel Like a Motherless Child
November 7, 1955	
	The Lord Is a Busy Man
	I'm Grateful
	Down by the Riverside
	Trouble in My Way

better quality of the recording itself also elevated the Columbia version over the earlier Apollo side.

With the sessions for her album prominently showcasing modern gospel songs, Jackson's Columbia signing was also an opportunity for the black gospel field. Russell noted in his journal that the previous month "Prof. Dorsey had sent a package of about a dozen songs" for Jackson's consideration, and a few weeks later Dorsey dropped by Jackson's apartment to personally plug two of his tunes. Russell recorded Dorsey on piano accompanying Jackson singing his 1951 song "Peace, It's Wonderful" and himself on "Walk Over God's Heaven." The 1954 sheet music for "Walk Over God's Heaven" credits both the words and music to Dorsey, but it is in fact an arrangement of the familiar spiritual "I Got Shoes," also known as "Heav'n Heav'n" as performed by a multitude of black concert recitalists. At her first session, Jackson recorded "Walk Over

God's Heaven"—oddly, released despite a near train wreck in the final stop-time section—as well as Dorsey's earlier composition "I'm Going to Live the Life I Sing About in My Song." In December, Dorsey was back again. Shortly before Christmas, Jackson told Terkel and his radio audience that Dorsey "was at my house this morning. Brought me some new music."[22] Another recent gospel song that Jackson recorded at her first session was "Oh Lord, Is It I?" published in 1954 and a signature number for its composer, Jackson's friend and musical colleague Robert Anderson, who recorded it on at least two different occasions himself.[23]

But Jackson's early work as a Columbia recording artist also bumped up against recurring questions about intellectual property in the black gospel field. In 1949, the Martin and Morris Music Studio published sheet music for "Jesus Met the Woman at the Well" that suggested it was an original song with music by Kenneth Morris and words by Pilgrim Travelers singer and manager James Woodie (J. W.) Alexander. But in a letter written to Avakian a week before Jackson recorded it for Columbia, Russell described the song as "a very old bounce spiritual ('bluesey' as Mahalia says) which she'd never used, or heard, for 20 years until about a month ago."[24] Jackson's recollection that the song, based on the biblical encounter be- tween Jesus and a Samaritan woman in John 4, long preceded the Morris and Alexander copyright is corroborated by a recording of the song for Apollo by the Two Gospel Keys in February 1947 that retains the basic identity of the song but renders it in a style closer to country blues. Morris and Alexander were opportun- istic in publishing the song under their names; shortly after World War II, "Jesus Met the Woman at the Well" entered the repertory of male gospel quartets and, in typical fashion, was recorded in succession by a multitude of groups. Perhaps the first was Thermon Ruth's Selah Jubilee Singers in 1946 or 1947, followed by the Pilgrim Travelers in 1948, but within the next three years recordings of the song by the Golden Gate Quartet, Fairfield Four, Famous Blue Jay Singers, and Swan Silvertones followed.[25] The ubiquity of the song on record and surely on programs in the late 1940s and early 1950s makes Jackson's claim that she did not hear it until 1954 slightly dubious, though not impossible. Perhaps the Pilgrim Travelers' manner of rendering the song became influential enough among quartets that Alexander wanted to legally protect their arrangement. But claiming the song as an original composition and not a novel take on an older tune was an overreach, if a shrewd move that increased the likelihood of getting paid every time a gospel singer recorded the song.

If Morris and Alexander could get paid for their interpretation of a public domain song, why not Jackson? At Apollo, Berman had already used Jackson's name extensively and improperly as a songwriter to avoid paying royalties. At Columbia, things were more above board, though Jackson was determined that if her performances of traditional songs were indeed distinctive, they should be acknowledged as arrangements for which she should receive a royalty, a provision to which Miller agreed. Jackson claimed that "Jesus Met the Woman at the Well" and five songs that she recorded at her first session—"When I Wake Up in Glory," "Didn't It Rain," "Amazing Grace," "When the Saints Go Marching In," and "Keep Your Hand on the Plow"—were her own arrangements and asked Russell to take care of the nitty-gritty of obtaining copyrights. "I helped copy down and registered in the copyright office her arrangements," Russell wrote Avakian. "I even sent in the 'notice of use' (for mechanical instruments) to the Copyright Register for these numbers, which is required by law, as well as the manuscript." From an objective standpoint, Jackson's understanding of an "arrangement" was liberal to the extreme. In all six cases, she sings the song with no markedly individuating musical decisions other than her own singing style. Her claim in the case of "Amazing Grace," which she recorded for both Apollo and for Columbia the way black Baptists would have sung it in church as a lined-out Dr. Watts hymn, seems particularly gratuitous. It is sometimes difficult to track claims Jackson made about authorship. In January 1955, she told an interviewer, rather curiously, and certainly inaccurately: "I write most of my own songs."[26]

The case that rankled Jackson the most was "Jesus Met the Woman at the Well," which Columbia, despite being aware of Jackson's copyrights, mistakenly credited to Morris and Alexander when her single came out in January. In following up with Avakian, Russell was doing Jackson's bidding to make sure she got paid, though he was also "wondering if all my work (and hers) was wasted" through a slip-up by "some dumb girl" in the Columbia labeling department when he had other things do, like finish his book on jazz drummer Warren "Baby" Dodds. But the conflict-averse Russell also realized that as the de facto intercessor between Columbia and a "quite upset" Jackson, he was beginning to be put in an uncomfortable position that, he explained to Avakian, also risked causing rifts within the densely interconnected Chicago gospel community.

> Since I am not on anyone's payroll I see no excuse for me to get into any unpleasant discussions with anyone. I'd just as soon keep all my contacts with Mahalia on the most happy basis possible, so I was glad I wasn't at the house when her copy of "Woman at the Well" was received, crediting the arrangement to Alexander and Morris. But I did tell her a few days later that I'd write to you about it and I'm finally getting around to it.
>
> I'm sure Mahalia hasn't anything against Morris and his music publishing company (in fact since January I've seen her appear at the church where Morris is director of music and he played for her and has sent her a

lot of sheet music since then) but I know Mahalia claims this is just an old tune from way back. . . .

On the other hand, if I were Morris and saw my name on a Columbia record I'd think they might owe me the royalty too. So a little matter like this could cause complications, loss of friends, etc., for Mahalia.[27]

Avakian shared Jackson's concern with Miller highlighting the crux of the issue: "Mahalia is very annoyed that other people's names are credited to what are her arrangements—in addition to the fact that they are getting paid for her arrangements!" In Avakian's view, "It would appear that Mahalia is not entitled to royalties, but then neither are the licensors."[28] But the kerfuffle yet again highlights a larger two-headed economic issue within the post-war black gospel field, both sides of which—perhaps contradictory, perhaps compensatory—were rooted in the myth of black culture as its own generator: black performances of anonymous traditional religious songs could acquire the status of legally protected intellectual property even as record companies were more than ready to assert that original songs by flesh-and-blood black composers were simply "traditional" and thus belonged to no one.

While recognizing that Jackson was "a pioneer in this whole field" of black gospel singing, Miller also had a broader vision born of self-confidence in his Midas touch in the 1950s pop market. "I wanted her artistry to spread over everything, because she had something to say in music and why limit her only to gospel?" Miller remembered. "We had nothing to lose. If it didn't turn out great we didn't have to release them. I wanted the people to hear the whole full range of her ability." In October, Miller recommended Franz Schubert's Latin-texted "Ave Maria," a setting that Falls also liked and had encouraged Jackson to sing on her radio show, but Russell told Avakian in late November "Mahalia doesn't seem to know this tune at all" and he doubted she "could get it ready, with words, etc., for next week."[29]

Miller's pop tastes were, however, never far in the background. Alongside the heavy dose of black church numbers recorded for Avakian at her first Columbia sessions, Jackson also cut a handful of religious popular songs for which she had been primed both at Apollo and on her radio show. Jackson recorded five such songs at her November sessions, repertory touching on the conventional themes of God's boundless love (Terry Gilkyson's "The Treasures of Love"), the plurality but essential unity of monotheistic believers (Ervin Drake and James Shirl's "One God," a spinoff of their 1953 hit "I Believe"), and the omnipotence of a higher entity (Johnny Lange, Hy Heath, and Sonny Burke's "Somebody Bigger Than You or I"). These three songs and Bob Merrill's novelty number "A Rusty Old Halo" had all been written since the breakout of religious pop in 1950. The oldest of the five was Rodgers and Hammerstein's "You'll Never Walk Alone" from the 1945 musical *Carousel*, though the song had acquired fresh interpretive possibilities and new salience among African American listeners with Roy Hamilton's popular 1954 cover for Columbia's new subsidiary label Epic Records. Jackson's magisterial performance of "You'll Never Walk Alone," sung with the metric freedom of her triple-meter hymns, builds on Hamilton's gospel-flavored reading of the song, one subsequently carried on by other black vocalists including Tommy Hunt of the Flamingos and Aretha Franklin.[30]

Jackson's ambivalence about Miller's selection of songs caused mild tension. She asked Russell to voice her displeasure to Miller via Avakian, who wrote back that Miller "was not happy to hear that Mahalia didn't care too much for the tunes" he sent her. In a late-December television interview, Jackson clarified that Miller was responsible for her non-gospel Columbia repertory. "I was a big fish in a little pond and I was grateful," she explained to the host tactfully. "I finally got with Columbia Records and I've made these songs—'Treasure of Love,' that was his selection, and 'Rusty Old Halo.' I think they're very good numbers."[31] Of "his" religious pop sides, Miller pushed "A Rusty Old Halo" the hardest. The recording was played again and again on her radio program and the producers of Jackson's television show had to ensure that "a verse or so of 'Rusty Old Halo' be included each week," at the request of sponsor Kelly Motors.[32] Jackson performed the song repeatedly in live appearances throughout 1955, perhaps at Columbia's behest though she surely understood that the more the record sold, the more she could earn. Recorded at roughly the same time as a version of the song by country singer and rockabilly pioneer Bonnie Lou for King Records, Jackson's "A Rusty Old Halo" reflects Miller's penchant for market-friendly pop gimmicks—a double-tracked Jackson sang in harmony with herself during the chorus—but it also gave evidence of another feature introduced in Jackson's early Columbia records. With "hillbilly" artists, like gospel voices, crossing over to the pop charts, it is notable that multiple songs recorded at Jackson's first sessions exhibit a country feel. The "boom chuck-chuck" barnyard waltz feel of "A Rusty Old Halo" and "Out of the Depths," complemented by Ryerson's gentle fills of harmonized thirds, nudge these sides toward a stylistically hybrid sound increasingly characteristic of mid-1950s pop.[33]

This new country feel is in evidence on the most outstanding product of Jackson's first Columbia sessions, and to my ears one of the crowning achievements of her career as a recording artist, "When I Wake Up in Glory," released on her debut album. The Columbia label identified "When I Wake Up in Glory" as a "traditional" song arranged by Jackson, though here again we encounter the liberties frequently taken along the frayed boundary between black composition and non-notated practices. The song's carefully crafted text should already be an indication that it does not present a case of anonymous folk poetry.

Verse

> I shall fall asleep someday
> And from earth shall pass away
> But my soul shall reach a better land
> For the things of life all fail
> And the hosts of sin prevail
> And God's ways we cannot understand

Chorus

> But I'll wake, wake, wake up in glory
> And to Jesus will sing redemption's story
> I shall see his blessed face
> Who has kept me by His grace
> When I wake up in glory by and by

In 1939, Roberta Martin published her own arrangement of the song, one that illustrates how sheet music was often a representation in notation—in a way, a souvenir—of a memorable live performance. In many cases, gospel sheet music registered remarkably specific social connections within and among black gospel communities. Martin credited herself as the arranger, but did not identify the composer. An inscription above the staff did, however, note that "When I Wake Up in Glory" had been arranged "As sung by Mme. Mary J. Davis, Nat'l Gospel Singer, Pittsburgh, Pa." and was dedicated to the singer's husband, "my Friend and Coworker, Prof. E. C. Davis, Songwriter."

This unattributed song was in fact composed by African American gospel songwriter, spiritual arranger, and choral director Edward C. Deas (1884–1944), a college-educated native of Florence, South Carolina. By 1920, Deas had relocated to Chicago, where he joined the congregation of historic Coppin Chapel and attained a position of leadership within the AME church. With the appearance of *Gospel Pearls* in 1921 and the *Baptist Standard Hymnal* in 1924, the 1920s were a fertile period for the publication of black hymnody and religious song. Deas added to this bounty by editing multiple collections of songs written by himself and other composers, among which were *Notes of Gold* (1921) and *Gems of Love* (1924). Both of these interdenominational songbooks, containing "Gospel songs and Jubilee melodies" but also "songs for Pentecostal meetings," included Deas's 1919 song "When I Wake Up in Glory," set to a text by Julian Alford.[34] Like Martin, the Methodist Deas was living on the South Side of Chicago when Martin's arrangement appeared, so the failure to acknowledge his cross-pollination of Baptist repertory is curious, though it may have also been symptomatic of what Robert Anderson described as denominationally "segregated" mainline black churches before the rise of gospel helped establish common ground.

Jackson seems to have been using the Martin sheet music, which simplified Deas's rhythmic notation but also made very minor changes to Alford's text that Jackson followed. The Ward Singers' 1950 recording of the song, by contrast, followed the original words. But we are also left to wonder how much Jackson's interpretation was influenced by the inspiration for Martin's arrangement, the song's performance by Mary Johnson Davis (*c.* 1900–1982). Black gospel music history is replete with groups and soloists who either never recorded or whose recordings are disproportionately sparse in comparison with their reputation and legacy; the first gospel choruses at Ebenezer and Pilgrim Baptist churches in Chicago, the Live Wire Singers of Cleveland, and Willie Mae Ford Smith of St. Louis are examples. Mary Johnson Davis is one of these. Born Mary Louise Johnson in Pittsburgh, where she was already on the church-singing circuit as a small child, she married E. Clifford Davis in 1937. The two became a gospel power couple in 1940s, he as assistant director of the National Baptist Convention chorus and a noted gospel song composer working out of his music store in Pittsburgh, and she as a "nationally known gospel singer," earning a reputation both as a dynamic soprano soloist and as the leader of her popular mixed gospel group. Boyer wrote that Davis moved to Philadelphia after the death of her husband, but in fact she initiated a highly public divorce in 1950 due to his drinking, chronic philandering, and squandering of their earnings, interfering, she told black newspapers, with his duties as an evangelist and a bread-winning husband and causing her "undue embarrassment." Taking her performance career into her own hands, Davis began a relentless touring schedule, surely to attain some financial stability, though these programs also showcased the power of gospel singing and elevated her own status in black church communities on the East Coast and in the South. Gospel singer Marion Williams, born and raised in Miami, remembered that Davis "would sing any hymn out of the Baptist hymnal, and tear up worse than anyone you ever saw." Like the Roberta Martin Singers, Mary Johnson and Her National Gospel Singers were an ensemble in which important young gospel vocalists cut their teeth, including future Ward Singers Frances Steadman and Thelma Jackson, Jeff and Charles Banks, who gained fame as the Banks Brothers, and the respected Pittsburgh-based singer, organist, and music director Ruby Gould. Davis later remarried to Reverend Benjamin J. Smalls and continued to be an influential performer and mentor in Pittsburgh and Philadelphia until her death in 1982.[35]

Unfortunately, fewer than a dozen recordings of Davis's group for the Lewis, Coleman, and Atlantic labels were released commercially—several of the Atlantic sides remain unreleased—and of these only a few feature her as a soloist. These do, however, offer a glimpse of a vocal control and delivery that could range from a punchy brassiness to an elegantly sculpted portamento. As a gospel singer Davis was unique, in part because of "sharp soprano bluesy vocals" in which Timothy Dodge heard the influence of 1920s sanctified singer Arizona Dranes,[36] but also because of a style that, somewhat like Georgia Peach, suggests her transitional positioning in gospel history. On her *c.* 1947 solo recording of "Come Ye Disconsolate," considered by some a signature number because she recorded it multiple times, Davis begins with a stately vibrato and conspicuously flipped Rs that gradually yield to bent notes, melismatic runs, and increased rhythmic activity. "Ain't That Good News" and "I'm Going to Wait on the Lord," both recorded in 1949 by Davis supported by her backing vocalists, feature a singer using more chest voice, swinging harder in the former and phrasing elastically in the latter. Her spacious reading of Roberta Martin's "Try Jesus, He Satisfies" draws on Davis's interpretation of the hymns for which she was so well known.

Davis never recorded "When I Wake Up in Glory" though her performance of the song in the 1930s was commemorated by Martin's arrangement. Goreau suggests that Jackson was also singing the song around the same time. Heilbut, who has been instrumental in keeping Davis's small handful of recordings in circulation through compilation reissues, hears her style, "equally bluesy and equally imbued with the strength of a testimony," as "one of Mahalia Jackson's vocal inspirations."[37] Still, judging from the little recorded evidence, Davis and Jackson were notably different singers. "When I Wake Up in Glory" was a song that Jackson sang in one of her favorite keys, B-flat, enabling her to crank up the blues urgency by opening up the throttle at climactic moments to wail on the blue third (D-flat) at the very top of her range. Yet her Columbia recording of the song is also notable for its leisurely pace and subtly intricate texture. The tempo, Jackson's phrasing, and Falls's accompaniment lean toward a gospel feel, with Jackson singing on the "4-1" end of the seesaw. (See my earlier discussion of Jackson's "B-flat tunes" and the "gospel seesaw" feel in Chapter 6.) At the same time, Shawker's steady brush strokes on the snare, marking each beat of the measure, undermine the "4-1" and "2-3" division of the bar associated with the "gospel feel" and shades slightly toward the four-beat feel of swing. Meanwhile, Carroll plays a bass line that hews closely to the first and third beat of the bar, shading the track unmistakably toward country. This subtle blend of gospel, swing, and country behind Jackson finds a satisfying coexistence in large part because of the wonderful symbiosis between Falls and Ryerson. Ordinarily the "2-3" segment of the bar would be relegated to Falls. But here she shares the space with Ryerson, enacting a graceful dance with continuous cooperation between the two musicians—sometimes trading off, other times in counterpoint—in executing these fills over the bed of Jones's quietly sustained organ harmonies.

This heterophonic interlace supports Jackson's exquisite vocal performance. Jackson sings two verses in alternation with the chorus, then, given the opportunity to stretch out on an over-four-minute LP track, concludes with a final repetition of the refrain. The melody sits perfectly in her range—her lowest notes expressively breathy yet supported and her upper register forceful but without a hint of strain—enabling her to play the two registers off of each other. In the verse, the melody remains largely within the lower half of the scale, between B-flat and F, ascending to the upper tonic only in the chorus. During the second verse,

> When my weary eyelids close
> And I sink to sweet repose
> Singing hallelujah as I go
> All my sorrows will be past
> I'll be free from sin at last
> And I'll leave my trouble here below

Jackson slightly modifies the words, including the third line, which she begins "Singing glory hallelujah" then, as if impatient, rockets a major seventh upward from E-flat to a D-natural on "*Yes,* as I go"—overshooting the blue third—and drifts melismatically back down to the lower tonic. This sudden and dramatic but completely controlled eruption complements the deft timing of Jackson's phrasing and the eloquent note selection in her ornamentation of the melody. Jackson saves what must be one of the most indulgently bluesy phrases she ever sung on record for the final repeat of the chorus on the line "I'm gon' *saaang* redemption's story," where she bends a G upward to the flat seventh with sly equivocation, continues the line with an almost haughty rhythmic nonchalance, and snaps back into the pocket of the groove with a punctuating "Oh, Lord." Whether or not we would consider this an "arrangement" in the strictest sense, and whatever Davis's possible influence, the performance of "When I Wake Up in Glory" by Jackson and by her backing ensemble transforms the decades-old song through an alloy of modern gospel, jazz, country, and a singer at the top of her game.

1955 Sessions

Jackson's November 1954 Columbia sessions resulted in one LP and three singles, two of them religious pop ("Rusty Old Halo" b/w "The Treasures of Love" and "You'll Never Walk Alone" b/w "One God") and the third gospel ("Walk Over God's Heaven" b/w "Jesus Met the Woman at the Well") (Figure 10.3). In his liner notes, Avakian explained his naming of the album in lofty terms.

> When it came time to think up a title for this album, it soon became apparent that the best thing was to call it what it was: just *Mahalia Jackson, The World's Greatest Gospel Singer.*
> This is one of the less extravagant phrases to emerge from this typewriter. One might as well say that Ty Cobb is a fair base runner, that Maurice Richard can handle a hockey stick, or that Adlai Stevenson makes sense. That's how much more Mahalia Jackson is than just "the world's greatest gospel singer."

FIG. 10.3 Mahalia Jackson at home, posing with the promotional double pack of her first two 45 RPM singles for Columbia Records, released in January 1955. Resting on the piano is the Liberace album package given to her by Columbia producer George Avakian. GTN Pictures.

With Jackson's first Columbia releases on the market, the division of labor producing her recordings continued in 1955. Miller ramped up his efforts to record Jackson singing recently written religious pop songs that would be attractive to a crossover market. On June 1, he recorded Jackson at the Church singing Murray Mencher and Raymond Leveen's "I See God," Stuart Hamblen's "His Hands," and Abner Silver and Al Hoffman's "You're Not Living in Vain." This was Jackson's grandest backing to date. She and Falls reported to Russell that "Mitch had arranged the songs for a 30 to 35 piece orchestra" with "full strings, brass, woodwinds (with sax, etc.)." The actual studio orchestra was smaller—six violins, three trumpets, two trombones, two alto saxophones, one tenor saxophone, one baritone saxophone, and a rhythm section of vibraphone, piano, guitar, bass, and drums—but it was the first taste of the setting that would in future years become characteristic of Mahalia Jackson the Columbia album artist. Notably, Falls and Jones did not play at this session. Miller also took a crack at Jackson singing "Stay on the Right Side, Sister," a tune from the 1930s sung by Doris Day in the 1955 Ruth Etting biopic *Love Me or Leave Me*, "but it was too jivy," Russell wrote, and the recording was apparently not preserved.[38]

Later in the summer, Miller returned to the countrified Jackson he had experimented with back in November. He sent her a pair of new songs to learn, "The Bible Tells Me So," a Dale Evans tune that Evans recorded with her singing-cowboy husband Roy Rodgers, and "A Satisfied Mind," written by Joe "Red" Hayes and Jack Rhodes. Hayes, a singing fiddler, made the first recording of the song for independent Starday Records in 1954, but it was Porter Wagoner's 1955 cover for RCA that reached number one on the *Billboard* country charts. Miller came to Chicago for an August 4 session to record Jackson singing the two country songs backed by the Jack Halloran Quartet as well as "The Lord's Prayer." Russell didn't think much of the material, calling the Hayes song "a hillbilly waltz" and dismissing the Evans ditty as "a catchy, but really cheap song." Miller's selections even perplexed Jackson, who "didn't seem to mind" singing them but "made some funny remarks about it" and "wondered where Mitch got all those songs."[39]

Finally, on November 3, 1955, Jackson cut three more religious pop songs: Raymond Allan and Jerry Joyce's peppy novelty number "The Lord Is a Busy Man," Johnny Lange and Jimmy Duncan's "I Asked the Lord," and Erwin Drake and Jimmy Shirl's "I'm Grateful." At this session, Miller also had Jackson record the reflective show tune "Without a Song," from the 1929 Vincent Youmans musical comedy *Great Day*. "Without a Song," which Jackson sang on her radio show, falls into the category of contemplative "Old South" black laborer soliloquies in the vein "Old Man River" and "That Lucky Old Sun." In *Great Day*, "Without a Song" was introduced by black baritone crooner Lois Deppe, who performed the role of plantation worker Lijah. As in the case of "You'll Never Walk Alone," however, Miller likely recorded Jackson singing "Without a Song" as a follow-up to its reinterpretation by Roy Hamilton released just the week before. After having been revived by Billy Eckstine in 1946, "Without a Song" gained considerable popularity in the late 1950s and 1960s among African American vocalists, including gospel singers on the lookout for tasteful crossover repertory. Miller fleshed out the November 3 session with two spirituals, "Down by the Riverside" and "Joshua Fit de Battle of Jericho," and the "Summertime"/"Sometimes I Feel Like a Motherless Child" medley that Jackson liked singing to reveal how Gershwin became "famous all over" after having "heard the Negroes singing" down South. At a lecture-demonstration presented by the erudite semantics professor S. I. Hayakawa at the University of Chicago the previous January, Jackson suggested that highlighting the similarities she heard between the two songs was her form of musicology, though she could make her argument by singing it "better than I can explain" in words, she told the audience: "A lot of times people can talk, but I have to sing mine 'cause I can't use all of them phrases Dr. Hayakaya uses [*sic*]."[40]

Miller's 1955 recordings of Jackson singing religious pop resulted in three singles—"I See God" b/w "His Hands," "A Satisfied Mind" b/w "The Bible Tells Me So," and "You're Not Living in Vain" b/w "The Lord Is a Busy Man." "I See God" exhibits the richness of Jackson's resonant chest voice and "The Bible Tells Me So" is a vehicle for the rhythmic verve of her phrasing. Perhaps the most satisfying of her early religious pop sides is "You're Not Living in Vain," a lovely record that despite minimal gospel ornamentation showcases Jackson's voice in the most relaxed part of her range, rendering the melody with easy delicacy. The madcap "The Lord Is a Busy Man" is off the charts, unlike anything Jackson had ever recorded, with brass flourishes that push her as close to the Copacabana or a 1950s movie musical as anything she would ever put on record.

Meanwhile, Avakian was envisioning a different venture, which he proposed to Jackson in a letter on February 24.

> I would like to have you record a 12" LP of Christmas songs, which we would entitle *O Come All Ye Faithful*. . . .Would you please let me know what Christmas songs you have in your repertoire; and if there are not enough to make up a 12" LP, we can decide between us what Christmas songs should be added to complete the album. . . .
>
> I have a feeling that this album will be extremely successful because there is nothing like it on the market as yet, and I know that it will be an exceptional one from the musical point of view as well.[41]

Avakian's point person in working out the logistics for the proposed album was yet again his old friend Russell, who was charged with determining what Christmas repertory Jackson could pull off and keeping Avakian abreast of her preparations. Jackson had presented two Christmas-themed radio programs and knew other seasonal repertory from church, which already equipped her with a healthy number of possibilities. After conferring with Jackson, Russell responded to Avakian on March 2 in a nine-page letter. Fortunately, he noted, Jackson's two best Christmas songs, "Silent Night" and "Go Tell It on the Mountain," had been recorded for Apollo outside of the negotiated five-year window. Russell assessed the viability of other repertory, including his strong recommendations "Children, Go and I Will Send Thee" and "There Wasn't No Room at the Inn," both of which, he said, Jackson performed with lively "bounce"; familiar carols like "O Come, All Ye Faithful" and "Joy to the World" that she already knew, though he felt less effectively highlighted her distinctiveness; and the standbys "White Christmas," "O Little Town of Bethlehem," "Hark! The Herald Angels Sing," and "It Came

Upon a Midnight Clear." Jackson had recommended "What Shall I Give Them for Christmas," a new song written by the sister of her PR manager Al Duckett, and another song that Russell said he did not know, "Sweet Little Jesus Boy," composed by Robert MacGimsey. MacGimsey, a white lawyer from Louisiana who published anthologies of African American spirituals, wrote songs, and performed as a virtuoso whistler on the side, composed "Sweet Little Jesus Boy" in 1934 and the song was quickly adopted as a seasonal number by African Americans, some of whom presumed that its stylized, pentatonic folk melody was of black vernacular origin. Jackson also floated the idea of including "Santa Claus Is Coming to Town" to fill out the album. "In December Mahalia once asked me to get the sheet music of this Tin Pan Alley ditty but she never got around to rehearsing it," Russell told Avakian. "Possibly the fact that the Quartet used it on the radio program saved us from hearing her do it."[42]

Jackson responded positively to Avakian's proposal, but her relentless schedule nearly bogged down the endeavor. On April 28, Russell updated Avakian, letting him know that Jackson had been too busy with her television show and with learning new songs for Miller to make much progress on her Christmas repertory. On May 16, he wrote again: "Just a line to let you know things are still going very slowly with the Christmas album, but Mahalia did finally start rehearsing the 'new' Xmas songs last Monday and Tuesday after her rush of trips to New York for Godfrey and Carnegie Hall and her two TV [shows] here each week." Jackson had also been preoccupied by a trip to Detroit for a *Pittsburgh Courier*–sponsored concert, performances in Youngstown, Ohio, and Evanston, Illinois, and "a lot of other things to take her attention, such as a revival meeting in which she's much interested." Falls speculated that "Mahalia doesn't feel the new Xmas songs yet, but when she does they will come out something new and different."

Eventually, Jackson did record the ten tracks for Avakian's Christmas album in two sessions sandwiched around her June 1 date for Miller. Jackson flew into New York Tuesday night, May 31, and immediately went to the Church for a six-hour session at which she recorded "Silent Night," "O Little Town of Bethlehem," "Go Tell It on the Mountain," "White Christmas," and another song from the 1930s written by a folk song–catching composer, John Jacob Niles's "I Wonder as I Wander." Two days later, she returned for another four-and-a-half hours to cut "Sweet Little Jesus Boy," "Children, Go and I Will Send Thee" (as "The Holy Babe"), "No Room at the Inn," "Joy to the World," and "O Come, All Ye Faithful." "Hark! The Herald Angels Sing" and "Silver Bells," were also considered in the studio, but were rejected when Avakian, Jackson, and Russell all agreed on their lack of enthusiasm for the songs.[43]

When Avakian proposed the album, Jackson suggested having "a quartet, or perhaps even a choir with her on some of the numbers." Avakian opted for a smaller backing ensemble, recording Jackson at the first session with Falls, Jones, jazz bassist Milt Hinton, vibraphonist Elden "Buster" Bailey (also a percussionist with the New York Philharmonic), and a male vocal quintet led by Johnny Bell. In post-production, however, Avakian overdubbed additional instrumentation and voices, adding strings to "I Wonder as I Wander," strings and woodwinds to "O Little Town of Bethlehem," and a male quartet and tubular bells to "Joy to the World," "O Come, All Ye Faithful," and "Sweet Little Jesus Boy." In Jackson's more improvisatory small group Columbia sessions, finding performers who could lock in on the feel of her music and follow her occasional extemporaneous detours seemed to be a challenge. The Bell group "didn't work out at all. They seemed entirely at a loss to get together on the harmony, etc., and perhaps this material was too unfamiliar to them or possibly they were scared to death," the musicians told Russell, who was not in New York for the session. "Mahalia said they just wasted about 4+ hours of everyone's time and never did cut anything with her." For the June 2 session, there was a new vibraphonist, Robert Prince, who struggled with some of the songs and had to be replaced by a fortuitous visitor to the 30th Street studio.

> On Thursday night when they were having trouble with vibraphone (he always wanted to know if he should play a G or F chord here and there) Lionel Hampton came by the studio and after greeting Milt and everyone and warming up, cut a couple numbers with them. "Go and I Will Send Thee" and possibly "No Room at the Inn."

Hampton also played lightly in the background on "O Come, All Ye Faithful." His appearance on the Christmas album was one of a series of encounters with Jackson in 1955. Hampton heard her perform in May at the *Courier* concert in Detroit, at which he led the house band, and in July they shared a more unusual collaboration. In Chicago for an engagement at the Blue Note, Hampton agreed to appear at a Jackson program hosted by Reverend Joseph Branham's South Shore Baptist Church. With only fifty people in attendance (including "a half dozen or so other white people")—much to the shock of Terkel, who had publicized the concert over the radio—Hampton played the three Columbia Christmas numbers plus extended versions of "When the Saints Go Marching In" and "Keep Your Hand on the Plow," during which he soloed for several choruses. Jackson and Hampton exchanged kudos during the South Shore program. Jackson shared the anecdote of Hampton subbing in at her recording session, declaring "some people criticize you for bringing jazz into the church, but I like it." Hearing Jackson sing "I Believe" in Detroit "thrilled him and renewed his belief," Hampton reciprocated, telling the audience that Jackson possessed "the greatest voice he'd ever heard."[44]

To finalize the album package, Columbia sent a photographer to Chicago to capture an image for the album cover. He arrived with explicit instructions from Avakian, who shared them with Jackson in advance: "A picture of you in one of your concert gowns (preferably white), bending over and smiling at a little boy dressed in a white altar boy's costume. This should be taken in your church, so it has the authentic background."[45] Released in November with Avakian's prescribed cover, Jackson's Christmas album, now given the title *Sweet Little Jesus Boy*, received positive reviews, including *Billboard*'s assessment that it was "outstanding, combining great technical skill with all the emotion inherent in the material."[46]

Avakian wrote the liner notes for his two Jackson LPs. Jackson's "attitude toward jazz and the blues is still respectful, but she remains firm in her devotion to gospel songs," he observed on the back cover of *The World's Greatest Gospel Singer*. Yet if Miller wanted to broaden Jackson's appeal through the prism of pop, Avakian's comments indicate a strategy of cultivating new admirers by pitching her music as close kin to jazz, as his college mate Stearns had done at the Music Inn four years earlier. "Gospel singing is something off the beaten track for many record buyers," Avakian acknowledged, though its connectedness to the more familiar Negro spiritual brought it closer to home. Whatever gospel's roots in the venerable spirituals, however,

> the emphasis is on newer songs which are similar in subject matter but somewhat more like good jazz tunes in their musical construction. Gospel singing, swings. The freedom in gospel singing, however, is even greater than in jazz, not only in the mechanics of variations on melody and rhythm, but in the emotional surge of a performance as well.[47]

Avakian lauded "I'm Going to Live the Life I Sing About in My Song" as "one of the greatest vocal performances I have ever heard," rendered by "the greatest jazz voice since the incomparable Bessie Smith."

In his liner notes for *Sweet Little Jesus Boy*, Avakian praised the personal qualities of Jackson, "a truly humble Christian" with a "knack of projecting not only a musical personality, but a warm humanity as well." And once again he continued to lure jazz fans by promising Christmas-themed songs "sung and played with a great swinging beat" and vouching that "these performances are wonderful jazz." But Avakian also provocatively and perceptively highlighted the shifting vocal practices in the performances of a woman he called "one of the finest artists in the world today."

> "Sweet Little Jesus Boy" is especially interesting; it combines in one performance several aspects of Mahalia's singing. At times (as in the opening measures) she chooses to swing, with a solid accompaniment by the Falls-Jones Ensemble and the chorus; at other times she becomes a concert singer, or she will break time with all the freedom of the reflective gospel style. Mahalia as ballad singer is heard in the Kentucky carol, "I Wonder as

I Wander." Her "White Christmas," taken with a steady light jazz beat, is a model of how to swing at an easy rocking tempo.[48]

A considerable consequence of Jackson signing with Columbia Records was the label's ability to shape how she was heard and understood as a vocalist. Independent record companies like Apollo, trafficking primarily in singles, often hung their hat on a minimalist presentation and a deliberately raw immediacy suggesting that the sound of the record spoke for itself. Backed by the resources of a major label, Jackson was marketed with a greater sense of purpose and a more specified framing of her recorded performances, a development made possible by the multimedia textuality of the LP itself, which juxtaposed musical sound with carefully chosen words and images. Avakian's liner notes for *Sweet Little Jesus Boy*, countered the rhetorical bluntness of "The World's Greatest Gospel Singer" with a rapid fire invocation of techniques that recast the master specialist as a consummate artist with a stylistic breadth encompassing jazz vocals, the classical recital stage, the folk ballad, and gospel singing straight out of the black church.

It is this layering of assigned identities—Jackson the paragon of gospel, Jackson the embodiment of holistic theories about the black vernacular, and Jackson the transcendent artist—that decisively staked out her exceptional position within the black gospel field and within American popular culture. Each of these claims is, of course, grounded in its own specific form of mythology: the notion of there being a "greatest" singer in a gospel tradition so reliant upon the in the-moment context of individual and collective spirits being moved represents as much a belief system as either the conviction that all legitimately black music has emerged from a "common root" or romantic metaphysical aesthetics grounded in German idealist philosophy.

Whatever she thought of Miller's material, Jackson's early career as a Columbia artist offered new opportunities for her to explore and demonstrate her full arsenal as a vocalist. This is an aspect of her singing career that Avakian hints at and that many regretful fans of her earlier Apollo recordings rarely acknowledge. It is also true, however, that the collateral result of recording Jackson with the supplement of pop material and production was a gradual sacrifice of that portion of her studio repertory reserved for the "true gospel songs" that she featured on her first album. We are left to ponder in hindsight the historical significance had Miller and subsequent Columbia producers, rather than steering Jackson toward familiar spirituals and crossover inspirational repertory, envisioned a project akin to Ella Fitzgerald's composer "songbook" albums for Verve Records—perhaps something along the lines of *Mahalia Jackson Sings the Black Gospel Songbook*—that would have enabled Jackson to document the extraordinary flood of outstanding gospel compositions published during the 1940s and early 1950s.[49] Nonetheless, Jackson believed that if "Move On Up a Little Higher" launched her to fame, being signed to a major label took her to new heights. "I had sold 8 to 10 million records with Apollo, but still they didn't know me other side of 12th Street in Chicago," she told Leonard Feather in 1964. "I'd been to London and then to Europe and they still didn't know me in this country. They didn't know me really until I got with Columbia."[50]

The investment of a major record label and media network had important ramifications for the black gospel field as well. As Jackson's career as a Columbia recording artist unfolded in 1954–1955, a broadening of her audience presented her with complex dynamics to negotiate while also paving new inroads for gospel singers on the American entertainment landscape.

"I'm Still Just Mahaly to You All"

THE MEANINGS OF FAME

EVEN AFTER NEARLY twenty-five years living on the South Side, Mahalia Jackson had probably never felt more fully embraced by the city of Chicago than she was in the summer of 1955. On Saturday, August 6, Jackson was a featured celebrity at the twenty-sixth annual Bud Billiken parade and picnic, sponsored by the *Chicago Defender*. Bud Billiken, "the legendary godfather of Chicago's Negro children," was the fictitious mascot of a club launched in 1921 from the *Defender*'s "Young Folks" pages. By 1929, Bud Billiken Club members and their families had a community holiday of their own, climaxed by a parade through the heart of the South Side and a picnic in Washington Park that became, and remains, the biggest summer celebration for black Chicago. Bud Billiken Day was an opportunity to fete a club that the *Defender* touted as "the largest children's organization in the world" but also to laud the newspaper itself. Nineteen fifty-five marked the *Defender*'s fiftieth anniversary and advance publicity promoted the "official greeting" for that year's Billiken Day: "Hi Bud! The *Defender* is 50!" The main attraction, however, was the three-hour, twenty-block-long parade down South Parkway (now Martin Luther King Jr. Drive), into Washington Park and past a reviewing stand on Ellsworth Drive holding an assemblage of public officials that included Chicago's newly elected Mayor Richard J. Daley. Festivities were somewhat muted by sporadic heavy rain, but the *Defender* reported the attendance of 9,000 picnicking families, participation of more than 50,000 marchers, and a parade route lined by 300,000 spectators representing "every element of the population racially, economically, socially," each enjoying a cavalcade of "some of the biggest stars and personalities of our times," including "that gospel singing sensation Mahalia Jackson."[1]

Two weeks later, Jackson was featured even more prominently at the city's most high-profile musical event. Held from 1930 to 1964 at Soldier Field, the *Chicago Tribune*'s annual Chicagoland Music Festival regularly drew massive crowds from throughout the Midwest region. The festival grew steadily in its pre-war iterations, promising to cater to all musical tastes and social classes and presenting a mix of local talent and a handful of nationally known stars. The Chicagoland Music Festival also sought to mitigate racial strife with an event intending "to create kindly feeling between Caucasians and Negroes" through its diverse, if in its early years still racially segregated, audiences.[2] Black musical performance was a consistent centerpiece. Patriotic audience sing-alongs were mainstay attractions, though the annual highlight of the Chicagoland Festival was the Negro spirituals sung by a thousand-voice African American chorus organized and directed by the city's most respected black choir directors.

Liam Ford has written that the Chicagoland Music Festival, established the same year as Bud Billiken Day, provided "some white Chicagoans with their first exposure to black music," and indeed advance publicity for Jackson's August 20 appearance crossed a new threshold of local promotion, consciously striving to introduce both her and black gospel music to a new audience base.[3] Nine days before the festival, Chicago's WBBM-TV broadcast an interview with Jackson and in the weeks leading up to the event the *Tribune* ran five feature stories on Jackson, two by festival director Philip Maxwell and a three-part series by Clay Gowran. Maxwell exuberantly lauded "the Queen of the Gospel Singers" as an "amazing artist, who has been acclaimed in the music halls of Europe and America, on radio and on television, by her record enthusiasts, and by those who sing with her in church." But his tone often took on the woodenness of a Mahalia Jackson 101 textbook: "her critics hold that her music has a bounce. She usually closes her eyes while she sings; she can 'see' better that way. Sometimes in the fervor of her singing, she claps her hands and her whole body sways to her emotion."[4]

Gowran's articles, on the other hand, based on his "long talks" with Jackson while visiting her apartment in early July, are important documents not only for their more personal touch and the prominence of Jackson's own voice, but also for their clear reinforcement of the plot points of Jackson's biographical narrative. The central thrust of the account offered by Gowran via Jackson—and surely vice versa—was again her "Louisiana Cinderella" story. *Tribune* readers unfamiliar with Jackson learned that she was born dirt poor in New Orleans, developed a singing style that voiced the melancholic world-weariness of her upbringing in the Jim Crow South, and paid her dues working service jobs in Chicago, all the while maintaining her unshakable religious devotion until, through the breakthrough of "Move On Up a Little Higher," she reached the apex of both popular and elite culture, despite having "never studied a note of music." Growing up in New Orleans, she "never had nuthin'," Jackson testified. "Down there, you see the white folks going on to school, but you don't get to go. You don't get anything." As Jackson's visibility grew, the ramifications of that increased exposure became an inescapable subplot of her reception. One black South Sider raised in New Orleans, a city where African American awareness of variations in class status was pronounced, disputed Jackson's depiction of her childhood. In a letter to the *Chicago Defender*, Octavia Randolph, who lived blocks away from Jackson in Chicago, rejected the broader conclusion that Jackson's self-narrative represented the prototypical black experience in New Orleans.

> Dear Editor: It appears to me that Mahalia Jackson is trying to make her rise to success a big achievement. I think she should tell the real facts about her childhood days in New Orleans. I am a product of the famous Crescent City and proud of it.
>
> She has given out erroneous statements when she said "down there you see white folks going to school but you don't get to go, you don't get anything."
>
> I graduated from high school at Southern University there in 1911.[5]

If Jackson reminisced about the rags, Gowran enumerated the riches. "Today," Gowran picked up the story, "Mahalia drives a baby blue Cadillac, owns the six apartment buildings in which she lives, and has fat bank accounts," earning "$1,000 and up per concert these days." She finally reached "the peak" with her appearance at Carnegie Hall. Jackson seemed to get a kick out of rolling the highlight reel of her emergent celebrity ("In France, they had to get out the law because the crowd was so heavy each night"), even as she marveled at the improbability of her journey: "Think of it—me a wash-woman standing where such people as Caruso and Lily Pons stood. I've never gotten over it." Underlying it all were her Christian beliefs. "I had faith," Jackson said, delivering the moral of the story, "and look at the things that have come true for me."[6]

Having failed to land their first choice, the Crew Cuts, the *Tribune* advertised Jackson's two co-headliners: violinist and television personality Florian ZaBach, the Chicago-born son of a Vienna Philharmonic clarinetist who specialized in pop-classical numbers "written to display his flair for fiddle pyrotechnics"; and twenty-two-year-old Eddie Fisher, the chart-topping crooner who rose from poor Philadelphia kid in the synagogue choir to perhaps the biggest male pop idol of the early 1950s.[7] Jackson, who received a fee of $1,200 for the engagement, admitted nervousness about singing for her largest live audience to date—a capacity crowd of 80,000 at Soldier Field, the blustery lakefront home of pro football's Chicago Bears—but also excitement that the concert would be broadcast nationally over the Mutual Broadcasting System, reaching all the way to New Orleans affiliate WTPS. "I've got lots of cousins down there," she told Maxwell, "and I've told them to keep close to the radio that Saturday night."[8] True to form, Bill Russell recorded Jackson's 19-minute, five-song set from the radio, capturing her performances of "You'll Never Walk Alone," "Didn't It Rain," "When the Saints Go Marching In,"

"Soon I Will Be Done With the Trouble of This World," and "His Hands," all backed by Mildred Falls, Ralph Jones, the Jack Halloran Quartet, and two members of the Chicago Symphony Orchestra. Familiar spirituals are well represented in Jackson's Chicagoland set list, though it is also notable that she had already recorded four of the five songs for Columbia, the first three at her initial session for the label in November and "His Hands" in June. Jackson's appearance at the festival thus served to present her to the city of Chicago as a hometown hero and to a national public as a new Columbia artist.

The close succession of Jackson's appearances at the Billiken Day Parade and at the Chicagoland Music Festival in the summer of 1955 call our attention to a highly visible seam in the chronology of her career. In a year that saw the release of her first Columbia recordings, the creation of her television show, a broadening public, and recovery from life-threatening illness, Jackson faced new metrics of self-assessment as she managed relationships with her record company, her television audience, new interracial configurations of fans, the city of Chicago, and her home base of black churches. Jackson primarily maneuvered these relationships through repertory, strategic deployment of her autobiographical narrative, personal charm, and charismatic musical performance. Meanwhile, through the activity of other celebrity gospel artists, above all the Clara Ward Singers, the gospel landscape was undergoing a process of transformation through novel forms of prestige and models of success with implications for our understandings of Jackson and the black gospel field at mid-century.

Mahalia Jackson Sings

The final episode of *The Mahalia Jackson Show* aired on February 6, 1955, but as the radio program was winding down preparations for a new television show were gearing up. "Speculation is rife among radio and television circles," black newspapers noted as early as January, that "CBS is said to be working out plans for a weekly show to feature the queen of the gospel singers" and that there was even a "dickering for sponsors." In March, *Jet* magazine reported that even with the radio show being cut to ten minutes and then canceled for lack of a sponsor, a half-hour Sunday night TV program starring Jackson was "very close to set." This time, Jackson's show, again created by Louis Cowan's production company, was local, airing on Chicago's CBS affiliate WBBM-TV at the direct request of station vice president H. Leslie Atlass, who "sent word down to find a slot for her."[9] Co-produced by veterans Les Weinrott and Chuck Strother and directed by Dick Liesendahl, *Mahalia Jackson Sings* premiered on Sunday, March 13, and aired two evening episodes a week, on Sundays at 11:00 and Thursdays at 10:30. John Lewellen, Cowan's Chicago representative who had cultivated a trusting relationship with Jackson and Russell through their work together on the radio show, was on set in a supervisory and consultative role. As on the radio, Jackson was backed by Falls, Jones, and the Jack Halloran Quartet, which was also featured in each episode performing two or three numbers on its own.

But the big news was the show's sponsorship by Martin J. Kelly, "Chicago's foremost Chrysler-Plymouth dealer." For black consumers of popular culture, any television show starring an African American was a major breakthrough, though particularly validating was clearing the recurring hurdle of finding commercial backing. Recognition of this achievement was communicated explicitly at a gospel program at Greater Salem Baptist Church just a week before the debut of *Mahalia Jackson Sings* during remarks by Jackson's close friend, the charismatic church and cultural leader Willa Saunders Jones (1901–1979) (Figure 8.4). Born in Little Rock, Arkansas, Jones became a prominent and respected member of the South Side community, perhaps best known for her Passion play, which she wrote in the 1920s and presented annually for six decades, often with such outstanding vocalists as Dinah Washington and Jackson. An accomplished musician, Jones was occasionally Jackson's piano or organ accompanist at church performances.[10] Jones saluted Jackson for having "started right here," for remaining "a faithful, regular member" for twenty-five years, and especially for her contributions to the purchase of a new organ, "a living, visible emblem of the service and the work she has done here in Greater Salem Baptist Church." She went on to passionately underscore the nexus of Jackson's community presence, her racial identity, and her accumulating prestige of recognition.

> We are sort of celebrating, and this is a prelude to Mahalia's show. I think come this Sunday night, if I am correct, she is beginning her television show. And I think that . . . regardless if you know her or if you don't know her, if you've never even met her, she has definitely made a distinct opening for our people, and we are proud of her. And she is the only woman of our group [*pounding the rostrum with her hand for emphasis*] with her own television show! [*applause*] I got news for you. . . .[*slight pause for effect, then raises her voice*] And the Chrysler Company is sponsoring Mahalia Jackson![11]

Jackson counted on the support of the black church community to make her new program a success, but logistically she relied heavily on a core inner circle— Falls, Jones, Cylestine Fletcher, and Russell—working with and for her daily to help her manage an increasingly complicated portfolio of responsibilities that now included a television show. Filming two episodes a week meant staying on top of rapidly repeating cycles of rehearsal and minute details of production. Jackson rehearsed at her home with Falls, Jones, and Russell multiple times during the week, polishing numbers that she knew and learning new material. Some of these rehearsals were recorded by Russell, but his most important job—on top of the regular spate of household chores—was to prepare and hold cue cards with song lyrics for Jackson, which he called "idiot sheets," and attend to her needs at the studio, bringing her food and coffee before the show. These tasks might explain why he was no longer able to record any episodes after the initial two. Cylestine Fletcher, whom Jackson gave the nickname "Polly," had worked for Jackson at her beauty shop and remained with her as a personal secretary as Jackson's career expanded. For the television show, Fletcher often chauffeured Jackson to the recently remodeled television studio at the Garrick Theater at 64 West Randolph Street in the Chicago Loop, fixed her hair, and ironed the choir robes that she wore on air for each episode. Russell seemed to enjoy recording Jackson's show-to-show selections from her growing wardrobe of choir gowns, noting whether she chose "her pink lace robe," "her new 'silk' white robe," or "her new green robe with a lot of spangles around the neck." Another pillar of the production process was Halloran. As he had for the radio show, Russell recorded demo tapes for Halloran so the quartet leader could produce arrangements of the chosen repertory. According to Russell's journal, Jackson expressed concern and raised questions about the quartet's commitment and, as they began to perform independently on the show, about whether the jaunty character of their selections ran contrary to the more reverential tone set by her own performances. When the Halloran Quartet flew to New York in June for appearances on the Arthur Godfrey and Milton Berle shows, Jackson had Fletcher send Halloran a telegram wishing them luck.

> However Mahalia was quite disgruntled about them because they get there too late to rehearse and aren't able to learn new numbers to back her up. Since they are paid for that work too she said some of that money could or should be used so they could have guests on the program. During one number, she said they almost got her off. . . .Mildred or someone agreed with me that their comic "MacNamara's Band" coming after "Precious Lord" ruined the mood.[12]

Jackson felt vindicated when Avakian visited the filming of an early episode of *Mahalia Jackson Sings* and observed "every time the quartet opened their mouths it seemed to slow things down." Weinrott "thought they could cut out the quartet entirely, which he thought was a let down" and even letters to the station indicated that some viewers could do without "the 'pop' songs the quartet sung after Mahalia's songs."[13] In Halloran's defense, he may have felt entitled to a little slack having been given the considerable task on both the radio and television shows of surfing the waves of Jackson's personal working style. His ability and willingness to translate the spirit of her vaguely worded preferences into singable parts and whip together last-minute arrangements when Jackson changed her mind about repertory the day of filming made him an invaluable asset. Still, tracing the three-year arc from her appearance on Sullivan's *Toast of the Town* to *Mahalia Jackson Sings*, it is a notable indicator of broader changes in U.S. entertainment that at this point it was Halloran, not Jackson, who was the "pace-changer," bridging performances of black gospel music curated by the show's featured star.

To my knowledge, no footage of *Mahalia Jackson Sings* has survived, but Russell recorded the sound from the first two Sunday broadcasts and documented the repertory performed on all thirty-four episodes, in addition to the regular observations in his journal. (In 1961, NBC launched a series of five-minute television programs that aired throughout the week featuring Jackson singing spirituals and gospel songs, also called *Mahalia Jackson Sings*. The complete run of 58 shows is available on DVD.)[14] The show varied somewhat in its specific content but largely remained consistent in format over the course of its run. There were clear continuities between the radio and TV shows, both of which began with Jackson, "a voice that has thrilled millions, from Albert Hall in London to thousands of humble churches throughout the land," singing what had become her theme song, "His Eye Is on the Sparrow," followed by four or five live performances in alternation with brief conversations. On television, these "dialogues," as the script called them, resembled mini-interviews with host Jim Conway, conducted, a *Variety* review described, "off camera, using a script by Studs Terkel whom she's adopted as her radio-TV mentor."[15] Conway was a versatile and ubiquitous on-air personality in Chicago for over thirty years, best known at the time for hosting the popular WBBM entertainment program *In Town Tonight*. Most of the questions on the debut episode were fluffy at best—How does it feel to be a Columbia recording star? How do you feel inside when you sing a spiritual? What do you see when you close your eyes?—but the interaction feels less mannered than the scripted exchanges on radio and Conway's more natural style seemed to relax the singer. Viewed from the production team's perspective, Jackson did still have her rough moments—she described how "Summertime" composer "George Gershman taken this song from a Negro spiritual"—and perhaps for this reason, the one-to two-minute dialogues on the first episode were shortened to more compact exchanges that Conway turned into introductions to the next song. The efficiency of the Jackson-Conway dialogue on Show #3 transitioning from her performance of "Down by the Riverside" to "That Lonesome Road," with Conway speaking for the star more than previously, is exemplary.

CONWAY: "Down by the Riverside." Mahalia, that song, in your words, would be considered gospel with a bounce, wouldn't it?

JACKSON: Yes. It's an old spiritual that has been revived with a little bounce to it.

CONWAY: Last week you said that gospel could be gay as well as sorrowful. But there was a time not too long ago when you felt low in spirit and ailing in body. When you were ill, your tour of Europe had to be cut short. The doctors were shaking their heads. Possibly at that time, echoing and re-echoing through your mind were the strains of "Lonesome Road."

The spoken commercials for the car dealership were delivered twice per show by Kelly spokesman Jack Callaghan. In later programs, Jackson said a sentence or two, read from cue cards prepared by Russell, to introduce Callaghan's pitch.

Repertory also provided a key link to the radio show. The first several episodes of *Mahalia Jackson Sings* drew almost exclusively on material from *The Mahalia Jackson Show*. Excluding Show #9, on which she tested out four new songs, all but three of the thirty-nine songs that Jackson sang on the first eleven television episodes had been heard on her radio program. These spanned the radio show's mix of gospel songs ("Jesus Met the Woman at the Well" and Akers's "God Spoke to Me"), religious pop ("I Believe" and "Somebody Bigger Than You or I"), sentimental oldies ("Trees" and "A Perfect Day"), and reverie-filled show tunes ("Summertime" and "The Lonesome Road"). In noticeably heavier rotation on these early shows, however, were traditional African American spirituals, which made up about a quarter of Jackson's selections.

With several shows worth of material behind her and with what seems to be her greater latitude in choosing repertory, Jackson began expanding her song list. Over time, the show pruned most of the sentimental parlor songs and musical theater numbers heard on the radio though it continued to ride the wave of such hot-off-the-presses religious pop as "The Holy Bible," "Whither Thou Goest," "I Asked the Lord," and "Have You Talked to the Man Upstairs," while also reaching back to the 1940s for the inspirational song "If I Can Help Somebody." Russell's journal reveals that Jackson was on the constant lookout for possible repertory. One of the biggest, if unlikeliest, hits of 1954–55 was religious pop specialist Stuart Hamblen's "Open Up Your Heart and Let the Sunshine In," which Hamblen recorded on his own television show with a group of small children identified as the Cowboy Church Sunday School. Released by Decca, the recording became a surprise smash and through subsequent cover versions and sheet music sales Hamblen's song became one of the best-known tunes in the country by early 1955. Perhaps to capitalize on this popularity, Jackson, whether by request or by choice, performed "Open Up Your Heart and Let the Sunshine In" on two separate shows that spring.

Jackson also turned to the interdenominational and interracial traditions of American hymnody, from which she selected "He Will Remember Me," "Alone," "The Old Rugged Cross," and "Hark the Voice of Jesus Calling." The latter hymn was one Jackson encountered in a vintage Moody-Sankey songbook that she borrowed when she sang at a benefit for Goodwill Industries in Chicago. A tape recording made at Jackson's home in April captures a husband-and-wife duet accompanied by piano singing a four-song set, at the end of which Jackson let out a hearty "Amen" and laughed with pleasure. Later in the run of program, Jackson performed one of the couple's selections, "Spread a Little Sunshine," as well as a new James Cleveland song that a younger, mixed gospel group with a soprano lead sang for her that same day, "Come into My Heart, Lord Jesus." The Roberta Martin Singers recorded "Come into My Heart, Lord Jesus" in 1955, a performance led by one of black gospel's greatest sopranos, Chicago's DeLois Barrett Campbell. The soloist at Jackson's apartment seems to closely model her performance on Campbell's. Russell's annotations identify this group as the "Cleveland Singers," raising the probability that Cleveland, who knew Jackson since childhood, was himself part of the performance.[16]

Gospel songs also had a prominent place on *Mahalia Jackson Sings*. Jackson reprised numbers that she recorded for Apollo but had not sung on the radio ("Dig a Little Deeper," "Do You Know Him," and "In the Upper Room") and folded in new ones, like Dorothy Love Coates's "You Must Be Born Again." On one of her final shows, she hoped to perform James Cleveland's "Trouble in My Way," but the producers balked when they could not clear the copyright in time.[17] The biggest beneficiary of Jackson's seeking out of material for *Mahalia Jackson Sings* was Dorsey. Jackson's relationship with Dorsey and his music went back to his heyday of celebrity in the late 1930s and early 1940s, when she toured with him to promote his songs, and extended into the late 1940s when she recorded his songs for Apollo. Jackson's signing by CBS and Columbia kindled a straw fire of new publicity for Dorsey, whom she recognized publicly on multiple occasions. With Dorsey in the studio audience for her radio show, Jackson introduced him on air as "my good friend" who was written "more gospel songs than I believe anybody in the world." At the Greater Salem organ dedication, Jackson hailed Dorsey as "one of the greatest songwriters of this modern time."[18] In January 1955, shortly after Jackson's first Columbia singles were released, black newspapers celebrated the new sides as a triumph for Jackson but also for Dorsey, whose "Walk Over God's Heaven" was said to have been "written especially for her," making the record a collaboration of "two of the best known names in contemporary gospel music" (Figure 11.1).[19]

Dorsey himself, who had his royalty battles with Bess Berman over Jackson's Apollo recordings of his songs, must have recognized that Jackson's new association with CBS and Columbia opened up possibilities. Dorsey's self-promotional offensive of sending Jackson parcels of his songs and dropping by her apartment to accompany her and sing them himself appears to have paid dividends. On her television show, Jackson performed twelve of Dorsey's songs, most of which she had already either recorded or sung on her radio program, though also others— "When I Do the Best I Can," "It Don't Cost Very Much," and "Standing Here Wondering Which Way to Go"—that were perhaps part of her church repertory but that she had yet to perform either on record or on air. Russell described a

FIG. 11.1 Mahalia Jackson singing at home, accompanied by Thomas A. Dorsey, probably January 1955. Laurraine Goreau Photograph Collection, Hogan Jazz Archive, Tulane University.

comical scene when Jackson planned to sing Dorsey's "Beautiful Tomorrow" and "Search Me Lord" on Show #12 but neither Jackson, Falls, or Jones could remember the complete lyrics for the latter, leading to a frantic series of last-minute phone calls—to Dorsey, to the NCGCC office at Pilgrim Baptist Church, to the Martin and Morris music shop, and finally to a friend who happened to know the words— that enabled Russell to prepare her cue cards.[20] Repertory provided connective tissue between Jackson's place in Chicago's black gospel community and her work as a mass-mediated musical celebrity, as did the filming sessions at the Garrick Theater. Though the studio audience was not a part of the show in the way it had been on the early episodes of the *Mahalia Jackson Show*, Jackson's church friends, including Willa Saunders Jones and Theodore Frye, attended the live broadcasts, lending support and offering immediate feedback on her performances and the show's production.

Over its thirty-four episodes, *Mahalia Jackson Sings* did undergo various changes, some modifying scheduling, others altering content. Beginning in early May with Show #17, Kelly and WBBM eliminated the Thursday episodes, cutting the program to once weekly. Two weeks later, Jackson's Sunday time slot was changed from 10:30 pm to one o'clock in the afternoon and filming was moved from the Garrick to Studio "G" on the twelfth floor of the State-Lake Theater, two blocks away. The ill-conceived Sunday midday air time—inconvenient for a church singer and her base audience—lasted only four weeks, after which the show was moved back to Sunday nights and the Garrick Theater. With the program being local and not a national broadcast, Jackson had more influence over the musical content. This became even more apparent when Kelly Motors dropped its sponsorship of the show. In the weeks leading up to the expiration of Kelly's thirteen-week contract, Jackson felt anxiety over the fate of the show. Jackson tweaked the audience during a program at First Church of Deliverance, telling them "her show might not last long. The white man said 'You folks ain't buying no Chryslers,' you still want those Cadillacs, so they may turn that light off on me." Privately, she fretted and even expected the worst, becoming increasingly "worried about losing her Kelly show sponsor" and even wondering to Russell if she had fallen victim to some good old-fashioned New Orleans hoodoo courtesy of somebody sprinkling "Goofer dust" in her path. Jackson admitted becoming less strict with her diet, an indulgence Russell perceived as being "because she figured her TV program was over and wasn't enjoying life." When the contract expired on June 5 at the conclusion of Show #21, she and Russell were initially led to believe that Kelly had renewed his support, but they found out the following week that he had in fact declined his option.[21] However, in a strong show of commitment—or perhaps to spare Columbia the embarrassment of their ballyhooed new star having two shows canceled in a span of four months—CBS picked up the tab and kept *Mahalia Jackson Sings* alive with the unusual step of making it a sustaining program, industry parlance for a show airing without sponsorship, in the manner of a public service broadcast.

As Russell observed, all of a sudden "there were fewer guys around the studio," though less sponsor oversight and no commercials also meant more elbow room in the allotted half-hour to probe new musical possibilities and preserve a more consistent mood.[22] To some, getting rid of the ads was itself a godsend. On "one of the most refreshing programs to originate from Chicago in a long time," griped Richard Orr of the *Tribune*, it seemed in irredeemably "poor taste . . . to hear a pitch man crying 'No money down! That's right, no money down!' after Miss Jackson has finished singing 'The Lord's Prayer.'"[23] From early on, Jackson had input on the set list for each episode—the repertory was reshuffled after she "complained about three wailing numbers in a row" on Show #3—but she also began mulling over the idea of adding guest performers to the program. When Sister Rosetta Tharpe and Marie Knight came to Chicago in May to play the Black Orchid nightclub, Jackson considered inviting the duo to make a cameo appearance. Jackson's passing judgments of the appropriateness of local gospel singers and pastors for the show offer a glimpse of her personal tastes. Though a great admirer of Willie Webb as a pianist, Jackson was less enthusiastic about his group: she told Russell "she wouldn't want them as guests on her program because they yelled too much and didn't sing in parts enough." In a car ride from State-Lake to a program at Greater Salem, Jackson and her circle brainstormed other possibilities, assessing the television promise of colleagues in Chicago's gospel community, including the chronic "show-off" Dorsey, while also remaining vigilant about opening the floodgates.

> On the way down, Mahalia talked about various guests for her TV [show]. She asked Polly to phone Rev. [J. C.] Austin (Sr.) of Pilgrim and ask if he could talk on program next Sunday for 1½ minutes. They planned to have Dorsey and his trio or if possible the full gospel choir. Mildred laughed and said Dorsey wouldn't want to play piano, he'd have to get on TV and direct. Mahalia said they let church out early so everybody could be on TV and Rev. Austin would do anything to get his face before the TV cameras. . . .
>
> Mahalia said there were a lot of Negro groups that yelled loud and were no good anyway. She said just like some of the white singers are no good they also have Negroes who can't sing. She wondered about the Salem choir (all the churches would be after her to get on, once she starts). . . .Ralph and Mahalia laughed about what [Greater Salem pastor] Rev. [Leon] Jenkins would do and both imitated him, as he responds during sermons—with "Yeah, Yeah."[24]

Eventually Jackson did invite other singers to perform on *Mahalia Jackson Sings*, including the Gayton Sisters, Robert Wooten Sr.'s youth choir from Beth Eden Baptist Church in Morgan Park, and Robert Johnson, a young boy affiliated with the Salvation Army. Lewellen arranged an appearance by Reverend Constance Elms from Methodist Church for the Deaf, who delivered the words of "The Lord's Prayer" in sign language while Jackson sang.

The show's host was a variable that enmeshed *Mahalia Jackson Sings* in mid-1950s Cold War politics. Within weeks of the program's debut, Conway's host duties were taken up by Terkel, already a scriptwriter for the show (Figure 11.2). Terkel's virtuosity as a raconteur and his close friendship with Jackson, whom he had interviewed on both radio and television numerous times, made him a natural for the job of conducting the show's between-song dialogues and adding "descriptive sidelights on the whys of gospel music."[25] With such an intimate connection to the show, Terkel was angered when he was abruptly replaced in mid-May by another popular Chicago media personality, Frank McCormick, because, he was told, the show was transitioning to a different vibe. When Jackson and her team showed up to the studio on May 29 for the filming of Show #20, Lewellen broke the news to her and Russell that Terkel's political leanings had exposed him to red baiting.

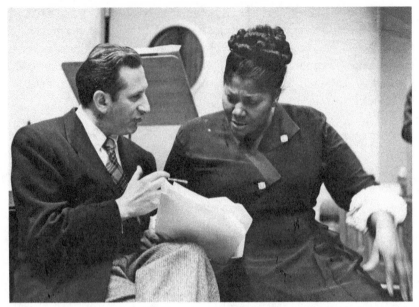

FIG. 11.2 Studs Terkel and Mahalia Jackson reviewing scripts for *The Mahalia Jackson Show*, 1954. Laurraine Goreau Photograph Collection, Hogan Jazz Archive, Tulane University. By permission of the National Association of Broadcast Employees and Technicians, Local 31.

> After [the] program he explained that Studs had been dropped from pro-
> gram because of pressure on the sponsor by the American Legion. Mahalia
> got pretty upset and mad and said she thought Studs had lived that down
> and John said he guessed not. Mahalia thought they shouldn't tell Studs the
> real reason to upset him, but let him continue to think as they explained
> before that the new announcer . . . would just ad lib and they wouldn't need
> a script, etc.
>
> The more Mahalia thought about it, the madder she got and wondered
> if anyone who liked Negroes was considered a communist.

An influential veterans service organization, the American Legion flexed its muscle in the early 1950s by aggressively promoting religious revival and uncompromising anticommunism, and Russell concluded that the television networks were "evidently plenty afraid of the Legion now too." Russell expressed his own disapproval of Kelly's treatment of Terkel, who had been under FBI surveillance since at least the 1940s for his purported coziness with the Left, by reminding Jackson of the speech three days earlier by Mississippi's Democratic senator and staunch segregationist James Eastland. From the Senate floor, a vitriolic Eastland denounced *An American Dilemma*, the 1944 study of U.S. race relations by Swedish

Nobel Laureate economist Gunnar Myrdal that provided a decisive rationale for the *Brown v. Board of Education* decision. Eastland introduced a resolution "to investigate the extent and degree of participation by individuals and groups identified with the communist conspiracy, communist front organizations, and alien ideologies, in the formation of the 'modern scientific authority' upon which the Supreme Court relied in the school integration cases." Even understanding the toxic political climate, Jackson pressed the matter of Terkel's firing further with Lewellen and, remaining upset the next day, "she still mentioned what a dirty trick she thought it was."[26]

There were fans of *Mahalia Jackson Sings* who shared the singer's disappointment over Terkel being replaced by McCormick—Russell noted "some mail complaining about the dumb questions Frank was forced (?) to ask Mahalia on TV"[27]—but other reception of the show highlighted its broader ramifications for Jackson's career. Both *Billboard* and *Variety* considered the television show to be an improvement on Jackson's radio program, one that "may well land her a network TV spot." This was attributed in part to the show's novel approach to lighting, which spotlit her against a simple dark backdrop, and to camera work that tended toward unconventional shooting angles and an unusual number of closeups—distorting her natural beauty, Russell and some of the crew thought. But reviewers also perceived that one of the show's strengths was its potential attractiveness to an audience that was certain to cross multiple vectors. Having "appeal for viewers of all types and ages," the program also bridged those who long knew Jackson and her music intimately and those who may have only recently heard her name, offering "a fine feast for the regular Mahalia fans and an exciting first bite for the new ones." More importantly, the show, delivering Judeo-Christian themes and black vernacular culture, was built around performances that were a showcase for both Jackson and for the gospel sound. "The music, altho aimed primarily at religious lyrics, contains the typical gospel music beat which is very listenable and relatively light in tempo," wrote *Billboard*'s Steve Schickel. "To top it off, Mahalia Jackson is a personality that presents a wealth of appeal by way of her style which mingles emotion with joy in an exhilarating manner." Orr's write-up of the show for the *Tribune* also dwelled upon on Jackson's "warmth and naturalness, a deep sincerity, that casts a sort of magic spell over her listeners."[28]

This strong emphasis on selling Jackson's vocal prowess side-by-side with her endearing personal charisma—"her devout yet happy-go-lucky outlook on life, which is as much a part of her wares as her mellow pipes," as the *Variety* reviewer put it—points to an important continuity between Jackson's multiply mediated performances for CBS. Early in the television run, Terkel's "Singing comes as natural as breathing" line was recycled from the radio show. This line, like the eventual TV slogan ("Her songs come from the heart"), persistently privileged unmediated purity over performance. In certain respects, highlighting a performer's personal qualities is a run-of-the-mill method for building a fan base for an emerging artist. But for a black entertainer and her African American fans—for "our people," Jones reminded the Greater Salem congregation—Jackson's public self in the 1950s carried nearly as much significance as her music.

Particularly telling are references to the "good taste" and "simple, yet dignified format" of Jackson's program. Whatever may have been communicated implicitly by these affirmations in the white press was expressed explicitly in a *Chicago Defender* editorial published the week Jackson's show went on the air. The commentary gave a caustic rundown of the pervasive racial prejudice in a television industry that instead of "spotlighting people like the amazing Mr. Nat Cole, the ever-acceptable Duke Ellington, and other proven and delightful stars" seemed more inclined toward figures like Louise Beavers's Beulah, "a presentation based on concepts unattractive to most Negroes." This was particularly unfortunate in light of the transformative potential of the medium: "We love television but there is something seriously wrong with such an important and rapidly growing industry which only finds a guest room in its house for the darker brother." *New York Age* columnist "Sonny" Murrain was dubious of the significance of *The Mahalia Jackson Show*, which to him satisfied CBS's desire to present "a 'Negro' program," but the *Defender* found a glimmer of optimism in *Mahalia Jackson Sings.*

> We are happy to note that the wonderful gospel star Mahalia Jackson has been able to crash television's glass curtain—at least locally . . .
>
> Miss Jackson is no "Beaulah," [sic] has innate dignity, tremendous talent and a spiritual message to convey which is as good for the souls of white folks as it is for Negroes.
>
> We hope that the boogey-man of racial stupidity will not scare off the plans of the Columbia Broadcasting System to expand this show nationally in the immediate future.[29]

Invoked as a gauge of cultural-political progress, verifiable comparisons of Jackson with the beleaguered black maid character—privately in the "Don't be a Beulah" note sent anonymously to Jackson and publicly on the editorial pages of a flagship black newspaper—raise the likelihood of more extensive, if undocumented, on-the-street discourse about the relationship between Jackson's mediated persona and perceptions of African Americans more broadly.

That the content and form of Jackson's success had meaning for black Americans seems clear, but it also mattered concretely to Jackson, who began to consider the state of her career in historical terms. If the referent for some was Beulah, Jackson, in the midst of her historic endeavor on television, communicated to Russell that her personal benchmark remained her childhood hero growing up in New Orleans, arguably the most famous black woman popular vocalist of the first half of the twentieth century.

> Sunday morning Mahalia seemed a little dejected about probably being off TV soon and said (as John had agreed) she'd done everything she could and expected of her and [Kelly had] still not signed up. Her rating had been good, etc. Anyway she'd done more than any other colored singer, even Bessie Smith. She asked if I didn't agree, which I did of course. When I mentioned that in the days I'd heard Bessie before her death in '37 she was reduced to tent shows, etc., Mahalia said of course don't forget in those days Negro artists didn't have a chance of good bookings.[30]

Thinking of herself in terms that outsized the category "gospel singer," Jackson's assessment of her gains as in 1955 suggest an artist who saw herself as having put together a body of work that was beginning to buttress her against the critical eye of respectability politics. But Jackson now had to learn how to operate within what had become tandem careers, as a Columbia recording artist and media celebrity and as a church singer, if one now exceptionally positioned within the black gospel field.

Some Things Old, Some Things New

On Wednesday, May 4, Jackson was in New York to appear on the CBS live variety television program *Arthur Godfrey and His Friends,* a show that in conjunction with the simultaneously airing *Arthur Godfrey's Talent Scouts* positioned Godfrey as a powerful star maker. Maneuvering a spot with Godfrey, who helped launch the careers of Tony Bennett, Eddie Fisher, Patsy Cline, and others, was a masterstroke, and even the Chicago crew of *Mahalia Jackson Sings* was buzzing as Jackson prepared for her trip East. Unlike Ed Sullivan, Godfrey gave Jackson a rapturous introduction, explaining how he had first been tipped off by Mitch Miller then finally got to hear her when CBS chairman Bill Paley sat him down to watch an episode of her television show. "I wept the whole half hour of it. I've never had anything take a hold of me so strongly as this did," Godfrey told the studio audience and millions viewing at home. "I do believe that you will agree with me when this show is over tonight that you feel a much better man and a much better woman and a much better child for having listened to her and watched her." Jackson, who sang "A Rusty Old Halo," a scorching "When the Saints Go Marching In," and "His Eye Is on the Sparrow," returned the compliment after "Saints," gushing breathlessly about the opportunity: "I never thought I'd have a chance to be on your show, Mr. Godfrey. The Lord has let my prayers be answered. Isn't it wonderful? I'm on the great Mr. Godfrey show." As always, black commentators like *Defender* columnist

Al Monroe recognized Jackson's appearance in such a context as another major step for both the singer and the music, calling it "the first time a gospel singer was presented in such a highly valued berth by an air personality."[31]

With her first Columbia singles and LP in circulation, a television show on the air, and engagements with Sullivan and Godfrey in her back pocket, Jackson was no longer just another gospel singer. Yet even as her national profile grew, she remained active on the local church circuit. Part of maintaining her credibility among her multiplying constituencies was verification from black congregations that she still had both feet on the ground, even as her presence brought extra charge to community events. Two weeks after the Godfrey show, Jackson made a cameo at the dedication of athletic facilities on the South Side; she didn't perform but was invited to take a bow and signed autographs. Then, with Russell in tow, she hustled to First Church of Deliverance for a gospel program featuring the Caravans. James Cleveland asked Jackson to say a few words, during which she remembered watching Cleveland and his fellow Caravans Albertina Walker and Gloria Griffin grow up as kids and "stressed that gospel singers were nothing unless they centered their activities around the church." According to Russell, this turned into public affirmation that success had not changed her.

> She told that she hadn't forgotten the church, would be around more since her TV program was to be earlier, said even when she used to "pull hair" six days a week everybody knows she went to church on Sundays. She wasn't getting grand now. Just the other day a woman called her up and wanted her to fix her hair, because she always used to do it. "I may be a big TV star to those white folks downtown, but I'm still just Mahaly to you all."[32]

Recognizing herself, in one breath, as "a big TV star" and as a prized local beautician, Jackson the singer sought to preserve a sense of what Michelle Scott, in her study of Bessie Smith's formation in early twentieth-century Chattanooga, has called black "working-class womanhood," its own form of in-group prestige.[33] One of the most compelling aspects of Russell's journal is in fact its illumination of the time and labor now required of Jackson to shuttle back and forth, both physically and in the act of performance, between black church gigs and "those white folks downtown," between becoming "a big TV star" and remaining "just Mahaly."

In effect, Jackson was managing two intersecting singing careers. The remarkable richness of Chicago's black gospel community emerges from Russell's documentation of Jackson's appearances at black church programs and live radio broadcasts on the South and West Sides, and even at the southernmost city limits. In July, she performed at Mount Joy Baptist Church with Robert Anderson and program presenter Maceo Woods, who boasted to the audience "a lot of people wouldn't believe she was coming out to Morgan Park." During 1955, Jackson still made church appearances at least once or twice a week, and often more, on top of *Mahalia Jackson Sings*, and even when she did not sing at events she was usually asked to speak. In some cases, she got double-booked, as on the Monday night in May when she was mistakenly scheduled to perform on a church program at St. Stephen's AME Church on the West Side the same evening she had agreed to appear on *In Town Tonight*. She pulled off both by singing a nine-song set at the beginning of the St. Stephens program then racing to the WBBM studio to perform another two on television. Jackson also kept up her involvement with community events. For the April 29 inauguration of fellow New Orleanian John Earl Lewis as Mayor of Bronzeville, Jackson sang at the victory ball and dinner at the Parkway Ballroom, which also raised funds to combat teenage delinquency.[34] Meanwhile her apartment continued to be a haven for gospel singers, as she regularly held court for a steady stream of visitors.

Flagging under the weight of her grueling schedule, Jackson confessed identifying with her good friend Ernestine Washington, for whom domestic life was making it difficult to summon the energy to "get around to churches much anymore." But she was responsible for presenting a week-long series of services from June 12–17 at Greater Salem Baptist Church to raise funds for a new Hammond organ.[35] At Sunday's opening program, attended by 400 to 500 people, Jackson apologized for not having "been able to devote much or any time to advertising and promoting" because "she's been so busy with TV and helping other concerts that she couldn't get around and see and remind everyone." Despite her regret that "she couldn't remember to invite all the different singers," Jackson was able to organize music for every night, including the Greater Salem Choir, Robert Anderson, Princess Stewart, Edward Robinson, Alice McClarity, and Willie Webb's South Side Community Chorus. Other prominent community figures, such as Bronzeville Mayor Lewis and Al Duckett, the African American journalist who also worked as Jackson's press agent, showed up to make brief remarks and pose for photographs for the *Defender*. Jackson also enlisted several prominent ministers to speak, including Reverend James Lofton of Church of Our Prayer in Detroit and well-respected local clergymen Reverend Leon Jenkins, her home pastor at Greater Salem, Reverend Elijah Thurston of 44th Street Baptist Church, Reverend James Stone of Stone Temple Baptist Church, and Reverend Joseph Branham from South Shore Baptist Church. Jackson sang throughout the week, both as a soloist and as the enthusiastic leader of the congregation during song service, and also offered extensive commentary. She spoke generously about Branham but expressed particular appreciation for his father, Reverend John L. Branham Sr., the right hand of the late Olivet Baptist Church pastor and National Baptist Convention president Reverend L. K. Williams, for having given her "the chance to make herself known through the National Baptist Convention."

Jackson seemed particularly nostalgic that week, reflecting on her early roots, lean years, and benefactors. At the opening program, she reminisced about former Bronzeville Mayor Bob Miller, an "undertaker" who gave her one of her first singing jobs, paying her $2 to sing at funeral services—"a lot of money" during the Depression. Jackson also paid tribute to Louise Lemon, a longtime Greater Salem member and a fellow Johnson Singer in the 1930s, with whom she then sang "He'll Understand (And Say 'Well Done')" as a duet. Jackson told the audience "how after her first paid concert with [the] Johnson Singers when she got $4 she quit her job working for white folks." The next night, June 13, she shared her recollections of Robert Johnson himself, the founder of the Johnson Singers who was there to perform with his choir and with whom Jackson also sang a duet. A professed member of Greater Salem since 1912, Johnson was the "man responsible for her starting out," said Jackson, who gave her own historical account of the germinal role played by their church and Johnson's group in the spread of black gospel music.

> Mahalia made quite a speech about Robert Johnson on Monday, telling how when she came to Chicago she joined the Salem Choir of Professor [John C.] Tompkins who said, "Girl, you holler too loud," but Robert he said you got a good voice. And she told how they organized the Johnson singers and how gospel music started in Chicago that way.
>
> Sunday or Monday she mention[ed] that many (or possibly, she said, most) of the Baptist Churches in Chicago, "came out of Salem." 44th St. [Baptist Church] was one of the first evidently and of course others like Stone Temple.

Though over the course of the week the Greater Salem services gradually saw more sparse crowds—Jackson counted only $471 total raised through collections—fellowship remained warm and spirited and Jackson seemed to relish the opportunity for bonding. Coming two weeks after her second Columbia session and the same week Kelly dropped his sponsorship of *Mahalia Jackson Sings*, the Greater Salem organ drive is a remarkable snapshot of Jackson on her home turf at a transitional phase of her career. On a personal level, the services functioned multiply: to rearticulate her self-narrative, to consolidate her base by certifying and performing her historical connections to Chicago's Baptist circles, and, despite becoming a pop-cultural figure, to assert the primacy of her identities as a church singer and a black community member. Jackson told the congregation that whatever her dalliances with white people "on the other side of the tracks," she "feels more at home in church than anyplace" and would continue to reject the glitz and glamour of secular venues. "This is our nightclub," she declared from the pulpit.

Still, Jackson's renewal of her vows to her church community was itself acknowledgment of a rapidly diversifying audience. Back on January 25, Jackson had been the featured performer at a lecture-demonstration on gospel music titled

"How Gospel Was Born—A Chicago Story," presented by Japanese-American se-
manticist Seymour Ichiye (S. I.) Hayakawa at the University of Chicago's Mandel
Hall. Born in Vancouver, Canada, and receiving his PhD in English from the
University of Wisconsin, Hayakawa (1906–1992) built a considerable reputation
in the 1940s with important books on general semantics. Hayakawa admitted to
becoming "a little bit of a lost soul" after an unsuccessful roll of the die, leaving a
tenured position at the Illinois Institute of Technology to try and land a job at the
University of Chicago, only to discover they "wouldn't have me." After teaching
as an adjunct at the University of Chicago from 1950 to 1955, he was hired by the
English Department at San Francisco State where he achieved his greatest noto-
riety in 1968 as acting university president, when he stood down a raucous crowd
of student strikers. The incident made him a darling of political conservatives, a
wave of popularity that the seventy-year-old Hayakawa rode on the way to election to the U.S. Congress in 1976 as a Republican representative of California.
In some ways, Hayakawa's first love was African American music, particularly
blues, jazz, and gospel, and in the 1950s he developed a personal friendship with
Jackson. Even before the Mandel Hall event, he devoted an episode of his eighteen-
part 1954 radio series on Chicago's WFMT, *Hayakawa's Jazz Seminar*, to an hour-
long conversation with Jackson in which they discussed her career, her Apollo
sides, and her response to recordings by Bessie Smith, Duke Ellington, Artie
Shaw, and Gerry Mulligan. Jackson developed a fondness for Hayakawa and, he
remembered, seemed impressed by his "highbrow way of talking," once barking
to a group of friends: "That Dr. Hayakawa, he knows more about Negrology than
any you niggers!"[36]

    "How Gospel Was Born" was the fourth in a series of mostly jazz-related events
presented by Hayakawa as fundraisers for a local cooperative nursery school. The
fascinating event, tape recorded by Russell, allows us to hear processes of translation and the negotiation of co-present forms of prestige.[37] Hayakawa's intent was
to introduce gospel music to what he described as "a highly educated, largely white
audience."[38] This was done both verbally, through Hayakawa's excursions on the
differences and overlaps of gospel music with spirituals and the blues, but also
through musical performances by Jackson, the three women in the Dorsey-directed
Celestial Trio (Julia Mae Smith, Marion Peoples, and Willie Ruffin Wadley), and a
duo of Chicago bluesmen, pianist Albert "Sunnyland Slim" Luandrew and bassist
Ernest "Big" Crawford. Hayakawa, seemingly intent to convey the scholarly seriousness of the evening's subject, conducted proceedings with a manner straddling
the boundary between priggishly pedantic and playfully professorial. "I would like
to illustrate what I mean and start the musical portion of our program tonight by
having what we call in semantics an 'extensional definition,'" he lectured learn-
edly to introduce compare-and-contrast performances of "I Got Shoes" by the
Celestial Trio and by Jackson (as "Walk Over God's Heaven"). "First, I would like

to define, extensionally, a spiritual and then I would like to define extensionally a gospel song." Yet Hayakawa also acknowledged the peculiarity of having to introduce Jackson to the audience in the first place.

> It sort of interests me that Mahalia Jackson, who is nationally famous in the Negro community and in 1952 began to acquire an international reputation through her European tour, tremendously successful tour, has got to be known in the white community in the United States only recently through her work in her radio program and her many television appearances.

Years later, Hayakawa confessed the message he hoped to send through his University of Chicago concerts: "You darn high people don't know how famous our Negro neighbors are! And what a profound cultural influence they are."[39] Admirably, Hayakawa hoped to acquaint the audience not just with Jackson but with the black gospel field, particularly the Chicago scene. He discussed at length "the development of a very considerable business in the publication and sales of music" by acknowledging the names, compositions, and business operations of Alex Bradford (to whom he mistakenly attributed "Move On Up a Little Higher"), Theodore Frye, Lillian Bowles, Kenneth Morris, Sallie Martin, and Roberta Martin. Hayakawa reserved his most extensive profile for Dorsey, delineating in detail the life and career of the "central hero" of the story of modern gospel music.

The event's dynamics were driven by an oscillation between forms of authority and prestige: from Hayakawa's verbally performed academic command, to Dorsey's gravitas as the reputed founding father of modern black gospel, to the dynamism of Jackson, the unquestioned star of the field, whose charismatic artistry eventually overshadowed both. It is revealing to hear the considerable stylistic gap between the somewhat dated (and at times ragged) performances of the Celestial Trio, accompanied by Dorsey on piano, and those of Jackson, by then the consummate pro. But the gamesmanship of jurisdiction was most in evidence in efforts to deliver the "story" of gospel. In a question-and-answer exchange, Jackson confirmed that she had once told Hayakawa that the most affecting black voices were those that possessed a "cry," a perspective that she began to echo in interviews shortly after hearing Spelman College professor Willis James outline his theory of the "Negro folk cry" at Stearns's "Definitions in Jazz" symposium in 1951.[40] When Hayakawa pushed Jackson to develop her thoughts on the topic further, she brusquely cut him off: "When I'm called on to talk, it takes me a long time to think about it, so you just keep talking and when I think what I'm gonna say, I'll say something." The ensuing peals of laughter and applause registered the audience's relief at the open acknowledgment of the awkward yet progressively amusing interface of communication styles.

Jackson, appearing among an assorted, interracial coterie of friends and associates on stage and in the audience—including Dorsey, Terkel, Big Bill Broonzy (who made a surprise appearance), and "Dr. Hayakaya," as she repeatedly called him—was strikingly comfortable calling attention to the elephant of cultural literacy in the room and she did not shy away from an "us" and "them" framing of her music. When asked if white choirs sing Dorsey's songs the same way as black choirs, Jackson replied: "Well, no. They don't sing it exactly like us. They sing it close to the notes that Professor Dorsey writes. But we don't never sing it the way he write it." Terkel—"the greatest man in the world," Jackson shouted as he came up on stage—tried tentatively to clarify the ambiguous sacred-secular divide exemplified by the circulation of such songs as "Just a Closer Walk with Thee" and "When the Saints Go Marching In" in New Orleans. Jackson abruptly intervened: "I want to help you because I know you white people don't quite understand what it's all about." If Hayakawa differentiated spirituals from gospel on the basis of gospel being a notated music of "relatively recent origin" cultivated among black Chicagoans, Jackson warned about prioritizing form over content, insisting that it was not just a matter of African American cultural production. "We might put a little bounce to it and become overemotional and let our body move with the rhythm, but gospel is as old as our Lord and Savior Jesus Christ," Jackson said emphatically. "Mr. Dorsey came along and put a little bounce to it, but it still is the gospel of Jesus Christ, and don't you forget that."

Becoming an increasingly public figure, Jackson appeared to develop a perception of two repertories, as she mused with greater openness about the preferences of white audiences. On record, on radio, and on television, song choices became one vehicle for negotiating her various performance settings and her roles as a church singer and a commercial recording artist. At Mandel Hall, Jackson finished up the evening by singing "Move On Up a Little Higher" to a tumultuous ovation. Jackson cut off the applause and mused out loud: "Now you know something, I don't understand it. I try to sing songs I think you like and you didn't do nothing. Then I sing the real old gospel songs—you liked that, didn't you?"

At the same time, whatever Jackson's desire to whet appetites for "the real old gospel songs," her focus was also on selling her Columbia recordings. When Jackson sang "Walk Over God's Heaven," Hayakawa joked that the song was on "her latest recording, by the way, so you can dash out and buy it afterwards." In her live performances, Jackson followed the standard pattern of promoting songs that were on the market. Hayakawa gave the last twenty minutes of his program to Jackson, who sang five songs, "Just a Closer Walk with Thee" and four Columbia songs, "When the Saints Go Marching In," "A Rusty Old Halo," "Keep Your Hand on the Plow," and "Move On Up a Little Higher." She refused repeated requests for "His Eye Is on the Sparrow." In other contexts, she (or Columbia) seemed determined to promote her religious pop sides, particularly at performances for the white or mixed audiences whom she perhaps believed were their intended market. Shortly after the release of "His Hands" b/w "I See God" in June, Jackson performed "His Hands" on three consecutive episodes of her television show. That Jackson began to make a point of singing her records in public was made explicit at a concert for an all-white audience in July, for whom Jackson sang "His Hands," then "said she'd sing 'the other side'—'I See God.'" In 1957, Terkel put Jackson on the spot in front of a live, predominantly white audience at Chicago's Morrison Hotel, asking: "Would you call 'Rusty Old Halo' a sweetenin' water song?" Using one of Jackson's own expressions, he clearly meant to suggest a type of diluted (or in Russell's words "cheap") pop tune pushed by Mitch Miller that was not part of her core gospel repertory. "Ohhhh!" she recoiled with a guffaw, chiding Terkel affably for airing dirty laundry from private conversation. "I got to sell my record, man! What you talkin' 'bout?"[41]

In 1955, more live engagements for majority white audiences began to appear on Jackson's schedule. She sang five songs at a Good Friday morning service presented by the Women's Auxiliary of Goodwill Industries, then two weeks later delivered a recital at Bethany Methodist Church on the North Side. Having had a television episode the night before the Bethany concert, Jackson admitted feeling a bit hoarse for the first half of the program, though Russell thought that "her voice was in unusually good form" and, witnessing the enthusiastic crowd, "she knew she'd gotten an unusual response from the all white audience." Jackson was struck by and also sought to maximize the growing mutual comfort at her concerts. At a July concert in the 1,200-seat auditorium at Des Plaines Methodist Camp Ground in northeastern Illinois, Jackson "asked them to clap so she'd feel like she was in her own church" and, swarmed by autograph seekers afterwards, "was much impressed at [the] reception and welcome she got (all white)." Increasingly, white fans were attending even black organized programs. At an event "run by a colored church" in Evanston, Illinois, and presented at a large gymnasium set up to seat well over a thousand people, Jackson received $900 (a $200 guarantee plus a percentage of the box office) for a concert at which she sang a dozen numbers. Again, she conferred with Russell about the response by white audience members: "Afterwards, she asked me to confirm that the white people (probably about 50+% of audience) there had never heard anything like it." The Evanston concert also revealed Jackson's consciousness of her own biographical self-presentation for different audiences. "When she looked at [the] program notes I'd written, she said 'what's this about the New Orleans levee,' etc., as if she was ashamed," Russell recorded. "I said, you read all those notes and only two nights before (at Caravan concert) I heard 'someone' talking about coming up from the 'swamps of Louisiana.'"[42]

Sometimes worlds collided. At the Downers Grove Fall Festival on Saturday, September 3, Jackson waved to crowds from the back seat of a convertible along the parade route to the culminating concert at a local high school football stadium.

With festival organizers having "asked for mostly bounce numbers," Jackson performed a six-song set of spirituals and religious pop, then came back onstage to sing "Battle Hymn of the Republic" as the grand finale. Jackson was driven to Downers Grove, a predominantly white community 25 miles west of down-town Chicago, by "Mr. Roy," one of the festival's staff members. Roy was slightly late picking her up because of unexpected traffic on the South Side. Jackson explained to an embarrassed Roy that the funeral for Emmett Till, the fourteen-year-old black Chicagoan who was brutally murdered and mutilated on August 28 by white supremacists while visiting relatives in Money, Mississippi, was being held that day at Roberts Temple of the Church of God in Christ, six blocks from her apartment. Driving home, Jackson discussed the lynching, condemning the tragedy though also sympathizing with "how bad Mr. Roy felt when she told him what [the] crowd was about, 'Just like we feel bad when a Negro does something.' She said something will have to be done about the Mississippi situation." Shortly thereafter, Jackson reached out to Emmett's mother Mamie Till and purchased the headstone for her son's grave.[43]

The centerpiece of Jackson's presentation to the entire city of Chicago in 1955 was her appearance at the Chicagoland Music Festival. Jackson's invitation to the *Tribune*-sponsored event was perhaps precipitated by her triumphant appearance the previous November at the Harvest Moon Festival, presented by the *Chicago Sun-Times* to benefit locally hospitalized veterans. Along with Terkel, Harvest Moon Festival co-emcee and respected *Sun-Times* columnist Irv Kupcinet was an important early champion of Jackson in Chicago, acknowledging her frequently in his "Kup's Column." Appearing alongside celebrities that included Mickey Rooney, Carol Channing, and Eartha Kitt, Jackson was called back onstage for multiple encores by a boisterous crowd at Chicago Stadium that "just wouldn't let her get off the stage." Kupcinet remarked how Jackson "rocked the Stadium" and "captivated the capacity 22,000 as have few performers," but he was even more struck by the equally rap-turous reception at a lavish after-party at the Ambassador East Hotel. Initially hesi-tant, Jackson was persuaded to attend by Kupcinet and stayed late into the night: "As Mahalia rose to leave everybody in the room joined in a spontaneous ovation."[44]

Opening for Eddie Fisher at Chicagoland for a crowd four times the size was, however, a major step up from Harvest Moon. The day after Chicagoland, Jackson gathered with Falls, Jones, and a small group of friends at her apartment to listen to Russell's reel-to-reel recording of the broadcast and assess the performance. Jackson thought that "You'll Never Walk Alone" was in too high a key (F) for her to hit the climactic high C comfortably, but Falls reassured her that the choice was appropriate. The weather conditions—"it was a wonder any tone at all [came] out with the wind hitting her in mouth," Jackson told Russell—and her difficulty feeling the crowd's energy at the much larger Soldier Field made her second-guess her performance. Jackson seemed to cut her strong rendering of "When the Saints

Go Marching In" and "Didn't It Rain" conspicuously short, partly, she admitted, "because she thought it wasn't going over so good, because of the wind, etc. Also thought that the audience clapping wasn't so good."

That some un-hip white audiences tend to clap along on beats one and three instead of on the backbeats, two and four, is somewhat of a running gag, if a stereotype, though it is striking how often Jackson remarked about this, complaining that it threw off her feel of a song. On some occasions, she would stop a song in the middle, demonstrate how to clap along, and then begin again. In her performance of "Saints" at Soldier Field, the crowd joined in enthusiastically, clapping as Jackson sang, but as their sense of the beat began to unravel, Jackson slammed on the brakes, brought it to an abrupt end, and moved on to the next song. In "Didn't It Rain," the audience can also be heard clapping rambunctiously on 1 and 3. "But when she heard the tape," Russell wrote, "she was pleased with the sound and the audience response" to her performances. Even "His Hands," one of the Miller-recommended religious pop numbers that Russell found distasteful, was to his ears "better than she usually did it." Perhaps her strongest song in the set was "Soon I Will Be Done," which she delivered with a gripping intensity and sense of conviction. A few years later, Jackson was featured singing the same song during her cameo in the 1959 remake of *Imitation of Life*. Jackson spoke briefly to the crowd to transition between selections. Listening to her effusive comments before "Saints"—"One day we're going to have a greater gathering than this when the Lord shall come to gather his own, when the saints go marching in! Hallelujah!"—they all "got the biggest kick [and] almost busted laughing" when Jackson "nearly started to preach a sermon" at the 50-yard line of Soldier Field.[45]

"You know," Jackson mused during an appearance on Kupcinet's television show *Chicago Story* on Christmas Eve 1954, "Chicago, I really think, loves me a lot." Together, the Harvest Moon and Chicagoland Music festivals marked an important milepost in the claiming of Jackson by the city of Chicago as a local treasure. Over the radio, the emcee at Soldier Field proclaimed to the "four million people in Chicago and . . . those millions of people listening" across the country, that Jackson had become "the toast of now her hometown of Chicago." Coming after her 1950 Carnegie Hall debut, her 1952 *Toast of the Town* performance, the 1954 launch of her radio program, and her appearance on the Arthur Godfrey show in May, Jackson's engagements at the two Chicago music festivals were the next in a series of highly visible crossover performances that further broadened her recognition and reputation within 1950s U.S. popular culture.

Sharing the Stage

Jackson steadily gained national recognition, though by the summer of 1955 her television show had already made her a local celebrity in Chicago. Russell observed

Jackson being "mobbed for autographs" at her appearances at Greater Salem and the Des Plaines camp meeting and by passersby on the street. In July, Jackson, Falls, Jones, and Russell spent a weekend at Riverview Park, the popular amusement park that stretched 74 acres along the Chicago River. Jackson, flashing the skills that made her a standout baseball player in her youth, "was a good thrower and won a doll by knocking over two dolls with brass balls. The man who ran it recognized her." Later, at a Riverview tent attraction featuring a woman wrestling an alligator, "the man running [the] show recognized Mahalia right away and introduced her. . . .People asked for autographs and they even announced outside that Mahalia Jackson was inside seeing the show." Meanwhile, a group of white society women brought together by Muriel Wagner and Winifred Hastings formed a Mahalia Jackson Fan Club that met regularly at Wagner's apartment in the exclusive Park Tower high-rise on Michigan Avenue in Chicago's Gold Coast neighborhood. The wife of a wealthy businessman and herself a voice teacher, Wagner developed a friendship with Jackson. She sang at the week-long revival at Greater Salem and invited Jackson, who admired the "old time look of [an] old millionaire's mansion," to her home to pitch her a song that she wrote. Wagner brought about a dozen members of the fan club to the filming of the final episode of *Mahalia Jackson Sings*, after which Jackson "stayed in [her] dressing room about 20 minutes . . . waiting for most people to go so they wouldn't mob her, although plenty got her autograph." Jackson seemed to enjoy the waves of attention, though it still took some getting used to. When a young girl living in one of the units of her apartment building knocked on her door with a pack of friends to prove to them that she lived in the same building as Mahalia Jackson, she wondered "what's gotten into people all of a sudden"?[46]

The group in the black gospel field who most closely rivaled Jackson in popularity in the mid-1950s were the Ward Singers, organized by Gertrude Ward with her two daughters, Willa, and eventual star of the group Clara (1924–1973). George and Gertrude Ward migrated from rural Anderson, South Carolina, to North Philadelphia, where the family attended Mutchmore Memorial Baptist Church while struggling to make ends meet.[47] In gospel lore, Gertrude Ward emerges as the quintessential stage mother and an indomitable force of nature, "a combination manager, major-domo and sargeant at arms," as one newspaper read.[48] Willa, the older sister by four years, described her mother as a woman not unlike Jackson's Aunt Duke, a domineering and a strict disciplinarian who liberally dispensed severe whippings for perceived infractions of inviolable rules, while also maintaining a grand vision of success for her daughters. Philadelphia was a gospel town, and in the mid-1930s, the three Ward women formed a family trio called the Consecrated Gospel Singers that sang on programs with Dorsey and Sallie Martin, the latter appearing with her accompanist Ruth Jones, who later changed her name to Dinah Washington. After the group grew by adding Louise Nixon Waters and Louise Jones, the ensemble, now called the Ward Singers, had their first major breakthrough at the 1943 National Baptist Convention in Chicago, where their performances of four songs, including Dorsey's "If We Never Needed the Lord Before," were enthusiastically received. Willa Ward remembered that while in Chicago for the Baptist gathering, they also spent time with "our friend Mahalia Jackson," who fed them and styled their hair for their convention debut at her beauty shop. They bolstered their reputation at the 1946 convention in Atlanta, after which they enjoyed an explosion of popularity that expanded their appearances beyond the Baptist church circuit, took them to the West Coast for the first time in the summer of 1948, and by the "milestone year" of 1949 made them stars. Gertrude had to take on a less central musical role when her singing voice was adversely affected by a goiter operation, but this only enabled her to be more active as a gospel promoter who booked other groups, choirs, and evangelists without losing her focus on elevating the Ward Singers, who some now called "the nation's leading exponents of gospel singing."[49]

In 1949, the Ward Singers initiated a remarkable recording career as a group, beginning a lengthy association with independent label Savoy Records in New Jersey. For the next three years Clara, Willa (now Ward-Moultrie), and their mother recorded as a quintet with Henrietta Waddy from South Carolina and Marion Williams from Miami. The most decisive addition was Williams, who joined the group in 1947 and immediately became one of its featured voices and its most charismatic presence, known for her trademark falsetto squalls that Boyer has called the "high whoo."[50] Clara Ward and Williams combined as switch leads on the 1950 recording "Surely God Is Able," a hit on par with Jackson's "Move On Up a Little Higher" in popularity and impact on the post-war gospel field.[51] Ward, who began her career in gospel primarily as a piano accompanist, became the most regular feature, recording several sides as a soloist under the group's name but without backing singers. Heilbut has written that Ward was most outstanding in her reading of hymns.[52] As a soloist, she can be heard to great effect in her recordings of "There Is a Fountain" from *Gospel Pearls* and the Dr. Watts hymn "The Day Is Passed and Gone," though also on the gospel songs "He Knows How Much We Can Bear," "I Know What He's Done for Me," and "Who Can Ask for Anything More," a loose adaptation of Gershwin's "I Got Rhythm."

In mid-1952, the Ward Singers made a clear turn toward consolidating their sound with an increasing number of arrangements featuring a more driving four-to-a-bar swing feel. This was established especially when they began recording with drums in November 1952 and with slide guitar in July 1953. The group also arrived at a configuration of personnel that pushed them to new heights of popular acclaim in the studio and as live performers: Ward, Ward-Moultrie, Waddy, Williams, and Frances Steadman, with Thelma Jackson and Kitty Parham alternately filling out the lineup (Figure 11.3). The Ward Singers' mid-1950s recordings are exceptional for the quality of the individual voices, which made each singer a strong lead while also producing electric backing harmonies. Some of the recordings from this period

FIG. 11.3 The Ward Singers in the mid-1950s: (clockwise from top left) Frances Steadman, Thelma Jackson, Henrietta Waddy, Marion Williams, Willa Ward-Moultrie, Clara Ward, Gertrude Ward. Michael Ochs Archive/Getty Images.

that showcase both the group's influential hard-swinging sound—recognizably different from the sound and feel of Mahalia Jackson's records—and the distinctive solo voices of their individual members are "Hold Back the Tears" (Clara Ward, lead), "I'm Climbing Higher and Higher" (Williams), "The Wonderful Counselor Is Pleading for Me" (Steadman), "I Want to Be More Like Jesus" (Waddy), "Farther On Up the Road" (Jackson), "I Feel the Holy Spirit" (Parham), and "Who Shall Be Able to Stand" (Ward-Moultrie). The tenacious steamrolling groove of the two-tempo, double-sided "I Know It Was the Lord," one of the Ward Singers's capstone recordings, unfolds in stages with three lead singers, prepared by the magisterial Steadman's free-feel opening, set in motion by Jackson, and driven home by Williams.

The Ward Singers were also instrumental in the recognition of black gospel music as a new type of phenomenon that was an unmistakable departure from the movement crafted by Dorsey, Frye, Butts, and Sallie Martin in the 1930s. The group played a central role in cultivating a new variety of prestige in the form of pop-cultural cachet, a species of cultural capital that was in many cases symbolic—having a hit record or a high profile television appearance, whatever financial reward one might recoup from it—though increasingly the rewards were materially profitable. An extraordinary surge in the demand for gospel singing in live performance in the early 1950s, triggered in part by the greater circulation of recordings, was a catalyzing factor. Larger gospel programs were regularly presented in high school auditoriums or churches that housed bigger congregations, but the sheer scale of concerts continued to grow to the point of becoming full-scale festivals described as "giant" and "mammoth" events. Underscored by the repeated refrain "gospel singing is big business," coverage linked this growth of gospel as "one of the most lucrative segments of the entertainment business" to a new proliferation of numbers documenting concert attendance, box office tallies, and artist earnings, however accurate. "Did you know that gospel singing festivals are climbing into the big money brackets?" the *Pittsburgh Courier* asked readers in 1952. "Well, the demand for religious music is simply astounding. Gospel singing groups like Sister Rosetta Tharpe, Mahalia Jackson, the Ward Singers, Clara Ward, Fairfield Four, Soul Stirrers, etc. are booked on a year-round basis." A 1954 article in *Billboard* by Joel Friedman describing "spiritual and gospel music" as a "growing bonanza" provided hard data for male quartets:

> During 1953 the Pilgrim Travelers racked up an estimated gross of $100,000 playing 173 dates at ball parks and auditoriums, drawing approximately 110,000 people. The group played to 10,000 at Columbus, Ga.; 5,000 at Dallas; 3,600 at Oakland, Calif., and 5,200 at Birmingham with tickets scaled at $1.25.
>
> The Original Blind Boys of Mississippi[,] considered to be one of the nation's top acts, pulled approximately $130,000 in grosses during 40 weeks in '53, while the Soul Stirrers drew $78,000.[53]

The face of the storehouse newly opened up by the growing popularity of gospel singing became Clara Ward and her group, which generated excitement through their ability "to stage a show and still maintain the dignity of singing this type of song." A packed house for the Wards at a January 1952 concert at the Golden Gate Auditorium in Harlem, presented by gospel promoter Edna Mae Crenshaw, was just a prelude to crowds exceeding 10,000 at both their anniversary concert in Philadelphia on Memorial Day and at Griffith Stadium in Washington DC in July. To many, as notable as the thronging crowds were the Ward Singers' earnings and the price tag for a lavish lifestyle made possible though business acumen, relentless touring, a commit-ment to showmanship, and sheer gumption. Such newspaper headlines as "25,000 Pay $40,000 to Hear Ward Singers Wearing $4,000 Wardrobes in Pa., N.J., Md." became the story itself. Black papers reported that the group grossed $100,000 in 1952, only to exceed that the following year, with total earnings of $125,000 by Clara Ward Enterprises from concert fees, recordings, and a newly launched publishing company, Ward's House of Music, that offered "religious music of all faiths" and signed W. Herbert Brewster as an in-house composer. By 1951, the Wards had in fact, formed a second spinoff group, the Clara Ward Specials, that enabled them to sat-isfy the deluge of performance requests and collect artist fees in two places at once. Ward staked out a unique position as the music celebrity and fashion diva who "has a $50,000 wardrobe, a pea-green limousine, and earns a quarter of a million dollars yearly," leading a hit-making group that earned "almost three times as much money as their nearest competitor in the gospel singing field."[54]

The relative positioning of Jackson and the Ward Singers in the early-1950s black gospel field merits some unpacking. When in 1952 the Ward Singers toured with Jackson, the Selah Jubilee Singers, and Reverend Abner Duncans as part of the highly publicized "Gospel Train," Jackson was the undisputed star of the package; the con-cert program identified Jackson as the "Gospel Singing Queen of the Nation" and the Wards, despite their considerable success nationwide, as an "up and coming" gospel group. Three years later, both Jackson and the Ward Singers brought more formi-dable reputations to the arena of popular culture. Shortly after Jackson left Apollo to sign with Columbia Records, she found herself in a pitched battle of song with the Ward Singers that illustrated not only how some observers continued to filter their perception of gospel singing through the thrill of competitive spectator sport, but also how the song battle remained a conceptual frame through which gospel music could occupy a place within popular culture in a way the concert spiritual never could.

In the early 1940s, the *Pittsburgh Courier*, which had by then surpassed the *Chicago Defender* as the most widely circulated African American newspaper, began conducting an annual poll for readers to vote for their favorite stars in several music and entertainment categories, with the winners and runners-up performing in a mega concert at a major venue. The star-studded "Command Performance Concert" on March 14 at Detroit's Olympia Stadium to celebrate the results of the 1955 Band Poll was attended by 11,000 and featured performances by Count Basie, Lionel Hampton, Dinah Washington, and Ella Fitzgerald. The *Courier* first instituted a gospel singing contest in 1952 and noted the new cate-gory had generated the most voting activity. In the "most spectacular race in the contest" in 1955, Ward edged out Jackson "with the almost unbelievable tabulation of 104,117 votes to 96,190 votes," capping "a driving finish which was not decided until the final day." To capitalize on the immense popularity of both singers, the newspaper folded a gospel song battle into the Detroit concert. This was a "new innovation," wrote William Nunn Sr., who was struck by how prominently featured were "the appearances of Clara Ward and her incomparable singers, plus the all-compelling personality and the all-enveloping voice of stately, dynamic, soul-stirring and heart-moving Mahalia Jackson."[55]

Russell was in Detroit for the event and offered his account of the scene: "The Ward Singers came in [the] first half. Mahalia said they really rocked as much as anyone could, did everything they could to make a hit, but still didn't go over very big with the audience." To Russell, Jackson's grandeur eclipsed the Wards' spectacle.

> As soon as Mahalia started "I Believe" the big crowd hushed as if by magic, then she broke them up with "Saints." They all yelled for "Halo" and responded so much they clapped for each word in a way and Mahalia had to stop and try to calm them down. It was a terrific response, then they yelled for "Move On Up." Each artist was supposed to sing only two songs each, but Mahalia had to sing four. She said [the] next day, "I just had a lucky night."[56]

Despite the galaxy of show business celebrities at the event, the *Courier*'s Dawn Francis, communicating the new pop-cultural resonance of gospel music, lingered on the faceoff between Ward and Jackson, who "gave the near-capacity [audience] a show to end all shows." Her review, however, determined the showdown to be a draw.

> But the highlight of the evening was the fulfillment of the promise made by the queens of the gospel singers, Miss Ward and Miss Jackson, to decide once and for all, which should have the title undisputed.
>
> The audience not only "rocked and rolled," it screamed and shouted when Mahalia opened up with a spine-tingling version of "I Believe," and followed it with "Rusty Ole Halo" and then wasn't allowed off the stage until she had done two encores, including "Move [On] Up a Little Higher." The audience had been waiting to see what Mahalia would pull out of the bag after the Clara Ward Singers completely captured the audience and held it in the palms of their hands almost from the first note. It was truly a battle!
>
> This writer can't say which won. The Clara Ward Singers as a group can't be touched in the gospel field, and Mahalia Jackson, the top "single" in this field, remains the undefeated champion.[57]

Francis's diplomatic apples-and-oranges verdict on the song battle in Detroit concluded that the Ward Singers and Jackson were qualitatively different gospel performers. This distinction had already been made during the voting for "this big, new lucrative field." The *Courier* acknowledged that Jackson and Ward "might have well been placed in different categories. As an individualist, they claim that Mahalia is supreme, but Clara Ward (with both the Ward Singers and the Ward Specials) is a show-woman without a peer."

But beyond being differentiated as a group leader and as a soloist, respectively, Ward and Jackson also came to represent other axes of comparison, both explicit and implicit. This often began with references to their physical body types and backgrounds: If "buxom Mahalia Jackson was born where the blues were born," Ward the Philadelphian "only weighs 98 pounds and stands a scant 5 feet 3" but possessed the goods to set off "a pandemonium of screaming, shouting and crying."[58] In subsequent years, Jackson and Ward were occasionally pitted as rivals, at least in the black press, particularly when Jackson voiced strong disapproval of the increasing number of Ward Singer appearances at unconventional venues for gospel like the luxury Fontainebleau Hotel in Miami Beach, the Village Vanguard nightclub in Manhattan's Greenwich Village, and Disneyland—even as Jackson herself made appearances at the Newport Jazz Festival. But by the mid-1950s, coverage had already introduced points of contrast—Jackson's humble sincerity versus the Wards' flamboyant glamour, Jackson's vocal artistry versus the Wards' showmanship, Jackson's repeated mantra of devout integrity versus Ward's unapologetic embrace of new pop-cultural opportunities—that were reductive but also signaled new and multiple avenues for participation and celebrity in the field as well as a dynamic cultural politics of black gospel divadom.

The End of the Beginning

Episode #34 of *Mahalia Jackson Sings* aired on Chicago's WBBM-TV on Sunday, September 4, 1955, and trotted out a new experiment. In addition to Jackson's solo numbers—"Walk Over God's Heaven," "Rock-A My Soul," and "I See God"—the show's producers decided to incorporate a "community sing," allowing the ticketed audience to join in on "When the Saints Go Marching In," "A Rusty Old Halo," and "Onward Christian Soldiers." The show continued to pursue arty production ideas, projecting images of church windows on the background behind Jackson. Russell estimated that the station received twenty letters a week "complaining of too much of one face" so the sing-along numbers enabled the crew to mix in a wider variety of shots with the usual close-ups of Jackson. Cameras shot the audience from behind Jackson's back with her in the foreground and scanned the crowd to show some of her friends, like organist Louise Overall Weaver, and several children, including one white boy who stuck out his tongue at the camera. The show closed with Jackson and the audience singing "Joshua Fit de Battle of Jericho." Jackson was initially skeptical of the sing-along idea, but "she threw herself into the program and everybody who saw the show on TV thought she enjoyed it more than usual." But whether because of her perception of the precariousness of the show's survival or the rising stakes of a career in which she now had much more to lose, Jackson was growing increasingly tense. "Mahalia was on edge all day," Russell noted the day of the show, and even Falls had observed that although "Mahalia doesn't really get nervous at concerts, she has been more nervous lately than at anytime in the eight years Mildred has worked with her."[59]

As it turned out, it would be Jackson's final television episode. Jackson's health had been a concern ever since the discovery of her sarcoidosis in 1952 and her hysterectomy following her European tour that fall. In June 1955, Jackson, who arrived in Chicago in 1931 skinny as a rail, became alarmed when her weight ballooned to 260 pounds, which she attributed to her insatiable consumption of fruit at home and in the studio during the past year. She began keeping a closer eye on her eating habits and three weeks later Russell reported that Jackson, with the help of Fletcher, had "been taking her diet seriously, counting her calories," and had lost 20 pounds, reducing to 240; Jackson hoped "to get to 200 but not 180 as Polly suggests."[60] The day after the community sing episode of *Mahalia Jackson Sings* was Labor Day and Jackson attended a barbecue. The next day Russell went by Jackson's home for his usual visit and was told by a somber Falls that Jackson was "quite sick" after being up all night with gas pains, perhaps from having "eaten too much junk on the holiday." By Wednesday, Jackson had been admitted to Billings Hospital where her regular doctor, William Barclay, suspected severe gallstones in need of immediate surgery.[61]

Dr. Philip Harper, who to Russell "looked so young I thought he was an intern," performed the operation to remove Jackson's gall bladder the following evening, Thursday, September 7, and informed Falls afterwards that "there was only a 50-50 chance Mahalia would live since her gall bladder had ruptured." Falls and Jackson's Aunt Hannah kept watch at her bedside in the days after surgery and Russell was finally allowed to visit on Monday. He noticed that Jackson, now down to 205 pounds, "looked very bad" and he helped her walk up and down the hospital corridors to relieve her still severe gas pains. She was cheered, however, by numerous large bouquets from friends, fans, Cowan, CBS, *Ebony* magazine, and even Bess Berman—no word from "Halloran and his boys," though, Russell noted.

Jackson was sent home on Monday, September 19. On his church radio broadcast the day before, Reverend Louis Boddie of Greater Harvest Baptist Church admonished over the air: "Now, 500 of you people will be wanting to go by and see Haly, but . . . Haly ain't never gonna get well if you don't let her alone." Privately, however, the prominent pastor was suggesting that Jackson's illness was divine retribution for her not following a narrower path. Word reached Russell through the grapevine that "Reverend Boddie talked so badly about Mahalia the week before and said if she'd stayed in the church to sing she'd be well right now."[62] Jackson laid low for several weeks and slowly recovered. On the Sunday after she fell sick, WBBM announced that due to illness, Jackson's show would be preempted by a movie. As it turned out, the program never returned to the air, and Russell's almost daily documentation of Jackson's activities also stopped abruptly after she returned from the hospital. With her activity dramatically curtailed, and surely anxious to return to his own raft of projects, Russell ended his Mahalia Jackson journal by listing Jackson's repertory at a November 25 concert at Mandel Hall and her television appearance on *Studs Terkel's Briefcase* on December 6. In 1956, Russell moved to New Orleans, where lived until his death in 1992.

In October, however, was Jackson's birthday. She was honored with a $25-a-plate dinner on October 28 at the Terrace Casino of the Morrison Hotel benefiting the campaign to build a Halfway House on the South Side supporting homeless and delinquent young women. Attended by three hundred of her friends and fans, "A Birthday Salute to Mahalia Jackson" brought into view a cross-section of Jackson's career in late 1955.[63] Terkel, whom Jackson acknowledged as "one of the finest persons that I know," someone who "has been like a brother" to her, was master of ceremonies for a program that featured delegates from the church, the black community, the media, and civic leadership. Each speaker represented a constituency in Chicago expressing their recognition of Jackson's accomplishments. Jackson received warm accolades from Mayor Daley, who brought "the greetings of all the people of Chicago to this fine and outstanding woman who has done so much to bring so much confidence and cheer and inspiration to all the people of America." Mayor of Bronzeville John Earl Lewis remarked that Jackson's personality and voice were beloved both in the United States and across the Atlantic, while joking that she was his "dear, beloved hometown girlfriend" from New Orleans. On behalf of newspapers and television, Kupcinet reminded the audience about how Jackson "really broke up the joint" at the Harvest Moon Festival and assured the audience that the local media "regard her as the number one shining light in Chicago." For the radio, pitchman and disk jockey Marty Faye described how having only recently been made aware of Jackson by Terkel, who brought him to the filming of an episode of *Mahalia Jackson Sings*, he found himself "dumbstruck" by her voice: "You stand in front of someone who is absolutely awe-inspiring and actually you don't know how to react." The most extensive and personal remarks were made by Duckett, who described her as a "race proud," pathbreaking artist who opened "the doors to Carnegie Hall, the doors to national radio and television, the doors to tremendous commercial success as a gospel singer, the doors of understanding between people all over America and throughout Europe."

In addition to the glowing tributes, Jackson's birthday salute featured several performances. Reverend Morris Harrison Tynes, pastor of Monumental Baptist Church sang "You'll Never Walk Alone" and "The Lord's Prayer" in a rich concert baritone, and Jackson's second cousin John Stevens gave a dramatic reading of James Weldon Johnson's 1922 poem "The Creation." Mahalia Jackson Fan Club president Muriel Wagner, introduced by Terkel as "a very close friend of Mahalia's," sang what she described as Jackson's "favorite song," the popular religious number from the 1930s "My God and I." But most of the musical performances were by aspiring, classically trained, local black talent, "young people," Willa Saunders Jones enthusiastically proclaimed, who "have gotten their pitch from Mahalia" and "are walking in the path that she has opened for them." These included twelve-year-old harp prodigy Gloria Burt, pianist Charlesetta Westbrook, who played "Malagueña" from Ernesto Lecuona's *Suite Andalucia*, and nineteen-year-old Charles Walker, a music student at DePaul University, who delivered an impressive performance of a modernist toccata. The Wooten Singers, who had appeared on Jackson's television program in July, captured the spirit of the event with a laudatory choral anthem written especially for the occasion, "A Dedication to Mahalia."

> Who's the queen of song?—Mahalia
> With a faith so strong?—Mahalia
> Who's that gospel voice that made our hearts rejoice
> Shouting "The Lord won't fail you?"
> Who can chime the soul?—Mahalia
> Make the spirit whole?—Mahalia
> We are here to say on this your birthday
> All our wishes true, Mahalia.
> Hail to Mahalia!

After the cutting of an elegant birthday cake, sent courtesy of Reverend James Lofton of Detroit, Jackson's mutual admirer who years earlier recommended her for State Department diplomatic duty (Figure 11.4), the sentimental climax came when six-year-old Rachel Lois Washington, "representing the children of America," gave Jackson the doll that she could never afford as a poor child in New Orleans. "I can't tell you how happy I am," said Jackson when she stepped to the podium to offer her thanks for such a spectacular affair. "The things that I prayed for are gonna be proved. You want to know how old I am. I'm forty-four years old and got a baby tonight." She then closed the evening by singing an intimate, half-voiced version of what had become her media theme song, "His Eye Is on the Sparrow," accompanied by Falls.

FIG. 11.4 Mahalia Jackson with Chicago Mayor Richard Daley at "A Birthday Salute to Mahalia Jackson," a benefit dinner at the Terrace Casino of the Morrison Hotel attended by 300 friends and admirers, October 28, 1955. The cake was provided by Rev. James Lofton of Detroit. Photo by Isaac Sutton. Laurraine Goreau Photograph Collection, Hogan Jazz Archive, Tulane University.

In many ways, "A Birthday Salute to Mahalia Jackson" marked a culmination and a point of departure. Attendees mapped out a network of advocates and associates that would have been inconceivable for any black gospel singer before her. Stevens, Jones, Lofton, Wooten, Tynes, and Duckett ratified Jackson's long familial and church ties, while Lewis and prominent attorney Edith Sampson, chosen by Harry Truman in 1950 to be the first African American delegate to the United Nations, certified her stature among Chicago's black citizenry. Terkel and Kupcinet had been instrumental in building Jackson's reputation and transporting her voice to the white Chicagoans for whom Bronzeville was out of earshot, drawing new admirers like Wagner and Faye. The performances by Burt, Westbrook, and Walker suggested that Chicago youth steeped in the cultivated tradition that aroused so much ambivalence for Jackson since her childhood in New Orleans now aspired to the artistry of the vernacular-steeped "Leontyne Price of the gospel community." And all the while, jazz junkie Bill Russell, silently and in the background, captured it all on his tape recorder, an expression of his admiration for "a person with her heart and body completely full of music." Recognizing her standing in black Chicago, Mayor Daley became Jackson's steadfast champion for the rest of her life, his presence at the birthday banquet indicating that even as she remained part of her family of Baptists, gospel singers, and South Siders, Jackson was now also cherished by the city of Chicago and by a country in which her grandparents had been born into slavery a century before. Still, what in October 1955 must have felt like a pinnacle was just a prelude to even greater triumphs that lay ahead, to dates with the Duke and Dr. King yet to come.

Conclusion

IN DECEMBER 1951, Columbia Records released a four-LP set produced by George Avakian, *The Bessie Smith Story*, offering a curated selection of remastered recordings that the great blues singer made for the label in the 1920s and 1930s. "To those who knew her and were familiar with her work," *Billboard*'s Hal Webman enthused about the archival set's historical importance, Smith "was the most distinctive, power-packed transmitter of vocal emotion that has ever graced the business."[1] Three years later, Avakian was days away from his first session with a new Columbia artist, gospel singer Mahalia Jackson, a woman who studied Smith's recordings when they first appeared and who for many commentators resurrected the power and the glory of her childhood idol. As a token of goodwill, Avakian sent Jackson a copy of his Smith anthology. Bill Russell confirmed that the gift had been received.

> Thanks very much for the tape and the Bessie records, which Mahalia appreciates very much and for which she wants me to thank you.
>
> As soon as I took the records down yesterday she played three sides (18 blues). Then suddenly she shut the phonograph off, saying something like "That's enough of you, Bessie; everybody has her day."[2]

Jackson recalled that as a child growing up in poverty in New Orleans' "Nigger Town" she "had this feeling that I could live better, and I used to dream of living better." By the mid-1950s, having achieved pathbreaking success that brought new visibility to the black gospel field and inspired broader horizons of imagination for gospel singers, Jackson may have sensed that her own day had indeed come, and in certain respects—particularly through the complementary media of radio, television, and the long-playing album—verged on surpassing Smith's zenith. The "Louisiana Cinderella" narrative that tracked Jackson as her reputation grew to international proportions in the early 1950s also functioned as an autobiographical vehicle through which she could mobilize testimony about her cultural authenticity, the rewards of steadfast Christian faith, South-to-North migration, and her complex working-class status as the self-identifying "wash-woman" who struck it big.

But as this book has shown, the themes of devout integrity, black vernacular triumph, and against-all-odds personal achievement, however central, mark a beginning, not the end, of how we might account for Jackson's career during the decade following World War II. Most fundamentally, it is revealing to discern the continuous work of making "Miss Jackson and her art" legible to expanding publics in ways that continued to speak to and for African American observers in the church pews, in the press, and as consumers of popular culture. We are constantly reminded that Jackson was a black woman. Observers repeatedly took the opportunity to read her public persona and performances against a range of African American woman entertainers, steering her reception through direct analogy or "this-not-that" comparison. Often, commentators juxtaposed Jackson with early twentieth-century blues vaudevillians like the "power-packed" Smith, though for those in the know the standards of measure were her gospel contemporaries, among them Frances Steadman, Queen C. Anderson, and Dorothy Love Coates, as well as other admired singers like Rosetta Tharpe, Ernestine Washington, Georgia Peach, Willie Mae Ford Smith, Mary Johnson Davis, Roberta Martin, Doris Akers, and Clara Ward. But we also see Jackson's name slotted in *Jet*'s 1951 list of the country's top black female vocalists, along with Ella Fitzgerald, Billie Holiday, Sarah Vaughan, Dinah Washington, Ruth Brown, Pearl Bailey, Lena Horne, Josephine Baker, and Hadda Brooks, and find her at the 1954 Harvest Moon Festival in Chicago sharing the stage with Eartha Kitt. Jackson's name circulated in counterpoint with the gravitas of classically trained recitalist Marian Anderson but also with the vexed politics of representation triggered by Beulah actors Hattie McDaniel and Louise Beavers. If a critical understanding of Jackson within the histories of black musical worship and the practice of gospel singing is paramount—and there remains much work to do even on this front—we must also register those moments when the reception of African American women entertainers more broadly was a reference point. Study of Jackson as a musical performer pushes us to consider how an unlettered and unmarried yet charismatic "classicist of the spiritual" offered a unique angle of vision onto the space of possibilities for black womanhood and public blackness in the post-war years.

Jackson was called upon to represent variably and her work situated her at multiple intersections: evangelical singing and pop-cultural celebrity, black vernacular folkways and highly formalized denominational institutions, the black experience and U.S. propaganda, spiritual calling and socioeconomic desires. Indeed, a primary theme of Jackson's life and career through the mid-1950s was her tireless mobility. Within her own family story, this mobility was literal. The Clarks' relocation from Pointe Coupée to New Orleans around the turn of the century, followed by Jackson's own move to Chicago in the early 1930s, traced familiar patterns of migration for African Americans seeking opportunities to stay afloat in the Jim Crow era and enacted transitions from rural to urban settings and from Southern to Northern lifestyles. Constant travel on the Chicago church circuit, along the nationwide gospel highway, and during a 1952 European tour that brought continental audiences face-to-face with black gospel singing also indicated how Jackson was perpetually on the move.

But Jackson lived and embodied other forms of mobility. Aligning herself strongly with the black Baptist church establishment, Jackson since her childhood also identified with and took inspiration from Sanctified worship, a charismatic form of religious expression that she brought to her performance of gospel songs. This initially drew consternation among some conservative Baptists in Chicago. Being a much in demand church singer providing musical worship for "different congregations" thus required close observance of the varying receptiveness to Pentecostal-influenced performance styles across denominations. "All of my folks don't like those type of songs, but to please my public I have to learn to sing them," she told her audience at the Music Inn in 1951, referring to her more driving numbers that made worshippers shout. "Now when I go to the Holy Rollers' church that's what they like, you know . . . [but] when I go to a Methodist church, I have to stand up and sing it easy."[3] Jackson's ambivalent class politics of voice, within which she openly calibrated vernacular models and black voice culture, also fostered a mobile sense of self as a singer and led her to alternately characterize her practice of singing gospel songs as "modern" and "primitive." Jackson both reinforces and complicates how we map cultivated-vernacular distinctions and presumptions about "natural" and "trained" voices onto our study of black music. Both are inescapably present, as they were for Jackson.

Making Jackson's mass mediated work and live appearances beyond black churches a central part of the story foregrounds additional forms of mobility. Most notable and woefully understudied in this regard, I believe, are questions pertaining to repertory. As an Apollo recording artist, Jackson sang gospel songs but was called upon to tap the vogue for religious pop amid the surge of religiosity in the early Cold War United States. At Columbia, she performed many songs in this vein while also adjusting to new methods of production and to the distinguishable commodity forms of the single and long-playing album. Jackson's radio program broadened this song list further, adding sentimental oldies, inspirational Tin Pan Alley numbers, and even semi-classical songs, rendered within a more tightly scripted format. On television, she was allowed more latitude, placing her in a more curatorial role that gave her choices in the types of religious material she sang to a more diverse audience. Bill Russell's recordings of Jackson's sometimes rugged rehearsals remind us that far from being "as natural as breathing," singing this increasingly wide-ranging repertory produced real labor and often struggle. This endeavor represented its own form of "training" and necessitated Jackson's continuous assessment of her strengths and limitations as a vocalist, not infrequently on a song-by-song basis. Moreover, these performances across media asked Jackson, who believed that singing gospel songs required "something else besides a voice," to develop flexible acclimation to a range of working methods that sometimes compromised the well-honed performance strategies that maximized her effectiveness in a church setting.[4] Jackson was keenly aware of the implications as her performances began to circulate more widely and as her fan base began to grow and diversify demographically. She was called upon repeatedly to be a cultural interpreter, explaining the significance of black sacred song, and, more critically, as she shuttled between the church and the world of popular culture, to negotiate and mediate the visceral pleasure new audiences took in the sound of gospel music vocality and her own testimony in song about devout Christian belief.

New forms of mobility influenced the post-war black gospel field more broadly. Priscilla Ferguson has delineated how a feature of emergent fields of cultural production—as in the transition from black gospel singing to a black gospel field—is precisely an increasingly "acute consciousness of positions and possibilities for social mobility" achieved in part through forged "links with adjacent and kindred institutions and fields, linkages that generate social prestige."[5] If Dorsey and his leadership partners in the National Convention of Gospel Choirs and Choruses sought to build an organizational platform for the gospel singing movement in the 1930s and early 1940s, he, Butts, and Frye also built bridges that enabled the NCGCC to converse fluently with other black institutions like the National Baptist Convention and the National Association of Negro Musicians while also appropriating the discourse of respectability politics and asserting the relevance of gospel singing to political events in the world beyond church walls. Jackson demonstrated new possibilities for building audiences for gospel singing through her commercial recordings and media engagements for Apollo, CBS, and Columbia, though she also accrued prestige through the live performance format of the song battle and Johnny Myers's spectacles at the Golden Gate. These linkages contributed to the reconfiguration of the black gospel field in ways that extended beyond Dorsey's vision—and even preference—entering the realm of popular culture.

Efforts by those active in the black gospel field as performers, presenters, entrepreneurs, and fans to make sense of the significance of the surprising parameters of Jackson's success also reconfigured the field. The work of the National Baptist Convention Publishing Board, the appearance of important new religious songbooks in the 1920s, the popularization and sale of gospel songs by Dorsey and others in the 1930s, and the proliferation of independent music outlets like Martin and Morris and Roberta Martin's studio in the 1940s are reminders that the commodification of black religious song and economic ambition within the gospel field were omnipresent. But these products were targeted specifically to black church folk. The transatlantic circulation of Jackson's recordings and live performances, her mediation through radio and television, and increasingly prominent bookings that made her a "star to those white folks downtown," along with the Ward Singers' distinctive brand of gospel glamour, introduced new forms of prestige, above all public recognition and pop-cultural cachet, that transformed what it meant to participate in the field. These activities have often been cast as ancillary to "real" gospel. But a more inclusive and relational understanding of the black gospel field brings into focus tensions and areas of contestation—between spiritual and commercial aspirations, between humble Christian service and fame, between an insular black vernacular and the extensive reach of mass culture—that open up infrequently pursued avenues of inquiry.

Jackson's seemingly contradictory yet deeply provocative self-description—a decidedly "modern gospel singer" who was at the same time "America's most primitive singer"—introduces another of these productive tensions while also highlighting ways in which multiple forms of desire remain an ever-reverberating centerpiece in the study of black music. Jackson's own desire for spiritual renewal, professional status, self-betterment, and recognition of her talents was a driving force in her career and reflected desires of African Americans in the 1940s and 1950s. For black citizens hungry for respect and for equal opportunities to flourish, Jackson's successes affirmed new forms of cultural recognition. It is easy to underplay the watershed of a black woman gospel singer born in a sequestered community within a city in the Deep South being acclaimed for having reached the acme of musical artistry. But these achievements also signaled possibilities for socioeconomic mobility associated less with uplift ideology than with modern, market-driven rewards of 1950s liberal possessive individualism and with the prestige attainable through the unprecedented visibility attainable through post-war media.

Meanwhile, Jackson's emergence as a public figure on the national and international stage pushes us to interrogate an issue raised at the outset: the terms under which black culture and black bodies can be recognized. As I insisted in my introductory chapter, and as I hope to have shown, Jackson's early career makes clear that "black gospel" matters. At the same time, and notwithstanding the far-reaching admiration for Jackson's vocal performances, the repeated celebration of her natural sensibilities, cultural authenticity, religious sincerity, and personal charisma remind us how for some she also satisfied longstanding and still lingering desires for preferred black culture and black subjects, particularly, though not exclusively, on the part of white audiences. Investment in a uniquely black approach to religious worship—and in the cultural-political significance of this difference—has enjoyed broad, time-honored endorsement, having been embraced by a diverse cast of historical actors, stretching from white abolitionists of the 1860s to black nationalists of the 1960s.[6] It is a romantic racialism that continues to shape writing on black gospel and African American musical traditions, even as it can place methodological and interpretive constraints upon our study of them. Jackson, the great exceptional case within the black gospel field, also embodied persistent predilections for exceptional blackness. But in acknowledging both the critical salience and the limits of such exceptionalism, we move toward an appreciation and study of black gospel music that allows us to savor the singularity and transformative power of Mahalia Jackson and the black gospel field within U.S. culture and beyond, while also recognizing the splendid entanglements of gospel voices with the broader world to which they belong and in which they continually resound.

Notes

PREFACE

1. Quoted in Alden Whitman, "Mahalia Jackson, Gospel Singer, and a Civil Rights Symbol, Dies," *New York Times* (January 28, 1972).

CHAPTER 1

1. James Maguire, *Impresario: The Life and Times of Ed Sullivan* (New York: Billboard Books, 2006), 126–66; Gerald Nachman, *Right Here on Our Stage Tonight!: Ed Sullivan's America* (Berkeley: University of California Press, 2009), 138–47; "Tele Followup Comment," *Variety* (January 23, 1952): 34.

2. Anthony Heilbut, *The Gospel Sound: Good News and Bad Times* (New York: Limelight, 1997), 67; "Mahalia Jackson Wins Top French Honors for Record," *Baltimore Afro-American* (May 5, 1951); Art Rosett, "Paris Peek," *Billboard* (March 31, 1951): 46; Mark Burford, "Mahalia Jackson Meets the Wise Men: Defining Jazz at the Music Inn," *Musical Quarterly* 96 (Winter 2014): 429–86; Publicity card for "Lift Every Voice and Sing: A Program of People's Music," WRC, Mss. 513, folder 438; "Ten Best Girl Singers," *Jet* (December 13, 1951): 58–62; "Mahalia Jackson to Head 1952 Gospel Concert Tour," *Norfolk New Journal and Guide* (February 23, 1952).

3. Ed Sullivan interview with Laurraine Goreau, November 19, 1972, transcript in LGC.

4. "CBS Ed Sullivan Show Has Featured Most Negro Artists," n.d. Clipping in WRC, Mss. 513, folder 305; "Television: Negro Performers Win Better Roles in TV Than in Any Other Entertainment Medium," *Ebony* (June 1950): 22–23.

5. Ed Sullivan interview with Laurraine Goreau, November 19, 1972, transcript in LGC; John Sellers, interview with Laurraine Goreau, July 11, 1973, transcript in LGC.

6. My thanks to Gema Interiano of SOFA Entertainment for enabling me to view the January 20, 1952, episode of *Toast of the Town*. Jackson's performance

of "These Are They" can also be seen in the documentary *Rejoice and Shout*, directed by Don McGlynn (Magnolia Pictures, 2010) and on YouTube [https:// www.youtube.com/watch?v=7TvAOoKNddQ, accessed May 10, 2018].

7. On Brewster, see Heilbut, *The Gospel Sound*, 97–105; Heilbut, "'If I Fail, You Tell the World I Tried': Reverend W. Herbert on Records," *Black Music Research Journal* 7 (1987): 119–26, reprinted in *We'll Understand It Better By and By: Pioneering African American Gospel Composers*, edited by Bernice Johnson Reagon (Washington, DC: Smithsonian Institution Press, 1992), 233–44. The latter collection also includes essays on Brewster by Reagon ("William Herbert Brewster: Rememberings," 185–209), Horace Clarence Boyer ("William Herbert Brewster: The Eloquent Poet," 211–31), and William Wiggins ("William Herbert Brewster: Pioneer of the Sacred Pageant," 245–51).

8. Another gospel standard that addresses this theme is Roberta Martin's "I'm Sealed ('Til the Day of Redemption)."

9. Mahalia Jackson 25th Anniversary Program, October 19, 1951, Mahalia Jackson Scrapbook, LGC.

10. Mary Johnson Davis Gospel Singers (Frances Steadman, lead) (Coleman 6026, 1949); Brewster Singers (Queen C. Anderson, lead) (Gotham 709, *c.* 1950–1952); Mahalia Jackson (Apollo 234, 1950); and the Original Gospel Harmonettes (Dorothy Love Coates, lead) (Specialty 816, 1951).

11. See also Heilbut, *The Gospel Sound*, 102.

12. My thanks to Anthony Heilbut for pointing out this textual connection.

13. John Sellers interview with Laurraine Goreau, January 13, 1973, transcript in LGC; "Blind Girl Wants to Sing on Ed Sullivan's 'Toast of the Town,'" *Chicago Review* (October 31, 1954), Clipping in WRC, Mss. 513, folder 270; "Mahalia Jackson Honored by Dayton Gospel Fans," *Pittsburgh Courier* (Local Edition), (September 13, 1952).

14. Photo with caption, *New York Amsterdam News* (February 2, 1952); E. B. Rea, "Encores and Echoes," *Baltimore Afro-American* (February 2, 1952); S. W. Garlington, "Radio-TV Highlights," *New York Amsterdam News* (January 26, 1952).

15. Pearl Williams-Jones, "Afro-American Gospel Music: A Crystallization of the Black Aesthetic," *Ethnomusicology* 19 (1975): 373–85; Horace Clarence Boyer, "Contemporary Gospel Music," *Black Perspective in Music* 7 (1979): 22–34. See also Andrew Legg, "A Taxonomy of Musical Gesture in African American Gospel Music," *Popular Music* 29 (2010): 103–29.

16. Williams-Jones, "Afro-American Gospel Music"; and Mellonee Burnim, *The Black Gospel Music Tradition: Symbol of Ethnicity* (PhD diss., Indiana University, 1980), Penny Von Eschen, *Satchmo Blows Up the World: Jazz Ambassadors Play the Cold War* (Cambridge, MA: Harvard University Press, 2004), 161.

17. For two perspectives on white reception of religious singing by enslaved African Americans, see Jon Cruz, *Culture on the Margins: The Black Spiritual and the*

Rise of American Cultural Interpretation (Princeton, NJ: Princeton University Press, 1999) and Ronald Radano, *Lying Up a Nation: Race and Black Music* (Chicago: University of Chicago Press, 2003), 164–229.

18. James Goff Jr., *Close Harmony: A History of Southern Gospel* (Chapel Hill: University of North Carolina Press, 2002); Douglass Harrison, *Then Sings My Soul: The Culture of Southern Gospel* (Urbana: University of Illinois Press, 2012).

19. Stephen Shearon, "Establishing the Fundamentals of Gospel Music History." Paper delivered at the National Conference of the Society for American Music, Lancaster, Pennsylvania, March 7, 2014.

20. Kenneth Morris, *Improving the Music in the Church* (Chicago: Martin and Morris, 1949), 24; "Singers Plan Tribute to Prof. Dorsey," *Chicago Defender* (May 29, 1943). On Dorsey, see also Heilbut, *The Gospel Sound*, 21–36; Michael Harris, *The Rise of Gospel Blues: The Music of Thomas Andrew Dorsey in the Urban Church* (New York: Oxford University Press, 1992); Horace Clarence Boyer, "Take My Hand, Precious Lord, Lead Me On," in *We'll Understand It Better By and By*, 141–63; and Robert Marovich, *A City Called Heaven: The Birth of Gospel Music in Chicago* (Champaign-Urbana: University of Illinois Press, 2015), 71–77.

21. Campbell Robinson, "A Quiet Exodus: Why Black Worshippers Are Leaving White Evangelical Churches," *New York Times* (March 9, 2018).

22. Heilbut quoted in the documentary *Rejoice and Shout*.

23. Heilbut, *The Gospel Sound*, 71. See also John Hammond, "Mahalia Dead at 60," *Rolling Stone* (March 2, 1972): 18–20.

24. "Mahalia's New Orleans: A Concert and Conference in Honor of Mahalia Jackson," Tulane University, March 7, 2015.

25. Heilbut, *The Gospel Sound*; Viv Broughton, *Black Gospel: An Illustrated History of the Gospel Sound* (Dorset, England: Blandford Press, 1985); Horace Clarence Boyer, *The Golden Age of Gospel* (Urbana: University of Illinois Press, 2000); Robert Darden, *People Get Ready: A New History of Black Gospel Music* (New York: Continuum, 2004).

26. Harris, *The Rise of Gospel Blues*; Reagon, ed., *We'll Understand It Better By and By*; Alan Young, *The Pilgrim Jubilees* (Jackson: University Press of Mississippi, 2001); Jerry Zolten, *Great God A'Mighty! The Dixie Hummingbirds: Celebrating the Rise of Soul Gospel Music* (New York: Oxford University Press, 2003); Bil Carpenter, *Uncloudy Days: The Gospel Music Encyclopedia* (San Francisco: Backbeat Books, 2005); Daniel Wolf, *You Send Me: The Life and Times of Sam Cooke* (New York: Quill, 1996), 37–142; Peter Guralnick, *Dream Boogie: The Triumph of Sam Cooke* (New York: Back Bay Books, 2006), 7–170; Anita McAllister, *The Musical Legacy of Dorothy Love Coates: African American Female Gospel Singer with Implications for Education and Theater Education* (EdD diss., Kansas State University, 1995); Gayle Wald, *Shout, Sister, Shout!: The Untold Story of Rock-and-Roll Trailblazer Rosetta Tharpe* (Boston: Beacon Press, 2007); Lynn Abbott, *I Got Two Wings: Incidents and Anecdotes of the Two-Winged Preacher and Electric*

Guitar Evangelist Elder Utah Smith (Montgomery, AL: CaseQuarter, 2008); Timothy Dodge, *The School of Arizona Dranes: Gospel Music Pioneer* (Lanham, MD: Lexington Books, 2013); Opal Louis Nations, *Sensational Nightingales: The Story of Joseph "Jo Jo" Wallace and the Early Days of the Sensational Nightingales* (San Francisco: Black Scat Books, 2014); Claudrena Harold, "'Lord, Let Me Be an Instrument': The Artistry and Cultural Politics of Reverend James Cleveland and the Gospel Music Workshop of America, 1963–1991," *Journal of Africana Religions* 5 (2017): 157–80; Kay Norton, "'Yes, [Gospel] Is Real': Half a Century with Chicago's Martin and Morris Company," *Journal of the Society for American Music* 11 (2017): 420–51.

27. Kerrill Rubman, *From "Jubilee" to "Gospel" in Black Male Quartet Singing*, PhD diss., University of North Carolina, 1980; Ray Allen, *Singing in the Spirit: African American Sacred Quartets in New York City* (Philadelphia: University of Pennsylvania Press, 1991); Kip Lornell, *"Happy in the Service of the Lord": African American Sacred Vocal Harmony Quartets in Memphis* (Knoxville: University of Tennessee Press, 1995); Cedric Dent, *The Harmonic Development of the Black Religious Quartet Singing Tradition*, PhD diss., University of Maryland, 1997; Idella Johnson, *Development of African American Gospel Piano Style (1926–1960): A Socio-Musical Analysis of Arizona Dranes and Thomas A. Dorsey* (PhD diss., University of Pittsburgh, 2009); Lynn Abbott and Doug Seroff, *To Do This, You Must Know This: Music Pedagogy in the Black Gospel Quartet Tradition* (Jackson: University Press of Mississippi, 2013).

28. Lynn Abbott, *The Soproco Spiritual Singers: A New Orleans Quartet Family Tree* (New Orleans: Jean Lafite National Historical Park, 1983); Doug Seroff, "On the Battlefield: Gospel Quartets in Jefferson County, Alabama," in *Repercussions: A Celebration of African-American Music*, edited by Geoffrey Haydon and Dennis Marks (London: Century, 1985), 10–53; Jacqueline DjeDje, "Gospel Music in the Los Angeles Black Community: A Historical Overview," *Black Music Research Journal* 9 (1989): 35–79; Jacqueline DjeDje, "Los Angeles Composers of African American Gospel Music: The First Generations," *American Music* 11 (1993): 412–57; Allen, *Singing in the Spirit*; Lornell, *Happy in the Service of the Lord*; Frederick Burton, *Cleveland's Gospel Music* (Charleston, SC: Arcadia, 2003); Thérèse Smith, *"Let the Church Sing": Music and Worship in a Black Mississippi Community* (Rochester, NY: University of Rochester Press, 2004); Carrie Allen, *"A Mighty Long Way": Community, Continuity, and Black Gospel Music on Television in Augusta, Georgia, 1954–2008* (PhD diss., University of Georgia, 2009); Carrie Allen, "'When We Send Up Praises': Race, Identity, and Gospel Music in Augusta, Georgia," *Black Music Research Journal* 27 (2007): 79–95; Jerrilyn McGregory, *Downhome Gospel: African American Spiritual Activism in Wiregrass County* (Jackson: University Press of Mississippi, 2010); Robert Marovich, *A City Called Heaven*.

29. Williams-Jones, "Afro-American Gospel Music"; Portia Maultsby, "The Influence of Gospel Music on the Secular Music Industry," in *Signifyin(g), Sanctifyin', and*

Slam Dunking: A Reader in African American Expressive Culture, edited by Gena Dagel Caponi (Amherst: University of Massachusetts Press, 1999), 172–90; Jerma Jackson, *Singing in My Soul: Black Gospel Music in a Secular Age* (Chapel Hill: University of North Carolina Press, 2003); Robert Darden, *Nothing but Love in God's Water: Black Sacred Music from the Civil War to the Civil Rights Movement* (University Park, PA: Pennsylvania University Press, 2014).

30. Burnim's contributions to black gospel music scholarship began with her 1980 dissertation *The Black Gospel Music Tradition: Symbol of Ethnicity* and has been sustained over the course of numerous articles, including "Culture Bearer and Tradition Bearer: An Ethnomusicologist's Research on Gospel Music," *Ethnomusicology* 29 (1985): 432–47; "The Black Gospel Music Tradition: A Complex of Ideology, Aesthetic, and Behavior," in *More than Dancing: Essays on Afro-American Music and Musicians*, edited by Irene Jackson (Westport, CT: Greenwood, 1985), 147–66; "Functional Dimensions of Gospel Music in Performance," *Western Journal of Black Studies* 12 (1988): 112–21; "The Performance of Black Gospel Music as Transformation," in *Music and the Experience of God*, edited by Mellonee Burnim, Mary Collins, and David Power (Edinburgh: Clark, 1989), 52–61; "The Gospel Music Industry," in *African American Music: An Introduction*, edited by Portia Maultsby and Mellonee Burnim (New York: Routledge, 2006), 416–29; "Voices of Women in Gospel Music," in *Issues in African American Music: Power, Gender, Race, Representation*, edited by Portia Maultsby and Mellonee Burnim (New York: Routledge, 2017), 201–15.

31. On black gospel's "Golden Age," see Heilbut, *The Gospel Sound*, 327, 340; Broughton, *Black Gospel*, 61–89; Boyer, *The Golden Age of Gospel*; and Darden, *People Get Ready*, 221ff. A significant body of mid-1990s compilations, and a handful of recent releases, all featuring recorded gospel performances from 1945 to 1965 by black gospel quartets, groups, soloists, and choirs, have been particularly instrumental in establishing the "Golden Age" as a brand for this era. The producers of these collections remain among the most respected and most-frequently consulted gospel music authorities. See Lee Hildebrand's and Opal Louis Nations's co-produced reissues of Specialty Record's vast gospel catalogue, *Women of Gospel's Golden Age* (Specialty 7056–2, 1994), *Golden Age Gospel Choirs (1954–1963)* (Specialty 7068–2, 1997), *Golden Age Gospel Quartets (1947–1954)*, vol. 1 (Specialty 7069–2, 1997), *Golden Age Gospel Quartets (1954–1963)*, vol. 2 (Specialty 7070–2, 1997); Nations's four-CD box set *Nuggets of the Golden Age of Gospel* (JSP 77126, 2009); and Anthony Heilbut's *Working the Road: The Golden Age of Chicago Gospel* (Delmark DE 702, 1997), and *How Sweet It Was: The Sights and Sounds of Gospel's Golden Age* (Shanachie/Spirit Feel CD and DVD, 2010). The taste of other compilations, such as those released by Mississippi Records in Portland, Oregon, have consciously tended toward earlier or less commercially polished amateur and semi-professional gospel performances. See, for example,

the three-CD box set *Fire in My Bones: Raw & Rare & Otherworldly African American Gospel Music, 1944–2007* (Tompkins Square, TSQ 2271 2009).

32. On the Gospel Roots of Rock and Soul project, see xpngospelroots.org (accessed May 10, 2018).

33. Black Gospel Restoration Project [http://www.baylor.edu/lib/gospel/].

34. Cedric Hayes and Robert Laughton, eds., *Gospel Discography, 1943–2000*, 3d ed. (Vancouver, Canada: Eyeball Productions, 2014).

35. Mahalia Jackson with Evan McLeod Wylie, *Movin' On Up* (New York: Hawthorne Books, 1966); Laurraine Goreau, *Just Mahalia, Baby: The Mahalia Jackson Story* (Waco, TX: Word Books, 1975); Jules Schwerin, *Got to Tell It: Mahalia Jackson, Queen of Gospel* (New York: Oxford University Press, 1992).

36. Hettie Jones, *Big Star Fallin' Mama: Five Women in Black Music* (New York: Viking Press, 1974), 65–87; Jean Gay Cornell, *Mahalia Jackson: Queen of Gospel Song* (Champaign, IL: Garrard, 1974); Kay McDearmon, *Mahalia: Gospel Singer* (New York: Dodd, Mead, 1976); Evelyn Witter, *Mahalia Jackson: Born to Sing Gospel Music* (Fenton, MI: Mott Media, 1985); Charles Wolfe, *Mahalia Jackson: Gospel Singer* (Philadelphia: Chelsea House, 1990); Darlene Donloe, *Mahalia Jackson* (Los Angeles: Melrose Square, 1992); Montrew Dunham, *Mahalia Jackson: Young Gospel Singer* (New York: Aladdin, 1995); Leslie Gourse, *Mahalia Jackson: Queen of Gospel Song* (New York: Franklin Watts, 1996); Roxanne Orgill, *Mahalia: A Life in Gospel Music* (Somerville, MA: Candlewick, 2002); Barbara Kramer, *Mahalia Jackson: The Voice of Gospel and Civil Rights* (New York: Enslow, 2003); Nina Nolan, *Mahalia Jackson: Walking with Kings and Queens* (New York: Amistad, 2015).

37. Don Evans and John Lewis's *Mahalia* (1972); Llewellyn Smith's *Mahalia's Song* (1983); Richard Smallwood, George Faison, and Wayne Davis's *Sing, Mahalia, Sing!* (1985); Queen Esther Marrow's *Truly Blessed: A Music Celebration of Mahalia Jackson* (1990); Tom Stolz's *Mahalia: A Gospel Musical* (1994); Sharon Scott's *Mahalia Jackson: Just as I Am* (2009), and Troi Bechet's *Flowers for Hallie* (2019).

38. Goreau, *Just Mahalia, Baby*, 83.

39. Goreau, *Just Mahalia, Baby*, 63.

40. Sam Staggs, *Born to Be Hurt: The Untold Story of* Imitation of Life (New York: St. Martin's, 2009), 20–21; Schwerin, *Got to Tell It*, 117–18.

41. Schwerin, *Got to Tell It*, 112, 118, 148. Emphasis added. The footage of Jackson singing a medley of "Summertime" and "Sometimes I Feel Like a Motherless Child" for Crosby and Martin can be seen at https://www.youtube.com/watch?v=dVcnO1hRnh4 (accessed May 10, 2018). Rosa Parks discusses her training as an activist in her autobiography, *Rosa Parks: My Story* (New York: Dial Books, 1992), 101–7. See also Jeanne Theoharis, *The Rebellious Life of Mrs. Rosa Parks* (Boston: Beacon Press, 2013).

42. Gerald Early, "Gospel's Unsung Heroine: A No-Souls-Bared Tribute to Mahalia Jackson," *Washington Post* (December 4, 1992).

43. See Adam Green, *Selling the Race: Culture, Community, and Black Chicago, 1940–1955* (Chicago: University of Chicago Press, 2007), 62–66; Johari Jabir, "On Conjuring Mahalia: Mahalia Jackson, New Orleans, and the Sanctified Swing," *American Quarterly* 61 (2009): 649–69; Emily Lordi, *Black Resonances: Iconic Women Singers and African American Literature* (New Brunswick, NJ: Rutgers University Press, 2013), 66–98; Marovich, *A City Called Heaven*; Burford, "Mahalia Jackson Meets the Wise Men."

44. These publications are highlighted by LeRoi Jones, *Blues People: Negro Music in White America* (New York: William Morrow, 1963); Charles Keil, *Urban Blues* (Chicago: University of Chicago Press, 1966); Bill C. Malone, *Country Music, U.S.A.* (Austin: University of Texas Press, 1968); Phyl Garland, *The Sound of Soul: The Story of Black Music* (Chicago: H. Regnery, 1969); Paul Hemphill, *The Nashville Sound: Bright Lights and Country Music* (New York: Simon and Schuster, 1970); Greil Marcus, *Mystery Train: Images of America in Rock 'n' Roll Music* (New York: E. P. Dutton, 1975); Jeff Todd Titon, *Early Downhome Blues: A Musical and Cultural Analysis* (Urbana: University of Illinois Press, 1977); and Arnold Shaw, *Honkers and Shouters: The Golden Age of Rhythm and Blues* (New York: Collier Books, 1978).

45. *Exiled in Paradise: German Refugee Artists and Intellectuals in America, from the 1930s to the Present* (New York: Viking, 1983); *Thomas Mann: Eros and Literature* (New York: Alfred A. Knopf, 1996); *The Fan Who Knew Too Much: Aretha Franklin, the Rise of the Soap Opera, Children of the Gospel Church, and Other Meditations* (New York: Knopf, 2012).

46. The most recent comprehensive history of black gospel, Darden's *People Get Ready*, includes some original research but for the most part weaves together existing secondary sources into the most cohesive, digestible, and reliably sourced narrative available, making it perhaps the most teaching-friendly option.

47. Heilbut, *The Fan Who Knew Too Much*, 317.

48. *The Gospel Sound* (Columbia LP G31086, 1971) and *The Gospel Sound*, vol. 2 (Columbia KG31595, 1972). The recent Jackson compilation CD produced by Heilbut is *Moving Up a Little Higher* (Shanachie 6066, 2016).

49. Though Heilbut does not use the term, "hidden transcript" is a formulation coined by James Scott "to characterize discourse that takes place 'offstage,' beyond direct observation by powerholders." Scott differentiates hidden transcripts from "public transcripts," a "shorthand way of describing the open interaction between subordinates and those who dominate." Scott, *Domination and the Arts of Resistance: Hidden Transcripts* (New Haven, CT: Yale University Press, 1990), 1–16.

50. Heilbut, "The Children and Their Secret Closet," in *The Fan Who Knew Too Much*, 3–91. Ethnomusicologist Alisha Lola Jones has undertaken groundbreaking work on the sexual politics of contemporary gospel music, focusing particularly on black masculinities. See, for example, "Are All the Choir

Directors Gay?: Black Men's Sexuality and Identity in Gospel Performance,"
in *Issues in African American Music: Power, Gender, Race, Representation*, edited by Portia Maultsby and Mellonee Burnim (New York: Routledge, 2017),
216–36.

51. Barney Hoskyns, "The Gospel According to Anthony," *Independent* (London),
June 25, 1996.

52. Jean-François Lyotard, *The Postmodern Condition: A Report on Knowledge*,
translated by Geoff Bennington and Brian Massumi (Minneapolis: University of
Minnesota Press, 1984).

53. Leonard Feather, "A Talk with Mahalia Jackson," *American Folk Music Occasional*
1 (1964): 48; Paul Silverstein and Jane Goodman, "Introduction: Bourdieu
in Algeria," in *Bourdieu in Algeria: Colonial Politics, Ethnographic Practices,
Theoretical Developments*, edited by Jane Goodman and Paul Silverstein (Lincoln
and London: University of Nebraska Press, 2009), 1.

54. Pierre Bourdieu, *The Field of Cultural Production* (New York: Columbia University
Press, 1993); Pierre Bourdieu and Loïc Wacquant, *An Invitation to Reflexive
Sociology* (Chicago: University of Chicago Press, 1992); David Schwartz, *Culture
and Power: The Sociology of Pierre Bourdieu* (Chicago and London: University of
Chicago Press, 1997), 121. Also influential on my thinking about field analysis
have been Priscilla Ferguson, "A Cultural Field in the Making: Gastronomy
in 19th-Century France," *American Journal of Sociology* 104 (1998): 597–641;
Michael Denning, *Culture in the Age of Three Worlds* (London: Verso, 2004); and
Sherry Ortner, *Anthropology and Social Theory: Culture Power, and the Acting
Subject* (Durham, NC: Duke University Press, 2006).

55. Bourdieu and Wacquant, *An Invitation to Reflexive Sociology*, 98–100.

56. Heilbut, *The Gospel Sound*, 80, 168, 196, 198.

57. Heilbut, *The Gospel Sound*, 135.

58. Marovich, *A City Called Heaven*, 150–51.

59. Otis Clay interview with the author, Chicago, June 4, 2009; Garnett Mimms interview with the author, September 18, 2009; Howard Tate interview with the
author, October 14, 2009; Therman Ruth Jr., interview with the author, July 15,
2009. On music pedagogy among earlier black gospel quartets, see Abbott and
Seroff, *To Do This, You Must Know How*.

60. Marovich, *A City Called Heaven*, 150; Stephen Hawkins interview with Robert
Marovich, *Gospel Memories*, June 7, 2014 (WLUW, Chicago), transcribed by the
author.

61. Marovich, *A City Called Heaven*, 189. On Sallie Martin, see Heilbut, *The Gospel
Sound*, 3–19; and DjeDje, "Gospel Music in the Los Angeles Black Community."

62. Harris, *The Rise of Gospel Blues*, 241–71; Marovich, *A City Called Heaven*, 112–31.

63. Mahalia Jackson at the "Definitions in Jazz" roundtable, Music Inn, Lenox,
Massachusetts, August 31, 1951, IJS, transcribed by the author.

64. "Mahalia Jackson to Head 1952 Gospel Concert Tour," *Norfolk New Journal and Guide* (February 23, 1952); "New Names . . . New Faces!" *Pittsburgh Courier* (April 5, 1952).

65. Von Eschen, *Satchmo Blows Up the World*, 5.

CHAPTER 2

1. "In Memoriam: Joseph Merrick Jones, 1903–1963," *Tulane Law Review* 37 (1963): 353–54.

2. The following discussion of the Merrick family draws on Emily Merrick King, "Merrick," in *A History of Pointe Coupée Parish and Its Families*, edited by Judy Riffel (Baton Rouge: Le Comité des Archives de la Louisiane, 1983), 263–64; J. I. Sanford, *Beautiful Pointe Coupée and Her Prominent Citizens* (New Orleans: American Printing Co., 1906); and U.S. Census data.

3. 1860 Slave Schedule for the State of Louisiana.

4. Caroline E. Merrick, *Old Times in Dixie Land: A Southern Matron's Memories* (New York: Grafton Press, 1901), 52.

5. Buddy Guy with David Ritz, *When I Left Home* (New York: Da Capo, 2012), 4.

6. Rosa Williams interview with Laurraine Goreau, April 26, 1972, transcript in LGC.

7. Goreau, *Just Mahalia Baby*, 7.

8. Thomas King interview with Laurraine Goreau, May 10, 1972, transcript in LGC; 1880, 1900, and 1910 censuses of the United States.

9. Rayford Logan, *The Negro in American Life and Thought: The Nadir, 1877–1901* (New York: Dial Press, 1954).

10. Mahalia Jackson interview with Studs Terkel on *Studs Terkel Almanac*, WFMT Chicago, September 14, 1954, WRC, Mss. 530, 1.48, transcribed by the author.

11. Dates of birth for the Clark children in parentheses are approximate, based on U.S. Census data gathered in Pointe Coupée between 1880 and 1910, though they are likely within a few years of accuracy. Porterfield, Cleveland, and Harrison do not appear in the census but were identified through Goreau's interviews with family members. Sarah and Ollie are listed in census data as daughters of Paul and Celia Clark, but are not mentioned by Goreau.

12. Allen Clark interview with Laurraine Goreau, February 6, 1973, transcript in LGC.

13. H. Llewellyn Smith and George Askwith, *Cost of Living in American Towns: Report of an Enquiry by the Board of Trade into Working Class Rents, Housing and Retail Prices, Together with the Rates of Wages in Certain Occupations in the Principal Industrial Towns on the United States of America* (London: His Majesty's Stationery Office, 1911), 288.

14. New Orleans Office of Policy Planning, Black Pearl Neighborhood Profile (December 1978), 3.01.

15. Email communication with Richard Campanella, July 26, 2016; Mahalia Jackson interview with Jules Schwerin, January 8, 1952, NSC, transcription by the author.

16. Allen Clark interview with Laurraine Goreau, February 6, 1973, transcript in LGC; Bessie Kimble interview with Laurraine Goreau, April 17, 1972, transcript in LGC; Alice Stamps Lawson interview with Laurraine Goreau, November 2, 1972, transcript in LGC; Marguerite Rightor Ellis interview with Laurraine Goreau, May 9, 1972, transcript in LGC; Thomas Ellis interview with Laurraine Goreau, May 10, 1972, transcript in LGC.

17. 1920 Census of the United States.

18. Mahalia Jackson interview with Jules Schwerin, January 8, 1952, NSC, transcription by the author; Jackson and Wylie, *Movin' On Up*, 11–12; Richard Campanella, *Geographies of New Orleans: Urban Fabrics before the Storm* (Lafayette, LA: Center for Louisiana Studies, 2006), 305.

19. Allen Clark interview with Laurraine Goreau, February 6, 1973, transcript in LGC; Cecile Taylor interview with Laurraine Goreau, April 15, 1972, transcript in LGC; Rosa Williams interview with Laurraine Goreau, April 26, 1972, transcript in LGC.

20. On early twentieth-century dock work in New Orleans, see Eric Arnesen, *Waterfront Workers of New Orleans: Race, Class, and Politics, 1863–1923* (Urbana and Chicago: University of Illinois Press, 1991).

21. Alice Stamps Lawson interview with Lorraine Goreau, April 9, 1973, transcript in LGC.

22. Brian Costello and Randy Decuir, *The Flood of 1912: 100th Anniversary Centennial Album of the Mississippi Valley Flood* (n.p.: CreateSpace, 2012).

23. Bessie Kimble interview with Lorraine Goreau, April 12, 1972, transcript in LGC.

24. Alice Lawson interview with Laurraine Goreau, April 9, 1973, transcript in LGC.

25. Darden, *People Get Ready*, 210.

26. Marovich, *A City Called Heaven*, 77.

27. Anthony Heilbut, liner notes to *Moving On Up a Little Higher* (Shanachie CD 6066) and personal communication with the author, April 11, 2015.

28. Goreau, *Just Mahalia, Baby*, 4–6; Hannah Robinson interview with Laurraine Goreau, April 5, 1973, transcript in LGC.

29. Sandy Polishuk, "Secrets, Lies, and Misremembering: The Perils of Oral History Interviewing," *Frontiers* 19/3 (1998): 14.

30. Marguerite Rightor Ellis interview with Laurraine Goreau, May 9, 1972, transcript in LGC; Richard Grady interview with Laurraine Goreau, May 11, 1972, transcript in LGC; Bessie Kimble interview with Lorraine Goreau, January 31, 1973, transcript in LGC. Blind Lemon Jefferson, "Rising High Water Blues" (Paramount 12487, 1927), Lonnie Johnson, "Broken Levee Blues" (Okeh, 8618, 1928), and Charley Patton, "High Water Everywhere (Paramount 12909, 1929). See also Richard Mizelle Jr., *Backwater Blues: The Mississippi Flood of 1927 in*

the African American Imagination (Minneapolis: University of Minnesota Press, 2014).

31. Mahalia Jackson interview with Jules Schwerin, January 8, 1952, NSC, transcribed by the author. An edited version of this oral history, interspersed with sung performances by Jackson, can be heard on the Schwerin-produced *I Sing Because I'm Happy*. The album originally appeared in 1979 in two volumes (Folkways 311010 and 31102) and has since been released on CD by Smithsonian Folkway Records (SFSP 90002). A recording of the complete interview is archived at the NSC. For another early twentieth-century account of black New Orleans, see Thomas Brothers, *Louis Armstrong's New Orleans* (New York: W. W. Norton, 2006).

32. Cecile Taylor interview with Laurraine Goreau, April 15, 1972, transcript in LGC.

33. Bessie Kimble interview with Laurraine Goreau, January 31, 1972, transcript in LGC.

34. "News from the Churches: Broadway Mission B.C.," *Louisiana Weekly* (October 30, 1926).

35. "News from the Churches: Plymouth Rock Baptist Church," *Louisiana Weekly* (September 14, 1925).

36. Marguerite Rightor Ellis interview with Laurraine Goreau, May 9, 1972, transcript in LGC; Henry Rightor interview with Laurraine Goreau, May 9, 1972, transcript in LGC; Thomas Ellis interview with Laurraine Goreau, May 10, 1972, transcript in LGC.

37. Allen Clark interview with Laurraine Goreau, February 6, 1973, transcript in LGC. For Goreau's account of Charity Clark's burial in Pointe Coupée, see *Just Mahalia, Baby*, 14–15.

38. Allen Clark interview with Laurraine Goreau, February 6, 1973, transcript in LGC; Richard Grady interview with Laurraine Goreau, May 11, 1972, transcript in LGC; Annise Jackson Scully interview with Laurraine Goreau, May 5, 1972, and February 10, 1973, transcript in LGC; Corrinne Looper and Rose Monica Levi interview with Laurraine Goreau, May 5, 1972, transcript in LGC; Marguerite Rightor Ellis interview with Laurraine Goreau, May 9, 1972, transcript in LGC.

39. Bessie Kimble interview with Laurraine Goreau, May 19, 1972, transcript in LGC.

40. Bessie Kimble interview with Laurraine Goreau, January 31, 1973, transcript in LGC.

41. Annise Jackson Scully interview with Laurraine Goreau, May 5, 1972, and February 10, 1973, transcript in LGC; "News from the Churches: Plymouth Rock Baptist Church," *Louisiana Weekly* (June 4, 1927); Mahalia Jackson Oral History, WRC, Mss. 530, 1.26, transcription by the author; Cecile Taylor interview with Laurraine Goreau, April 18, 1972, transcript in LGC; Bessie Kimble interview with Laurraine Goreau, May 9, 1972, transcript in LGC; Marian Pearl

Hunter Robinson interview with Laurraine Goreau, February 5, 1973, transcript in LGC.

42. "News from the Churches: Plymouth Rock Baptist Church," *Louisiana Weekly* (June 30, 1927).

43. Mahalia Jackson interview with Jules Schwerin, January 8, 1952, NSC, transcription by the author.

44. Annise Jackson Scully interview with Laurraine Goreau, May 5, 1972, and February 10, 1973, transcript in LGC; Isabella Duskin Lazard interview with Laurraine Goreau, April 22, 1972, transcript in LGC.

45. Mahalia Jackson interview with Jules Schwerin, January 8, 1952, NSC, transcription by the author.

46. Cecile Taylor interview with Laurraine Goreau, April 18, 1972, transcript in LGC; Annise Jackson Scully interview with Laurraine Goreau, May 5, 1972 and February 10, 1973, transcript in LGC; Edward Burnette interview with Laurraine Goreau, June 7, 1972, transcript in LGC; Richard Grady interview with Laurraine Goreau, May 11, 1972, transcript in LGC.

47. Mahalia Jackson interview with Jules Schwerin, January 8, 1952, NSC, transcription by the author.

48. O. C. W. Taylor, "The Public School Your Child Attends," *Louisiana Weekly* (March 5, 1927); O. C. W. Taylor interview with Laurraine Goreau, April 2, 1972, transcript in LGC.

49. "Bon Jour," *New Orleans Herald* (September 19, 1925).

50. On this remapping of the "Harlem Renaissance," see especially the essays in the collection edited by Davarian Baldwin and Minkah Makalani, *Escape from New York: The New Negro Renaissance beyond Harlem* (Minneapolis: University of Minnesota Press, 2013). On the productive juxtaposition in black political thought of integration and black separatism often associated with the NAACP and the UNIA, respectively, see Steven Hahn, *Political Worlds of Slavery and Freedom* (Cambridge, MA: Harvard University Press, 2009), 115–62.

51. Annise Jackson Scully interviews with Laurraine Goreau, May 5, 1972 and February 10, 1973, transcript in LGC.

52. Tom Castine interview with Laurraine Goreau, May 11, 1972, transcript in LGC Bessie Kimble interview with Laurraine Goreau, May 9, 1972, transcript in LGC; Allen Clark interview with Laurraine Goreau, February 6, 1973, transcript in LGC.

53. Bessie Kimble interviews with Laurraine Goreau, January 31, 1973, transcript in LGC; Alice Stamps Lawson interview with Laurraine Goreau, February 7, 1972, LGC, transcript in LGC; Annise Jackson Scully interview with Laurraine Goreau, May 5, 1972 and February 10, 1973; Cecile Taylor interview with Laurraine Goreau, April 15, 1972, transcript in LGC; Allen Clark interview with Laurraine Goreau, February 6, 1973, transcript in LGC.

54. Marguerite Rightor Ellis interview with Laurraine Goreau, May 9, 1972, transcript in LGC.

55. Bessie Kimble interviews with Laurraine Goreau, June 7, 1972 and January 31, 1973, transcripts in LGC.

56. For writers citing 1927, following Goreau, see Heilbut, *The Gospel Sound*, 59–60; Schwerin, *Got to Tell It*, 36; Boyer, *The Golden Age of Gospel*, 85; Darden, *People Get Ready*, 211; Marovich, *A City Called Heaven*, 79; Lordi, *Black Resonances*, 73. Jackson's claim of 1928 in *Movin' On Up* (41), is echoed in Carpenter, *Uncloudy Days*, 207, and Green, *Selling the Race*, 62.

57. Isabella Duskin Lazard interview with Laurraine Goreau, April 22, 1972, transcript in LGC.

58. Goreau, *Just Mahalia, Baby*, 99.

59. Ethel Adams interview with Laurraine Goreau, February 5, 1973, transcript in LGC.

60. Marian Pearl Hunter Robinson interview with Laurraine Goreau, February 5, 1973, transcript in LGC.

61. Alice Stamps Lawson interview with Laurraine Goreau, April 9, 1973, LGC, transcribed by the author.

62. Jerry Brock has also noted the discrepancy between 1930 census data and published accounts of Jackson's departure from New Orleans. See "Hallelujah, Mahalia," *Louisiana Cultural Vistas* (Summer 2012): 10–19, which includes valuable original research on Jackson's New Orleans years.

63. Jackson and Wylie, *Movin' On Up*, 12–16.

CHAPTER 3

1. Gospel scholars remain grateful for the rich body of material gathered by Laurraine Goreau and for the further context provided by more recent studies for what we know about Mahalia Jackson's early years in Chicago. The following summary of Jackson's early years in Chicago draws on Goreau, *Just Mahalia, Baby*, 51–103 and transcripts of her numerous interviews, as well as Jackson and Wylie, *Movin' On Up*, 39–89; Schwerin, *Got to Tell It*, 36–62; Green, *Selling the Race*, 51–91; and Marovich, *A City Called Heaven*.

2. Marovich, *A City Called Heaven*, 79–80; Thomas Dorsey quoted in Harris, *The Rise of Gospel Blues*, 258; Robert Anderson interview with Laurraine Goreau, November 4, 1972, transcript in LGC; Ernestine Washington interview with Laurraine Goreau, April 9, 1973, transcript in LGC; Sallie Martin interview with Laurraine Goreau, November 4, 1972, transcript in LGC. On Jackson's reputation as a "sexy" singer, see also Heilbut, *The Gospel Sound*, 62.

3. Goreau, *Just Mahalia, Baby*, 54.

4. For views on this convention, see Austin Curtis in *Untold Tales, Unsung Heroes: An Oral History of Detroit's African American Community, 1918–1967*, ed. Elaine Moon (Detroit: Wayne State University Press, 1994), 253–54; Andrew Manis, *Southern Civil Religions in Conflict: Civil Rights and the Culture*

Wars (Macon, GA: Mercer University Press, 2002), 28; William Dargan, *Lining Out the Word: Dr. Watts Hymn Singing in the Music of Black Americans* (Berkeley: University of California Press, 2006), 279, n. 13; Randall Jimerson, *Shattered Glass in Birmingham: My Family's Fight for Civil Rights, 1961–1964* (Baton Rouge: Louisiana State University Press, 2014), 171.

5. Allen Clark Sr., interview with Laurraine Goreau, February 6, 1973, transcript in LGC; Cecile Taylor interview with Laurraine Goreau, April 19, 1972, transcript in LGC; Elliott Beal interview with Laurraine Goreau, September 14, 1966, transcript in LGC.

6. Goreau, *Just Mahalia, Baby*, 58, 61.

7. "Insurance Groups Banquet New Head of Unity Mutual," *Chicago Defender* (May 1, 1937); "Marriage Licenses," *St. Louis Star-Times* (December 9, 1941).

8. Sallie Martin interview with Laurraine Goreau, November 4, 1972, transcript in LGC. For a discussion of Jackson's ethos of entrepreneurship, see Green, *Selling the Race*, 62–66.

9. On the early history of the National Baptist Convention, see Joseph H. Jackson, *A Story of Christian Activism: The History of the National Baptist Convention, U.S.A., Inc.* (Nashville: Townsend Press, 1980); Luvenia George, "Lucie E. Campbell: Baptist Composer and Educator," *Black Perspective in Music* 15 (1987): 23–49; Thomas Kidd and Barry Hankins, *Baptists in America: A History* (New York: Oxford University Press, 2015), 149–65.

10. William Rosborough, J. H. Carter, and J. W. Tobias, *National Anthem Series, Prepared Especially for Church Choirs and Young People's Meetings* (Nashville: National Baptist Publishing Board, 1906). On uplift ideology, see Kevin Gaines, *Uplifting the Race: Black Leadership, Politics, and Culture in the Twentieth Century* (Chapel Hill and London: University of North Carolina Press, 1996).

11. Mark Hyman, "Convention Hall Seethes with Baptist Activity," *Philadelphia Tribune* (September 9, 1950).

12. Williams-Jones, "Roberta Martin: Spirit of An Era," in Reagon, *We'll Understand It Better By and By*, 259; Becky Garrison, "National Baptist Convention," in *Encyclopedia of American Gospel Music*, edited by W. K. McNeil (New York: Taylor & Francis, 2005), 270; Kenneth Morris, "I'll Be a Servant for the Lord" (interview conducted and edited by Bernice Johnson Reagon), in *We'll Understand It Better By and By*, 332.

13. James Lee interview with Laurraine Goreau, November 11, 1972, transcript in LGC.

14. Mahalia Jackson at the "Definitions in Jazz" roundtable, Music Inn, Lenox, Massachusetts, August 27, 1951, recording at IJS, transcribed by the author.

15. George, "Lucie E. Campbell," 34; Boyer, *The Golden Age of Gospel*, 138–40; J. Robert Bradley interview with Laurraine Goreau, September 9, 1973, LGC, transcribed by the author.

16. Goreau, *Just Mahalia, Baby*, 95.

17. *Proceedings of the Sixtieth Annual Session of the National Baptist Convention, U.S.A., Inc.*, September 4–9, 1940, Birmingham Alabama.

18. Porter Phillips, "Prominent Pastor Deplores 'Whooping Singers,'" *Pittsburgh Courier* (September 28, 1940).

19. For accounts of the impact of South-to-North migration and ensuing class conflicts over black church music in Chicago during the 1930s and 1940s, see Harris, *The Rise of Gospel Blues*; Best, *Passionately Human, No Less Divine*, 94–117; Davarian Baldwin, *Chicago's New Negroes: Modernity, the Great Migration, and Black Urban Life* (Chapel Hill: University of North Carolina Press, 2007), 155–92; Marovich, *A City Called Heaven*, 11–57.

20. Gwynn Kuhner Brown, "The Serious Spirituals of William L. Dawson," paper delivered at the National Conference of the American Musicological Society, Rochester, New York, November 11, 2017.

21. "Says Choir Directors Apathetic," *Norfolk Journal and Guide* (August 12, 1944); Wilson King, "Says Pastor and Church Organist Pay Startlingly Out of Proportion," *Norfolk Journal and Guide* (September 8, 1945); Wilson King, "Jazzing of Church Music Not Always Sacrilegious," *Norfolk Journal and Guide* (September 3, 1949); "Wilson King Resigns Post at Church," *Norfolk Journal and Guide* (October 14, 1950).

22. Orrin Suthern II, "Too Much Jazz; Too Little Pay, Politics, Says Organist," *Baltimore Afro-American* (February 24, 1940); Orrin Suthern II, "Noted Negro Organist Writes on Church Music," *Pittsburgh Courier* (November 9, 1940); Edwin Harleston, "Too Much Jazz in Modern Church Music, Says Ex-John Wesley Organist," *Baltimore Afro-American* (February 21, 1942).

23. On Dorsey, see also Heilbut, *The Gospel Sound*, 21–35; Boyer, "Take My Hand, Precious Lord, Lead Me On," in *We'll Understand It Better By and By*, 141–63; Kathryn Kemp, *Anointed to Sing the Gospel: The Levitical Legacy of Thomas A. Dorsey* (Chicago: Joyful Noise Press, 2015); and George Nierenberg's documentary *Say Amen, Somebody* (GTN Pictures, 1982). Boyer offers the most thorough analysis of Dorsey's style as a gospel song composer.

24. Boyer, "Take My Hand Precious Lord," 143; Goreau, *Just Mahalia, Baby*, 62.

25. On Sallie Martin, see Heilbut, *The Gospel Sound*, 319; Marovich, *A City Called Heaven*, passim; Sallie Martin interview with Laurraine Goreau, November 4, 1972, transcript in LGC; Kay Norton, "'Yes, [Gospel] Is Real': Half a Century with Chicago's Martin and Morris Company."

26. Harris, *The Rise of Gospel Blues*, 191–96.

27. Tragically, Pilgrim Baptist Church was destroyed by a fire in 2006 that also consumed Dorsey's invaluable personal papers housed there. In December 2017, representatives of the Stellar Gospel Music Awards announced plans to build a National Museum of Gospel Music at Pilgrim's former location, to

be opened in 2020. See Steve Johnson, "National Museum of Gospel Music Planned for Bronzeville Site," *Chicago Tribune* (December 7, 2017).

28. Harris, *The Rise of Gospel Blues*, 299; Marovich, *A City Called Heaven*, 85. There is woefully little information on the ubiquitous Frye and Butts, though for some brief background, see Marovich, *A City Called Heaven*, 83–86.

29. Rev. Esther Greer quoted in Harris, *The Rise of Gospel Blues*, 187.

30. Abbott and Seroff, *To Do This, You Must Know How*, 252.

31. "To Be Hosts to Gospel Singers," *Chicago Defender* (August 19, 1933); "Gospel Choruses Plan Gala Songfest Aug. 29," *Chicago Defender* (August 19, 1933); "Gospel Singers Close National Meeting," *Chicago Defender* (September 9, 1933); "Gospel Choirs Prepare for National Confab," *Chicago Defender* (January 27, 1934).

32. Mahalia Jackson interview with Studs Terkel, *Studs Terkel's Almanac* (WFMT-Chicago) (September 14, 1954); Goreau, *Just Mahalia, Baby*, 56.

33. Goreau, *Just Mahalia, Baby*, 58.

34. Loreta Garrett interview with the author, July 14, 2016; "Dorsey Leads Gospel Chorus to Convention," *Chicago Defender* (August 24, 1935). See also Harris, *The Rise of Gospel Blues*, 268–69.

35. "Gospel Singers Will Hold Annual Meet in Chicago," *Atlanta Daily World* (July 20, 1940); "Chicago Gospel Choruses Honor Founders in Lavish Anniversary Celebration," *Chicago Defender* (July 6, 1935).

36. Harris, *The Rise of Gospel Blues*, 187, 208.

37. "Gospel Singers Close National Meeting"; "Gospel Singers Close Second Annual Meet," *Chicago Defender* (August 11, 1934); "Gospel Singers in Mid-Winter Meet," *Chicago Defender* (March 2, 1935); "Gospel Choirs in Detroit to National Meet," *Chicago Defender* (August 22, 1936); "3,000 at Gospel Chorus Annual Convention," *Atlanta Daily World* (September 5, 1936); "Gospel Choruses Hold Nat'l Convention in Indianapolis," *Chicago Defender* (Aug 21, 1937); Arnold Taschereau, "Capacity Audiences Attending National Singing Convention," *Atlanta Daily World* (March 20, 1942); "Gospel Singers Will Hold Annual Meet in Chicago"; "Accredited Gospel Singer," *Pittsburgh Courier* (August 30, 1941); "National Choral Body Convenes in Charleston," *Chicago Defender* (April 13, 1946); "Gospel Singers Board to Meet at Louisville," *Pittsburgh Courier* (March 22, 1947). See also Marovich, *A City Called Heaven*, 115.

38. On the NANM, see Willis Patterson, *A History of the National Association of Negro Musicians: The First Quarter Century, 1919–1943* (PhD diss., Wayne State University, 1993); Doris McGinty, *A Documentary History of the National Association of Negro Musicians* (Chicago: Center for Black Music Research, 2004); Lawrence Schenbeck, *Racial Uplift and American Music, 1878–1943* (Jackson: University Press of Mississippi, 2014), 195–201.

39. "Gospel Singers Close National Meeting"; "Gospel Singers in Mid-Winter Meet"; Grace Tompkins, "Music News," *Chicago Defender* (February 17, 1940).

40. "Says 'Swinging Spiritual' Is Disgrace to Race," *Pittsburgh Courier* (March 11, 1939); Rev. George W. Harvey, "Let's Fight to Keep Our Spirituals Sacred," *Pittsburgh Courier* (March 18, 1939); Thomas Dorsey, Letter to the George Harvey, *Pittsburgh Courier* (April 1, 1939).

41. W. E. B. Du Bois, *The Souls of Black Folk* (Chicago: McClurg, 1903); James Weldon Johnson, ed., *The Book of American Negro Spirituals* (New York: Viking Press, 1925); Alain Locke, ed., *The New Negro: An Interpretation* (New York: Boni, 1925).

42. "Gospel Singers Ready for Confab," *Chicago Defender* (July 21, 1934); "Gospel Music Leaders Hold Board Meet," *Chicago Defender* (February 29, 1936); "Gospel Singers Close National Meeting"; "Chicago Gospel Choruses Honor Founders in Lavish Anniversary Celebration."

43. "Chicago Gospel Choruses Honor Founders in Lavish Anniversary Celebration"; "Gospel Choruses Hold Nat'l Convention in Indianapolis," *Chicago Defender* (August 21, 1937); "Canadian Unit, Mich. Singers Close Confab," *Chicago Defender* (January 21, 1939); "National Gospel Singers Close Annual Meeting," *Pittsburgh Courier* (August 29, 1942); "National Gospel Singers Close Meet in Cleveland," *Pittsburgh Courier* (August 28, 1943).

44. "Singers Plan Tribute to Prof. Dorsey," *Chicago Defender* (May 29, 1943); Photo caption, *Chicago Defender* (September 23, 1939); Sallie Martin interview with Laurraine Goreau, November 4, 1972, transcript in LGC; Dorothy Love Cates quoted in Heilbut, *The Gospel Sound*, 63–64; John Sellers interview with Laurraine Goreau, December 22, 1972, transcript in LGC; Hattie Brown, "Brooklyn Social Notes," *New York Age* (March 22, 1941).

45. Bill Russell journal, June 13, 1955, WRC, Mss. 513, fol. 472; "Chicago Gospel Singers Visit Philly," *Chicago Defender* (September 23, 1939); "National Baptist Convention, Inc. Holds 66th Convention in Atlanta," *Pittsburgh Courier* (September 7, 1946); "Program Arranged for Baptist Annual Convention," *Norfolk New Journal and Guide* (September 4, 1948); Mahalia Jackson interview with Studs Terkel, *Studs Terkel's Almanac* (WFMT-Chicago), September 14, 1954. WRC, Mss. 530, 1.48, transcribed by the author.

46. Goreau, *Just Mahalia, Baby*, 116. Goreau's account is the source for Marovich's restatement of the claim in his recent and exhaustively researched history of black gospel music in Chicago. See *A City Called Heaven*, 182.

47. J. Robert Bradley interview with Laurraine Goreau, September 9, 1973, LGC, transcribed by the author.

48. Mildred Falls interview with Laurraine Goreau, November 9, 1972, LGC, transcribed by the author.

49. Photo with caption, *Atlanta Daily World* (December 6, 1946).

50. Albert Barnett, "Expect 15,000 Baptists for Chicago Conclave," *Chicago Defender* (June 22, 1946).

51. Theodore Frye, Georgiana Rose, and Mahalia Jackson, "First Annual Report of the National Baptist Music Convention," *Proceedings of the Sixty-eighth Annual Session of the National Baptist Convention, U.S.A., Inc.*, September 8–12, 1948, Houston, Texas; "The Defender News Reel," *Chicago Defender* (May 1, 1948); "2,000 Jam Shiloh Baptist for Local Meet of Church Musicians," *Chicago Defender* (February 24, 1951).

52. Mildred Falls interview with Laurraine Goreau, November 9, 1972, transcript in LGC; "Board of Directors of Nat'l Baptist Music Convention to Meet in Memphis June 23," *Atlanta Daily World* (June 18, 1949); "Lay Plans for National Baptist Convention in Philadelphia," *Chicago Defender* (August 12, 1950).

53. Kenneth Morris, *Improving the Music in the Church*.

54. "Top Gospel Singer Attends Bapt. Meet," *Baltimore Afro-American* (June 11, 1949); *Proceedings of the Sixty-ninth Annual Session of the National Baptist Convention, U.S.A., Inc.*, September 7–11, 1949, Los Angeles; "Musical Bosses," *Pittsburgh Courier* (September 17, 1949); "Baptists Cram Music, Banquets Into Crowded Convention Agenda," *Chicago Defender* (September 20, 1952).

55. *Proceedings of the Seventy-second Annual Session of the National Baptist Convention, U.S.A., Inc.*, September 10–14, 1952, Chicago, Illinois.

56. "Gospel Queen Began Life in Humble Home: Now Top Paid," *New York Amsterdam News* (October 11, 1952).

57. Ferguson, "A Cultural Field in the Making," 599.

58. Norton, "Yes, [Gospel] Is Real," 423.

CHAPTER 4

1. Mahalia Jackson at the "Definitions in Jazz" roundtable at the Music Inn, Lenox, Massachusetts, August 31, 1951, recording at IJS, transcribed by the author.

2. Bill Russell journal, August 2, 1954, WRC, Mss. 513, folder 459.

3. Mahalia Jackson interview with Studs Terkel, *Studs Terkel's Almanac* (WFMT-Chicago), September 14, 1954. WRC, Mss. 530, 1.48, transcribed by the author.

4. John Sellers interview with Laurraine Goreau, December 22, 1972, transcript in LGC.

5. Allen, *Singing in the Spirit*, x–xiv, 76–96, 238. For other oral-historical and ethnographic documentation of gospel programs, see Burt Feintuch, "A Non-Commercial Black Gospel Group in Context: We Live the Life We Sing About," *Black Music Research Journal* 1 (1980): 37–50; Daniel Patterson, "'Going Up to Meet Him': Songs and Ceremonies of a Black Family's Ascent," in *Diversity of Gifts: Field Studies in Southern Religion*, edited by Ruel Tyson Jr., James Peacock, and Daniel Patterson (Urbana: University of Illinois Press, 1988), 91–102; Lornell, "Happy in the Service of the Lord," 49–66; Glenn Hinson, *Fire in My Bones: Transcendence*

and the Holy Spirit in African American Gospel (Philadelphia: University of Pennsylvania Press, 2000); Young, *The Pilgrim Jubilees*. Lornell traces the development of gospel quartet performances from the 1930s to the mid-1950s, tracking the encroachment of professionalization and commercialization.

6. Robert Anderson interview with Laurraine Goreau, November 4, 1972, transcript in LGC.

7. "Honored," *Chicago Defender* (October 6, 1945); Abbott and Seroff, *To Do This, You Must Know How*, 234–71; Marovich, *A City Called Heaven*, 160–64.

8. Quoted in Horace Clarence Boyer, "Roberta Martin: Innovator of Modern Gospel Music," in *We'll Understand It Better By and By*, 276.

9. Williams-Jones, "Roberta Martin: Spirit of An Era," 255–74; Boyer, "Roberta Martin: Innovator of Modern Gospel Music," 275–86; Boyer, *The Golden Age of Gospel Music*, 66–79.

10. A flyer for the program is reprinted in Marovich, *A City Called Heaven*. Marovich has determined that the flyer mistakenly lists the year of the program as 1945.

11. Brother Sellers, "Move On Up a Little Higher" b/w "Just Wait a Little While" (Miracle 107, 1946).

12. John Sellers interview with Laurraine Goreau, December 22, 1972, transcript in LGC.

13. John Sellers interview with Laurraine Goreau, January 13, 1973, transcript in LGC.

14. John Sellers interview with Laurraine Goreau, December 22, 1972, transcript in LGC.

15. For a sampling of this copious body of literature, see Dafni Tragaki, ed., *Empire of Song: Europe and Nation in the Eurovision Song Contest* (Lanham, MD: Scarecrow Press, 2013); Katherine Walker, "Cut, Carved, and Served: Competitive Jamming in the 1930s and 1940s," *Jazz Perspectives* 4 (2010): 183–208; Christopher Wells, *"Go Harlem!": Chick Webb and His Dancing Audience during the Great Depression* (PhD diss., University of North Carolina at Chapel Hill, 2014), 220–58; Marcyliena Morgan, "After . . . Word!: The Philosophy of Hip-Hop Battle," in *Hip Hop and Philosophy: Rhyme 2 Reason*, edited by Derrick Darby and Tommie Shelby (Chicago: Open Court, 2005), 205–12; Mark Katz, *Groove Music: The Art and Culture of the Hip-Hop DJ* (New York: Oxford University Press, 2012), 153–78; Chris Goertzen, "Balancing Local and National Approaches at American Fiddle Contests," *American Music* 13 (1996): 352–81; Sharon Graf, *Traditionalization at the National Oldtime Fiddler's Contest: Politics, Power, and Authenticity* (PhD diss., Michigan State University, 1999); Lisa McCormick, *Performing Civility: International Competitions in Classical Music* (Cambridge: Cambridge University Press, 2015); Kiril Tomoff, *Virtuosi Abroad: Soviet Music and Imperial Competition during the Early Cold War, 1945–1958* (Ithaca: Cornell University Press, 2015); Brenda Fauls, "Some Thoughts about International Choral Competitions," *Choral Journal* 48 (March 2008): 18–39; William Braun, "You

Came Here to Win, Didn't You?" *Opera News* 76 (December 2011): 22–23; Shannon Dudley, *Music From Behind the Bridge: Steelband Spirit and Politics in Trinidad and Tobago* (New York: Oxford University Press, 2007).

16. Doug Seroff, "Old-Time Black Gospel Quartet Contests," *Black Music Research Journal* 10 (1990): 27–28. Emphasis in the original.

17. James Weldon Johnson, Introduction to *The Book of American Negro Spirituals*, 35–36; James Weldon Johnson, "The Origin of the Barbershop Chord," *Mentor*, February 29, 1929; Lynn Abbott, "Play that Barbershop Chord," 29; Doug Seroff and Lynn Abbott, "The Origins of Ragtime," *78 Quarterly* 1/10 (*c.* 1999): 130–31. I will discuss "voice culture" in more detail in Chapter 7.

18. Allen, *Singing in the Spirit*, 79; "Quartet Contest Attracts Close to 500 Spectators," *Norfolk Journal and Guide*, February 27, 1943. For a historical overview of African American sacred quartets see Lornell, *Happy in the Service of the Lord*, 1–41.

19. "Gospel Quartettes Hold Contest," *Pittsburgh Courier* (April 1, 1939).

20. See the 1910 "singing contest between Olivet Baptist Church and St. Mark's M. E. Church" in Chicago cited in Abbott and Seroff, *To Do This, You Must Know How*, 223; Photograph with caption in *Chicago Defender* (March 15, 1930); Maude Roberts George, "News of the Music World," *Chicago Defender* (April 26, 1930).

21. See, for example, the recollections of Thermon Ruth in Allen, *Singing in the Spirit*, 79, and Ira Tucker in Zolten, *Great God A'mighty! The Dixie Hummingbirds*, 64–65.

22. "Live Wire Quartet Offers Six Programs," *Cleveland Call and Post* (April 17, 1943); "Hapeville News," *Atlanta Daily World* (February 26, 1950); I. P. Reynolds, "What Sam of Auburn Says," *Atlanta Daily World* (September 8, 1943); "Royal Singers to Appear at Church of Christ," *Pittsburgh Courier* (September 21, 1946); "House of Prayer Will Stage Musical Program August 20," *Norfolk Journal and Guide* (July 31, 1948); "Mt. Pleasant Baptist Church," *Cleveland Call and Post* (January 16, 1943); Photo with caption, *Chicago Defender* (December 13, 1947).

23. "Gospel Singers in Unique Contest," *Pittsburgh Courier* (December 10, 1938); Jacqueline DjeDje, "Gospel Music in the Los Angeles Black Community," 47; Gwendolyn Lightner interview with Laurraine Goreau, September 19, 1972, transcript in LGC; Heilbut, *The Gospel Sound*, 3–19; "Song Battle Scheduled By Gospel Singers," *Los Angeles Sentinel* (August 12, 1948); "Song Battle at Tabernacle Sun.," *Cleveland Call and Post* (November 1, 1947).

24. "Methodists to Hold Revival Meetings," *Cleveland Call and Post* (March 12, 1936); Wallace Best, *Passionately Human, No Less Divine: Religion and Culture in Black Chicago, 1915–1952* (Princeton: Princeton University Press, 2005), 112–17, 178–80; Seroff, "On the Battlefield: Gospel Quartets in Jefferson County, Alabama"; Abbott and Seroff, *To Do This, You Must Know How*, 113–216; Kimberley Phillips, *AlabamaNorth: African-American Migrants, Community, and Working-Class Activism in Cleveland, 1915–45* (Urbana and Chicago: University of Illinois Press, 1999), 161–80.

25. "Tune In First Unity Church of God, WHK Every 2nd & 4th Sun.," *Cleveland Call and Post* (June 23, 1945); Advertisement in *Cleveland Call and Post* (July 28, 1945); "Great Song Battle," *Cleveland Call and Post* (May 24, 1947); "Great Song Battle at First Unity Church," *Cleveland Call and Post* (May 31, 1947); "Greatest Song Battle of All Times!!" *Cleveland Call and Post* (July 5, 1947); "Song Battle," *Cleveland Call and Post* (July 17, 1948). For an introduction to some of the principal gospel groups in Cleveland, see Burton, *Cleveland's Gospel Music.*

26. "Old Favorite Group in Contest," *Cleveland Call and Post* (March 21, 1942); "Five Soul Stirrers Here for Contest," *Cleveland Call and Post* (March 21, 1942); Untitled photo and caption, *Cleveland Call and Post* (December 5, 1942); Zolten, *Great God A'mighty! The Dixie Hummingbirds,* 138; "Present Dixie Humming Birds," *Cleveland Call and Post* (June 22, 1946); "Live Wire Quartet to Celebrate Its 13th Anniversary; Starts Sept. 21," *Cleveland Call and Post* (September 19, 1942); "Song Battle! Live Wire Singers vs. the Dixie Humming Birds Sunday, Feb. 24th at Friendship," *Cleveland Call and Post* (February 23, 1946); Untitled photo with caption, *Cleveland Call and Post* (November 20, 1948).

27. "To Feature Five Male Quartettes in Pla-Mor Song Battle Jan. 14," *Cleveland Call and Post* (January 6, 1945); Christopher Lornell, "Thermon Ruth and the Selah Jubilee Singers: An Interview," *Journal of Black Sacred Music* 2 (1988): 47; "20 Quartets to Take Part in Greensboro Contest July 18," *Norfolk Journal and Guide* (July 19, 1943); Seroff, "Old-Time Black Gospel Quartet Contests," 27; Untitled photo with caption, *Pittsburgh Courier* (June 3, 1950); "Silvertones to Appear on a $1,000 Program," *Pittsburgh Courier* (June 17, 1950).

28. "Clergy Compete in Song Fest at Zion Baptist Church," *Norfolk Journal and Guide* (May 11, 1946).

29. "Philco Amateurs," *Variety* (January 22, 1936); 48 " 'Applause Meter' Used by Tech Boys," *Boston Globe* (February 1936); Trend Is to Novelties—Favor Programs for Audiences," *Variety* (August 26, 1936): 47, 64; Robert Heinl, "Radio Dial Flash," *Washington Post* (June 11, 1932); "Hoover Rings Bell on Applause Meter," *Washington Post* (June 11, 1936); "Willkie Outruns Roosevelt on Fair Applause Meter," *Chicago Tribune* (July 20, 1940); "Applause-Meter at S.F. Expo OK's Wealth Draft," *Variety* (August 21, 1940): 63; "Musicians to Vie on 'Talent Night,'" *Atlanta Constitution* (May 20, 1938); "Bowes Mantle to Godfrey in New Air Talent Hour," *Billboard* (June 29, 1946): 5; George Berkowitz, "Network Program News and Analyses," *Billboard* (August 9, 1947); "They're 'Taking It Off' Again at the Gayety," *Washington Post* (August 17, 1947); "Mahalia and Jersey Joe in Benefit for Boys Club," *Chicago Defender* (August 14, 1954).

30. Marovich, *A City Called Heaven,* 155.

31. "Quartet Contest," *Pittsburgh Courier* (July 15, 1939); Blanche Van Hook, "Columbus Society: 3,000 Hear Concert," *Cleveland Call and Post* (May 9, 1942); "Swans Slate Junior Writers, Famous Harmonizing Four," *Pittsburgh Courier*

(December 16, 1950); Advertisement in the *New York Amsterdam News* (October 21, 1944); Advertisement in *New York Amsterdam News* (November 8, 1947).

32. Lornell, "Thermon Ruth and the Selah Jubilee Singers," 46–47; "Calvery Baptist Church" [*sic*], *Cleveland Call and Post* (April 10, 1943); "Quartets Sing in Big Event," *Pittsburgh Courier* (July 29, 1944); Zolten, *Great God A'mighty! The Dixie Hummingbirds*, 99–100.

33. "Stars Galore to Entertain Kiddies—20-Ring Circus on Picnic Bill," *Chicago Defender* (July 9, 1949); "To Pick Best Gospel Group," *Chicago Defender* (July 23, 1949).

34. Boyer, *The Golden Age of Gospel*, 87, 242–43; Carpenter, "Gay Sisters," in *Uncloudy Days*, 150–53; Marovich, *A City Called Heaven*, 164–66; Evelyn Gay interview with Laurraine Goreau, July 28, 1973, transcript in LGC; Fannie Gay interview with Laurraine Goreau, August 5, 1973, transcript in LGC; "Director," *Chicago Defender* (August 18, 1945).

35. John Sellers interview with Laurraine Goreau, January 13, 1973, transcript in LGC.

36. On Tindley, see the essays by Bernice Johnson Reagon and by Horace Boyer in *We'll Understand It Better By and By*.

37. On Tharpe's 1947 recording of "Beams of Heaven," see Wald, *Shout, Sister, Shout!*, 86–87.

38. My thanks to Bob Marovich for sharing a copy of this very rare Jackson recording with me, which has since been released on the 2016 compilation *Moving On Up a Little Higher* (Shanachie CD 6066).

39. John Sellers interview with Laurraine Goreau, December 28, 1972, transcript in LGC; Ernestine Washington and the Southern Sons, "I Thank You Lord" b/w "The Lord Will Make a Way" (Manor 1084, 1947).

40. John Sellers interview with Laurraine Goreau, December 28, 1972, transcript in LGC; Boyer, *The Golden Age of Gospel*, 161–63; Ernestine Washington interview with Laurraine Goreau, April 9, 1973, transcript in LGC; "Ex-Boy Pastor Is Temple Head," *New York Amsterdam News* (June 14, 1958); Elizabeth Kolbert, "The People's Preacher," *New Yorker* (February 18, 2002): 156–67.

41. Boyer, *The Golden Age of Gospel*, 161–63; Bill Russell journal, January 1946, WRC, Mss. 513, fol. 436; "Blues for Bessie Due at Town Hall," *New York Amsterdam News* (December 27, 1947); E. B. Rea, "Encores and Echoes," *Baltimore Afro-American* (November 1, 1947); Photo with caption in *Norfolk Journal and Guide* (October 23, 1948); "Meet Sister Washington," *Baltimore Afro-American* (October 30, 1948); Sister Ernestine B. Washington with the Bunk Johnson Jazz Band, "Does Jesus Care" b/w "Where Could I Go But to the Lord" (Disc, 6038, 1947) and "The Lord Will Make a Way Somehow" b/w God's Amazing Grace" (Disc 6039, 1947); Ernestine Washington, *Gospel Singing in Washington Temple* (Westminster WAST 15032, 1958). Episodes of *TV Gospel Time* are archived at SCRBC.

42. B. Dexter Allgood, "Black Gospel in New York City and Joe William Bostic, Sr.," *Black Perspective in Music* 18 (1990): 105; Hilary Moore, "New York,

Gospel in," in *Encyclopedia of American Gospel Music*, edited by W. K. McNeil (New York: Routledge, 2005), 274–76.

43. "John Myers, Mahalia's Pilot, Dies," *New York Amsterdam News* (December 3, 1966).

44. John Sellers interview with Laurraine Goreau, December 28, 1972, transcript in LGC.

45. "Classiest Ballroom Due Soon," *New York Amsterdam News* (October 21, 1939); "Harlem's New Ballroom," *Variety* (October 25, 1939); "Harlem's New Golden Gate Promises Stiff Competish for Savoy," *Billboard* (October 29, 1939); "Golden Gate Has Record Crowds," *New York Amsterdam News* (November 25, 1939); Leonard Feather, "New York News," *Down Beat* (March 15, 1940), 2, 20; "Savoy Corp. Buys Out Golden Gate Ballroom," *New York Amsterdam News* (April 6, 1940).

46. "Negro Playwrights Company in Debut," *New York Amsterdam News* (July 20, 1940); "Hail Willkie in Harlem Talk," *New York Amsterdam News* (October 12, 1940); "Michaux Sets Huge Meeting," *New York Amsterdam News* (November 2, 1940); "Says F.D.R. Is Divine Gift—Evangelist and Choir Appear Here at Golden Gate Ballroom Rally," *New York Amsterdam News* (November 9, 1940); "Famous People's Singer to Appear in Harlem," *New York Amsterdam News* (March 29, 1941); "Huge Victory Fete Planned," *New York Amsterdam News* (November 29, 1941); "Thomas W. Lamb, 71; A Noted Architect," *New York Times* (February 27, 1942); "First Lady Praises Mrs. Bethune," *New York Times* (May 3, 1943); Scott DeVeaux, *The Birth of Bebop: A Social and Musical History* (Berkeley and Los Angeles: University of California Press, 1997), 138–40; Warren Weaver Jr., "Albany Bill Seeks 'Subversives' Curb," *New York Times* (January 16, 1952); "Jack Asks Subversive Law for NY," *New York Amsterdam News* (January 26, 1952).

47. "Johnny Myers Presents" advertisements in the *New York Amsterdam News* on July 31, 1943, July 15, 1944, September 16, 1944, October 19, 1946, November 9, 1946, and June 28, 1947; "National Quartet Convention Coming to Borough," September 2, 1944; "100 Quartets Expected at Brooklyn Songfest," *Baltimore Afro-American* (September 2, 1944).

48. Photo with caption, *Chicago Defender* (March 22, 1947); "Atlanta's Own Sons, the Reliable Jubilee Singers, In 'Home-Coming' Here Tonite," *Atlanta Daily World* (April 17, 1947); Ken Romanowski, Liner notes for Two Gospel Keys and Sister O. M. Terrell, *Country Gospel: The Post War Years (1946–1953)* (Document DOCD-5221, 1993); John Sellers interviews with Laurraine Goreau, December 28, 1972 and July 14, 1973, transcripts in LGC.

49. Biographical information on the Thrasher Wonders, MFAC; "Other Music: 'Jubilee Program Given," *New York Times* (May 22, 1941); "Coffee Concert Offers Jubilee," *New York Amsterdam News* (May 24, 1941); "We're the Thrasher Wonders," *New York Amsterdam News* (May 31, 1941); Ruth Miller, "Mapping Brooklyn," *Chicago Defender* (June 3, 1944); "Spotlighter Stages

Revue," *New York Amsterdam News* (July 14, 1945); Abbott, *I Got Two Wings*, 54–53; Frederic Ramsey Jr., Liner notes for the Thrasher Wonders and Two Gospel Keys, *Spirituals* (Disc 658, 1946).

50. Unless otherwise indicated, the following information on Georgia Peach comes from "Interview with Georgia Peach" (1960), Mura Dehn Papers on Afro-American Social Dance NYPLPA-D, box 4, fol. 102; and from 1910 and 1930 U.S. census data.

51. Boyer, *The Golden Age of Gospel*, 159–61. On Johnson, see Dargan, *Lining Out the Word*, 169–72.

52. " 'Rev. Snowball' to Preach Tonight," *Atlanta Constitution* (August 23, 1931); L. D. Reddick, "Educational Programs for the Improvement of Race Relations: Motion Pictures, Radio, the Press, and Libraries," *Journal of Negro Education* 13 (1944): 383.

53. Sister Clara Hudmon, "Now Is the Needy Time" b/w "My Loved Ones Are Waiting for Me" (Okeh 8851, 1930) and "Stand By Me" b/w "I Want to See Jesus" (Okeh 8882, 1930); Snowball and Sunshine, "Leave It There" (Columbia 152021, 1931); Clara Belle Gholston, the Georgia Peach and Her Gospel Singers, "When the Saints Go Marching In" b/w "Who's That Knocking" (Banner 32654, 1932); Rev. J. M. Gates, "There's Something About the Lord Mighty Sweet" (Bluebird B5660, 1934); "Jesus Knows How Much We Can Bear" b/w "Do Lord, Send Me" (Decca 8648, 1942).

54. On Mann, see Nora Holt, "Music: " 'POP' Opera Spices Summer Music," *New York Amsterdam News* (June 21, 1947) and "Music: A Backlog of Reviews Re: Concerts, Student Recitals, Chorus, Dance," *New York Amsterdam News* (June 30, 1951).

55. "Atlanta to Honor Mrs. Clara G. Brock," *Atlanta Daily World* (July 2, 1953); "Bury 'Georgia Peach,' 1,500 Attend Funeral," *New York Amsterdam News* (January 16, 1965).

56. "Elder Broadie Scores Success," *New York Amsterdam News* (October 4, 1941); Val Adams, "Something New in Radio: The One-Day Week," *New York Times* (November 6, 1949); "Johnny Myers Presents" advertisements in the *New York Amsterdam News* on August 13, 1944, March 28, 1948, and April 24, 1948; Rev. Frederick D. Washington, "The Wildest Creature (That Ever Lived)" (Manor 1091, 1947); Elder Benjamin H. Broadie, World Wonder Preacher and the Famous Ivory Gospel Singers, "Come on Back Home, Baby, Papa Ain't Mad at You" (Coleman 5859, *c*. 1948).

57. "Johnny Myers Presents" advertisements in the *New York Amsterdam News* on November 11, 1944, December 23, 1944, October 19, 1946, January 11, 1947, December 13, 1947, January 11, 1948, March 27, 1948, and December 25, 1948.

58. "CRC, U. S. Record Plans," *Billboard* (September 2, 1939): 9; "Bart Forms Disking Org," *Billboard* (May 19, 1945): 21; "Lenetska and Bart, Both Ex-Gale, Form Office; Guide Spots," *Billboard* (May 26, 1945): 18; "Asch Sells Signature Disks,"

Billboard (July 1, 1944): 19; "Thiele Inks Eng. Firm to Record Ban-Skirt Wax," *Billboard* (July 17, 1948): 18; "Signature Buys Haven Masters," *Billboard* (August 21, 1948): 16; "Signature to Release New Red-Black Label," *Billboard* (August 21, 1948): 16; "Another Disc Film Readying Catalog," *Billboard* (December 5, 1942): 25; "Another Disk Mfr.; Spirituals Only," *Billboard* (February 20, 1943): 21; "Regis Label Starts Releasing Platters," *Billboard* (March 27, 1943): 25; "Manor Record Execs Set Up Talent Agency in N.Y.," *Variety* (March 5, 1947): 46; "Arco Signs Artists, Buys Disc Platters, Sets Release Dates," *Billboard* (November 5, 1949): 44; "Haven Signs New Wax Luminaries," *Pittsburgh Courier* (September 14, 1946); "Diskeries to Set Up Org," *Billboard* (March 8, 1947): 15, 24; Tony Olmstead, *Folkways Records, Moses Asch and His Encyclopedia of Sound* (New York and London: Routledge, 2003); Arnold Shaw, *Honkers and Shouters*, 129–40; John Broven, *Record Makers and Breakers: Voices of the Independent Rock 'n' Roll Pioneers* (Urbana and Chicago: University of Illinois Press, 2009), 53–72; Barbara Kukla, *Swing City: Newark Nightlife, 1925–50* (New Brunswick, NJ: Rutgers University Press, 1991), 147–52.

59. Letter from Sally Jones and Emma Daniel (per Fred Jones) to Asch Record Company, March 14, 1946, MFAC.

60. "Johnny Myers Presents" advertisements in the *New York Amsterdam News* on August, 19, 1944, October 14, 1944, October 21, 1944, and December 23, 1944; "Music Events," *New York Amsterdam News* (November 4, 1944).

61. "Concert Planned for Boro Church," *New York Amsterdam News* (April 14, 1945); "Johnny Myers Presents" advertisements in the *New York Amsterdam News* on April 14, 1945; " 'Spirituals at Midnight' to Headline Famed Singers," *New York Amsterdam News* (March 15, 1947); Robbie Lieberman, *"My Song Is My Weapon": People's Songs, American Communism, and the Politics of Culture, 1930–50* (Champaign: University of Illinois Press, 1995); Photo with caption, *New York Amsterdam News* (March 22, 1947); "Atlanta's Own Sons, the Reliable Jubilee Singers, In 'Home-Coming' Here Tonite," *Atlanta Daily World* (April 17, 1947).

62. Bernice Bass, "Louisiana Cinderella Still Empress of Chicago Gospel," Mahalia Jackson 25th Anniversary Program, October 19, 1951, Mahalia Jackson Scrapbook, page 427, LGC.

63. "Famed Gospel Singer Draws Record Crowd," *Norfolk Journal and Guide* (January 22, 1949).

64. Luis John, "Mahalia Jackson Concert Crowded," *Philadelphia Tribune* (May 20, 1950); "Taps Files AFM Pleas vs. Myers," *Billboard* (May 6, 1950): 18. The flyer for the 1950 concert is reproduced in Boyer, *The Golden Age of Gospel*, 8.

65. Goreau, *Just Mahalia, Baby*, 129.

66. Joe Bostic quoted in Met Tapley, " 'Gospel Train' Conductor Bostic on Express Track," *New York Amsterdam News* (January 15, 1983), 23.

67. "Negro Gospel Fete Held," *New York Times* (October 2, 1950); "Concert and Recital: Music Festival," *New York Herald Tribune* (October 2, 1950); "Mahalia Jackson Gospel Song Diva," *Amsterdam News* (October 7, 1950); "8,000 Witness First Negro Gospel Concert at Carnegie Hall," *Chicago Defender* (October 14, 1950).

CHAPTER 5

1. On this stylistic transition in gospel quartet performance, see Heilbut, *The Gospel Sound*, 42–53; Lornell, *Happy in the Service of the Lord*, 1–41; Marovich, *A City Called Heaven*, 120–22.

2. Robert Miller interview with Laurraine Goreau, November 11, 1970, transcript in LGC; Goreau, *Just Mahalia, Baby*, 58–59.

3. Moon, "Mahalia Jackson: A Great Gospel Singer," 16.

4. Cedric Hayes and Bob Laughton, *The Gospel Discography, 1943–1970* (West Vancouver, British Columbia, Canada: Eyeball Productions, 2007).

5. Marovich, *A City Called Heaven*, 230.

6. Russell Sanjek and David Sanjek, *American Popular Music Business in the 20th Century* (New York: Oxford University Press, 1991), 58–78.

7. Mahalia Jackson at the "Definitions in Jazz" roundtable at the Music Inn, Lenox, Massachusetts, August 31, 1951, recording in IJS, transcribed by the author.

8. Broven, *Record Makers and Breakers*, 53–55; Goreau, *Just Mahalia, Baby*, 109; Arnold Shaw, *Honkers and Shouters*, 133, 138; Heilbut, *The Gospel Sound*, 64; Kempton, *Boogaloo*, 49; Christopher Lornell, "Thermon Ruth and the Selah Jubilee Singers," 48.

9. Unless otherwise indicated, the following discussion of Bess Berman's family history is based on data gathered from U.S. and New York State censuses from 1900 to 1940.

10. "Economy Opens Baltimore Branch," *Billboard* (October 3, 1942): 61; "Economy Supply to Open Branch Office for Baltimore Ops," *Billboard* (February 16, 1946): 113.

11. DeVeaux, *The Birth of Bebop*, 308.

12. Marovich, *A City Called Heaven*, 179.

13. John Sellers interview with Laurraine Goreau, December 28, 1972, transcript in LGC.

14. "Apollo Exits: Prexy Siegal and Schneider," *Billboard* (May 29, 1948): 20; "Apollo Names Mrs. Berman to Head Firm," *Billboard* (June 5, 1948): 17; Ron Merenstein interview with the author, May 12, 2015; "Forms Pop Lable [*sic*]," *Cash Box* (June 5, 1954): 24.

15. Mahalia Jackson interview with S. I. Hayakawa on *Hayakawa's Jazz Seminar* (WFMT), March 12, 1954, transcribed by the author.

16. See also Marovich, *A City Called Heaven*, 179–85.

17. Ward-Royster and Rose, *How I Got Over*, 77.

18. James Francis interview with Laurraine Goreau, April 11, 1973, transcript in LGC; John Sellers interview with Laurraine Goreau, January 13, 1973, transcript in LGC; Robert Anderson Interview with Laurraine Goreau, November 4, 1972, transcript in LGC.

19. Goreau, *Just Mahalia, Baby*, 117–18.

20. Robert Anderson interview with Laurraine Goreau, November 4, 1972, transcript in LGC.

21. Nat Hentoff, "You Can Still Hear Her Voice When the Music Has Stopped," *Reporter* (June 27, 1957), 34.

22. George F. Brown, "King, Apollo Denounce Wax Race Tags," *Pittsburgh Courier* (May 14, 1949).

23. David Albert Francis, *Panama's Story: My History as a Jazz Drummer* (n.p.: Xlibris, 2013), 26.

24. John Sellers interview with Laurraine Goreau, January 13, 1973, transcript in LGC.

25. "People Are Talking About," *Jet* (June 18, 1953): 48.

26. Jackson and Wylie, *Movin' On Up*, 87–88.

27. Mahalia Jackson at the "Definitions in Jazz" roundtable, Music Inn, Lenox, Massachusetts, August 30, 1951, recording at IJS, transcribed by the author.

28. Dr. William Barclay interview with Laurraine Goreau, July 31, 1973, transcript in LGC.

29. J. Robert Bradley interview with Laurraine Goreau, September 9, 1973, LGC, transcribed by the author.

30. Personal communication with Lewis Merenstein, April 15, 2015.

31. "Mahalia Jackson Feted by Apollo Records," Apollo Records press release, January 13, 1950, DRMC, *Amsterdam News* Photograph Archive, Series B, Box B-4, folder 21; "25 Years in Gospel," *Philadelphia Tribune* (July 5, 1952).

32. Morris, "I'll Be a Servant for the Lord" (interview conducted by Bernice Johnson Reagon) in *We'll Understand It Better By and By*, 333, 336–37; Marovich, *A City Called Heaven*, 169. Sheet music publishing remains an understudied but enormously significant topic in black gospel scholarship. For a notable recent contribution, see Norton, "Yes [Gospel Music] Is Real: Half a Century with Chicago's Martin and Morris Company."

33. "Court Halts Steal of Dorsey's Hymns," *Chicago Defender* (November 8, 1947); Dorsey, "Ministry of Music in the Church," in Morris, *Improving the Music in the Church*, 43.

34. "War Brewing on Peace Tune," *Billboard* (July 14, 1951): 15.

35. "Forms Pop Lable" [*sic*].

36. "Hill & Range Claiming 'Consideration' Infringe," *Variety* (November 11, 1953): 15; "Hill & Range Sues, on 'Consideration,'" *Billboard* (November

14, 1953): 22; "Writer Wins Credit for Mahalia Jackson Song," *Jet* (August 5, 1954): 60.

37. "H&R in Infringe Suit vs. Apollo," *Variety* (May 14, 1955): 47; "H&R 18-count Suit Versus Apollo, Lloyd," *Billboard* (May 7, 1955): 24, 30.

38. James Lee interview with Laurraine Goreau, November 10, 1972, transcript in LGC; John Sellers interview with Laurraine Goreau, 1973 (Tape 7B), transcript in LGC; Schwerin, *Got to Tell It*, 66–68; Jackson and Wylie, *Movin' On Up*, 86. Wylie also mistakenly claims the record was cut for Decca.

39. John Sellers interview with Laurraine Goreau, December 12, 1972, transcript in LGC.

40. Benjamin Aaron, "Amending the Taft-Hartley Act: A Decade of Frustration," in *The Taft Hartley Act after Ten Years: A Symposium*, a special issue of *Industrial and Labor Relations Review* 11/3 (April 1958): 327–38; Freeman Champney, "Taft-Hartley and the Printers," *Antioch Review* 8/1 (1948): 49–62; James Gross, *Broken Promises: The Subversion of U.S. Labor Relations Policy, 1947–1994* (Philadelphia: Temple University Press, 1995), 1–14; Troy Rondinone, *The Great Industrial War: Framing Class Conflict in the Media, 1865–1950* (New Brunswick, NJ: Rutgers University Press, 2011), 151–65; *Labor Management Relations Act of 1947*, §9(h).

41. "Record Ban Edict Issued in Chicago," *Broadcasting* (October 27, 1947), 16; "Featherbedding and Taft-Hartley," *Columbia Law Review* 52/8 (December 1952): 1020–21; Joe Carlton, "Petrillo Nix On Recordings Held Certain," *Billboard* (October 18, 1947): 17; "Indie Diskeries Mulling South of Border Trek to Beat Petrillo Ban," *Variety* (October 29, 1947): 51.

42. Scott DeVeaux, "Bebop and the Recording Industry: The 1942 AFM Recording Ban Reconsidered," *Journal of the American Musicological Society* 41 (1988): 126–65. On the AFM recording bans, see also Tim Anderson, "'Buried Under the Fecundity of His Own Creations': Reconsidering the Recording Bans of the American Federation of Musicians, 1942–44 and 1948," *American Music* (2004); 231–69; Tim Anderson, *Making Easy Listening: Material Culture and Postwar American Recording* (Minneapolis: University of Minnesota Press, 2006), 1–47; and Marina Peterson, "Sound Work: Music as Labor and the 1940s Recording Bans of the American Federation of Musicians," *Anthropological Quarterly* 86 (2013): 791–824.

43. Hayes and Laughton, *The Gospel Discography, 1943–1970*.

44. "Rhythm Kings Wax Noel Tune," *Baltimore Afro-American* (November 25, 1950); Mahalia Jackson interview with Laurraine Goreau, June 22, 1967, transcript in LGC.

45. "Stafford-MacRae P.D., Catching On, Has Eight Versions Being Pushed," *Variety* (September 7, 1949): 1; "Como's 'Ave Maria,' 'Lord's Prayer' Give Push to RCA's 45," *Variety* (November 16, 1949): 53.

46. "Decca to Launch Religioso Series," *Variety* (March 1, 1950): 39; "Decca Puts Andrews Sisters, Bing on Religious Wax Series," *Billboard* (March 4, 1950);

"Crosby Cuts 16 Hymns, 8 Pop & Xmas Platters," *Billboard* (May 14, 1949): 21; "Col. in Religious Field with Shore-Autry Disks," *Variety* (April 26, 1950): 52; "Col Shore-Autry Gospel Package," *Billboard* (April 29, 1950): 16; "Col. Records to Expand Religioso Catalog," *Variety* (June 7, 1950): 41.

47. "RCA Releases 15 Disks with Religious Air," *Billboard* (May 6, 1950): 18.

48. "Capitol to Push 'Church' Waxing," *Billboard* (April 1, 1950): 13.

49. Reinhold Niebuhr, "Is There a Revival of Religion?" *New York Times* (November 19, 1950); "Nation Is Warned Against Atheism," *New York Times* (September 19, 1954); Billy Graham, "Satan's Religion," *American Mercury* (August 1954): 42; Thomas Aiello, "Constructing 'Godless Communism': Religion, Politics, and Popular Culture, 1954–1960," *Americana* (Spring 2005): http://www.americanpopularculture.com/journal/articles/spring_2005/aiello.htm (accessed May 10, 2018); Stephen Bates, "'Godless Communism' and Its Legacies," *Society* 41/3 (March/April 2004): 29–33. The McCarthy quote is from the "Wheeling Speech" that thrust the senator and his anticommunist crusade onto the national stage. See Joseph McCarthy, "'Enemies from Within' (February 9, 1950)," in *Infamous Speeches: From Robespierre to Osama bin Laden*, edited by Bob Blaisdell (New York: Dover, 2011), 139–46.

50. Lisle Rose, *The Cold War Comes to Main Street: America in the 1950s* (Lawrence: University Press of Kansas, 1999); Robert Ellwood, *1950: Crossroads of American Religious Life* (Louisville: Westminster John Knox Press, 2000).

51. "Accent Is on Religioso Records as New Pops Get the Brushoff," *Variety* (June 28, 1950): 43; "Robbins Stressing 'Lady' for Religioso Standard," *Variety* (August 23, 1950): 42; "Religious Music Gets Buildup as Sales Soar," *Variety* (October 18, 1950): 22; "Tin Pan Alley Develops Religious Song Trend to Fullscale Scramble," *Variety* (November 22, 1950): 41; "Hamblen Finding Out Religiosos Pay Off," *Variety* (December 13, 1950): 54; "Willson's Semi-Religioso Gets Fabulous Pop Plugs," *Billboard* (December 15, 1950): 14; "Pop-Flavored Religioso Tunes Flood Publishers," *Variety* (June 27, 1951): 45.

52. "Music Notes: Matthew's First Harlem Recital Captivates Audience," *New York Amsterdam News* (December 12, 1936).

53. "Bibletone Sets Disk Deal to Test Choir Works," *Variety* (December 6, 1950): 48.

54. "Religioso Songs Again Clicking on Sheets, Disks," *Variety* (July 29, 1953): 1.

55. John Wm. Riley, "Popular Records: Hymns by Crooner and Hillbilly Singers," *Boston Globe* (October 8, 1950).

CHAPTER 6

1. Max Jones, "Magnificent Mahalia—The Greatest Gospel Voice," *Melody Maker* (June 2, 1951), 9; "New Company Formed to Issue Jazz-Disques Here," *Melody Maker* (April 7, 1951), 6.

2. "Mahalia Jackson Wins Top French Honors for Record," *Baltimore Afro-American* (May 5, 1951); Art Rosett, "Paris Peek," *Billboard* (March 31, 1951): 46.

3. For two studies of Jackson as a singer, see Katherine White, *Analysis of the Singing Style of Gospel Singer Mahalia Jackson*, M.A. thesis, Washington University, 1982; and Horace Clarence Boyer, "The Vocal Style of Mahalia Jackson, Gospel Singer," *Rejoice* 2/3 (Spring 1990): 3–9.

4. Ingrid Monson, *Saying Something: Jazz Improvisation and Interaction* (Chicago: University of Chicago Press, 1996), 26–72; Albert Murray, *Stomping the Blues* (New York: Da Capo Press, 1976), 93–128.

5. "Mildred Falls, Pianist for Mahalia Jackson, Artistic 'Proof' of Claim," *Chicago Defender* (October 30, 1954); Mildred Falls Interview with Laurraine Goreau, November 9, 1972, transcript in LGC.

6. The following discussion of Ruth is drawn from Lornell, "Thermon Ruth and the Selah Jubilee Singers"; Allen, *Singing in the Spirit*, 30–37; Marv Goldberg, "The Larks," http://www.uncamarvy.com/Larks/larks.html (accessed May 10, 2018); and Therman Ruth Jr. interview with the author, July 15, 2009.

7. Lornell, "Thermon Ruth and the Selah Jubilee Singers," 42, 45.

8. "Forms Pop Lable [*sic*]"; The Larks, "My Reverie" (Apollo 1184, 1951) and "If It's a Crime (Lloyds 110, 1954).

9. "Mahalia Jackson Heads Tour Featuring Gospel, Spiritual Singers," *Chicago Defender* (February 23, 1952).

10. Eileen Southern, "Hymnals of the Black Church," in *Readings in African American Church Music and Worship*, edited by James Abbington (Chicago: GIA Publications, 2001), 146–47.

11. *Gospel Pearls* (Nashville: Sunday School Publishing Board, Black Baptist Convention, U.S.A., 1921); *The Baptist Standard Hymnal* (Nashville: Sunday School Publishing Board, Black Baptist Convention, U.S.A., 1924).

12. Boyer, *The Golden Age of Gospel*, 41–44.

13. Goreau, *Just Mahalia, Baby*, 56, 78–79. On *Gospel Pearls*, see also Harris, *The Rise of Gospel Blues*, 68–69, 75. On Parker, see Abbott and Seroff, *To Do This, You Must Know How*, 255–56; Marovich, *A City Called Heaven*, 50–57.

14. For a recent study on the topic, see Idella Johnson, *Development of African American Gospel Piano Style*.

15. The best and most easily accessible source for Jackson's Apollo recordings is *Complete Mahalia Jackson* (Intégrale Mahalia Jackson), vols. 1–4, from the series of compact discs released by Frémeaux & Associés.

16. Hentoff, "You Can Still Hear Her Voice When the Music Has Stopped"; Larry Wolters, "Television News and Views," *Chicago Tribune* (August 6, 1953); Izzy Rowe, "Izzy Rowe's Notebook," *Pittsburgh Courier* (September 25, 1954); "More Ounce to Her Bounce," *People Today* (December 1, 1954).

17. Mahalia Jackson interview with Studs Terkel on *Studs Terkel Almanac*, WFMT Chicago, September 14, 1954, WRC, Mss. 530, 1.48, transcribed by the author.

18. *The Mahalia Jackson Show*, WBBM, episode 7, recorded October 22, 1954, aired November 7, 1954, WRC, Mss. 530, 1.32, transcribed by the author.

19. Burford, "Mahalia Jackson Meets the Wise Men," 470–73.

20. Harris, *The Rise of Gospel Blues*, 197–98, 204–5.

21. Boyer, "Take My Hand, Precious Lord, Lead Me On," in *We'll Understand It Better By and By*, 149, 156, 158.

22. Jackson and Wylie, *Movin' On Up*, 89.

23. Matthew Butterfield, "Why Do Jazz Musicians Swing Their Eighth Notes?" *Music Theory Spectrum* 33 (2011): 3–4.

24. Ralph Ellison, "As the Spirit Moves Mahalia," *Saturday Review* (September 27, 1958): 43.

25. James Lee interview with Laurraine Goreau, November 10, 1972, transcript in LGC.

26. Christopher Washburne, "The Clave of Jazz: A Caribbean Contribution to the Rhythmic Foundation of an African-American Music," *Black Music Research Journal* 17 (1997): 59–80.

27. Boyer, *The Golden Age of Gospel Music*, 208–9; Carpenter, *Uncloudy Days*, 12; DjeDje, "Los Angeles Composers of African American Gospel Music," 433–34; Opal Louis Nations, "Doe and Dove: The Doris Akers Singers Story," self-published, 2005. For a reading of the scholarly implications of the black gospel-Southern gospel divide, see Shearon, "Establishing the Fundamentals of Gospel Music History."

28. William Tallmadge, "Dr. Watts and Mahalia Jackson—The Development, Decline, and Survival of a Folk Style in America," *Ethnomusicology* 5/2 (1961): 98; Heilbut, *The Gospel Sound*, 61; Boyer, *The Golden Age of Gospel*, 87.

29. Dargan, *Lining Out the Word*. On the singing of lined-out hymns by black congregations, see also Walter Pitts, *Old Ship of Zion: The Afro-Baptist Ritual in the African Diaspora* (New York: Oxford University Press, 1993); Ben Bailey, "The Lined Hymn Tradition in Black Mississippi Churches," *Black Perspective in Music* 6/1 (1978): 3–17; Carl Smith, *The Lined Hymn Tradition in Selected Black Churches of Eastern Kentucky* (PhD diss., University of Pittsburgh, 1987). Performances of lined-out hymnody are plentiful online. For examples of testimonies of memory as prefaces to Dr. Watts hymn singing, see Pastor T. L. James leading the singing of "I Love the Lord He Heard My Cry" (https://www.youtube.com/watch?v=6xP2D Ypy2DQ&list=PLUWj43Lsq4onDjBXqw4Uo277mY-I8kJ_F); Rev. Randy Brewer leading "Before This Time Another Year" (https://www.youtube.com/watch?v =rqHFfg8Loac&index=7&list=PLUWj43Lsq4onDjBXqw4Uo277mY-I8kJ_F); Pastor Jerome Jackson leading "Before This Time Another Year" (https://www. youtube.com/watch?v=FfsPiFesq34&list=PLUWj43Lsq4onDjBXqw4Uo277mY-I8kJ_F&index=8); and Rev. Lonnie Weaver leading "When I Can Read My Title Clear" https://www.youtube.com/watch?v=wVw_ncYU8wc&index=23&list= PLUWj43Lsq4onDjBXqw4Uo277mY-I8kJ_F).

30. Annise Jackson interview with Laurraine Goreau, May 5, 1972, transcript in LGC.

31. Bill Russell letter to George Avakian, November 17, 1954, JHP, box 15, fol. 257; Mahalia Jackson, "Father, I Stretch My Hand to Thee," "Before This Time Another Year," and "Dark Was the Night and Cold Was the Ground," WRC, Mss. 530, 1.19. Two of these Jackson home recordings, "Dark Was the Night and Cold Was the Ground" and "Before This Time Another Year," are included on the recent compilation *Moving Up a Little Higher* (Shanachie CD 6066).

32. Chosen Gospel Singers, "Before This Time Another Year" (Specialty SP 838, 1952). For comparison, see the notated variant of this lined-out hymn in the *African American Heritage Hymnal: 575 Hymns, Spirituals, and Gospel Songs* (Chicago: GIA Publications, 2011).

33. Marshall Stearns, *The Story of Jazz* (New York: Oxford University Press, 1956), 1–11.

34. "Mahalia Jackson Sets European Tour," *Billboard* (August 23, 1952): 21; "Jackson Religioso Disk Top Dane Foreign Seller," *Variety* (October 29, 1952): 11; Bob Rolontz, "Rhythm and Blues Notes," *Billboard* (December 6, 1952): 36; Unidentified television show, WRC, Mss. 530, 1.49, transcribed by the author.

35. In an extended discussion drawing on Dorsey's recollection of the 1921 convention, Michael Harris offers his reconstruction of Nix's performance of "I Do, Don't You." See *The Rise of Gospel Blues*, 68–77.

36. Dixie Hummingbirds, "Amazing Grace" (Apollo 108, 1946); Swan Silvertones, "Amazing Grace" (Vee Jay 909, 1962); Caravans, "Amazing Grace" on *Seek Ye the Lord* (Vee Jay LP 5026, 1962); Sister Rosetta Tharpe, "Amazing Grace" (Decca 14575, 1951); J. Robert Bradley, "Amazing Grace" on *When Gospel Was Gospel* (Shanachie 6064, 2005). The frequently reiterated Jackson quote about Bradley's rendering of "Amazing Grace" seems to have first appeared in print in John Pareles's obituary for Bradley in the *New York Times* ("J. Robert Bradley, 87, Charismatic Gospel Singer, Dies," May 4, 2007), passed on to Pareles via conversation with Heilbut. In my own email communication with Heilbut (May 28, 2015), Heilbut remembered becoming aware of the Jackson comment when "Bradley and the community quoted her." We have no reason to question or doubt the essential accuracy of the sentiment attributed to Jackson. But for the purposes of recognizing the bedeviling challenges of sourcing gospel knowledge, it is instructive to register the fact that what has circulated widely as a direct quotation attributed to Jackson is in fact a paraphrase of a third-hand anecdote. Put more bluntly, and at the risk of seeming pedantic, it is the salient difference between "Jackson said . . . " and "According to Heilbut, Bradley and others remembered that Jackson once said. . . ."

37. For another discussion of Jackson's performance of "Amazing Grace" and her relationship to the Dr. Watts tradition, see Tallmadge, "Dr. Watts and Mahalia Jackson," 95–99.

38. "The Gospel Singers," Mura Dehn Papers on Afro-American Social Dance, box 4, fol. 101, NYPLPA-D.

39. Recording of *Mahalia Jackson Sings*, WBBM-TV Chicago, episode broadcast on March 13, 1955, WRC, Mss. 530, 1.46, transcribed by the author.

CHAPTER 7

1. "Gospel with a Bounce," *Time* (October 4, 1954); Edward Kitch, "'Queen of Gospel Singers' Had No Musical Training," *St. Louis Globe-Democrat* (September 11, 1955); "Gospel With a Bounce," *Milwaukee Journal* (c. October 1954), clipping in WRC, Mss. 513, f. 199.

2. Mildred Falls interview with Laurraine Goreau, November 9, 1972, LGC, transcribed by the author; Goreau, *Just Mahalia, Baby*, 96; Robert Anderson interview with Laurraine Goreau, November 4, 1972, transcript in LGC.

3. John Kouwenhoven, *Made in America: The Arts in Modern Civilization* (New York: Doubleday, 1948), 15–95.

4. H. Wiley Hitchcock, *Music in the United States: A Historical Introduction*, 3rd edition (Englewood Cliffs, NJ: Prentice-Hall, 1988), 53–63. Hitchcock's textbook was first published in 1969 and his definitions of "cultivated" and "vernacular" remained virtually identical through three editions. For a classic account of the evolving relationship between "high culture" and the "popular" in the United States, extending to the nineteenth century and spanning a wide range of expressive forms, see Lawrence Levine, *Highbrow/Lowbrow: The Emergence of Cultural Hierarchy in America* (Cambridge: Harvard University Press, 1988).

5. Theodore Kalem, "Can America Claim Cultural Isolationism?" *Christian Science Monitor* (December 2, 1948); Charles Adams, "Some Aspects of Black Worship," *Andover Newton Journal* 63/3 (1971), reprinted in *Readings in African American Church Music and Worship*, ed. James Abbington (Chicago: GIA Publications, 2001), 299; Thomas Dorsey, "Ministry of Music in the Church," in Morris, *Improving the Music of the Church*, 42.

6. For a discussion of how ideological assumptions underlying the distinction of "natural" and "encultured" voices shape even how listeners hear "voice," see Nina Eidsheim, "Race and the Aesthetics of Vocal Timbre," in *Rethinking Difference in Music Scholarship*, edited by Olivia Bloechl, Melanie, Lowe, and Jeffrey Kallberg (Cambridge: Cambridge University Press, 2015), 338–65.

7. Jackson and Wylie, *Movin' On Up*, 32.

8. Mahalia Jackson interview with Jules Schwerin, January 8, 1952, NSC, transcribed by the author.

9. Mahalia Jackson radio interview with S. I. Hayakawa on *Hayakawa's Jazz Seminar*, WFMT Chicago, broadcast March 12, 1954, transcribed by the author; Bill Russell journal, September 25, 1954, WRC, Mss. 513, fol. 490; Clay Gowran, "Gospel Singing Queen Lonely, Sad as a Child," *Chicago Tribune* (August 7,

1955); Gowran, "Language No Bar as Mahalia Sings," *Chicago Tribune* (August 14, 1955); Mahalia Jackson interview with unknown Swedish interviewer, January 24, 1955, Chicago, WRC, Mss. 530, 1.25, transcribed by the author.

10. Mahalia Jackson interview with Jules Schwerin, January 8, 1952, NSC, transcribed by the author. For a recent study of the New Orleans brass band tradition and its communal meanings, see Matt Sakakeeny, *Roll with It: Brass Bands in the Streets of New Orleans* (Durham: Duke University Press, 2013).

11. Bucklin Moon, "Mahalia Jackson: A Great Gospel Singer," *The Record Changer* (April 1949), 15–16; Jackson and Wylie, *Movin' On Up*, 29–30.

12. Mahalia Jackson interview with Studs Terkel on *Studs Terkel Almanac*, WFMT Chicago, September 14, 1954, WRC, Mss. 530, 1.48, transcribed by the author.

13. Mahalia Jackson interview with Studs Terkel on *Studs Terkel Almanac*, September 14, 1954, WRC, Mss. 530, 1.48, transcribed by the author; Mahalia Jackson interview with Jules Schwerin, January 8, 1952, January 8, 1952, NSC, transcribed by the author. For another discussion of Jackson's musical life in New Orleans, see also Robert Marovich, "*Bon Temps* and Good News: The Influence of New Orleans on the Performance Style of Mahalia Jackson," *Association for Recorded Sound Collections Journal* 42 (2011): 50–62.

14. Mahalia Jackson interview with Studs Terkel on *Studs Terkel Almanac*, WFMT Chicago, December 21, 1955, WRC, Mss. 530, 1.47, transcribed by the author.

15. Mahalia Jackson interview with Jules Schwerin, January 8, 1952, NSC, transcribed by the author.

16. Isaac Sutton, "Mahalia Talks About Things," *Jet* (March 29, 1962): 58.

17. Moon, "Mahalia Jackson: A Great Gospel Singer," 15–16.

18. Bill Russell journal, July 6, 1955, WRJ, Mss. 513, fol. 472.

19. Richard Meryman, *Louis Armstrong: A Self-Portrait* (New York: Eakins, 1971), 24. On Armstrong's relationship to opera and its impact on his trumpet playing, see Joshua Berrett, "Louis Armstrong and Opera," *Musical Quarterly* 76 (1992): 416–41; and Peter Ecklund, "The Influence of Opera and the Light-Classical Tradition on the Improvisational Language of Louis Armstrong," Paper delivered at the Musical Intersections conference, Toronto, November 3, 2000.

20. Mura Dehn, "Interview with Georgia Peach," Mura Dehn Papers on African American Social Dance, NYPLPA-D, box 4, fol. 102.

21. Harris, *The Rise of Gospel Blues*, 106–16, 127. For another, more nuanced analysis of the historical processes linking black migration to the emergence of modern gospel, see Best, *Positively Human, No Less Divine*.

22. Scott Carter, "Forging a Sound Citizenry: Voice Culture and the Embodiment of the Nation, 1880–1920," *American Music Research Center Journal* 22 (2013): 11–34.

23. Juanita Karpf, "The Vocal Teacher of Ten Thousand: E. Azalia Hackley as Community Music Educator, 1910–1922," *Journal of Research in Music Education* 47 (1999): 319–30; Juanita Karpf, "For Their Musical Uplift: Emma Azalia Hackley and Voice Culture in African American Communities," *International*

Journal of Community Music 4 (2011): 237–56; Sarah Schnalenberger, "Shaping Uplift through Music," *Black Music Research Journal* 28 (2008): 57–83; Abbott and Seroff, *To Do This, You Must Know How*, 26–33. On another conjunction of European concert music and the African American spiritual, see Mark Burford, "Black and White, then 'Red' All Over: Chicago's American Negro Music Festival," *American Music Review* 44/2 (Spring 2015): 1–6.

24. Jackson and Wylie, *Movin' On Up*, 58.

25. Louise Hutchinson, "Mahalia Jackson—Big Voice, Big Body, and a BIG Spirit," *Chicago Tribune* (September 26, 1965).

26. Recording of Mahalia Jackson at the "Definitions in Jazz" Roundtable, Music Inn, Lenox, Massachusetts, August 30, 1951, IJS, transcribed by the author.

27. Mahalia Jackson interview with Jules Schwerin, January 8, 1952, NSC, transcribed by the author.

28. Sallie Martin interview with Laurraine Goreau, November 4, 1972, transcribed by the author; Mahalia Jackson interview with Laurraine Goreau, June 22, 1967, transcript in LGC.

29. Harris, *The Rise of Gospel Blues*, 259–61.

30. "National Musicians Group's Honor Night to Attract Country's Leading Figures," *Indianapolis Recorder*, July 18, 1953; Mahalia Jackson oral history, recorded by Bill Russell, probably September 1954, WRC, Mss. 530, 1.26, transcribed by the author; Robert Nolan, "Mahalia Jackson Penetrating, Warm," *Detroit Chronicle* (October 3, 1953); Bill Russell interview with Laurraine Goreau, January 30, 1974, transcript in LGC.

31. Max Jones, "Magnificent Mahalia—the Greatest Gospel Voice," *Melody Maker* (June 2, 1951), 9.

32. "Certo, Mahalia non è una cantante di jazz: è una *gospel singer*; canta, cioè, soltanto pezzi religiosi e soppratutto *spirituals*. Non si creda tuttavia che essa abbia dei punti in commune con la celebre Marian Anderson, che, per quanto negra, si è avvicinata alla tradizione del canto europeo. La Jackson, che è nata a New Orleans una quarantina di anni fa, è rimasta viceversa fedele alle tradizioni della sua razza; il suo canto ha conservato tutta la violenta espressività del folklore musicale negro, quella stessa espressività che caratteristica essenziale del canto blues." Review of "Since the Fire Starting Burning in My Soul" b/w "In My Home Over There," *Musica Jazz* 7/10 (October 1951): 16. Translation by the author. Emphasis in the original.

33. "Evangelist in Recital at Cleveland," *Chicago Defender* (December 17, 1938); Feather, "A Talk with Mahalia Jackson," 47; Izzy Rowe, "Izzy Rowe's Notebook: The Postman Always Rings Twice," *Pittsburgh Courier* (May 2, 1953); Ollie Stewart, "Report from Europe," *Baltimore Afro-American* (November 15, 1952).

34. Moon, "Mahalia Jackson: A Great Gospel Singer," 15–16.

35. Bill Russell journal, October 10, 1954, WRC, Mss. 513, fol. 440.

36. Jackson and Wylie, *Movin' On Up*, 58–59, 88.
37. Goreau, *Just Mahalia, Baby*, 60–61.
38. For two examples of recent scholarship on this topic, see Abbott and Seroff, *To Do This You Must Know How* and Laurence Schenbeck, *Racial Uplift and American Music*.
39. Mahalia Jackson interview with Studs Terkel on *Studs Terkel Almanac*, WFMT Chicago, September 14, 1954, WRC, Mss. 530, 1.48, transcribed by the author.
40. Bill Russell journal, May 12, 1955, WRC, Mss. 513, fol. 472.
41. J. Robert Bradley interview with Laurraine Goreau, September 9, 1973, LGC, transcribed by the author; J. Robert Bradley interview with the National Visionary Leadership Project, n.d., http://www.visionaryproject.org/bradleyrobert/ (accessed May 10, 2018), transcribed by the author.
42. J. Robert Bradley interview with Laurraine Goreau, September 9, 1973, LGC, transcribed by the author; Boyer, *The Golden Age of Gospel*, 145; Boyer, "Lucie Campbell: Composer for the National Baptist Convention," in *We'll Understand It Better By and By*, 85. See also J. Robert Bradley (as told to Amos Jones Jr.), *In the Hands of God: An Autobiography of the Life of Dr. J. Robert Bradley* (Nashville, TN: Townsend Press, 1993).
43. Goreau, *Just Mahalia, Baby*, 138.
44. Mahalia Jackson interview with Laurraine Goreau, June 22, 1967, transcript in LGC; J. Robert Bradley interview with Laurraine Goreau, September 9, 1973, LGC, transcribed by the author; Bill Russell journal, May 18, 1955, WRC, Mss. 513, fol. 472.
45. Recording of Mahalia Jackson home rehearsal, September 18, 1954, WRC, Mss. 530, 1.2.
46. Larry Wolters, "Grand Opera's Glamor Girl," *Chicago Sunday Tribune Grafic Magazine* (March 29, 1953).
47. Many black popular musicians in the 1950s experienced the frustration of their commercial success being undercut by nearly identical cover versions of their recordings by white artists, sometimes with the same backing band, that consistently outsold their own releases, a practice sometimes referred to as "whitewashing." In her autobiography, written with David Ritz, Etta James discussed how Gibbs cashed in by re-recording her original, released with the title "Roll with Me, Henry." The substitution of "Dance" for "Roll" was apparently intended to eliminate any hint of sexual innuendo: "Georgia's cutesy-pie do-over went over big. My version went underground and continued to sell while Georgia's whitewash went through the roof. Her Henry became a million seller. I was happy to have any success, but I was enraged to see Georgia singing the song on *The Ed Sullivan Show* while I was singing it in some funky dive in Watts." Etta James and David Ritz, *Rage to Survive: The Etta James Story* (New York: Da Capo, 1995), 49–50. Gibbs in many ways became the poster child for whitewashing. Singer LaVern Baker seethed in 1955 after watching Gibbs's

cover of her "Tweedle Dee" rise to number three on the pop charts. "I bitterly resent their arrogance in thefting my music note for note," said Baker. "We worked all night to get the arrangement; it didn't seem fair to have someone get all the gravy for nothing." Quoted in Chip Defaa, *Blue Rhythms: Six Lives in Rhythm and Blues* (Urbana: University of Illinois Press, 1996), 181–86. Russell overheard Jackson express the opinion that technology became a crutch that leveled the playing field for white singers like Gibbs: "Mahalia said the white folks don't need the colored singers with their big voices anymore (it was during a Georgia Gibbs' TV program), that they can use their mikes to turn up the little voices and make them sound good." Bill Russell journal, July 24, 1955, WRC, Mss. 513, fol. 472.

48. Bill Russell journal, May 12, 1955, WRC, Mss. 513, fol. 472. Emphasis in the original. The *Shower of Stars* episode "High Pitch" can be viewed at www .youtube.com/watch?v=Na9mv42qI5s (accessed May 10, 2018). The "Dance with Me, Henry" segment begins at 29:20.

49. "Mahalia Jackson Joins Stars for Harvest Fete," *Chicago Sun-Times* (October 1954); Mahalia Jackson, "I Sing for the Lord," *Music Journal* (January 1963), 19, 30; Mahalia Jackson interview with Laurraine Goreau, February 20–24, 1970, transcript in LGC.

50. Eddie Kendrix interview with author, September 29, 2009.

CHAPTER 8

1. Publicity card for "'Lift Every Voice and Sing': A Program of People's Music," WRC, Mss. 513, fol. 438; "Season's Biggest Gospel Sing Today," *Atlanta Daily World* (April 22, 1951); "Mahalia Jackson Fails to Show Up in Texarkana," *Arkansas State Press* (May 11, 1951).

2. Robbie Lieberman, *"My Song Is My Weapon"*; Ronald Cohen, *Rainbow Quest: The Folk Music Revival and American Society, 1940–1970* (University of Massachusetts Press, 2002), 37, 43, 63; Richard Reuss, *American Folk Music and Left-Wing Politics, 1927–1957* (Lanham, MD: Scarecrow, 2000), 221–64.

3. "E.C. Music Festival Slated for April 20," *Chicago Defender* (April 26, 1947); "Progressives Open 4th Ward Campaign at Party Tuesday," *Chicago Tribune* (April 4, 1948); Thomas Doherty, *Cold War, Cool Medium: Television, McCarthyism, and American Culture* (New York: Columbia University, 2003), 25; Conrad Clark, "Gospel Queen Threatens to Sue Leftists," *Philadelphia Tribune* (August 5, 1952).

4. Recording of Mahalia Jackson at "Lift Every Voice and Sing: A Program of People's Music," Wendell Phillips High School, Chicago, April 28, 1951, WRC, Mss. 530, 1.23, transcribed by the author. Jackson's performance of "Savior More Than Life to Me" is also included on the recent compilation *Moving On Up a Little Higher* (Shanachie CD 6066). See also Willie Webb Singers (Alex Bradford, lead), "Every Day and Every Hour" (Gotham 671, 1950); Princess Stewart, "Savior More Than Life to Me" on *That's God* (Vee Jay LP 5018, 1962);

Doris Akers, "Closer to Thee" on *Doris Akers Sings in Church for Missions* (Crusade LP 2703, 1963). Contemporary gospel superstar Kirk Franklin also wrote a song titled "Savior More Than Life to Me," the opening track of his 1996 album *Whatcha Lookin' 4*, with music and lyrics that are entirely different from the older hymn.

5. Unless otherwise indicated, information on Russell's early life is drawn from his personal papers in WRC, Mss. 533 and 756, as well as Ed Nylund, "William Russell," *Jazz Information* (August 9, 1940): 15–16; Michael Slatter, "A Portrait of William Russell," *Jazz Journal* (September 1959): 28–29; George Kay, "Bill Russell Reminisces," *Mississippi Rag* (September 1979): 1–4; and Mike Hazeldine, *Bill Russell's American Music* (New Orleans: Jazzology Press, 1993), ix–xi.

6. Carol Oja, *Making Music Modern: New York in the 1920s* (New York: Oxford University Press, 2000).

7. "Who's Who in the Critics Row, Part Three" *Down Beat* (December 15, 1940): 7; Frederic Ramsey and Charles Edward Smith, eds., *Jazzmen* (New York: Harcourt, Brace and Co., 1939). On the significance of *Jazzmen*, see John Gennari, *Blowin' Hot and Cool: Jazz and Its Critics* (Chicago: University of Chicago Press, 2006), 122–30.

8. Ruth Chamberlain, "Allendale School to See Chinese Shadow Pictures Tomorrow," *Rochester Evening Journal and Post Express* (April 16, 1934) (clipping in WRC, Mss. 756); Grant Hayter-Menzies, *Shadow Woman: The Extraordinary Career of Pauline Benton* (Montreal and Kingston: McGill-Queens University Press, 2013), 51–52, 65, 92.

9. Michael Hicks, "John Cage's Studies with Schoenberg," *American Music* 8 (1990): 126.

10. John Cage and William Russell, "Percussion Music an Its Relation to the Modern Dance," *Dance Observer* 6 (October 1939): 266, 274; Hicks, "John Cage's Studies with Schoenberg," 126; William Russell, "Schoenberg the Teacher," *Tempo* 8/12 (April 1, 1940): 6, 13; Alfred Frankenstein, "A Splendid Performance Opens Red Cross Series," *San Francisco Chronicle* (July 19, 1940); John Cage, *Silence* (Hanover, NH: Wesleyan University Press, 1973), 72–73.

11. Frances Hamilton, "Here's Real Dr. Rhythm," *San Francisco News* (July 18, 1940); Marjory Fisher, "Composer's Search Proved Profitable," *San Francisco News* (August 17, 1940); Bill Russell's studies with Arnold Schoenberg, WRC, Mss. 756, fol. 91.

12. Gennari, *Blowin' Hot and Cool*, 80–81; John de Toledano, Introduction to *Frontiers of Jazz*, edited by John de Toledano (New York: Frederick Ungar, 1947), xii.

13. Bill Russell journal, December 28, 1945 and January 1, 1946, WRC, Mss. 497, fol. 17; "Program of Jazz Traces Its History," *New York Times* (January 2, 1946).

14. Bill Russell journal, January 1946, WRC, Mss. 513, fol. 436.

15. Bill Russell journal, January 1946, WRC, Mss. 513, fol. 436.

16. Bill Russell journal, January 13, 1946, WRC, Mss. 497, fol. 17.

17. Bill Russell journal, January 13, 1946, WRC, Mss. 497, fol. 17; Russell quoted in Moon, "Mahalia Jackson: A Great Gospel Singer," 16.

18. Kay, "Bill Russell Reminisces," 2.

19. Draft of Bill Russell letter to "C," May 2, 1951, WRC, Mss. 533, fol. 638.

20. Draft of Bill Russell letter to "C," May 17, 1951, WRC, Mss. 533, fol. 639.

21. Bill Russell journal, July 2, August 12, and August 14, 1951, WRC, Mss. 513, fol. 440; Marovich, *A City Called Heaven*, 157.

22. Bill Russell journal, January 1952, Spring 1952, and March 8, 1954, WRC, Mss. 513, fol. 440.

23. Bill Russell journal, October 19, 1952, WRC, Mss. 513, fol. 440; Bernice Bass, "Louisiana Cinderella Still Empress of Chicago Gospel," Mahalia Jackson 25th Anniversary Program, October 19, 1951, Mahalia Jackson Scrapbook, page 427, LGC.

24. Bill Russell journal, March 18, 1954, WRC, Mss. 513, fol. 442.

25. Bill Russell journal, May 9, 1954, WRC, Mss. 513, fol. 444.

26. Letter from Bill Russell to Mahalia Jackson, July 16, 1954, WRC, Mss. 513, fol. 2; Letter from Frederic Ramsey to Bill Russell, September 28, 1954; WRC, Mss. 519, Frederic Ramsey, fol. 55; Bill Russell letter to Glenn Kittler, March 26, 1958, WRC, Mss. 513, fol. 16. On Russell's interactions with Jackson, see also Kristine Somerville, Speer Morgan, and Maritza McCauley, eds., "Traveling with Mahalia: The Notebooks of Bill Russell," *Missouri Review* 39/2 (2016): 129–59.

27. Bill Russell journal, June 16, 1955, WRC, Mss. 513, fol. 472.

28. Alice McClarity interview with author, April 5, 2011 and January 30, 2015; Mahalia Jackson interview with Studs Terkel, *Studs Terkel's Almanac* (WFMT-Chicago), September 14, 1954, WRC, Mss. 530, 1.48, transcribed by the author.

29. St. Clair Drake and Horace Cayton, *Black Metropolis: A Study of Negro Life in a Northern City* (New York: Harcourt, Brace, and Company, 1945); Arnold Hirsch, *Making the Second Ghetto: Race and Housing in Chicago, 1940–1960* (Chicago: University of Chicago Press, 1983).

30. Bill Russell journal, April 1, 1955, WRC, Mss. 513, fol. 472.

31. Bill Russell journal, June 30, 1954, WRC, Mss. 513, fol. 449.

32. Bill Russell journal, July 12, 1954, WRC, Mss. 513, fol. 454.

33. Bill Russell interview with Laurraine Goreau, January 30, 1974, transcript in LGC.

34. Bill Russell journal, July 2, 1954, WRC, Mss. 513, fol. 449.

35. Bill Russell journal, August 26, 1954, WRC, Mss. 513, fol. 440.

36. "Chicago Music Lovers Honor Willie Webb in 4th Anniversary Musical Celebration," clipping in WRC, Mss. 513, fol. 239; Bill Russell journal, June 21, 1954, WRC, Mss. 513, fol. 446; Ibid., July 4, 1954, WRC, Mss. 513, fol. 450; Ibid., August 29, 1955, WRC, Mss. 513, fol. 472; *The Great 1955 Shrine Concert* (Specialty 7045–2, 1993). See also the National Public Radio story on the Shrine concert, "Marking a Great Gospel Concert's 50th Anniversary"

[http://www.npr.org/templates/story/story.php?storyId=4766085, accessed May 10, 2018].

37. Bill Russell journal, August 10, 1955, WRC, Mss. 513, fol. 472.

38. Bill Russell journal, May 18, 1955, WRC, Mss. 513, fol. 472; Caravans with James Cleveland, "The Solid Rock" (States 1531, 1955).

39. Bill Russell journal, July 4, 1954, WRC, Mss. 513, fol. 450.

40. Marovich, *A City Called Heaven*, 172.

41. Philip Maxwell, "Music Festival to Star Famed Gospel Singer," *Chicago Tribune* (June 26, 1955).

42. Alice McClarity interviews with author, April 5, 2011 and January 30, 2015.

43. J. Robert Bradley interview with Laurraine Goreau, September 9, 1973, LGC, transcribed by the author. On Mahalia's Beauty Shop as a "fellowship hot spot" for gospel singers, see also Marovich, *A City Called Heaven*, 123.

44. Bill Russell journal, May 19, 1955, WRC, Mss. 513, fol. 472; Bill Russell journal, July 26, 1955, WRC, Mss. 513, fol. 472; Bill Russell journal, May 4, 1955, WRC, Mss. 513, fol. 472.

45. Alice McClarity interview with the author, April 5, 2011.

46. Bill Russell journal, August 2, WRC, Mss. 513, fol. 459.

47. Bill Russell journal, June 12, 1955, WRC, Mss. 513, fol. 472.

48. Reverend James Lofton and His Church of Our Prayer 250 Voice Choir, "Great Day" (Vee-Jay 3419 A/B, 1955).

49. Brotherhood Award, February 27, 1955, Chicago Conference for Brotherhood, CHM, box 3, fol. 3.

50. Letter from James Lofton to John Foster Dulles, August 20, 1955, and letter from Howard Cook to James Lofton, September 1, 1955, USNARS; "Clergy Wants Mahalia Jackson Sent to Russia," *Memphis World* (August 26, 1955); "State Department Considers Mahalia Jackson Peace Tour," *Atlanta Daily World* (October 1, 1955).

51. Bill Russell journal, May 18, 1955, WRC, Mss. 513, fol. 472.

52. Bill Russell journal, September 2, 1955, WRC, Mss. 513, fol. 472.

53. Goreau, *Just Mahalia, Baby*, 185, 205–6, 216–18, 257, 265; Ed Harris, "On the Town," *Philadelphia Tribune* (April 10, 1954) and (May 1, 1954); "Ward Sisters Faith Crusade," *Baltimore Afro-American* (April 24, 1954); "'Faith Crusade' Is Launched in Baltimore," *Atlanta Daily World* (May 2, 1954); "Report from Atlantic City," *Baltimore Afro-American* (January 8, 1955); "'Bonus' Offered by Shore Hotel," *Baltimore Afro-American* (November 19, 1955); Rev. Russell Roberts (as told to Al Duckett), "Jersey Joe and His Christian Crusade," *Chicago Defender* (October 2, 1954); "2,000 Attend Rites for Rev. Russell Roberts," *Jet* (March 5, 1959): 22; Mildred Falls interview with Laurraine Goreau, November 9, 1972, LGC, transcribed by the author.

54. Al Duckett, "Why Celebs Often 'Lose Tempers' Funny to Everyone but the Aces," *Chicago Defender* (August 13, 1955).

55. Bill Russell journal, June 13, 1955, WRC, Mss. 513, fol. 472.

56. Bill Russell journal, June 12, 1955, WRC, Mss. 513, fol. 472.

57. "Contralto Singer Sunday Afternoon at Bethel Church," *Jacksonville Journal* (October 7, 1955).

58. Recording of Mahalia Jackson at the "Definitions in Jazz" roundtable at the Music Inn, Lenox, Massachusetts, August 27, 1951, IJS, transcribed by the author.

59. Bill Russell journal, July 27, 1955, WRC, Mss. 513, fol. 472; Recording of various singers and Mahalia Jackson, April 12, 1955, WRC, Mss. 530, 1.26; B. H. Logan, "Around with the Churches," *Pittsburgh Courier* (July 24, 1954); Bill Russell journal, January 13, 1946, WRC, Mss. 497, fol. 17; Bill Russell journal, June 12, 1955, WRC, Mss. 513, fol. 472.

60. Bill Russell journal, May 10, 1955, WRC, Mss. 513, fol. 472.

61. Bill Russell journal, May 23, 1955, WRC, Mss. 513, fol. 472.

62. Bill Russell journal, August 10, 1955, WRC, Mss. 513, fol. 472.

63. Bill Russell journal, June 15, 1955, WRC, Mss. 513, fol. 472.

64. Bill Russell journal, July 3, 1955, WRC, Mss. 513, fol. 472.

65. Bill Russell journal, April 21, 1955, WRC, Mss. 513, fol. 472.

66. Bill Russell journal, June 13, 1955, WRC, Mss. 513, fol. 472.

67. Bill Russell journal, April 23, 1955, WRC, Mss. 513, fol. 472.

68. Bill Russell journal, August 10, 1955, WRC, Mss. 513, fol. 472.

69. Bill Russell interview with Laurraine Goreau, January 30, 1974, transcript in LGC.

70. Bill Russell journal, June 13 and 14, 1955, WRC, Mss. 513, fol. 472.

71. Bill Russell journal, May 19, 1955, WRC, Mss. 513, fol. 472.

72. Bill Russell letter to Glenn Kittler, March 26, 1958, WRC, Mss. 513, fol. 16.

73. Bill Russell letter to George Avakian, November 17, 1954, JHP, box 15, fol. 257.

74. "Mahalia Jackson Scores New Hit," *Chicago Defender* (January 22, 1955).

CHAPTER 9

1. Helen Phillips became the first African American to sing onstage at the Met in December 1947 when she was a last-minute substitution for a regular chorus member in five performances of Pietro Mascagni's *Cavalleria rusticana*.

2. Lin Holloway, "Marian Anderson–Met Pact Story was 1954's Biggest," *Norfolk New Journal and Guide* (January 1, 1955); "Dream Come True—Marian Anderson to Sing Opera," *Baltimore Afro-American* (October 16, 1954).

3. "Warning to 1955: Your Predecessor Was on the Ball," *Chicago Defender* (January 1, 1955); Earl Brown, "Time for Goose Pimples," *New York Amsterdam News* (October 16, 1954). For representative coverage of the Anderson signing, see "Miss Anderson to the Met," *New York Times* (October 9, 1954); Evelyn Cunningham, "Marian to *Courier*: 'Never Gave Up Hope,'" *Pittsburgh Courier*

(October 16, 1954); Olin Downes, "A Door Opens," *New York Times* (October 17, 1954); "Marian Anderson and the Met," *Chicago Defender* (October 23, 1954); Paul Hume, "Miss Anderson Fells a Barrier," *Washington Post* (October 24, 1954).

4. For another consideration of *The Mahalia Jackson Show*, see Charles Wolfe, "Mahalia on the Air, 1954," *Rejoice* 2/3 (Spring 1990): 10–13.

5. Faye Emerson, "Mahalia, A Radio Phenomenon," *New York World-Telegram* (September 25, 1954); "Exclusives in the News: Gospel Star on TV," *Pittsburgh Courier* (June 12, 1954); "A Show for Mahalia," *Chicago Defender* (July 24, 1945); "Big U.S. Radio Plans for Mahalia," *Melody Maker* (July 31, 1954); CBS Press Release, August 12, 1954, Mahalia Jackson File, NYPLPA-M.

6. Randall Vogt, "Louis Cowan," in the *Encyclopedia of Radio*, vol. 1, edited by Christopher Sterling (New York: Routledge, 2004), 664–65; Martin Gardner, *Quiz Kids: The Radio Program with the Smartest Children in America, 1940–1953* (Jefferson, NC: McFarland, 2013); "6-Year-Old Prodigy Makes Quiz Kid TV Debut," *Jet* (March 27, 1952): 55; Goreau, *Just Mahalia, Baby*, 182–83.

7. Lucia Carter, "Mahalia Heading for Stardom Sept. 26," *Chicago Sun-Times* (September 16, 1954); Tony Weitzel, "The Town Crier," *Chicago Daily News* (September 27, 1954); Goreau, *Just Mahalia, Baby*, 189; Sara Love, "Mostly About Women," *Chicago Defender* (October 2, 1954).

8. David Metzer, "Shadow Play: The Spiritual in Duke Ellington's 'Black and Tan Fantasy,'" *Black Music Research Journal* 17 (1997) 137–59.

9. Bill Russell journal, September 6, 1954, WRC, Mss. 513, fol. 478; Recording of Mahalia Jackson rehearsal, September 6, 1954, WRC, Mss. 530, 1.1.

10. Recording of Mahalia Jackson rehearsal, September 18, 1954, WRC, Mss. 530, 1.2; Williams Arms Fisher Preface to "Goin' Home" (Oliver Ditson, 1922). Marked influence on Dvořák's famous symphony, which premiered in 1893, came from the spirituals he heard sung by Henry Thacker Burleigh, an African American composition student at New York's National Conservatory of Music. See Jean Snyder, *Harry T. Burleigh: From the Spiritual to the Harlem Renaissance* (Urbana: University of Illinois Press, 2016), 65–112.

11. David Chevan, "Musical Literacy and Jazz Musicians in the 1910s and 1920s," *Current Musicology* 71–73 (Spring 2001–Spring 2002): 200–31.

12. Recording of *Mahalia Jackson Show* rehearsal, September 22, 1954, WRC, Mss. 530, 1.8.

13. Bill Russell journal, September 8, 1954, WRC, Mss. 513, fol. 479.

14. Mahalia Jackson interview with Studs Terkel on *Studs Terkel Almanac* (WFMT Chicago), September 14, 1954, WRC, Mss. 530, 1.48, transcribed by the author.

15. Goreau, *Just Mahalia, Baby*, 63; "Mahalia Jackson to Sing at CBS Fete," *Baltimore Afro-American* (August 21, 1954); "National News," *Chicago Defender* (August

28, 1954); Ben Stegner column, *Chicago Sun-Times* (September 3, 1954); "Izzy Rowe's Notebook," *Pittsburgh Courier* (September 25, 1954).

16. CBS Radio Network, *Mahalia Jackson Show* press packet, Mahalia Jackson file, IJS; Edward "Sonny" Murrain, "Front and Center," *New York Age* (October 16, 1954).

17. Bill Russell journal, October 10, 1954, WRC, Mss. 513, fol. 440.

18. Evelyn Cunningham, "The Women: Mahalia the Mystery," *Pittsburgh Courier* (October 9, 1954). See also Izzy Rowe, "The Rootin' Section," *Pittsburgh Courier* (October 9, 1954).

19. Al Monroe, "Swinging the News," *Chicago Defender* (September 25, 2014); Richard Orr, "Mahalia's Songs Sell the Gospel," *Chicago Tribune* (November 16, 1954); "Gospel with a Bounce," *Time* (October 4, 1954): 46; Mason Sargent, "Meet Mahalia Jackson—Classicist of the Spiritual," *Down Beat* (November 17, 1954); Mason Sargent, "Mahalia to Keep to Her Own Pattern on Discs," *Down Beat* (December 1, 1954); "Mahalia Jackson—CBS Singing Star," CBS Radio Biographical Service press release, September 29, 1954, copy in IJS; Walter Winchell, "The Broadway Lights," *Washington Post* and *Times Herald* (September 13, 1954).

20. "Duke Proposes Mr. B. as Head of Nat'l Group to Aid Show Biz Tyros," *Variety* (August 12, 1953): 50; "Artist Group to Aid Youngsters Make Mark," *Philadelphia Tribune* (September 22, 1953); "Not Divorced from Church, Mahalia Jackson Says," *Atlanta Daily World* (September 30, 1953). "Duke Ellington Officially Dedicates New Talent Group," *Atlanta Daily World* (October 4, 1953).

21. Goreau, *Just Mahalia Baby*, 171; Duke Ellington, *Music Is My Mistress* (New York: Da Capo, 1973), 255–56.

22. "Gospel Queen Mahalia," *Life* (November 29, 1954): 63–66; Jimmy Brown, "These Foolish Things," *Philadelphia Tribune* (December 4, 1954).

23. Arnold de Mille, "Mahalia Jackson Network Show Scheduled for Airing Sept. 26," *Chicago Defender* (August 14, 1954); "3000 Hear Mahalia Jackson," *Los Angeles Sentinel* (October 7, 1954).

24. Bill Russell journal, September 8, 1954, WRC, Mss. 513, fol. 479.

25. Russell's recordings of the entire run of *The Mahalia Jackson Show*, with the exception of episodes #1 and #9, are archived in WRC, Mss. 530, 1.27–1.42. All transcriptions are by the author, unless otherwise indicated.

26. Mahalia Jackson interview with Studs Terkel on *Studs Terkel Almanac* (WFMT Chicago), September 14, 1954, WRC, Mss. 530, 1.48.

27. Rosemary Clooney, "Brahms's Lullaby (Close Your Eyes)" (Columbia CO 48861, 1953).

28. Ward-Royster and Rose, *How I Got Over*, 19–20.

29. Ed Sullivan interview with Laurraine Goreau, November 19, 1972, transcript in LGC; Lucia Carter, "Mahalia Heading for Stardom," *Chicago Sun-Times* (September 16, 1954); Dan Burley, "Talking About," *Jet* (November 4, 1954): 51.

30. Arthur Bronson, "Lanza Proves Hottest Draw with $177,720 Gross in 22 Concerts," *Variety* (May 9, 1951): 1, 16; Eddie Gallaher, "On Record," *Washington Post* (June 10, 1951); Mario Lanza on *Two Hours of Stars*, 1948, https://www.youtube.com/watch?v=eFhhwNG3N74 (accessed May 10, 2018), transcribed by the author; Howard Thompson, "Lanza, the Bonanza," *New York Times* (May 6, 1951); Mario Lanza interview with Dick Simmons, 1951, https://www.youtube.com/watch?v=BObiFGX4BcA (accessed May 10, 2018), transcribed by the author.

31. Dan Burley, "Talking About." *The American Caruso* is the title of a 1983 PBS documentary on Lanza.

32. Therman Ruth Jr. interview with the author, July 15, 2009.

33. Recording of Mahalia Jackson rehearsal, September 18, 1954, WRC, Mss. 530, 1.2. See Chapter 7.

34. Bill Russell journal, September 21, 1954, WRC, Mss. 513, fol. 489.

35. "Gospel with a Bounce," *Time* (October 4, 1954).

36. Curtis Evans, *The Burden of Black Religion* (New York: Oxford University Press, 2008), 10.

37. Sargent, "Mahalia to Keep to Her Own Pattern on Discs."

38. "Gospel with a Bounce," *Time* (October 4, 1954).

39. Bill Russell journal, September 24, 1954, WRC, Mss. 513, fol. 490.

40. Mahalia Jackson interview with unknown Swedish interviewer, January 24, 1955, Chicago, WRC, Mss. 530, 1.25, transcribed by the author.

41. Tony Weitzel, "The Town Crier," *Chicago Daily News* (September 27, 1954); Review of *Mahalia Jackson Show*, *Variety* (September 29, 1954): 35.

42. Recording of *The Mahalia Jackson Show* #5, recorded October 8, 1954, aired October 24, 1954, WRC, Mss. 530, 1.30.

43. Recording of *The Mahalia Jackson Show* #6, recorded October 15, 1954, aired October 31, 1954, WRC, Mss. 530, 1.31.

44. Bill Russell journal, October 14, 1954, WRC, Mss. 513, fol. 440.

45. Quoted in Donald Bogle, *Prime Time Blues: African Americans on Network Television* (New York: Farrar, Straus and Giroux, 2001), 33.

46. On *The Beulah Show*, *Amos 'n' Andy*, and early-1950s controversy about them, see J. Fred MacDonald, *Blacks and White TV: African Americans in Television since 1948*, 2nd ed. (Chicago: Nelson-Hall, 1992), 27–35; Herman Gray, *Watching Race: Television and the Struggle for Blackness* (Minneapolis: University of Minnesota Press, 1995), 73–77; William Barlow, *Voice Over: The Making of Black Radio* (Philadelphia: Temple University Press, 1999), 35–46; Bogle, *Prime Time Blues*, 19–41; Doherty, *Cold War, Cool Medium*, 70–80; James Baughman, *Same Time, Same Station: Creating American Television, 1948–1961* (Baltimore: Johns Hopkins University Press, 2007), 162–65; Aniko Bodroghkozy, *Equal Time: Television and the Civil Rights Movement* (Champaign: University of Illinois Press, 2012), 17–37; Jennifer Frost, "Hedda Hopper, Hollywood Gossip, and

the Politics of Racial Representation in Film, 1946–1948," *Journal of African American History* 93/1 (2008): 36–63; Victoria Sturtevant, "'But Things Is Changin' an' Mammy's Gettin' Bored': Hattie McDaniel and the Culture of Dissemblance," *Velvet Light Trap*, no. 44 (Fall 1999): 68–79; Melvin Patrick Ely, *The Adventures of Amos 'n' Andy: A Social History of an American Phenomenon* (New York: The Free Press, 1991); Jenny Woodley, *Art for Equality: The NAACP's Cultural Campaign for Civil Rights* (Lexington: University Press of Kentucky, 2014), 159–89; Jason Chambers, *Madison Avenue and the Color Line: African Americans in the Advertising Industry* (Philadelphia: University of Pennsylvania Press, 2008), 106–9; Donald Bogle, *Heat Wave: The Life and Career of Ethel Waters* (New York: HarperCollins, 2011), 457–61; "'Amos 'n' Andy,' 'Beulah' Blasted by NAACP Board," *Atlanta Daily World* (June 30, 1951); Paul Jones, "Amos 'n' Andy Television Show Offends Some, Pleases Others," *Pittsburgh Courier* (July 28, 1951); John Crosby, "The Video 'Beulah' Is Mostly Unblessed," *New York Herald Tribune* (April 29, 1951); Joseph Bibb, "'Beulah' Flayed," *Pittsburgh Courier* (May 19, 1951); Rebecca Sharpless, "Servants and Housekeepers," in *The New Encyclopedia of Southern Culture*, vol. 13: *Gender*, edited by Nancy Bercaw and Ted Ownby (Chapel Hill: University of North Carolina Press, 2014), 246–51. The features of the black maid popularized over radio and television overlap with and are in a basic sense derivative from the "Mammy" figure. On the latter character, see Kimberly Wallace-Sanders's critical-historical study *Mammy: A Century of Race, Gender, and Southern Memory* (Ann Arbor: University of Michigan Press, 2008).

47. Frost, "Hedda Hopper, Hollywood Gossip, and the Politics of Racial Representation in Film," 56.

48. Crosby, "The Video 'Beulah' Is Mostly Unblessed"; Bibb, "'Beulah' Flayed"; Bogle, *Heat Wave*, 457–61.

49. Bodroghkozy does, however, offer a perceptive analysis of the distinctly individuated ways that Waters, McDaniel, and Beavers approached and interpreted the role on television. See *Equal Time*, 29–32.

50. Carlton Jackson, *Hattie: The Life of Hattie McDaniel* (Lanham, MD: Madison Books, 1990), 30. As Carlton Jackson points out, this quote has also been attributed to other black actresses relegated to maid roles, including Waters, Beavers, and Butterfly McQueen.

51. Schwerin, *Got to Tell It*, 117–18; Barbara Coopersmith letter to Roy Wilkins, December 14, 1959, NAACP, Mahalia Jackson, 1958–1959; Farah Jasmine Griffin, "When Malindy Sings: A Meditation on Black Women's Vocality," in *Uptown Conversation: The New Jazz Studies*, edited by Robert O'Meally, Brent Edwards, and Farah Jasmine Griffin (New York: Columbia University Press, 2004), 104.

52. Edward "Sonny" Murrain, "Front and Center," *New York Age Defender* (January 1, 1955).

53. Murrain, "Front and Center," *New York Age Defender* (January 8, 1955).

54. Murrain, "Front and Center," *New York Age Defender* (January 15, 1955).

55. Carol Lee, "Hattie McDaniel, Radio's 'Beulah,' Sees Little Point in Row over Role," *Philadelphia Tribune* (February 14, 1948).

56. Recording of *The Mahalia Jackson Show* #10, recorded November 5, 1954, aired November 28, 1954, WRC, Mss. 530, 1.34.

57. Recording of *The Mahalia Jackson Show* #15 (script #16), recorded December 22, 1954, aired January 2, 1955, WRC, Mss. 530, 1.39. The scripts for Shows #15 and #16 indicate that this show and the next were originally intended to be aired in reverse order. Russell's notes record that this show, though designated in its script as #16, aired first as show #15. A rationale for the switch was likely that the release of Jackson's first Columbia singles, scheduled for January 1, apparently got pushed back a week. Therefore, the show featuring these new recordings (the original Show #15) was postponed and aired on January 9 to coincide with their release.

58. Nat Hentoff, "You Can Still Hear Her Voice When the Music Has Stopped."

59. My thanks to Christopher Reynolds for making me aware of the Four Coins' cover and of the song's lasting popularity as a wedding song.

60. "Salt Peanuts" is a bebop tune written and recorded by Dizzy Gillespie that features a recurring fill sung and played to the rhythm of "salt peanuts, salt peanuts." The famous riff can also, however, be heard in a number of earlier jazz recordings. See Gunther Schuller, *The Swing Era: The Development of Jazz, 130–1945* (New York: Oxford University Press, 1989), 371.

61. Mahalia Jackson (with Al Duckett), "God Spared Me to Sing," *Chicago Defender* (September 11, 1954).

62. Recording of *The Mahalia Jackson Show* #11, recorded November 19, 1954, aired December 5, 1954, WRC, Mss. 530, 1.35.

63. Joseph McCarthy, "Enemies from Within" in *Infamous Speeches*.

64. Recording of *The Mahalia Jackson Show* #8, recorded October 29, 1954, aired November 4, 1954, WRC, Mss. 530, 1.33.

65. Recording of *The Mahalia Jackson Show* #10, recorded November 5, 1954, aired November 28, 1954, WRC, Mss. 530, 1.34.

66. Quoted in Heilbut, *The Gospel Sound*, 62.

67. Ella J. Baker interview with John Britten, June 19, 1968, transcript in RBOHC.

68. Recording of *The Mahalia Jackson Show* #14, recorded December 8, 1954, aired December 26, 1954, WRC, Mss. 530, 1.38.

69. For work on the showcasing of black culture and the management of civil rights claims as a Cold War strategy, see Mary Dudziak, *Cold War Civil Rights: Race and the Image of American Democracy* (Princeton, NJ: Princeton University Press, 2000); Von Eschen, *Satchmo Blows Up the World*; and Danielle Fosler-Lussier, *Music in America's Cold War Diplomacy* (Berkeley: University of California Press, 2015).

70. Lucia Carter, "The Professor Gets an 'A,'" *Chicago Sun-Times* (January 12, 1955); Herb Lyon, "Tower Ticker," *Chicago Daily Tribune* (January 11, 1955).

71. "This Gordon's in Demand!" *Washington Post* (February 20, 1955); "CBS Radio Cancels Mahalia Jackson," *Variety* (February 9, 1955): 27; Izzy Rowe, "Izzy Rowe's Notebook: The Sons and Daughters of Harlem," *Pittsburgh Courier* (February 5, 1955).

CHAPTER 10

1. John S. Wilson, "Some Jazz Vocalists on LP Disks," *New York Times* (May 8, 1955).
2. Review of Mahalia Jackson, "A Rusty Old Halo" b/w "The Treasures of Love," *Variety* (January 12, 1955): 50.
3. "Negro Artists Rise as Solid Pops Sellers," *Billboard* (July 23, 1955): 18, 56.
4. Jerry Wexler quoted in David Simons, *Studio Stories—How the Great New York Records Were Made: From Miles to Madonna, Sinatra to the Ramones* (San Francisco: Backbeat Books, 2004), 34. On Miller's production philosophy, see also Albin Zak, *I Don't Sound Like Nobody: Remaking Music in 1950s America* (Ann Arbor: University of Michigan Press, 2010), 47–54.
5. "Columbia Wraps Up Best Phono Year," *Billboard* (January 8, 1955): 22; "Columbia's 'Pajama' Tops; Flock of Other Cast Album Sets Hit Market, *Variety* (June 9, 1954): 39; "Columbia Hits Folk Market," *Billboard* (June 7, 1952): 18; "Columbia Expands Its Hillbilly Roster," *Variety* (September 8, 1954): 56.
6. John Hammond interview with Laurraine Goreau, July 30, 1973, transcript in LGC; Goreau, *Just Mahalia, Baby*, 118.
7. Gennari, *Blowing Hot and Cool*, 43–55. For more on Hammond, see John Hammond and Irving Townsend, *John Hammond on Record: An Autobiography* (New York: Ridge Press, 1977); Count Basie (as told to Albert Murray), *Good Morning Blues: The Autobiography of Count Basie* (New York: Random House, 1985); Lewis Erenberg, *Swingin' the Dream: Big Band Jazz and the Rebirth of American Culture* (Chicago: University of Chicago Press, 1998); Paul Allan Anderson, *Deep River: Music in Harlem Renaissance Thought* (Durham, NC: Duke University Press, 2001), 226–47; Dunstan Prial, *The Producer: John Hammond and the Soul of American Music* (New York: Farrar, Straus, and Giroux, 2006).
8. John Hammond interview with Laurraine Goreau, July 30, 1973, transcript in LGC.
9. Mitch Miller interviews with Laurraine Goreau, July 19 and 23, 1973, transcript in LGC; Goreau, *Just Mahalia, Baby*, 177–82
10. John Hammond interview with Laurraine Goreau, July 30, 1973, transcript in LGC.
11. "Columbia Records Inks Mahalia Jackson," Columbia Records press release, August 12, 1954, Mahalia Jackson vertical file, NYPLPA-M.
12. "Col, Apollo in Mahalia Hassle," *Variety* (August 18, 1954): 47; "Apollo and Columbia in Pact Hassle," *Billboard* (August 21, 1954): 18; "Mahalia Jackson

Nears Columbia Record Contract," *Billboard* (September 18, 1954): 18; "Col, Apollo Settle Tiff Over Mahalia," *Variety* (September 22, 1954): 45; Columbia Records memo from Alfred Lorber to Mitch Miller et al., September 20, 1954, JHP, box 15, folder 257.

13. Mitch Miller interview with Laurraine Goreau, July 23, 1973, transcript in LGC.

14. See archival documents on Elvis Presley's signing by RCA on the website of Presley's guitarist Scotty Moore, http://www.scottymoore.net/article551122.html (accessed May 10, 2018).

15. George Avakian Letter to Bill Russell, November 8, 1954, WRC, Mss. 513, fol. 5.

16. Bill Russell letter to George Avakian, November 17, 1954, JHP, box 15, fol. 257.

17. Repertory on *Great Songs of Love and Faith* that Jackson first learned for and performed on *The Mahalia Jackson Show* were "Because," "Trees," "My Task," "My Friend," "The House I Live In," "Danny Boy," "The Rosary," "Crying in the Chapel," and "A Perfect Day."

18. Jim Carlton, *Conversations with Great Jazz and Studio Guitarists* (Pacific, MO: Mel Bay, 2009), 52.

19. Bill Russell journal, May 20, 1955, WRC, Mss. 513, fol. 472.

20. Simons, *Studio Stories*, 22–44.

21. Mahalia Jackson interview with Laurraine Goreau, June 22, 1967, transcript in LGC.

22. Bill Russell journal, October 14, 1954, WRC, Mss. 513, fol. 440; Recording of Mahalia Jackson rehearsal, October 24, 1954, WRC, Mss. 530, 1.18; Mahalia Jackson interview with Studs Terkel, *Studs Terkel's Almanac* (WFMT-Chicago), December 21, 1954. WRC, Mss. 530, 1.47, transcribed by the author.

23. Robert Anderson, "Oh Lord, Is It I?" (United 134, 1952); Robert Anderson, "Oh Lord, Is It I?" (Apollo 300, 1955).

24. Bill Russell letter to George Avakian, November 17, 1954, JHP, box 15, fol. 257.

25. Selah Jubilee Quartet, "Jesus Met the Woman at the Well" (Lenox 509, *c.* 1946–47); Two Gospel Keys, "Jesus Met the Woman at the Well" (Apollo 137, 1947); Pilgrim Travelers, "Jesus Met the Woman at the Well" (Specialty 329, 1948), Golden Gate Quartet, "Jesus Met the Woman at the Well" (Mercury 8124, 1949), Fairfield Four, "Jesus Met the Woman at the Well" (Dot 1003, 1949); Famous Blue Jay Singers, "Jesus Met the Woman at the Well" (Decca 48178, 1950); Swan Silvertones, "Jesus Met the Woman at the Well" (King LP 578, 1951).

26. Mahalia Jackson interview with unknown Swedish interviewer, January 24, 1955, Chicago, WRC, Mss. 530, 1.25, transcribed by the author.

27. Bill Russell letter to George Avakian, March 2, 1955, JHP, box 15, fol. 257.

28. Columbia Records memo from George Avakian to Mitch Miller, March 29, 1955, JHP, box 15, folder 257.

29. Mitch Miller interview with Laurraine Goreau, July 23, 1973, transcript in LGC; Bill Russell letter to George Avakian, November 17, 1954, JHP, box 15, fol. 257.

30. Roy Hamilton, "You'll Never Walk Alone" (Epic 9015, 1954); Flamingos, "You'll Never Walk Alone" on *Requestfully Yours* (End LP 308, 1960); Aretha Franklin, "You'll Never Walk Alone" on *Amazing Grace* (Atlantic SD 2-906, 1972).

31. George Avakian Letter to Bill Russell, November 8, 1954, WRC, Mss. 513, fol. 5; Mahalia Jackson interview with "Stu" on an unidentified television program, December 24, 1954, recorded by Bill Russell, WRC, Mss. 530, 1.49.

32. Bill Russell journal, March 20, 1955, WRC, Mss. 513, fol. 472.

33. For a discussion of 1950s pop eclecticism at the level of sound and feel, see Mark Burford, "Sam Cooke as Pop Album Artist: A Reinvention in Three Songs," *Journal of the American Musicological Society* 65 (2012): 133–41. See also Albin Zak, *I Don't Sound Like Nobody*, 53.

34. Tesro Galanti, "Bishop's Council Highlights," *Atlanta Daily World* (February 15, 1940); "Writer of Religious Songs Dies in Chicago," *Baltimore Afro-American* (July 8, 1944); "Mary Brown Deas Dies in Florida," *Pittsburgh Courier* (February 22, 1947); Edward C. Deas, ed., *Notes of Gold* (Chicago: Edward C. Deas, 1921); Edward C. Deas, ed., *Gems of Love* (Chicago: Edward C. Deas, 1924).

35. "Mary Louise Johnson," *Pittsburgh Courier* (August 24, 1982); "Professor Davis to Sponsor Mammoth Musical Program," *Pittsburgh Courier* (December 22, 1945); Boyer, *The Golden Age of Gospel*, 117–18; "Evangelist Divorces Husband," *Pittsburgh Courier* (March 11, 1950); "Coming Home," *Pittsburgh Courier* (June 4, 1950); Marion Williams quoted in Heilbut, *The Fan Who Knew Too Much*, 257.

36. Dodge, *The School of Arizona Dranes*, 148.

37. Goreau, *Just Mahalia, Baby*, 54, 60; Heilbut, "If I Fail, You Tell the World I Tried," 243.

38. Bill Russell journal, June 3, 1955, WRC, Mss. 513, fol. 472.

39. Bill Russell journal, August 2, 1955, WRC, Mss. 513, fol. 472.

40. Recording of "How Gospel Was Born—A Chicago Story," University of Chicago, Mandel Hall, January 25, 1955, OTSFM. On November 7, Jackson returned to the studio to re-record "The Lord Is Busy Man," "I'm Grateful," "Down by the Riverside" and "Trouble in My Way." For an analysis of various instances of "troping" the spiritual "Sometimes I Feel Like a Motherless Child," including Gershwin's "Summertime," see Samuel Floyd, *The Power of Black Music: Interpreting Its History from Africa to the United States* (New York: Oxford University Press, 1995), 216–20.

41. Letter from George Avakian to Mahalia Jackson, February 24, 1955, WRC, Mss. 513, fol. 8.

42. Letter from Bill Russell to George Avakian, March 2, 1955, JHP, box 15, fol. 257.

43. Bill Russell journal, June 3, 1955, WRC, Mss. 513, fol. 472.

44. Bill Russell journal, July 5, 1955, WRC, Mss. 513, fol. 472.

45. George Avakian letter to Mahalia Jackson, June 3, 1955, JHP, box 15, fol. 257.

46. Review of Mahalia Jackson, *Sweet Little Jesus Boy*, *Billboard* (November 19, 1955): 46.

47. George Avakian, Liner notes for Mahalia Jackson, *The World's Greatest Gospel Singer* (Columbia CL 644, 1955).

48. George Avakian, Liner notes for Mahalia Jackson, *Sweet Little Jesus Boy* (Columbia CL 702, 1955).

49. Between 1956 and 1964, Fitzgerald recorded a series of eight albums for Verve, each, respectively, featuring songs written by Cole Porter, Richard Rodgers and Lorenz Hart, Duke Ellington, Irving Berlin, George and Ira Gershwin, Harold Arlen, Jerome Kern, and Johnny Mercer.

50. Leonard Feather, "A Talk with Mahalia Jackson," *American Folk Music Occasional* 1 (1964): 45.

CHAPTER 11

1. "Half Million Await Parade, Picnic Aug. 6," *Chicago Defender* (July 9, 1955); Marion Campfield, "Mostly About Women," *Chicago Defender* (July 16, 1955); "Bud's 1955 Parade to Be Greatest in History," *Chicago Defender* (July 23, 1955); "Parade Highlights Annual Bud Billiken Day Festivities, *Chicago Tribune* (August 7, 1955); "75,000 Billiken Marchers Defy Rain," *Chicago Defender* (August 9, 1955); Meredith Johns, "Largest Children's Organization in the World and Still Growing," *Chicago Defender* (August 13, 1955).

2. Monica Reed, "Music Festivals and the Formation of Chicago Culture," *Journal of the Illinois State Historical Society* 103 (Spring 2010): 73.

3. Liam Ford, *Soldier Field: A Stadium and Its City* (Chicago: University of Chicago Press, 2009), 145.

4. Philip Maxwell, "Music Festival to Star Famed Gospel Singer," *Chicago Tribune* (June 26, 1955); Philip Maxwell, "Mahalia Keyed Up for Music Festival Debut," *Chicago Tribune* (July 24, 1955).

5. Octavia Randolph, "For the Record," *Chicago Defender* (November 5, 1955).

6. Bill Russell journal, July 7, 1955, WRC, Mss. 513, fol. 472; Clay Gowran, "Gospel Singing Queen Lonely, Sad as a Child," *Chicago Tribune* (July 31, 1955); Clay Gowran, "Mahalia's Rise to Fame Rapid," *Chicago Tribune* (August 7, 1955); Clay Gowran, "Language No Bar as Mahalia Sings," *Chicago Tribune* (August 14, 1955).

7. Philip Maxwell, "Florian ZaBach to be Star at Music Festival," *Chicago Tribune* (July 3, 1955); Larry Wolters, "Eddie Fisher to Soar Anew at Music Fete," *Chicago Tribune* (August 11, 1955).

8. Bill Russell journal, July 3, 1955, WRC, Mss. 513, fol. 472; Maxwell, "Mahalia Keyed Up."

9. "CBS Said Planning Mahalia TV Show," *Philadelphia Tribune* (January 18, 1955); Al Monroe, "Swinging the News," *Chicago Defender* (January 15, 1955); "Mahalia

Jackson Leaves Radio, TV Show Planned," *Jet* (March 3, 1955): 60; "Mahalia Remains Berthed on Chi TV," *Variety* (February 16, 1955): 25.

10. On Jones, see Brian Hallstoos, *Windy City, Holy Land: Willa Saunders Jones and Black Sacred Music and Drama* (PhD diss., University of Iowa, 2009).

11. Willa Saunders Jones remarks at Greater Salem Baptist Church, Chicago, March 7, 1955, WRC, Mss. 530, 1.14, transcribed by the author.

12. Bill Russell journal, June 12, 1955, WRC, Mss. 513, fol. 472.

13. Bill Russell journal, April 4, August 7, and September 4, 1955, WRC, Mss. 513, fol. 472.

14. "Mahalia to Star in New T.V. Series Over WBKB," *Chicago Defender* (October 14, 1961); *A Gospel Calling: Mahalia Jackson Sings* (Hollywood Select Video DVD 2010).

15. "Dave," Review of *Mahalia Jackson Sings, Variety* (March 16, 1955): 35.

16. Bill Russell journal, May 29 and July 7, 1955, WRC, Mss. 513, fol. 472; Recording of Mr. and Mrs. Bell singing "Spread a Little Sunshine," "Highway of Happiness," "Sow Seed in Your Garden," and "He Is Here" and the Cleveland Singers singing "Come into My Heart," April 12, 1955, WRC, Mss. 530, 1.9.

17. Bill Russell journal, August 28, 1955, WRC, Mss. 513, fol. 472.

18. Recording of *The Mahalia Jackson Show* #6, recorded October 15, 1954, aired October 31, 1954, WRC, Mss. 530, 1.31; Mahalia Jackson at Greater Salem Baptist Church, Chicago, March 7, 1955. WRC, Mss. 530, 1.14, transcribed by the author.

19. "Mahalia Jackson Scores New Hit," *Chicago Defender* (January 22, 1955); "Gospel Greats" (photo with caption), *Norfolk Journal and Guide* (January 22, 1955).

20. Bill Russell journal, April 21, 1955, WRC, Mss. 513, fol. 472.

21. Bill Russell journal, May 12, May 18, May 19, June 5, and June 12 1955, WRC, Mss. 513, fol. 472.

22. Russell journal, June 15,1955, WRC, Mss. 513, fol. 472.

23. Richard Orr, "'Mahalia Sings' Is TV Magic," *Chicago Tribune* (March 17, 1955).

24. Russell journal, March 20, May 17, July 3, and June 12, 1955, WRC, Mss. 513, fol. 472.

25. Steve Schickel, "Mahalia TV Stint Tops Radio Effort," *Billboard* (April 16, 1955): 4.

26. Bill Russell journal, May 21, May 29, and May 30, 1955, WRC, Mss. 513, fol. 472; Robert Lichtman, *The Supreme Court and McCarthy-Era Repression: One Hundred Decisions* (Urbana: University of Illinois Press, 2012), 75–76; Jeff Woods, *Black Struggle, Red Scare: Segregation and Anti-Communism in the South, 1948–1968* (Baton Rouge: Louisiana State University Press, 2004), 52–56.

27. Bill Russell journal, August 7, 1955, WRC, Mss. 513, fol. 472.

28. Steve Schickel, "Mahalia TV Stint Tops Radio Effort"; "Dave," Review of *Mahalia Jackson Sings*; Orr, "'Mahalia Sings' Is TV Magic."

29. "TV Ain't the Thing," *Chicago Defender* (March 19, 1955).

30. Bill Russell journal, May 21, 1955, WRC, Mss. 513, fol. 472.

31. Recording of Mahalia Jackson on *Arthur Godfrey and His Friends*, May 4, 1955, WRC, Mss. 530, 1.44; Al Monroe, "Swinging the News," *Chicago Defender* (May 7, 1955).

32. Bill Russell journal, May 18, 1955, WRC, Mss. 513, fol. 472.

33. Michelle Scott, *Blues Empress in Black Chattanooga: Bessie Smith and the Emerging Urban South* (Urbana: University of Illinois Press, 2008).

34. Bill Russell journal, July 27 and May 23, 1955, WRC, Mss. 513, fol. 472; "Millions of Votes Pour In for 'Bronzeville Mayor,'" *Atlanta Daily World* (March 30, 1955); Herb Lyon, "Tower Ticker," *Chicago Tribune* (April 21, 1955).

35. The following discussion of the week of services at Greater Salem Baptist Church is based on Bill Russell journal, June 12–17, 1955, WRC, Mss. 513, fol. 472.

36. S. I. Hayakawa interview with Laurraine Goreau, September 25, 1972, transcript in LGC.

37. Unless otherwise indicated, the discussion that follows is based on the recording of "How Gospel Was Born—A Chicago Story," University of Chicago, Mandel Hall, January 25, 1955, OTSFM, transcribed by the author.

38. S. I. Hayakawa interview with Laurraine Goreau, September 25, 1972, transcript in LGC.

39. S. I. Hayakawa interview with Laurraine Goreau, September 25, 1972, transcript in LGC.

40. Burford, "Mahalia Jackson Meets the Wise Men," 443–45

41. Bill Russell journal, July 18, 1955, WRC, Mss. 513, fol. 472; Mahalia Jackson live WFMT radio broadcast from the Morrison Hotel, Chicago, September 20, 1957, http://www.wfmt.com/2017/03/15/stream-rare-live-recording-queen-gospel-mahalia-jackon-will-take-church (accessed May 10, 2018), transcribed by the author.

42. Bill Russell journal, April 8, April 22, May 20, July 18, 1955, WRC, Mss. 513, fol. 472.

43. Bill Russell journal, September 3, 1955, WRC, Mss. 513, fol. 472; Devery Anderson, *Emmett Till: The Murder that Shocked the World and Propelled the Civil Rights Movement* (Jackson: University of Mississippi Press, 2015), 292.

44. "Mahalia Jackson Joins Stars for Harvest Fete," *Chicago Sun-Times* (October 24, 1954); Irv Kupcinet, "Kup's Column," *Chicago Sun-Times* (November 22, 1954); Irv Kupcinet, "Kup's Column," *Chicago Sun-Times* (November 23, 1954); Comments by Irv Kupcinet at "A Birthday Salute to Mahalia Jackson," October 28, 1955, WRC, Mss. 530, 1.17, transcribed by the author.

45. Mahalia Jackson at the Chicagoland Music Festival, August 20, 1955, WRC, Mss. 530, 1.17, transcribed by the author; Bill Russell journal, August 21, 1955, WRC, Mss. 513, fol. 472.

46. Bill Russell journal, May 22, June 12, June 16, July 18, July 28, and August 1, 1955, WRC, Mss. 513, fol. 472.

47. Unless otherwise indicated, the following discussion of the Ward family background draws on Willa Ward-Royster (as told to Toni Rose), *How I Got Over: Clara*

Ward and the World-Famous Ward Singers (Philadelphia: Temple University Press, 1997).

48. George Bennett, "One Million Gospel Lovers Couldn't Be Wrong," *Baltimore Afro-American* (May 22, 1954).

49. "Ward Singers at Auditorium Tonight," *Atlanta Daily World* (December 4, 1949).

50. Boyer, *The Golden Age of Gospel*, 107. Williams's greatest champion, Anthony Heilbut, has written extensively about the singer and has re-released or produced multiple albums of her music. See, for example, *The Gospel Sound*, 221–36.

51. For Boyer's assessment of the significance of the Ward Singers' "Surely God Is Able," see *The Golden Age of Gospel*, 107–10.

52. Heilbut, *The Gospel Sound*, 105–13.

53. "New Names . . . New Faces!" *Pittsburgh Courier* (April 5, 1952); George Brown, "No Cover Charge," *Pittsburgh Courier* (April 25, 1953); "Gospel Singing! . . . It's Big Business!" *Pittsburgh Courier* (April 30, 1955); "Clara Ward Triumphs on Tour of Dixieland," *Pittsburgh Courier* (September 20, 1952); "Night Lite Review," *Atlanta Daily World* (October 2, 1952); Joel Friedman, "Religious Field Growing Bonanza," *Billboard* (February 6, 1954): 13, 44.

54. "25,000 Pay $40,000 to Hear Ward Singers Wearing $4,000 Wardrobes in Pa., N.J., Md.," *Baltimore Afro-American* (June 20, 1953); " 'I'm Sticking to Gospel Singing'—Clara Ward," *Pittsburgh Courier* (April 11, 1953); "Clara Ward Proves Gospel Is Still Big Business," *Baltimore Afro-American* (February 20, 1954); "Gospel Singer Opens House in Penn.," *Chicago Defender* (February 7, 1953); George Bennett, "One Million Gospel Lovers Couldn't Be Wrong."

55. "New Names . . . New Faces!" *Pittsburgh Courier* (April 5, 1952); William Nunn Sr., "11,000 Jam Giant Courier Band Concert," *Pittsburgh Courier* (May 21, 1955).

56. Bill Russell journal, May 14, 1955, WRC, Mss. 513, fol. 472.

57. Dawn Francis, "Mahalia & Clara Battle to Draw in Hot Contest of Gospel Singers," *Pittsburgh Courier* (May 21, 1955).

58. "New Names . . . New Faces!"; "Miss Gospel Singer," *Our World* (June 1949): 40–42; "Clara Ward . . . Gospel Singer," *Our World* (December 1953): 38–41.

59. Bill Russell journal, September 4, 1955, WRC, Mss. 513, fol. 472.

60. Bill Russell journal, June 19 and July 10, 1955, WRC, Mss. 513, fol. 472.

61. Bill Russell journal, September 6, 1955, WRC, Mss. 513, fol. 472; Dr. William Barclay interview with Laurraine Goreau, July 31, 1973, transcript in LGC.

62. Bill Russell journal, September 6–18, 1955, WRC, Mss. 513, fol. 472.

63. "Birthday Salute to Mahalia Jackson Will Kick Off Halfway House Drive," *Chicago Defender* (October 29, 1955); "Fete TV Gospel Singer in $25 a Plate Fund Dinner," *Chicago Tribune* (October 29, 1955). My discussion of "A Birthday Salute to Mahalia Jackson" is based on Russell's audio recording of the event, WRC, Mss. 530, 1.17, transcribed by the author.

CONCLUSION

1. *The Bessie Smith Story* (Columbia GL 503–506, 1951); Hal Webman, "Bessie Smith Lives Again on Disks, Bringing Back Her Rich, Hot Blues," *Billboard* (December 5, 1951): 3.
2. Bill Russell letter to George Avakian, November 17, 1954, JHP, box 15, fol. 257.
3. Mahalia Jackson at the "Definitions in Jazz" roundtable, Music Inn, Lenox, Massachusetts, August 27, 1951, transcribed by the author.
4. Cunningham, "Mahalia the Mystery."
5. Ferguson, "A Cultural Field in the Making," 602, 634.
6. Evans, *The Burden of Black Religion*, 9–13, 17–20.

Bibliography

ARCHIVES AND RESEARCH COLLECTIONS

CHM   Mahalia Jackson Papers, Chicago History Museum
DRMC   Division of Rare Manuscript Collections, Cornell University
IJS   Institute for Jazz Studies, Rutgers University–Newark
JHP   John Hammond Papers, Gilmore Music Library Archives, Yale University
LGC   Laurraine Goreau Collection, Hogan Jazz Archive, Tulane University
MFAC   Moses and Frances Asch Collection, Center for Folklife and Cultural Heritage, Smithsonian Institution
NAACP   National Association for the Advancement of Colored People Administrative Files, 1956–1965
NSC   Norman Studer Collection, Special Collections and Archives, State University of New York–Albany
NYPLPA-D Jerome Robbins Dance Division, New York Public Library for the Performing Arts
NYPLPA-M Music Division, New York Public Library for the Performing Arts
OTSFM   Old Town School of Folk Music Resource Center (Chicago)
RBOHC   Ralph J. Bunche Oral History Collection, Moorland-Spingarn Library, Howard University
SCRBC   Schomburg Center for Research in Black Culture, New York Public Library
USNARS   United States National Archives and Record Service
WRC   William Russell Collection, Williams Research Center, Historic New Orleans Collection

MAGAZINES AND PERIODICALS

American Mercury
Billboard

Broadcasting
Cash Box
Chicago Review
Dance Observer
Down Beat
Ebony
Jazz Information
Jazz Journal
Jet
Life
Melody Maker
Mentor
Mississippi Rag
Music Journal
Musica Jazz
Newsweek
Opera News
Our World
People Today
Record Changer
Rejoice
Reporter
Rolling Stone
Saturday Review
Tempo
Time
Variety

NEWSPAPERS

Arkansas State Press
Atlanta Constitution
Atlanta Daily World
Baltimore Afro-American
Boston Globe
Chicago Daily News
Chicago Defender
Chicago Sun-Times
Chicago Tribune
Christian Science Monitor
Cleveland Call and Post

Detroit Chronicle

Independent (London)

Indianapolis Recorder

Jacksonville Journal

Los Angeles Sentinel

Louisiana Weekly (New Orleans Herald)

Memphis World

Milwaukee Journal

New York Age Defender

New York Amsterdam News

New York Herald Tribune

New York Times

New York World-Telegram

Norfolk New Journal and Guide

Philadelphia Tribune

Pittsburgh Courier

Rochester Evening Journal and Post Express

St. Louis Globe-Democrat

St. Louis Star-Times

San Francisco Chronicle

San Francisco News

Washington Post

BOOKS, ARTICLES, AND PAPERS

Aaron, Benjamin. "Amending the Taft-Hartley Act: A Decade of Frustration," *Industrial and Labor Relations Review* 11/3 (April 1958): 327–38.

Abbington, James, ed. *Readings in African American Church Music and Worship.* Chicago: GIA Publications, 2001.

Abbott, Lynn. *The Soproco Spiritual Singers: A New Orleans Quartet Family Tree.* New Orleans: Jean Lafitte National Historical Park, 1983.

—————. *I Got Two Wings: Incidents and Anecdotes of the Two-Winged Preacher and Electric Guitar Evangelist Elder Utah Smith.* Montgomery, AL: CaseQuarter, 2008.

Abbott, Lynn, and Doug Seroff. *To Do This, You Must Know This: Music Pedagogy in the Black Gospel Quartet Tradition.* Jackson: University Press of Mississippi, 2013.

Aiello, Thomas. "Constructing 'Godless Communism': Religion, Politics, and Popular Culture, 1954–1960," *Americana* (Spring 2005): http://www.americanpopularculture.com/journal/articles/spring_2005/aiello.htm (accessed May 31, 2017).

Allen, Carrie. "'When We Send Up Praises': Race, Identity, and Gospel Music in Augusta, Georgia," *Black Music Research Journal* 27 (2007): 79–95.

——————. *"A Mighty Long Way": Community, Continuity, and Black Gospel Music on Television in Augusta, Georgia, 1954–2008.* PhD diss., University of Georgia, 2009.

Allen, Ray. *Singing in the Spirit: African American Sacred Quartets in New York City.* Philadelphia: University of Pennsylvania Press, 1991.

Allgood, B. Dexter. "Black Gospel in New York City and Joe William Bostic, Sr.," *Black Perspective in Music* 18 (1990): 101–15.

Anderson, Devery. *Emmett Till: The Murder that Shocked the World and Propelled the Civil Rights Movement.* Jackson: University of Mississippi Press, 2015.

Anderson, Paul Allen. *Deep River: Music in Harlem Renaissance Thought.* Durham, NC: Duke University Press, 2001.

Anderson, Tim. "'Buried Under the Fecundity of His Own Creations': Reconsidering the Recording Bans of the American Federation of Musicians, 1942–44 and 1948," *American Music* (2004): 231–69.

——————. *Making Easy Listening: Material Culture and Postwar American Recording.* Minneapolis: University of Minnesota Press, 2006.

Arnesen, Eric. *Waterfront Workers of New Orleans: Race, Class, and Politics, 1863–1923.* Urbana and Chicago: University of Illinois Press, 1991.

Bailey, Ben. "The Lined Hymn Tradition in Black Mississippi Churches," *Black Perspective in Music* 6/1 (1978): 3–17.

Baldwin, Davarian. *Chicago's New Negroes: Modernity, the Great Migration, and Black Urban Life.* Chapel Hill: University of North Carolina Press, 2007.

Baldwin Davarian, and Minkah Makalani, eds. *Escape from New York: The New Negro Renaissance beyond Harlem.* Minneapolis: University of Minnesota Press, 2013.

Barlow, William. *Voice Over: The Making of Black Radio.* Philadelphia: Temple University Press, 1999.

Basie Count (as told to Albert Murray). *Good Morning Blues: The Autobiography of Count Basie.* New York: Random House, 1985.

Bates, Stephen. "'Godless Communism' and Its Legacies," *Society* 41/3 (March/April 2004): 29–33.

Baughman, James. *Same Time, Same Station: Creating American Television, 1948–1961.* Baltimore: Johns Hopkins University Press, 2007.

Bercaw, Nancy, and Ted Ownby, eds. *The New Encyclopedia of Southern Culture*, vol. 13: *Gender.* Chapel Hill: University of North Carolina Press, 2014.

Berrett, Joshua. "Louis Armstrong and Opera," *Musical Quarterly* 76 (1992): 416–41.

Best, Wallace. *Passionately Human, No Less Divine: Religion and Culture in Black Chicago, 1915–1952.* Princeton, NJ: Princeton University Press, 2005.

Blaisdell, Bob. *Infamous Speeches: From Robespierre to Osama bin Laden.* New York: Dover, 2011.

Bodroghkozy, Aniko. *Equal Time: Television and the Civil Rights Movement.* Champaign: University of Illinois Press, 2012.

Bogle, Donald. *Prime Time Blues: African Americans on Network Television.* New York: Farrar, Straus and Giroux, 2001.

—————. *Heat Wave: The Life and Career of Ethel Waters*. New York: Harper Collins, 2011.

Bontemps, Arna. "Rock, Church, Rock!" *Common Ground* 3 (Fall 1942): 74–80.

Bourdieu, Pierre. *The Field of Cultural Production*. New York: Columbia University Press, 1993.

Bourdieu, Pierre, and Loïc Wacquant. *An Invitation to Reflexive Sociology*. Chicago: University of Chicago Press, 1992.

Boyer, Horace Clarence. "Contemporary Gospel Music," *Black Perspective in Music* 7 (1979): 22–34.

—————. "The Vocal Style of Mahalia Jackson, Gospel Singer," *Rejoice* 2/3 (Spring 1990): 3–9.

—————. *The Golden Age of Gospel*. Urbana: University of Illinois Press, 2000.

Bradley, J. Robert, with Amos Jones, Jr. *In the Hands of God: An Autobiography of the Life of Dr. J. Robert Bradley*. Nashville, TN: Townsend Press, 1993.

Brock, Jerry. "Hallelujah, Mahalia," *Louisiana Cultural Vistas* (Summer 2012): 10–19.

Brothers, Thomas. *Louis Armstrong's New Orleans*. New York: W. W. Norton, 2006.

Broughton, Viv. *Black Gospel: An Illustrated History of the Gospel Sound*. Dorset, England: Blandford Press, 1985.

Broven, John. *Record Makers and Breakers: Voices of the Independent Rock 'n' Roll Pioneers*. Urbana and Chicago: University of Illinois Press, 2009.

Brown, Gwynn Kuhner. "The Serious Spirituals of William L. Dawson." Paper delivered at the National Conference of the American Musicological Society, Rochester, New York, November 11, 2017.

Burford, Mark. "Sam Cooke as Pop Album Artist—A Reinvention in Three Songs," *Journal of the American Musicological Society* 65 (2012): 113–78.

—————. "Mahalia Jackson Meets the Wise Men: Defining Jazz at the Music Inn," *Musical Quarterly* 96 (2014): 429–86.

—————. "Black and White, then 'Red' All Over: Chicago's American Negro Music Festival," *American Music Review* 44/2 (Spring 2015): 1–6.

Burnim, Mellonee. *The Black Gospel Music Tradition: Symbol of Ethnicity*, PhD diss., Indiana University, 1980.

—————. "The Black Gospel Music Tradition: A Complex of Ideology, Aesthetic, and Behavior" in *More than Dancing: Essays on Afro-American Music and Musicians*, edited by Irene Jackson, 147–66, Westport, CT: Greenwood, 1985.

—————. "Culture Bearer and Tradition Bearer: An Ethnomusicologist's Research on Gospel Music," *Ethnomusicology* 29 (1985): 432–47.

—————. "Functional Dimensions of Gospel Music in Performance," *Western Journal of Black Studies* 12 (1988): 112–21.

—————. "The Performance of Black Gospel Music as Transformation" in *Music and the Experience of God*, edited by Mellonee Burnim, Mary Collins, and David Power, 52–61, Edinburgh: Clark, 1989.

—————. "The Gospel Music Industry" in *African American Music: An Introduction*, edited by Portia Maultsby and Mellonee Burnim, 416–29, New York: Routledge, 2006.

—————. "Voices of Women in Gospel Music" in *Issues in African American Music: Power, Gender, Race, Representation*, edited by Portia Maultsby and Mellonee Burnim, 201–15, New York: Routledge, 2017.

Burton, Frederick. *Cleveland's Gospel Music*. Charleston, SC: Arcadia, 2003.

Butterfield, Matthew. "Why Do Jazz Musicians Swing Their Eighth Notes?" *Music Theory Spectrum* 33 (2011): 3–26.

Cage, John. *Silence*. Hanover, NH: Wesleyan University Press, 1973.

Campanella, Richard. *Geographies of New Orleans: Urban Fabrics before the Storm*. Lafayette: Center for Louisiana Studies, 2006.

Carlton, Jim. *Conversations with Great Jazz and Studio Guitarists*. Pacific, MO: Mel Bay, 2009.

Carpenter, Bil. *Uncloudy Days: The Gospel Music Encyclopedia*. San Francisco: Backbeat Books, 2005.

Carter, Scott. "Forging a Sound Citizenry: Voice Culture and the Embodiment of the Nation, 1880–1920," *American Music Research Center Journal* 22 (2013): 11–34.

Chambers, Jason. *Madison Avenue and the Color Line: African Americans in the Advertising Industry*. Philadelphia: University of Pennsylvania Press, 2008.

Champney, Freeman. "Taft-Hartley and the Printers," *Antioch Review* 8 (1948): 49–62.

Chevan, David. "Musical Literacy and Jazz Musicians in the 1910s and 1920s," *Current Musicology* 71–73 (Spring 2001–Spring 2002): 200–31.

Cohen, Ronald. *Rainbow Quest: The Folk Music Revival and American Society, 1940–1970*. Amherst: University of Massachusetts Press, 2002.

Cornell, Jean Gay. *Mahalia Jackson: Queen of Gospel Song*. Champaign, IL: Garrard, 1974.

Costello, Brian, and Randy Decuir. *The Flood of 1912: 100th Anniversary Centennial Album of the Mississippi Valley Flood*. n.p.: CreateSpace, 2012.

Cruz, Jon. *Culture on the Margins: The Black Spiritual and the Rise of American Cultural Interpretation*. Princeton: Princeton University Press, 1999.

Darden, Robert. *People Get Ready: A New History of Black Gospel Music*. New York: Continuum, 2004.

—————. *Nothing but Love in God's Water: Black Sacred Music from the Civil War to the Civil Rights Movement*. University Park: Pennsylvania State University Press, 2014.

Dargan, William. *Lining Out the Word: Dr. Watts Hymn Singing in the Music of Black Americans*. Berkeley: University of California Press, 2006.

Defaa, Chip. *Blue Rhythms: Six Lives in Rhythm and Blues*. Urbana: University of Illinois Press, 1996.

Denning, Michael. *Culture in the Age of Three Worlds*. London: Verso, 2004.

Dent, Cedric. *The Harmonic Development of the Black Religious Quartet Singing Tradition*, PhD diss., University of Maryland, 1997.

de Toledano, John. *Frontiers of Jazz*. New York: Frederick Ungar, 1947.

DeVeaux, Scott. "Bebop and the Recording Industry: The 1942 AFM Recording Ban Reconsidered," *Journal of the American Musicological Society* 41 (1988): 126–65.

———. *The Birth of Bebop: A Social and Musical History*. Berkeley and Los Angeles: University of California Press, 1997.

DjeDje, Jacqueline. "Gospel Music in the Los Angeles Black Community: A Historical Overview," *Black Music Research Journal* 9 (1989): 35–79.

———. "Los Angeles Composers of African American Gospel Music: The First Generations," *American Music* 11 (1993): 412–57.

Dodge, Timothy. *The School of Arizona Dranes: Gospel Music Pioneer*. Lanham, MD: Lexington Books, 2013.

Doherty, Thomas. *Cold War, Cool Medium: Television, McCarthyism, and American Culture*. New York: Columbia University Press, 2003.

Donloe, Darlene. *Mahalia Jackson*. Los Angeles: Melrose Square, 1992.

Drake, St. Clair, and Horace Cayton. *Black Metropolis: A Study of Negro Life in a Northern City*. New York: Harcourt, Brace, and Company, 1945.

Du Bois, W. E. B. *The Souls of Black Folk*. Chicago: McClurg, 1903.

Dudley, Shannon. *Music From Behind the Bridge: Steelband Aesthetics and Politics in Trinidad and Tobago*. New York: Oxford University Press, 2007.

Dudziak, Mary. *Cold War Civil Rights: Race and the Image of American Democracy*. Princeton: Princeton University Press, 2000.

Dunham, Montrew. *Mahalia Jackson: Young Gospel Singer*. New York: Aladdin, 1995.

Ecklund, Peter. "The Influence of Opera and the Light-Classical Tradition on the Improvisational Language of Louis Armstrong." Paper delivered at the Musical Intersections conference, Toronto, November 3, 2000.

Eidsheim, Nina. "Race and the Aesthetics of Vocal Timbre" in *Rethinking Difference in Music Scholarship*, edited by Olivia Bloechl, Melanie, Lowe, and Jeffrey Kallberg, 338–65, Cambridge: Cambridge University Press, 2015.

Ellington, Duke. *Music Is My Mistress*. New York: Da Capo, 1973.

Ellwood, Robert. *1950: Crossroads of American Religious Life*. Louisville: Westminster John Knox Press, 2000.

Ely, Melvin Patrick. *The Adventures of Amos 'n' Andy: A Social History of an American Phenomenon*. New York: Free Press, 1991.

Erenberg, Lewis. *Swingin' the Dream: Big Band Jazz and the Rebirth of American Culture*. Chicago: University of Chicago Press, 1998.

Evans, Curtis. *The Burden of Black Religion*. New York: Oxford University Press, 2008.

Fauls, Brenda. "Some Thoughts about International Choral Competitions," *Choral Journal* 48 (March 2008): 18–39.

Feather, Leonard. "A Talk with Mahalia Jackson," *American Folk Music Occasional* 1 (1964): 45–49.

Feintuch, Burt. "A Non-Commercial Black Gospel Group in Context: We Live the Life We Sing About," *Black Music Research Journal* 1 (1980): 37–50.

Ferguson, Priscilla. "A Cultural Field in the Making: Gastronomy in 19th-Century France," *American Journal of Sociology* 104 (1998): 597–641.

Floyd, Samuel. *The Power of Black Music: Interpreting Its History from Africa to the United States.* New York: Oxford University Press, 1995.

Ford, Liam. *Soldier Field: A Stadium and Its City.* Chicago: University of Chicago Press, 2009.

Fosler-Lussier, Danielle. *Music in America's Cold War Diplomacy.* Berkeley: University of California Press, 2015.

Francis, David Albert. *Panama's Story: My History as a Jazz Drummer.* n.p.: Xlibris, 2013.

Frost, Jennifer. "Hedda Hopper, Hollywood Gossip, and the Politics of Racial Representation in Film, 1946–1948," *Journal of African American History* 93 (2008): 36–63.

Gaines, Kevin. *Uplifting the Race: Black Leadership, Politics, and Culture in the Twentieth Century.* Chapel Hill and London: University of North Carolina Press, 1996.

Gardner, Martin. *Quiz Kids: The Radio Program with the Smartest Children in America, 1940–1953.* Jefferson, NC: McFarland, 2013.

Garland, Phyl. *The Sound of Soul: The Story of Black Music.* Chicago: H. Regnery, 1969.

Gennari, John. *Blowin' Hot and Cool: Jazz and Its Critics.* Chicago: University of Chicago Press, 2006.

George, Luvenia. "Lucie E. Campbell: Baptist Composer and Educator," *Black Perspective in Music* 15 (1987): 23–49.

Goertzen, Chris. "Balancing Local and National Approaches at American Fiddle Contests," *American Music* 13 (1996): 352–81.

Goff Jr., James. *Close Harmony: A History of Southern Gospel.* Chapel Hill: University of North Carolina Press, 2002.

Goodman, Jane, and Paul Silverstein, eds. *Bourdieu in Algeria: Colonial Politics, Ethnographic Practices, Theoretical Developments.* Lincoln and London: University of Nebraska Press, 2009.

Goreau, Laurraine. *Just Mahalia, Baby: The Mahalia Jackson Story.* Waco, TX: Word Books, 1975.

Gourse, Leslie. *Mahalia Jackson: Queen of Gospel Song.* New York: Franklin Watts, 1996.

Graf, Sharon. *Traditionalization at the National Oldtime Fiddler's Contest: Politics, Power, and Authenticity.* PhD diss., Michigan State University, 1999.

Gray, Herman. *Watching Race: Television and the Struggle for Blackness.* Minneapolis: University of Minnesota Press, 1995.

Green, Adam. *Selling the Race: Culture, Community, and Black Chicago, 1940–1955.* Chicago: University of Chicago Press, 2007.

Griffin, Farah Jasmine. "When Malindy Sings: A Meditation on Black Women's Vocality" in *Uptown Conversation: The New Jazz Studies*, edited by Robert O'Meally, Brent Edwards, and Farah Jasmine Griffin, 102–125. New York: Columbia University Press, 2004.

Gross, James. *Broken Promises: The Subversion of U.S. Labor Relations Policy, 1947–1994*. Philadelphia: Temple University Press, 1995.

Guralnick, Peter. *Dream Boogie: The Triumph of Sam Cooke*. New York: Back Bay Books, 2006.

Guy, Buddy, with David Ritz. *When I Left Home*. New York: Da Capo, 2012.

Hahn, Steven. *Political Worlds of Slavery and Freedom*. Cambridge: Harvard University Press, 2009.

Hallstoos, Brian. *Windy City, Holy Land: Willa Saunders Jones and Black Sacred Music and Drama*. PhD diss., University of Iowa, 2009.

Hamilton, Marybeth. *In Search of the Blues*. New York: Basic Books, 2008.

Hammond, John, with Irving Townsend. *John Hammond on Record: An Autobiography*. New York: Ridge Press, 1977.

Harold, Claudrena. "'Lord, Let Me Be an Instrument': The Artistry and Cultural Politics of Reverend James Cleveland and the Gospel Music Workshop of America, 1963–1991," *Journal of Africana Religions* 5 (2017): 157–80.

Harris, Michael. *The Rise of Gospel Blues: The Music of Thomas Andrew Dorsey in the Urban Church*. New York: Oxford University Press, 1992.

Harrison, Douglass. *Then Sings My Soul: The Culture of Southern Gospel*. Urbana: University of Illinois Press, 2012.

Hayes, Cedric, and Bob Laughton. *The Gospel Discography, 1943–1970*. West Vancouver, British Columbia, Canada: Eyeball Productions, 2007.

Hayter-Menzies, Grant. *Shadow Woman: The Extraordinary Career of Pauline Benton*. Montreal and Kingston: McGill-Queens University Press, 2013.

Hazeldine, Mike. *Bill Russell's American Music*. New Orleans: Jazzology Press, 1993.

Heilbut, Anthony. *The Gospel Sound: Good News and Bad Times*. Twenty-fifth anniversary edition. New York: Limelight, 1997. First published 1971.

———. "'If I Fail, You Tell the World I Tried': Reverend W. Herbert on Records," *Black Music Research Journal* 7 (1987): 119–26.

———. *The Fan Who Knew Too Much: Aretha Franklin, the Rise of the Soap Opera, Children of the Gospel Church, and Other Meditations*. New York: Knopf, 2012.

Hemphill, Paul. *The Nashville Sound: Bright Lights and Country Music*. New York: Simon and Schuster, 1970.

Hicks, Michael. "John Cage's Studies with Schoenberg," *American Music* 8 (1990): 125–40.

Higginbotham, Evelyn. *Righteous Discontent: The Women's Movement in the Black Baptist Church, 1880–1920*. Cambridge: Harvard University Press, 1994.

Hinson, Glenn. *Fire in My Bones: Transcendence and the Holy Spirit in African American Gospel*. Philadelphia: University of Pennsylvania Press, 2000.

Hirsch, Arnold. *Making the Second Ghetto: Race and Housing in Chicago, 1940–1960*. Chicago: University of Chicago Press, 1983.

Hitchcock, H. Wiley. *Music in the United States: A Historical Introduction*, 3d edition. Englewood Cliffs, NJ: Prentice-Hall, 1988.

Jabir, Johari. "On Conjuring Mahalia: Mahalia Jackson, New Orleans, and the Sanctified Swing," *American Quarterly* 61 (2009): 649–69.

Jackson, Carlton. *Hattie: The Life of Hattie McDaniel*. Lanham, MD: Madison Books, 1990.

Jackson, Jerma. *Singing in My Soul: Black Gospel Music in a Secular Age*. Chapel Hill: University of North Carolina Press, 2003.

Jackson, Joseph H. *A Story of Christian Activism: The History of the National Baptist Convention, U.S.A., Inc.* Nashville: Townsend Press, 1980.

Jackson Mahalia, with Evan McLeod Wylie. *Movin' On Up*. New York: Hawthorne Books, 1966.

James, Etta, and David Ritz. *Rage to Survive: The Etta James Story*. New York: Da Capo, 1995.

Jimerson, Randall. *Shattered Glass in Birmingham: My Family's Fight for Civil Rights, 1961–1964*. Baton Rouge: Louisiana State University Press, 2014.

Johnson, Idella. *Development of African American Gospel Piano Style (1926–1960): A Socio-Musical Analysis of Arizona Dranes and Thomas A. Dorsey*. PhD diss., University of Pittsburgh, 2009.

Johnson, James Weldon, ed. *The Book of American Negro Spirituals*. New York: Viking Press, 1925.

Jones, Alisha Lola. "Are All the Choir Directors Gay?: Black Men's Sexuality and Identity in Gospel Performance" in *Issues in African American Music: Power, Gender, Race, Representation*, edited by Portia Maultsby and Mellonee Burnim, 216–36, New York: Routledge, 2017.

Jones, Hettie. *Big Star Fallin' Mama: Five Women in Black Music*. New York: Viking, 1974.

Jones, LeRoi. *Blues People: Negro Music in White America*. New York: William Morrow, 1963.

Karpf, Juanita. "The Vocal Teacher of Ten Thousand: E. Azalia Hackley as Community Music Educator, 1910–1922," *Journal of Research in Music Education* 47 (1999): 319–30.

──────. "For Their Musical Uplift: Emma Azalia Hackley and Voice Culture in African American Communities," *International Journal of Community Music* 4 (2011): 237–56.

Katz, Mark. *Groove Music: The Art and Culture of the Hip-Hop DJ*. New York: Oxford University Press, 2012.

Keil, Charles. *Urban Blues*. Chicago: University of Chicago Press, 1966.

Kemp, Kathryn. *Annointed to Sing the Gospel: The Levitical Legacy of Thomas A. Dorsey*. Chicago: Joyful Noise Press, 2015.

Kidd, Thomas, and Barry Hankins. *Baptists in America: A History*. New York: Oxford University Press, 2015.

Kouwenhoven, John. *Made in America: The Arts in Modern Civilization*. New York: Doubleday, 1948.

Kramer, Barbara. *Mahalia Jackson: The Voice of Gospel and Civil Rights*. New York: Enslow, 2003.

Kukla, Barbara. *Swing City: Newark Nightlife, 1925–50*. New Brunswick, NJ: Rutgers University Press, 1991.

Legg, Andrew. "A Taxonomy of Musical Gesture in African American Gospel Music," *Popular Music* 29 (2010): 103–29.

Levine, Lawrence. *Highbrow/Lowbrow: The Emergence of Cultural Hierarchy in America*. Cambridge: Harvard University Press, 1988.

Lichtman, Robert. *The Supreme Court and McCarthy-Era Repression: One Hundred Decisions*. Urbana: University of Illinois Press, 2012.

Lieberman, Robbie. *"My Song Is My Weapon": People's Songs, American Communism, and the Politics of Culture, 1930–50*. Champaign: University of Illinois Press, 1995.

Locke, Alain, ed. *The New Negro: An Interpretation*. New York: Boni, 1925.

Logan, Rayford. *The Negro in American Life and Thought: The Nadir, 1877–1901*. New York: Dial Press, 1954.

Lordi, Emily. *Black Resonances: Iconic Women Singers and African American Literature*. New Brunswick, NJ: Rutgers University Press, 2013.

Lornell, Christopher (Kip). "Thermon Ruth and the Selah Jubilee Singers: An Interview," *Journal of Black Sacred Music* 2 (1988): 29–51.

————. *"Happy in the Service of the Lord": African American Sacred Vocal Harmony Quartets in Memphis*. Knoxville: University of Tennessee Press, 1995.

Lyotard, Jean-François. *The Postmodern Condition: A Report on Knowledge*, translated by Geoff Bennington and Brian Massumi, Minneapolis: University of Minnesota Press, 1984.

MacDonald, J. Fred. *Blacks and White TV: African Americans in Television since 1948*, 2d ed. Chicago: Nelson-Hall, 1992.

Maguire, James. *Impresario: The Life and Times of Ed Sullivan*. New York: Billboard Books, 2006.

Malone, Bill C. *Country Music, U.S.A.* Austin: University of Texas Press, 1968.

Manis, Andrew. *Southern Civil Religions in Conflict: Civil Rights and the Culture Wars*. Macon, GA: Mercer University Press, 2002.

Marcus, Greil. *Mystery Train: Images of America in Rock 'n' Roll Music*. New York: E. P. Dutton, 1975.

Marovich, Robert. "*Bon Temps* and Good News: The Influence of New Orleans on the Performance Style of Mahalia Jackson," *Association for Recorded Sound Collections Journal* 42 (2011): 50–62.

————. *A City Called Heaven: The Birth of Gospel Music in Chicago*. Champaign-Urbana: University of Illinois Press, 2015.

Maultsby, Portia. "The Influence of Gospel Music on the Secular Music Industry" in *Signifyin(g), Sanctifyin', and Slam Dunking: A Reader in African American Expressive Culture*, edited by Gena Dagel Caponi, 172–90, Amherst: University of Massachusetts Press, 1999.

McAllister, Anita. *The Musical Legacy of Dorothy Love Coates: African American Female Gospel Singer with Implications for Education and Theater Education.* EdD diss., Kansas State University, 1995.

McCormick, Lisa. *Performing Civility: International Competitions in Classical Music.* Cambridge: Cambridge University Press, 2015.

McDearmon, Kay. *Mahalia: Gospel Singer.* New York: Dodd, Mead, 1976.

McGinty, Doris. *A Documentary History of the National Association of Negro Musicians.* Chicago: Center for Black Music Research, 2004.

McGregory, Jerrilyn. *Downhome Gospel: African American Spiritual Activism in Wiregrass County.* Jackson: University Press of Mississippi, 2010.

McNeil, W. K., ed. *Encyclopedia of American Gospel Music.* New York: Taylor & Francis, 2005.

Merrick, Caroline E. *Old Times in Dixie Land: A Southern Matron's Memories.* New York: Grafton Press, 1901.

Meryman, Richard. *Louis Armstrong: A Self-Portrait.* New York: Eakins, 1971.

Metzer, David. "Shadow Play: The Spiritual in Duke Ellington's 'Black and Tan Fantasy,'" *Black Music Research Journal* 17 (1997): 137–59.

Mizelle Jr., Richard. *Backwater Blues: The Mississippi Flood of 1927 in the African American Imagination.* Minneapolis: University of Minnesota Press, 2014.

Monson, Ingrid. *Saying Something: Jazz Improvisation and Interaction.* Chicago: University of Chicago Press, 1996.

Moon, Elaine, ed. *Untold Tales, Unsung Heroes: An Oral History of Detroit's African American Community, 1918–1967.* Detroit: Wayne State University Press, 1994.

Morgan, Marcyliena. "After . . . Word!: The Philosophy of Hip-Hop Battle" in *Hip Hop and Philosophy: Rhyme 2 Reason*, edited by Derrick Darby and Tommie Shelby, 205–12, Chicago: Open Court, 2005.

Morris, Kenneth. *Improving the Music in the Church.* Chicago: Martin and Morris, 1949.

Murray, Albert. *Stomping the Blues.* New York: Da Capo Press, 1976.

Nachman, Gerald. *Right Here on Our Stage Tonight!: Ed Sullivan's America.* Berkeley and Los Angeles: University of California Press, 2009.

Nations, Opal Louis. "Doe and Dove: The Doris Akers Singers Story." Self-published, 2005.

—————. *Sensational Nightingales: The Story of Joseph "Jo Jo" Wallace and the Early Days of the Sensational Nightingales.* San Francisco: Black Scat Books, 2014.

Nolan, Nina. *Mahalia Jackson: Walking with Kings and Queens.* New York: Amistad, 2015.

Norton, Kay. "'Yes, [Gospel] Is Real': Half a Century with Chicago's Martin and Morris Company," *Journal of the Society for American Music* 11 (2017): 420–51.

Oja, Carol. *Making Music Modern: New York in the 1920s.* New York: Oxford University Press, 2000.

Olmstead, Tony. *Folkways Records, Moses Asch and His Encyclopedia of Sound.* New York and London: Routledge, 2003.

Orgill, Roxanne. *Mahalia: A Life in Gospel Music.* Somerville, MA: Candlewick, 2002.

Ortner, Sherry. *Anthropology and Social Theory: Culture Power, and the Acting Subject.* Durham, NC: Duke University Press, 2006.

Parks, Rosa. *My Story.* New York: Dial Books, 1992.

Patterson, Daniel. "'Going Up to Meet Him': Songs and Ceremonies of a Black Family's Ascent" in *Diversity of Gifts: Field Studies in Southern Religion,* edited by Ruel Tyson Jr., James Peacock, and Daniel Patterson, 91–102, Urbana: University of Illinois Press, 1988.

Patterson, Willis. *A History of the National Association of Negro Musicians: The First Quarter Century, 1919–1943.* PhD diss., Wayne State University, 1993.

Peterson, Marina. "Sound Work: Music as Labor and the 1940s Recording Bans of the American Federation of Musicians," *Anthropological Quarterly* 86 (2013): 791–824.

Phillips, Kimberley. *AlabamaNorth: African-American Migrants, Community, and Working-Class Activism in Cleveland, 1915–45.* Urbana and Chicago: University of Illinois Press, 1999.

Pitts, Walter. *Old Ship of Zion: The Afro-Baptist Ritual in the African Diaspora.* New York: Oxford University Press, 1993.

Polishuk, Sandy. "Secrets, Lies, and Misremembering: The Perils of Oral History Interviewing," *Frontiers* 19/3 (1998): 14–23.

Prial, Dunstan. *The Producer: John Hammond and the Soul of American Music.* New York: Farrar, Straus, and Giroux, 2006.

Radano, Ronald. *Lying Up A Nation: Race and Black Music.* Chicago: University of Chicago Press, 2003.

Ramsey Frederic, and Charles Edward Smith, eds., *Jazzmen.* New York: Harcourt, Brace and Co., 1939.

Reagon, Bernice Johnson, ed. *We'll Understand It Better By and By: Pioneering African American Gospel Composers.* Washington, DC: Smithsonian Institution Press, 1992.

Reddick, L. D. "Educational Programs for the Improvement of Race Relations: Motion Pictures, Radio, the Press, and Libraries," *Journal of Negro Education* 13 (1944): 367–89.

Reed, Monica. "Music Festivals and the Formation of Chicago Culture," *Journal of the Illinois State Historical Society* 103 (Spring 2010): 76–89.

Reuss, Richard. *American Folk Music and Left-Wing Politics, 1927–1957.* Lanham, MD, Scarecrow, 2000.

Riffel, Judy, ed. *A History of Pointe Coupee Parish and Its Families.* Baton Rouge: Le Comité des Archives de la Louisiane, 1983.

Rondinone, Troy. *The Great Industrial War: Framing Class Conflict in the Media, 1865–1950.* New Brunswick, NJ: Rutgers University Press, 2011.

Rose, Lisle. *The Cold War Comes to Main Street: America in the 1950s.* Lawrence: University Press of Kansas, 1999.

Rubman, Kerrill. *From "Jubilee" to "Gospel" in Black Male Quartet Singing,* PhD diss., University of North Carolina, 1980.

Sakakeeny, Matt. *Roll with It: Brass Bands in the Streets of New Orleans.* Durham: Duke University Press, 2013.

Sanford, J. I. *Beautiful Pointe Coupee and Her Prominent Citizens.* New Orleans: American Printing Co., 1906.

Sanjek, Russell, and David Sanjek. *American Popular Music Business in the 20th Century.* New York: Oxford University Press, 1991.

Schenbeck, Lawrence. *Racial Uplift and American Music, 1878–1943.* Jackson: University Press of Mississippi, 2014.

Schnalenberger, Sarah. "Shaping Uplift through Music," *Black Music Research Journal* 28 (2008): 57–83.

Schuller, Gunther. *The Swing Era: The Development of Jazz, 130–1945.* New York: Oxford University Press, 1989.

Schwartz, David. *Culture and Power: The Sociology of Pierre Bourdieu.* Chicago and London: University of Chicago Press, 1997.

Schwerin, Jules. *Got to Tell It: Mahalia Jackson, Queen of Gospel.* New York: Oxford University Press, 1992.

Scott, James. *Domination and the Arts of Resistance: Hidden Transcripts.* New Haven, CT: Yale University Press, 1990.

Scott, Michelle. *Blues Empress in Black Chattanooga: Bessie Smith and the Emerging Urban South.* Urbana: University of Illinois Press, 2008.

Seroff, Doug. "On the Battlefield: Gospel Quartets in Jefferson County, Alabama" in *Repercussions: A Celebration of African-American Music,* ed. Geoffrey Haydon and Dennis Marks), 10–53, London: Century, 1985.

——————. "Old-Time Black Gospel Quartet Contests," *Black Music Research Journal* 10 (1990): 27–28.

Seroff, Doug and Lynn Abbott, "The Origins of Ragtime," *78 Quarterly* 1/10 (c. 1999): 130–31.

Shaw, Arnold. *Honkers and Shouters: The Golden Age of Rhythm and Blues.* New York: Collier Books, 1978.

Shearon, Stephen. "Establishing the Fundamentals of Gospel Music History." Paper delivered at the National Conference of the Society for American Music, Lancaster, Pennsylvania, March 7, 2014.

Simons, David. *Studio Stories—How the Great New York Records were Made: From Miles to Madonna, Sinatra to the Ramones.* San Francisco: Backbeat Books, 2004.

Smith, Carl. *The Lined Hymn Tradition in Selected Black Churches of Eastern Kentucky.* PhD diss., University of Pittsburgh, 1987.

Smith, H. Llewellyn, and George Askwith. *Cost of Living in American Towns: Report of an Enquiry by the Board of Trade into Working Class Rents, Housing and Retail Prices, Together with the Rates of Wages in Certain Occupations in the Principal Industrial Towns on the United States of America*. London: His Majesty's Stationery Office, 1911.

Smith, Thérèse. *"Let the Church Sing": Music and Worship in a Black Mississippi Community*. Rochester, NY: University of Rochester Press, 2004.

Snyder, Jean. *Harry T. Burleigh: From the Spiritual to the Harlem Renaissance*. Urbana: University of Illinois Press, 2016.

Somerville, Kristine, Speer Morgan, and Maritza McCauley, eds. "Traveling with Mahalia: The Notebooks of Bill Russell," *Missouri Review* 39/2 (2016): 129–59.

Staggs, Sam. *Born to Be Hurt: The Untold Story of* Imitation of Life. New York: St. Martin's, 2009.

Stearns, Marshall. *The Story of Jazz*. New York: Oxford University Press, 1956.

Sterling, Christopher, ed. *Encyclopedia of Radio*, vol. 1. New York: Routledge, 2004.

Sturtevant, Victoria. "'But Things Is Changin' an' Mammy's Gettin' Bored': Hattie McDaniel and the Culture of Dissemblance," *Velvet Light Trap*, no. 44 (Fall 1999): 68–79.

Tallmadge, William. "Dr. Watts and Mahalia Jackson—The Development, Decline, and Survival of a Folk Style in America," *Ethnomusicology* 5/2 (1961): 95–99.

Theoharis, Jeanne. *The Rebellious Life of Mrs. Rosa Parks*. Boston: Beacon Press, 2013.

Titon, Jeff Todd. *Early Downhome Blues: A Musical and Cultural Analysis*. Urbana: University of Illinois Press, 1977.

Tomoff, Kiril. *Virtuosi Abroad: Soviet Music and Imperial Competition during the Early Cold War, 1945–1958*. Ithaca: Cornell University Press, 2015.

Tragaki, Dafni, ed. *Empire of Song: Europe and Nation in the Eurovision Song Contest*. Lanham, MD: Scarecrow Press, 2013.

Von Eschen, Penny. *Satchmo Blows Up the World: Jazz Ambassadors Play the Cold War*. Cambridge: Harvard University Press, 2004.

Wald, Gayle. *Shout, Sister, Shout!: The Untold Story of Rock-and-Roll Trailblazer Rosetta Tharpe*. Boston: Beacon Press, 2007.

Walker, Katherine. "Cut, Carved, and Served: Competitive Jamming in the 1930s and 1940s," *Jazz Perspectives* 4 (2010): 183–208.

Wallace-Sanders, Kimberly. *Mammy: A Century of Race, Gender, and Southern Memory*. Ann Arbor: University of Michigan Press, 2008.

Ward-Royster, Willa (as told to Toni Rose). *How I Got Over: Clara Ward and the World-Famous Ward Singers*. Philadelphia: Temple University Press, 1997.

Washburne, Christopher. "The Clave of Jazz: A Caribbean Contribution to the Rhythmic Foundation of an African-American Music," *Black Music Research Journal* 17 (1997): 59–80.

Wells, Christopher. *"Go Harlem!": Chick Webb and His Dancing Audience during the Great Depression*. PhD diss., University of North Carolina, 2014.

White, Katherine. *Analysis of the Singing Style of Gospel Singer Mahalia Jackson.* M.A. thesis, Washington University, 1982.

Williams-Jones, Pearl. "Afro-American Gospel Music: A Crystallization of the Black Aesthetic," *Ethnomusicology* 19 (1975): 373–85.

Witter, Evelyn. *Mahalia Jackson: Born to Sing Gospel Music.* Fenton, MI: Mott Media, 1985.

Wolf, Daniel. *You Send Me: The Life and Times of Sam Cooke.* New York: Quill, 1996.

Wolfe, Charles. *Mahalia Jackson: Gospel Singer.* Philadelphia: Chelsea House, 1990.

——————. "Mahalia on the Air, 1954," *Rejoice* 2/3 (Spring 1990): 10–13.

Woodley, Jenny. *Art for Equality: The NAACP's Cultural Campaign for Civil Rights.* Lexington: University Press of Kentucky, 2014.

Woods, Jeff. *Black Struggle, Red Scare: Segregation and Anti-Communism in the South, 1948–1968.* Baton Rouge: Louisiana State University Press, 2004.

Young, Alan. *The Pilgrim Jubilees.* Jackson: University Press of Mississippi, 2001.

Zak, Albin. *I Don't Sound Like Nobody: Remaking Music in 1950s America.* Ann Arbor: University of Michigan Press, 2010.

Zolten, Jerry. *Great God A'Mighty! The Dixie Hummingbirds: Celebrating the Rise of Soul Gospel Music.* New York: Oxford University Press, 2003.

Index

Note: Italic page numbers refer to figures.